W9-AQY-956

PRACTICE
MAKES
PERFECT®

Complete
English All-in-One
for ESL Learners

PRACTICE
MAKES
PERFECT®

Complete
English All-in-One
for ESL Learners

Ed Swick

McGraw Hill

New York Chicago San Francisco Athens London Madrid
Mexico City Milan New Delhi Singapore Sydney Toronto

ISBN   978-1-260-45524-3
MHID   1-260-45524-6

e-ISBN   978-1-260-45525-4
e-MHID   1-260-45525-0

This book consists of content from previously published titles in the Practice Makes Perfect series. Substantial portions of the following books make up this All-in-One volume:
• Ed Swick/*Practice Makes Perfect English Grammar for ESL Learners, 3rd Edition*
• Mark Lester/*Practice Makes Perfect English Verb Tenses Up Close*
• Loretta Gray/*Practice Makes Perfect English Verbs, 2nd Edition*
• Robin Torres-Gouzerh/*Practice Makes Perfect Intermediate English Grammar for ESL Learners, 3rd Edition*
• Ed Swick/*Practice Makes Perfect English Pronouns and Prepositions, 2nd Edition*
• Ed Swick/*Practice Makes Perfect English Sentence Builder, 2nd Edition*
• Jean Yates/*Practice Makes Perfect English Conversation, 2nd Edition*

McGraw-Hill Education Language Lab App
Audio recordings of conversations (in chapters 27–29) are available to support your study of this book. Go to www.mhlanguagelab.com to access the online version of this application, or search "McGraw-Hill Education Language Lab" in the iTunes app store or Google Play app store (for Android) for the free mobile app.
Note: Internet access is required for streaming audio via the app.

Contents

Preface

Practice Makes Perfect: Complete English All-in-One for ESL Learners, aimed especially at self-taught learners, is designed to serves two purposes for acquiring the skills needed to be a confident user of English as a second language. Firstly, it is an excellent instrument for practicing the many intricacies of the grammar and structure of the English language. Secondly, the book is a resource that contains the answers to questions most frequently on the minds of ESL-learners.

The book is a compilation of seven ESL books that cover the major grammar topics that describe and explain how the various parts of speech function in a sentence, and, most importantly, it also provides abundant exercises for practice.

- Ed Swick/*Practice Makes Perfect English Grammar for ESL Learners, 3rd Edition*
- Mark Lester/*Practice Makes Perfect English Verb Tenses Up Close*
- Loretta Gray/*Practice Makes Perfect English Verbs, 2nd Edition*
- Robin Torres-Gouzerh/*Practice Makes Perfect Intermediate English Grammar for ESL Learners, 3rd Edition*
- Ed Swick/*Practice Makes Perfect English Pronouns and Prepositions, 2nd Edition*
- Ed Swick/*Practice Makes Perfect English Sentence Builder, 2nd Edition*
- Jean Yates/*Practice Makes Perfect English Conversation, 2nd Edition*

In just this one book, the student has a tool for learning and practicing his or her new language and a valuable resource that provides immediate answers to questions.

Technical terminology has been kept to a minimum but is introduced and explained when it is needed to describe an important concept. But the goal of the book is to hold such terminology to a minimum. For example, the term *elliptical clause* is a concept that must be memorized because those two words together have no precise meaning at first glance and merely *stand for* a special kind of clause. They describe a clause, in which something has been omitted. For example:

You are just as smart as Jim. = *You are just as smart as Jim* **is**.

The verb (*is*) is left out of the final clause because it is understood. In this book, the term *elliptical clause* is avoided as much as possible, and the clause is more simply described as *omitting the verb* or *leaving out the verb*. Those replacement phrases provide simplicity and an instantaneous understanding of how the clause is structured. Avoiding technical terminology provides ESL-learners with a more immediate understanding of material.

This English *All-in-One* book provides a comprehensive look at English grammar and its usage. In addition, the large abundance of exercises provides a generous opportunity to practice what has been learned or a concept that learners may wish to master. ESL-learners are encouraged to use the extensive answer key to check for accuracy and as an aid to assess the skill level that has been achieved.

One of the great advantages of using a compiled book like this is having access to an all-inclusive collection of English grammar topics, thorough explanations of those topics, and a generous amount of exercises with an answer key. It is to the user's advantage to review both small concepts and complete chapters until the ESL-learner's new skills can be used comfortably and confidently.

Nouns

Nouns can be either *proper* or *common*. Proper nouns are those that refer to a *particular* person, place, thing, or idea. Such nouns are capitalized: *America, George Washington, Mr. Neruda, October.*

Nouns that do not refer to a particular person, place, thing, or idea are common nouns. They are not capitalized: *land, girls, money, test.* Compare the following list of proper and common nouns:

Proper Nouns	Common Nouns
Mexico	country
Ms. Finch	woman
English	language
McGraw-Hill	publisher
American Airlines	company
December	month

EXERCISE

1·1

Next to each noun write the word proper *or* common.

1. _____ France

2. _____ rope

3. _____ United States

4. _____ Professor Hall

5. _____ professor

6. _____ the stadium

7. _____ the Olympics

8. _____ horses

9. _____ Dr. Blanchard

10. _____ our school

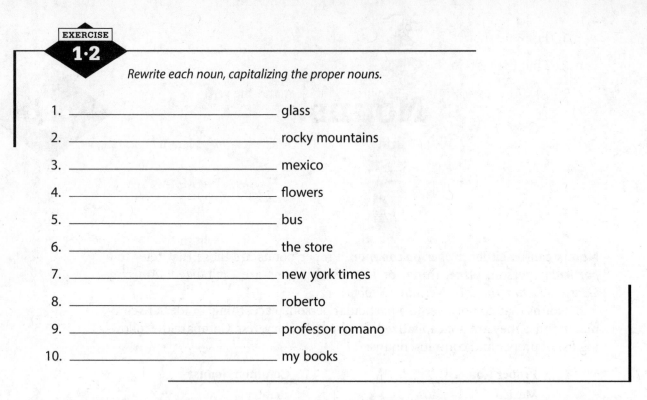

EXERCISE

1·2

Rewrite each noun, capitalizing the proper nouns.

1. _____ glass

2. _____ rocky mountains

3. _____ mexico

4. _____ flowers

5. _____ bus

6. _____ the store

7. _____ new york times

8. _____ roberto

9. _____ professor romano

10. _____ my books

Nouns can be used as the *subject of a sentence*. The subject is the word that is performing the action in the sentence. The subject can be a proper noun or a common noun, and it can be singular or plural:

> *Juanita* is a friend of mine.
> *The boys* like to play soccer.
> Where is the *school*?

Nouns can also be used as *direct objects*. The direct object in a sentence is the noun that receives the action of the verb. To find the direct object in a sentence, do three things:

1. Find the subject of the sentence.

2. Find the verb in the sentence.

3. Ask whom or what with the subject and the verb.

Look at these sample sentences:

"Sara likes my brother."   "The girls find a book."

1. subject = *Sara*   1. subject = *girls*

2. verb = *likes*   2. verb = *find*

3. ask whom = Whom does   3. ask what = What do the
   Sara like?   girls find?

The direct object is *my brother*.   The direct object is *book*.

Nouns are sometimes *indirect objects*. They stand before the direct object in the sentence. It is the person to whom or for whom something is provided. To find the indirect object in a sentence, do three things:

1. Find the subject of the sentence.

2. Find the verb in the sentence.

3. Ask to whom or for whom with the subject and the verb.

Look at these sample sentences:

"Justin buys the girl a magazine."   "Mother gives Nate five dollars."

1. subject = *Justin*

2. verb = *buys*

3. ask to whom or for whom = For whom does Justin buy a magazine?

The indirect object is *girl*.

1. subject = *Mother*

2. verb = *gives*

3. ask to whom or for whom = To whom does Mother give five dollars?

The indirect object is *Nate*.

Note: It is rare that something inanimate is used as an indirect object.

When a noun is used as a *predicate noun*, it follows the predicate in the sentence. The predicate can be a single verb or a verb phrase:

Verb as the predicate: Maria *helps* us.
Verb phrase as the predicate: Maria *usually helps with the gardening*.

Predicate nouns most often follow the verbs *to be* and *to become*:

My mother wants to be *a doctor*.
Celine became *an actress*.
Are you *the manager* of this building?

EXERCISE

1·3

Look at the italicized word in each sentence. Decide how it is used, then write subject, direct object, indirect object, *or* predicate noun *in the blank.*

1. _____ Claudia likes *Bret*.

2. _____ *The boys* found some money.

3. _____ The girls found *some money*.

4. _____ My father is *an engineer*.

5. _____ I sent *my sister* a telegram.

6. _____ Tomas buys *Serena* three red roses.

7. _____ Is *the woman* at home now?

8. _____ Mr. Jimenez became *a pilot*.

9. _____ He needs *a new car*.

10. _____ Carmen gives them *the books*.

Write a sentence using the noun given as a direct object.

EXAMPLE: the boy

*Barbara sees **the boy** in the park.*

1. my sister

   _____

2. a new car

   _____

3. Jackie

   _____

Write a sentence using the word given as an indirect object.

4. the children

   _____

5. a puppy

   _____

6. Grandfather

   _____

Using the phrase in parentheses, answer each question using that phrase as the direct or indirect object.

EXAMPLE: (Yolanda) Whom does Gerry meet?

Gerry meets Yolanda.

1. (the boys) Whom does the girl not trust?

   _____

2. (his wallet) What does Father often misplace?

   _____

3. (the landlord) To whom does she always give the rent money?

   _____

4. (her new computer) What does Anita want to sell soon?

   _____

5. (her grandchildren) For whom does she buy the toys?

_____

6. (Ms. Johnson) Whom must you visit in New York?

_____

7. (their new house) What do they like so much?

_____

8. (little Johnny) To whom can she give the present?

_____

9. (Dr. Lee) Whom does he need to see today?

_____

10. (Michael) To whom does she throw the ball?

_____

EXERCISE

1·6

Rewrite each verb phrase as a complete sentence by adding a subject.

EXAMPLE   Is a real bargain.   *That coat is a real bargain.*

1. Were eating an Italian specialty. _____

2. Have worked in Austin for two years.

_____

3. Purchased it last week. _____

4. Is awful. _____

5. Looks comfortable. _____

6. Went to the theater. _____

Underline the subject(s) in each sentence.

1. Children ought to be more careful.

2. Water is good for you.

3. Prague is an amazing and historic Eastern European city.

4. The furry, clean, calm cat slept on the couch.

5. The furry, clean, calm, black cat ran outside.

6. The furry, clean, calm, black cat with a scar jumped on the counter.

7. The big, ugly, dirty, brown bear with long ears and large claws attacked a hunter.

8. She read a magazine yesterday.

9. Peter went to the circus.

10. Lending money and giving too much advice can cause problems.

Definite and Indefinite Articles

The English **definite article** is *the*. It is used to identify a *particular* person or thing. If you are speaking about someone or something you are already familiar with, you use *the* with the noun. Look at these examples:

> I already know *the man*.
> She met *the women* who won the lottery.
> This is *the book* that I told you about.

The **indefinite article** is used to describe someone or something that is unfamiliar to you or about which you are speaking *in general*. There are two forms: *a* and *an*. Use *a* before a word beginning with a consonant. Use *an* before a word beginning with a vowel. Look at these examples:

> He sees *a stranger* on the corner.
> Did you buy *an apple* or *an orange*?
> Is the woman *a good lawyer*?
> She has *an idea*.

Compare the difference between the definite and indefinite article by using these sentences:

> I want *an* apple. (I do not see an apple. But I feel hungry for one.)
> I want *the* apple. (I am choosing between the apple and the orange that I see before me.)

The definite article for plural nouns is also *the*. But there is no indefinite article for plural nouns. The plural articles are used in the same way as the singular articles.

Singular Definite	Singular Indefinite	Plural Definite	Plural Indefinite
the boy	a boy	the boys	boys
the house	a house	the houses	houses
the idea	an idea	the ideas	ideas

Fill in the blank with either the definite or indefinite article, whichever makes the best sense.

1. Did you buy a Ford or _____ Chevy?

2. Does he know _____ man on the corner?

3. She has _____ secret to tell you.

4. What time does _____ train leave?

5. We need _____ hot dogs and a bottle of Coke.

6. Did you see _____ accident?

7. He met _____ guests as they arrived.

8. _____ teacher is angry with us.

9. I can't find _____ keys.

10. Is that _____ snake in that tree?

Rewrite each sentence, changing the singular nouns in each sentence to plural nouns. Make any changes to the articles and verbs that are necessary.

1. They gave us an orange.

   _____

2. I like the book very much.

   _____

3. Do you often visit the farm there?

   _____

4. A rabbit is hiding behind it.

   _____

5. Katrina likes to play with the kitten.

   _____

Follow the same directions, but change the plural nouns to singular.

6. Montel has dogs and cats.

   _____

7. I want to buy the roses.

   _____

8. There are gifts for you.

   _____

9. Can you hear the babies crying?

   _____

10. Do you have brothers or sisters?

    _____

Adjectives

Adjectives are words that describe nouns. They tell the size, color, or quality of something: a *big* room, the *red* car, four *interesting* books. Here are some commonly used adjectives:

beautiful	fast	loud	tall
big	funny	old	terrible
black	handsome	quiet	thirsty
boring	interesting	right	ugly
careful	late	sad	young
careless	little	short	white
early	long	slow	wrong

EXERCISE

3·1

Circle the adjective that makes more sense in the sentence.

1. I often go to a **green/late** movie.

2. Their **little/right** boy is six years old.

3. The **wrong/young** teacher is very smart.

4. We took the **fast/loose** train to New York.

5. The **old/funny** story made me laugh.

6. Do you know that **handsome/early** man?

7. She had an **early/careless** breakfast.

8. I saw the **long/terrible** accident.

9. The new house has **boring/white** doors.

10. The **green/short** boy is my cousin.

Just like nouns, adjectives can follow the predicate. They most often come after forms of the verbs *to be* and *to become*:

> My sister was very *sad*.
> The horse suddenly became *thirsty*.
> My grandfather is *old*.

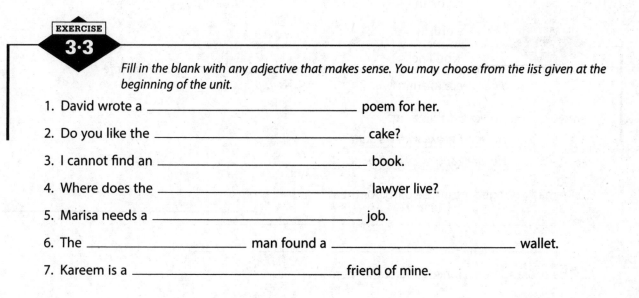

EXERCISE 3·2

Look at the example sentences. Change each sentence so that the adjective follows the predicate.

EXAMPLE: The white house is on the hill.

> *The house on the hill is white.*

1. The sad song was from Mexico.

   _____

2. The funny story is about a clown.

   _____

3. The careless waiter is out of work.

   _____

4. The ugly snake is from Egypt.

   _____

5. The beautiful woman is from Spain.

   _____

EXERCISE 3·3

Fill in the blank with any adjective that makes sense. You may choose from the list given at the beginning of the unit.

1. David wrote a _____ poem for her.

2. Do you like the _____ cake?

3. I cannot find an _____ book.

4. Where does the _____ lawyer live?

5. Marisa needs a _____ job.

6. The _____ man found a _____ wallet.

7. Kareem is a _____ friend of mine.

8. There is a _____ test tomorrow.

9. When can you come to our _____ farm?

10. That is a _____ question.

Adjectives

Adjectives describe or modify a noun or pronoun. They provide more information about a noun or pronoun, and they can provide additional meaning for a noun phrase.

> Joseph is a **famous** guitar player.
> The **elderly** couple slept at last.

The list of English adjectives is, of course, quite long. Here are some frequently used examples.

appropriate	generous	lonely	Spanish
beautiful	good	modern	spicy
bitter	intelligent	poor	tall
brown	lazy	rich	tasty
forgetful	local	scary	vintage

An English adjective has only one form, whether the noun or pronoun it modifies is masculine, feminine, or neuter, or singular or plural. This is true for predicate adjectives, as well as for adjectives that stand before a noun.

> The new professor is quite **intelligent**.
> **Intelligent** people don't brag about their talents.

> His youngest son is terribly **lazy**.
> A **lazy** person probably won't go far in life.

> Even the baby giraffe is **tall**.
> That **tall** girl is the star of her basketball team.

EXERCISE

3·4

Rewrite each sentence, placing never *in the appropriate position. Then, rewrite the sentence with* rarely.

EXAMPLE   He spoke with his aunt.

He never spoke with his aunt.

He rarely spoke with his aunt.

1. We had arranged a surprise party for them.

_____

_____

2. The soprano from France sang at the Met.

_____

_____

3. Grandfather was in a good mood.

_____

_____

4. My brother could fix his own car.

_____

_____

5. They will go to Alaska in the winter.

_____

_____

EXERCISE
3·5

Underline the adjective(s) in each sentence.

1. This book is hard to read.

2. This is the best article I have ever read.

3. She was beautiful and happy at her wedding.

4. If we are fast, we will find good seats for the movie.

5. The humid breezes blew across the plain.

6. They were beaming and radiant at their anniversary.

Now, underline the adverb in each sentence.

7. We hurriedly ran out of the burning building.

8. I rarely take any breaks in the morning.

9. Loudly, the teenagers moved through the school corridors.

10. She finally went to the grocery store after running out of toilet paper.

11. He often read the Bible in the morning.

12. The library receives a copy of the newspaper biweekly.

13. Our manager spoke to us seriously about behavioral issues.

14. The children ended by playing indoors.

15. Catherine regularly brings coffee to her co-workers.

16. I was still stuck in traffic.

17. Perhaps we will fly to Atlanta next month.

Using adjectives

Adjectives are words that modify nouns or pronouns. A variety of adjectival forms must be understood in order for you to write accurately. The most common type is the *descriptive adjective*.

Descriptive adjectives

Precisely as their name suggests, descriptive adjectives describe someone or something. The following list contains high-frequency descriptive adjectives. Consider what they tell about a noun they might modify.

beautiful	funny	kind	short
big	handsome	little	soft
blue	happy	red	tall
evil	hard	sad	ugly

The complete listing of all descriptive adjectives would be much longer. You can probably think of many other words that fit this category.

Predicative and attributive adjectives

Adjectives are used primarily in two different ways: *predicatively* and *attributively*. A predicate adjective is one that follows a linking verb and modifies a noun or pronoun "from a distance"—that is, separated from the noun itself by the verb.

subject + linking verb + predicate adjective

Mr. Price is **handsome**.
My vision seems **blurred**.
That really smells **good**!
It suddenly got **cold**.

Here are some commonly used linking verbs.

act	fall	look	smell
appear	feel	prove	sound
become	get	remain	taste
come	grow	seem	

Naturally, adjectives can be modified by any variety of adverbs. For example:

Mr. Price is **very** handsome.
Today the weather became **quite** terrible.

Attributive adjectives, on the other hand, stand before a noun. It is common to use more than one adjective to modify nouns in this position.

attributive adjective + subject + verb

The **young** officer came up to me.
The **frightened young** officer came up to me.
An **old** man sat down to rest.
A **tired old** man sat down to rest.

You can view attributive adjectives as replacements for relative clauses that contain the linking verb **to be**. Compare the following two sentences with the previous two examples:

> The officer, **who was** frightened and young, came up to me.
> A man, **who was** tired and old, sat down to rest.

Let's look at an example of how a relative clause is changed to become an attributive adjective. Here's the original sentence, with the relative clause set off by commas:

> The story, **which is** silly, amused the children.

To convert this sentence, the adjective **silly** is removed from the relative clause. The remaining words in the relative clause are omitted (as are the commas), and the adjective is placed before the noun. The result is a sentence with an attributive adjective, and that sentence conveys the same meaning as the sentence in which there was a relative clause:

> The **silly** story amused the children.

When a noun follows a linking verb, it is called a *predicate nominative*. The predicate nominative is a noun that further describes the subject of the sentence. Adjectives can modify the subject, the predicate nominative, or both. For example:

> The winner was a man from Holland.
> The **eventual** winner was a man from Holland.
> The winner was an **athletic** man from Holland.
> The **eventual** winner was an **athletic** man from Holland.

A sentence with a predicate nominative can be changed by reversing the positions of the subject and the predicate nominative and *still make complete sense*. This can occur only with linking verbs.

> An **athletic** man from Holland was the **eventual** winner.

Some adjectives can be used only as predicate adjectives. They sound awkward if used attributively. Some of the most commonly used ones are these:

afraid	glad	safe
alive	ill	sorry (meaning *apologetic*)
alone	likely	sure
apart	ready	unable
aware		

Let's look at a couple of sentences illustrating correct versus incorrect usage:

The boy was quite **alone**.	*correct usage*
The **alone** boy waited in the hall.	*incorrect usage*

Certain other adjectives should be used only as attributive adjectives. If they are used as predicate adjectives, they should be followed by predicate nominatives.

atomic	north/south
east/west	northern/southern
eastern/western	northern/western
indoor/outdoor	supplementary
maximum	woolen
nationwide	

If **indoor** and **outdoor** are used predicatively, they take the adverbial form **indoors** and **outdoors**. If **supplementary** is used predicatively, its form changes to a noun: **a supplement**. In the case of **woolen**, when used predicatively, it becomes the phrase **made of wool**.

Let's again look at a pair of sentences illustrating correct usage versus incorrect usage:

An **occasional** rain kept the streets   *correct usage*
wet and slick.
The rain today was only **occasional**.   *incorrect usage*

EXERCISE
3·6

Complete each sentence that follows with an appropriate predicate adjective. Then, write a sentence using the same adjective attributively.

EXAMPLE: Mark was very <u>sad</u>.

The <u>sad</u> look in her eyes brought me to tears.

1. a. Are the boys _____ again?

    b. _____

2. a. Grandma's kitchen smelled _____.

    b. _____

3. a. How long has this woman been _____?

    b. _____

4. a. Your report is _____.

    b. _____

5. a. Your new tie looks _____.

    b. _____

6. a. Professor Garcia seemed _____ yesterday.

    b. _____

7. a. Were you _____ as a child?

    b. _____

8. a. The young lawyer seemed rather _____.

    b. _____

9. a. Your rose garden smells _____!

    b. _____

10. a. Why does her voice sound so _____?

    b. _____

Limiting adjectives

There are nine types of limiting adjectives: definite and indefinite articles, possessive adjectives, demonstrative adjectives, indefinite adjectives, interrogative adjectives, cardinal adjectives, ordinal adjectives, proper adjectives, and nouns used as adjectives. The obvious function of any limiting adjective is to limit or to specify some aspect of the noun it modifies.

Definite and indefinite articles

The definite and indefinite articles illustrate this limitation function well. The definite article (**the**) specifies *someone or something as already known or mentioned*. Indefinite articles (**a, an**) identify *an unknown person or thing* and *persons or things in general*. For example:

The man on the corner is my friend.	*A specific man is the topic here. He is known to the speaker.*
A man on the corner was hit by a car.	*An unspecified man is the topic here. He is unknown to the speaker.*
The heavy suitcase belongs to Mary.	*A specific suitcase is the topic here. The speaker knows that it is heavy.*
A heavy suitcase is not allowed.	*Heavy suitcases in general are the topic here.*

Indefinite articles are not used with plural nouns. The complete omission of an article with a plural noun indicates that the meaning is *indefinite*. Compare the following pairs of sentences:

Singular	Plural
The boy plays chess.	**The** boys play chess.
A good student must behave.	Good students must behave.

Possessive adjectives

Possessive adjectives limit the nouns they modify in terms of the ownership implied: **my**, **your**, **his**, **her**, **its**, **our**, and **their**. The possessive **whose**, which inquires into ownership, is also an interrogative adjective but belongs in this group, as well.

My new car is a Ford.	*Ownership of the car is limited to me.*
Her kitten became quite ill.	*Ownership of the kitten is limited to her.*
Our garden did well this year.	*Ownership of the garden is limited to us.*

Demonstrative adjectives

The demonstrative adjectives—**this**, **that**, **these**, and **those**—limit the modified noun to the one identified by the speaker: **this one**, **that one**. The demonstrative adjectives show *closeness* (**this**, **these**) or *distance* (**that**, **those**) in the same way as the demonstrative pronouns.

This book is hard to understand.
That remark was uncalled for.
These men need a job.
Do you know **those** people?

*Write three original sentences containing the noun or phrase provided. Use a definite article or an indefinite article (or both) in the first sentence; use a possessive adjective in the second sentence; and use a demonstrative adjective in the third. If a question mark (**?**) is also provided, make at least one of your sentences a question.*

EXAMPLE: jacket ?

<u>The jacket on the bed belongs to him.</u>

<u>Have you seen my jacket?</u>

<u>This jacket is just what I've been looking for.</u>

1. CD player ?

   a. _____

   b. _____

   c. _____

2. young children

   a. _____

   b. _____

   c. _____

3. yacht ?

   a. _____

   b. _____

   c. _____

4. new lobby

   a. _____

   b. _____

   c. _____

5. pillows ?

   a. _____

   b. _____

   c. _____

6. friends and relatives

   a. _____

   b. _____

   c. _____

7. grammar

    a. _____

    b. _____

    c. _____

8. mathematical formula ?

    a. _____

    b. _____

    c. _____

9. calendar

    a. _____

    b. _____

    c. _____

10. unusual painting

    a. _____

    b. _____

    c. _____

Indefinite adjectives

Indefinite adjectives provide general information about the nouns they modify. They often answer the questions *how much?* or *how many?* Among the most common indefinite adjectives are **all**, **any**, **each**, **every**, **few**, **many**, and **some**. Let's look at some sentences that illustrate their use:

All work must be completed by noon.	*how much work?*
Each candidate will have ten minutes to speak.	*how many candidates?*
Are **some** companies in financial trouble?	*how many companies?*

Interrogative adjectives

The interrogative adjectives are **what**, **which**, and **whose** (as noted earlier, **whose** is also a possessive adjective). They modify nouns in the same way as other limiting adjectives. **What** and **which** inquire into a choice between two persons or things and from among a group of persons or things. **Whose** asks about ownership. Here are some examples:

What airline are you taking to Brazil?
What cities do you want to visit?
What day will you arrive back in the States?

Which game do you like best?
Which candidate appeals to you more?
Which dessert did you order?

Whose limousine is parked in front of the house?
Whose husband is a famous rap star?
Whose cake won first prize at the fair?

Cardinal adjectives

Cardinal adjectives are simply numbers used as adjectives. They limit the nouns they modify by specifying an amount. That amount can be as little as "zero" or as great as any number you can conceive of. For example:

One boy scraped his knee on the ground.
Fifteen girls are in the contest.
Eighty dollars was too much for the blouse.

Notice that the subject of the last of these sentences is plural, but it is considered a single quantity and therefore takes a singular verb: **Eighty dollars was . . . .** Let's consider the difference between the use of a singular verb and a plural verb with such quantities.

If there are eighty *individual* dollar bills on the floor, you can say: **Eighty dollars are on the floor.** If, instead, you wish to refer to the entire quantity of eighty dollars as a single sum of money, you can say: **Eighty dollars is more than I want to spend.**

Ordinal adjectives

Numbers are used in a slightly different adjectival form with ordinal adjectives. These adjectives limit the nouns they modify by specifying numerical order. For example:

The **first** question on the test was simple.
They're celebrating their **fiftieth** wedding anniversary.
Jake is the **twelfth** boy in line.

The majority of ordinal adjectives are formed by adding **-th** to the end of a number: **fourth, thirtieth, hundredth,** and so on. There are only a few irregular forms, as follows:

CARDINAL NUMBER	ORDINAL NUMBER
one	first
two	second
three	third
five	fifth

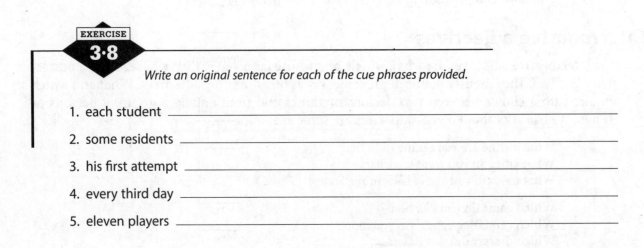

EXERCISE 3·8

Write an original sentence for each of the cue phrases provided.

1. each student _____

2. some residents _____

3. his first attempt _____

4. every third day _____

5. eleven players _____

6. many complaints _____

7. few demands _____

8. our daughter _____

9. the fifth row _____

10. too much noise _____

Using each cue phrase provided, write a question with **what** as an interrogative adjective. Then write a response to your question.

EXAMPLE: color

What color is Jim's new suit?

Jim's new suit is bright green.

1. wristwatch

a. _____

b. _____

2. blanket

a. _____

b. _____

3. set of towels

a. _____

b. _____

4. length

a. _____

b. _____

Follow the same directions, but write your questions with **which** as an interrogative adjective.

5. writing implements

a. _____

b. _____

6. path

a. _____

b. _____

7. breakfast menu

   a. _____

   b. _____

*Follow the same directions, but write your questions with **whose** as an interrogative adjective.*

8. passport and visa

   a. _____

   b. _____

9. Cuban relatives

   a. _____

   b. _____

10. coin purse

   a. _____

   b. _____

Proper adjectives and nouns used as adjectives

Proper adjectives are words that are proper nouns but act as modifiers of other nouns. Since proper nouns are capitalized, capitalization is also required when they are used as adjectives. A large category of proper adjectives comprises words that come from country or language names and that can be used both attributively and predicatively. Here are some examples:

> I love **Italian** food.
> Is **French** champagne the best?
> He said the **American** cars are less expensive.
> I believe this drawing is **Japanese**.

The same need for capitalization applies to proper names; however, proper names tend to be used only attributively. For example:

> We read a **Shakespearean** play.
> The **Hilton** mansion is hidden by trees.
> The **Bush** administration ended in 2009.
> Isn't that a **Streisand** song?

Many other nouns can also act as modifiers. If they are not proper nouns, they do not need to be capitalized and can be used only attributively. For example:

> Several **party** gifts were identical.
> The **wedding** guests were starting to get tipsy.
> I think I lost my **credit** card.

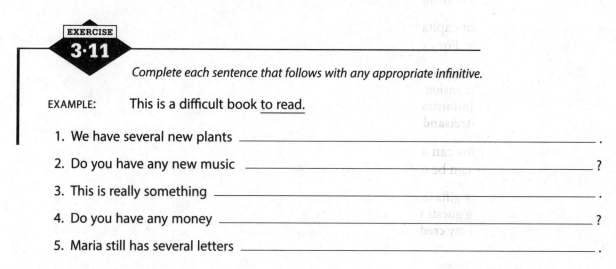

Using the noun cues provided, write original sentences with the nouns functioning as adjectives.

Example: Ford <u>There's a Ford dealership over there.</u>

1. Elizabethan _____

2. divorce _____

3. Kennedy _____

4. recreation _____

5. chemistry _____

6. faculty _____

7. White House _____

8. movie _____

9. baseball _____

10. Jack London _____

Infinitives

In some cases, an infinitive can function as an adjective. The infinitive usually immediately follows the noun or pronoun it modifies. For example:

This is always a fun show **to watch**.
We still haven't found anyone **to hire** for this position.
Professor Keller's class would be a great one **to take**.

Complete each sentence that follows with any appropriate infinitive.

EXAMPLE: This is a difficult book <u>to read.</u>

1. We have several new plants _____ .

2. Do you have any new music _____ ?

3. This is really something _____ .

4. Do you have any money _____ ?

5. Maria still has several letters _____ .

Using the infinitives that follow as adjectives, write original sentences.

6. to develop _____

7. to clean up _____

8. to grade _____

9. to defend _____

10. to be praised _____

Personal Pronouns

Pronouns are words that take the place of nouns. The English personal pronouns are:

	Singular	**Plural**
First Person	I	we
Second Person	you	you
Third Person	he, she, it	they

Notice that *you* is both singular and plural. When speaking to one person, say *you*. When speaking to two or more persons, say *you*:

Tim, *you* are a very good student.
Bruno and Rene, *you* have to study more.

Just as nouns have gender, pronouns also do. *I*, *we*, and *you* can be used by males or females. *He* is always masculine, *she* is always feminine, and *it* is always neuter. The plural of the third-person pronouns is always *they*, whether masculine, feminine, or neuter. And just like nouns, pronouns can be used as:

1. the subject of a sentence

2. a direct object

3. an indirect object

But when used as a direct object or indirect object, some of the pronouns change:

Subject	**Direct Object**	**Indirect Object**
I	me	me
you	you	you
he	him	him
she	her	her
it	it	it
we	us	us
you (plural)	you	you
they	them	them

If a pronoun replaces a noun in the sentence, it must have the same characteristics as the noun: the same number (singular or plural), the same gender (masculine, feminine, or neuter), and the same use in the sentence (subject, direct object, or indirect object). Look at these examples where the pronoun replaces the italicized noun:

Joseph is a hard worker. → *He* is a hard worker.
(singular masculine noun/subject)   (singular masculine pronoun/subject)

Do you know *the girls*? → Do you know *them*?
(plural noun/direct object)   (plural pronoun/direct object)

We gave *Mrs. Jones* some flowers. → We gave *her* some flowers.
(singular feminine noun/   (singular feminine pronoun/
indirect object)   indirect object)

Notice that the nouns and pronouns are in the third person. This is true when a pronoun replaces a noun. But when a noun or pronoun is combined with the first-person singular pronoun *I*, it is replaced by the first-person plural pronoun *we*:

You and I have work to do. → *We* have work to do.
He helps *the girls and me*. → He helps *us*.

EXERCISE
4·1

Look at the pronoun given in parentheses. Fill in the blank in the sentence with its correct form.

1. (you) How are _____ today?

2. (he) Caleb gave _____ a gift.

3. (she) _____ lives on Main Street.

4. (it) I really don't like _____.

5. (I) She met _____ in the city.

6. (Kris and I) Please give _____ the magazines.

7. (you and I) _____ worked in the garden.

8. (they) Are _____ your friends?

9. (we) The puppy followed _____ home.

10. (they) My brother saw _____ in New York.

11. (you) Mikhail wants to visit _____ today.

12. (I) When can _____ move into the apartment?

13. (it) Derrick bought _____ in Mexico.

14. (you and I) The children are helping _____.

15. (she) I like _____ a lot.

Change the italicized noun in each sentence to the corresponding pronoun.

1. *The students* came to class late. _____

2. I found *the money* in the closet. _____

3. Her brother sent *Jennifer and me* a postcard. _____

4. Do *your parents* live in Florida? _____

5. *My landlady* is very nice. _____

6. Do you know *my landlady*? _____

7. *Boys* can get so dirty. _____

8. Did you lose *your wallet*? _____

9. Juan visits *his uncle* often. _____

10. May I borrow *your watch*? _____

Change the italicized pronoun in each sentence to any appropriate noun.

1. *We* often speak English. _____

2. Do you like *it*? _____

3. Where did you find *them*? _____

4. *She* is from Puerto Rico. _____

5. Patricia never met *him* before. _____

6. Is *he* sick today? _____

7. We sent *them* a box of candy. _____

8. *It* costs twenty dollars. _____

9. The boys watched *her*. _____

10. Do *they* understand us? _____

When you change a direct object noun to a direct object pronoun, you must add *to* or *for* before the indirect object noun or pronoun. The indirect object becomes the object of the preposition *to* or *for*. Place the prepositional phrase after the direct object. For example:

I gave Jay **a book**. → I gave **it** to Jay.
We buy her **flowers**. → We buy **them** for her.

Rewrite each sentence, changing the italicized direct object to a pronoun. Add to or for appropriately.

1. I sent my friends *a letter*.

_____

2. She is giving us *two cakes*.

_____

3. Trey sold her *his car*.

_____

4. I didn't buy Ella *the scarf*.

_____

5. My brother will bring me *my gloves*.

_____

Nouns or pronouns can be used to complete *a prepositional phrase*. That is a phrase made up of a preposition and a noun or a pronoun. Here are some of the most commonly used prepositions:

after, behind, between, for, from, in, near, on, of, through, to, with, without

Look at these sample prepositional phrases:

after the concert	behind me
between the girls	for you
from a friend	in him
near the city	on it
of a book	through her
to a student	with us
without the money	without them

In a prepositional phrase, use the same form of the pronoun that is used as a direct or indirect object:

Subject Pronoun	Direct or Indirect Object	Prepositional Phrase
I	me	after me
you	you	behind you
he	him	for him
she	her	from her
it	it	in it
we	us	between us
they	them	near them

Complete the sentences, changing the subject pronoun in parentheses to an object pronoun.

1. (I) They have a gift for _____.

2. (you) I sent some flowers to _____.

3. (he) Karen often comes home without _____.

4. (she) I like dancing with _____.

5. (it) We found something in _____.

6. (we) Teresa sits near _____.

7. (they) This is a letter from _____.

8. (Dwayne and I) He is speaking of _____.

9. (you and I) Someone is standing behind _____.

10. (he) You can come in after _____.

Change the italicized noun to a pronoun.

1. We are driving through *the tunnel*. _____

2. A wolf was standing between *the boys*. _____

3. Do you want to ride in *my car*? _____

4. The guests have something for *Julia*. _____

5. I like singing with *Mr. Garcia*. _____

6. Maria is sitting near *Ali and me*. _____

7. I get postcards from *the tourists*. _____

Pronouns as the subject of a sentence

The *first person* pronouns refer to one's self. The *second person* pronouns refer to others to whom you are speaking. And the *third person* pronouns are substitutes for all other nouns. The pronouns that can act as the subject of a sentence (and are for this reason called subject, or personal, pronouns) are listed in the chart below.

	Singular	Plural
First Person	I	we
Second Person	you	you
Third Person	he, she, it	they

Note that *you* has both a singular and plural meaning: "Mary, you are a great athlete." "Tom and Mary, you have to study more."

In addition, there are two more pronouns that are used to ask questions about people (*who*) and about things (*what*).

The pronoun *he* can replace nouns that refer to males:

> the man → he
> a boy → he
> the doctor → he

The pronoun *she* can replace nouns that refer to females:

> the woman → she
> a girl → she
> the doctor → she

The pronoun *it* can replace nouns that refer to objects:

> the rock → it
> a building → it
> his nose → it

The pronoun *they* can replace nouns that refer to plurals:

> the girls → they
> men → they
> two rocks → they

The pronoun *who* can replace animate nouns to form a question:

> The man became ill. → **Who** became ill?
> A few women went shopping. → **Who** went shopping?

The pronoun *what* can replace inanimate nouns to form a question:

> Our house burned down. → **What** burned down?
> His tools are in the garage. → **What** is in the garage?

There is one notable exception to the rule that pronouns are derived by the gender of nouns. It is common to refer to a boat or sometimes an automobile as a female:

> "What a beautiful sailboat! **She's** a real beauty."
> "What about the *Titanic*?" "**She** sank in the Atlantic in 1912."
> "**She's** been a good old car, but it's time to trade her in."

Note that a noun or pronoun combined with *I* can be replaced by *we*:

> you and I = we
> she and I = we
> the boy and I = we
> the girls and I = we

The subject pronouns determine the form of the verb in the sentence. In the present tense most verbs require an *-s* ending when the subject is a third person singular pronoun or noun: *he has,* *the girl sings.* The other pronouns do not require an ending on the verb. The only exception to this is the verb *to be*, which has a more complicated conjugation than other verbs:

	to come	to help	to be
I	come	help	am
you	come	help	are
he, she, it	comes	helps	is
we	come	help	are
you	come	help	are
they	come	help	are

In the past tense the subject pronouns do not require an additional ending on the verb beyond the past tense formation. There is only one exception to this rule, and, again, it is the verb *to be*. Look at these examples in the past tense:

	to come	to help	to be
I	came	helped	was
you	came	helped	were
he, she, it	came	helped	was
we	came	helped	were
you	came	helped	were
they	came	helped	were

There is another second person singular pronoun. It is *thou*. It is considered archaic and is only found in very old documents or literature and in certain versions of the Bible. Its forms are:

Subject pronoun: *thou*
Object pronoun: *thee*
Possessive pronouns: *thy, thine*

As the subject of a present tense sentence, *thou* requires an *-st* ending on the verb: *thou hast, thou canst.* You should be aware of this pronoun's existence, but it will not be considered further in this book.

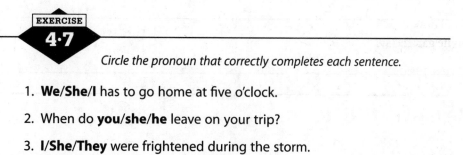

EXERCISE
4·7

Circle the pronoun that correctly completes each sentence.

1. **We/She/I** has to go home at five o'clock.

2. When do **you/she/he** leave on your trip?

3. **I/She/They** were frightened during the storm.

4. **I/You/We** am planning on early retirement.

5. Why are **it/you/he** crying?

6. **They/Who/We** wants to arrange a surprise party for her?

7. **He/You/We** was sound asleep.

8. **What/I/They** needs to be repaired right away?

9. Where does **I/you/she** go every afternoon?

10. **They/She/He** earn a very good salary.

Rewrite each sentence, changing the italicized noun phrase to the appropriate pronoun.

1. *My little sister* is such a sweet child.

   _____

2. *These boys* just can't seem to get along.

   _____

3. Where did *the sleepy soldiers* find a place to rest?

   _____

4. *My friends and I* spent a week camping in the mountains.

   _____

5. *The new school* burned down last night.

   _____

6. Where is *John* from?

   _____

7. *Two jet planes* roared overhead.

   _____

8. Why is *Ms. Brown* laughing?

   _____

9. Does *your arm* still hurt?

   _____

10. *Tom and I* can help you today.

    _____

You should be aware that personal pronouns used as subjects can form contractions. Contractions are formed with pronouns and certain verbs. Look at the examples that follow:

Pronoun	have	has	is	are	am	would	will
I	I've				I'm	I'd	I'll
you	you've			you're		you'd	you'll
he		he's	he's			he'd	he'll
she		she's	she's			she'd	she'll
it		it's	it's				
we	we've			we're		we'd	we'll
they	they've			they're		they'd	they'll
who		who's	who's			who'd	who'll
what		what's	what's				

There is one special contraction formed from the words *let us*: *let's*.

Other contractions are a combination of a verb and the negative word *not*:

Verb	Contraction	Verb	Contraction
are	aren't	must	mustn't
can	can't	need	needn't
could	couldn't	should	shouldn't
did	didn't	was	wasn't
do	don't	were	weren't
has	hasn't	will	won't
have	haven't	would	wouldn't
is	isn't		

Pronouns in a contraction should only be used in complete utterances and not in an elliptical phrase (a phrase in which information is understood):

> He'll arrive here on the five-thirty bus.
> I'm sure tomorrow will be a better day for you.

But it is common to respond to someone's question with an elliptical phrase. An elliptical phrase is one that leaves out certain words that are understood *from the words in the question*. In elliptical phrases contractions should *not* be used, unless the contraction is the combination of a verb and the negative word *not*. Let's look at some examples:

> Question: Is he going to work today?
> Answer: Yes, **he's** going to work today.
> Elliptical answer: Yes, **he is**. (no contraction)

> Question: Are you afraid of mice?
> Answer: Yes, **I'm** afraid of mice.
> Elliptical answer: Yes, **I am**. (no contraction)

> Question: Did she have enough money?
> Answer: No, **she didn't** have enough money.
> Elliptical answer: No, **she didn't**. (combination of a verb and *not*)

EXERCISE

4·9

Write an elliptical answer to each of the following questions.

1. Do you like living in San Francisco?

   _____

2. Is she a good programmer?

   _____

3. Have they ever seen the Grand Canyon?

   _____

4. Was he always such a complainer?

   _____

5. Am I permitted to study in this room?

_____

6. Aren't we spending too much time on this problem?

_____

7. Should she really buy such an expensive car?

_____

8. Can you understand what he's talking about?

_____

9. Shouldn't he rest for a while?

_____

10. Will they have to spend the night here?

_____

Pronouns as direct objects

Although nouns do not change when they are used as direct objects in a sentence, most pronouns do.

Subject	Direct Object
I	me
you (singular)	you (singular)
he, she, it	him, her, it
we	us
you (plural)	you (plural)
they	them
who	whom
what	what

You should be aware that in casual language, most people substitute *who* for *whom* as the direct object form.

Now look at the pronouns when they are used as direct objects in a sentence:

Bill saw **me** at the bank yesterday.

I like **you** a lot. (singular *you*)

Mom sent **her** to the store.

We bought **it** a week ago.

She found **us** hiding in the garage.

I'll help **you**. (plural *you*)

Michael warned **them** about the danger.

Whom did you meet at the party? (or, in casual language, **Who** did you meet at the party?)

What are they making for supper?

Look at these examples that show what occurs when direct object nouns are changed to direct object pronouns:

Jim tried to kiss **the girl**. → Jim tried to kiss **her**.
They really like **their former coach**. → They really like **him**.
Who threw **the ball** to him? → Who threw **it** to him?
You'll find **the new tools** in the shed. → You'll find **them** in the shed.

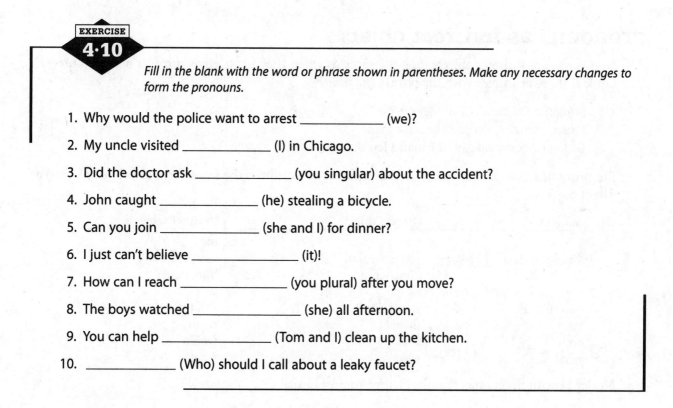

EXERCISE
4·10

Fill in the blank with the word or phrase shown in parentheses. Make any necessary changes to form the pronouns.

1. Why would the police want to arrest _____ (we)?

2. My uncle visited _____ (I) in Chicago.

3. Did the doctor ask _____ (you singular) about the accident?

4. John caught _____ (he) stealing a bicycle.

5. Can you join _____ (she and I) for dinner?

6. I just can't believe _____ (it)!

7. How can I reach _____ (you plural) after you move?

8. The boys watched _____ (she) all afternoon.

9. You can help _____ (Tom and I) clean up the kitchen.

10. _____ (Who) should I call about a leaky faucet?

EXERCISE
4·11

Rewrite each sentence and change the direct object noun phrase to a pronoun.

1. My sister liked Jim's roommate a lot.

_____

2. Can you understand that foreign language?

_____

3. I bought several CDs at the mall.

_____

4. When did you first meet my brother and me?

_____

5. I spent a lot of money.

_____

6. We used to visit the twins regularly.

_____

7. I'd like to introduce my girlfriend Anita.

_____

Pronouns as indirect objects

Nouns used as indirect objects look the same as when they are used as subjects or direct objects. Look at these examples with the phrase *the man*.

> SUBJECT: The man is a stranger to me.
> DIRECT OBJECT: Do you know the man?
> INDIRECT OBJECT: I gave the man a few dollars.

But pronouns change. Pronouns used as indirect objects have the same form as pronouns used as direct objects.

Subject	Direct Object	Indirect Object
I	me	me
you (singular)	you (singular)	you (singular)
he, she, it	him, her, it	him, her, it
we	us	us
you (plural)	you (plural)	you (plural)
they	them	them
who	whom	whom
what	what	what

Notice how indirect object nouns change to pronouns:

> Mike gave **the girls** the tickets. → Mike gave **them** the tickets.
> I bought **James** a new shirt. → I bought **him** a new shirt.
> Did Bill send **your sister** a postcard? → Did Bill send **her** a postcard?

EXERCISE

4·12

Change the italicized indirect objects to pronouns.

1. He won't sell *Jim* the car.

_____

2. Did you bring *your girlfriend* a gift?

_____

3. I loaned *the Smith family* a hundred dollars.

_____

4. Please give *Ms. Garcia* a copy of the will.

_____

5. I'm going to buy *the children* some new pajamas.

_____

6. James sent *his elderly aunt* a bouquet of roses.

_____

7. She wrote *her boyfriend* several letters.

_____

EXERCISE
4·13

Fill in the blank with the word or phrase shown in parentheses. Make any necessary changes to form the pronouns.

1. I wanted to give _____ (you singular) something nice.

2. Please send _____ (she) a telegram with the news.

3. They brought _____ (we) breakfast in bed.

4. Can you lend _____ (I) a few dollars until tomorrow?

5. You ought to write _____ (he) a letter every week.

6. She'll buy _____ (you plural) new socks and underwear.

7. Mr. Brown gave _____ (Jim and I) a lecture on politics again.

8. I'm sending _____ (they) the directions to our new house.

9. Tell _____ (I) a story.

10. Who bought _____ (we) these tools?

Pronouns in a prepositional phrase

Nouns do not change their form when used in a prepositional phrase. But pronouns do, and they take the same form they do as direct or indirect objects.

Form of Pronouns That Follow Prepositions

me	us	whom
you (singular)	you (plural)	what
him, her, it	them	

In sentences, the pronouns following a preposition look like this:

Repeat this sentence **after me**.

She wants to speak **with you**. (singular)

I took a picture **of him**.

What do you know **about her**?

There's something hiding **in it**.

What do they want **from us**?

The thief was sitting **between you**. (plural)

Is that a deer coming up **to them**?

If the pronoun is *who* or *what*, the preposition often stands at the end of the question in casual speech, and *who* may be substituted for *whom*.

With whom were you chatting?

Who were you chatting **with**?

On what did you place the book?

What did you place the book **on**?

EXERCISE 4·14

Fill in the blank with the word or phrase shown in parentheses. Make any necessary changes to form the pronouns.

1. They were asking questions about _____ (you singular).

2. I received several letters from _____ (she).

3. From _____ (who) did you borrow the money?

4. _____ (What) were they all laughing about?

5. Someone threw a rock at _____ (I).

6. This problem has nothing to do with _____ (you plural).

7. That shirt really looks good on _____ (he).

8. A crow was flying directly over _____ (they).

9. An old woman came up to _____ (we).

10. Those stories were written by _____ (the girls and I).

EXERCISE 4·15

Fill in the blank with any preposition from the list below.

about	after	at	by	for	from
in	near	of	on	to	with

1. Three of the girls wanted to dance _____ me.

2. The artist painted a wonderful portrait _____ her.

3. _____ whom did you send the manuscript?

4. A little bird was sitting _____ it.

5. What did you put it _____ ?

6. I entered the building right _____ him.

7. There's a new bank _____ it.

8. The frightened dog came slowly up _____ us.

Direct and indirect object pronouns in the same sentence

When a direct object and an indirect object are used in the same sentence and *both are nouns*, the indirect object (IO) always precedes the direct object (DO).

> Father showed **Mr. Garcia** (IO) **his new car** (DO).
> Will you give **the dogs** (IO) **some water** (DO)?

If only the indirect object is changed to a pronoun, the same word order occurs:

> Father showed **him** (IO) **his new car** (DO).
> Will you give **them** (IO) **some water** (DO)?

But if the direct object is changed to a pronoun, there is a significant change in the word order and the indirect object becomes the object of the preposition *to* or *for*. This occurs whether the indirect object is a noun or a pronoun. Look at these examples:

Direct Object as Noun	Direct Object as Pronoun
I sent the men **some fresh coffee**.	I sent **it** *to the men*.
Who gave him **these gifts**?	Who gave **them** *to him*?
We bought the girls **a few flowers**.	We bought **them** *for the girls*.
Bring me **a hammer**.	Bring **it** *to me*.

EXERCISE 4·16

Rewrite each sentence, changing the direct object to a pronoun.

1. The magician showed us a fantastic trick.

   _____

2. Don't give the children the cookies.

   _____

3. I can't lend you the money.

   _____

4. Who sent your cousin this awful letter?

   _____

5. Tom is going to buy them a kitten.

   _____

6. The lawyer did him a favor.

   _____

7. The lonely soldier wrote his girlfriend four long letters.

   _____

8. She gave me her phone number.

_____

9. Uncle Robert bought us a new TV.

_____

10. Do you send them a check every week?

_____

EXERCISE
4·17

Rewrite each sentence, changing the direct and indirect objects to pronouns.

1. The judge sent the lawyers the documents.

_____

2. Why did you show Mary that picture?

_____

3. I can't lend my boyfriend so much money.

_____

4. Dr. Brown gave the nurse the surgical instruments.

_____

5. Show the police officer your license.

_____

6. They're going to buy their nephew several CDs.

_____

7. Will you save Maria a seat at this table?

_____

EXERCISE
4·18

Rewrite each sentence, changing the italicized word or phrase to a pronoun. Make all other necessary changes.

1. *Several boys* were standing on the corner and laughing.

_____

2. Someone threw *a rock* through that window!

_____

3. Bill wants to buy his mother *a birthday present*.

_____

4. You shouldn't speak about *your brother* in that terrible way.

_____

5. Where did you buy *such a beautiful necklace*?

_____

6. Ms. Smith has moved out of *her apartment*.

_____

7. Do you know *these women*?

_____

8. *Bill and I* were on our way to the party when it happened.

_____

9. I bought you *some flowers*.

_____

10. Do you want to go there with *my sister and me*?

_____

11. *That young lady* has been elected chairperson of the committee.

_____

12. He hates *spiders*.

_____

13. Put *those old clothes* in the attic, please.

_____

14. Is *that tall man* the new boss?

_____

15. We love *beautiful warm weather*.

_____

EXERCISE
4·19

Write three original sentences with the pronoun given in parentheses. In the first sentence, use the pronoun as a direct object. In the second sentence, use the pronoun as an indirect object. In the third sentence, use the pronoun as the object of a preposition.

1. (I) _____

_____

_____

2. (she) _____

_____

_____

3. (we) _____

_____

_____

4. (they) _____

_____

_____

5. (who) _____

_____

_____

A Word of Caution

You will sometimes hear native speakers use pronouns incorrectly. This is particularly true when two pronouns are used together or a noun and a pronoun are used together—for example, *you and I, Tom and he*.

You have seen examples in this book that show which pronouns are used as the subject of a sentence. But compare what is correct with what you might hear a native say:

Correct: Tom and **she** are playing baseball tomorrow.

Incorrect: Tom and **her** are playing baseball tomorrow.

Correct: **He** and **I** have the same birthday.

Incorrect: **Him** and **me** have the same birthday.

Similar errors occur when such phrases are used as a direct or indirect object or the object of a preposition. In order to sound loftier, some speakers "overcorrect" the pronoun and use a nominative case pronoun where an objective case pronoun is really required. This seems most prevalent with the first person singular pronoun *I*:

Correct: Martha gave Barbara and **me** a list of chores.

Incorrect: Martha gave Barbara and **I** a list of chores.

Correct: Did he want to speak with both you and **me**?

Incorrect: Did he want to speak with both you and **I**?

Demonstrative pronouns

It is easy to identify a demonstrative pronoun. It is a pronoun that points out the noun that is being spoken or written about. It modifies the noun like an adjective. The four demonstrative pronouns are *this*, *that*, *these*, and *those*.

This and *these* indicate something that is close by. *This* is used with singular nouns, and *these* is used with plural nouns:

> **This** man is a good friend of mine. (The man is here.)

> **These** books are on sale now. (The books are here.)

That and *those* indicate something that is far away. *That* is used with singular nouns, and *those* is used with plural nouns:

> **That** woman is my teacher. (I see the woman in the distance.)

> Did you see **those** airplanes? (Did you see the airplanes in the distance?)

EXERCISE
4·20

Using the information in parentheses, fill in the blank with the appropriate demonstrative pronoun.

1. (located next to me) I found puppy behind a _____ bush.

2. (on my lap) She thought magazines were _____ interesting.

3. (two blocks from here) tall building is the city _____ hall.

4. (in my hand) Would you like some of _____ nuts?

5. (above the city) dark clouds mean a storm is _____ coming.

6. (in another state) town is about two hundred miles from _____ here.

7. (in the apartment down the hall) Why do _____ people make so much noise?

8. (around my neck) I bought necklace on _____ sale.

9. (out in the yard) swing set is just for _____ children.

10. (back at the school) boys played soccer all _____ afternoon.

Indefinite pronouns

The indefinite pronouns are used to refer to a person or thing that has been mentioned earlier. Their list is rather long:

all	either	neither	several
another	everybody	no one	some
any	everyone	nobody	somebody
anybody	everything	none	someone
anyone	few	nothing	something
anything	many	one	
both	most	other	
each	much	others	

Like any other pronoun, an indefinite pronoun replaces a noun, but it is usually a noun that has appeared earlier in an utterance. Look at these examples:

> **The children** were in an accident. But **all** are safe and sound now.
> Were **the robbers** finally caught? Only **some** of them.
> **Mary and Barbara** were born on the same day. Yes, but **each** has a separate birthday party.

You need to be aware that a few of the indefinite pronouns can be used as a singular or plural: *all*, *any*, *more*, *most*, *none*, and *some*. Here are a few examples:

Singular	Plural
All is well.	**All** speak English and Spanish.
Most was done by John.	**Most** aren't going to vote for him.
Some was left on the table.	**Some** think she's very beautiful.

EXERCISE
4·21

Circle the indefinite pronoun that best completes each sentence.

1. He has three brothers. **Some/Much/Each** served in the navy for three years.

2. I bought seven tickets. **All/Something/Neither** were purchased at a discount.

3. The children didn't like her, and **most/none/any** would play with her.

4. **Nobody/Other/Either** put in enough time on the project.

5. **Someone/Many/Everything** he said turned out to be a lie.

6. Many of them enjoyed the concert. **Others/Each/Another** went home early.

7. They invited a hundred guests. **Much/Several/Anybody** are already in the reception hall.

8. The two girls took part in the competition, but **any/somebody/neither** had a chance of winning.

9. **Anyone/Another/Few** found without proper identification will be arrested.

10. **Many/Anything/Much** has been said about the problem, but nothing has been done.

Interrogative pronouns

The interrogative pronouns are *who*, *whom*, *whose*, *which*, and *what*. They are called *interrogative* because they ask a question. And like other pronouns, they replace nouns.

> **Who** invited these people to the party? (**Tom** invited these people.)
> **Whom** can I rely upon in these difficult times? (I can rely upon **Tom**.)
> **Whose** was voted the best cake at the fair? (**Tom's** cake was voted best.)
> **Which** is the hat you decided to buy? (I decided to buy that **gray** hat.)
> **What** is he talking about? (He is talking about **the theory of relativity**.)

These pronouns can be separated into *nominative*, *objective*, and *possessive* forms:

Nominative	Objective	Possessive
who	whom	whose
which	which	
what	what	

The nominative is used as the subject of a sentence. The objective is used as the direct object, indirect object, or object of a preposition. The possessive form shows ownership. Look at these examples with *who* and *which*:

> Nominative: **Who** rented your apartment?
> Objective: **Whom** will they elect as president?
> Possessive: **Whose** is the brightest child?

> Nominative: **Which** came first, the chicken or the egg?
> Objective: **Which** do you want to sell?

Just like indefinite pronouns, interrogative pronouns are used when the noun in question is understood.

EXERCISE
4·22

Change the italicized word or phrase to the appropriate interrogative pronoun and form a question.

1. *This gentleman* would like to order some dinner.

   _____

2. She found *some old documents* in the drawer.

   _____

3. *Mr. Brown's* is the fastest horse in the race.

   _____

4. They were discussing *the last one*.

   _____

5. Several women were talking about *the coming election*.

   _____

6. We met *him* while traveling in Mexico.

   _____

7. *Maria and James* spent a lot of time in the mountains.

   _____

8. They prefer *the new one*.

   _____

9. *A long, black snake* slithered across the road.

   _____

10. They received several letters *from their attorney*.

   _____

Numbers as pronouns

If a pronoun is a word that replaces a noun, then *a number* that does the same thing can be considered a pronoun. If the number stands alone, it is no longer just a numerical value or an adjective modifying a noun. It functions as a pronoun. Look at some examples:

Number Modifying a Noun	Number Used as a Pronoun
One boy was crying.	**One** felt sad but would not cry.
Three kittens played with the ball.	**Three** were born just a few minutes apart.
Ten soldiers watched the enemy approach.	**Ten** fled the battlefield in fear.

Just like indefinite pronouns, numbers are used as pronouns when the noun in question is understood.

Numbers as Nouns

Careful! A number can also act as a noun. When it is a noun, the verb used is singular. When it is a pronoun, the verb is plural (except with *one*):

Noun: **Thirteen** is an unlucky number.
Pronoun: **Thirteen** are hiding in the brush.

Noun: *One* is pronounced like the word *won*.
Pronoun: **One** is still in the nest.

EXERCISE
4·23

Rewrite each sentence, changing the noun phrase to a number used as a pronoun.

1. Five little boys were playing in the mud.

   _____

2. I have eleven pairs of socks in that drawer.

   _____

3. The two older gentlemen are friends of mine.

   _____

4. One excellent suggestion came from Ms. Garcia.

   _____

5. There were five clean plates on the table a moment ago.

_____

6. The new sales clerk sold her eight beautiful skirts.

_____

7. Three people applied for the same job.

_____

8. There were at least fifty pennies scattered about the floor.

_____

The Pronoun *one*

Many people use the pronoun *one* in a more traditional or formal style. But it can be replaced by *you* in casual speech. Either pronoun—*one* or *you*—is used when someone does not want to use a pronoun that identifies a specific person; they are used to speak *in general*. If you substitute the pronoun *someone* for *one*, you will have the approximate meaning of *one*. Like other pronouns, *one* and *you* have four functions:

Nominative	Objective	Possessive	Reflexive
one	one	one's	oneself
you	you	your	yourself

(The reflexive will be taken up separately in Unit 11.)

Look how they are used in sentences:

> FORMAL: If **one** believes in ghosts, **one** might be considered superstitious.

> APPROXIMATE MEANING: If **someone** believes in ghosts, **someone** might be considered superstitious.

> CASUAL: If **you** believe in ghosts, **you** might be considered superstitious.

One is a third person pronoun and, therefore, verbs used with this pronoun require the same ending as any other third person pronoun: *he talks, one talks; she goes, one goes; it is, one is*. But if *you* replaces *one*, the ending *-s* is not required in the present tense.

> FORMAL: If **one plays** fairly, **one** always **wins**.

> CASUAL: If **you play** fairly, **you** always **win**.

Do not confuse this special use of *you* with the second person pronoun *you*. They can be used in identical sentences, but the meaning of each sentence is different.

Second person pronoun: John, **you** should always wash your hands.
Replacement for third person pronoun *one*: **You** should always wash your hands. (One should always wash one's hands. Someone should always wash his hands.)

Rewrite each sentence, changing the pronoun one *in each sentence to* you.

1. One must have strength to carry on.

   _____

2. Should one always be on time for one's lessons?

   _____

3. If one loses one's wallet, one should report that to the police.

   _____

4. One ought to try to stay in shape.

   _____

5. When one drinks too much, one gets drunk.

   _____

6. One has little choice when it comes to love.

   _____

7. One should always behave oneself.

   _____

8. How can one be so mean to her?

   _____

9. If one has too much time on one's hands, one needs to find a job.

   _____

10. When one has humility, one also has respect.

    _____

Rewrite each sentence below twice: once with the pronoun one *and once with the casual replacement pronoun* you.

1. She might get into a lot of trouble.

   _____

   _____

2. If they speak slowly, they are better understood.

   _____

   _____

3. My friends ought to consider taking the train there.

_____

_____

4. Should he criticize his own mistakes?

_____

_____

5. Children learn slowly when they are very young.

_____

_____

6. In time, people accept their limitations.

_____

_____

7. If the man carries on like a fool, he'll be considered a fool.

_____

_____

8. When the girls get a little too heavy, they should begin to exercise.

_____

_____

Using pronouns in sentences

In the category of pronouns, people tend to be most familiar with personal pronouns, since these parts of speech are widely used in the English language. Other types of pronouns also exist, however, and they must be identified and practiced in order for you to be able to use them well in sentence writing. This chapter addresses the following types of pronouns: personal pronouns, relative pronouns, demonstrative pronouns, reflexive pronouns, indefinite pronouns, reciprocal pronouns, and intensive pronouns.

All pronouns are used as a replacement for a form of a noun. For example:

♦ Pronoun as a subject

   the man is → **he** is

♦ Pronoun as an object

   we saw **the man** → we saw **him**

♦ Possessive pronoun

   the man's → **his**

Personal pronouns

The personal pronouns have a subjective form, an objective from, and a possessive form. The subjective form is used in place of a noun subject of a sentence. The objective form is used in place of a noun serving as either a direct object, an indirect object, or the object of a preposition. The possessive form replaces a possessive noun formed with an apostrophe plus *s* (for example, **Bill's**) or in a prepositional phrase introduced by **of** (for example, **of Bill**). The personal pronouns are as follows:

Subjective	Objective	Possessive
I	me	my/mine
you	you	your/yours
he	him	his/his
she	her	her/hers
it	it	its/its
we	us	our/ours
they	them	their/theirs
who	whom	whose/whose
what	what	whose/whose

When a possessive modifies a noun, the first possessive form in the preceding list of pairs is used:

My car is new.
Her books were on the floor.
Their tent blew over in the wind.

When the possessive is used in place of the possessive word and the noun it modifies, the noun is omitted, and the second form of the pairs is used.

Mine is new.
Hers were on the floor.
Theirs blew over in the wind.

It is only the third-person pronouns (**he, she, it, they, who,** and **what**) that are substitutions for a noun. **He, she,** and **it** replace singular nouns.

The doctor is young.	**He** is young.
Their daughter was ill.	**She** was ill.
Jim opened the cage.	**He** opened it.

They replaces plural nouns—both animate and inanimate.

Are **the boys** home?	Are **they** home?
Did you meet **our visitors**?	Did you meet **them**?

Both **who** and **what** are used in questions.

Jack broke his arm.	**Who** broke his arm?
The dog ate **the pie**.	**What** did the dog eat?

The first- and second-person pronouns (**I, you, we**) are not replacements for nouns but rather function on their own. However, **I** can be combined with nouns or other pronouns, and that combination can be replaced by a form of **we**. For example:

Jane and I live on the same street.	**We** live on the same street.
The girls saw **Tom and me**.	The girls saw **us**.
You and I will always be friends.	**We** will always be friends.
She and I started a club.	**We** started a club.

A pronoun serves as the subject in each of the following sentences. Using that pronoun as your cue, write one sentence with that pronoun serving as a direct or indirect object; write a second sentence using the pronoun as the object of a preposition; and write a third sentence using the pronoun as a possessive. Link the content of each sentence so that you create a simple story line.

EXAMPLE: She developed a friendship with John.

<u>Did John take her out on a date?</u>

<u>Not really, but John spoke with her every day.</u>

<u>Her father never really grew to like John.</u>

1. They broke down on a regular basis.

   a. _____

   b. _____

   c. _____

2. It destroyed several houses on the edge of town.

   a. _____

   b. _____

   c. _____

3. We never allowed the dogs in the dining room during meals.

   a. _____

   b. _____

   c. _____

4. I want to travel to Mexico during winter vacation.

   a. _____

   b. _____

   c. _____

5. You bought new clothes and shoes but never went to the party.

   a. _____

   b. _____

   c. _____

6. He had to laugh when he saw his brother dressed as a clown.

   a. _____

   b. _____

   c. _____

7. She caught a bad cold and had to stay home a few days.

a. _____

b. _____

c. _____

Relative pronouns

Relative pronouns are used to combine two sentences that contain identical nouns or pronouns. The sentence in which the noun is replaced by a relative pronoun becomes a subordinating clause. As such, that clause cannot stand alone; it functions as part of the main clause. The person and number of the antecedent of the relative pronoun will determine the person and number of the relative pronoun.

person and number of antecedent → person and number of relative pronoun

The English relative pronouns are **who**, **whom**, **whose**, **which**, **that**, and an elliptical form, in which the relative pronoun is omitted but understood. The forms of **who** and **which** are used to introduce a *nonrestrictive* relative clause—that is, a clause that gives *parenthetical information*. Nonrestrictive relative clauses are set off from the rest of the sentence by commas. **That** introduces a *restrictive* relative clause—that is, a clause that defines the antecedent in the main clause. Let's look at some example sentences:

◆ Nonrestrictive relative clauses

He met the mayor, **who** was elected in a landslide.

The primary information is that *he met the mayor*. The writer of this sentence is giving incidental information (*the mayor was elected in a landslide*) that is not necessarily pertinent to the fact that *he met the mayor*.

She approached the officer, **whom** her brother knew from college.

The primary information is that *she approached the officer*. The writer of this sentence is giving incidental information (*her brother knew the officer from college*) that is not necessarily pertinent to the fact that *she approached the officer*.

I opened the ledger, **which** had two large ink stains on it.

The primary information is that *I opened the ledger*. The writer of this sentence is giving incidental information (*the ledger had two large ink stains on it*) that is not necessarily pertinent to the fact that *I opened the ledger*.

The relative clauses just illustrated merely provide parenthetical information; the information is not necessary for the meaning of the main clause. Those clauses could be omitted, because they do not enhance the meaning of the main clause:

He met the mayor.
She approached the officer.
I opened the ledger.

◆ Restrictive relative clauses

He met the mayor **that** was accused of unethical practices.

He didn't meet just any mayor. The relative clause explains more about its antecedent: *this mayor was accused of unethical practices.*

She approached the officer **that** had given her a ticket.

She didn't approach just any officer. The relative clause explains more about its antecedent: *this officer had given her a ticket.*

I opened the ledger **that** was hidden in the back of my boss's closet.

I didn't open just any ledger. The relative clause explains more about its antecedent: *this ledger was hidden in the back of my boss's closet.*

When writing sentences with relative clauses in them, it is necessary to choose the appropriate relative pronoun. If you wish to make a parenthetical statement, choose a nonrestrictive relative pronoun. If you wish to add information that explains the antecedent in the main clause, choose a restrictive relative pronoun. For example:

David danced with the woman, **who** has a summer house on the shore.
David danced with the woman **that** had been flirting with him.
David danced with the woman **who** had been flirting with him.

Be aware that **who** can function as a restrictive relative pronoun and can replace **that.**

♦ Elliptical relative pronouns

I found the little ashtray (**that**) you made in junior high school.
We finally arrived at the corner (**that**) John had been waiting on for hours.
Here's the jacket (**that**) I bought yesterday.

Notice that the word **that** can be omitted in these clauses only when they are used as objects. When **that** is used as the subject of the clause, it must be retained.

Here's the jacket **that** was made in France.   *subject*
Have you met our new neighbors **that** live on Hyde Street?   *subject*

An elliptical relative pronoun can be derived from a clause containing either **that** or **which**. However, when the relative pronoun is omitted, the tone of the clause becomes restrictive.

Here's the jacket, **which** I bought yesterday.   → Here's the jacket I bought yesterday.
Here's the jacket **that** I bought yesterday.   → Here's the jacket I bought yesterday.

It is correct to use **whose** to refer to either an animate or an inanimate antecedent. With inanimate antecedents, the prepositional phrase **of which** can replace **whose**. For example:

♦ Animate antecedents

Tim liked the girl, **whose** eyes were following him wherever he went.
Have you interviewed the man **whose** house burned down?

♦ Inanimate antecedents

She bought a sweater, **whose** dark color didn't flatter her.
She bought a sweater, the dark color **of which** didn't flatter her.

The judge studied the document, **whose** content was extremely vague.
The judge studied the document, the content **of which** was extremely vague.

Prepositions in relative clauses require a special look. Their position is not static; they can occupy two different places in the clause. In formal style, the preposition precedes a nonrestrictive relative pronoun. For example:

The lawyer, **from whom** he received the information, is under investigation.
I cannot explain the circumstances **under which** she gradually lost her wealth.
They innocently hiked toward the woods **in which** cannibals were said to dwell.

In a less formal style, the preposition can be placed at the end of the clause:

The lawyer, **whom** he received the information **from**, is under investigation.

In a still less formal style, the correct use of **whom** is avoided:

The lawyer, **who** he received the information **from**, is under investigation.

When **that** and **who(m)** are used as restrictive relative pronouns, prepositions always appear at the end of the relative clause. This is also true with elliptical relative pronouns.

The dress **that** she slipped into was much too big for her.
The dress she slipped into was much too big for her.

That's the old man **whom** Thomas works for.
That's the old man Thomas works for.

EXERCISE
4·27

Complete each sentence that follows with an appropriate nonrestrictive relative clause.

EXAMPLE: Henry ordered a cheese pizza, <u>which is not his girlfriend's favorite food.</u>

1. The soldiers stormed the fort, _____ .

2. We spent a week in the capital, _____ .

3. I'd like to introduce you to our new coach, _____ .

4. Dr. Flores, _____ , has to return to Madrid.

5. Can you explain this formula, _____ ?

Follow the same directions, but provide a restrictive relative clause.

6. He hurried up to the boys _____ .

7. I need a laptop _____ .

8. The man _____ is a friend of mine.

9. I'd prefer to speak to the clerk _____ .

10. Send me a copy of the message _____ .

Complete each sentence that follows with (a) a clause that is introduced by a preposition, (b) a nonrestrictive clause that places the preposition at the end of the clause, (c) a restrictive clause with a preposition, and (d) an elliptical pronoun with a preposition.

EXAMPLE: He found a large chest

a. <u>, in which someone had hidden a map.</u>

b. <u>, which he found some money in.</u>

c. <u>that a cat was sleeping on.</u>

d. <u>his father had paid a hundred dollars for.</u>

1. The girls had to find accommodations in a village

a. _____

b. _____

c. _____

d. _____

2. Mr. Dean hoped to speak with the owners

a. _____

b. _____

c. _____

d. _____

3. She made her way to the bed

a. _____

b. _____

c. _____

d. _____

4. Sally believed she was in love with the actor

a. _____

b. _____

c. _____

d. _____

5. I avoid meetings

a. _____

b. _____

c. _____

d. _____

Demonstrative pronouns

The singular demonstrative pronouns are **this** and **that**. **This** refers to someone or something nearby or part of the present topic of conversation. **That** points to someone or something in the distance or referred to in the past. Their plural forms are **these** and **those** and refer, respectively, to something nearby or in the distance. These pronouns also function as adjectives.

located nearby + this/these

located in the distance + that/those

This fellow is in a lot of trouble.   *He is nearby. We're talking about him now.*
That fellow was rather arrogant.   *He is in the distance. We talked about him earlier.*

These people are friends of mine.   *They are nearby. We're talking about them now.*
Those people work for Mr. Paine.   *They are in the distance. We talked about them earlier.*

When these pronouns are not accompanied by a noun, they function as pronouns rather than as adjectives, but their meaning of closeness or distance from a person or thing is maintained.

This is the one I want.
That was the last one.

I borrowed **these** from Jim.
Were **those** once a different color?

As is true of other pronouns, demonstrative pronouns can be subjects or objects. To indicate a possessive, a demonstrative pronoun becomes the object of the preposition **of**. Here are examples:

This really wasn't necessary.   *subject*
Did you buy **those** in Mexico?   *object*
We spoke about **that** a moment ago.   *object of preposition*
What is the meaning of **this**?   *possession with* of

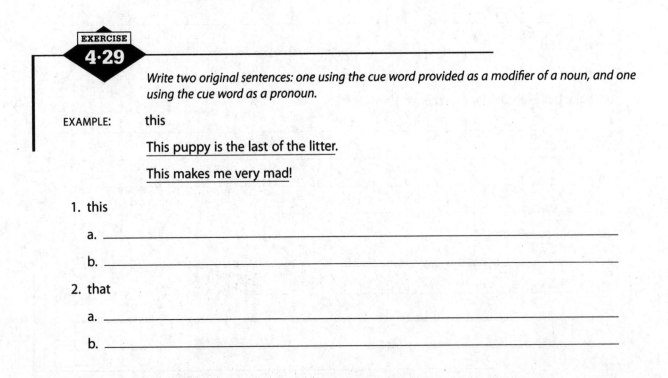

EXERCISE
4·29

Write two original sentences: one using the cue word provided as a modifier of a noun, and one using the cue word as a pronoun.

EXAMPLE: this

This puppy is the last of the litter.

This makes me very mad!

1. this

    a. _____

    b. _____

2. that

    a. _____

    b. _____

3. these

   a. _____

   b. _____

4. those

   a. _____

   b. _____

Reflexive pronouns

Reflexive pronouns are used only as objects and never as subjects of a sentence. They can be direct objects, indirect objects, or the objects of prepositions.

> He cut **himself** shaving.   *direct object*
> He bought **himself** some new ties.   *indirect object*
> He was talking to **himself**.   *object of preposition*

Compare the English personal pronouns with their reflexive-pronoun counterparts:

Personal pronouns	Reflexive pronouns
I	myself
you	yourself
he	himself
she	herself
it	itself
we	ourselves
you	yourselves
they	themselves

When the subject and object are different persons or things, the object is a personal pronoun. For example:

> The **man** asked **her** what happened.
> **We** bought **them** some ice cream.

It is when the subject and object are the same person or thing that a reflexive pronoun is used.

> The **man** asked **himself** what happened.
> **We** bought **ourselves** some ice cream.

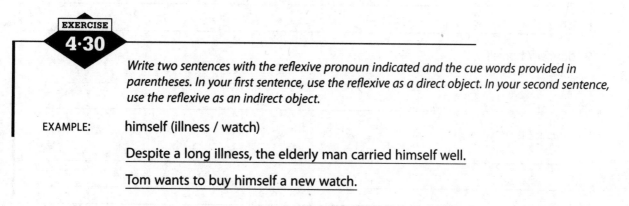

EXERCISE

4·30

Write two sentences with the reflexive pronoun indicated and the cue words provided in parentheses. In your first sentence, use the reflexive as a direct object. In your second sentence, use the reflexive as an indirect object.

EXAMPLE: himself (illness / watch)

      Despite a long illness, the elderly man carried himself well.

      Tom wants to buy himself a new watch.

1. herself (spring / ring)

   a. _____

   b. _____

2. yourself (rarely / soon)

   a. _____

   b. _____

3. ourselves (dinner / dessert)

   a. _____

   b. _____

4. myself (angrily / similar)

   a. _____

   b. _____

5. themselves (sandwiches / wine)

   a. _____

   b. _____

Using the first cue provided, write a sentence with that cue as the object of a preposition. Then, using the reflexive pronoun provided, write a sentence with that pronoun as the object of a preposition.

EXAMPLE: sister / herself

        <u>Maria is going to buy a used car for her sister.</u>

        <u>Maria is going to buy a used car for herself.</u>

6. grandfather / himself

   a. _____

   b. _____

7. soldier / yourselves

   a. _____

   b. _____

8. flight attendant / myself

   a. _____

   b. _____

9. dancer / herself

   a. _____

   b. _____

10. guests / themselves

   a. _____

   b. _____

Indefinite pronouns

The indefinite pronouns have a unique function. They act in a sentence like other pronouns—that is, they are substitutions for nouns; however, the indefinite pronouns are not a replacement for a *specific noun*. Instead, they refer to *anyone, everyone,* or *no one in particular.* Here are some of the most commonly used indefinite pronouns that are always singular:

anyone/anybody	neither
each	no one/nobody
either	one
everyone/everybody	someone/somebody
much	

Each pronoun in the four pairs of indefinite pronouns (**anyone/anybody, everyone/everybody, no one/nobody, someone/somebody**) is identical in meaning to its companion pronoun.

Anyone can play this game.	→ **Anybody** can play this game.
No one understands me.	→ **Nobody** understands me.

Also, do not confuse the indefinite pronoun **one** (a number) with the personal pronoun **one** (*a person*).

Indefinite	**One** of you will have to stay on duty tonight.
Personal	**One** might at first assume that his theory is correct.

It's important to recognize these pronouns as singular, because some of them are used with prepositional phrases that can contain a plural. This construction sometimes causes confusion and results in the use of a plural verb where a singular verb is needed.

> **Each** of the dismissed employees **receives** a termination bonus.

Since **each** is a singular, the singular verb **receives** is needed in this sentence. The plural noun in the prepositional phrase **of the dismissed employees** is not the subject of the sentence.

Here is another example:

> **One** of you **has** to take responsibility.

Since **one** is a singular, the singular verb **has** is needed in this sentence. The plural pronoun **you** is not the subject of the sentence.

Even when more than one person or thing is understood, these pronouns still always use only a singular verb. For example:

> These two ties are the right price, but **neither** really **appeals** to me.

A few indefinite pronouns are plural, such as **both**, **few**, **many**, and **several**, and they require a plural verb when used as the subject of a sentence. For example:

> **Both** of these women **are** candidates for mayor.
> **Few understand** his motives.
> **Many** of his opponents **lie** about his record.

There are also indefinite pronouns that are considered either singular or plural:

all	most
any	none
more	some

The choice of a singular or plural verb with these indefinite pronouns depends on their usage in the sentence and on any accompanying prepositional phrase:

♦ Singular

All is lost!
You can take the last piece of pie. **More is** coming.
Don't eat the whole cake. **Some is** for Bill.

♦ Plural

I met John's fraternity brothers. **Most are** quite nice.
All of the children **have had** their inoculations.
There are several magazines on the floor, but **none are** mine.

EXERCISE
4·31

Using the indefinite pronoun provided, write an original sentence with the pronoun as the subject of the sentence.

1. much _____

2. either _____

3. each _____

4. neither _____

5. one _____

6. everybody _____

7. no one _____

8. few of them _____

9. many _____

10. each of the contestants _____

Reciprocal pronouns

There are only two reciprocal pronouns: **one another** and **each other**. Either one is correct, and each can replace the other in a sentence. They are used to combine two sentences that say that two persons or things are carrying out the same action. For example:

John loves Mary. Mary loves John.	→ John and Mary love **one another**.
The dog glares at the cat. The cat glares at the dog.	→ The dog and cat glare at **each other**.
She kissed me. I kissed her.	→ We kissed **each other**.

When pronouns are used in pairs of sentences as in the last example (**She kissed me. I kissed her.**), the pronoun I indicates that a second-person-plural pronoun (**we**) will be used with a reciprocal pronoun. If the pronoun is in the third person, a third-person-plural pronoun (**they**) will be used with a reciprocal pronoun.

He sees her. She sees him.　　　　　→ They see **one another**.

Intensive pronouns

Intensive pronouns are often mistaken as reflexive pronouns because they look like reflexive pronouns.

Personal pronouns	Intensive pronouns
I	myself
you	yourself
he	himself
she	herself
it	itself
we	ourselves
you	yourselves
they	themselves

Intensive pronouns function differently from reflexive pronouns. Their purpose is to emphasize the subject of the sentence. Compare the following pairs of sentences, in which the subject is emphasized in the second pair.

I believe that war with them can be avoided.
I **myself** believe that war with them can be avoided.

You said that you could afford it.
You **yourself** said that you could afford it.

They are the ones to blame.
They **themselves** are the ones to blame.

EXERCISE 4·32

Rewrite each sentence that follows with the appropriate intensive pronoun.

1. William tried to free the car from the muddy rut.

   _____

2. Several of the men heard the strange sounds in the attic.

   _____

3. I longed to return to my homeland.

   _____

4. Ms. Thomas and I were rather good dancers.

   _____

5. The administration is responsible for our improved economy.

   _____

6. Nancy broke down in tears upon hearing the news.

   _____

7. You tried to get some help for them.

   _____

8. He felt ashamed for what had happened that day.

   _____

9. They attempted to exploit the situation.

   _____

Verbs

The present tense

The present tense has a diverse range of meanings. There are no fewer than seven distinct meanings for the present tense distributed across not only present time but also past and future time as well. Here is a brief summary of the seven different meanings divided into three groups—the first group dealing with present time, the second group dealing with past time, and the third group dealing with future time:

Present time

1. Makes assertions or generalizations about ongoing conditions or states

2. Describes existing habits or customs

3. Comments on present-time actions

Past time

4. Recounts ideas or information from the past that affects us in the present

5. Comments on or paraphrases the works of others

Future time

6. Refers to future events if those events are fixed or scheduled

7. Refers to future events in adverb clauses when the main clause uses *will*

We will now discuss the present, past, and future uses of the present tense in detail.

Using the present tense for present time

Not surprisingly, the most common use of the present tense is for the present period of time. It is critical to understand that there are two fundamentally different ways of conceptualizing what we mean by "present time": (1) the present moment of time, or (2) a span or period of time that is not bound to the present moment of time; that is, the verb describes an ongoing "timeless" state or condition.

If we want to refer to the present moment of time, we do not use the present tense at all; instead, we use the present progressive. If we want to refer to a span or period of present time, we use the present tense.

Here is an example that shows the difference between the two tenses:

Present progressive	Bill is walking the dog.
Present	Bill walks to help control his blood pressure.

The implication of the present progressive sentence is that Bill is out walking at this present moment of time. The present tense sentence does not tell us what Bill is doing at the moment. It tells us that Bill takes walks for his health, but it implies nothing about what Bill is doing at the present moment. In fact, Bill might not have walked for weeks.

EXERCISE

5·1

Each pair of sentences uses the same verb in its infinitive form (in parentheses). One of the sentences uses the verb to talk about an existing present condition; the other sentence uses the verb to talk about the present moment of time. Replace the verb in parentheses with the present tense if the verb is talking about an existing condition. Replace the verb in parentheses with the present perfect if the verb is talking about the present moment of time. The first is done as an example.

treat

Doctors ~~(treat)~~ this type of infection with broad-spectrum antibiotics.

is treating

The doctor ~~(treat)~~ the infection with a broad-spectrum antibiotic.

1. I can't see you. The light (shine) in my eyes.

   The light (shine) against the paintings on the wall.

2. The kids (play) in the living room.

   The kids (play) indoors when it rains.

3. The company (publish) my first novel.

   The company (publish) works by new authors.

4. Bad news always (spread) faster than good news.

   The news (spread) all over town.

5. We (gain) weight as we get older.

   We (gain) weight on this trip.

6. The board (make) the final decision on hiring.

   The board (make) a bad mistake.

7. Conflicts about immigration always (divide) communities.

   The conflict on immigration (divide) the community into factions.

8. The garage always (check) the oil.

   The mechanic (check) the oil now.

9. John (smile) whenever he thinks about what you said.

   John (smile) at what you just said.

10. We (walk) every chance we get.

    We (walk) to the park. Want to come along?

The present tense verbs that treat the present as a "timeless" span or period of time fall into two distinct categories: (1) verbs that make assertions or generalizations about ongoing conditions or states and (2) verbs that describe habits or customs. We will discuss both ways of treating present time.

Assertions or generalizations about ongoing conditions or states. As noted in Chapter 1, verbs in English (and most other languages, for that matter) can be divided into two large families: **dynamic** and **stative**; 99 percent of all verbs belong to the dynamic family. The traditional definition of verb (a word that shows action) refers exclusively to dynamic verbs. Dynamic verbs do things; for example: *run, jump, sing, work, sleep.*

Stative verbs, on the other hand, don't really do anything. Instead, they describe conditions or states. While there are only a relative handful of stative verbs, they are among the most frequently used verbs. For example, *be* and *have* are stative verbs. Here are some examples:

> *Be* Mary is cold.
> Mary is a farmer.
> *Have* Mary has a little lamb.
> The lamb has a ribbon around its neck.

In these example sentences, the subjects (*Mary* and the *lamb*) are not doing anything. Rather, the stative verbs *be* and *have* are used to describe or tell us something about the subjects.

The reason why the distinction between dynamic and stative verbs is relevant to this discussion is that the present tenses of *all* stative verbs make assertions or generalizations about presently existing conditions or states, and as such, they must be used in the present tense because that is what the function of the present tense is: to make assertions about ongoing conditions or states. In fact, if we try to use stative verbs in the present progressive, the result is predictably ungrammatical:

> *Be* **X** Mary is being cold.
> **X** Mary is being a farmer.
> *Have* **X** Mary is having a little lamb.
> **X** The lamb is having a ribbon around its neck.

The inherently different meanings of these two types of verbs cause them to interact very differently with the present tense. The timeless meaning of stative verbs is a perfect match with the timeless meaning of the present tense. Conversely, the time-bound meaning of dynamic verbs makes them incompatible with the basic "timeless" meaning of the present tense; for example, when we use the dynamic verb *buy* in the present, the result is ungrammatical:

> **X** John buys a truck.

As we will see, we can make this and other dynamic verbs grammatical in the present tense, but only if we use them in sentences that make "timeless" assertions or generalizations, or use the verbs to describe habitual or customary actions.

Most stative verbs can be grouped into the following six semantic categories (with examples):

Appearance: appear, be, look, seem
Cognition: believe, know, mean, think, understand
Emotions: appreciate, desire, dislike, doubt, hate, like, need, prefer, want, wish
Measurement: consist of, contain, cost, have, measure, weight
Sense: feel, hear, see, seem, smell, taste
Ownership: belong, have, own, possess

(**Note:** some verbs appear twice because they can be used with different meanings.)

The underlined verbs in the following sentences are all in the present tense. The sentences that use stative verbs are grammatical; the sentences that use dynamic verbs are ungrammatical. In the space provided, write "OK" if the sentence is grammatical; write "Not OK" if the sentence is not grammatical. The first two sentences are done as examples.

I <u>like</u> how you have arranged your office.

ANSWER: OK

We <u>compare</u> the results from the two samples.

ANSWER: Not OK

1. I <u>shake</u> the tree to make the nuts fall off. _____

2. I <u>doubt</u> that we can get to the meeting on time. _____

3. The police <u>identify</u> the suspect. _____

4. His proposal <u>sounds</u> pretty attractive to me. _____

5. We <u>arrange</u> a meeting between the two groups. _____

6. I <u>gain</u> two pounds over the holiday. _____

7. We <u>know</u> what you mean. _____

8. The whole project <u>costs</u> more than we can afford to pay. _____

9. I <u>fill</u> the tank with gas. _____

10. The results in the study closely <u>resemble</u> the result predicted in the model.

_____

11. When the water in the tank <u>equals</u> the water outside the tank, the gate will open.

_____

12. Their lawyer <u>explains</u> the problem. _____

13. The job <u>entails</u> a great deal of travel. _____

14. I <u>watch</u> TV. _____

15. I <u>hear</u> what you are saying. _____

Dynamic verbs can also be used in the present tense, but only if one of the following two conditions on the meaning of the sentence are met: (1) the sentence makes an assertion or generalization about existing conditions or states, or (2) the sentence describes existing habits or customs. Let us take these conditions in order:

The assertions/generalizations can be of an objective, scientific nature; for example:

The planets <u>revolve</u> around the sun.
Fresh water <u>floats</u> on top of sea water.

They can be publicly verifiable; for example:

The semesters at our school <u>last</u> 15 weeks.
He <u>gives</u> private piano lessons.

They can be totally subjective personal opinions; for example:

> Kids today <u>spend</u> too much time playing computer games.
> Greenhouse gases <u>cause</u> global warming.
> Cable TV <u>costs</u> too much.

Notice that none of these examples of dynamic verbs is tied to a specific moment in time. All are essentially "timeless" generalizations.

Existing habits or customs. Here are some examples of verbs in this category:

> I always <u>take</u> my lunch to work.
> We <u>go</u> to the movies every chance we get.
> She normally <u>checks</u> her messages first thing in the morning.
> The westbound train <u>stops</u> here only in the morning.
> The kids usually <u>do</u> their homework right after school.

Verbs in this category describe a behavior that is typical or normal. It does not mean that the action is being performed at the present moment. For example:

> We usually <u>eat</u> dinner at my mother's house on Sunday.

This sentence does not mean that we are eating at my mother's house now. In fact, the sentence would still be a valid statement if we haven't seen my mother in a month.

One of the characteristics of this use of the present tense is that the sentence typically contains an adverb of frequency such as *usually, always, every day, normally,* or *every weekend.*

EXERCISE
5·3

All of the following sentences use the present tense of dynamic verbs, some sentences correctly, some incorrectly. If the sentence is grammatical, write "OK" in the space provided and then give the reason that justifies using the present tense. Use either "assertion" or "habitual." If the use of the present tense is ungrammatical, write "Not OK." The first three sentences are done as examples.

> We usually <u>start</u> around 8:00.

ANSWER: OK habitual

> I <u>ask</u> the same question.

ANSWER: Not OK

> Cold winters <u>kill</u> the beetles that attack pine trees.

ANSWER: OK assertion

1. Eating too much always <u>makes</u> me sleepy.

   _____

2. Garlic <u>lowers</u> one's blood pressure.

   _____

3. The two parties <u>discuss</u> the agreement.

   _____

4. Research <u>proves</u> that listening to loud music permanently damages teenagers' hearing.

   _____

5. The janitor normally <u>locks</u> up after everyone leaves.

   _____

6. The flood waters spread throughout the valley.

_____

7. The nurse treats the wound now.

_____

8. Journalists never tell who their sources are.

_____

9. The company publishes my first book.

_____

10. Ravens and crows recognize people they have seen before.

_____

Finally, there is a third use of the present tense that refers to present time. However, this use is completely different from the first two because this third use actually does refer to the present moment of time (unlike the other two already discussed). We can use the present tense to comment on or describe an ongoing present time action. Obviously, the situations in which we would use the present tense in this manner are highly restricted. The most common situations are sports events, demonstrations, and speech act commentaries. Here are some examples of each type:

Sports event	Here comes the pitch. Johnston swings and misses.
	Rodriguez is tripped in midfield. The referee blows his whistle and gives a yellow card to the defender.
Demonstration	Next, I add a cup of flour and stir in thoroughly.
	Finally, I close all open windows and reboot the computer.
Speech act commentary	I hereby resign from the council.
	We accept your offer.

We have now identified three different ways present tense verbs refer to present time:
- By making assertions or generalizations about ongoing conditions or states
- By describing presently existing habits or customs
- By commenting on present-time ongoing actions

EXERCISE
5·4

The underlined present tense verbs are all used correctly. Identify which of the three ways of using the present tense best describes the verb in each sentence using the following shorthand labels: (1) making assertions; (2) describing habits; (3) commenting on present-time actions. The first is done as an example.

The dog wants to go out for a walk.

ANSWER: (1) making assertions

1. Clothes dry a lot faster in hot weather.

_____

2. Today I announce my candidacy for the presidency of the United States.

_____

3. Houston, we <u>have</u> a problem.

_____

4. This children's cereal <u>contains</u> nothing but sugar and refined carbohydrates.

_____

5. Smith <u>scores</u> from 10 feet out.

_____

6. Janet <u>gets</u> the weather forecast every morning before she decides what to wear.

_____

7. My wife always <u>reads</u> the ending of books first.

_____

8. I really <u>like</u> the food here.

_____

9. New cars <u>cost</u> a fortune to repair because of all the electronics they have in them.

_____

10. The company sends <u>cards</u> to all its employees at Christmas every year.

_____

11. First, we <u>combine</u> all the dry ingredients together in a large bowl.

_____

12. Many people <u>vote</u> for whoever promises to lower their taxes the most.

_____

13. Every night my father <u>locks</u> up the house before he goes to bed.

_____

14. The bus <u>is</u> late this morning.

_____

15. The pond <u>attracts</u> a lot of mosquitoes.

Using the present tense for past time

We use the present tense for referring to the past in two ways: (1) recounting ideas or information from the past that affects us in the present, and (2) commenting on or paraphrasing the works of others.

Recounting ideas or information from the past that affects us in the present

Normally, when we talk or write about specific events, we do so in the past tense. For example, virtually all novels and short stories are written in the past tense. As we will see in the next section of this chapter, the basic meaning of the past tense is that the action described in the past tense is finished—over and done with.

But what if we want to talk about something that happened in the past that directly affects us in the present moment of time? Suppose, for example, that you heard on the evening news that a bad storm was predicted for your area. You could tell other people about the threatening weather in either the past tense or the present tense:

Past tense	The evening news <u>said</u> that a big storm <u>was</u> coming.
Present tense	The evening news <u>says</u> that a big storm <u>is</u> coming.

There is no real difference in meaning, but there is a difference in emphasis: the present tense version is much more immediate and urgent.

Even where there is no sense of urgency, the present tense still implies that the information is new and immediate. For example, compare the following sentences:

Past tense	I <u>heard</u> that you might be moving.
Present tense	I <u>hear</u> that you might be moving.

The use of the present tense suggests that the information is new and relevant to the speaker.

We often use the present tense in discussing older material to emphasize that the content is still relevant to us in the present time. Here are some examples:

St. Paul <u>says</u>, "If I <u>have</u> not charity I <u>am</u> nothing."
Darwin <u>emphasizes</u> that the world <u>is</u> not a static place.
Shakespeare <u>says</u> that all the world <u>is</u> a stage.

Commenting on or paraphrasing the works of others

When we write about the works of others, we often write in the present tense. Reviews of books, plays, movies, and TV programs are typically written in the present tense. For example, here is a brief summary of *The Milagro Beanfield War*. Notice that all of the verbs are in the present tense.

This 1988 fable about community solidarity <u>takes</u> place in the small town of Milagro, New Mexico (population 426). The movie <u>revolves</u> around the attempt by a large corporation to buy enough land in this small town to develop a tourist resort. The main obstacle <u>is</u> Joe Mondragon. Joe <u>takes</u> water that <u>runs</u> by his land to irrigate a field of beans that he <u>plants</u>. Technically, the water <u>is</u> reserved for the corporation, setting in motion a conflict over water rights between the local residents and the corporation. Colorful local characters and beautiful New Mexico scenery along with an intelligent, good-natured script <u>make</u> this a highly successful film.

Reports and summaries are usually written in the present tense. For example, here is a summary of a company's leave policy:

Our current leave policy <u>makes</u> no distinction between vacation leave, sick leave, or personal time. All employees <u>have</u> a base of two weeks leave in their first year with the company. For each subsequent year of continuous employment, employees <u>gain</u> an additional day of leave. The maximum amount of leave that can be accumulated <u>is</u> three weeks per year.

Using the present tense for future time

There are two different grammatical constructions in which the present tense is used to refer to future time: one in main clauses and one in dependent adverb clauses.

In main clauses, we use the present tense to refer to future events if those events are already fixed or scheduled; for example:

The full moon <u>occurs</u> Wednesday night.
The train <u>departs</u> at 11:35.
Tomorrow's *New York Times* <u>covers</u> the Senate race in California.
Next Tuesday <u>is</u> the twenty-third.
I <u>see</u> the dentist tomorrow at 11:00.

There is a colloquial extension of the use of the present tense for proposing a course of action; for example: "OK, here's the plan. I <u>pick</u> up Mary at work, you <u>get</u> the car, and we all <u>meet</u> at the restaurant." In effect, this is a tentative proposal for a schedule of future activities.

We use the present tense for asking questions about predictable future events; for example:

When <u>does</u> the movie start?
When <u>is</u> the tide full?
What <u>day</u> of the week <u>is</u> Christmas this year?
When <u>does</u> the kids' summer program begin?

We would not use the present tense for future events that are less than certain; for example:

X It <u>rains</u> tomorrow.
X I believe that Italy <u>wins</u> the World Cup.
X Our CEO thinks that we <u>get</u> the contract.

EXERCISE

5·5

In all of the following sentences, the present tense is used to refer to the future. If the usage is appropriate, write "OK." If the usage is not appropriate, write "Not OK." The first two sentences are done as examples.

Your presentation <u>begins</u> at 3:30.

ANSWER: OK

The senator easily <u>wins</u> reelection.

ANSWER: Not OK

1. The exam <u>ends</u> in exactly 45 minutes.

_____

2. He <u>washes</u> the dishes.

_____

3. The gates <u>close</u> at 10:00 tonight.

_____

4. Susan <u>finds</u> the missing car keys.

_____

5. We <u>get</u> off the freeway if the traffic gets any worse.

_____

6. The moon <u>rises</u> just after sunset.

_____

7. In order to be competitive, the store <u>drops</u> its prices.

_____

8. When <u>is</u> the game?

   _____

9. Mrs. Brown <u>returns</u> on Monday.

   _____

10. They <u>meet</u> in Los Angeles next week, I believe.

   _____

The other use of the present tense for future time is in adverb clauses when the main clause uses *will* to talk about future time; for example:

A neighbor will look after our cat, while we <u>are</u> away.

   main clause   adverb clause

I will call you if I <u>hear</u> anything.

   main clause   adverb clause

They will start work as soon as they <u>get</u> the necessary permits.

   main clause   adverb clause

They won't win the war even if they <u>win</u> this battle.

   main clause   adverb clause

In all these examples it is very easy to see that the verb in the present tense form is referring to the future just as much as the verb in the main clause that uses *will*.

One of the characteristics of adverb clauses is that they are easily moved in front of the main clause. As a result, the present tense used for future time can come before the main clause with *will*; for example:

While we <u>are</u> away, a neighbor will look after our cat.

   adverb clause   main clause

If I <u>hear</u> anything, I will call you.

   adverb clause   main clause

As soon as they <u>get</u> the necessary permits, they will start work.

   adverb clause   main clause

Even if they <u>win</u> this battle, they won't win the war.

   adverb clause   main clause

Note that when an adverb clause is moved from its normal position following the main clause and placed in front of the main clause, the adverb clause is set off from the main clause by a comma. This use of the comma is obligatory.

The following sentences contain both a main clause and an adverb clause (in either order), with blank spaces where the verbs go. Underneath each sentence are two verbs in their infinitive forms. Insert the verbs into the appropriate clauses as directed. Make sure that each verb is used in the correct form to refer to future time. The first sentence is done as an example. Hint: the adverb clause always begins with an adverb or adverb phrase (for example: when, if, before).

Whatever they <u>need</u> us to do, we <u>will do</u>.

main clause: <u>do</u>; adverb clause: <u>need</u>

1. If I _____ him, I _____ hello.

   main clause: <u>say</u>; adverb clause: <u>see</u>

2. Until they _____ some more money, they _____ trouble paying for it.

   main clause: <u>have</u>; adverb clause: <u>save</u>

3. We definitely _____ if they _____ us the job.

   main clause: <u>accept</u>; adverb clause: <u>offer</u>

4. As soon I _____ home, I _____ dinner.

   main clause: <u>start</u>; adverb clause: <u>get</u>

5. We _____ a movie after we _____ eating.

   main clause: <u>watch</u>; adverb clause: <u>finish</u>

6. Once I _____ my check, I _____ for a new apartment.

   main clause: <u>look</u>; adverb clause: <u>get</u>

7. The game still _____ played, even if it _____.

   main clause: <u>be</u>; adverb clause: <u>rain</u>

8. We _____ ahead as planned, even though there _____ some objections.

   main clause: <u>go</u>; adverb clause: <u>be</u>

9. Unless there _____ a problem, we _____ you in Denver tomorrow.

   main clause: <u>meet</u>; adverb clause: <u>be</u>

10. I _____ to visit them next time I _____ to Phoenix.

    main clause: <u>try</u>; adverb clause: <u>go</u>

In this section we have identified the following seven meanings and uses of the present tense (numbered for use in the following exercise):

Present time

1. Makes assertions or generalizations about ongoing conditions or states

2. Describes existing habits or customs

3. Comments on present-time actions

Past time

4. Recounts ideas or information from the past that affects us in the present

5. Comments on or paraphrases the works of others

Future time

6. Refers to future events if those events are fixed or scheduled

7. Refers to future events in adverb clauses when the main clause uses *will*

EXERCISE
5·7

Each one of the following sentences contains an underlined present tense verb. Identify which of the seven uses best describes the meaning and use of that present tense verb using the numbers previously given. The first is done as an example.

The weather <u>seems</u> unusually hot for this time of year. (1)

1. Hurry up! The game <u>starts</u> in five minutes. _____

2. Anne's white paper <u>warns</u> against the risk of inflation. _____

3. As Freud <u>says</u>, "Sometimes a cigar is only a cigar." _____

4. In his essay, Whitehill <u>argues</u> for a return to the gold standard. _____

5. Good advance planning <u>saves</u> a lot of time in the long run. _____

6. Hardship <u>teaches</u> self-reliance. _____

7. I usually <u>decline</u> getting the extended warranties on things I buy. _____

8. When we <u>know</u> the date, we will send out the invitations. _____

9. I hereby <u>nominate</u> Joe Smith for Congress. _____

10. Raising children <u>requires</u> a lot of patience. _____

11. We <u>fly</u> back to Madison on Wednesday. _____

12. My mother always <u>saves</u> empty plastic containers. _____

13. The goalie <u>blocks</u> a hard shot from the left corner. _____

14. The pilots will take off just as soon as they <u>get</u> clearance. _____

15. Darwin's research <u>rests</u> on a wealth of observational studies. _____

The past tense

The main use of the past tense is for events, conditions, or states that once existed in or during some past time but that do not exist in the present. There are two other non-past-time uses for the past tense: (1) hypothetical statements and (2) polite questions and deferential requests.

Using the past tense for past time

The past tense is used for events, conditions, or states that are now over and done with. So, for example:

> Samantha <u>went</u> to school at Berkeley.

This sentence not only tells us where Samantha went to school but also tells us that Samantha is no longer going to school there.

The past tense is quite broad in the sense that it can refer to variety of past-time uses; for example:

A single point of past time
The power <u>went</u> out at 7:15 this morning.
I <u>picked</u> up the kids after school.

A span of time
I <u>worked</u> in that office from 2001 to 2006.
The most recent ice age <u>lasted</u> for about 13,000 years.

Habitual or repeated events
We always <u>got</u> the *New York Times* when we lived in the city.
They <u>went</u> to the same hotel every anniversary.

States or conditions that existed at some past time
Jason always <u>admired</u> his father's achievements.
I <u>hated</u> having to take piano lessons when I was in grade school.

In all these different uses of the past tense, there is always the implication that it is no longer true today. Even ongoing states and conditions are tied (and limited) to the past. For example:

> The children <u>loved</u> being read to at bedtime.

This sentence implies that the children are no longer being read to: either they have outgrown being read to or for some other reason no one reads to them anymore.

Other uses of the past tense

There are two other uses of the past tense:

* Hypothetical statements
* Polite questions and deferential requests

We will discuss these two uses of the past tense in turn.

Hypothetical statements

The past tense in modern English has inherited some of the functions of the subjective mood that existed in older forms of the language. One of these functions is making statements that are hypothetical or even contrary to fact. Needless to say, the past tense form in this subjunctive use does not mean past time; quite the contrary: this use of the subjunctive is often used to talk about the present or future (but in a tentative, hypothetical way).

The most distinctive use of the past tense for hypothetical statements is seen in constructions that preserve the historical subjunctive use of *were* instead of the expected *was*. Here are some examples:

> If I <u>were</u> you, I would try harder.
> I wish I <u>were</u> feeling better.
> It's not as though he <u>were</u> guilty of a crime.
> Suppose we <u>were</u> to quit our jobs.

If clauses have an unusual feature: all the verbs in the main clause that accompany the adverbial *if* clause must also be in the past tense. Here is an example of an *if* clause with multiple verbs in the main clause:

> If I <u>were</u> you, I <u>would</u> be careful of what I <u>said</u>.
>
>   main clause

Both verbs in the main clause, *would* and *said*, are in the past tense. In fact, if the verbs in the main clause were in the present or future tense, the sentence would become ungrammatical:

Present tense	**X** If I <u>were</u> you, I <u>am</u> careful of what I <u>say</u>.
Future tense	**X** If I <u>were</u> you, I <u>will</u> be careful of what I <u>will say</u>.

This is the only instance in English in which the subordinate clause controls the verb tense of the main clause.

EXERCISE
5·8

Add the hypothetical if *clause* if I were you *to the following sentences, making the necessary changes to the verb tenses in the main clause. The first sentence is done as an example.*

I will tell them what they need to do.

ANSWER: If I were you, I <u>would</u> tell them what they <u>needed</u> to do.

1. I will watch what I eat.

   _____

2. I will talk only about what I know.

   _____

3. I will remind them what they agree to pay.

   _____

4. I will be worried about where I park my car.

   _____

5. I will start working only when I have enough light to see what I am doing.

   _____

Polite questions and deferential requests

The past tense also inherits another feature of the subjunctive: deference or polite indirectness. This form of the subjunctive is used in asking questions and making requests when we want to show consideration or even polite deference to the person we are talking to. The use of the past tense form signals the person we are talking to that that person has no obligation to agree to or approve our request (which is put in the form of a question). Another way to think of it is that we are signaling that we are not acting as a superior talking to a subordinate as might be the implication of a direct question in the present tense. For example, if we were talking to friends or social equals, we would probably invite them to lunch in the present tense:

> <u>Do</u> you want to go out for lunch?

However, if we were talking to a superior or a person we did not know well, we would probably phrase the invitation in a more indirect manner using the past tense:

> <u>Did</u> you want to go out for lunch today?

Here is another example. We would probably ask a colleague for some time by saying:

> <u>Can</u> you give me a minute?

But we would make the same request of a superior in the past tense:

> <u>Could</u> you give me a minute?

We would ask equals if they were ready to leave in the present tense:

> <u>Are</u> you ready to leave?

But we would ask a superior the same thing in the past tense:

> <u>Were</u> you ready to leave?

EXERCISE
5·9

Here are ordinary questions that one might ask of equals. Change the questions to the corresponding polite or deferential form. The first sentence is done as an example:

Do you need to get something?

ANSWER: <u>Did</u> you need to get something?

1. What do you think about it?

   _____

2. Will you join us for lunch?

   _____

3. Can you stop by my office before you leave?

   _____

4. Will you be free this evening?

_____

5. May I make an alternative proposal?

_____

The future tense

In traditional grammar, the future tense consists of the helping verb *will* followed by a verb in its **base form**. The base form of a verb is the dictionary entry form of the verb. It is an infinitive without the *to*; for example:

> I will call you as soon as I get a chance.

In this example, *call* is in its base form. *Will* plus the base-form verb *call* is thus the future tense of *call*.

The way traditional grammar defines the future tense (helping verb plus base-form verb) is radically different from the way that the present and past tenses are defined. The present and past tenses are defined by a change in the verb itself, either by adding an ending (*-s* in the case of the present; *-ed* in the case of the past tense) or by a change in the form of the verb, as in the case of irregular verbs. To understand the implications of the traditional definition of the future tense, we need to understand a bit about the very peculiar history of the future tense in English.

In the past, the ancestor language of English (called Indo-European) formed the future tense as all other verb tenses: by a change in the verb itself. This future tense is related to the future tenses that survive today in most modern-day languages of Indo-European origin, for example, French, Italian, Greek, Russian, and the languages of northern India.

Later, the common Indo-European language broke apart into separate branches. The branch that ultimately leads to English is Germanic (the Germanic languages besides English are Dutch, German, and the Scandinavian languages). One of the main characteristics of the Germanic branch that sets it apart from all the other branches of Indo-European is that the future tense verb ending totally disappeared. That is, none of the Germanic languages (including English) has a verb tense form that means future time.

The disappearance of the future tense verb form in the ancestral Germanic language was probably the result of another development unique to the Germanic languages: the creation of a remarkable set of helping verbs called **modal verbs.** These modal verbs provided speakers with a more sophisticated and flexible way of talking about the future. It is entirely likely that the future verb tense form was driven into extinction by the rise of these modal verbs. The modern English forms of the modal verbs are the following: *can, may, must, shall,* and *will.*

These five verbs can all be used with infinitives to talk about the future:

> I can call him later.
> I may call him later.
> I must call him later.
> I shall call him later.
> I will call him later.

We can even use the past tense forms of these verbs (except *must*, which has no past tense) to talk about the future:

> I could call him later.
> I might call him later.
> I should call him later.
> I would call him later if I were you.

As you can see, these nine verb forms allow English speakers to talk about the future in a number of highly nuanced ways—much more than a single future tense verb form would ever allow.

If all of these helping verbs have evolved to become the way that English speakers talk about future time, then why was *will* singled out by traditional grammar as "the future tense" in English? There are two reasons: (1) *will* is the closest in meaning of all nine modal forms to the meaning of the future tense in Latin (Latin is the basis of traditional grammars of English), and (2) the basic meaning of *will* is simple futurity; all of the other modal verbs have a variety of additional meanings such as necessity, possibility, and obligation. Because Latin has nothing similar to modal verbs, traditional Latin-based grammars of English simply ignored the remaining modal verbs.

In this chapter we will examine *will* because (1) it is the traditional marker of the future tense, and (2) it is by far the most common way of talking about future time. We will also examine the four nonmodal ways that English speakers commonly use to refer to future time.

Using *will* to talk about future time

We use *will* in two quite different ways: (1) prediction and (2) intention.

Will is used to make predictions about some future event, behavior, or outcome. Here are some examples:

> The weatherman says that it will rain all day tomorrow.
> You will feel better after a good night's sleep.
> The stock market will react negatively to such bad economic news.
> They will never agree to such a proposal.
> Who knows how soon the volcano will erupt again?
> Will the store be open on Sunday?

We can also use *will* in a somewhat different way to talk about characteristic behaviors or actions (which, of course, we predict will reoccur in the future); for example:

> Sally will play with that toy all day.
> They will end up arguing about politics as usual.
> My father will want to pick up the check.
> The market will, as usual, overreact to any unexpected development.
> On vacation we will get up late every morning and go for a walk before breakfast.

Will is also used to make a statement of someone's intention to carry out some future action. This use of *will* requires an animate subject that acts volitionally to carry out a purposeful future act. Here are some examples:

> I will give you a hand with that.
> He will call you back as soon as he gets a chance.
> I will stop by after work if it is not too late.
> Jerry will never allow that to happen.
> The company will petition the court for an injunction to stop the strike.

This meaning of *will* is used for requests for future actions and questions about a person's intentions or willingness to do something in the future; for example:

> Will you answer the phone?
> Will you set the table, please?
> Will you be able to attend the meeting?
> Will the union cooperate?

Will used as an expression of intention is often replaced in questions or requests by *would* as a form of respect or politeness; for example:

> Will/would you help me with this?
> Will/would that be OK with you?
> Will/would you take care of that?
> Would you like to dance?

(For a detailed discussion of polite questions and deferential requests, see Chapter 3, "The past tense.")

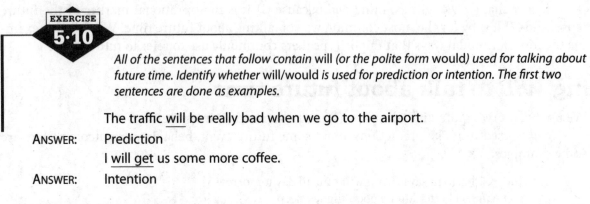

EXERCISE
5·10

All of the sentences that follow contain will *(or the polite form* would*) used for talking about future time. Identify whether* will/would *is used for prediction or intention. The first two sentences are done as examples.*

The traffic will be really bad when we go to the airport.

ANSWER: Prediction

I will get us some more coffee.

ANSWER: Intention

1. I think that the committee will not approve his application the way it is written now.

_____

2. The maintenance staff will have finished by now.

_____

3. We will certainly do our best to meet your expectations.

_____

4. Would you like to leave a message?

_____

5. They are so good that I think they will qualify for the World Cup this year.

_____

6. I will go home the back way so you can see the river.

_____

7. The lawyer thinks that they will settle out of court.

_____

8. We <u>would like</u> some more coffee, please.

   _____

9. You <u>will have</u> a hard time selling the house in this economy.

   _____

10. I <u>will think</u> about it.

    _____

Other ways of talking about future time

There are four nonmodal ways to talk about future time:

Present progressive tense
Present tense
- *Be going to* plus base form
- *Be about to* plus base form

The present progressive and present tenses are similar in meaning, but the present progressive tense is much broader in its use than the present tense. We will discuss the present progressive tense first, then we will turn to the more restricted present tense, and finally we will discuss the differences and similarities between these two ways of talking about the future.

Present progressive tense

The present progressive tense refers to future events that arise directly (and often immediately) from present plans, arrangements, or commitments; for example:

We <u>are continuing</u> the presentation after lunch.
The children <u>are going</u> to the park this afternoon.
They <u>are taking</u> a taxi to the airport.
The president <u>is making</u> a speech here next month.
My parents <u>are staying</u> in Arizona this winter.

As you can see from these examples, the present progressive tense is often used with animate subjects; these subjects are the ones who make the plans, the arrangements, or the commitments that cause the future action. The present progressive can also be used with inanimate subjects, but only if the action or event is arranged, scheduled, or highly predictable; for example:

The play <u>is opening</u> Friday night.
According to the weather channel, it'<u>s getting</u> warmer tomorrow.
The trains <u>are running</u> on a holiday schedule Monday.
The cherry trees in Washington <u>are blooming</u> next week.
Our team <u>is playing</u> at home next week.

There is one important restriction on the use of the present progressive: many stative verbs cannot be used in the present progressive. Here are some examples with stative verbs:

X We <u>are needing</u> to change trains at the next station.
X They <u>are wanting</u> to talk to us.
X The kids <u>are feeling</u> bad if we don't come.

We often use the present progressive for announcing imminent actions or events; for example:

> We are ordering takeout; let me know what you want.
> Your coffee is getting cold.
> Kids, we're leaving soon.
> Come to the table; we're eating in just a minute.
> Hurry, the game is starting right after this commercial.
> The market is opening in five minutes.

Present tense

The present tense can refer to future events, but only if those events have already been determined. It is the tense we would use for scheduled or fixed events; for example:

> Jayne's wedding is June 18.
> Our plane departs at 8:15.
> I see the dentist next Tuesday.
> They get back next week.
> The plays there start at 8:30.

We cannot use the present tense for unscheduled future actions or events; for example:

> X It rains tomorrow.
> X They are upset if we don't get the contract.
> X I come back early unless there is a problem.
> X We go home soon.

The use of the present tense for future time is more restricted than the present progressive. For example, all of the following sentences in the present progressive are grammatical:

> We are ordering takeout; let me know what you want.
> Your coffee is getting cold.
> Kids, we are leaving now.
> Come to the table; we are eating in just a minute.
> Hurry, the game is starting right after this commercial.
> The market is opening in a few minutes.

When we use the present tense in these same examples, the results are surprisingly diverse: some (marked with **X**) are flatly ungrammatical, some (marked with **?**) are probably grammatical but sound odd, and some are perfectly grammatical:

> X We order takeout; let me know what you want.
> X Your coffee gets cold.
> ? Kids, we leave now.
> ? Come to the table; we eat in just a minute.
> Hurry, the game starts right after this commercial.
> The market opens in a few minutes.

The degree of grammaticality in using the present tense is a function of how formally the future event is scheduled. In the first two examples, there is no scheduling or planning at all; they are extemporaneous, unplanned statements about the future, and, as such, they are clearly incompatible with the present tense:

> X We order takeout; let me know what you want.
> X Your coffee gets cold.

The last two examples refer to formally scheduled future events:

> Hurry, the game <u>starts</u> right after this commercial.
> The market <u>opens</u> in a few minutes.

These are completely grammatical in the present tense.

The middle two examples are in between planned and unplanned. That is, they are not formally planned, but they are not really extemporaneous either. The borderline grammaticality of these two sentences reflects the fact that they are quasi-planned.

> **?** Kids, we <u>leave</u> now.
> **?** Come to the table; we <u>eat</u> in just a minute.

Here is another pair of sentences that illustrates the difference between the present and present progressive for future time:

Present	**X** I <u>take</u> a group picture after class.
Present progressive	I <u>am taking</u> a group picture after class.

Both of these sentences are talking about carrying out a future-time activity. The problem with using the present tense is that the activity is not formally scheduled. Its extemporaneous nature makes it incompatible with the present tense. Using the present tense this way is a common mistake for even advanced nonnative speakers of English.

The much tighter restrictions on the use of the present tense mean that many verbs that can be used quite normally in the present progressive for future time cannot be used in the present tense.

EXERCISE
5·11

All of the following sentences contain grammatical uses of the present progressive tense. Change each use of the present progressive into the present tense, and then determine the grammatical validity of the result. If the result is fully grammatical, write "OK." If the result is not grammatical or is distinctly odd, write "Not OK." The first two sentences are done as examples.

She <u>is having</u> a baby next June.

ANSWER: She <u>has</u> a baby next June. Not OK

She <u>is going</u> into the hospital next week.

ANSWER: She <u>goes</u> into the hospital next week. OK

1. Everyone <u>is staying</u> with friends until the water recedes.

_____

2. They <u>are moving</u> out of the apartment at the end of the month.

_____

3. I <u>am waxing</u> the car as soon as the water dries.

_____

4. We <u>are helping</u> the public radio fund-raising program Saturday from noon till 4:00.

_____

5. Loretta is presenting the keynote at this year's conference.

   _____

6. They are selling their house as soon as they get a reasonable offer.

   _____

7. The course is covering that material in the last week.

   _____

8. Because of global warming, some insurance companies are raising their flood insurance rates next year.

   _____

9. The contractor is laying the carpet as soon as he can get the pad installed.

   _____

10. I am teaching that class next semester.

   _____

The difference we have seen between present progressive and present tense carries over to situations in which both the present progressive and present tenses are grammatical. For example, compare the following sentences:

Present progressive	Our flight is leaving at 8:15.
Present	Our flight leaves at 8:15.

These two sentences mean the same thing, but there is a difference in their implications. Using the present progressive implies that this is new information: either it is new information to the person being spoken to, or the original flight departure time has been changed, and thus it is new information for everybody. If it is the latter, there is the additional implication that this new time is not firmly scheduled and is thus subject to further change.

Using the present tense implies that the flight is definitely scheduled to leave at 8:15. If this is a new time, it implies that this new time is a formal rescheduling of the original departure time, and as such we have some expectation that this departure time is reliable information.

Finally, we need to mention another, unrelated use of the present tense for future time. We use it in adverb clauses when the main clause uses *will* to indicate future time; for example:

If she pushes this button, the outdoor lights will go on.

adverb clause   main clause

When he moves there next month, he will need to get new furniture.

adverb clause   main clause

The adverb and main clause can be used in either order:

The outdoor lights will go on if she pushes this button.

main clause   adverb clause

He will need to get new furniture when he moves there next month.

main clause   adverb clause

See Chapter 2 for a detailed discussion of this rather specialized use of the present tense.

Be going to plus base form

This idiomatic construction uses some form of *be* in the present tense to express future action; for example:

> I am going to take the 5:45 train.
> The price of gold is going to fall dramatically.

An alternative analysis would be to describe this construction as follows:

> *be going* plus infinitive

An infinitive consists of *to* plus a base-form verb. Obviously, either description will work. The reason that linguists prefer *be going to* plus base-form verb is that is it easy to break the construction apart between the *to* and the base-form verb, suggesting that the *to* is more like a preposition than the marker of an infinitive. Here is a brief dialogue that separates the *to* from the base-form verb:

> A: Do you think George will ever retire?
> B: Yes, I think he actually is going to this summer. (*Retire* is understood.)

If *to retire* were a single grammatical unit, we would not expect to separate the *to* and *retire* so easily.

Here are some more examples of this construction:

> Aunt Mae and Uncle Jim are going to sell the farm.
> The storm is going to hit sometime tomorrow morning.
> Our mayor is going to run for Congress this fall.

When the subject is an animate noun, *be going to* plus base-form verb signals a strong intention of the subject to carry out the future action specified, almost as a statement of commitment. Here are some more examples with animate subjects:

> We are going to get married.
> The company is going to open a new branch in Seattle.
> They are going to meet us at the park.
> I am going to mow the lawn now.

With inanimate subjects, the speaker is asserting confidence that the described future event is highly likely to actually happen; for example:

> It's going to start raining any minute.
> The reception is going to be at her aunt's house.
> His speech is going to create a lot of controversy.
> The train is going to be half an hour late.

We can even use this construction with non-referential, existential subjects like *there* and *it* as long as the speaker has confidence in the validity of what is said:

> There is going to be a staff meeting Friday.
> It's going to be really hot tomorrow.

Be about to plus base form

This is another idiomatic construction that also uses some form of *be* in the present tense to express future action; for example:

> Hurry, the light is about to change.
> Let's sit down. The presentation is about to begin.

I'm about to give up.
The boat is about to leave.

The *to* in this construction also acts as a preposition rather than the marker of an infinitive because we can so easily separate the *to* and the verb; for example:

A: Are you going to quit soon?
B: Yes, I am just about to. (*Quit* is understood.)

Be about to plus base form is used to emphasize that something is on the verge of happening. It is used to emphasize the immediacy of what is going to happen in the very near future. *Be about to* plus base form can be used only with verbs that convey a strong sense of immediate action. As we would expect, this construction is most often used with verbs that have animate subjects that perform the action of the verb; for example:

John is about to look for a new job.
The company is about to open a new plant in Mexico.
Can't it wait? We're just about to leave.
The president is about to make an important announcement.
We are about to buy our first new car.

Be about to plus base form can be used with inanimate subjects but only if there is a sense of immediacy in the sentence. The action does not need to be caused by the subject of the sentence. Here are some examples:

The house is about to go on the market.
Their job description is about to change drastically.
The field is about to be flooded for irrigation.

We can also use impersonal subjects; for example:

It's about to start raining.
There is about to be a big fight over the proposed new law.

Summary of ways of talking about the future

In this chapter we have identified the following six ways of talking about the future:

♦ *Will* plus base form (prediction)
  Animate   They will call us as soon as they hear anything.
  Inanimate   It will take about 45 minutes to get to the airport.

♦ *Will* plus base form (intention)
  Animate   I will take you to the airport.
  Inanimate   (rarely used)

  Comment: *will* plus base form is used for normal expectations about future actions or events.

♦ Present progressive tense
  Animate   I am taking them to the airport.
  Inanimate   The meeting is starting at 4:30.

  Comment: with animate nouns, the present progressive refers to future events that arise directly from present plans, arrangements, or commitments. With inanimate nouns, the present progressive refers to events that are arranged or highly predictable. We often use the present progressive for announcing imminent actions or events, especially if the actions or events are new information.

- Present tense

Animate	Alice <u>takes</u> the kids to camp tomorrow.
Inanimate	Their flight <u>leaves</u> at 6:30.

Comment: the present tense is used to describe an action or event that has been scheduled or prearranged.

- *Be going to* plus base form

Animate	I<u>'m going to give</u> them a call right now.
Inanimate	Their flight <u>is going to be</u> a little late.

Comment: with animate nouns, *be going to* plus base form signals a strong intention or even commitment to carry out a future action. With inanimate nouns, *be going to* plus base form asserts confidence that the described future event will actually happen.

- *Be about to* plus base form

Animate	They <u>are about to board</u> their plane.
Inanimate	The plane <u>is about to take</u> off.

Comment: with both animate and inanimate subjects, *be about to* plus base form emphasizes the immediacy of the action of the verb.

In deciding what form to use for talking about future time, here are some things to keep in mind:

- *Will* plus base form is the default way of talking about the future. That is, we use *will* plus base form unless we have a particular reason for using one of the other forms.
- The present progressive and *be going to* plus base form are used very frequently in conversation because they both imply information that is new to the audience. For example, compare the following uses of *will* plus base form, present progressive, and *be going to* plus base form:

Will plus base form	I<u>'ll take</u> the bus to work tomorrow.
Present progressive	I<u>'m taking</u> the bus to work tomorrow.
Be going to plus base form	I<u>'m going to take</u> the bus to work tomorrow.

All three sentences have the same basic meaning. However, they do not have the same implications. The use of *will* plus base form implies that taking the bus to work is something that the speaker does frequently so that the sentence is merely confirming a normal practice. Both the present progressive and the *be going to* plus base form, however, are announcing something that is new to the audience and/or is worth singling out for special emphasis.

Here is the opposite situation where the "new information" aspect of the present progressive and *be going to* plus base form are inappropriate. Imagine it's the end of the workday; two colleagues are leaving the office at the same time, and each says "good-bye" to the other with the following verb forms:

Will plus base form	I<u>'ll see</u> you tomorrow.
Present progressive	I<u>'m seeing</u> you tomorrow.
Be going to plus base form	I<u>'m going to see</u> you tomorrow.

The "new information" verb forms are utterly socially inappropriate because they (incorrectly) imply that seeing the other person at work the next day is the result of some special arrangement; it is not something that just normally happens.

- ◆ The remaining two verb forms, present tense and *be about to* plus base form, are essentially special-purpose verb forms: the present tense is used solely for future events that are already scheduled or fixed; *be about to* plus base form is used to emphasize the immediacy of the future action or event.

To summarize:

- ◆ Normal expectations about future actions or events: *will* plus base form
- ◆ New information about future actions or events: present progressive or *be going to* plus base form
- ◆ Scheduled or fixed future events: present tense
- ◆ Immediate future actions or events: *be about to* plus base form

EXERCISE
5·12

Based on the previous discussion of future verb forms, identify the meaning of the underlined verb forms using the following terms: "normal expectations," "new information," "scheduled or fixed future event," "immediate future action." The first two sentences are done as examples:

I <u>am going to go</u> swimming as soon as we get there.

ANSWER: New information

The copy machine <u>will</u> automatically <u>sort</u> the pages.

ANSWER: Normal expectations

1. They <u>are</u> just <u>about to announce</u> the winners.

   _____

2. The play <u>closes</u> after Saturday's performance.

   _____

3. The days <u>will be</u> longer in April.

   _____

4. We <u>are staying</u> a few nights in Paris on our way back.

   _____

5. They <u>are about to make</u> a really big mistake.

   _____

6. The new law <u>goes</u> into effect tomorrow.

   _____

7. Remember, I <u>present</u> the committee's recommendations to the board on Friday.

   _____

8. Naturally, they <u>will resist</u> any last-minute changes.

   _____

9. I <u>am about to leave</u>; do you want a ride?

_____

10. They <u>are selling</u> their house as soon as they can get a buyer.

_____

Based on the previous discussion of future verb forms, pick the best future-time form for the underlined verb to represent the future-time meanings that appear in parentheses. The first two sentences are done as examples.

(normal expectations) I <u>believe</u> that when I see it.

ANSWER: I <u>will believe</u> that when I see it.

(new information) We <u>make</u> them a new offer.

ANSWER: We <u>are making/are going to make</u> them a new offer.

1. (immediate future action) Careful, you <u>sit</u> in a wet chair.

_____

2. (scheduled or fixed future event) The tournament <u>begin</u> this Saturday.

_____

3. (new information) I <u>need</u> to rent a car.

_____

4. (normal expectations) I <u>turn</u> the lights off when I leave the building.

_____

5. (immediate future action) We <u>replace</u> the countertops in the kitchen.

_____

6. (new information) They <u>launch</u> a search for the overdue hikers.

_____

7. (scheduled or fixed future event) The news <u>come</u> on at 10:00 tonight.

_____

8. (immediate future action) The storm <u>hit</u> the coast with heavy rains.

_____

9. (normal expectations) The aides <u>handle</u> all the registration details.

_____

10. (new information) He <u>try</u> a totally new approach.

_____

More about Verbs

Simple present

When you refer to habitual actions, customs, and facts, use simple present verb forms.

HABITUAL ACTION: I **work** in the library.

CUSTOM: Most Americans **eat** turkey on Thanksgiving Day.

FACT: The earth **revolves** around the sun.

If you include a time reference, you can also use the simple present to indicate future time.

FUTURE ACTION: The concert **starts** in five minutes.

Except for *be* and *have*, verbs in the simple present follow this pattern:

	Singular	Plural
First Person	I **verb**	we **verb**
Second Person	you **verb**	you **verb**
Third Person	he, she, it **verb + s/es**	they **verb**

As you can see, the base form of the verb is used with the subject pronouns *I*, *you*, *we*, and *they* and with the nouns these pronouns can replace. For example, *the students* takes the same verb form as *they*. An ending, either *-s* or *-es*, is added to the verb when the subject pronoun is *he*, *she*, or *it* or a noun these pronouns can replace. The *-s* ending is used most frequently. The *-es* ending is used after certain letters or letter combinations.

Letters	Examples
s	pass + es
sh	push + es
ch	march + es
x	box + es
o	do + es
When a verb ends in a consonant and *y*, change the *y* to *i* and add *-es*.	bury → buries

The verb *be* is described in Unit 2. In the following chart are the forms of the verb *have*:

	Singular	Plural
First Person	I **have**	we **have**
Second Person	you **have**	you **have**
Third Person	he, she, it **has**	they **have**

Notice that *has* is the verb form used with *he*, *she*, *it*, and the nouns these pronouns can replace.

Complete each sentence with the simple present form of the verb in parentheses. Circle the reason that the simple present is used.

1. I _____ (eat) lunch in the cafeteria every day but Friday.

   Habitual action   **Custom**   **Fact**   **Future time**

2. Julia _____ (carry) a heavy backpack to school every day.

   Habitual action   **Custom**   **Fact**   **Future time**

3. You _____ (speak) English well.

   Habitual action   **Custom**   **Fact**   **Future time**

4. The state of Florida _____ (produce) a great deal of citrus fruit.

   Habitual action   **Custom**   **Fact**   **Future time**

5. During the holidays, we always _____ (make) special meals.

   Habitual action   **Custom**   **Fact**   **Future time**

6. He _____ (watch) television every night.

   Habitual action   **Custom**   **Fact**   **Future time**

7. My roommate _____ (say) a prayer before he eats.

   Habitual action   **Custom**   **Fact**   **Future time**

8. The game _____ (begin) in an hour.

   Habitual action   **Custom**   **Fact**   **Future time**

9. My friends and I _____ (live) near a park.

   Habitual action   **Custom**   **Fact**   **Future time**

10. Trees _____ (grow) tall in the Pacific Northwest.

    Habitual action   **Custom**   **Fact**   **Future time**

11. We _____ (wear) traditional dress on holidays.

    Habitual action   **Custom**   **Fact**   **Future time**

12. Most people _____ (shake) hands when they first _____ (meet)

    Habitual action   **Custom**   **Fact**   **Future time**

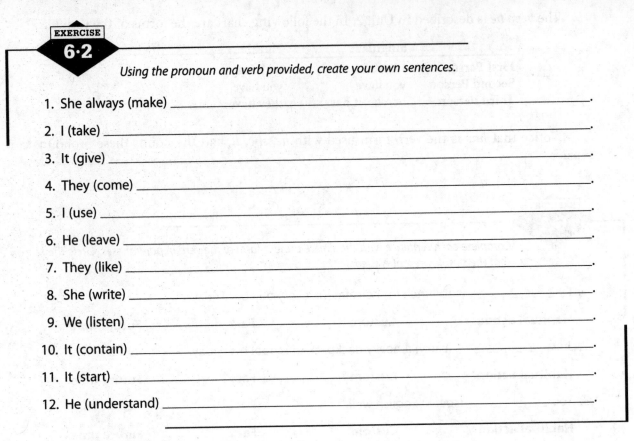

Using the pronoun and verb provided, create your own sentences.

1. She always (make) _____.

2. I (take) _____.

3. It (give) _____.

4. They (come) _____.

5. I (use) _____.

6. He (leave) _____.

7. They (like) _____.

8. She (write) _____.

9. We (listen) _____.

10. It (contain) _____.

11. It (start) _____.

12. He (understand) _____.

Forming negatives

To make a verb negative, add the auxiliary verb *do* and the word *not* before the main verb.

do not go   does not like

Remember that *does* is used with the pronouns *he*, *she*, and *it*. When *does* is used, the main verb has no *-s* or *-es* ending.

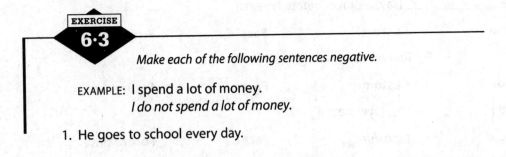

Make each of the following sentences negative.

EXAMPLE: I spend a lot of money.
I do not spend a lot of money.

1. He goes to school every day.

   _____

2. My roommate likes snakes.

   _____

3. You know my family.

   _____

4. The owner opens the store every day at 8:00.

   _____

5. We help our neighbors.

_____

6. My friends send me letters.

_____

7. I feel tired.

_____

8. She speaks five different languages.

_____

9. They study in the library.

_____

10. We listen to pop music.

_____

11. They grow tomatoes in their backyard.

_____

12. This car runs well.

_____

Present of *be*

The verb *be* has three different forms in the simple present: *am*, *is*, and *are*.

	Singular	Plural
First Person	I **am**	we **are**
Second Person	you **are**	you **are**
Third Person	he, she, it **is**	they **are**

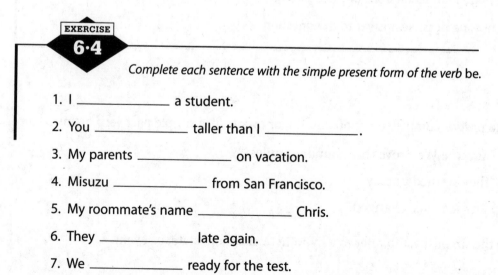

EXERCISE
6·4

Complete each sentence with the simple present form of the verb be.

1. I _____ a student.

2. You _____ taller than I _____.

3. My parents _____ on vacation.

4. Misuzu _____ from San Francisco.

5. My roommate's name _____ Chris.

6. They _____ late again.

7. We _____ ready for the test.

8. I _____ interested in all kinds of sports.

9. It _____ easy.

10. Your coat _____ in the closet.

11. She _____ the director.

12. They _____ in class together.

The word *there* is often used with the verb *be* to acknowledge the existence of someone or something. The form of the *be* verb is based on the subject that follows it.

SINGULAR SUBJECT: There **is a concert** in the park tonight.

PLURAL SUBJECT: There **are four rooms** in the house.

EXERCISE
6·5

Circle the verb that agrees in number with the subject that follows it.

1. There **is/are** someone at the door.

2. There **is/are** several parks in the town.

3. There **is/are** fifty-two cards in a deck.

4. There **is/are** a restroom at the end of the hall.

5. There **is/are** sixteen students in the class.

6. There **is/are** a bank on the corner of Lincoln and Ash.

7. There **is/are** an information booth in the lobby.

8. There **is/are** many specialty stores in the Mall of America.

9. There **is/are** still tickets available.

10. There **is/are** a typo on page 3.

11. There **is/are** a huge fountain in front of the building.

12. There **is/are** only one possible answer to the question.

Simple past

When you refer to past or completed actions, states, or events, use simple past verb forms.

COMPLETED ACTION: We **drove** three hundred miles.

PAST STATE: They **seemed** uneasy.

PAST EVENT: The schedule **changed**.

You can also use the simple past to refer to a hypothetical action, state, or event.

HYPOTHETICAL ACTION: If you **joined** our team, we could win the championship.

Sentences such as this one will be discussed in more detail in Part IV.

The simple past for regular verbs consists of the verb and the ending *-ed*.

	Singular	Plural
First Person	I **verb + ed**	we **verb + ed**
Second Person	you **verb + ed**	you **verb + ed**
Third Person	he, she, it **verb + ed**	they **verb + ed**

For regular verbs, the simple past form and the perfect/participles are the same.

When a one-syllable word or a word with a stressed final syllable ends in a single consonant sound, double the last letter before adding *-ed*.

One-syllable word: plan → planned

Word ending in a stressed syllable: occur → occurred

BUT row → rowed [This word ends in a vowel sound.]

Irregular verbs have a variety of simple past forms, which can be found in the appendix.

The following are common irregular verb patterns. Some of these irregular simple past forms are the same as the perfect/passive forms.

- Pattern 1: The final *d* becomes a *t*. (Same as perfect/passive)

send	sent
lend	lent
spend	spent

- Pattern 2: A *-d* or *-t* suffix is added. The vowel changes. (Same as perfect/passive)

feel /fil/	felt /fɛlt/
sleep /slip/	slept /slɛpt/
tell /tɛl/	told /told/

- Pattern 3a: The vowel changes. (Different from perfect/passive)

eat /it/	ate /et/
speak /spik/	spoke /spok/
know /no/	knew /nu/

- Pattern 3b: The vowel changes. (Same as perfect/passive)

hold /hold/	held /hɛld/
meet /mit/	met /mɛt/
sit /sɪt/	sat /sæt/

- Pattern 4: The base form and the simple past form are the same. (Same as perfect/passive)

put	put
hit	hit
cut	cut

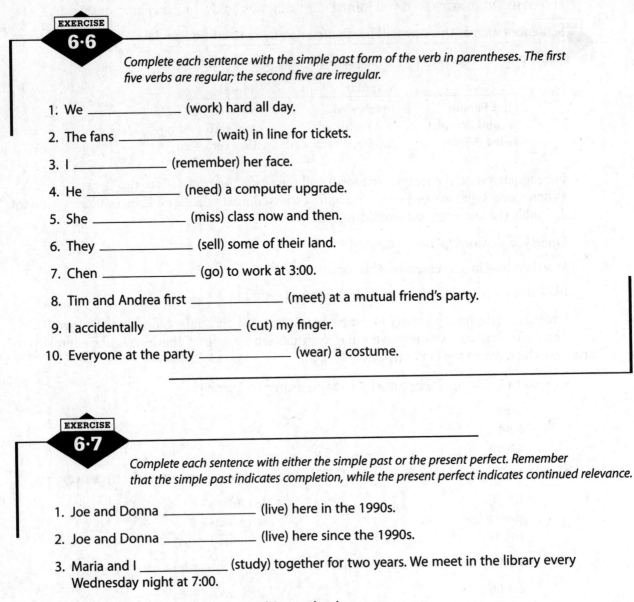

EXERCISE

6·6

Complete each sentence with the simple past form of the verb in parentheses. The first five verbs are regular; the second five are irregular.

1. We _____ (work) hard all day.

2. The fans _____ (wait) in line for tickets.

3. I _____ (remember) her face.

4. He _____ (need) a computer upgrade.

5. She _____ (miss) class now and then.

6. They _____ (sell) some of their land.

7. Chen _____ (go) to work at 3:00.

8. Tim and Andrea first _____ (meet) at a mutual friend's party.

9. I accidentally _____ (cut) my finger.

10. Everyone at the party _____ (wear) a costume.

EXERCISE

6·7

Complete each sentence with either the simple past or the present perfect. Remember that the simple past indicates completion, while the present perfect indicates continued relevance.

1. Joe and Donna _____ (live) here in the 1990s.

2. Joe and Donna _____ (live) here since the 1990s.

3. Maria and I _____ (study) together for two years. We meet in the library every Wednesday night at 7:00.

4. Maria and I _____ (study) together last year.

5. We _____ (travel) to London in April.

6. We _____ (travel) to many countries, but this year we're staying home.

7. I _____ (work) for Safeway since May.

8. I _____ (work) for Safeway in 2003.

9. He _____ (build) many houses. He is currently building one on Madison Street.

10. He _____ (build) a house for his sister.

Forming negatives

To make a verb negative, add the auxiliary verb *did*, which is the simple past form of *do*, and the word *not* before the main verb.

> did not believe

Make each of the following sentences negative.

EXAMPLE: I made a mistake.

I did not make a mistake.

1. He came to work on time.

   _____

2. My roommate liked the movie.

   _____

3. She understood the problem.

   _____

4. We took a wrong turn.

   _____

5. The students needed help with the homework.

   _____

6. The driver blamed me for the accident.

   _____

7. I listened to the directions.

   _____

8. She earned a degree in economics.

   _____

9. He calculated the taxes.

   _____

10. They complained about the weather.

    _____

Past of *be*

The verb *be* has two different forms in the simple past: *was* and *were*.

	Singular	Plural
First Person	I **was**	we **were**
Second Person	you **were**	you **were**
Third Person	he, she, it **was**	they **were**

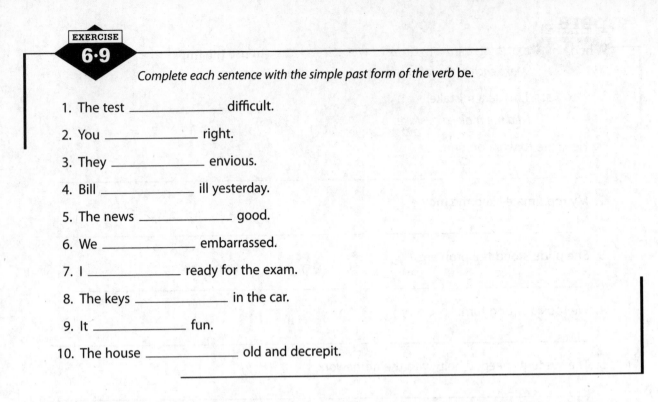

EXERCISE
6·9

Complete each sentence with the simple past form of the verb be.

1. The test _____ difficult.

2. You _____ right.

3. They _____ envious.

4. Bill _____ ill yesterday.

5. The news _____ good.

6. We _____ embarrassed.

7. I _____ ready for the exam.

8. The keys _____ in the car.

9. It _____ fun.

10. The house _____ old and decrepit.

The word *there* is often used with the verb *be* to acknowledge the existence of someone or something. The form of the verb is based on the subject that follows it.

Singular subject: There **was a storm** last night.
Plural subject: There **were** twelve people in the cast.

EXERCISE
6·10

Circle the verb that agrees in number with the subject that follows it.

1. There **was/were** a parade yesterday.

2. There **was/were** many celebrities at the rally.

3. There **was/were** a lot of traffic.

4. There **was/were** pizza for everyone.

5. There **was/were** several buildings in need of repair.

6. There **was/were** no more tickets left.

7. There **was/were** a four-hour delay.

8. There **was/were** an empty seat in the back row.

9. There **was/were** many tourists at this year's festival.

10. There **was/were** a nice breeze earlier this morning.

Imperative

When you want to give instructions or directions, you can use the imperative:

> INSTRUCTION: **Mix** the ingredients together.

> DIRECTION: **Turn** right at the corner.

Imperatives are used for other purposes as well:

> REQUEST: **Close** the window, please.

> WARNING: **Watch** out!

> INVITATION: **Come** over to our house tonight.

> WISH: **Have** a nice time.

Using the verb in the imperative construction is easy because there are no endings. Just use the base form (the form found in the dictionary).

Because imperatives are directed toward another person or other persons, the subject *you* is understood; that is, it is not mentioned except for emphasis.

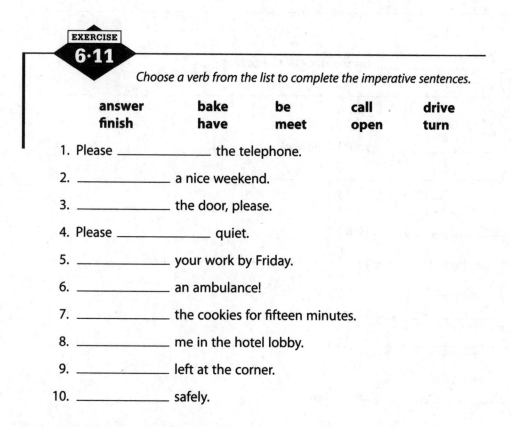

EXERCISE 6·11

Choose a verb from the list to complete the imperative sentences.

answer	bake	be	call	drive
finish	have	meet	open	turn

1. Please _____ the telephone.

2. _____ a nice weekend.

3. _____ the door, please.

4. Please _____ quiet.

5. _____ your work by Friday.

6. _____ an ambulance!

7. _____ the cookies for fifteen minutes.

8. _____ me in the hotel lobby.

9. _____ left at the corner.

10. _____ safely.

Forming negatives

To form a negative imperative, place the auxiliary verb *do* and the word *not* before the base form of the verb.

> do not go

Forming contractions: *Don't*

In informal or conversational situations, use a contraction.

don't go

EXERCISE 6·12

Complete the following sentences using the negative form of the verb provided. Then rewrite the sentence using a contraction.

EXAMPLE: walk

Do not walk on the grass.
Don't walk on the grass.

1. Be

_____ late!

_____

2. Run

_____ on the deck of the pool.

_____

3. Forget

_____ your homework.

_____

4. Lie

_____ to me.

_____

5. Shout

_____ at us.

_____

6. Drink

_____ the water.

_____

7. Start

_____ the car yet.

_____

8. Blame

_____ me.

_____

9. Boil

_____ the water too long.

_____

10. Break

_____ anything.

_____

Using imperatives

Imperatives, or commands, are as important in good sentence writing as any other grammatical element. It is essential to differentiate among the various types of imperatives in order to use them appropriately and effectively.

You as the subject of an imperative

Most imperatives are made to the second-person singular or plural (**you**), although the pronoun is not stated.

> imperative form of a verb + predicate → command

Certain gruff or impolite-sounding imperatives cannot be used in every situation. Some of these are said in a casual manner, while others are said in anger or out of belligerence. For example:

Shut up!	Get out!
Be quiet!	Don't ever say that again!
Don't ever do that again!	Stop it!
Hurry up!	Leave me alone!
Shut your mouth!	Give me that!
Let go!	Take your time!

The exclamation point

Most imperatives of this nature are punctuated with an exclamation point, but imperatives can also be punctuated with a period. An exclamation point in writing is a signal that the imperative is stated with great emphasis. For example:

Stand up!	*emphatic, perhaps angry in tone*
Stand up.	*milder but still casual and a bit gruff in tone*

Other short imperatives can be written with an exclamation point when they are pleas or urgent requests. For example:

Have a heart!	Be patient!
Stand back!	Keep moving!
Don't joke about that!	Hold on tight!
Don't excite the dog!	Make some room for me!

Respond to each incident described with a gruff or angry imperative.

1. Someone approaches you menacingly and says, "I'm going to get you."

   _____

2. Someone has unlocked your diary and is reading through it.

   _____

3. Someone continues to refuse to leave your home.

   _____

4. Someone is acting foolishly and is teasing you.

   _____

5. Someone is packing a suitcase slowly although the hour of departure is near.

   _____

6. Someone is pestering you and making you annoyed.

   _____

Follow the same directions, but respond with a plea or an urgent request.

7. A child is leaning down to pet a vicious dog.

   _____

8. You're riding fast on a motorcycle and you tell your passenger to be careful.

   _____

9. You are thirsty and would like a soft drink.

   _____

10. You feel that someone should be kinder.

   _____

Please

Most imperatives are usually said with a certain amount of courtesy. The inclusion of **please** softens the tone of the command. Certainly, **please wait here** sounds nicer than **wait here**. Therefore, it is wise to include the word **please** in most commands. However, its position in a sentence and the addition or lack of a comma can change the general meaning of the sentence significantly. If an imperative begins with **please**, it has the same meaning as when it ends with **please**.

> *please* + **imperative verb** + **predicate**
>
> Please + lend + me a dollar.

> **imperative verb** + **predicate** + *please*
>
> Lend + me a dollar +, please.

If **please** is written at the end of an imperative, as in the example just shown, it is preceded by a comma. Here are more examples:

Please sign here.	Sign here, please.
Please fill out this form.	Fill out this form, please.
Please fasten your seat belts.	Fasten your seat belts, please.

A comma placed after an initial **please** changes the courteous meaning to one that suggests impatience or exasperation. In speech, the word **please** would be followed by a pause before the imperative is given. In writing, the pause is indicated by a comma.

Courteous	**Impatient**
Please keep back from the fire.	Please, keep back from the fire.
Please don't feed the animals.	Please, don't feed the animals.
Please move along quickly.	Please, move along quickly.

If the imperative is meant to show impatience or exasperation, it can be punctuated with an exclamation point:

Please, control your temper!

EXERCISE
6·14

*Using the cue word provided, write an imperative sentence twice, beginning it once with **please** and ending it once with **please**.*

EXAMPLE: stay

Please stay in your room.
Stay in your room, please.

1. enjoy

   a. _____

   b. _____

2. find

   a. _____

   b. _____

3. remember

   a. _____

   b. _____

4. choose

   a. _____

   b. _____

5. explain

   a. _____

   b. _____

6. remain

   a. _____

   b. _____

7. pretend

   a. _____

   b. _____

8. join

   a. _____

   b. _____

9. follow

   a. _____

   b. _____

10. hurry

   a. _____

   b. _____

Let's and *let*

While most imperatives are said to the second-person-singular or second-person-plural pronoun **you**, some can include the person giving the command. Imperatives of this type begin with the contraction **let's** (**let us**) and are followed by an infinitive phrase. Infinitive phrases that follow **let's** omit the particle word **to**. **Let's** conveys that the person giving the command will participate in the action of the command; for example, **Let's listen to some music.** In this sentence, the speaker suggests that you listen to some music, and the speaker will join you in that activity. **Let's** is the contraction of **let us**, but the uncontracted form is used less often.

> ***let's*** + **infinitive phrase**
>
> Let's + go home.

Here are a few more examples:

> **Let's take** a look at that scratch on your arm.
> **Let's work** on a new way of blocking unwanted e-mails.
> **Let's see** what's on today's agenda.

If the verb **let** is used without the contraction of **us** (**let's**), it still is an imperative, but it has a different meaning. In this case, the person giving the command is suggesting that "you" allow someone or something to perform an action. The structure consists of **let** followed by a direct object and an infinitive phrase with the particle word **to** omitted.

> **let** + **direct object** + **infinitive phrase**
>
> Let + them + sleep until ten.

For example:

> **Let John** help you with the project.
> **Let me** know whether you need more time for the job.
> **Let the problem** just go away.
> **Let the soldiers** find some shade and get a little rest.

EXERCISE
6·15

*Rewrite the following sentences as an imperative with **let's**. Then, after adding an appropriate direct object, rewrite the imperative with **let**.*

EXAMPLE: You drove Maria to the bus station.

Let's drive Maria to the bus station.
Let Henry drive Maria to the bus station.

1. You spent about two hundred dollars.

   a. _____

   b. _____

2. You send Jim a text.

   a. _____

   b. _____

3. You should send them another e-mail.

   a. _____

   b. _____

4. You report the burglary to the police.

   a. _____

   b. _____

5. You have repaired the rickety steps.

   a. _____

   b. _____

6. You tried to signal the boat struggling in the swift current.

   a. _____

   b. _____

7. You will send for the paramedics.

   a. _____

   b. _____

8. You drove to the edge of the cliff.

   a. _____

   b. _____

9. You have to put up a privacy fence.

a. _____

b. _____

10. You solve the difficult equation.

a. _____

b. _____

How about

Another version of an imperative appears in the form of a question. It begins with the phrase **how about** and is followed by a gerund and its complement. This kind of imperative sounds more like a suggestion than a command, and since it is in the form of a question, it gives the impression that it is no command at all. Also, it includes the command giver in the action. Let's peruse some examples:

How about going to the movies tonight?
How about having dinner at the Bella Luna Café?
How about giving me a hand with this heavy chest?

Why don't you

Yet another version of an imperative also appears in the form of a question. It begins with **why don't you** and is followed by an infinitive phrase. Unlike imperatives with **how about**, this imperative does not include the command giver in the action of the verb.

Why don't you go out and play for a while?
Why don't you get dressed and come down for breakfast?
Why don't you think about what you just said?

If you change the pronoun **you** to **we** in this imperative, the command giver is now included in the action of the verb. For example:

Why don't we try to get along a little better?
Why don't we set a trap for that pesky raccoon?
Why don't we take a little trip downtown and do some shopping?

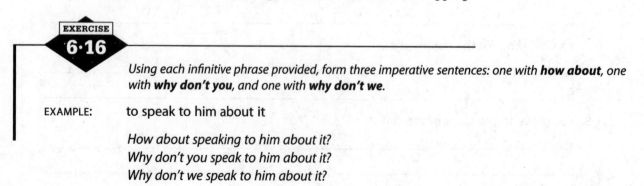

EXERCISE
6·16

*Using each infinitive phrase provided, form three imperative sentences: one with **how about**, one with **why don't you**, and one with **why don't we**.*

EXAMPLE: to speak to him about it

How about speaking to him about it?
Why don't you speak to him about it?
Why don't we speak to him about it?

1. to sit down under a shady tree

   a. _____

   b. _____

   c. _____

2. to come to an understanding about this matter

   a. _____

   b. _____

   c. _____

3. to let them work it out for themselves

   a. _____

   b. _____

   c. _____

4. to grant her permission to take the trip

   a. _____

   b. _____

   c. _____

5. to sing a song for Grandma

   a. _____

   b. _____

   c. _____

6. to refrain from using such language

   a. _____

   b. _____

   c. _____

7. to fertilize the fields with dung

   a. _____

   b. _____

   c. _____

8. to open a business on State Street

   a. _____

   b. _____

   c. _____

9. to register to vote in the next election

    a. _____

    b. _____

    c. _____

10. to try to behave a little better

    a. _____

    b. _____

    c. _____

EXERCISE

6·17

Using the cues provided, write original imperative sentences.

1. please

_____

2. let's

_____

3. let

_____

4. Please, . . . !

_____

5. how about

_____

6. why don't you

_____

7. spend more time

_____

8. work out

_____

9. Please keep . . .

_____

10. why don't

_____

Modal auxiliary verbs

Modal auxiliary verbs appear before main verbs. They are used for a number of purposes. Here are some of the most common:

> INDICATE ABILITY: She **can** speak English.
>
> GIVE ADVICE: You **should** see a doctor.
>
> EXPRESS CERTAINTY: We **will** finish by 8:00.
>
> INDICATE POSSIBILITY: It **may** rain tonight.
>
> INDICATE OBLIGATION: You **must** attend the last class.
>
> GIVE PERMISSION: You **may** use your dictionaries during the exam.
>
> INDICATE PAST HABIT: When I was little, we **would** go swimming every day.

Unlike other verbs, modal verbs have only one form. In other words, no -*s* is added to modal verbs to indicate third-person singular.

> He/she/it **can/should/will/may/must** move.

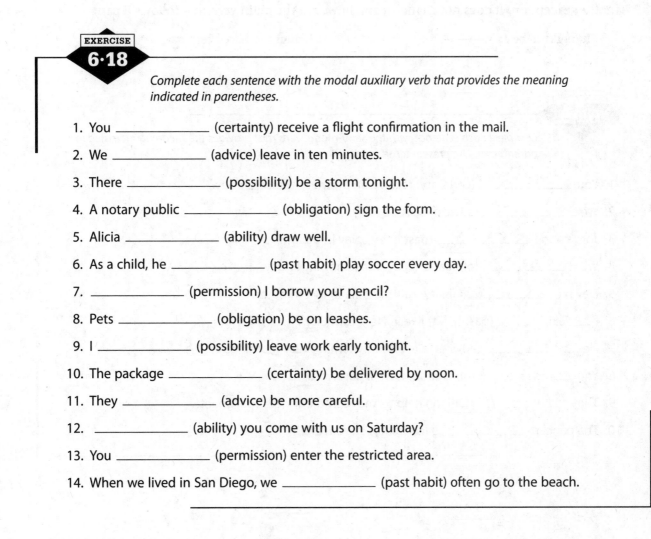

EXERCISE 6·18

Complete each sentence with the modal auxiliary verb that provides the meaning indicated in parentheses.

1. You _____ (certainty) receive a flight confirmation in the mail.

2. We _____ (advice) leave in ten minutes.

3. There _____ (possibility) be a storm tonight.

4. A notary public _____ (obligation) sign the form.

5. Alicia _____ (ability) draw well.

6. As a child, he _____ (past habit) play soccer every day.

7. _____ (permission) I borrow your pencil?

8. Pets _____ (obligation) be on leashes.

9. I _____ (possibility) leave work early tonight.

10. The package _____ (certainty) be delivered by noon.

11. They _____ (advice) be more careful.

12. _____ (ability) you come with us on Saturday?

13. You _____ (permission) enter the restricted area.

14. When we lived in San Diego, we _____ (past habit) often go to the beach.

Semi-modal auxiliary verbs

English also has semi-modal auxiliary verbs. They are used for many of the same purposes as modal auxiliary verbs.

INDICATE ABILITY: He **is able to** speak three different languages.

GIVE ADVICE: You **ought to** finish the report.

EXPRESS CERTAINTY: We **are going to** complete the project tonight.

INDICATE OBLIGATION: You **have to** attend the meeting.

INDICATE PAST HABIT: We **used to** play basketball together.

Unlike one-word modal verbs, most semi-modals are marked for number and tense.

I **am** able to go.   I **was** able to go.
You **have** to give a speech.   You **had** to give a speech.
We **are** going to leave.   We **were** going to leave.
They **have** to work late.   They **had** to work late.

Used to is an exception. It has only one form and always refers to the past. *Ought to* is another exception. It does not change form; however, the main verb that follows it can.

It **ought to** be easy.   It **ought to** have been easy.

EXERCISE
6·19

Complete each sentence with the semi-modal verb that provides the meaning indicated in parentheses. Use present tense forms.

1. You _____ (certainty) receive an award at the ceremony.

2. We _____ (advice) exercise daily.

3. Jorge and I _____ (past habit) play in a band.

4. We _____ (obligation) pay our tuition by Friday.

5. Devin _____ (ability) run the mile in five minutes.

6. I _____ (past habit) live in New York City.

7. He _____ (advice) take a multivitamin every morning.

8. You _____ (obligation) have a password.

9. They _____ (ability) help us move into our new apartment.

10. The concert _____ (certainty) start at 8:00.

Complete each sentence with the semi-modal verb that provides the meaning indicated in parentheses. Use the past tense if possible.

1. It _____ (certainty) rain, so we left early.

2. She _____ (advice) have rested.

3. We _____ (obligation) pay a service charge.

4. The teacher _____ (ability) remember everyone's name.

5. I _____ (certainty) go with them, but then I got sick.

6. My father _____ (advice) have had a checkup yesterday.

7. Amber _____ (obligation) retype her paper, because she lost her disk.

8. They _____ (ability) hike long distances when they were young.

Combining semi-modals

Sometimes semi-modals can be used with other semi-modals or after some regular modals.

> They **are going to have to** finish their papers by Friday. [semi-modal + semi-modal]
> I **will have to** call you back later. [modal + semi-modal]

Underline the modals and circle the semi-modals in the following sentences.

1. I might be able to help you on Thursday.

2. They are going to be able to take a vacation next month.

3. She might have to quit her job.

4. You are going to have to work hard.

5. We will have to take notes at the lecture.

Auxiliary Verbs

·7·

Introduction to the perfect tenses

What is so "perfect" about the perfect tenses? Nothing. The use of *perfect* as a grammatical term comes from the Latin verb *perficere*, "to do something completely or to bring something to a successful completion." The modern English word *perfect* is normally used as an adjective, but we still keep one of the original Latin verb meanings of *perficere*, "to bring to a successful completion." For example, a tennis player might say, "I am trying to perfect my backhand." (Note: The verb *perfect* is even pronounced differently from the adjective *perfect*. The verb is stressed on the second syllable, "perFECT," while the adjective is stressed on the first syllable, "PERfect.") Over time the English verb *perfect* developed a secondary meaning of "to finish or complete." It is this meaning that the grammatical term *perfect* draws on: the perfect tenses have a stated or implied finishing point.

There are three perfect tenses: the **present perfect**, the **past perfect**, and the **future perfect**. All three are formed in exactly parallel manner: the appropriate present, past, or future tense form of the helping verb *have* followed by a verb in the past participle form; for example:

Present perfect	Joan has lived in Denver for five years.
Past perfect	Joan had lived in Denver for five years before she moved last May.
Future perfect	Joan will have lived in Denver for five years this May.

The most common use of the **present perfect** is for past-time actions or events whose actions or consequences continue until they are terminated, for example, "perfected," at the present moment of time.

Joan has lived in Denver for five years.

In our example sentence, the use of the present perfect *has lived* means that Joan moved to Denver five year ago and has continued to live in Denver right up to the present moment of time.

The **past perfect** is used for some more distant past time, or past actions or events that were terminated, "perfected," at some more recent moment of past time, or by some more recent past-time event.

Joan had lived in Denver for five years before she moved last May.

In our example sentence, the use of the past perfect *had lived* means that Joan lived in Denver for five years until she moved in May. Joan's moving in May is the more recent past-time event that terminated the action of the past perfect verb *had lived*.

The **future perfect** is used for future-time actions or events that will be terminated, "perfected," by an even more distant moment of time or defining event.

Joan <u>will have lived</u> in Denver for five years this May.

In our example sentence, the use of the present perfect *will have lived* means that as of this coming May, Joan has lived in Denver for five years. *This May* is the more distant future-time expression that terminates the action of the future perfect verb *will have lived*.

EXERCISE
7·1

Underline and identify the perfect tenses in the following sentences. The first is done as an example.

We had just finished dinner when the phone rang.

ANSWER: We <u>had</u> just <u>finished</u> dinner when the phone rang.

past perfect

1. Fortunately, I had checked the weather before we started on the hike.

   _____

2. The storm has delayed all inbound flights.

   _____

3. By then, the market will have closed.

   _____

4. During the night, the electricity had gone out so the clocks were all wrong.

   _____

5. It looks as though they have already started on the project.

   _____

6. Fortunately, I had gotten some euros before I flew to Rome.

   _____

7. Some politicians have maintained friendships with members of the opposing party.

   _____

8. We hope that we will have finished by noon.

   _____

9. No one had anticipated how difficult the problem would be.

   _____

10. The resistance movement will have armed itself as soon as they heard the news.

   _____

Replace the underlined infinitive verb with the perfect verb form identified in parentheses. The first is done as an example.

(past perfect) They <u>hire</u> extra security for the concert.

ANSWER: They <u>had hired</u> extra security for the concert.

1. (present perfect) I <u>ask</u> them to provide more information.

_____

2. (future perfect) Surely the lake <u>freeze</u> by now.

_____

3. (past perfect) We <u>tell</u> them about what they said.

_____

4. (future perfect) They <u>clear</u> customs by now.

_____

5. (present perfect) The court <u>rule</u> on many similar cases over the years.

_____

6. (past perfect) Before they moved in, they <u>repaint</u> the entire apartment.

_____

7. (future perfect) They <u>invite</u> more people than they have space for.

_____

8. (past perfect) Fortunately, we <u>adjust</u> the insurance before the accident happened.

_____

9. (present perfect) Surely, he <u>retire</u> by now.

_____

10. (future perfect) His announcement <u>attract</u> a lot of attention.

_____

One of the mildly unusual features of the perfect tenses is that they can be used with both stative and dynamic verbs. The basic meaning of stative verbs, states that continue over time, is a perfect match for the ongoing nature of the perfect tenses. Here are the three perfect tenses with examples of both stative and dynamic verbs:

Present perfect
Stative   John <u>has been</u> a good friend.
Dynamic   John <u>has signed</u> the agreement.

Past perfect
Stative   John <u>had been</u> in graduate school at the time.
Dynamic   John <u>had majored</u> in accounting before he
                   switched to music.

Future perfect

Stative	John <u>will have been</u> at the airport for hours.
Dynamic	John's plane <u>will have landed</u> by now.

The present perfect tense

The present perfect tense consists of a present tense form of the helping verb *have* followed by a verb in the past participle form; for example:

> He <u>has been</u> out sick all week.
> The business <u>has expanded</u> steadily for the past several years.
> I think that I <u>have guessed</u> the answer.
> <u>Have</u> you <u>seen</u> Harry recently?
> We <u>have had</u> a busy day.
> I've just <u>heard</u> the news.

The present perfect tense is used to talk about past-time events that directly affect the present. Notice that none of the previous examples actually mentions the present moment of time; they do not need to because the linkage to the present moment of time is inherent in the meaning of the present perfect. To confirm that this is the case, note what happens when we use past-time adverbs in the examples; they all become ungrammatical:

> X He <u>has been</u> out sick all last week.
> X The business <u>has expanded</u> steadily several years ago.
> X I think that I <u>have guessed</u> the answer last week.
> X <u>Have</u> you <u>seen</u> Harry yesterday?
> X We <u>have had</u> a busy day last Monday.
> X I've <u>heard</u> the news last week.

We use the present perfect tense in two different ways: the main use of the present perfect is for past-time events that have continued over past time up to the present moment of time. We will call this the **continuous** use of the present perfect.

We also use the present perfect for very recent single past-time events that directly impact the present. We will call this the **noncontinuous** use of the present perfect. We will discuss the noncontinuous use of the present perfect after we have discussed the more frequent continuous use.

The continuous use of the present perfect

Here are some examples of the continuous present perfect:

> My parents <u>have lived</u> in their house for 30 years.
> I <u>have worked</u> there for two years.
> She <u>has delivered</u> papers at many major conferences.
> Their company <u>has been</u> in business for more than 100 years.
> He <u>has owned</u> that truck for as long as I <u>have known</u> him.
> I <u>haven't seen</u> my cousin in years.

As was mentioned in Chapter 5, one of the characteristics of all the perfect tenses is that both stative and dynamic verbs can be used freely in all of them. However, there is a difference in the way that the two types of verbs are used. In the present perfect, stative verbs, because of their inherent meaning of an ongoing state or condition, always are normally used with the meaning of an unbroken span of time up to the present moment. Here are some examples of stative verbs:

> I <u>have</u> always <u>disliked</u> broccoli.
> Our family <u>has</u> always <u>had</u> dogs.
> Americans <u>have</u> always <u>loved</u> happy endings in their movies.

John has been a close friend ever since college.
This project has cost us a small fortune.
We have always wanted to go to Hawaii.

Dynamic verbs, on the other hand, typically describe actions that are necessarily intermittent because they start and stop over a period of time. For example, we can legitimately describe the following sentence as continuous in the very real sense that Sam's voting is an activity that is repeated regularly over time, even though he can vote only when elections are held—every two years.

Sam has voted in every election since he was 18.

In the following sentence, Barbara's actions are continuous in the sense that we can imagine Barbara systematically climbing one peak after another until she has climbed them all.

Barbara has climbed every major peak in the Rockies.

In the next sentence, the speaker's infrequent use of his tuxedo still constitutes an activity that has been performed multiple times up to the present moment.

I have worn my tuxedo only three times in the past 20 years.

Here are some more examples of dynamic verbs used in the continuous present perfect:

The kids have gone to the same camp for the past four years.
Our basement has flooded every spring.
I have always parked on the street when I visit them.
Over the years, hail storms have damaged a lot of crops in the area.
She has directed more than 20 plays in her long career.
Our baseball team has won about half of its games.

EXERCISE
7·3

Determine whether the present perfect sentences that follow show a continuously ongoing state (stative verb) or sustained intermittent action (dynamic verb). The first two are done as examples.

Heavy snow has closed the road a dozen times this winter.

ANSWER: Intermittent action (dynamic)

I have always believed that hard work pays off in the end.

ANSWER: Continuously ongoing state (stative)

1. It has rained a lot this week.

_____

2. The train has always been on time before.

_____

3. I have never possessed a good sense of direction.

_____

4. We have spent a lot of money getting ready for this trip.

_____

5. <u>Have</u> we <u>covered</u> all the topics that are going to be on the final?

_____

6. The team <u>has</u> never <u>looked</u> better than it has this season.

_____

7. That car <u>has passed</u> us half a dozen times in the past hour.

_____

8. I <u>have</u> always <u>felt</u> that his work was not sufficiently appreciated.

_____

9. We <u>have lost</u> too many games this season because of poor preparation.

_____

10. We <u>have</u> always <u>eaten</u> there when we are in town.

_____

The noncontinuous use of the present perfect

The present perfect also allows for a noncontinuous or single-event use of the perfect tense. Here are some examples of noncontinuous uses:

> The printer <u>has</u> just <u>run</u> out of ink.
> The meeting <u>has been</u> canceled.
> The committee <u>has demanded</u> a second vote.
> The team <u>has picked</u> a new captain.
> We <u>have found</u> the problem, and we can fix it in a few hours.

As you can see, all of these examples describe a one-time only action or event. There is no continuous state or repeated action across a span of time.

In the noncontinuous use of the present perfect, this single, recently completed, past-time event or action directly and immediately affects the present moment of time. This is in contrast to the normal continuous use of the present perfect, which describes a series of events or actions that span a period of past time up to the present moment. For example, compare the following:

Continuous	There <u>have been</u> a lot of bad accidents on the freeway lately.
Noncontinuous	There <u>has been</u> a bad accident on the freeway.

The first sentence with the continuous use of the present perfect describes a situation in which a number of accidents have occurred on the freeway over a span of time. The second sentence with the noncontinuous use of the present perfect describes a single recent accident on the freeway. Using the noncontinuous present perfect emphasizes that (1) the information about the accident is new (and quite possibly not previously known to the audience) and (2) this information impacts the present situation in some way; in our example, the freeway might be closed for hours.

As we would expect, the noncontinuous present perfect is closely tied to the present moment of time. If we shift the time frame of a noncontinuous present perfect sentence to a more distant point in past time, the sentence becomes ungrammatical. For example, compare the following pairs of sentences:

Present time	Their daughter <u>has</u> just <u>graduated</u> from NYU.
Past time	**X** Their daughter <u>has</u> just <u>graduated</u> from NYU last week.
Present time	I've just <u>read</u> your letter.
Past time	**X** I've just <u>read</u> your letter last night.
Present time	We <u>have enjoyed</u> meeting your family.
Past time	**X** We <u>have enjoyed</u> meeting your family yesterday.

In all these examples, the use of the noncontinuous present perfect is totally incompatible with a past-time adverb.

EXERCISE
7·4

Label the underlined present participle verb form as either continuous or noncontinuous. The first two sentences are done as examples:

The Chinese and Americans <u>have argued</u> about trade policies for years.

ANSWER: Continuous

The Chinese and the Americans <u>have agreed</u> on a new trade policy.

ANSWER: Noncontinuous

1. The company <u>has replaced</u> the branch manager.

   _____

2. We <u>have seen</u> several of his plays on Broadway.

   _____

3. He <u>has</u> certainly <u>put</u> on some weight since the last time I saw him.

   _____

4. The conference <u>has arranged</u> transportation for you.

   _____

5. I've <u>found</u> the reference I had been looking for.

   _____

6. I see that they <u>have built</u> an outdoor pool.

   _____

7. We <u>have paid</u> by credit card before whenever we have stayed here.

   _____

8. Wages <u>have increased</u> about 3 percent a year for the past 20 years.

_____

9. They <u>have</u> finally <u>made</u> up their minds.

_____

10. We <u>have</u> always <u>used</u> premium gas in that car.

_____

To understand the meaning and function of the noncontinuous use of the present perfect, we need to contrast it with its alternative: the past tense. In many cases the noncontinuous present perfect and the past tense are interchangeable from a strictly grammatical point of view. For example, we can use the noncontinuous present perfect or the past tense equally well in the following sentences:

Present perfect	There <u>has been</u> a mistake on my income tax.
Past tense	There <u>was</u> a mistake on my income tax.
Present perfect	I've <u>seen</u> the final report.
Past tense	I <u>saw</u> the final report.
Present perfect	Elvis <u>has left</u> the building.
Past tense	Elvis <u>left</u> the building.

However, the implications of the noncontinuous and the past tenses can be quite different.

As we saw in Chapter 3, the past tense is used for events, conditions, or states that are now over and done with. To illustrate this point, we used this example:

Samantha <u>went</u> to school at Berkeley.

The sentence not only tells us where Samantha went to school, but the use of the past tense also tells us that Samantha is no longer going to school there. The key point in understanding the difference between the noncontinuous present perfect tense and the past tense is that the past tense erects a wall between past-time events (even ones that occurred in the immediate past) and the present moment of time.

The noncontinuous present perfect, on the other hand, highlights the connection between an event in the immediate and the present moment of time. Often we use the noncontinuous present perfect to emphasize that the past-time information is new to the audience and that the information is of immediate relevance to the present moment. The following pair of sentences is a good illustration of the differences between the noncontinuous present perfect and the past tense:

Present perfect	I've <u>lost</u> my car keys.
Past tense	I <u>lost</u> my car keys.

Both sentences mean the same thing. However, the present perfect sentence implies (1) that the fact that the speaker lost the keys is new information to the audience and (2) that it is important to the present moment of time. In other words, we all need to help the speaker look for the missing car keys. The past tense is simply a neutral statement of fact about something that happened in the past. There is no necessary implication that this is new information or that the listeners should do anything about it.

Using the noncontinuous present perfect rather than the past tense is a way of telling the audience that what we are saying is new and worth paying attention to. In this sense, it is a kind of emphatic form we might choose over the more standard and expected past tense. For this reason we are more likely to use the noncontinuous present perfect in casual conversation than in writing.

EXERCISE

7·5

Determine whether the underlined verb tense is emphatic (that is, the verb tense emphasizes new and important information) or neutral (that is, the verb tense is a statement of fact). The first two sentences are done as examples.

We <u>have fixed</u> the problem.

ANSWER: Emphatic

We <u>fixed</u> the problem.

ANSWER: Neutral

1. I've <u>got</u> an idea.

_____

2. We <u>made</u> a wrong turn.

_____

3. The witness <u>has admitted</u> mistaking the date of the accident.

_____

4. It <u>has encouraged</u> me to try again.

_____

5. The electricity <u>went</u> out.

_____

6. John <u>has insisted</u> on meeting with the board.

_____

7. I <u>twisted</u> my ankle playing soccer with the kids.

_____

8. We've just <u>got</u> an e-mail from the head office.

_____

9. The news <u>surprised</u> everyone.

_____

10. We've <u>decided</u> to host a party for their anniversary.

_____

Rewrite the underlined verb using both emphatic and neutral tenses. If it is emphatic, use the noncontinuous present perfect tense; if it is neutral, use the past tense. The first sentence is done as an example.

The senator <u>claim</u> that he was misquoted.

EMPHATIC: The senator <u>has claimed</u> that he was misquoted.

NEUTRAL: The senator <u>claimed</u> that he was misquoted.

1. The senator <u>refuse</u> to retract his statement.

Emphatic: _____

Neutral: _____

2. A big tree <u>fall</u> in the backyard.

Emphatic: _____

Neutral: _____

3. A reporter <u>reveal</u> the source of the money.

Emphatic: _____

Neutral: _____

4. They <u>tell</u> me what happened.

Emphatic: _____

Neutral: _____

5. I <u>turn</u> down the offer.

Emphatic: _____

Neutral: _____

6. We <u>buy</u> a new car.

Emphatic: _____

Neutral: _____

7. I <u>find</u> my car keys.

Emphatic: _____

Neutral: _____

8. The CEO <u>saw</u> the new sales figures.

Emphatic: _____

Neutral: _____

9. Our flight <u>be</u> canceled.

Emphatic: _____

Neutral: _____

10. The game <u>end</u> in a tie.

Emphatic: _____

Neutral: _____

The same distinction between the noncontinuous present perfect and past tenses carries over into questions. However, in questions the difference in implications between the noncontinuous present perfect and past tenses can be more significant, sometimes even amounting to a shift in meaning. For example, compare the noncontinuous present perfect and past tense versions of the same question:

Present perfect tense	Have you <u>seen</u> the play at the Civic Theater?
Past tense	<u>Did</u> you <u>see</u> the play at the Civic Theater?

The noncontinuous present perfect with its present-time relevancy implies (among other things) that the play is still running at the Civic Theater and the person being addressed still has a chance to see it if he or she hasn't done so already. The past tense in the second sentence definitely implies that the play's run is over and that the person being addressed has no further opportunity to see the play even if he or she wanted to.

The previous pair of sentences is a dramatic example of how distinct the implications of questions in the noncontinuous present perfect and past tenses can be. The difference between them is usually more modest. Here is a typical example:

Present perfect tense	Have you <u>reported</u> the accident to the police?
Past tense	<u>Did</u> you <u>report</u> the accident to the police?

The first question with the noncontinuous present perfect tense reflects a built-in expectation that reporting an accident to the police is something that people would normally do. Thus, asking the question in the present perfect conveys a tacit expectation that the answer would be "yes." The past tense question, on the other hand, is much more neutral. The past tense question does not voice the same expectation about reporting the accident to the police. It is a simple, factual question without the built-in positive implications of the noncontinuous present perfect question.

Here is a second example:

Present perfect tense	Have you <u>ordered</u> the pizza?
Past tense	<u>Did</u> you <u>order</u> the pizza?

The two questions have the same basic meaning. The differences in implication, however, are substantial. The first question with the noncontinuous present perfect tense implies that there was a definite plan to order pizza. The question functions as a confirmation of the fact that the pizza has already been ordered as expected: the person asking this question anticipates either of two possible answers: "yes" or "not yet."

The past tense question is much more neutral. Maybe the person ordered the pizza or maybe not—either answer is equally plausible. The use of the past tense is more like a genuine open-ended question than the present perfect version.

Decide whether the following questions have affirmative or neutral expectations. The first two are done as examples.

<u>Have</u> you just <u>got</u> here?

ANSWER: Affirmative expectation

<u>Did</u> you just <u>get</u> here?

ANSWER: Neutral expectation

1. <u>Did</u> they <u>find</u> out how the fire started?

   _____

2. <u>Has</u> the medication <u>helped</u> relieve the pain?

   _____

3. <u>Have</u> you <u>met</u> everyone?

   _____

4. <u>Did</u> the plumber finally <u>show</u> up?

   _____

5. <u>Has</u> the jury <u>reached</u> a verdict?

   _____

6. <u>Did</u> they <u>grow</u> these vegetables themselves?

   _____

7. <u>Did</u> you <u>remember</u> to walk the dog before you left?

   _____

8. <u>Have</u> you <u>learned</u> anything from this experience?

   _____

9. <u>Have</u> they <u>decided</u> what they are going to do?

   _____

10. <u>Did</u> you <u>drive</u> to work this morning?

    _____

Turn the following statements into questions with both affirmative and neutral expectations. If the question has an affirmative expectation, use the noncontinuous present perfect tense. If the question has a neutral expectation, use the past tense. The first sentence is done as an example.

They <u>replied</u> to the e-mail.

ANSWER: Affirmative expectation: <u>Have</u> they <u>replied</u> to the e-mail?

NEUTRAL: <u>Did</u> they <u>reply</u> to the e-mail?

1. The Coast Guard <u>warned</u> boaters about the storm.

   Affirmative expectation: _____

   Neutral: _____

2. The paint <u>dried</u>.

   Affirmative expectation: _____

   Neutral: _____

3. The committee <u>adopted</u> the proposal.

   Affirmative expectation: _____

   Neutral: _____

4. He <u>buy</u> the tickets.

   Affirmative expectation: _____

   Neutral: _____

5. The garage <u>checked</u> the battery.

   Affirmative expectation: _____

   Neutral: _____

6. You <u>stayed</u> there before.

   Affirmative expectation: _____

   Neutral: _____

7. She <u>kept</u> the receipts.

   Affirmative expectation: _____

   Neutral: _____

8. They <u>responded</u> to our offer.

   Affirmative expectation: _____

   Neutral: _____

9. You <u>get</u> enough to eat.

   Affirmative expectation: _____

   Neutral: _____

10. They <u>started</u> to work.

    Affirmative expectation: _____

    Neutral: _____

The past perfect tense

The past perfect tense consists of the helping verb *had* (the past tense of *have*) followed by a verb in the past participle form. Here are some examples:

> I called her, but she <u>had</u> already <u>left</u> for the day.
> The passes were all closed because we <u>had had</u> so much snow.
> The caller <u>had</u> already <u>hung</u> up by the time I answered the phone.
> I told him that I <u>had</u> already <u>made</u> up my mind.
> They bought an old house that <u>had been</u> built in the 1920s.

Time, the old joke goes, was invented to keep everything from happening all at once. Likewise, the past perfect tense was invented to keep two different past-time events from happening all at once. For this reason, the past perfect tense is sometimes called "the past in the past."

The two past-time events are almost always clauses—usually an independent clause and a subordinate clause but sometimes two independent clauses. The clause in the past perfect tense describes an action or event that has been completed before the action or event in the clause in the past tense takes place. Here are some examples of both types of clauses:

Independent clause and subordinate clause

(Note that some types of independent and subordinate clauses can be in either order. That is, the clause with the past perfect tense can either precede or follow the past tense clause.)

> They sold the house after they <u>had remodeled</u> it extensively.
>   more recent past-time event   older past-time event

> I <u>had</u> just <u>stepped</u> into the shower when the phone rang.
>   older past-time event   more recent past-time event

> We got a new rug because the old one <u>had faded</u> so badly.
>   more recent past-time event   older past-time event

> The landscapers removed the trees that <u>had grown</u> too big.
>   more recent past-time event   older past-time event

Two independent clauses

> They asked us to go with them, but we <u>had</u> already <u>made</u> other plans.
>   more recent past-time event   older past-time event

> I wanted to get a ride with Jim, but he <u>had</u> already <u>left</u>.
>   more recent past-time event   older past-time event

EXERCISE 7·9

Each of the following sentences contains two past-time clauses. Underline the past perfect tense. Then label the older clause as "older past-time event" and the newer one as "more recent past-time event." The first two sentences are done as examples.

We asked them to redo the tests that had been done last week.

ANSWER: We asked them to redo the tests that <u>had been done</u> last week.

    more recent past-time event   older past-time event

We went for a drive as soon as we had finished washing the car.

ANSWER: We went for a drive as soon as we <u>had finished</u> washing the car.

    more recent past-time event   older past-time event

1. We revised the estimates that we had made earlier.

2. He went into the hospital after his temperature had reached 103 degrees.

_____

3. They had patented the device before they put it on the market.

_____

4. I tried to get tickets, but they had already sold out.

_____

5. We fell into bed utterly exhausted as soon as we had eaten.

_____

6. The sun came out for the first time in days after the storm had finally passed.

_____

7. I knew the answer as soon as she had asked the question.

_____

8. I had picked up a cold when I was traveling.

_____

9. We had lived there some time before we met them.

_____

10. The bakery stopped making the cake that everyone had liked so much.

_____

The meaning and use of the past perfect tense is quite straightforward. The main difficulty using the past perfect tense is with sentences that contain an independent clause and an adverb clause because adverb clauses, unlike other types of clauses, can be moved around, making it more difficult to determine which clause should be in the past perfect tense and which should be in the past tense. Accordingly, we will focus the remaining discussion of the past perfect tense on sentences containing an independent clause and an adverb subordinate clause.

Let us begin by looking closely at an example of a sentence with an adverb clause:

I <u>had been</u> an intern for two years before they made me a job offer.
main clause   adverb clause

The past perfect portion of the sentence in the main clause expresses the older time—the two-year period that the speaker was an intern. The past tense portion of the sentence in the adverb clause expresses a second, more recent event—the speaker's being offered a job. The whole point of using the past perfect tense is to separate this sentence, all of which takes place in the past, into two distinct past-time frames—the older time period of the internship and the more recent event of the job offer. The use of the two different tenses enables us to place the two past-time events into a clear and unequivocal chronological sequence.

Sometimes the time sequencing imposed by the two different tenses can even imply a cause-and-effect relationship between the two clauses. For example:

They <u>had had</u> a big fight just before they broke up.
main clause   adverb clause

This sequencing leads us to think that their fight may have caused their subsequent breakup.

Adverb clauses are dependent clauses that play the role of adverbs. As with single-word adverbs, adverb clauses modify verbs by giving more information about the time, place, manner, or cause of the action of the verb. Here we are concerned only with adverb clauses that give information about time or (occasionally) cause.

In our first set of examples of past perfect tenses in adverb clauses, all of the past perfect tenses will be in the main clause:

The driver <u>had suffered</u> a heart attack before the car ran off the road.
main clause   adverb clause

The plane <u>had been</u> airborne for about two hours when the left engine quit.
main clause   adverb clause

He <u>had committed</u> himself to the plan before he knew all the facts.
main clause   adverb clause

We <u>had repainted</u> the house before we put it on the market.
main clause   adverb clause

One of the characteristics of adverb clauses is that they can be moved from their normal position following the main clause to a position in front of the main clause. (When we move the adverb clause in front of the main clause, the adverb clause is said to be **inverted**.) We must separate the inverted introductory adverb clause from the main clause by a comma. (We do not use a comma to separate the main clause from the adverb clause when the adverb clause is in a position following the main clause.) Here are the previous example sentences now with the adverb clauses in inverted positions:

Before the car ran off the road, the driver <u>had suffered</u> a heart attack.
adverb clause   main clause

When the left engine quit, the plane <u>had been</u> airborne for about two hours.
adverb clause   main clause

Before he knew all the facts, he <u>had committed</u> himself to the plan.
adverb clause   main clause

Before we put it on the market, we <u>had repainted</u> the house.
adverb clause   main clause

Inverting adverb clauses has no effect on the grammatical meaning of the sentence. The only difference is in emphasis: putting the adverb clause first gives it greater relative emphasis, following the general rhetorical principle that any grammatical structure moved out of its normal position (especially when it is moved to the first position in the sentence) automatically becomes more prominent.

EXERCISE
7·10

All of the following sentences contain a main clause in the past perfect tense followed by an adverb clause in the past tense. Invert the two clauses so that the adverb clause is given greater emphasis. Be sure to use a comma with the inverted adverb clause. The first sentence is done as an example.

It <u>had stopped</u> snowing by the time we got to airport.

ANSWER: By the time we got to the airport, it <u>had stopped</u> snowing.

1. We <u>had adjusted</u> the car seats before we started driving.

_____

2. The waiter <u>had started</u> clearing the dishes before everyone finished eating.

_____

3. The ice cream <u>had</u> already <u>melted</u> by the time we cut the cake.

_____

4. The house <u>had been</u> empty for years when we first moved in.

_____

5. We <u>had</u> already <u>finished</u> setting the table before I noticed the dirty glasses.

_____

6. He <u>had advertised</u> the job opening before the position was approved.

_____

7. The sun <u>had risen</u> long before we got on the road.

_____

8. The rebels <u>had</u> already <u>abandoned</u> the fort before the soldiers arrived.

_____

9. The rain <u>had stopped</u> by the time we got our tents set up.

_____

10. I <u>had heard</u> the loud music even before I reached the door.

_____

EXERCISE

7·11

Here are pairs of simple sentences in the past tense, one labeled "Older" and the other labeled "More recent." Combine the two simple sentences to produce a single sentence containing a present perfect tense in the "older" main clause and a past tense in the "more recent" adverb clause. Write two versions. In the first version, the adverb clause is in normal order following the main clause. In the second version, the adverb clause is inverted. Use the word in parentheses to help form the adverb clause. The first sentence is done as an example.

OLDER: I <u>hid</u> the presents.

            More recent: The children <u>got</u> up. (*before*)

ANSWER: Normal order: I <u>had hidden</u> the presents before the children <u>got</u> up.

            Inverted: Before the children <u>got</u> up, I <u>had hidden</u> the presents.

1. Older: We <u>taped</u> all the windows and doors.

   More recent: We <u>started</u> painting. (*before*)

   Normal order: _____

   Inverted: _____

2. Older: John already <u>swam</u> competitively.

   More recent: He <u>went</u> to college. (*before*)

   Normal order: _____

   Inverted: _____

3. Older: Everyone <u>put</u> on protective headgear.

   More recent: They <u>went</u> bicycle riding. (*before*)

Normal order: _____

Inverted: _____

4. Older: I <u>skipped</u> lunch.

   More recent: I <u>had</u> an important conference call at noon. (*because*)

   Normal order: _____

   Inverted: _____

5. Older: The lawyers totally <u>revised</u> their strategy.

   More recent: The court <u>reconvened</u> after lunch. (*before*)

   Normal order: _____

   Inverted: _____

6. Older: The cook <u>rubbed</u> the roast with herbs.

   More recent: He <u>put</u> it in the oven. (*before*)

   Normal order: _____

   Inverted: _____

7. Older: He <u>hesitated</u> noticeably.

   More recent: He <u>answered</u> the question. (*before*)

   Normal order: _____

   Inverted: _____

8. Older: They <u>drained</u> a lot of water out of the reservoir.

   More recent: The heavy rains <u>came</u>. (*before*)

   Normal order: _____

   Inverted: _____

9. Older: The company <u>analyzed</u> the proposal carefully.

   More recent: They <u>invested</u> money in it. (*before*)

   Normal order: _____

   Inverted: _____

10. Older: They <u>got</u> extra car insurance.

    More recent: Their son <u>was</u> old enough to drive. (*as soon as*)

    Normal order: _____

    Inverted: _____

To this point, all of our examples of past perfect tenses used in sentences with adverb clauses have had the past perfect verb in the main clause. However, the past perfect verb is actually more often used in the adverb clause. Here are some examples:

We cleared off the driveway as soon as it <u>had stopped</u> snowing.
main clause   adverb clause

My bicycle got a flat tire before we <u>had gone</u> two miles.
  main clause   adverb clause

I wasn't able to play because I <u>had injured</u> my leg last week.
  main clause   adverb clause

The janitor always locked the gym up after the team buses <u>had departed</u>.
  main clause   adverb clause

These adverb clauses can also be inverted, putting the past perfect verb in the first clause:

As soon as it <u>had stopped</u> snowing, we cleared off the driveway.
  adverb clause   main clause

Before we <u>had gone</u> two miles, my bicycle got a flat tire.
  adverb clause   main clause

Because I <u>had injured</u> my leg last week, I wasn't able to play.
  adverb clause   main clause

After the team buses <u>had departed</u>, the janitor always locked the gym up.
  adverb clause   main clause

EXERCISE
7·12

All of the following sentences contain a main clause in the past tense followed by an adverb clause in the past perfect tense. Invert the two clauses so that the adverb clause is given greater emphasis. Be sure to use a comma with the inverted adverb. The first sentence is done as an example:

I knew my wallet was on the dresser because I <u>had put</u> it there the night before.

ANSWER: Because I <u>had put</u> it there the night before, I knew my wallet was on the dresser.

1. I called them on my cell phone as soon as the plane <u>had landed</u>.

   _____

2. I knew the answer even before he <u>had finished</u> asking me the question.

   _____

3. Our team scored even before we <u>had found</u> our seats.

   _____

4. We hung the clothes on the line after the sun <u>had come</u> out.

   _____

5. We could declare a thesis topic after we <u>had passed</u> the qualifying exam.

   _____

6. I had to come up with a plan even before we'd <u>had</u> a chance to talk about it.

   _____

7. We looked for better seats after we <u>had reboarded</u> the bus.

   _____

8. General Lee became a college president after the Civil War <u>had ended</u>.

   _____

9. It functioned much better after they had repaired it.

_____

10. The plane finally took off after we had sat on the tarmac for an hour.

_____

_____

Here are pairs of simple sentences in the past tense, one labeled "More recent" and the other labeled "Older." Combine the two simple sentences to produce a single sentence containing a past tense in the "More recent" main clause and a present perfect tense in the "Older" adverb clause. Write two versions. In the first version, the adverb clause is in normal order following the main clause. In the second version, the adverb clause is inverted. The first sentence is done as an example. (Your answers may have slightly different wording.)

MORE RECENT: Bob was able to play again. (main clause)

OLDER: He had surgery on his injured knee. (adverb clause)

ANSWER: Normal order: Bob was able to play again after he had had surgery on his injured knee.

INVERTED: After he had had surgery on his injured knee, Bob was able to play again.

1. More recent: They were eligible to play professional football. (main clause)

   Older: Their class graduated from college. (adverb clause)

   Normal order: _____

   Inverted: _____

2. More recent: The airlines instituted a new policy. (main clause)

   Older: There was a near collision on the tarmac. (adverb clause)

   Normal order: _____

   Inverted: _____

3. More recent: He was arrested. (main clause)

   Older: He lied to the grand jury under oath. (adverb clause)

   Normal order: _____

   Inverted: _____

4. More recent: Ralph quit his job and moved to Florida. (main clause)

   Older: Ralph won the lottery. (adverb clause)

   Normal order: _____

   Inverted: _____

5. More recent: The cloth shrunk badly. (main clause)

   Older: The cloth got wet. (adverb clause)

   Normal order: _____

   Inverted: _____

6. More recent: The protesters <u>were</u> arrested. (main clause)

   Older: The protesters <u>disrupted</u> a city council meeting. (adverb clause)

   Normal order: _____

   Inverted: _____

7. More recent: The witness <u>was</u> excused from testifying. (main clause)

   Older: The witness <u>invoked</u> her right against self-incrimination. (adverb clause)

   Normal order: _____

   Inverted: _____

8. More recent: Someone <u>called</u> the fire department. (main clause)

   Older: The residents <u>were</u> alerted by the smell of smoke. (adverb clause)

   Normal order: _____

   Inverted: _____

9. More recent: The meetings <u>were</u> better attended. (main clause)

   Older: They <u>started</u> serving refreshments. (adverb clause)

   Normal order: _____

   Inverted: _____

10. More recent: The dog <u>chewed</u> up all the furniture. (main clause)

    Older: They <u>left</u> for work that morning. (adverb clause)

    Normal order: _____

    Inverted: _____

Summary of sentences with adverb clauses

Using the past perfect tenses with sentences that contain adverb clauses is confusing for two reasons: (1) adverb clauses can be either in their normal positions after main clauses or they can be inverted, and (2) it is quite common for the past perfect tense to be used in the main clause rather than the adverb clause. Thus, there are no fewer than four possibilities for where the past perfect tense can occur:

- The past perfect tense is in a main clause in its normal initial position.
  Example: We <u>had packed</u> a picnic lunch before we left.
      main clause   adverb clause
- The past perfect tense is in a main clause, but the main clause is in the second position following an inverted adverb clause.
  Example: Before we left, we <u>had packed</u> a picnic lunch.
- The past perfect tense is in the adverb clause in its normal position following the main clause.
  Example: It took a while to clean the pot because the rice <u>had boiled</u> over.
- The past perfect tense is in an adverb clause inverted to a position in front of the main clause.
  Example: Because the rice <u>had boiled</u> over, it took a while to clean the pot.

The future perfect tense

The future perfect tense verb form consists of *will have* (the future tense form of *have*) followed by a verb in the past perfect form. Here are some examples:

> By then, everyone <u>will have finished</u> eating.
> The office <u>will have closed</u> before we can get there.
> They <u>will have lived</u> in Japan for six years this coming January.

The future perfect tense, as all of the perfect tenses, must be terminated or "perfected" by an even more distant moment of time or defining event. In the case of the future perfect tense, this more distant moment is defined by an adverb prepositional phrase (usually beginning with the preposition *by*) or by an adverb clause of time. Here are some examples:

Terminating adverb prepositional phrase
The moon <u>will have set</u> by midnight.
The team <u>will have come</u> out onto the field by now.
Amazon <u>will have shipped</u> our order by the end of next week.

Terminating adverb clause of time
They <u>will have rented</u> a place to stay before school starts in the fall.
He <u>will have figured</u> out the answer as soon as he gets all the clues.
The chairman <u>will have replaced Harry</u> before the board meets on Monday.

The future perfect tense is used to talk about future-time events or conditions that will be completed or concluded no later than some specified future time or future event; for example:

Specified future time
I <u>will have entered</u> all the data before the end of the day.
The kitchen <u>will have stopped</u> serving by 10:00.
I <u>will have earned</u> $5,000 by the end of the summer.
The storm <u>will have blocked</u> all the roads by nightfall.

Specified future event
The painters <u>will have finished</u> the interior before the carpets are laid.
We <u>will have paid</u> the developers a fortune by the time we are finished.
They <u>will have gotten</u> the tents up before it starts raining.
I <u>will have graded</u> the papers before class begins.

When we talk about future conditions, we often use stative verbs with an adverb of duration; for example:

> They <u>will have been</u> married <u>for 10 years</u> this June.
>   adverb of duration

> I <u>will have owned</u> my truck <u>for two years</u> this coming Labor Day.
>   adverb of duration

> I <u>will have had</u> a cold <u>for two weeks</u> now.
>   adverb of duration

The difference between the future tense and the future perfect tense is that the future perfect tense is used to emphasize the completion of the future event. For example, compare the following sentences:

Future tense	We <u>will have</u> dinner by 7:00.
Future perfect tense	We <u>will have</u> had dinner by 7:00.

The future tense sentence implies that dinner will start by 7:00. The future perfect tense implies that dinner will be over by 7:00.

Here is another example:

| Future tense | The clouds <u>will break</u> up by noon. |
| *Future perfect tense* | The clouds <u>will have broken</u> up by noon. |

The future tense sentence implies that we will have at least partial sun by noon. The future perfect sentence implies that the clouds will be completely gone by noon.

Here is an example where the difference is more subtle:

| *Future tense* | Larry <u>will get</u> to the office around 9:00. |
| *Future perfect tense* | Larry <u>will have gotten</u> to the office around 9:00. |

The sentence with the future tense envisions Larry arriving at the office at or before 9:00. The sentence with the future perfect tense envisions that at or before 9:00, Larry will already have been settled in his office for some time.

In general, we can say that the future tense envisions a future event happening. The future perfect tense envisions that future event as already being completed.

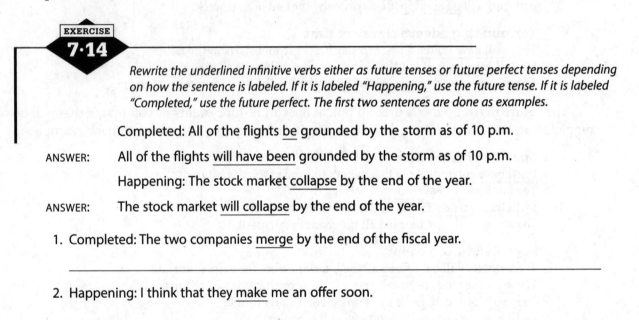

EXERCISE

7·14

Rewrite the underlined infinitive verbs either as future tenses or future perfect tenses depending on how the sentence is labeled. If it is labeled "Happening," use the future tense. If it is labeled "Completed," use the future perfect. The first two sentences are done as examples.

Completed: All of the flights <u>be</u> grounded by the storm as of 10 p.m.

ANSWER: All of the flights <u>will have been</u> grounded by the storm as of 10 p.m.

Happening: The stock market <u>collapse</u> by the end of the year.

ANSWER: The stock market <u>will collapse</u> by the end of the year.

1. Completed: The two companies <u>merge</u> by the end of the fiscal year.

_____

2. Happening: I think that they <u>make</u> me an offer soon.

_____

3. Completed: They <u>trace</u> the source of the leak in a few hours.

_____

4. Happening: The carpets <u>fade</u> quickly if they are not protected from the sun.

_____

5. Completed: Surely any message they sent <u>reach</u> us by now.

_____

6. Completed: Hurry, or they <u>sell</u> all the good seats by the time we get our orders in.

_____

7. Happening: The doctor <u>prescribe</u> a different medication after seeing what happened.

_____

8. Completed: Her heirs <u>gain</u> control of their estate when they turned 18.

_____

9. Completed: The chair <u>cut</u> off discussion after two hours.

_____

10. Completed: The police <u>inform</u> him of his rights the moment he was arrested.

_____

Present perfect

Use the present perfect when you want to refer to a situation that originated in the past but continues into the present or to refer to a past experience that has current relevance.

> PAST SITUATION CONTINUING INTO THE PRESENT: I **have lived** in Dallas for six years.
> PAST EXPERIENCE WITH CURRENT RELEVANCE: We **have traveled** to Alaska three times.

For an experience to be relevant, it is usually related to a possible future experience. In the example "We have traveled to Alaska three times," the speaker may be considering another trip. The present perfect is often used in job interviews when an employer asks a prospective employee about his or her experience: "Have you ever driven a large vehicle?" "Have you ever used a cash register?"

The present perfect consists of the auxiliary verb _have_ and the perfect/passive form of the main verb. The auxiliary verb is marked for tense. The perfect/passive verb form is used to indicate either the perfect aspect or the passive voice. (The passive voice will be discussed in Part IV.) The perfect/passive form for regular verbs consists of the base form of the verb and the ending _-ed_.

	Singular	**Plural**
First Person	I **have verb + ed**	we **have verb + ed**
Second Person	you **have verb + ed**	you **have verb + ed**
Third Person	he, she, it **has verb + ed**	they **have verb + ed**

When a one-syllable word or a word with a stressed final syllable ends in a single consonant sound, double the last letter before adding _-ed_.

One-syllable word: pet → petted

Word ending in a stressed syllable: admit → admitted

BUT sew → sewed [This word ends in a vowel sound.]

The perfect/passive forms of irregular verbs can be found in the appendix.

The following are common irregular verb patterns:

- Pattern 1: The final _d_ becomes a _t_.

buil**d**	buil**t**
len**d**	len**t**
spen**d**	spen**t**

- Pattern 2: A _-d_ or _-t_ suffix is added. The vowel changes.

feel /fil/	felt /fɛlt/
keep /kip/	kept /kɛpt/
sell /sɛl/	sold /sold/

♦ Pattern 3: An *-n* or *-en* suffix is added.

eat	eaten
fall	fallen
know	known

Sometimes the vowel changes.

speak /spik/	spoken /spokɛn/
wear /wɛr/	worn /worn/

♦ Pattern 4: Just the vowel changes.

hold /hold/	held /hɛld/
meet /mit/	met /mɛt/
sit /sɪt/	sat /sæt/

♦ Pattern 5: The base form and perfect/passive form are the same.

put	put
hit	hit
cut	cut

EXERCISE
7·15

Complete each sentence with the present perfect form of the verb in parentheses. If you are unsure of the perfect/passive form, check the chart in the appendix.

1. Pat and Tom _____ (build) two houses this summer.

2. I _____ (eat) already.

3. His parents _____ (lend) him some money.

4. We _____ (speak) to the director about our concerns.

5. The company's stock _____ (fall).

6. You _____ (know) me for a long time.

7. They _____ (sell) their house.

8. It _____ (rain) every day for a week.

9. I _____ (keep) your secret.

10. He _____ (spend) too much money this month.

11. The bride and groom _____ (cut) the wedding cake.

Past perfect

Use the past perfect when you want to refer to a past action, state, or event that occurred prior to another time in the past. The more recent past time may be expressed as a prepositional phrase or as a clause in which another action, state, or event is mentioned.

PAST ACTION BEFORE PAST TIME: They **had finished** the project *by Friday.*

PAST STATE BEFORE PAST ACTION: He **had been** depressed *before he went on vacation.*

You can also use the past perfect to refer to a hypothetical action, state, or event.

HYPOTHETICAL ACTION: If they **had come** earlier, they would have received free tickets.

Sentences such as this one will be discussed in more detail in Part IV.

The past perfect consists of the auxiliary verb *have* and the perfect/passive form of the main verb. The auxiliary verb is marked for past tense. The perfect/passive verb form is used to indicate either the perfect aspect or the passive voice. (The passive voice will be discussed in Part IV.) The perfect/passive form for regular verbs consists of the base form of the verb and the ending *-ed*.

	Singular	Plural
First Person	I **had verb + ed**	we **had verb + ed**
Second Person	you **had verb + ed**	you **had verb + ed**
Third Person	he, she, it **had verb + ed**	they **had verb + ed**

When a one-syllable word or a word with a stressed final syllable ends in a single consonant sound, double the last letter before adding *-ed*.

One-syllable word: pat → patted

Word ending in a stressed syllable: occur → occurred

BUT tow → towed [This word ends in a vowel sound.]

The present/passive forms of irregular verbs can be found in the appendix.

EXERCISE
7·16

Complete each sentence with the past perfect form of the verb in parentheses. If you need help with irregular verb forms, check the appendix.

1. Before 2009, they_____(attend) college in Philadelphia.

2. After we _____(hold) a meeting, we announced our decision.

3. They _____ (sell) most of their furniture before they moved.

4. The employees _____ (meet) the new director already.

5. I _____ (feel) uneasy before I gave my speech.

6. He _____ (hit) twenty home runs before the All-Star Game.

7. We_____(sit) down right before the concert began.

8. She_____(run) three marathons by the age of twenty.

9. It _____ (snow) so much that school was canceled.

10. She _____ (be) there so often that everyone knew her.

EXERCISE

7·17

Using the verbs in parentheses, complete each sentence with either the simple past or the past perfect.

1. The taxi _____ (arrive) after he _____ (left).

2. After we _____ (finish) the dishes, we _____ (go) for a walk.

3. The teacher _____ (assign) twenty problems, but most students _____ (complete) only fifteen of them.

4. She _____ (be) tired because she _____ (work) late the night before.

5. He _____ (wear) the ring that his grandfather _____ (give) him.

6. I _____ (revise) a paper that I _____ (write) a year ago.

7. She _____ (knock) on the door before she _____ (enter).

8. All of a sudden we _____ (know) that we _____ (take) the wrong exit off the freeway.

9. He _____ (read) aloud from a new book he _____ (receive) as a gift.

10. They _____ (celebrate) because they _____ (pass) all their classes.

Introduction to the progressive tenses

There are three progressive tenses: the **present progressive**, the **past progressive**, and the **future progressive**. The three progressive tenses are all formed in exactly parallel manner: the appropriate present, past, or future tense form of the helping verb *be* followed by a verb in the present participle form; for example:

Present progressive	They <u>are working</u> in the garden now.
Past progressive	They <u>were working</u> in the garden earlier.
Future progressive	They <u>will be working</u> in the garden this afternoon.

The basic meaning of the progressive tense is an action in progress (thus the name **progressive** tense) at a particular moment in time. The present progressive is an action in progress at the present moment or period of time. The past progressive is an action in progress at some moment or period in the past. The future progressive is an action in progress at some moment or period in the future.

EXERCISE

7·18

Underline and identify the progressive tenses in the following sentences. The first sentence is done as an example.

My parents will be staying with us this weekend.

ANSWER: My parents <u>will be staying</u> with us this weekend.
future progressive

1. Our company is sponsoring a number of charity auctions.

   _____

2. We were just admiring your garden.

   _____

3. Our pets will be going to the vet for their annual shots.

   _____

4. I am translating some technical manuals into Spanish.

   _____

5. The kids will be staying overnight at a friend's house.

   _____

6. Am I interrupting anything?

   _____

7. They will be completing their training in June.

   _____

8. I was falling asleep at my desk so I took a little walk to wake up.

   _____

9. I don't know why they are blaming me for what happened.

   _____

10. Remember, they will be relying on you.

    _____

EXERCISE
7·19

*Replace the underlined verb with the progressive verb form identified in parentheses.
The first sentence is done as an example.*

(past progressive) The farmers <u>load</u> sacks of grain onto their trucks.

ANSWER: The farmers <u>were loading</u> sacks of grain onto their trucks.

1. (future progressive) You <u>waste</u> your time if you do that.

   _____

2. (present progressive) I <u>make</u> some coffee; would you like some?

   _____

3. (past progressive) The polls <u>lean</u> toward the incumbent candidate.

   _____

4. (future progressive) I <u>teach</u> part-time next year.

   _____

5. (past progressive) The heat <u>kill</u> all of our shade plants.

   _____

6. (future progressive) Their flight <u>arrive</u> at 9:45.

   _____

7. (present progressive) They <u>refer</u> the whole matter to their legal department.

   _____

8. (past progressive) I thought that they <u>deal</u> with the situation very well.

   _____

9. (future progressive) We <u>discuss</u> that issue at our next meeting.

   _____

10. (present progressive) His doctor <u>treat</u> the infection with a new antibiotic.

   _____

The present progressive tense

The present progressive tense consists of the helping verb *be* in a present tense form followed by a verb in the present participle *–ing* form. Here are some examples:

> Our builder <u>is leasing</u> some heavy equipment to clear the site.
> The heavy rain <u>is washing</u> ruts into our front yard.
> I <u>am telephoning</u> all of the committee members.
> We <u>are going</u> to my parents' home for Christmas.
> It seems that traffic <u>is getting</u> worse every month.
> I<u>'m hoping</u> that I could see you for a few minutes this afternoon.
> He <u>is</u> always <u>coming</u> in late to meetings.

The present progressive tense has two main meanings: (1) action in progress and (2) future. In addition, there are two idiomatic uses of the present progressive that we will discuss at the end of the chapter.

Using the present progressive for action in progress

"Action in progress" accounts for around 80 percent of the occurrences of the present progressive. The term *action in progress* refers to the fact that we use the present progressive tense to narrate or depict an action or event that takes place or "progresses" (hence the name of the tense "progressive") over some span of current time. What constitutes "some span of current time" is very broad.

The action can take place during the actual time of speaking; for example:

> I<u>'m</u> just <u>calling</u> to say hello.
> The children <u>are opening</u> their presents even as we speak.

Or, the action can take place over great periods of time; for example:

> The Pacific plate <u>is</u> slowly <u>diving</u> under the North American plate.
> The two galaxies <u>are passing</u> through each other over a period of millennia.

On the face of it, the present progressive tense in the sense of "action in progress" seems perfectly straightforward. In many ways it is, but it is surprisingly difficult for nonnative speakers to use correctly. In fact, advanced nonnative speakers of English probably make more errors with this meaning of the present progressive tense than with any other single verb form in English.

The problem is not in forming the present progressive correctly or in using it in appropriate situations. The main problem is that there are some aspects of the progressive tenses (the present progressive in particular) that lead nonnative speakers to use the present progressive tense with stative verbs, verbs that are incompatible with the progressive tenses.

There are two important areas of differences between dynamic verbs and stative verbs that are especially relevant to the progressive tenses: the nature of subject-verb relationships and how the two types of verbs treat time.

Subject-verb relationships

Dynamic and stative verbs enter into very different relationships with their subjects. Dynamic verbs require the subject to be the performer or "doer" of the action of the verb. For example:

> Frank answered the phone.
> Janet taught English in China for a few years.
> Farmer Brown planted potatoes this year.

In these dynamic verb sentences, the subjects are the performers of the action of the verbs: Frank performed the action of answering the phone; Janet performed the action of teaching English; Farmer Brown performed the action of planting potatoes.

Stative verbs enter into a different kind of relationship with their subjects, describing the ongoing condition or state of their subjects; for example:

> Frank has a cell phone but no landline.
> Janet knows a lot about teaching English in China.
> Farmer Brown owns 500 acres of land in Idaho.

None of the subjects in these examples are doing anything. Instead, the verbs are describing something about the nature or situation of the subjects: Frank's ownership of telephones is described; Janet is described as knowing a lot about teaching English in China; and Farmer Brown is described as owning land in Idaho (where he can grow his potatoes).

Sometimes, especially with mental or cognitive verbs, the subject-verb difference between stative and dynamic verbs is not obvious at first glance. Compare the following two sentences:

> Betty figured out the answer to the question.
> Betty knew the answer to the question.

Often with mental or cognitive verbs the difference between stative and dynamic comes down to this question: Is the subject intentionally performing the action of the verb? In the first example, Betty has actively engaged in the process of coming up with the answer to the question. The solution came about only because Betty intentionally made it happen. The second example is different. We don't necessarily choose to know things. For example, all of us have the lyrics to hundreds of idiotic pop songs from our teenage years cluttering up our brains. We would all be happy to get rid of these lyrics to free up more mental storage space if only we could.

Figure (out) is thus a dynamic verb, and *know* is thus a stative verb. When we use the two verbs in the present progressive, we see the difference in grammaticality:

> Betty is figuring out the answer to the question.
> X Betty is knowing the answer to the question.

Another challenge is that many verbs can be either stative or dynamic verbs depending on the way they are used. For example, the verb *appear* can be used as either a dynamic verb or a stative verb (note that both are grammatical in the past tense):

Dynamic verb	Jerome <u>appeared</u> in a Hollywood film.
Stative verb	Jerome <u>appeared</u> to be a little distracted.

In the dynamic verb sentence, *appear* means "play a role." In the stative verb sentence, *appear* means "seem to other people." As we would expect, the dynamic verb use is grammatical in the present progressive tense, while the stative verb use is not:

Dynamic verb	Jerome <u>is appearing</u> in a Hollywood film.
Stative verb	**X** Jerome <u>is appearing</u> to be a little distracted.

In the dynamic verb sentence, the subject *Jerome* is an agent performing the action of the verb *appear*. In the stative verb sentence, the same subject is not doing anything. Instead, the sentence comments on how the subject *Jerome* seems to other people.

EXERCISE

7·20

Each of the following items has two sentences, one with a stative verb and one with a dynamic verb. Relying solely on the relationship between the subject and the verb, identify which verb is the stative verb and which is the dynamic verb. The stative verb will describe the nature of the subject; the dynamic verb will carry out the action of the subject. Confirm your answers by using both sentences in the present progressive tense. The first sentence is done as an example.

The children always <u>like</u> to play outside.

The children always <u>ask</u> to play outside.

ANSWER: The children always <u>like</u> to play outside. **Stative**

The children always <u>ask</u> to play outside. **Dynamic**

Present progressive: **X** The children <u>are</u> always <u>liking</u> to play outside.

Present progressive: The children <u>are</u> always <u>asking</u> to play outside.

1. The sausages <u>weigh</u> two pounds.

   The butcher <u>weighs</u> the sausages.

   Present progressive: _____

   Present progressive: _____

2. College graduates <u>pile up</u> a lot of debt.

   College graduates <u>owe</u> a lot of money.

   Present progressive: _____

   Present progressive: _____

3. Bill <u>has</u> a broken toe.

   Bill <u>has</u> some friends over to celebrate his promotion.

   Present progressive: _____

   Present progressive: _____

4. The children <u>appear</u> to be ready to go.

The situation <u>changes</u> by the minute.

Present progressive: _____

Present progressive: _____

5. The kids always <u>turn</u> their bedroom into a playground.

The kids' bedroom <u>resembles</u> the scene of a natural disaster.

Present progressive: _____

Present progressive: _____

6. Her new hairstyle <u>suits</u> her very well.

Her new hairstyle <u>takes</u> a lot of time to maintain.

Present progressive: _____

Present progressive: _____

7. Everyone <u>tells</u> me to be careful.

Everyone <u>needs</u> to be careful.

Present progressive: _____

Present progressive: _____

8. The public <u>doubts</u> what the congressman is claiming.

The public <u>agrees</u> with what the congressman is claiming.

Present progressive: _____

Present progressive: _____

9. A big payment <u>comes</u> due at the end of the month.

A big problem <u>exists</u> in our cash flow.

Present progressive: _____

Present progressive: _____

10. The students <u>discussed</u> how to thank you.

The students <u>appreciate</u> all that you have done for them.

Present progressive: _____

Present progressive: _____

Time

The second major difference between dynamic and stative verbs is how they relate to time. Dynamic verbs are time bound; that is, the action of the verb always takes place in real time. Accordingly, the time of a dynamic verb's action can always be expressed by an adverb of time (either an adverb prepositional phrase or an adverb clause). For example:

Jennifer <u>bought</u> a leather jacket.

This is a grammatically complete sentence without any overt expression of time. However, because the action of buying a jacket must take place in time, we *always* have the option of adding an adverb of time (either an adverb prepositional phrase or an adverb clause) to specify the time of the action; for example:

> Jennifer <u>bought</u> a leather jacket **last week**. (adverb prepositional phrase)
> Jennifer <u>bought</u> a leather jacket **when she was in Denver**. (adverb clause)

Stative verbs, on the other hand, are not time bound—just the opposite. Stative verbs are not limited at all by time.

> Jennifer <u>owns</u> a leather jacket.

In this stative sentence, the stative verb *owns* describes something about the nature or character of the subject (Jennifer). In this case the verb tells us that she has a leather jacket. When somebody owns something, that state of ownership is not time bound. Ownership is an ongoing state with no built-in time limitation. When we own something, we own it indefinitely; we own it until we decide to get rid of it or otherwise lose possession of it.

If we try to modify a stative verb with an adverb of time, we are essentially mixing two incompatible systems: the inherently unlimited time of the stative verb with the limitation of the adverb of time. The result is necessarily both ungrammatical and nonsensical:

> **X Jennifer owns a leather jacket at five this afternoon.** (adverb prepositional phrase)
> X Jennifer owns a leather jacket **when she goes to dinner**. (adverb clause)

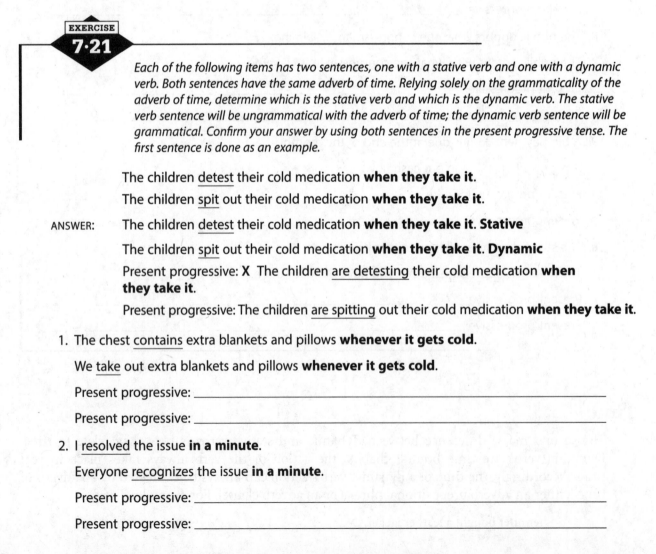

EXERCISE
7·21

Each of the following items has two sentences, one with a stative verb and one with a dynamic verb. Both sentences have the same adverb of time. Relying solely on the grammaticality of the adverb of time, determine which is the stative verb and which is the dynamic verb. The stative verb sentence will be ungrammatical with the adverb of time; the dynamic verb sentence will be grammatical. Confirm your answer by using both sentences in the present progressive tense. The first sentence is done as an example.

The children <u>detest</u> their cold medication **when they take it**.

The children <u>spit</u> out their cold medication **when they take it**.

ANSWER: The children <u>detest</u> their cold medication **when they take it**. **Stative**

The children <u>spit</u> out their cold medication **when they take it**. **Dynamic**

Present progressive: **X** The children are <u>detesting</u> their cold medication **when they take it**.

Present progressive: The children are <u>spitting</u> out their cold medication **when they take it**.

1. The chest <u>contains</u> extra blankets and pillows **whenever it gets cold**.

   We <u>take</u> out extra blankets and pillows **whenever it gets cold**.

   Present progressive: _____

   Present progressive: _____

2. I <u>resolved</u> the issue **in a minute**.

   Everyone <u>recognizes</u> the issue **in a minute**.

   Present progressive: _____

   Present progressive: _____

3. We <u>track</u> the paths of protons **when we are in the lab**.

   Atoms <u>consist</u> of protons **when we are in the lab**.

   Present progressive: _____

   Present progressive: _____

4. They <u>seem</u> to be reliable **all the time**.

   We <u>check</u> on their reliability **all the time**.

   Present progressive: _____

   Present progressive: _____

5. He <u>finds</u> out what the answer is **on Wednesday**.

   He <u>understands</u> what the answer is **on Wednesday**.

   Present progressive: _____

   Present progressive: _____

6. The new shoes <u>fit</u> well **every weekend**.

   I <u>wear</u> the new shoes **every weekend**.

   Present progressive: _____

   Present progressive: _____

7. We <u>buy</u> a new car **next week**.

   A new car <u>costs</u> more than we can afford **next week**.

   Present progressive: _____

   Present progressive: _____

8. The children <u>love</u> their new school **in the fall**.

   The children <u>enter</u> their new school **in the fall**.

   Present progressive: _____

   Present progressive: _____

9. Their new apartment <u>looks</u> like their old place **when they move in**.

   They <u>plan</u> to remodel their new apartment **when they move in**.

   Present progressive: _____

   Present progressive: _____

10. Everyone <u>helps</u> to rearrange the layout of our office **every Monday morning**.

    Everyone <u>dislikes</u> the layout of our office **every Monday morning**.

    Present progressive: _____

    Present progressive: _____

Different verb tenses interact with dynamic and stative verbs in different ways. The past tense is unusual in that it is equally accepting of both dynamic and stative verbs; for example:

Dynamic verb	Jennifer <u>bought</u> a leather jacket last week.
Stative verb	Jennifer <u>owned</u> a leather jacket when she lived in Denver.

The fact that the past tense can be freely used with both kinds of verbs is undoubtedly why most novels and other works of fiction are written in the past tense: writers can mix dynamic and stative verbs without problems of grammatical or semantic incompatibility.

The present tense will readily permit stative verbs but not dynamic verbs unless they are used in special ways; for example:

Stative verb	Jennifer <u>owns</u> a leather jacket.
Dynamic verb	**X** Jennifer <u>buys</u> a leather jacket.

We can use dynamic verbs in the present tense, but only if we use adverbs of frequency to make the action of the verb habitual or customary (and thus not time bound as dynamic verbs normally are):

Dynamic verb	Jennifer <u>buys</u> a leather jacket every time she goes to Italy.

We now return to the question of why it is so difficult for nonnative speakers to correct errors with stative verbs in the present progressive tense.

The answer probably lies in the unique way that the present progressive tense treats time. The very meaning of the tense name "**progressive**" emphasizes that the whole purpose of the tense is to describe things that span (progress) across time. It would then seem that the span of time that is always implicit in the actions described in the present progressive tense would be perfectly compatible with the continuous nature of stative verbs. The fact that nonnative speakers so persistently use stative verbs in the present perfect tense shows that this idea makes sense to them.

However, this is not the case at all. The present progressive is always time limited and therefore totally incompatible with the timeless nature of stative verbs. To see why this is the case, let us look at some typical present progressive sentences (with dynamic verbs, naturally):

Our team <u>is</u> really <u>getting</u> beat!
We <u>are</u> completely <u>revising</u> our landscape plan.
Did you hear that Janet Jones <u>is running</u> for mayor?

Note that none of these examples has any overt mention of an ending point or even of any expression of time. Instead, there is something much more subtle going on in these sentences. Whenever we use the present progressive tense, the action of the sentence exists in its own implied self-defined, self-limiting time frame. For example:

Our team <u>is</u> really <u>getting</u> beat!

In this sentence, the action exists only as long as the game lasts.

We <u>are</u> completely <u>revising</u> our landscape plan.

In this example, the action lasts however long it takes the speakers to revise their landscaping plan.

Did you hear that Janet Jones <u>is running</u> for mayor?

In this third example, the action lasts however long Janet Jones's mayoral campaign lasts.

The most striking demonstration of the self-defined, self-limiting time frame of verbs in the present progressive is with verbs whose meaning would seem to make them inherently unlimited in terms of time. One such verb is *live*. Compare the meaning of the verb *live* in the present tense with the meaning of the same verb in the present progressive tense:

Present tense   The Johnstons live in San Diego.
(Meaning: The Johnstons permanently reside in San Diego.)

Present progressive   The Johnstons are living in San Diego.
(Meaning: The Johnstons are staying in San Diego at the moment, but it is not their permanent residence.)

Here is a second example with the verb *store*:

Present tense   We store all of our equipment in a warehouse.
(Meaning: We always keep our equipment in a warehouse.)

Present progressive   We are storing all of our equipment in a warehouse.
(Meaning: We are temporarily keeping our equipment in a warehouse.)

As you can see, when we change the tense of the verb from the present tense to the present progressive tense, the implicit time frame of the sentence also changes from unlimited to limited or temporary; that is, it becomes time bound.

As we have seen in this subsection on the use of the present progressive tense to express action in progress, the present progressive describes actions that span a period of time. Some nonnative speakers apparently think of this span of time as being equivalent to the "timeless" nature of tenses such as the present tense, which also describes action that spans across time. Accordingly, nonnative speakers assume that the present progressive tense, as with the present tense, is compatible with stative verbs. The difference is that the present progressive has a somewhat unusual self-limiting time frame that makes the present progressive time bound and therefore incompatible with the basic timeless meaning of stative verbs.

The key, then, for avoiding the highly persistent error of using stative verbs in the present progressive tense is twofold: (1) clearly understanding the odd way that the present progressive uses a self-limiting time frame, and (2) knowing how to reliably recognize stative verbs. This presentation suggested two specific features of stative verbs to be aware of: by far the most important is the different relationship between verb and subject. Stative verbs describe their subjects. Dynamic verbs carry out the actions that their subjects perform. The second feature of stative verbs is the incompatibility of stative verbs with most adverbs of time. Determining whether adverbs of time can be used with a verb is a helpful way of testing to see whether the verb is a timeless stative verb or a time-bound dynamic verb.

EXERCISE
7·22

All of the following sentences are written in the present progressive tense. If the sentence is grammatical, write "OK." If the sentence is ungrammatical, mark the sentence with an "X" and replace the present progressive with an appropriate tense. The first two sentences are done as examples.

The girls are adoring their new baby sister.   **X**

ANSWER: The girls **adore** their new baby sister.

The actors are still stumbling over their lines rather badly.

ANSWER: The actors are still stumbling over their lines rather badly.   OK

1. The baby <u>is being</u> hungry all the time.

_____

2. Fortunately, we <u>are having</u> a laptop at our disposal.

_____

3. I <u>am supervising</u> a new construction project.

_____

4. The estimate <u>is including</u> all taxes and fees.

_____

5. The kids <u>are mowing</u> the backyard this afternoon.

_____

6. I <u>am hating</u> the fact that we are having so much trouble.

_____

7. I don't think it <u>is harming</u> anyone.

_____

8. The ceremony <u>is beginning</u> at 4 p.m.

_____

9. They <u>are</u> all <u>liking</u> the company's new logo.

_____

10. The heavy rain <u>is ruining</u> everyone's gardens.

_____

Replace the base-form verb in parentheses with the present progressive if possible. If the present progressive is not correct, then use the appropriate tense. The first two sentences are done as examples.

The traffic (merge) from four lanes down to just one because of an accident.

ANSWER: The traffic **is merging** from four lanes down to just one because of an accident.

I (need) to get a haircut today.

ANSWER: I **need** to get a haircut today.

1. The babysitter (warm) the kids' dinner in the oven.

_____

2. The kids (want) to watch TV until bedtime.

_____

3. Their approval (mean) a lot to us.

   _____

4. I told the waiter that we (celebrate) a birthday.

   _____

5. George (know) where the restaurant is.

   _____

6. The children (quarrel) again.

   _____

7. We (soak) all of our dirty hiking clothes in the washing machine.

   _____

8. The purse (belong) to that young lady over there.

   _____

9. The tire (seem) a little flat to me.

   _____

10. The flowers in the garden (bloom).

   _____

The past progressive tense

The past progressive tense consists of the helping verb *be* in a past tense form followed by a verb in the present participle *–ing* form. Here are some examples:

> We <u>were driving</u> downtown when the storm hit.
> The train <u>was</u> just <u>pulling</u> into the station when we got there.
> We <u>were thinking</u> about going out for dinner.
> I <u>was thinking</u> I might go camping this weekend.
> I <u>was talking</u> to Janet yesterday, and she told me that you were retiring.
> We <u>were working</u> on that project all morning!

Major use of the past progressive tense

The major function of the past progressive tense is very much like the basic function of the present progressive tense: to talk about something that takes place (i.e., "progresses") over some span of time—present time for the present progressive, past time for the past progressive. There are also a number of other, more idiomatic uses of the past progressive that we will discuss at the end of the chapter.

Another important point of similarity between the two tenses is that the past progressive (as with the present progressive) can be used only with **dynamic** verbs. (Chapter 10 has a detailed explanation of why.) Dynamic verbs are verbs whose action takes place in real time (as opposed to the inherently timeless nature of **stative** verbs). Consequently, dynamic verbs are compatible with the time-bound meaning of the past progressive tense. For example, notice that all of the examples of the past progressive given at the beginning of this chapter are dynamic verbs.

By the same token, the timeless nature of stative verbs makes them incompatible with the time-bound meaning of the past perfect tense. (Please see Chapter 1 if you need to review the characteristics of dynamic and stative verbs.) For example, the verb *like* is a typical stative verb that describes an ongoing state or condition. We cannot use this stative verb in the past progressive tense:

> **X** I <u>was</u> always <u>liking</u> homemade ice cream.

EXERCISE
8·1

All of the following sentences are in the past progressive tense. If the sentence uses a dynamic verb, write "OK" and put "Dynamic" above the verb. If the sentence uses a stative verb, write "X," draw a line through the stative verb, and write "Stative" above the verb. The first two sentences are done as examples.

We learned that Kathy <u>was teaching</u> English in Singapore.

Dynamic
ANSWER: OK We learned that Kathy <u>was teaching</u> English in Singapore.
            The company <u>was involving</u> us from the start.

Stative
ANSWER: **X** The company <u>~~was involving~~</u> us from the start.

1. We <u>were knowing</u> all along that the job would be difficult.

   _____

2. Because of the kitchen repairs, we <u>were eating</u> out a lot.

   _____

3. Clearly, all of the politicians <u>were avoiding</u> the issue.

   _____

4. Frank <u>was</u> always <u>possessing</u> a great sense of humor.

   _____

5. The kids <u>were sleeping</u> in a tent in the backyard.

   _____

6. The orchestra <u>was consisting</u> of a string section and some woodwinds.

   _____

7. I <u>was training</u> everyone in the office to use the new accounting software.

   _____

8. The government <u>was encouraging</u> everyone to get flu shots.

   _____

9. After it started raining, the kids <u>were wanting</u> to go home.

   _____

10. Everyone <u>was needing</u> to take a break because of the heat.

   _____

Both the past tense and the past progressive describe actions that took place in past time. The difference between the two is that the past tense treats the past-time action as a finished event—completely over and done with—whereas the past progressive treats the past-time action as an ongoing process that continues through some span of past time. For example, compare the following sentences:

Past tense	Fred <u>mowed</u> the lawn this afternoon.
	(event)
Past progressive	Fred was mowing the lawn this afternoon.
	(process)

The past tense sentence describes an action that was completed in the past. The past progressive sentence describes an action that was in process during the time frame of the sentence. We have no way of knowing whether or not Fred ever finished mowing the lawn. The past progressive sentence is not about what happened as a completed event; the sentence is about what was going on at or during some particular moment or period of past time.

EXERCISE
8·2

Each of the following sentences contains an underlined verb in its base form. Put the verb into its proper past tense or past progressive form according to whether the sentence describes an event (past tense) or a process (past progressive tense). The first two sentences are done as examples.

Some people <u>talk</u> all during the movie. (process)

ANSWER: Some people <u>were talking</u> all during the movie.

We <u>collect</u> the samples only in the early morning. (event)

ANSWER: We <u>collected</u> the samples only in the early morning.

1. The cold weather <u>threaten</u> to ruin the entire crop. (event)

_____

2. The country slowly <u>emerge</u> from financial chaos. (process)

_____

3. During the whole time, I <u>try</u> to get a word in edgewise. (process)

_____

4. The company rapidly <u>expand</u> into Asian markets. (event)

_____

5. As it turned out, the police <u>record</u> the entire conversation. (process)

_____

6. The heavy truck traffic <u>damage</u> the road surfaces. (process)

_____

7. The company <u>represent</u> some of the firms in the industry. (event)

_____

8. All the noise <u>frighten</u> the children. (process)

_____

9. The kids <u>swim</u> at the pool in the community center. (process)

_____

10. Their lawyer <u>advise</u> them not to say anything about what happened. (event)

_____

As we have seen, the past progressive functions much as does the present progressive in that they both describe actions in progress. There is, however, one way in which the two types of progressive tenses are not the same, especially when they use verbs with a strong sentence of action.

Compare the following examples of present progressive and past progressive sentences. Assume that there is no previous mention of these sentences, that is, you are seeing each sentence for the first time:

Present progressive	My parents <u>are traveling</u> in India.
Past progressive	My parents <u>were traveling</u> in India.

The present progressive sentence seems perfectly normal. However, the past progressive sentence as it stands seems unfinished or inconclusive in a way the present progressive sentence does not.

The difference is in the time of the action. Sentences in the present progressive tense take place in a time that is automatically defined: now—at the present moment of time. We always know when sentences in the present progressive tense take place: they take place *now*.

Sentences in the past progressive, however, are different. There is nothing that automatically defines when they took place in the past *unless* the producers of the sentences provide that information for us. That is why the example sentence about traveling in India seems incomplete in the past progressive. We have no way to place the trip to India in past time.

To make the sentence seem complete, we need to add what is called a "temporal frame." A temporal frame is an adverbial time expression that locates the action of the sentence in past time—either by providing a point in time or a span of time during which the action took place. Here are some examples of the same sentence with the temporal frame added (in italics):

My parents <u>were traveling</u> in India *recently*.
My parents <u>were traveling</u> in India *during my junior year*.
My parents <u>were traveling</u> in India *when the attack in Mumbai happened*.

The sentences with the temporal frame added now seem complete and perfectly normal. Note that the three examples of temporal frames use all three different types of adverbials:

Recently is an adverb.
During my junior year is an adverb prepositional phrase.
When the attack in Mumbai happened is an adverb clause.

All temporal frames are adverbials of time—adverbs, adverb prepositional phrases, or adverb clauses. Adverbials of time (as with most other adverbials) typically follow the verb in what is called **normal order**. One of the defining characteristics of adverbials of time (again, as with most adverbials) is that they can be moved to the beginning of the sentence in what is called **inverted order**. Here are the three example sentences again, both in normal order and in inverted order:

Adverb

Normal order	My parents <u>were traveling</u> in India *recently*.
Inverted order	*Recently* my parents <u>were traveling</u> in India.

Adverb prepositional phrase

Normal order	My parents <u>were traveling</u> in India *during my junior year*.
Inverted order	*During my junior year*, my parents <u>were traveling</u> in India.

Adverb clause

Normal order	My parents <u>were traveling</u> in India *when the attack in Mumbai happened*.
Inverted order	*When the attack in Mumbai happened*, my parents <u>were traveling</u> in India.

Note that when an adverb clause is inverted, that is, the adverb clause is moved from its normal place following the main clause to a position in front of the main clause, the inverted adverb clause is set off with a comma. Unlike in British English where the use of commas with inverted adverb clauses is optional, in American English the commas are obligatory.

EXERCISE
8·3

Each of the following sentences is in the past progressive tense. Each sentence contains an adverbial of time that functions as a temporal frame for that sentence. Underline the entire temporal frame. Confirm that your answer is correct by moving the entire temporal frame adverbial to the beginning of the sentence. (Remember, if you invert an adverb clause, be sure to use a comma.) The first sentence is done as an example.

A film crew was shooting a commercial in front of our building all morning.

ANSWER: A film crew was shooting a commercial in front of our building <u>all morning</u>.

CONFIRMATION: <u>All morning</u>, a film crew was shooting a commercial in front of our building.

1. I was listening to the radio on the way to work.

_____

Confirmation: _____

2. Everybody was completely on edge after what happened.

_____

Confirmation: _____

3. The water was flooding the lower fields after all the heavy rains.

_____

Confirmation: _____

4. They were performing at schools around the state during the fall.

_____

Confirmation: _____

5. The police were still questioning witnesses even after the trial started.

_____

Confirmation: _____

6. The wind was blowing faster than 100 miles an hour during the worst of the storm.

_____

Confirmation: _____

7. The manager was interviewing ski instructors over the Thanksgiving break.

_____

Confirmation: _____

8. She was working on her master's degree then.

_____

Confirmation: _____

9. I was just quitting for the night when the alarm sounded.

_____

Confirmation: _____

10. Things were looking pretty bad for our candidate before we got the new poll results.

_____

Confirmation: _____

Sentences with adverb clauses can be quite confusing. One thing that makes them confusing, as we have seen, is that the main clause and the adverb clause can be in either order; for example:

The teams <u>were</u> already <u>playing</u> *by the time we got to the stadium.*

  main clause   adverb clause

By the time we got to the stadium, the teams <u>were</u> already <u>playing</u>.

  adverb clause   main clause

There is a second reason why sentences with adverb clauses can be confusing. So far, all of our examples with adverb clauses have had the past perfect verb tense in the main clause and the temporal frame in the adverb clause. However, there is no grammatical requirement that the past perfect verb tense be in the main clause. It can be (and often is) in the adverb clause; for example:

I got interested in Asian art *when I <u>was living</u> in San Francisco.*

  main clause   adverb clause

And, of course, to add to the confusion, the adverb clause with the past progressive tense can also be inverted; for example:

When I <u>was living</u> in San Francisco, I got interested in Asian art.

  adverb clause   main clause

EXERCISE 8·4

This is a different type of exercise that mimics the options we have when we actually form real sentences. Each of the following sentences consists of two clauses, the first labeled "main clause" and the second labeled "adverb clause." Follow these steps to create two versions of the same sentence:

 Step 1: Identify and underline the two verbs that make up the past progressive tense (hint: they can be in either clause).

 Step 2: Attach the adverb clause to the end of the main clause to create a complete sentence with the adverb clause in the normal position following the main clause.

 Step 3: Form an inverted version of the same sentence by attaching the adverb clause to the beginning of the sentence (hint: check the punctuation).

 The first sentence is done as an example.

Main clause: I was just getting into the shower

Adverb clause: When the phone rang

ANSWER: Step 1: I <u>was</u> just <u>getting</u> into the shower

Step 2: I <u>was</u> just <u>getting</u> into the shower when the phone rang.

Step 3: When the phone rang, I <u>was</u> just <u>getting</u> into the shower.

1. Main clause: I was reading a book on my Kindle

   Adverb clause: While everyone else relaxed by the pool

   Step 1: _____

   Step 2: _____

   Step 3: _____

2. Main clause: My father suffered a minor stroke

   Adverb clause: When he was undergoing surgery

   Step 1: _____

   Step 2: _____

   Step 3: _____

3. Main clause: The troops were storing ammunition

   Adverb clause: When the big explosion happened

   Step 1: _____

   Step 2: _____

   Step 3: _____

4. Main clause: They were shutting the door

   Adverb clause: After the horse was stolen

   Step 1: _____

   Step 2: _____

   Step 3: _____

5. Main clause: The campers were packing up all their gear

   Adverb clause: When the storm finally broke

   Step 1: _____

   Step 2: _____

   Step 3: _____

6. Main clause: I got all the dishes done

   Adverb clause: While you were talking on the phone

   Step 1: _____

   Step 2: _____

   Step 3: _____

7. Main clause: The fund was investing in Swiss francs

   Adverb clause: Whenever the dollar was overvalued

   Step 1: _____

   Step 2: _____

   Step 3: _____

8. Main clause: We would make the kids give us their cell phones

   Adverb clause: Every time they were doing their homework

   Step 1: _____

   Step 2: _____

   Step 3: _____

9. Main clause: The birds were building nests

   Adverb clause: Whenever they could find a protected place

   Step 1: _____

   Step 2: _____

   Step 3: _____

10. Main clause: Our flights were always late

    Adverb clause: When we were flying in or out of Newark

    Step 1: _____

    Step 2: _____

    Step 3: _____

The future progressive tense

The future progressive tense consists of the helping verb *be* in its future tense form *will be* followed by a verb in the present participle *–ing* form. Here are some examples:

> We will be staying with some friends in Los Angeles.
> I will be waiting for you in the baggage claim area.
> The painters will be finishing up the kitchen tomorrow.
> The storm will be hitting the coast around midnight.
> Everyone will be watching the big game.
> I'll be loading the car while you check out of the motel.

Major use of the future progressive tense

The basic meaning of the future progressive tense is to talk about something that is expected to take place (i.e., "progresses") over some span of future time. There are also four other, more idiomatic uses of the future progressive tense that we will discuss at the end of the chapter.

The future progressive tense, as with the other two progressive tenses, can generally be used only with **dynamic** verbs and not with **stative** verbs.

Strangely enough, there is a special and quite limited use of the future progressive tense that does permit it to be used with some stative verbs. We will ignore this highly restricted use of the future progressive until we get to the discussion of idiomatic uses at the end of the chapter.

Here are some examples of the future progressive using both types of verbs:

Dynamic verbs
The fish <u>will be biting</u> after all this rain.
I'll <u>be working</u> downstairs if you need me.
It <u>will be snowing</u> all afternoon.

Stative verbs
X You <u>will be loving</u> your new kitchen when it is finished.
X They <u>will be agreeing</u> with you.
X I am afraid that it <u>will be costing</u> more than we can afford.

EXERCISE
8·5

All of the following sentences are in the future progressive tense. If the sentence uses a dynamic verb, write "OK" and put "Dynamic" above the verb. If the sentence uses a stative verb, write "X," draw a line through the stative verb, and write "Stative" above the verb. The first two sentences are done as examples.

They <u>will be discussing</u> the agreement for hours yet.
Dynamic
ANSWER: OK They <u>will be discussing</u> the agreement for hours yet.

He <u>will be belonging</u> to a fraternity when he is in college.
Stative
ANSWER: X He ~~will be belonging~~ to a fraternity when he is in college.

1. I <u>will be seeing</u> about it and let you know what I find out.

2. The electrician <u>will be rewiring</u> the kitchen on Monday.

3. Their children <u>will be looking</u> just like them.

4. They <u>will not be minding</u> it if we park in their driveway.

5. The committee <u>will be counting</u> votes tomorrow.

6. The team <u>will be deserving</u> its reputation if they can win today.

7. The kids <u>will be playing</u> on the swings all afternoon.

8. The dinner <u>will not be including</u> dessert or beverage.

9. The company <u>will be expanding</u> its online information system.

10. Ruth <u>will be playing</u> tennis this afternoon with some of her friends.

The future progressive is like the past progressive in one important way: the need to define when the action takes place by adding what is called a "temporal frame" to the sentence. (See Chapter 11 for a detailed discussion of temporal frames.) For example:

My parents <u>will be visiting</u> us.

This sentence seems incomplete without giving more information about the visit, either when the visit will take place (time) or how long the visit will be (duration). When we revise the sentence by adding a temporal frame (in italics), the sentence seems complete:

My parents <u>will be visiting</u> us *after Christmas*. (time)
My parents <u>will be visiting</u> us *for a couple of days*. (duration)

Temporal frames are always adverbials of time or duration; they can be adverbs, adverb prepositional phrases, or adverb clauses. Here is an example of each type in italics:

We <u>will be backpacking</u> in the Sierras *next week*. (adverb)
We <u>will be backpacking</u> in the Sierras *during spring break*. (adverb prepositional phrase)
We <u>will be backpacking</u> in the Sierras *while we are on vacation*. (adverb clause)

All of these adverbials of time and duration share the characteristic that they can be moved from their normal position at the end of the sentence to an **inverted** position at the beginning of the sentence; for example:

Next week, we <u>will be backpacking</u> in the Sierras.
During spring break, we <u>will be backpacking</u> in the Sierras.
While we are on vacation, we <u>will be backpacking</u> in the Sierras.

Note that the inverted adverb clause is followed by a comma. The use of commas with inverted adverb clauses is obligatory in American English.

EXERCISE 8·6

Each of the following sentences is in the future progressive tense and contains an adverbial of time that functions as a temporal frame for that sentence. Underline the entire temporal frame. Confirm that your answer is correct by moving the entire temporal frame adverbial to the beginning of the sentence. (Remember, if you invert an adverb clause, be sure to use a comma.) The first sentence is done as an example.

The band will be playing in Denver next Friday and Saturday.

ANSWER: The band will be playing in Denver <u>next Friday and Saturday</u>.

CONFIRMATION: <u>Next Friday and Saturday</u>, the band will be playing in Denver.

1. The principal will be judging the spelling competition at 1 p.m.

   _____

2. They will be living in Spain until the end of the summer.

   _____

3. We will be continuing the discussion after everyone finishes dinner.

   _____

4. We will be closing down the beach house after Labor Day.

   _____

5. The sales staff will be showing the apartment as soon as it is vacant.

   _____

6. Department heads will be meeting with the CFO every Monday morning.

   _____

7. They will be expecting us to begin discussions the minute we get off the plane.

_____

8. I will be teaching Accounting 101 in the winter quarter.

_____

9. They will be getting married after she graduates.

_____

10. Maintenance will be replacing all the old carpets over the holidays.

_____

Both the future tense and the future progressive are used to describe an action that will take place in future time, but the two tenses look at the future action in two very different ways: the future tense describes the action as a unitary **event** that happens at a single point in future time. The future progressive tense, however, is used to emphasize that the future action is a **process** that occurs across a span or period of future time; for example:

Future tense	We <u>will host</u> a reception for the sales force tomorrow.
Future progressive tense	We <u>will be hosting</u> a reception for the sales force tomorrow.

Even if the two sentences are talking about the same reception, the two tenses look at it in two different ways: the future tense sentence sees the reception as a single event (as opposed to all other possible events or not doing an event at all); the future progressive tense sees the reception as a process or sustained action that takes place across a period of time.

**EXERCISE
8·7**

Each of the following sentences contains an underlined verb in its base form. Put the verb into its proper future tense or future progressive form according to whether the sentence describes an event (future tense) or a process (future progressive). The first two sentences are done as examples.

The marketing department <u>fund</u> tomorrow's reception. (event)

ANSWER: The marketing department <u>will fund</u> tomorrow's reception.

The light <u>fade</u> by the time we get to the campground. (process)

ANSWER: The light <u>will be fading</u> by the time we get to the campground.

1. Everyone <u>rush</u> to get their taxes in before the April 15 deadline. (process)

_____

2. This last payment <u>fulfill</u> the terms of the contract. (event)

_____

3. Everyone <u>check</u> their roofs for damage as soon as this terrible wind lets up. (process)

_____

4. The governor <u>announce</u> the winners of the state awards at the banquet. (event)

_____

5. On the first day of school all the kids <u>cling</u> to their parents. (process)

   _____

6. Henry <u>edit</u> the white paper before we send it out for review. (process)

   _____

7. Everyone <u>notice</u> that Pat is gone. (event)

   _____

8. They <u>fish</u> until it gets too dark to bait their hooks. (process)

   _____

9. I <u>grab</u> a bite at the cafeteria before I go to the meeting. (event)

   _____

10. All the rivers <u>overflow</u> their banks after all this rain. (process)

    _____

The perfect progressive tenses

The perfect progressive tenses are a combination of one of the three perfect tenses (past perfect, present perfect, future perfect) with the progressive tense.

The perfect tenses consist of the helping verb *have* (in some form: present, past, or future) followed by a verb in the past participle form. In the following examples, the verb *fade* is in the past participle form.

Present perfect	The carpet **has** <u>faded</u> near the windows.
Past perfect	The carpet **had** <u>faded</u> near the windows.
Future perfect	The carpet **will have** <u>faded</u> near the windows.

The progressive tense consists of the helping verb *be* in some form followed by a verb in the present participle form; for example:

They <u>are celebrating</u> his birthday today.

When we combine the perfect and the progressive tenses, the perfect tense portion of the sentence consists of *have* (in one of its three forms) followed by *been* (the past participle form of *be*). *Been* plays a double role. In addition to being the past participle verb form required to form the perfect tense, *been* is at the same time the helping verb *be* required to form the progressive tense. For example:

I <u>have **been** working</u> in the garden all morning.

In this present perfect progressive sentence, we can see that *been* is linked with the verb in front of it (*have*) to form the perfect tense, and it is linked with the verb following it (*working*) to form the progressive tense. We might imagine the two roles of *been* as being played by two separate superimposed verbs, one *been* forming the present perfect tense with *have* and the other *been* forming the progressive tense with *working*:

<u>have **been**</u>	forms the present perfect portion of the sentence
<u>**been** working</u>	forms the progressive portion of the sentence

There are three different forms that the perfect progressive can take depending on the form that the verb *have* takes: present, past, or future. Here is an example of each:

Present perfect progressive	They **have** been protesting against the new taxes.
Past perfect progressive	They **had** been protesting against the new taxes.
Future perfect progressive	They **will have** been protesting against the new taxes.

EXERCISE
8·8

Each of the following items contains a grammatically correct sentence in one of the three forms of the perfect progressive. Underline all of the verbs that make up the perfect progressive tense and identify which type of perfect progressive tense it is: present perfect progressive, past perfect progressive, or future perfect progressive. The first sentence is done as an example.

She has been introducing all the speakers at the main sessions.

ANSWER: She has been introducing all the speakers at the main sessions.
present perfect progressive

1. He had been scoring nearly half of the team's goals.

2. The painters will have been stripping off all the old paint.

3. They had been washing all the dishes by hand during the power outage.

4. I have been smelling gasoline for days.

5. She will have been studying English since she was in elementary school.

6. Fortunately, I had been keeping a good record of all our building expenses.

7. The wild pigs had been reproducing at a rapid rate.

8. Apparently, they have been posing as reporters.

9. She will have been administering the fund for more than 20 years.

10. The doctor has been prescribing an antifungal drug for me.

The perfect progressive tenses, as with the other progressive tenses, cannot be used with stative verbs. Here are examples for the three perfect progressive tenses using the stative verbs *own, like, understand,* and *sound*:

Present perfect progressive
X Roberta has been owning several sailing boats.
X I have always been liking working in the garden.
X The children have all been understanding what to do in case of fire.
X The idea of a fall vacation has always been sounding like fun.

Past perfect progressive
X Roberta had been owning several sailing boats.
X I had always been liking working in the garden.
X The children had all been understanding what to do in case of fire.
X The idea of a fall vacation had always been sounding like fun.

Future perfect progressive

X Roberta <u>will have been owning</u> several sailing boats.

X I <u>will have</u> always <u>been liking</u> working in the garden.

X The children <u>will have</u> all <u>been understanding</u> what to do in case of fire.

X The idea of a fall vacation <u>will have</u> always <u>been sounding</u> like fun.

EXERCISE
8·9

All of the following sentences are in one of the perfect progressive tenses. If the sentence uses a dynamic verb, write "OK" and put "Dynamic" above the verb. If the sentence uses a stative verb, write "X," draw a line through the stative verb, and write "Stative" above the verb. The first two sentences are done as examples.

The heat <u>will be melting</u> the butter that we left out on the table.

ANSWER: OK The heat <u>will be melting</u> *(Dynamic)* the butter that we left out on the table.

They <u>had been needing</u> to get some gas for some time.

ANSWER: X They <s>had been needing</s> *(Stative)* to get some gas for some time.

1. They <u>have been waiting</u> for a final decision for months.

2. Their decision to get married <u>will have been pleasing</u> to both families.

3. My uncle <u>will have been fishing</u> every day this summer.

4. They were warned that they <u>had been exceeding</u> their budget.

5. He <u>had been recognizing</u> some old friends.

6. I'm afraid that I <u>have been lacking</u> enough money to do it.

7. They <u>have</u> certainly <u>been putting</u> up with a lot lately.

8. Henry <u>had been loving</u> pistachio ice cream ever since he was a child.

9. My old suits <u>had been fitting</u> me again after I had lost all that weight.

10. The government <u>had been exerting</u> a lot of pressure on them to reform.

We will now turn to a detailed examination of the three types of perfect progressive tenses.

Present perfect progressive

The present perfect progressive consists of a present tense form of the helping verb *have* (*has* or *have*) followed by *been* and the main verb in the present participle form (*–ing*). Here are some examples:

I <u>have been thinking</u> about what you said.
They <u>have been working</u> on this project for weeks now.
She <u>has been exhibiting</u> her work in galleries all over the world.
The head office <u>has</u> really <u>been interfering</u> with our day-to-day operations lately.
It <u>has been snowing</u> for hours.

The basic function of the present perfect progressive tense is to describe an action or condition that began in the past and has continued in an unbroken manner up to the present time and may continue on into the future; for example:

Their family <u>has been making</u> wine for five generations.

This definition of the present perfect progressive is virtually the same as the definition of the present perfect tense, and, indeed, with verbs that describe ongoing action, the two tenses can be quite similar in meaning; for example:

Present perfect progressive	The kids <u>have been watching</u> TV all afternoon.
Present perfect	The kids <u>have watched</u> TV all afternoon.

There is, however, something of a difference in emphasis between the two sentences. The present perfect progressive sentence emphasizes the ongoing duration of the TV watching more than does the present perfect sentence.

We can see a real difference between the two tenses quite clearly with most action verbs; for example:

Present perfect progressive	I <u>have been repairing</u> the gear shift on my bike.
Present perfect	I <u>have repaired</u> the gear shift on my bike.

The present perfect progressive sentence describes a work still in progress, while in the present perfect sentence, the job has already been completed. In general, present perfect progressive senses always place a strong emphasis on a process being carried out over time. Present perfect sentences, on the other hand, may or may not imply action in process.

EXERCISE
8·10

Each of the following sentences contains a base-form verb (underlined). Judging by the meaning of the sentence, decide which tense is more appropriate: the present perfect progressive or the present perfect. Then replace the base-form verb with the chosen tense. The first two sentences are done as examples.

The dog <u>chew</u> a hole in the living room couch.

ANSWER: Present perfect: The dog <u>has chewed</u> a hole in the living room couch.

The dog <u>sleep</u> on the living room couch for years.

ANSWER: Present perfect progressive: The dog <u>has been sleeping</u> on the living room couch for years.

1. I <u>made</u> a reservation for dinner at that new restaurant.

   _____

2. Grandfather <u>tell</u> that story ever since I was a child.

   _____

3. Jackson <u>injured</u> his leg again.

   _____

4. The dean <u>recommend</u> her for promotion.

   _____

5. Beginning with the Industrial Revolution, the climate steadily <u>warm</u>.

   _____

6. The reception <u>be</u> canceled because of the storm.

_____

7. My cousin <u>restore</u> old cars as long as I have known him.

_____

8. The company <u>start</u> a new internship program you might be interested in.

_____

9. Remind me who he is. I <u>forgot</u> his name.

_____

10. It seems as though it <u>rain</u> forever.

_____

The present perfect progressive tense also resembles its other parent, the present progressive. For example, compare the following two sentences:

Present perfect progressive	We <u>have been remodeling</u> our kitchen.
Present progressive	We <u>are remodeling</u> our kitchen.

At first glance, there does not seem to be any real difference between the two tenses. Both sentences describe an action (remodeling the kitchen) that is taking place over a span of present time.

The difference is in how the two tenses treat the meaning of "present time." For the present progressive, "present time" is nothing more or less than the present moment of time; it is an endless "now." The present moment of time is dimensionless: there is no earlier or later. There is no starting the remodeling process in the past; there is no movement across time to the completion of the remodeling project. The present progressive treats time as an indivisible, unitary block.

The present perfect progressive treats time in a different manner. It emphasizes that the action of the verb continues over a span of time up to the present moment.

A particularly striking demonstration of the "timeless" nature of the present progressive tense is the fact that we cannot use adverbs of time that imply duration for the simple reason that there is no duration in present progressive tense sentences. Look what happens when we attempt to add an adverbial of duration (in italics) to our example sentence:

X We <u>are remodeling</u> our kitchen _for the past two weeks_.
X We <u>are remodeling</u> our kitchen _recently_.
X We <u>are remodeling</u> our kitchen _ever since the tree fell on it_.
X We <u>are remodeling</u> our kitchen _since last week_.

These same adverbials of duration are perfectly grammatical with our example present perfect progressive sentence:

We <u>have been remodeling</u> our kitchen _for the past two weeks_.
We <u>have been remodeling</u> our kitchen _recently_.
We <u>have been remodeling</u> our kitchen _ever since the tree fell on it_.
We <u>have been remodeling</u> our kitchen _since last week_.

Past progressives and _be_

When you refer to a past action, state, or event that is incomplete or in progress, use the past progressive.

PAST ACTION: In 2002, **I was working** for a large company in Houston.
PAST STATE: **I was feeling** fine ten minutes ago.
PAST EVENT: Something strange **was happening**.

A specific time reference is often used with the past progressive. This reference is generally a prepositional phrase or another clause with a simple-past verb form.

> PREPOSITIONAL PHRASE: *By 5:00*, all the participants **were packing** their bags.
> CLAUSE: While **I was preparing** breakfast, *I heard the news on the radio.*

When you want to indicate two simultaneous ongoing actions, use the past progressive for both.

> SIMULTANEOUS ACTIONS: While **I was preparing** breakfast, **I was listening** to the news.

The past progressive consists of the auxiliary verb *be* and the *-ing* form of the main verb. The auxiliary verb is marked for tense.

	Singular	Plural
First Person	I **was verb + ing**	we **were verb + ing**
Second Person	you **were verb + ing**	you **were verb + ing**
Third Person	he, she, it **was verb + ing**	they **were verb + ing**

When a one-syllable word or a word with a stressed final syllable ends in a single consonant sound, double the last letter before adding *-ing*.

> One-syllable word: swim → swimming
> Word ending in a stressed syllable: permit → permitting
> BUT show → showing [This word ends in a vowel sound.]

When a word ends with the letter *e*, drop the *e* before adding *-ing*.

EXERCISE
8·11

Complete each sentence with the past progressive form of the verb in parentheses.

1. The customer _____ (be) rude.

2. The telephone _____ (ring) all day long.

3. While I _____ (wait), I _____ (dream) of distant places.

4. When you visited last year, they _____ (live) in a different apartment.

5. My roommate _____ (take) a nap while I _____ (study).

6. She _____ (put) on her coat when I walked in.

7. Someone _____ (knock) at the door just as I _____ (get) out of bed.

8. It _____ (rain) a few minutes ago.

9. They saw an accident while they _____ (go) to work.

10. We found old books and toys when we _____ (clean).

EXERCISE
8·12

The verb forms in the following sentences are either simple past or past progressive. Decide whether the verb in each sentence indicates a complete action or an ongoing past action. If you need help, review pages 47–48 and 61.

1. He *played* the piano beautifully.

    Complete action   **Action in progress**

2. He *was playing* the piano as the guests were arriving.

    Complete action   **Action in progress**

3. I *was cooking* dinner when I remembered his name.

    Complete action   **Action in progress**

4. I *cooked* dinner for everyone.

    Complete action   **Action in progress**

5. They *were shopping* for a new lamp, but they couldn't find a nice one.

    Complete action   **Action in progress**

6. They *shopped* for a lamp until they found a nice one.

    Complete action   **Action in progress**

7. When we lived in the suburbs, we *commuted* to work.

    Complete action   **Action in progress**

8. While we *were commuting* to work, we talked about our families.

    Complete action   **Action in progress**

9. She *was working* for Apex Law Firm when she received a new job offer.

    Complete action   **Action in progress**

10. She *worked* for Apex Law Firm from 1999 to 2002.

    Complete action   Action in progress

Forming negatives

To make a past progressive verb negative, place *not* after the auxiliary verb.

was not going   were not going

Make each of the following sentences negative.

EXAMPLE: We were visiting our relatives.

We were not visiting our relatives.

1. He was attending a conference.

   _____

2. They were laughing.

   _____

3. I was complaining about the work.

   _____

4. She was helping us.

   _____

5. Ted was studying last night.

   _____

6. They were paying attention.

   _____

7. I was talking to myself.

   _____

8. You were speaking loud enough.

   _____

9. They were doing their homework.

   _____

10. We were trying hard.

    _____

Past perfect progressive

When you want to refer to an action, a state, or an event that originated prior to another time in the past but is still ongoing or incomplete, use the past perfect progressive.

> ONGOING STATE: I **had been having** frequent headaches, so I decided to visit a doctor.
> INCOMPLETE ACTION: We **had been making** plans when someone interrupted us.

You can also use the past perfect progressive to refer to a hypothetical action or event.

> HYPOTHETICAL ACTION: If they **had been paying** attention, they would have found the clues.

Sentences such as this one will be discussed in more detail in Part IV.

The past perfect progressive consists of two auxiliary verbs, *have* and *be*, and the *-ing* form of the main verb. The auxiliary verb *had* comes first, and it is marked for tense.

Next comes the perfect/passive form of the verb *be*—*been*. The final element of the past perfect progressive is the *-ing* form of the main verb.

	Singular	Plural
First Person	**I had been verb + ing**	we **had been verb + ing**
Second Person	you **had been verb + ing**	you **had been verb + ing**
Third Person	he, she, **it had been verb + ing**	they **had been verb + ing**

EXERCISE

8·14

Complete each sentence with the past perfect progressive form of the verb in parentheses.

1. I _____ (work) ten-hour days, so I was very tired.

2. We _____ (discuss) that issue when the supervisor walked in.

3. They _____ (study) English since they came in 2001.

4. The company's profits _____ (increase) until they dropped in December.

5. They _____ (play) soccer together for years.

6. It _____ (rain) all day, so the game was postponed.

7. The children _____ (watch) television before we arrived.

8. He _____ (write) newspaper editorials for twenty years.

9. Sally _____ (study) since 6:00 A.M.

10. I _____ (work) for the telephone company before I came here.

Forming negatives

To make a past perfect progressive verb negative, place *not* after the auxiliary verb *had*.

had not been going

Complete each of the following sentences with the negative form of the past perfect progressive. Use the subject and verb provided.

EXAMPLE: We, expect, not
We had not been expecting your call.

1. The supervisor, assign, not

   _____ much work lately.

2. The weather, improve, not

   _____, so we returned home.

3. Jodi and I, follow, not

   _____ his directions.

4. They, check, not

   _____ the oil in their car frequently enough.

5. She, ignore, not

   _____ the phone messages.

6. You, get, not

   _____ to work on time.

7. I, exercise, not

   _____, so I was feeling sluggish.

Forming contractions

Contractions are often formed by combining pronouns and the auxiliary verb *had* or by combining the auxiliary verb *had* and *not*. You will often hear these contractions in conversation or see them in informal writing, but you will rarely find them used in formal contexts.

Notice that an apostrophe indicates that at least one letter is omitted:

I'd been going	I hadn't been going
You'd been going	You hadn't been going
He'd been going	He hadn't been going
She'd been going	She hadn't been going
It'd been going	It hadn't been going
We'd been going	We hadn't been going
They'd been going	They hadn't been going

Use the pronoun and verb given to create a sentence that contains a contraction. If not is also given, use a negative contraction.

EXAMPLE: We, hope
We'd been hoping for a nice day.

1. He, expect, not

    _____a phone call.

2. It, change

    _____slowly.

3. We, hope

    _____for good news.

4. They, look, not

    _____in the right places.

5. She, lie

    _____on the couch when the doorbell rang.

6. You, joke, not

    _____about the possible danger.

7. I, think

    _____about you when your letter arrived.

Simple future

When you are referring to a future action, state, or event, use the simple future.

FUTURE ACTION: We **will take** our final exam on Friday.
FUTURE STATE: They **will be** late.
FUTURE EVENT: The weather **will improve.**

To form the simple future for both regular and irregular verbs, place the modal auxiliary verb *will* before the base form of the verb.

	Singular	**Plural**
First Person	**I will verb**	we **will verb**
Second Person	you **will verb**	you **will verb**
Third Person	he, she, **it will verb**	they **will verb**

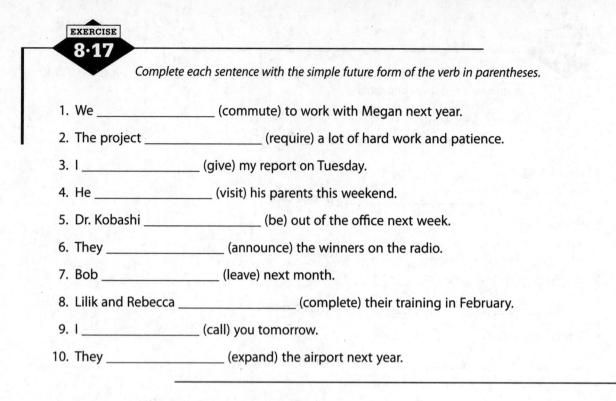

Complete each sentence with the simple future form of the verb in parentheses.

1. We _____ (commute) to work with Megan next year.

2. The project _____ (require) a lot of hard work and patience.

3. I _____ (give) my report on Tuesday.

4. He _____ (visit) his parents this weekend.

5. Dr. Kobashi _____ (be) out of the office next week.

6. They _____ (announce) the winners on the radio.

7. Bob _____ (leave) next month.

8. Lilik and Rebecca _____ (complete) their training in February.

9. I _____ (call) you tomorrow.

10. They _____ (expand) the airport next year.

Forming contractions: pronouns with the auxiliary verb *will*

In English, verbs are often combined with other words to form contractions. These shortened forms include an apostrophe (') to indicate missing letters. It is important to learn contractions because you will often hear them in conversation or see them in informal writing. Formal writing, though, rarely contains contractions.

The modal auxiliary verb *will* is often combined with a pronoun to form a contraction. Notice that an apostrophe indicates that the letters *w* and *i* are omitted:

I + will = I'll   we + will = we'll
he + will = he'll   you + will = you'll
she + will = she'll   they + will = they'll
it + will = it'll

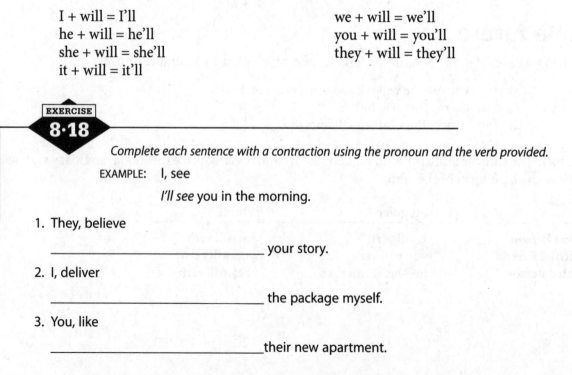

Complete each sentence with a contraction using the pronoun and the verb provided.

EXAMPLE: I, see

I'll see you in the morning.

1. They, believe

_____ your story.

2. I, deliver

_____ the package myself.

3. You, like

_____their new apartment.

4. It, end

_____ soon.

5. He, help

_____ us.

6. She, introduce

_____ you.

7. We, sit

_____ together.

Forming negatives

To form a negative, place *not* between the modal auxiliary verb *will* and the main verb.

will not go

EXERCISE
8·19

Make each of the following sentences negative.

EXAMPLE: You will find your book over there.
You will not find your book over there.

1. He will finish by tomorrow.

_____

2. You will have a lot of fun there.

_____

3. She will know the answer.

_____

4. We will ignore the problem.

_____

5. They will keep your secret.

_____

6. He will lie to you.

_____

7. I will need help with my homework.

_____

8. Marian will be alone.

_____

9. I will mention your name.

_____

10. They will be late.

_____

Forming contractions: *won't*

In conversation and informal writing, *will* and *not* are often contracted. The letter *i* in *will* changes to *o* in *won't*. The apostrophe indicates that at least one letter is omitted:

will + not = won't

EXERCISE 8·20

Rewrite the sentences you wrote in exercise 11-3 using contractions.

1. _____

2. _____

3. _____

4. _____

5. _____

6. _____

7. _____

8. _____

9. _____

10. _____

Be going to

The phrasal modal auxiliary verb *be going to* is also used to indicate future time.
   The verb *be* takes three different forms: *am, is,* and *are.*

	Singular	Plural
First Person	I **am going to** verb	we **are going to** verb
Second Person	you **are going to** verb	you **are going to** verb
Third Person	he, she, it **is going to** verb	they **are going to** verb

Be going to is less formal than *will*.

> Friend to friend: **I'm going to finish** the project by Friday.
> Employee to supervisor: **I'll finish** the project by Friday.

Although sometimes *be going to* and *will* can be used interchangeably, there are two special uses. *Be going to* signals that something is imminent.

> The alarm **is going to sound** in a second.

Will is used to make commitments.

> **I'll meet** you at 5:00.

You will learn more about modal auxiliary verbs in Part V.

EXERCISE 8·21

Complete each sentence with a form of be going to *and the main verb.*

1. This job _____ (be) difficult.

2. Our neighbors _____ (build) a new garage.

3. My roommate _____ (buy) a new printer.

4. I _____ (cancel) my magazine subscription.

5. Members of the Outing Club _____ (climb) Mt. Hood.

6. We _____ (celebrate) tonight.

7. He _____ (call) me today.

8. Matt _____ (come) over this evening.

9. Someone from the firm _____ (deliver) the letter tomorrow.

10. They _____ (elect) a new prime minister this year.

EXERCISE 8·22

Complete each sentence with either will *or a form of* be going to. *Circle the reason that supports your answer.*

1. Watch out. It _____ fall.

   Imminent action   **Commitment**

2. I _____ work for you on Friday.

   Imminent action   **Commitment**

3. I _____ sit down right now.

   Imminent action   **Commitment**

4. Sit down. The movie _____ start.

   Imminent action　　　　　　　　**Commitment**

5. Beth and I _____ help you next week.

   Imminent action　　　　　　　　**Commitment**

Forming negatives

To make the phrasal modal verb *be going to* negative, just add *not* after *be*.

　　am not going to　　　　　　is not going to　　　　　　are not going to

EXERCISE
8·23

Complete each of the following sentences using a negative form of be going to *and the subject and verb provided.*

EXAMPLE:　He, accept

　　　　　He *is not going to accept* the job offer.

1. Taxes, increase

   _____ this year.

2. It, snow

   _____ tonight.

3. We, go

   _____ to the party.

4. He, listen

   _____ to your advice.

5. She, travel

   _____ alone.

6. You, have

   _____ enough time.

7. I, forget

   _____ you.

Forming contractions

Contractions are often formed by combining pronouns and the verb *be* or by combining the verb *be* and *not*. You will often hear these contractions in conversation or see them in informal writing, but you will rarely find them used in formal contexts.

Notice that an apostrophe indicates that a letter is omitted:

I'm going to	I'm not going to	
You're going to	You're not going to	You aren't going to
He's going to	He's not going to	He isn't going to
She's going to	She's not going to	She isn't going to
It's going to	It's not going to	It isn't going to
We're going to	We're not going to	We aren't going to
They're going to	They're not going to	They aren't going to

EXERCISE

8·24

Complete the following sentences using contractions. For some sentences, more than one form can be used.

EXAMPLE: He, appear
He's going to appear on television this evening.

1. He, come, not

_____ with us.

2. It, rain

_____ soon.

3. I, clean

_____ my room tonight.

4. They, believe, not

_____ your story.

5. She, call, not

_____ tonight.

6. You, do

_____ well on the exam.

7. I, cook, not

_____ anything special.

Future progressive (*will be* verb + *ing*)

Use the future progressive when you refer to an action or event that will be ongoing at some time or for some period of time in the future.

> FUTURE ACTION OCCURRING FOR A PERIOD OF TIME: **I will be studying** *all night.*
> FUTURE EVENT OCCURRING AT A POINT IN TIME: *At approximately 7:30,* the sun **will be sinking** behind the horizon.

The future progressive consists of the auxiliary verbs *will* and *be* and the *-ing* form of the main verb.

	Singular	Plural
First Person	**I will be verb + ing**	we **will be verb + ing**
Second Person	you **will be verb + ing**	you **will be verb + ing**
Third Person	he, she, it **will be verb + ing**	they **will be verb + ing**

When a one-syllable word or a word with a stressed final syllable ends in a single consonant sound, double the last letter before adding *-ing*.

> One-syllable word: plan → planning
> Word ending in a stressed syllable: emit → emitting
> BUT sew → sewing [This word ends in a vowel sound.]

When a word ends with a consonant and the letter *e*, drop the *e* before adding *-ing*: come → coming. The letter *e* is not dropped from words such as *be, see,* and *free*.

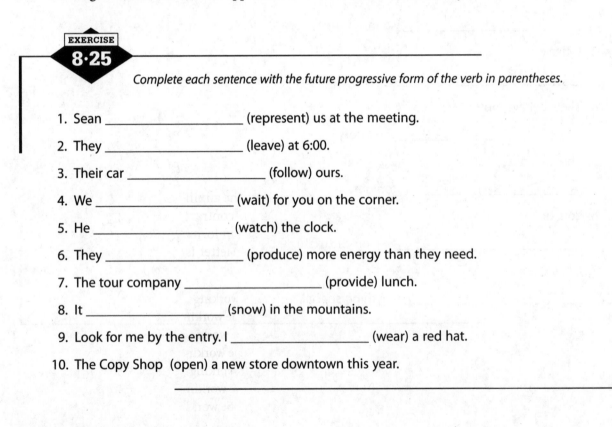

EXERCISE
8·25

Complete each sentence with the future progressive form of the verb in parentheses.

1. Sean _____ (represent) us at the meeting.

2. They _____ (leave) at 6:00.

3. Their car _____ (follow) ours.

4. We _____ (wait) for you on the corner.

5. He _____ (watch) the clock.

6. They _____ (produce) more energy than they need.

7. The tour company _____ (provide) lunch.

8. It _____ (snow) in the mountains.

9. Look for me by the entry. I _____ (wear) a red hat.

10. The Copy Shop (open) a new store downtown this year.

Forming negatives

To make a future progressive verb negative, place *not* after *will*.

> will not be flying

Complete each of the following sentences with a negative form of the future progressive. Use the subject and verb provided.

EXAMPLE: I, attend
            I will not be attending the meeting.

1. They, appear

   _____ on television.

2. It, start

   _____ on time.

3. We, read

   _____ that novel this term.

4. He, arrive

   _____ in time for the party.

5. She, stay

   _____ in a hotel.

6. You, live

   _____ by yourself.

7. I, make

   _____ much money next year.

Forming contractions

Contractions are often formed by combining pronouns and the auxiliary verb *will* or by combining the auxiliary verb *will* and *not*. You will often hear these contractions in conversation or see them in informal writing, but you will rarely find them used in formal contexts.

Remember that an apostrophe indicates that at least one letter is omitted and that the letter *i* in *will* changes to *o* in the negative contraction *won't*:

I'll be working	I won't be working
You'll be working	You won't be working
He'll be working	He won't be working
She'll be working	She won't be working
It'll be working	It won't be working
We'll be working	We won't be working
They'll be working	They won't be working

Use the pronoun and verb given to create a sentence that contains a contraction. If not is also given, use a negative contraction.

EXAMPLE: She, come, not

She won't be coming to the party.

1. He, joining, not

_____ us this evening.

2. It, affect

_____ everyone.

3. I, treat

_____ for dinner tonight.

4. They, need, not

_____ any more help.

5. She, arrive, not

_____ until midnight.

6. You, fly

Tomorrow _____ to Honolulu.

7. I, think, not

_____ of much besides the exam.

Future perfect

Use the future perfect when you want to refer to a future action, state, or event that will be completed by a specific time in the future.

> FUTURE ACTION: *By next week*, she **will have completed** the course.
> FUTURE STATE: *In 2020*, we **will have known** each other for twenty years.
> FUTURE EVENT: The ship **will have sunk** *by then*.

The future perfect consists of the modal auxiliary verb *will*, the auxiliary verb *have*, and the perfect/passive form of the main verb. The perfect/passive verb form is used to indicate either the perfect aspect or the passive voice. (The passive voice will be discussed in Part IV.) The perfect/passive form for regular verbs consists of the base form of the verb and the ending *-ed*.

	Singular	Plural
First Person	I **will have verb + ed**	we **will have verb + ed**
Second Person	you **will have verb + ed**	you **will have verb + ed**
Third Person	he, she, it **will have verb + ed**	they **will have verb + ed**

When a one-syllable word or a word with a stressed final syllable ends in a single consonant sound, double the last letter before adding *-ed*.

> One-syllable word: flip → flipped
> Word ending in a stressed syllable: refer → referred
> BUT bow → bowed [This word ends in a vowel sound.]

The perfect/passive forms of irregular verbs can be found in the appendix.

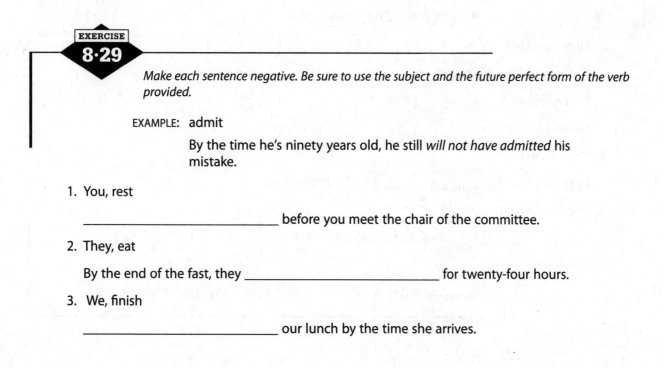

EXERCISE
8·28

Complete each sentence with the future perfect form of the verb in parentheses. If you need help with irregular verb forms, check the appendix.

1. By the time you arrive, most guests _____ (leave).

2. I _____ (write) the report by the time you get here.

3. By 10:00 A.M., all the participants _____ (introduce) themselves.

4. By the time they reach Sydney, they _____ (fly) four thousand miles.

5. We _____ (eat) dinner by the time they get here.

Forming negatives

To make a future perfect verb negative, place *not* after *will*.

> will not have gone

EXERCISE
8·29

Make each sentence negative. Be sure to use the subject and the future perfect form of the verb provided.

EXAMPLE: admit

By the time he's ninety years old, he still *will not have admitted* his mistake.

1. You, rest

_____ before you meet the chair of the committee.

2. They, eat

By the end of the fast, they _____ for twenty-four hours.

3. We, finish

_____ our lunch by the time she arrives.

4. Mark, sleep

_____ much before he makes his presentation.

5. She, save

_____ enough money for college by the time classes begin.

Forming contractions

Contractions are often formed by combining pronouns and the auxiliary verb *will* or by combining the auxiliary verb *will* and *not*. You will often hear these contractions in conversation or see them in informal writing, but you will rarely find them used in formal contexts.

Remember that an apostrophe indicates that at least one letter is omitted and that the letter *i* in *will* changes to *o* in the negative contraction *won't*:

I'll have moved	I won't have moved
You'll have moved	You won't have moved
He'll have moved	He won't have moved
She'll have moved	She won't have moved
It'll have moved	It won't have moved
We'll have moved	We won't have moved
They'll have moved	They won't have moved

EXERCISE
8·30

Use the pronoun and verb given to create a sentence that contains a contraction. If *not* is also given, use a negative contraction.

EXAMPLE: It, change

By next year, *it'll have changed.*

1. They, complete

By the time the director arrives, _____ the report.

2. He, finish, not

By the time I return, _____ the work.

3. You, recover

By the end of May, _____ completely.

4. They, make, not

_____ much progress without our help.

5. She, give

_____ the job to someone else by the time my application arrives.

Future perfect progressive

When you want to refer to an ongoing action, state, or event or to a habitual action that will continue until or through a specific time, use the future perfect progressive.

> HABITUAL ACTION: *In October*, we **will have been commuting** together for twenty years.
> ONGOING EVENT: *By that time*, the temperature **will have been increasing** steadily for five years.

The future perfect progressive consists of three auxiliary *verbs—will, have,* and *be*—and the *-ing* form of the main verb. The auxiliary verbs *will* and *have* come first. Next is the perfect/passive form of the verb *be—been*. The final element of the future perfect progressive is the *-ing* form of the main verb.

	Singular	Plural
First Person	I **will have been verb + ing**	we **will have been verb + ing**
Second Person	you **will have been verb + ing**	you **will have been verb + ing**
Third Person	he, she, it **will have been verb + ing**	they will **have been verb + ing**

EXERCISE 8·31

Complete each sentence with the future perfect progressive form of the verb in parentheses.

1. In December, we _____ (live) in this house for ten years.

2. By the time of our next meeting, we _____ (discuss) this plan for three years.

3. By the time of the recital, I _____ (practice) four hours a day, seven days a week.

4. When the Mariners meet the Red Sox, they _____ (play) on the road for six days already.

5. In June, they _____ (work) together for thirty years.

Forming negatives

To make a future perfect progressive verb negative, place *not* after the auxiliary verb *will*.

> will not have been going

EXERCISE
8·32

Complete each of the following sentences with a negative form of the future perfect progressive. Use the subject and verb provided.

EXAMPLE: He, answer, not

By the end of today, *he will not have been answering* his phone for a week.

1. They, talk, not

By Thursday, _____ to each other for a week.

2. The subways, run, not

By the end of the strike, _____ for six days.

3. They, produce, not

In January, _____ that type of car for three years.

4. The dance troupe, perform, not

At the end of the December, _____ for a whole year.

5. She, work, not

On Monday, _____ for three months.

Forming contractions

Contractions are often formed by combining pronouns and the auxiliary verb *will* or by combining the auxiliary verb *will* and *not*. You will often hear these contractions in conversation or see them in informal writing, but you will rarely find them used in formal contexts.

Remember that an apostrophe indicates that at least one letter is omitted and that the letter *i* in *will* changes to *o* in the negative contraction *won't*:

I'll have been going	I won't have been going
You'll have been going	You won't have been going
He'll have been going	He won't have been going
She'll have been going	She won't have been going
It'll have been going	It won't have been going
We'll have been going	We won't have been going
They'll have been going	They won't have been going

Use the pronoun and verb given to create a sentence that contains a contraction. If not is also given, use a negative contraction.

EXAMPLE: The foundation, donate

By next year, the foundation *will have been donating* money to that organization for five years.

1. They, work, not

   By the end of February, _____ the same shift for two months.

2. They, broadcast

   By the end of this year, _____ for fifty years.

3. We, rent

   On Friday, _____ this apartment for ten years.

4. They, return

   In June, _____ to the same place every summer for ten years.

5. He, assist, not

   By the end of this month, _____ us for a full year.

Passive voice

The **passive voice** is a structure that allows you to make a statement without knowing who performed the action of the sentence: *The house was destroyed.* Or the person who performed the action is placed in a *passive position* in the sentence: *The house was destroyed by soldiers.*

An *active* sentence is commonly structured *subject + verb + direct object.* A *passive* sentence changes that structure to *direct object* used as the *subject + to be + past participle + by + subject* used as the *object of the preposition.* Let's compare the two structures:

Active Sentences	Passive Sentences
Kim finds the dog.	The dog is found by Kim.
We buy his car.	His car is bought by us.
The girls stole the purse.	The purse was stolen by the girls.
They solved the problem.	The problem was solved by them.

The verb *to be* in the passive sentences is conjugated in the same tense as the verb in the active sentences. Look how the various tenses appear in the passive:

Tense	Passive Sentences
Present	The house is destroyed by the soldiers.
Past	The house was destroyed by the soldiers.
Present Perfect	The house has been destroyed by the soldiers.
Past Perfect	The house had been destroyed by the soldiers.
Future	The house will be destroyed by the soldiers.
Future Perfect	The house will have been destroyed by the soldiers.

Only in the present and past tenses is there a difference between the habitual form of the conjugation and the conjugation for an action in progress or incomplete:

the house is destroyed/the house is being destroyed
the house was destroyed/the house was being destroyed

Rewrite the passive sentences below as an action in progress. Keep the same tense.

1. Glenda is kissed by Stuart.

   _____

2. She was spoiled by her parents.

   _____

3. My eyes are tested in the clinic.

   _____

4. They were arrested for a crime.

   _____

5. Monique is awarded a medal.

   _____

6. The treasure was buried on an island.

   _____

7. The dog is punished again.

   _____

8. Was the old barn burned down?

   _____

Rewrite the passive sentences below in the present perfect tense.

1. We were punished by Father.

   _____

2. The men are taken prisoner.

   _____

3. She is thanked by the happy tourists.

   _____

4. I was beaten by a robber.

   _____

5. The car was not washed again.

   _____

6. Tony is examined by the doctor.

_____

7. They are surrounded by the enemy.

_____

8. Was your sister fired from her job?

_____

9. Was the baby carried to his bedroom?

_____

10. She is congratulated by her boss.

_____

Rewrite the following active sentences as passive sentences. Keep the same tense.

1. A storm destroyed the cottage.

_____

2. Did Columbus discover the New World?

_____

3. They will buy our house.

_____

4. My grandmother has baked the cakes.

_____

5. Phil is cutting the bread.

_____

6. Sergio was selling the newspapers.

_____

7. Has Iris taken the money?

_____

8. She will kiss the baby.

_____

9. Is Max building the fence?

_____

10. Her brother forgot the map.

_____

Using the passive

The passive voice occurs in all tenses and can even be used in a progressive tense. The following examples show active sentences and their corresponding passive formations.

	ACTIVE	PASSIVE
SIMPLE PRESENT	Eric **carries** Pam.	Pam **is carried** by Eric.
PRESENT PROGRESSIVE	Eric **is carrying** Pam.	Pam **is being carried** by Eric.
SIMPLE PAST	Eric **carried** Pam.	Pam **was carried** by Eric.
PAST PROGRESSIVE	Eric **was carrying** Pam.	Pam **was being carried** by Eric.
PRESENT PERFECT	Eric **has carried** Pam.	Pam **has been carried** by Eric.
PAST PERFECT	Eric **had carried** Pam.	Pam **had been carried** by Eric.
SIMPLE FUTURE	Eric **will carry** Pam.	Pam **will be carried** by Eric.
FUTURE PERFECT	Eric **will have carried** Pam.	Pam **will have been carried** by Eric.
"be going to" FORM	Eric **is going to carry** Pam.	Pam **is going to be carried** by Eric.

When a sentence is changed from active to passive, the tense of the active sentence is retained in the passive sentence.

Patrick **paints** a picture.	A picture **is painted** by Patrick.
Samantha **is teaching** the class.	The class **is being taught** by Samantha.
Robin **borrowed** a dollar.	A dollar **was borrowed** by Robin.
Tyler **has seen** this episode.	This episode **has been seen** by Tyler.
Alicia **will prepare** a salad.	A salad **will be prepared** by Alicia.

EXERCISE
9·4

Rewrite each active sentence as a passive sentence, retaining the tense of the original sentence.

1. Maria found a hundred dollars.

   _____

2. The students will memorize the Preamble to the Constitution.

   _____

3. Did you purchase the tickets?

   _____

4. They have discovered some ancient ruins.

   _____

5. Bill is measuring the room.

   _____

Sentences that cannot be written in the passive voice

Only transitive verbs—verbs followed by an object—can be used in the passive. It is not possible to use intransitive verbs, such as *happen, sleep, come, go, live, occur, rain, rise, depart, walk,* and *seem,* in the passive.

ACTIVE VOICE	PASSIVE VOICE
Marie helped Peter.	Peter was helped by Marie. (TRANSITIVE VERB)
The baby slept soundly.	— (INTRANSITIVE VERB)
The student came to class.	— (INTRANSITIVE VERB)

Forming the passive voice without a *by* phrase

The passive voice is often used when it is unimportant to know who or what performs the action. In the sentence "Coffee *is grown* in Colombia," we are informed where coffee is grown. Yet the coffee could be grown by villagers, by children, by immigrants, or by any other group of people. Following are examples that illustrate the most common ways of using the passive voice without a prepositional phrase introduced with *by*.

> Rice **is grown** throughout Asia.
> That car **was built** in the 1930s.
> This watch **was imported** from Geneva, Switzerland.
> Poor Mr. Lowry **is going to be fired**!

When the subject of an active sentence is some vague entity (*they, someone, people*), it is common to avoid using a *by* phrase in the passive.

ACTIVE	**They** cultivate grapes in southern France.
PASSIVE	Grapes are cultivated in southern France.

By is used in the passive when it is important to inform the reader or listener who is responsible for the action: "*Perfume* was written by Patrick Süskind." In this case, it is important to know that a specific author (and not just any author) wrote this particular book.

As a general rule, if the writer knows who performs the action, it's preferable to use the active voice: "My neighbor made the strawberry pie." Stylistically, the writer could use the passive, but it would mean that he or she is trying to direct the reader's attention to the new subject: "The strawberry pie was made by my neighbor."

EXERCISE
9·5

Rewrite each active sentence as a passive sentence. Don't use a prepositional phrase with by.

1. They manufactured a thousand cars at that plant.

   _____

2. Many people are developing theories about that.

   _____

3. Someone will buy that painting today.

   _____

4. They have postponed the opening of the new store.

   _____

5. No one respects his work.

   _____

Rewrite each active sentence as a passive sentence.

EXAMPLE   Two horses were pulling the princess's carriage.

  The princess's carriage was being pulled by two horses.

1. Kevin has suggested a new design for the logo.

   _____

2. The professor is going to explain the formula.

   _____

3. Bartenders serve people at the bar.

   _____

4. Noam Chomsky is preparing a speech.

   _____

5. Alex will invite Marie to the party.

   _____

6. Neil Gaiman wrote the novel *American Gods*.

   _____

Complete the second sentence of each pair with the correct passive form of the verb phrase in the first sentence. Retain the tense of the original sentence.

EXAMPLE   William was driving the car.

  The car ___*was being*___ driven by William.

1. William will have driven the car.

   The car _____ driven by William.

2. William drives the car.

   The car _____ driven by William.

3. William is driving the car.

   The car _____ driven by William.

4. William has driven the car.

   The car _____ driven by William.

5. William is going to drive the car.

   The car _____ driven by William.

6. William will drive the car.

   The car _____ driven by William.

7. William had driven the car.

   The car _____ driven by William.

Rewrite each passive sentence as an active sentence. If an active sentence is not possible, mark an "X" in the blank.

EXAMPLE   The karate tournament is being sponsored by Pepsi.

   Pepsi is sponsoring the karate tournament.

1. Technical skills are taught by every professional school in New York.

   _____

2. The ping-pong tournament is being broadcast by TF1.

   _____

3. The Inner Movement Symphony is being televised all over New Zealand.

   _____

4. This poem was written by Keats. The other one was written by García Lorca.

   _____

5. Paper was invented in China. Later, paper was produced in Baghdad by Arabs.

   _____

6. The new bridge will be completed sometime next year.

   _____

7. My socks were made in Scotland.

   _____

Rewrite each active sentence as a passive sentence, retaining the tense of the original sentence. Use a by *phrase wherever possible. If a passive sentence is not possible, mark an "X" in the blank.*

EXAMPLE   Somebody took my chair.

   My chair was taken by somebody.

1. Someone stole my purse.

   _____

2. Garret came to New York three days ago.

   _____

3. Gabriel borrowed my fork at lunch.

   _____

4. Someone made this antique sewing machine in 1834.

   _____

5. An accident happened on Loop 1 yesterday morning.

   _____

6. Steve was watering the plants when I walked into the garden this morning.

   _____

7. The jury is going to judge the president on the basis of his testimony.

   _____

8. When did America invent the atomic bomb?

   _____

9. Caroline slept until two o'clock!

   _____

10. Is Maureen organizing a reunion this week?

    _____

11. Professionals have translated the Bible into many languages.

    _____

The passive form of modal auxiliaries

The passive voice of modal auxiliaries is formed by the modal + *be* + past participle. This formation can be used to express the present and future tenses.

> The door **can't be opened**.
> Children **should be taught** how to read poetry.
> This package **ought to be sent** by tomorrow.
> Fred **has to be told** about the meeting.
> Jason **was supposed to be informed** about the changes.

The future tense

With some modals, the future tense is expressed with the auxiliary *will*.

> Fred **will have to be told** about the meeting.

The past tense

The past tense of certain modal auxiliaries in the passive voice is formed by the modal + *have been* + past participle.

> The letter **should have been sent** yesterday!
> This car **must have been stolen** two months ago.
> Andrew **ought to have been told** about the meeting.

With other modal auxiliaries, the past tense of the modal is used together with *to be* + past participle.

> Fred **had to be told** about the meeting.
> The door **couldn**'t **be opened**.

EXERCISE
9·10

Complete each sentence, using the correct forms of the verbs in parentheses. For some sentences, more than one tense may be used.

EXAMPLE   Tom ___*may have already been given*___ (may + already + give) this card by one of his friends.

1. Ronald _____ (should + tell) the good news as soon as possible.

2. Angela _____ (should + drive) to the airport half an hour ago.

3. Someone _____ (should + clean) the kitchen before dinner.

4. Butter _____ (must + keep) in the refrigerator or it will go bad.

5. We tried talking to him, but he _____ (could + not + convince). He had already made up his mind.

6. We tried, but we _____ (could + not + open) the window.

7. I am so excited! IBM called me, and I _____ (may + offer) a job with them soon.

8. The computer firm that Stephanie interviewed with last week

   _____ (may + not + offer) her a job, even though

   she had a good feeling about it.

9. I hope Bob accepts our job offer. He _____ (may + already + offer) a job with another company.

10. It might be too late to call her with an offer. Another competing company

    _____ (may + already + hire) her.

11. Peter didn't expect to see his little brother at the party. He

    _____ (must + surprise) when he saw him drinking.

12. Today is the 8th, and his birthday was on the 2nd. Her birthday card

    _____ (should + send) a week ago.

13. His birthday is coming up next week. His present _____
    (should + send) to his house soon.

14. Tricia _____ (had better + clean) her room before Mom
    gets back home.

15. Tricia, your room _____ (had better + clean) by the time
    I get home.

16. Tyler _____ (have to + return) these videos by tomorrow
    night.

17. These videos _____ (have to + return) to the video store
    by this afternoon.

18. There are too many people in this class. It _____
    (ought to + divide) in two, but there are no more available classrooms.

19. Last semester's class was too large. It _____
    (ought to + divide) in half.

*Complete each sentence with the correct form of the verb in parentheses together
with an appropriate modal auxiliary or similar expression.*

1. He is crying. He _____ (be) sad.

2. The entire forest _____ (see) from their balcony.

3. According to our teacher, all our calculators _____ (put) into
   our bags before she passes out the test.

4. A child _____ (not + get) everything he asks for.

5. Your son draws quite poorly. His interest in painting _____
   (not + encourage).

6. Five of the players on the team missed their plane. In my opinion, the game

   _____ (postpone).

7. Try to speak slowly when you give your lecture. Otherwise, some of your sentences

   _____ (misunderstand).

8. Some sightings of Elvis _____ (not + explain).

9. She is wearing a ring on the fourth finger of her left hand. She

   _____ (marry).

10. I found a wallet on the table. It _____ (left) by one of the
    students who was having lunch.

11. What! You lost your final paper draft? Your professor _____ (displease) once you've told him about it.

12. He is very lazy. If you need him to do something, he _____ (push).

13. The classrooms in this school are old, but the municipality gave us money and a new school _____ (build) by next summer.

14. Blue whales _____ (save) from extinction.

15. We can no longer sit here with our arms crossed! Something _____ (do)!

16. In my opinion, he _____ (elect), because he is honest and organized.

The stative passive

Past participles in a passive-voice sentence can act like adjectives, in the sense that they describe a noun.

> The car is **old**.
> The car is **locked**.

In the first example, the word *old* is an adjective and describes *car*. In the second example, *locked* is a past participle; it functions as an adjective and also describes *car*.

Essentially, the participle is derived from passive-voice sentences like the following.

> The car **has been locked** by someone. (The car is **locked**.)
> The window **was repaired** by someone. (The window is **repaired**.)

Adjectives and participles

The passive past participle can be used to describe an existing state or situation; when it does, it is called the **stative passive**. Consider the following examples.

> I locked the car door five minutes ago. Now the car door **is locked**.
> Peter broke the window two days ago. Now the window **is broken**.
> We were without water for a week. Now the pipe **is** finally **fixed**.

In all three examples, the action took place earlier, as described in the first sentence, and the state of that action in the present is expressed in the second sentence of each pair. In these second sentences, the past participle functions as an adjective.

Notice that there is no *by* phrase in any of the sentences. However, the stative passive is often followed by prepositions other than *by*.

> She is satisfied **with** her job.
> Marc is married **to** Vanessa.

There are many other common adjectives in English that are, in reality, stative passive structures.

Frank is **interested**. I'm **bored**.
The store was **closed**. He saw nothing but **closed** stores.
The work was **finished**. He took the **finished** work home.

Following is a list of commonly used adjectives that are derived from present and past participles.

amazing/amazed
boring/bored
confusing/confused
disappointing/disappointed
exciting/excited
exhausting/exhausted
frightening/frightened
interesting/interested
satisfying/satisfied
surprising/surprised
terrifying/terrified
tiring/tired

The present participle is used as a modifier for the active voice. The past participle is used as a modifier for the passive voice.

The athlete was **amazing**. (*This adjective describes what the athlete is.*)
The athlete was **amazed**. (*This adjective describes what happened to the athlete.*)

This book is **boring**. (*This adjective describes what the book is.*)
This student is **bored**. (*This adjective describes what happened to the student.*)

EXERCISE
9·12

Underline the correct participle in each sentence.

1. The journalist was **disappointing | disappointed** that the newspaper didn't accept her article.

2. Tokyo is an **exciting | excited** international city.

3. I am very **interesting | interested** in astrology.

4. Reading good novels is **gratifying | gratified**.

5. I am sorry for messing up the sauce. The recipe was really **confusing | confused**.

6. Peter was also **confusing | confused** when he read the instructions.

7. Susan is **exciting | excited**, because she will see her parents soon.

8. Richard hoped that his family would be **exciting | excited** to meet his new girlfriend.

EXERCISE 9·13

Complete each sentence, using the simple present or simple past tense of be with the stative passive form of the verb in parentheses.

EXAMPLE   It's getting warm in here, because the heater __is fixed__ (fix) again.

1. It smells bad in this kitchen, because the ventilator _____ (break).

2. It is hot in this car, because the window _____ (close).

3. Yesterday it was hot in this room, because the window _____ (close).

4. Peter is wearing a winter hat. It _____ (make) of cotton.

5. The door to the castle _____ (shut).

6. Bob looks worried. He is sitting all by himself. His elbows _____ (bend) and his hands _____ (fold) in front of him.

7. We can leave now, since the movie _____ (finish).

8. The headlights on his car _____ (turn) on.

9. This theater _____ (not + crowd).

10. Don't look under the stairs! Your Christmas present _____ (hide) there.

11. Oh no! How did this happen? My dress _____ (tear).

12. Where are my keys? They _____ (go)! Did you take them?

13. Mother just called us, because dinner is ready. The table _____ (set), the chicken and beans _____ (finish), and the candles _____ (light).

14. His room is finally looking cleaner. The bed _____ (make), the floor _____ (vacuum), and the windows _____ (wash).

15. We were trapped in a canyon for two days, because the car _____ (stick) in mud.

16. We are trapped here. The car _____ (stick) in mud.

Adverbs

·10·

You already know that adjectives modify nouns. For example: the *blue* house, our *little* brother, a *silly* poem. **Adverbs** are also modifiers, but they modify verbs, adjectives, and other adverbs. You can easily identify adverbs because most end in *-ly*: *happily, quickly, slowly, beautifully.*

Most adjectives can be changed to an adverb by adding *-ly* to the end of the adjective. If the adjective ends in *-y*, change the *-y* to *-i* and then add *-ly*.

Adjective	Adverb
bad	badly
bright	brightly
cold	coldly
happy	happily
merry	merrily
speedy	speedily
sudden	suddenly
wrong	wrongly

There are a few adjectives and adverbs that have special forms and uses. One important one is *good*. If *good* means "kind," it is only used as an adjective. Use *kindly* in place of it as an adverb. If *good* means "talented," use *well* as its adverb. Careful! If *well* means "healthy," it is not an adverb; it is an adjective.

good = kind: He is a *good* man.
 He spoke to us *kindly*.
good = talented: Hayley is a *good* tennis player.
 Hayley plays tennis *well*.
well = healthy: I am glad that your father is *well* again.

There is only one form for the word *fast*. It is both an adjective and an adverb:

Lee is a *fast* talker. (adjective)
Lee talks *fast*. (adverb)

And note that the adverb *home* does not end in *-ly*:

We went *home* after work.

You can also identify adverbs by asking certain questions of the verb in a sentence. Ask *how, where,* or *when.* The answer is an adverb.

How? Where? When?	The Answer = Adverb
Jamal got quickly to his feet.	
"How did Jamal get to his feet?"	quickly
She went home on the bus.	
"Where did she go on the bus?"	home
They arrived punctually.	
"When did they arrive?"	punctually

Some adverbs of time, which answer the question *when*, do not always end in *-ly*. Consider these words: *today, tomorrow, yesterday, tonight, late, early, never*.

Certain adverbs, which often do not end in *-ly*, qualify *the degree* of the meaning of an adjective or adverb: *quite, rather, very, somewhat, too*:

somewhat slowly = the slowness is not great but evident
rather slowly = the slowness is emphasized, but it is not extreme
quite slowly = the slowness is emphasized here
very slowly = the slowness is extreme
too slowly = the slowness is more than desired

Let's look at how adverbs can modify verbs, adjectives, and other adverbs:

Verbs	Adjectives	Adverbs
Justin walked *slowly*.	It is an *extremely* strange idea.	She ran *very* fast.
The boys drove *home*.	I have a *very* bad cold.	He sang *too* quietly.
Hannah laughed *loudly*.	It was a *rather* stupid question.	I sighed *rather* sadly.
Carmen writes *carelessly*.	He was *partially* dressed.	He smiled *quite* cheerfully.

EXERCISE

10·1

Change the adjective in parentheses to an adverb. Place it appropriately in the sentence.

1. My sister walked into the room. (timid)

_____

2. We sat down next to the bed. (quiet)

_____

3. Harvey spoke angrily to the man. (rather)

_____

4. The children entered the classroom. (noisy)

_____

5. He said that my story was boring. (too)

_____

6. She talked to the little girl. (harsh)

_____

7. Julia followed the pretty girl. (home)

_____

8. My uncle is a smart man. (very)

_____

9. My cousin plays the piano. (good)

_____

10. The animal stared into my face. (cold)

_____

Using the adverbial phrases in parentheses, write appropriate sentences.

1. (very neatly) _____

2. (well) _____

3. (sadly) _____

4. (too) _____

5. (rather quickly) _____

6. (yesterday) _____

7. (never) _____

8. (quite strongly) _____

9. (too carelessly) _____

10. (so beautifully) _____

A primary function of **adverbs** is to modify verbs. Many adverbs are formed by adding the suffix -*ly* to adjectives: *quick ~ quickly, happy ~ happily, careful ~ carefully, bitter ~ bitterly*.

> She swims **quickly**.
> He opened the window **carefully**.

Adverbs can also modify adjectives, thereby augmenting their meaning.

> They are **extremely** sad.
> The crowd soon became **rather** unruly.

Several adverbs express time, for example, *tomorrow, today, never, soon, yesterday, yet*.

> My parents are supposed to arrive **tomorrow**.
> Will you be off the phone **soon**?
> Has Jimmy taken his shower **yet**?

Some adverbs can be placed in the middle of a sentence, and they generally have a set position there. Mid-sentence adverbs stand in front of verbs in the simple present and simple past tenses. They follow forms of *be* in simple present and simple past tenses, and they stand between an auxiliary verb and a main verb.

BEFORE SIMPLE PRESENT AND PAST TENSES

> We **seldom** have dessert after dinner.
> My brother **often** spent his free time playing his guitar.
> I **rarely** talk on the phone for more than a few minutes.
> Tom **frequently** asks an embarrassing question.

FOLLOWING SIMPLE PRESENT AND PAST TENSES OF *BE*

> Anna is **always** there on time.
> Bill was **sometimes** late for an appointment.
> Her husband is **never** around when she needs him.
> The children are **apparently** in very good health.

BETWEEN AN AUXILIARY VERB AND MAIN VERB

> John can **never** face his parents again.
> Anna has **always** gotten there on time.
> They have **often** traveled abroad.
> Do you **regularly** shop in this store?

The word *well* can be used as an adverb or as an adjective. As an adverb, *well* means "in a good manner" or "capably" and describes how someone does something. As an adjective, *well* means "healthy."

Using adverbs

Adverbs modify verbs, adjectives, or other adverbs. They can be individual words, phrases, or clauses.

> adverb + verb
> adverb + adjective
> adverb + adverb

Adverb types and forms

There is more than one type of adverb. This chapter provides you with information on adverbs of manner, time, frequency, degree, and place, as well as adverbs that provide a comment on a situation.

Individual adverbs are formed simply by adding the suffix **-ly** to an adjective. Naturally, the English rules of spelling apply; for example, a final *y* is changed to *i* when an adverb is formed (**happy** → **happily**). Let's look at some example adjectives and their adverbial formation:

ADJECTIVE	ADVERB
careful	carefully
quick	quickly
simple	simply

A few adverbs are identical to their adjectival counterparts. For example:

ADJECTIVE	ADVERB
early	early
fast	fast
late	late

Adjectives that describe certain increments of time *look like adverbs* but are true adjectives. For example:

> We're paid on an **hourly** basis.
> I take a **daily** vitamin supplement.
> Grandma has a **weekly** appointment with her doctor.
>
> Your **monthly** salary is going to be increased.
> My **yearly** physical exam always makes me nervous.

Still other adjectives that look like adverbs are not related to the ones that describe increments of time. Examples are **deadly**, **early**, **lively**, and **only**.

When an adverb is used in the comparative or superlative, the suffix **-ly** is generally not added. However, if the comparative and superlative are formed with **more** and **most**, the suffix **-ly** is added.

POSITIVE	COMPARATIVE	SUPERLATIVE
quickly	quicker	(the) quickest
softly	softer	(the) softest
well	better	(the) best
awkwardly	more awkwardly	most awkwardly
beautifully	more beautifully	most beautifully
carefully	more carefully	most carefully

Don't confuse **late** with **lately**. Both are adverbs, but they have different meanings.

> The girls arrived **late**.   *the opposite of* early
> He's been rather moody **lately**.   *recently*

Adverbs of manner

Adverbs of manner form a large category. They tell how something is done. Consider the following sentences:

Martin drove **slowly**.	*How did he drive? Slowly.*
I **carefully** removed the battery.	*How did I remove the battery? Carefully.*
She kissed the baby **gently**.	*How did she kiss the baby? Gently.*

Adverbs of manner can be individual words or phrases. Let's look at some of these:

INDIVIDUAL WORDS	PHRASES
badly	in anger
politely	with a sly grin
sarcastically	with great sadness

Adverbs of manner tend to follow the predicate of a sentence.

subject + predicate + adverb of manner

Bill + spoke to her + angrily.
The team played **badly**.
He tried to speak **politely**.
She gave them the news **with great sadness**.
Tom began to shout **in anger**.

Adverbs of time

Adverbs such as **now, still, yesterday, just, finally,** and **Sunday** tell when something occurred. These adverbs of time are part of a category that includes individual words, phrases, and clauses. For example:

INDIVIDUAL WORDS	PHRASES	CLAUSES
finally	during the exam	after the game ended
recently	in the spring	I got on the bus
today	on Monday before	since she arrived here

Adverbs of time can introduce a sentence or follow it.

subject + predicate + adverb of time

He + left for work + at seven.

adverb of time + subject + predicate

At seven + he + left for work.
Recently, I bought a new laptop.
I bought a new laptop **recently**.

During the exam, Tina began to feel ill.
Tina began to feel ill **during the exam**.

Before I got on the bus, I realized I had lost my ticket.
I realized I had lost my ticket **before I got on the bus**.

Using each set of words and phrases provided, write a sentence with the adverb of manner in the appropriate position.

EXAMPLE: men / drive / carefully / mountains

The men had to drive carefully through the mountains.

1. children / run / school / with joy

_____

2. baritone / sing / better / soprano

_____

3. brother / lounge / lazily / sofa / TV

_____

4. Michael / show / car / with great pride

_____

5. she / act / responsibly / accident

_____

6. woman / mutter / weakly / that / ill

_____

7. professor / congratulate / with a bit of sarcasm

_____

8. eight-year-old / play / beautifully

_____

9. little James / recite / capably / bow

_____

10. Ellen / slap / with rage

_____

Using each adverb of time provided, write two original sentences: one in which the adverb introduces the action, and one in which it follows it.

EXAMPLE: recently

Recently, I found an old picture of Dad.

I found an old picture of Dad recently.

1. during the storm

a. _____

b. _____

2. yesterday

   a. _____

   b. _____

3. on the weekend

   a. _____

   b. _____

4. soon

   a. _____

   b. _____

5. next Friday

   a. _____

   b. _____

6. in time

   a. _____

   b. _____

7. after Paul gets here

   a. _____

   b. _____

8. in June

   a. _____

   b. _____

9. last year

   a. _____

   b. _____

10. before I studied English

   a. _____

   b. _____

Adverbs of frequency

Adverbs of frequency tell *how often* something occurs. They can be individual words or phrases. For example:

INDIVIDUAL WORDS	PHRASES
never	at times
sometimes	in the rarest of moments
usually	with great frequency

When an adverb of frequency is an individual word, it tends to stand just before the verb. If it is a phrase, it usually can either introduce the sentence or follow it. Let's look at some example sentences:

We **rarely** stay out very late.
My sister **often** invites her friends over to listen to music.

At times, I just want to drop everything and go out.
Mr. Johnson showed up at our door **with great regularity**.

Adverbs of degree

Adverbs of degree tell *to what extent* something is done. Some of the most commonly used adverbs of degree are listed here:

adequately	perfectly
almost	practically
entirely	profoundly
extremely	really
greatly	strongly
highly	totally
hugely	tremendously
immensely	very
moderately	virtually
partially	

The adverbs in this category are used to modify verbs, adjectives, or other adverbs. The position of the adverb in a sentence is determined by the word it modifies:

◆ Verbs

The children enjoyed the circus **immensely**.
The lawyer **strongly** advocated suing the company.

◆ Adjectives

She was an **extremely** beautiful woman.
Bill had become **profoundly** depressed.

◆ Adverbs

They sang **really** badly.
The project was progressing **moderately** well.

Rewrite the following sentences with an appropriate adverb of frequency.

EXAMPLE: She spoke with John.

<u>She never spoke with John.</u>

1. We supported our troops fighting overseas.

   _____

2. Larry had to work on the weekend.

   _____

3. I planned to take art courses at the college.

   _____

4. Do you work at the new plant in the suburbs?

   _____

5. Martin renews his subscription to this magazine.

   _____

6. We drink coffee with breakfast.

   _____

7. Did your parents live in Europe?

   _____

8. My sister and I baked a cake or cookies.

   _____

9. Jim and Ellen went to a dance.

   _____

10. Have you thought of becoming a doctor?

    _____

Write an original sentence using each adverb of degree and the accompanying verb, adjective, or adverb provided.

EXAMPLE: very strong <u>My cousin Jake is a very strong man.</u>

1. highly emotional _____

2. totally irrelevant _____

3. recommend highly _____

4. immensely proudly _____

5. hugely successful _____

6. weep profoundly _____

7. really stubbornly _____

8. really stubborn _____

9. entirely false _____

10. partially true _____

Adverbs of place

Adverbs of place tell *where* an action occurs. Some of these adverbs are single words. For example:

abroad	inside
anywhere	somewhere
downstairs	there
here	underground

Other adverbs of place appear in phrase form, particularly in prepositional phrases.

alongside the road	next door
at home	on the hearth
in the bedroom	over there

Let's look at some example sentences:

They lived **abroad** for five years.
They were working **somewhere** on a secret project.

Jack was making up the bed **in the bedroom**.
We spend a lot of time **at home**.

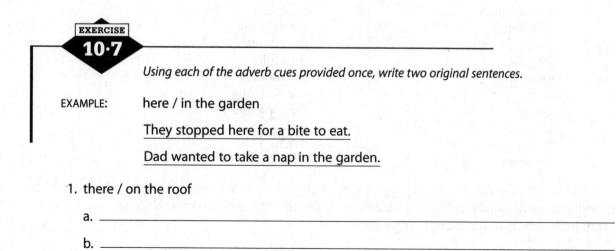

EXERCISE
10·7

Using each of the adverb cues provided once, write two original sentences.

EXAMPLE: here / in the garden

They stopped here for a bite to eat.

Dad wanted to take a nap in the garden.

1. there / on the roof

a. _____

b. _____

2. outside / next door

   a. _____

   b. _____

3. anywhere / over the mantle

   a. _____

   b. _____

4. upstairs / in a small box

   a. _____

   b. _____

5. underground / beyond the river

   a. _____

   b. _____

6. somewhere / under a leafy tree

   a. _____

   b. _____

Adverbs that make a comment

Some adverbs make a comment on a situation. They identify the speaker's or writer's *viewpoint* or *opinion* on the subject matter of a sentence. Some commonly used comment or viewpoint adverbs follow:

bravely	presumably
carelessly	seriously
certainly	simply
clearly	stupidly
cleverly	surely
confidentially	technically
definitely	theoretically
disappointingly	thoughtfully
foolishly	truthfully
generously	unbelievably
happily	undoubtedly
kindly	(un)fortunately
naturally	(un)luckily
obviously	wisely
personally	wrongly

When adverbs of this category are used in context, they show the degree to which the speaker or writer agrees or disagrees with a statement. These adverbs can also show disapproval or skepticism. Let's look at some example sentences:

She **clearly** has no understanding of the topic.

The speaker has doubts about her understanding.

| | **Theoretically**, the project should be completed by May. | *The speaker is skeptical that the completion date can be met.* |
| | **Wisely**, he chose to drop out of the competition. | *The speaker believes the decision to drop out was a good one.* |

Some adverbs of this type are placed only at the beginning of the sentence. For example:

Confidentially, I think that Martha is being dishonest.
Presumably, the storm is going to let up and we'll be able to leave.
Happily, the child was found unharmed.

Certain of these adverbs can either introduce the sentence or follow the subject. For example:

Naturally, I thought I had done the right thing.
I **naturally** thought I had done the right thing.

Certainly, Jean understands why you can't go tonight.
Jean **certainly** understands why you can't go tonight.

Personally, I believe the election came off quite smoothly.
I **personally** believe that the election came off quite smoothly.

Be careful with the adverb **happily**. It is both an adverb of manner and an adverb of viewpoint or comment. If it tells *how* something is done, it is an adverb of manner.

Tina spoke **happily** about her engagement.

If it expresses a point of view, suggesting that the subject matter of the sentence is good news, then the adverb is one of viewpoint or comment.

Happily, the man found his wallet and could buy the tickets.

EXERCISE
10·8

Rewrite each of the following sentences twice: first placing the adverb provided in parentheses at the beginning of the sentence, and then placing it after the subject.

EXAMPLE: (obviously) The blizzard is worse than expected.

Obviously, the blizzard is worse than expected.

The blizzard obviously is worse than expected.

1. (surely) You don't believe his story.

   a. _____

   b. _____

2. (undoubtedly) The man is a genius.

   a. _____

   b. _____

3. (personally) I feel I can place my trust in this woman.

   a. _____

   b. _____

4. (presumably) Mr. Lee has a wonderful new job in Boston.

   a. _____

   b. _____

5. (cleverly) Daniel found a seat next to the pretty girl from Korea.

   a. _____

   b. _____

Adverb placement in a sentence

Adverbs tend to be placed in a specific position in a sentence. This is merely a tendency, however, and some adverbs are more flexible and make sense in more than one position. In some cases, the position of an adverb in a sentence is determined by what element is stressed or by the actual function of the adverb. Also, some adverbs can be used in more than one way. For example:

Disappointingly, Mark received another bad grade.	*adverb of viewpoint introducing the sentence*
Bill **disappointingly** missed making a goal.	*adverb of viewpoint following the subject*
She gave a **disappointingly** weak response.	*adverb of degree modifying an adjective*

Following are some general rules for determining adverb placement in a sentence:

* Adverbs of manner, adverbs of time, and adverbs of place stand after the verb or the predicative expression at the end of the sentence.

   subject + verb + manner/time/place

The boys stared **glumly** at the scoreboard.	*adverb of manner*
They'll arrive in town **next week**.	*adverb of time*
Phillip stood **near the door**.	*adverb of place*

* Adverbs of frequency are placed before the main verb in a sentence.

   subject + frequency + verb

   Jack **often** visits us when he's in town.
   She **rarely** spoke of life in her village.

   An exception is that if the sentence contains an auxiliary verb, an adverb of frequency usually follows that auxiliary.

   Maria has **never** been to Canada.
   My dad will **usually** cry at a sad movie.
   You should **regularly** floss your teeth.

   Also, if the verb **to be** is used as the main verb of a clause, an adverb of frequency will follow that verb.

   She was **seldom** in class.
   You are **always** the best musician in the orchestra.

◆ Adverbs of degree follow the verb or verb phrase they modify—but if they modify an adjective or another adverb, they are placed before them.

The good news about Dad's health pleased them **tremendously**.   *modified verb*

He had a **profoundly** infected wound.   *modified adjective*

They had to drive **really** slowly.   *modified adverb*

◆ Adverbs of viewpoint or comment commonly begin the sentence—though, some can follow the subject. For example:

viewpoint + subject + verb

Wisely, they left the stalled car and walked to town.
Undoubtedly, you have no confidence in yourself.

subject + viewpoint + verb

She **clearly** has no intention of paying me back.
Bob **obviously** overslept again.

The explanations of adverb placement in this chapter have been qualified by words such as *commonly used* or *tendency*, because there can be exceptions to the rules. The rules are not finite.

One frequent exception to the rules is the placement of an adverb at the beginning of a sentence, rather than in its normal position, for emphasis. For example:

Now you finally come up with an answer to my question!
Rarely do I ever watch such television programs!
Sometimes I think about my days back on the farm.

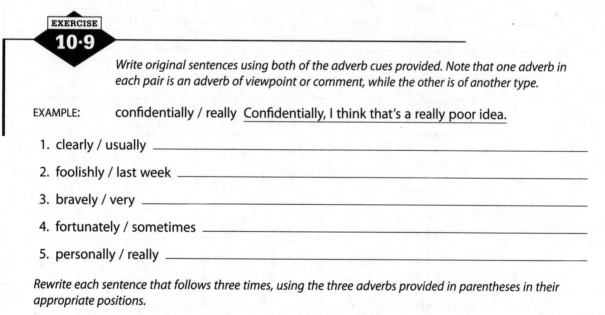

EXERCISE
10·9

Write original sentences using both of the adverb cues provided. Note that one adverb in each pair is an adverb of viewpoint or comment, while the other is of another type.

EXAMPLE: confidentially / really   Confidentially, I think that's a really poor idea.

1. clearly / usually _____

2. foolishly / last week _____

3. bravely / very _____

4. fortunately / sometimes _____

5. personally / really _____

Rewrite each sentence that follows three times, using the three adverbs provided in parentheses in their appropriate positions.

EXAMPLE: She bought a pretty sweater. (naturally / on Monday / really)

Naturally, she bought a pretty sweater.

She bought a pretty sweater on Monday.

She bought a really pretty sweater.

6. I ran to the window and saw Bill. (quickly / fortunately / suddenly)

   a. _____

   b. _____

   c. _____

7. Juanita destroyed the strange object. (wisely / immediately / very)

   a. _____

   b. _____

   c. _____

8. They carried her into the living room. (after she fainted / carefully / around five o'clock)

   a. _____

   b. _____

   c. _____

9. The old men sat around the little table. (presumably / extremely / silently)

   a. _____

   b. _____

   c. _____

10. Her left leg is broken. (seriously / once again / in two places)

   a. _____

   b. _____

   c. _____

Contractions

Contractions are a combination of two words. Often they are a pronoun and a verb. But not all verbs can be combined with a pronoun to form a contraction. Use only these verbs: *have, has, is, are, am, would,* and *will*. Look how these verbs form contractions with the pronouns:

Pronoun	have/has	is/are/am	would/will
I	I've	I'm	I'd/I'll
you	you've	you're	you'd/you'll
he	he's	he's	he'd/he'll
she	she's	she's	she'd/she'll
it	it's	it's	N/A
we	we've	we're	we'd/we'll
they	they've	they're	they'd/they'll
who	who's	who's	who'd/who'll

Certain verbs form contractions with the negative word *not*:

Verb	Contraction
are	aren't
can	can't
could	couldn't
did	didn't
do	don't
does	doesn't
has	hasn't
have	haven't
is	isn't
must	mustn't
need	needn't
should	shouldn't
was	wasn't
were	weren't
will	won't
would	wouldn't

Rewrite the pronoun and verb in each sentence as a contraction.

1. You have been very unhappy. _____

2. I am not going to work today. _____

3. He would enjoy this movie a lot. _____

4. They are my best friends. _____

5. It is very cold today. _____

6. She will stop by for a visit tomorrow. _____

7. Who has been using my computer? _____

8. He is a very fine teacher. _____

9. We have never seen anything like this. _____

10. I will join you for dinner tomorrow. _____

11. She is a great soccer player. _____

12. Who would want to live in this neighborhood? _____

13. You are spending too much money. _____

14. They have gone to the United States. _____

15. It has been a very humid day. _____

Rewrite the verb and not *in each sentence as a contraction.*

1. You must not act surprised. _____

2. He cannot go to school today. _____

3. Mother will not allow that to happen. _____

4. The boys could not know what danger there was. _____

5. They are not acting properly. _____

6. Did you not do the housework? _____

7. My cousin was not at work today. _____

8. The girls do not like Mark. _____

9. Is that man not your uncle? _____

10. We should not spend so much time together. _____

Write original sentences with the contractions given in parentheses.

1. (hasn't) _____

2. (mustn't) _____

3. (shouldn't) _____

4. (needn't) _____

5. (weren't) _____

6. (I've) _____

7. (he'll) _____

8. (they're) _____

9. (you'd) _____

10. (she's) _____

Plurals

Most English **plurals** are formed quite simply. Just add -*s* to the end of a noun:

> dog → dogs
> building → buildings

However, if the noun ends in -*s*, -*ss*, -*z*, -*x*, -*ch*, or -*sh*, add -*es* to form the plural:

> boss → bosses
> box → boxes
> witch → witches
> dish → dishes

If the noun ends in a consonant plus -*y*, change the -*y* to -*i*, then add -*es*:

> lady → ladies
> penny → pennies

Words that end in -*o* are a special problem. Some form their plural by adding -*s*, and others form their plural by adding -*es*. Look at these examples:

Singular	Plural + -*s*	Singular	Plural + -*es*
auto	autos	potato	potatoes
piano	pianos	hero	heroes
alto	altos	echo	echoes
zoo	zoos	veto	vetoes
solo	solos	cargo	cargoes

Consult a dictionary to know precisely which plural ending to use with words that end in -*o*.

There are a few words that form the plural with an -*s* ending but also require a consonant change in which *f* changes to *v*:

> knife → knives
> leaf → leaves
> shelf → shelves
> wife → wives
> wolf → wolves

Certain other nouns form their plural in completely irregular ways. Fortunately, the list is quite brief:

child → children
mouse → mice
foot → feet
person → people (or persons)
goose → geese
deer → deer [no change!]
man → men
woman → women
tooth → teeth
ox → oxen

EXERCISE
12·1

Write the plural form of the following words.

1. house _____

2. wife _____

3. ox _____

4. fox _____

5. tooth _____

6. mouse _____

7. fez _____

8. person _____

9. candy _____

10. veto _____

11. deer _____

12. factory _____

13. leaf _____

14. university _____

15. jury _____

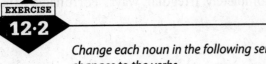
Change each noun in the following sentences to the plural. Make any necessary changes to the verbs.

1. The boy is chasing the little mouse.

   _____

2. His brother is putting the pot in the box.

   _____

3. Does the teacher know the man?

   _____

4. The hero of the story was a child.

   _____

5. My friend wants to buy the knife, spoon, and dish.

   _____

6. A goose is flying over the field.

   _____

7. The clumsy person hurt my foot.

   _____

8. The poor woman has a broken tooth.

   _____

9. We saw a wild ox in the zoo.

   _____

10. The ugly witch wanted the trained wolf.

   _____

Punctuation

The **period** is a commonly used signal that a sentence has ended. It is used after two types of sentences: (1) *the declarative sentence*, which is a statement about something, and (2) *the imperative sentence*, which is a request or command:

> **Statement**: I have five dollars in my pocket.
> **Command**: Give me the five dollars that you have in your pocket.

The period is also used after an abbreviation. Some abbreviations are titles: *Mr.*, *Mrs.*, *Ms.*, *Dr.*, *Rev.* Others are short versions of specific expressions: *A.M.*, *P.M.*, and so on. If you end a sentence with one of these abbreviations, *do not add a second period*. For example:

> Phillip arrived at exactly 8:00 P.M.

The **question mark** at the end of a sentence signals that the sentence is asking a question. You already know how to position verbs to form a question. Some examples:

Statement	Question
Carlotta is at home.	Is Carlotta at home?
You have a problem.	Do you have a problem?
They were in Rome.	Were they in Rome?

The **exclamation point** at the end of a sentence signals that the information in the sentence is stated strongly or with emotion. Some ordinary statements and exclamations look identical. But if the sentence ends in an exclamation point, it is expressed with emotion:

Ordinary Statement	Strong Statement
Jason is sick.	Jason is sick!
I saw a stranger there.	I saw a stranger there!
It has started to snow.	It has started to snow!
He didn't leave.	He didn't leave!

Place either a period, an exclamation point, or a question mark at the end of each sentence.

1. She took a book from the shelf and began to read _____

2. Do you like living in California _____

3. She asked me if I know her brother _____

4. Sit down and make yourself comfortable _____

5. Shut up _____

6. How many years were you in the army _____

7. I can't believe it's storming again _____

8. When did they arrive _____

9. Watch out _____

10. Her little brother is about eight years old _____

The **comma** is the signal in the middle of a sentence that ideas are being separated. This can be done to avoid confusing the ideas or to separate things in a list. For example, compare the sentence "When he came in the house was cold." to "When he came in, the house was cold." You do not mean that "he came in the house." There are two ideas here in two clauses. They are separated by a comma: (1) He came in. (2) The house was cold.

As an example of a list, consider the sentence "He bought pop, tarts, and candy." If you omit the comma after *pop*, someone might think that he bought *pop tarts*.

In a list, there should be a comma after every item until you use the word *and*: *a boy, a girl, two dogs,* and *a cat*. Some English writers prefer to omit the comma before *and*.

> I need paint, brushes, a yardstick, and some tape.

> **OR**

> I need paint, brushes, a yardstick and some tape.

Commas are also used to separate the name of a person to whom an imperative or a question is directed:

> Janelle, call Mr. Montoya on the telephone.
> Dr. Gillespie, will my husband be all right?
> Boys, try to be a little quieter.

They are also often needed to separate two or more adjectives that modify a noun:

> She wore a red, woolen jacket.
> The tall, muscular man was a weightlifter.

You should use a comma to separate two independent clauses combined as a compound sentence. They are most often combined with these conjunctions: *and, but, for, not, or, so,* and *yet*.

An independent clause is one that has a subject and predicate and makes sense when it stands alone. Some examples:

> DeWitt is baking a cake, and Allison is preparing the roast.
> Do you want to go to a movie, or should we just stay home?
> It began to rain hard, yet they continued on the hike.

You should separate exclamations and common expressions from the rest of the sentence with a comma:

> Oh, I can't believe you said that!
> No, I don't live in Germany anymore.
> Yes, you can go outside now.
> Well, you really look beautiful tonight.
> By the way, my mother is coming for a visit.

A comma is required to separate the day of the week from the date, and the day of the month from the year. The comma is omitted if only the month and year are given.

> He arrived here on Monday, June 1st.
> My birthday is January 8, 1989.
> The war ended in May 1945.

A **decimal point** looks like a period. In some languages, a decimal amount is separated by a comma: 6,25 or 95,75. But in American English, a decimal amount is separated by a period (a decimal point): 6.25 or 95.75.

In long numbers, amounts of thousands are separated by a comma in English. In other languages, they are often separated by a decimal point or by leaving a space:

English Numbers	Numbers in Other Languages
1,550,600	1.550.600 or 1 550 600
22,000,000	22.000.000 or 22 000 000

EXERCISE 13·2

Rewrite each sentence, and place commas where they are needed.

1. Ms. Muti please have a seat in my office.

   _____

2. She bought chicken ham bread and butter.

   _____

3. By the way your mother called about an hour ago.

   _____

4. Paul was born on May 2 1989 and Caroline was born on June 5 1989.

   _____

5. No you may not go to the movies with Rich!

   _____

6. Well that was an interesting discussion.

_____

7. The men sat on one side and the women sat on the other.

_____

8. Oh the dress hat and gloves look beautiful on you Jane.

_____

9. It happened on April 5 1999.

_____

10. Yes I have a suitcase and flight bag with me.

_____

The **colon** signals that a list of things or special related information follows. For example:

> You'll need certain tools for this project: a hammer, screwdriver, hacksaw, and chisel.
> I suddenly understood the plot of the story: A man steals a thousand dollars to help
>   his dying son.

It is also used to separate the hour from the minutes when telling time: 5:30, 6:25 A.M., 11:45 P.M.

The **semicolon** is a punctuation mark that is similar to both a comma and a period. It signals that there is a pause between ideas, and those ideas are closely linked. It often combines two related independent clauses into one sentence:

> Jamal is a powerful runner; he is determined to win the race today.
> Loud music filled the room; everyone was dancing as if entranced.

EXERCISE

13·3

In the blank, place either a colon or a semicolon.

1. There are some things you need for this recipe _____ sugar, salt, and flour.

2. She understood the meaning of the story _____ Thou shalt not kill.

3. Peter is an excellent swimmer _____ he coaches a team at our pool.

4. This document is important _____ it will prove his innocence.

5. Add these names to the list _____ Irena, Helen, Jaime, and Grace.

Quotation marks enclose the words that are said by someone. They indicate a direct quote. Look at the difference between a direct and indirect quote:

Direct Quote	Indirect Quote
He said, "Stay where you are."	He said that I should stay where I am.
She asked, "Is that Tran's brother?"	She asked if that is Tran's brother.

Remember that all punctuation marks that belong to the quoted sentence are enclosed *inside* the quotation marks:

Correct: He asked, "Does she often visit you?"
Incorrect: He asked, "Does she often visit you"?

The title of a short story or magazine article should be enclosed by quotation marks: *I just read "My Life on a Farm" by James Smith.* If a quote is located within a quote, it should be enclosed by *single* quotation marks: *He said, "I just read 'My Life on a Farm' by James Smith."*

EXERCISE
13·4

Rewrite each sentence, and add quotation marks where they are needed.

1. She asked, Why do you spend so much money?

_____

2. I learned that from Tips for Dining Out in a restaurant magazine.

_____

3. Rafael said, Elena's grandfather is very ill.

_____

4. This is going to be a big problem, he said sadly.

_____

5. Kurt will say, I already read The Ransom of Red Chief in school.

_____

You already know that the **apostrophe** is used in forming contractions:

I am → I'm
we are → we're

The apostrophe is also used to form possessives. To make the meaning of a singular noun possessive, add -'s. For plural nouns that end in an -s, just add the apostrophe. All other plurals will end in -'s.

Noun	Possessive Form	Meaning
boy	the boy's dog	the dog that belongs to the boy
boys	the boys' games	the games that belong to the boys
house	the house's roof	the roof of the house
Tom	Tom's aunt	an aunt of Tom's
book	a book's pages	the pages of a book
men	the men's work	the work that the men do

If a word ends in an -s, you can add -'s to form the possessive when the pronunciation of the word requires another syllable in the possessive:

Lois → Lois's
Thomas → Thomas's
actress → actress's

If another syllable is not pronounced to form the possessive, just add an apostrophe; this tends to be the case in the plural:

actresses → actresses'
railings → railings'
classes → classes'

It is common to use an apostrophe to form the plural of abbreviations: *two Dr.'s, three M.D.'s, four Ph.D.'s.* The same is true when forming the plural of a number or letter: "You had better mind your *p's* and *q's.*"

EXERCISE
13·5

Rewrite each sentence, and add apostrophes where they are needed.

1. The geeses eggs are well hidden.

   _____

2. She cant understand you.

   _____

3. Is Mr. Hancocks daughter still in college?

   _____

4. The two girls performance was very bad.

   _____

5. Ms. Yonans aunt still lives in Mexico.

   _____

6. She met several M.D.s at the party.

    _____

7. Do you know Mr. Richards?

    _____

8. The womens purses were all stolen.

    _____

9. He wont join the other Ph.D.s in their discussion.

    _____

10. It isnt right to take another mans possessions.

    _____

EXERCISE
13·6

In the blank, write in the missing form of punctuation.

1. Blake _____ will you please try to understand my problem?

2. They went to England _____ Wales, and Scotland.

3. Someone stole my money _____

4. She asked, _____ When is the train supposed to arrive?"

5. Mr. Wilson _____ s son wants to buy a house in Wisconsin.

6. I have the following documents _____ a will, a passport, and a visa.

7. Grandmother died September 11 _____ 1999.

8. Jack is a pilot _____ he flies around the world.

9. Well _____ I can't believe you came home on time.

10. Are you planning another vacation _____

To review, **punctuation** is used to make text easier to read and to convey clear and specific meaning. It is used to divide words into grammatical units, like clauses within sentences. Punctuation marks consist of a set of standardized symbols: periods, commas, semicolons, colons, question marks, exclamation points, apostrophes, quotation marks, hyphens and dashes, and parentheses and brackets. The proper use of these symbols is governed by grammatical and stylistic guidelines.

The period

A **period** is used to end a **declarative** sentence or **imperative** sentence. The period stands inside quotation marks.

> They are going to the mall.
> Hand me the book next to you, please.
> Finish your dinner so you can go to sleep.
> She said, "I'm not leaving my purse on the table unattended."

Periods are also often used with abbreviations and acronyms.

> Massachusetts Ave. begins in Dorchester.
> The U.S. and China are the countries most responsible for greenhouse gas emissions.

If a sentence ends with an abbreviation or acronym, no additional period is required.

> They will bring the dishes, serving pieces, flatware, etc.
> The train arrives at ten P.M.
> Their son recently received his B.S.

EXERCISE 13·7

Add periods where needed.

1. The city council requested that Gov Madison allocate more funds to the development of children's playgrounds

2. Richard told his parents, "I enjoy having dinner before eight o'clock, because it gives me enough time to finish my homework before going to sleep"

3. Meet them at Whole Foods for breakfast

4. Nathan said to his professor, "I can't be done with my paper by Monday"

5. I thanked Mrs Bronco for giving us a ride to school this morning

6. Sgt Pepper was called to the conference room for an important membership meeting

The comma

A **comma** is used to separate two independent clauses joined by any of the following coordinating conjunctions: *and, but, for, or,* and *nor.*

> The men remained in the kitchen, and the women went out to the garden.
> We were supposed to go boating, but the storm changed our plans.
> Should we stay home tonight, or should we go out to dinner?

A comma is used to separate a dependent clause from the main clause that follows.

> Even though the concert was great, we had to leave early.
> When I was through with the dishes, I sat down with a glass of wine.

If the dependent clause follows the main clause, the comma is often not used.

I sat down with a glass of wine when I was through with the dishes.

A comma is used to separate an introductory element from the main clause of a sentence.

Running as fast as he could, Chris finished second in the marathon.
Taken completely by surprise, the enemy was forced to surrender.

A comma is used after a wide range of introductory words, including *yes, no, oh,* and *well,* at the beginning of a sentence.

No, I can't tell you why she left so suddenly.
Well, they may stay in the guest room if they leave by tomorrow afternoon.

A comma is used to separate an apposite phrase from the rest of a sentence. An **apposition** is a word or phrase placed after another to provide additional information about it or to explain it.

Erin likes that dress, which she bought at a Macy's sale, because it fits so well.
We saw that blue car, the one that is parked right over there on the street, the last time
we ate here.
My game console, an Xbox, offers crystal clear graphics.

A comma is used to separate declarative elements from a clause that poses a question.

She is depending on those grades, isn't she?
That movie was beautiful, don't you think?

A comma is used to separate groups of numbers, the different elements of an address, and the date from the year. A comma ordinarily is not used to separate the name of a month from the year.

Their twentieth wedding anniversary was on March 10, 2000.
Barbara and I lived at 232 Lorraine Road, Austin, Texas for roughly ten years.
He left South Korea in May 1977.

A comma is used to separate interrupting elements from the rest of a sentence.

If Shawn writes more than 20 pages by the end of this weekend, and we doubt he will,
he will treat himself to a smoothie.
When John finishes his degree, which would be some kind of a miracle, he plans to start
his own business.
Karen won a prize in the lottery and, with any luck, will be able to pay off her debts.

A comma is used at the end of the greeting of a personal letter and at the end of the closing.

Dear Mr. Mustar,
Sincerely yours,

A comma is used to separate numbers composed of four or more digits (except for years).

The company made more than $8,000,000 in the last fiscal year.
We need 1,500 cubic yards of concrete for the parking lot.

A comma is sometimes used when the meaning of a sentence needs to be preserved and to avoid confusion.

> She asked me why I hadn't kissed her, and giggled. (to make clear that it is she who giggled)

A comma is used to separate direct quotations from the rest of a sentence.

> Mr. Wilson told me, "There is no gain without some loss."
> The president always said, "To protect our freedom, I must be conservative."

A comma is used to separate the person or persons being addressed from the rest of the sentence.

> Ladies and gentlemen of the jury, may I have your attention?
> Jack, turn down the volume on the TV.

A comma is used to separate items in a series.

> We bought apples, plums, and a bushel of tomatoes.
> They hope to visit France, Germany, and the Netherlands.

EXERCISE
13·8

For each sentence, explain the use of the comma(s).

1. Although we got there on time, we missed the train.

_____

2. She had lived at 6745 East Pinch Street, Austin, Texas since January 17, 1998.

_____

3. I went to the concert, but I had forgotten the tickets.

_____

4. The foundation gave $1,876,937 to the education council of Burundi.

_____

5. Albert did his homework, as promised, and should not be failed.

_____

6. Distinguished ladies and gentleman, it is with pride that I appear before you tonight.

_____

7. She was fascinated by his gentle, polite, elegant ways.

_____

Add commas where needed.

1. Taylor asked "How are we supposed to cook this with no oven?"

2. She packed two blouses a black skirt and a new business suit.

3. According to the U.S. Census Bureau the world population reached 6500000000 on February 25 2006.

4. Dear Mrs. Dimple

5. The Persian Gulf War officially ended on February 28 1991.

6. They were so excited by the soccer game which went into three overtimes that they hardly noticed the afternoon go by.

7. Marie Catherine and Chris are all going to the theater together.

8. IBM not Apple will build a fast computer.

9. If you've never been to the craft show there will be selected sales and bargain bins.

10. She will be participating won't she?

11. Yes I think there is enough time for you to pick it up and get back home before dinner.

12. If I could get a nickel for every time he lies I would be a billionaire.

13. He had intended to stay home but he decided instead to go running.

The semicolon

A **semicolon** is used to mark a break between independent clauses in the same sentence. It links clauses that are closely related.

> She has asked them to leave several times; they had a habit of overstaying their welcome.
> For the second time, he rescued a drowning child; his bravery is well known.

A semicolon is also used before conjunctive adverbs and transitional phrases that join independent clauses.

> They had been walking around the neighborhood for hours, looking for the lost dog; at the same time, they talked to neighbors they had never met before.
> The salesman let the man take the car for a drive; soon after, he had the eager buyer signing the purchase papers.

A semicolon is used to join independent clauses connected by a coordinating conjunction (*and, but, for, or, nor, so,* or *yet*) when at least one of the clauses contains a comma.

> It was time for the football team to take a break, drink some water, and stretch; but there were so many different exercises, and they had such a limited space, that they would need to be on break for too long to really stretch properly.

A semicolon is used to separate a series of elements from the rest of the sentence when at least one of the elements is long and contains commas. These elements can be phrases or clauses.

> In his analytical thesis on the Ninth Symphony, the author decided to include information about Beethoven's father, Johann, who was his first music teacher; Christian Gottlob Neefe, his most important teacher in Bonn; and Giulietta Guicciardi, his fiancée.

A semicolon is placed outside quotations marks.

> Sheryl told them, "You might be scared when you watch this movie"; still, I don't think it's scary enough to prevent you from watching it.

Semicolons are never used to join dependent to independent clauses.

EXERCISE
13·10

Add semicolons where needed.

1. The computers at my job have large monitors, loud speakers, CD burners, DVD players, and all sorts of other useful hardware are equipped with the most recent software and have the most sophisticated firewall.

2. Peter was amazed by the talent of the opposing team's poetry skills at the same time, he knew his team could win the poetry contest.

3. Greg was the first to run out of the burning house however, Elizabeth was the one who made it to a pay phone to call the fire department.

4. Each of us had enough time to get in the hotel's swimming pool nevertheless, we were all there on business.

5. There are moments when one needs to think about a situation calmly and for a long time likewise, there are moments when one needs to make decisions quickly and instinctively.

6. Gina said, "Let's work as a group" Peter said, "We should work individually instead" and Andrew said, "Let's split the team, and while some can work as a group, others can work individually."

7. Karen has been painting the kitchen for three hours all the while, she has been cooking and playing with the dogs.

The colon

A **colon** connects clauses that are closely linked in meaning or topic. Typically, the second clause continues or develops the thought of the first clause, or it contains an illustration or explanation of a topic in the first clause. If a complete sentence follows a colon, the first word of that sentence should be capitalized.

> Bill has 20 paintings on his wall: Ten of them he painted himself.
> The dictator was overthrown: The cruelty of his methods and the corruption of his government were finally exposed.
> Everything in his life seemed to be coming apart and collapsing: his marriage, his career, his confidence in himself.
> The economic sustainability of Bangladesh depends on three factors: the production of tea and rice, the export of garments, and foreign investment.

A colon is sometimes used to introduce dialogue or formal statements. In this case, the first word after the colon is capitalized.

> Julien could not help himself when the teacher asked him what was wrong: "There is no reason for all of us to be punished because Fred won't stop acting silly in class!"
> If she wants my opinion, this is what I shall tell her: "You need to raise your own kids when they're that little and stop leaving them in day care."

A colon is used after the greeting in formal or business letters.

> Dear Mrs. Jackson:
> Dear Governor:

A colon is used to separate hours and minutes in statements of time.

> 8:15 A.M.
> 11:37 P.M.

EXERCISE

13·11

Add colons where needed.

1. She told me what her favorite colors were blue, red, and light olive green.

2. Dear Madam President

3. It is 530 A.M.; why are you calling me so early?

4. There are three main ingredients in a cake sugar, flour, and eggs.

5. It was time for the lawyer to make his closing statement "My client is an honest man, a hardworking man, a good husband, and he should not be sitting in this court today."

6. Nixon said "Looting and pillaging have nothing to do with civil rights. Starting riots to protest unfair treatment by the state is not the best of solutions."

7. John has five trophies on his bookshelf Four of them are from basketball tournaments.

8. The professor made an interesting statement during class "We have not yet addressed the topic of social revolutions, which is a key component of our present argument."

The question mark

A **question mark** is used at the end of a sentence to signal a question; it can be a direct question, an interrogative series, or an expression of editorial doubt.

> When are you coming?
> Peter waved his hands while jumping up and down. What if they failed to see him?
> What do you think of his paintings? sculptures? drawings?
> Despite his participation in the 1934 riots (?), we do not know which organization
> he was marching with.

The exclamation point

An **exclamation point** or **mark** is used to signal an interjection, which is often associated with fear, surprise, shock, excitement, or disbelief. An exclamation point can also be used instead of a question mark to indicate that the overall emotion of a question is surprise, not interrogation.

> That's amazing!
> Great!
> He stops short, shoots, and scores!
> Did they really believe we were that stupid!

EXERCISE

13·12

Insert questions marks and exclamation points where needed.

1. Are you serious

2. Get out of here now

3. What do you think of the president's decision to go to war his views on foreign policy his thoughts on the economy

4. Quickly What are you waiting for

5. Are you in a hurry

6. When were you going to tell me

7. Super

8. That's so cool

9. Do you think the corporation will apologize for unjustly firing those employees taking away their retirement not providing them with a severance package

10. Are you out of your mind

The apostrophe

An **apostrophe** is used in one of two ways: to form a contraction (a shortened version of two words) or to express possession. Following are some common English contractions.

cannot → **can't**
do not → **don't**
it is → **it's**
what is → **what's**
who is → **who's**

In the same way that the apostrophe is used to replace letters that have been omitted, it can also be used to indicate that numbers have been omitted.

1990 → **'90**
2008 → **'08**

The following examples illustrate the use of the apostrophe to express possession.

Damien's car is really fast.
Rosie's roses are so pretty.
The roller skates are **Helen's**.
Have the **employees'** paychecks come in yet?

When an apostrophe is used to indicate joint ownership, only the last word has the apostrophe.

My grandmother and grandfather's paintings are in the attic.
Bill and Peter's car dealership is at the next intersection.

If joint ownership is not involved, each party has an apostrophe.

Tim and Barbara's pets (*All the pets belong to both Tim and Barbara.*)
Tim's and Barbara's pets (*Tim has his pets, and Barbara has hers.*)

It's is a contraction of *it is*, whereas *its* is a possessive pronoun.

It's the most complicated problem I've had to solve.
Its art collection was lost in the fire.

For each sentence, explain why the apostrophe is used (or not used).

1. Paul's and Janet's painting techniques are very different.

   _____

2. The cassettes were sent overseas by a company in Florida.

   _____

3. It's time the dog had its walk.

   _____

4. Wireless keyboards have been used since the 1990s.

_____

5. The Doors' second single was an instant hit.

_____

6. Peter and Margaret's car is navy blue.

_____

EXERCISE

13·14

*Insert apostrophes where needed. If no apostrophe is needed,
mark it with an "X.*

1. The sergeants boots were always the shiniest of all.

2. She really likes that about the 80s.

3. A doctors quick intervention can save a life.

4. There are times when the UNs presence has prevented armed conflict.

5. Whos winning today?

6. Our planes took off at the same time.

7. By the 1940s, jazz was already becoming an important musical movement.

8. Natalies new bicycle is red and yellow.

9. The Cutlips cat wandered into our garage this morning.

10. Her mothers and fathers wills were drafted by the lawyer.

Quotation marks

Quotation marks are used for the title of a short work, to indicate direct quotations, to indicate a part of a large work, and to emphasize certain, often ironic words. Quotation marks indicate the direct comments of a speaker or remarks taken from written material.

"The Raven" is the title of a poem written by Edgar Allan Poe. (TITLE OF A SHORT WORK)
Mark Twain first became known for his short story "The Celebrated Jumping Frog of Calaveras County." (TITLE OF A SHORT WORK)
She said, "There they go again," as the children raced back outside to play. (DIRECT QUOTATION)
In an article from last week's *Economist*, I read that "10% of the world's population controls 90% of the wealth." (DIRECT QUOTATION)
"When Business Mergers No Longer Work" was an article published in the *New Yorker*. (PART OF A LONGER WORK)
I agree, the theater play was so "entertaining" that I slept through most of it.
His latest painting is proof of "his creative skills" and worth every cent of the $20 he wants for it.

Single quotation marks are used to enclose a quotation within another quotation. The first quote is noted in the standard way, with double quotation marks, and the embedded quote is noted with single quotation marks.

> In his speech, Charles brought up an interesting point: "If Adam Smith wrote that 'the subjects of every state ought to contribute towards the support of the government, as nearly as possible, in proportion to their respective abilities,' then why are people clamoring for a flat tax?"

EXERCISE 13·15

Insert quotation marks where needed. If none are needed, mark it with an "X".

1. I met a woman who said she could make magic potions.

2. From what I hear, Joseph said the turning point in the novel is when Carlito tells his cousin, You should have never worked with Francisco in the first place; he's not to be trusted.

3. She read The Palm-Tree and was very moved by the poem.

4. What do you think of John Coltrane's tune My Favorite Things?

5. The morning newspaper mentioned that there might be snow tonight with a chance of hail and strong winds.

6. His father asked him, What would you like to do this summer, work or travel?

7. As Patrick walked away, she hesitated and then screamed, Will you go out with me?

8. The title of the book, How to Find Happiness Quickly, intrigued me.

9. We analyzed the play The Flies by Jean-Paul Sartre and his famous essay Americans and Their Myths.

10. The song Organ Donor is best qualified as groundbreaking.

11. The photographer encouraged the model by telling her, You're doing really well, but I want you to relax a little more. When the camera is pointed at you, just imagine someone is saying to you, You're the only one that can do this, and I want you to believe it!

The hyphen and the dash

A **hyphen** is used to divide or syllabify words at the end of a line when the word runs over to the beginning of the next line. It also connects individual words to form a compound word.

Hyphens cannot be used to divide one-syllable words: *thought, through, weight,* and so on. Hyphens can be used to divide words of two or more syllables.

> fun-damental
> funda-mental
> fundamen-tal

If a word already contains a hyphen, it is generally syllabified using that hyphen.

> a **mid-life** crisis
> a **cross-cultural** conference

A number of everyday words and expressions are hyphenated: U.S. Social Security numbers (*666-86-3454*), telephone numbers (*555-342-4536*), and certain compound nouns (*two-step*) and adjectives (*two-way*). Following are examples of hyphenated everyday words.

> hard-driving
> long-winded
> out-of-pocket
> pitch-dark
> six-cycle
> twice-told
> Yves Saint-Laurent

When dividing words at the end of a line, leave at least two letters at the end of the line and bring at least three letters down to the beginning of the next line.

A **dash** interrupts the flow of a sentence and sets a separate thought off from the rest of a sentence.

> If you find yourself in a dangerous situation, use the two Bs method—back off and breathe in—because otherwise you might panic.
> She was thinking of ways of running away—how could she have agreed to be part of this nonsense—but she was stuck.

**EXERCISE
13·16**

Insert hyphens and dashes where needed.

1. Eric could not figure out how to get out of the maze how silly and useless he felt!

2. The touchdown scored by the Patriots was an 83 yard play.

3. They were once considered wishy washy.

4. Carla was about to close the front door and thought to herself do I have everything I need in the bag?

5. The tight lipped receptionist told the reporters nothing.

6. She detests animal testing, so she never buys Yves Saint Laurent products.

7. Thirty two of the 52 figure skaters missed at least one of their jumps.

8. The Security Council voted against three crucial resolutions an armed attack, a forced embargo, and unified retaliation.

Parentheses and brackets

Parentheses enclose explanatory material, supplemental material, or any added information that could clarify the text it refers to. They are placed at the beginning and end of the enclosed text.

> The museum demolition that began in 1993 (and ended in 1996) was a sad reminder of how suddenly historical buildings can be taken away.

Parentheses can be used in text references.

> The death toll of Hurricane Katrina was staggering (see Table 5.7).

Parentheses can be used to set off a list of elements.

> The green screen on your left indicates (1) the wind speed, (2) the outside temperature, (3) the atmospheric pressure, and (4) the humidity ratio.

Brackets enclose editorial comments and corrections.

> These painting copies [reproduced from the original artworks that burned in the fire of 1954] are listed as some of the most expensive art of the exposition.
> The students prefer Milton over him [Shakespeare].
> The president said, "The illiteracy level of our children are [*sic*] appalling."

Brackets can also be used to replace a set of parentheses within a set of parentheses.

> During his trial, Fidel Castro stated, "None of you are entitled to condemn, you'll see, history will absolve me!" (See Fidel Castro's speech "History Will Absolve Me" [October 16, 1953].)

EXERCISE 13·17

Insert parentheses and brackets where needed.

1. *The Skibby Chronicle* published anonymously in the 1530s but now believed to be the work of Poul Helgesen describes Danish history from 1047 to 1534.

2. As members of the book club, we had to read *The Stranger* Albert Camus 1913–1960 and discuss the novelist's concept of the absurd.

3. According to historical accounts, the first bridge over the Chattahoochee River there Columbus, Georgia was built by John Goodwin in 1832–1833.

4. They were told there was a heavy load of work that they would have to deal with during the semester: They would have to 1 take two three-hour exams, 2 read 13 books, and 3 write a 50-page essay.

5. Thomas Hart Benton 1888–1975 finished his famous *Indiana Murals* in 1932.

6. Some scholars argue that Michelangelo noted Italian painter and sculptor 1475–1564 was the quintessential Renaissance man.

·14· Infinitives and gerunds

You have already discovered **infinitives** and how they are used as verbs. But infinitives can be used in other ways as well.

> They can be used as nouns: *To run would be cowardly.* (subject of the sentence)
> They can be used as adverbs: *We came here to thank you.* (why we came)
> They can be used as adjectives: *He is the man to trust.* (modifies *man*)

Gerunds look like present participles: a verb plus an *-ing* ending (*running, looking, buying,* etc.). But gerunds are different from present participles. Present participles are used to form an action in progress or incomplete: *I was running, she is speaking, they are helping.* And as a participle they can be used as adjectives. But a gerund is used as a noun. Look at these examples:

Present Participle	Gerund
She was baking cookies.	Baking takes a lot of time.
I am living alone.	I don't like living alone.
We have been relaxing at home.	Relaxing will help relieve the tension.
He was spelling the new words.	Spelling is my best subject.

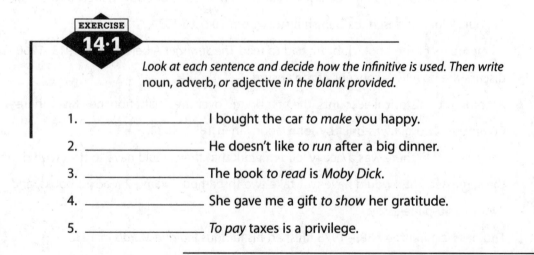

EXERCISE

14·1

Look at each sentence and decide how the infinitive is used. Then write noun, adverb, *or* adjective *in the blank provided.*

1. _____ I bought the car *to make* you happy.

2. _____ He doesn't like *to run* after a big dinner.

3. _____ The book *to read* is *Moby Dick*.

4. _____ She gave me a gift *to show* her gratitude.

5. _____ *To pay* taxes is a privilege.

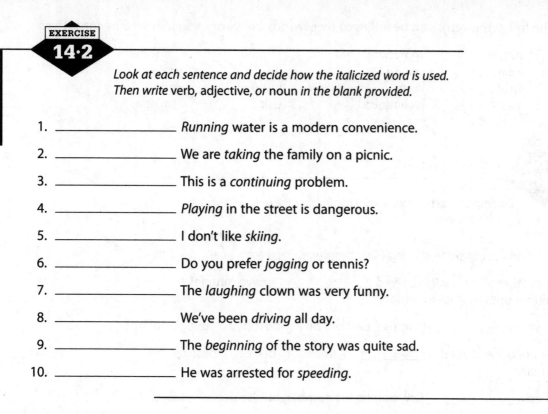

EXERCISE
14·2

Look at each sentence and decide how the italicized word is used.
Then write verb, adjective, *or* noun *in the blank provided.*

1. _____ *Running* water is a modern convenience.

2. _____ We are *taking* the family on a picnic.

3. _____ This is a *continuing* problem.

4. _____ *Playing* in the street is dangerous.

5. _____ I don't like *skiing*.

6. _____ Do you prefer *jogging* or tennis?

7. _____ The *laughing* clown was very funny.

8. _____ We've been *driving* all day.

9. _____ The *beginning* of the story was quite sad.

10. _____ He was arrested for *speeding*.

Gerund and infinitive complements

Gerunds and infinitives are verb forms, but they are not used as the main verbs in sentences. Gerunds are formed by adding *-ing* to the base form of a verb: *running, talking, doing.* (The *-ing* form is often called the *present participle.*) Infinitives consist of two parts: the infinitive marker *to* and the base form of a verb: *to run, to talk, to do.* Gerunds and infinitives can follow main verbs.

> She enjoys **playing** the guitar.
> He promised **to sing** for us.

Some verbs, such as *enjoy*, are followed by gerunds. Others, such as *promise*, are followed by infinitives. But some verbs can be followed by either gerunds or infinitives.

> I like **reading** mysteries.
> I like **to read** mysteries.

Generally, gerunds signal that an action has happened or is especially vivid. Infinitives indicate future or hypothetical events.

Using gerunds

Gerunds have four forms:

> SIMPLE: She avoids **driving** during rush hour.
> PERFECT: He admits **having taken** the documents.
> PASSIVE: They dislike always **being put** in the last row.
> PASSIVE PERFECT: I appreciate **having been given** this opportunity.

The following verbs can be followed by gerunds but cannot be followed by infinitives:

admit	appreciate	avoid	consider
delay	deny	dislike	enjoy
finish	keep	mind	miss
quit	recommend	risk	suggest

EXERCISE
14·3

Complete each sentence with the form of the gerund indicated in parentheses.

EXAMPLE: Albert considered *living* (live, simple) abroad for a year.

1. My brother and his wife delayed _____ (have, simple) children until they were settled.

2. I miss _____ (surprise, passive) on my birthday by my grandfather.

3. The politician denied _____ (mention, perfect) a possible tax increase.

4. I keep _____ (try, simple) his number, but he doesn't answer.

5. They didn't mind _____ (invite, passive perfect) at the last minute.

6. The doctor recommended _____ (eat, simple) more fruits and vegetables.

7. I appreciate _____ (choose, passive perfect) as your representative.

8. The committee finished _____ (review, simple) the applications yesterday.

9. We admitted _____ (be, perfect) the source of the trouble.

10. He dislikes _____ (treat, passive) as a child.

11. The tour guide suggested _____ (stop, simple) for lunch at this restaurant.

12. Fortunately, we avoided _____ (give, passive) a ticket.

13. For some reason, she quit _____ (play, simple) the piano a year ago.

14. When he made the repair, he risked _____ (damage, simple) the whole system.

15. We enjoyed _____ (introduce, passive) to your family.

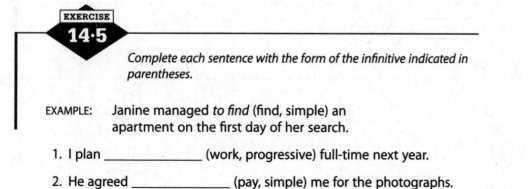

EXERCISE 14·4

Use gerunds to answer the following questions.

EXAMPLE: What sport do you like playing?
I like playing soccer.

1. What do you enjoying doing on holidays?

   _____

2. What have you avoided doing in the past year?

   _____

3. What do you dislike doing on the weekend?

   _____

4. What story did you like being told when you were a child?

   _____

5. Whom do you miss seeing whom you cannot see now?

   _____

Using infinitives

Infinitives have a number of forms. These are the most common:

SIMPLE: Eva wants **to become** a lawyer.
PROGRESSIVE: They seem **to be telling** the truth.
PERFECT: He hopes **to have finished** his work by next Friday.
PASSIVE: Anna deserves **to be promoted**.
PASSIVE PERFECT: We pretended **to have been surprised**.

The following verbs can be followed by infinitives but cannot be followed by gerunds:

agree	choose	decide	deserve
expect	fail	hope	intend
manage	need	offer	plan
pretend	promise	seem	want

EXERCISE 14·5

Complete each sentence with the form of the infinitive indicated in parentheses.

EXAMPLE: Janine managed *to find* (find, simple) an apartment on the first day of her search.

1. I plan _____ (work, progressive) full-time next year.

2. He agreed _____ (pay, simple) me for the photographs.

3. She hopes _____ (earn, perfect) a raise by the end of this year.

4. The child pretended _____ (faint, perfect).

5. Shoba deserves _____ (hire, passive) for the new position.

6. Everyone offered _____ (help, simple) us.

7. The announcement seems _____ (leak, passive perfect) to the press.

8. In order to get that job, he needs _____ (network, progressive).

9. The director expected _____ (receive, perfect) the report by now.

10. The reporter had wanted _____ (give, passive) a different assignment.

11. I promise _____ (meet, simple) you there at 5:00.

12. My parents decided _____ (stay, simple) an extra week.

13. He failed _____ (turn in, simple) the work on time.

14. Our neighbors intend _____ (move, simple) next year.

15. The company chose _____ (close, simple) one of the plants.

EXERCISE
14·6

Use infinitives to answer the following questions.

EXAMPLE: What did you expect to learn in this book?
             I expected to learn about English verbs.

1. Where do you plan to go this weekend?

   _____

2. Where do you intend to be next year at this time?

   _____

3. What do you need to buy this week?

   _____

4. What do you want to have for dinner?

   _____

5. What do you expect to study next term?

   _____

Verbs followed by a noun phrase and an infinitive

Some verbs are followed by both a noun phrase (a pronoun or a noun and any of its modifiers) and an infinitive:

advise	allow	cause	encourage
invite	order	permit	persuade
require	teach	tell	urge

EXERCISE

14·7

Complete each of the following sentences using the noun phrase provided and the simple form of the infinitive.

EXAMPLE: us, go
           The teacher encouraged *us to go* to the lecture.

1. him, exercise

   Dr. Olson advised _____ more frequently.

2. us, attend

   Carl invited _____ his piano recital.

3. my sister, ride

   My brother taught _____ a bike.

4. me, turn

   He told _____ left at the corner.

5. people, touch

   The museum guide permitted _____ some of the exhibits.

6. Brent and me, be

   The accident caused _____ more careful the next time.

7. local artists, hang

   Laura Adams allowed _____ their paintings in her restaurant.

8. the protesters, leave

   The police ordered _____.

9. me, rethink

   My parents persuaded _____ my plan.

10. employers, provide

    The new law required _____ safety training.

11. Robyn, major

   Mr. Pruett encouraged _____ in biology.

12. everyone, conserve

   The president urged _____ energy.

Gerunds or infinitives

Some verbs can be followed by either gerunds or infinitives. Sometimes there is no significant difference in meaning between a sentence with a gerund and a sentence with an infinitive.

   He began **humming**.
   He began **to hum**.

The most common verbs falling into this category are the following three verbs dealing with time:

   begin   continue   start

The verb *stop*, however, is used to express two different meanings.

   We stopped singing. [The singing has ended.]
   We stopped to sing. [The singing has not started yet.]

After verbs dealing with emotion, the gerund is generally used to express the vividness of an action, an event, or a state or to indicate its actual occurrence. The infinitive usually indicates a future, potential, or hypothetical action, event, or state.

   I usually prefer cooking my own food, but tonight I would prefer to go out.

The following verbs fall into this category:

   hate   like   love   prefer

Some verbs dealing with memory signal different time sequences, depending on whether a gerund or an infinitive is used.

   I remember **locking** the door. [The door was locked; then the action of locking was remembered.]
   I remembered **to lock** the door. [The remembering of a responsibility took place before the action of locking was performed.]

The following verbs fall into this category:

   remember   forget   regret

Underline the gerund or infinitive. Circle the reason that the gerund or the infinitive is used. If either a gerund or infinitive could be used, circle "No significant change in meaning."

1. It started to rain.

   Memory of action   **Vivid depiction**   **No significant change in meaning**

2. I remembered to bring a lunch.

   Memory to perform action   **Vivid depiction**   **No significant change in meaning**

3. He regretted quitting that job.

   Memory of action   **Memory to perform action**   **Vivid depiction**

4. They continued to talk during the entire movie.

   Actual occurrence   **Vivid depiction**   **No significant change in meaning**

5. My friends and I love going to the beach.

   Memory of action   **Vivid depiction**   **No significant change in meaning**

6. I would hate to clean up that mess.

   Actual occurrence   **Hypothetical occurrence**   **Vivid depiction**

7. Laxmi remembers returning the books to the library.

   Memory of action   **Memory to perform action**   **Vivid depiction**

8. My neighbors like throwing huge parties.

   Actual occurrence   **Vivid depiction**   **Potential occurrence**

9. The car began to make strange noises.

   Actual occurrence   **Vivid depiction**   **No significant change in meaning**

10. I prefer to take classes at night.

    Vivid depiction   **Potential occurrence**   **No significant change in meaning**

More on gerunds

Gerunds are verb forms that function as nouns. They are formed by adding the suffix *-ing* to the base form of the verb: *talking, running, building, developing,* and so on.

Gerunds can function as subjects or objects.

GERUND AS SUBJECT

Working has never been John's strong point.
Swimming is really great exercise.

GERUND AS OBJECT

I enjoy **working** at the plant, but I prefer **gardening**.
She always liked **knitting** and has made a good business out of it.

Complete each sentence with an appropriate gerund.

EXAMPLES   I don't care for ___*boating*___ .

I don't care for ___*dancing*___ .

1. My sister never liked _____ .

    My sister never liked _____ .

    My sister never liked _____ .

    My sister never liked _____ .

2. The boys were interested in _____ .

    The boys were interested in _____ .

    The boys were interested in _____ .

    The boys were interested in _____ .

Distinguishing gerunds from present participles

Although gerunds look like present participles, they function in a different way. Present participles are typically part of a progressive verb phrase and follow the auxiliary verb *be*. Gerunds are only used as nouns.

PRESENT PARTICIPLES

She **was cooking** and **cleaning** all day long. (PAST PROGRESSIVE)
Tom and Marie **have been jogging** for over an hour. (PRESENT PERFECT PROGRESSIVE)

GERUNDS

Jogging is always healthy. (SUBJECT)
Dad had to do the **cooking** and **cleaning** by himself. (DIRECT OBJECT)

Relative pronouns

Relative pronouns are used to link two sentences that have the same noun or pronoun in them. Relative pronouns form the beginning of a *relative clause*. In English there are five basic relative pronoun forms:

that = used when referring to either an animate or inanimate noun
who = used when referring to an animate noun
which = used when referring to an inanimate noun
whose = used as a possessive
elliptical relative pronoun = occurs when the relative pronoun is omitted

The noun in the introductory clause is called the *antecedent*. A relative pronoun replaces the noun in the second clause—the relative clause.

Let's look at how relative pronouns connect two sentences. If the same noun or pronoun is found in both sentences, the second one can be omitted and replaced by a relative pronoun. Then the two sentences are stated as one. Notice how the animate and inanimate nouns change to relative pronouns.

Two Sentences: He likes *the girl. The girl* comes from Alaska.
Relative Clause: He likes the girl **who** *comes from Alaska.* **OR**
He likes the girl **that** *comes from Alaska.*

Two Sentences: I bought *the car. The car* needs repairs.
Relative Clause: I bought the car **that** *needs repairs.* **OR**
I bought the car, **which** *needs repairs.*

Nouns can be used as subjects, direct objects, indirect objects, objects of prepositions, and possessives; so, too, can relative pronouns that replace them.

There are specific uses for *that*, *who*, and *which*; however, in casual speech the relative pronoun *that* can be substituted for *who* or *which* except when the relative pronoun shows possession. Look at these examples with inanimate nouns:

Use in a Sentence	Pairs of Sentences	Relative Clauses Formed
subject	I found the money. The *money* was lost.	I found the money that was lost. I found the money, which was lost.
direct object	I found the money. Bree lost the *money.*	I found the money that Bree lost. I found the money, which Bree lost.
indirect object	N/A	N/A
preposition	I found the money. They spoke *about the money.*	I found the money that they spoke about. I found the money about which they spoke.

possessive	I found the money. The color *of* the money is green.	I found the money, the color of which is green.

It is possible to substitute *whose* for a prepositional phrase starting with *of* with inanimate objects: *I found the money whose color is green.*

Now look at similar examples with animate nouns:

Use in a Sentence	Pairs of Sentences	Relative Clauses Formed
subject	I found the boy. The *boy* was lost.	I found the boy that was lost. I found the boy who was lost.
direct object	I found the boy. Kim met the *boy*.	I found the boy that Kim met. I found the boy whom Kim met.
indirect object	I found the boy. They gave the *boy* a gift.	I found the boy that they gave a gift to. I found the boy to whom they gave a gift.
preposition	I found the boy. They spoke *about the boy*.	I found the boy that they spoke about. I found the boy about whom they spoke.
possessive	I found the boy. The *boy's* father is a soldier.	I found the boy whose father is a soldier.

Careful! If *whom* or *which* is part of a prepositional phrase, the preposition can stand in front of *whom* or *which*, or it can stand at the end of the relative clause:

I like the man *for whom* I work.
I like the man *whom* I work for.

These are the books *about which* she spoke.
These are the books, *which* she spoke *about*.

When the relative pronoun is *that*, the preposition always stands at the end of the relative clause:

I like the man *that* I work *for*.
These are the books *that* she spoke *about*.

When an indirect object noun is changed to a relative pronoun, the preposition *to* or *for* should be added to give the meaning of the original sentence. Examples:

Do you know the man? I gave the man ten dollars.
Do you know the man *to whom* I gave ten dollars?

Andre saw the girl. I bought the girl some flowers.
Andre saw the girl *that* I bought some flowers *for*.

If the relative pronoun is used as a direct object or object of a preposition, it can be omitted. It is then called *elliptical*. If a preposition is involved, it must stand at the end of the relative clause.

Usage	Relative Pronoun Used	Elliptical Relative Pronoun
direct object	He's the man that I met in Canada.	He's the man I met in Canada.
preposition	Where's the car in which she was sitting?	Where's the car she was sitting in?

Note: You should be aware that in casual speech many English speakers regularly substitute *who* for *whom*.

There are two types of relative clauses: *restrictive clauses* and *nonrestrictive clauses*. Restrictive relative clauses contain information that is essential to the meaning of the sentence. If that information is omitted, the sentence cannot be understood as intended. The restrictive relative clause identifies the person or thing talked about in the other clause. Here are two examples:

The woman who stole the ring was soon arrested. (*who stole the ring* is essential information)
What's the make of the car that you bought? (*that you bought* is essential information)

Nonrestrictive relative clauses merely give additional information but do not define the person or thing talked about in the other clause. The relative pronoun *that* should not be used in nonrestrictive relative clauses. However, in casual speech there is often substitution between *that* and the relative pronouns *who* and *which*. Here are two examples of nonrestrictive clauses:

The mayor, who is out of town right now, will give a speech on Friday. (*who is out of town right now* is additional but nonessential information)
The play, which lasted over three hours, was given rave reviews. (*which lasted over three hours* is additional but nonessential information)

Commas are used to separate a nonrestrictive relative clause from the other clause in the sentence.

EXERCISE
15·1

Combine the following sentences by changing the second sentence to a relative clause. Use **that** *as the relative pronoun.*

1. I found the money. The money belonged to Jack.

   _____

2. She has a good memory. Her memory always serves her well.

   _____

3. This is the woman. I told you about the woman.

   _____

4. I have a document. The document proves my innocence.

   _____

5. They want to visit the country. Marsha comes from the country.

   _____

Follow the same directions, but use who, whom, *or* whose *as the relative pronoun.*

6. This is the doctor. The doctor saved my life.

   _____

7. Do you know the musician? I met the musician in Hawaii.

   _____

8. She likes the gentleman. I was telling her about the gentleman.

   _____

9. I visited the sisters. The sisters' father had recently died.

_____

10. Jerod noticed the stranger. All the neighbors were staring at the stranger.

_____

Follow the same directions, but use which *as the relative pronoun.*

11. Pablo threw away the picture. The boys had found the picture.

_____

12. I live in the house. My grandfather was born in the house.

_____

13. He bought a suit. The suit is navy blue.

_____

14. Anna has a new hat. I like the new hat very much.

_____

15. He wanted to paint the bench. A man was sitting on the bench.

_____

EXERCISE

15·2

Complete each sentence with any appropriate phrase.

1. This is the lady about whom _____.

2. We visited a country that _____.

3. I don't like the people whom _____.

4. Where's the basket in which _____?

5. Peter laughed at the story that _____.

6. My aunt met the writer whom _____ about.

7. Sammie spoke with the teacher whose _____.

8. I met the manager whom _____ for.

9. She hates the blouse that _____.

10. Tell me about the tourists whose _____.

Rewrite each sentence, changing the relative clause to its elliptical form. Omit the relative pronoun.

EXAMPLE: She's the girl whom I met there.

She's the girl I met there.

1. He was in the city that I visited last year.

_____

2. Did you finally meet the woman about whom I was telling you?

_____

3. Ron sold the house that he was born in.

_____

4. My father lost the checkbook that he kept his credit card in.

_____

5. Did you find the ball that I threw over the fence?

_____

6. That's the pretty girl for whom I wrote this poem.

_____

7. I don't know the people whom he gave the flowers to.

_____

8. The hat from which the magician pulled a white rabbit was empty.

_____

9. She forgot the tickets that she had placed next to her briefcase.

_____

10. They live in a tiny village, which we finally located on a map.

_____

Using relative pronouns

To review, two sentences can be combined by using a relative pronoun. If the same noun appears in two sentences, one of the nouns can be changed to a relative pronoun and the two sentences can be stated as one, the one with the relative pronoun being called a *relative clause*.

He likes the car. His father bought the car. = He likes the car ***that* his father bought**.

The English relative pronouns are:
who, whom, whose → used to replace animate nouns
which → used to replace inanimate nouns
that → used to replace animate or inanimate nouns

In casual speech *whom* is almost always replaced by *who*.

There is also an *elliptical* relative pronoun form, which omits the use of a relative pronoun entirely.

> RELATIVE PRONOUN *THAT*: He likes the car **that** his father bought.
> ELLIPTICAL FORM: He likes the car his father bought.

Although there are some traditional rules for choosing between *that* and the forms of *who* and *which*, in casual speech they are often used interchangeably:

> This is the man **that** I told you about.
> This is the man **who** I told you about.

The general rule for more formal usage requires using *that* if the relative clause is *restrictive*. A restrictive relative clause is one that defines or identifies the antecedent (the word to which the relative pronoun refers). Look at this example:

> The house **that his grandfather built many years ago** burned down last night.

The relative clause (in bold type) identifies *which house* burned down last night. The sentence would not have the same meaning if the relative clause were omitted. The meaning of *house* is restricted by the information provided in the relative clause.

The relative pronouns *who* and *which* tend to be used in relative clauses that provide nonessential information. Nonrestrictive clauses are set off by commas. The meaning of the original sentence is not affected by such relative clauses:

> Our mayor, **who has been in office for two years**, is traveling to Canada.
> Some articles, **which appeared in newspapers across the country**, ridiculed the mayor.

In these nonrestrictive relative clauses, the *mayor* and the *articles* are not identified by the relative clauses. They do not answer the questions, *Which mayor? Which articles?* The sentences make complete sense when the relative clauses are omitted:

> Our mayor is traveling to Canada.
> Some articles ridiculed the mayor.

When changing a noun to a relative pronoun, the function of the noun must remain the function of the relative pronoun: subject, direct object, indirect object, object of a preposition, or possessive. Here are some examples that use the sentence, *The boxer was the champ*:

> Subject: The boxer won the bout. → The boxer **that** won the bout was the champ.
> Direct object: He knocked out the boxer. → The boxer **that** he knocked out was the champ.
> Object of preposition: I spoke with the boxer. → The boxer **that** I spoke **with** was the champ.
> Possession: The boxer's training was best. → The boxer **whose** training was best was the champ.

If a noun is used as an indirect object, the relative pronoun becomes the object of the preposition *to* or *for* in the relative clause:

> Indirect object: I gave the boxer some good advice. → The boxer **that** I gave some good advice **to** was the champ.

When the relative pronoun is *that* and is the object of a preposition, the preposition must stand at the end of the clause:

> We found the scientist **that** Professor Jones had written **about**.

If the relative pronoun is *who(m)* or *which*, the preposition will stand before the relative pronoun in formal style but at the end of the clause in more casual style. Notice again that non-restrictive relative clauses are separated by commas:

Formal: It was a terrible event, **about which** much had been written.
Casual: It was a terrible event, **which** much had been written **about**.

Formal: The criminal, **from whom** they received several threats, was finally located.
Casual: The criminal, **who** they received several threats **from**, was finally located.

Use *whose* for the possessive of an animate. Use *of which* or *whose* for the possessive of an inanimate:

They visited their grandfather, **whose** farm is located in Maryland.
She bought a dreadful hat, the color **of which** was green.
She bought a dreadful hat, **whose** color was green.

The elliptical form of a relative clause occurs when the relative pronoun is a direct object or the object of a preposition. Look at these examples:

Direct object: They spoke with the thief **that** the police arrested yesterday.
Elliptical form: They spoke with the thief the police arrested yesterday.

Object of preposition: I found the document that you inquired **about**.
Elliptical form: I found the document you inquired **about**.

In the elliptical form of a relative pronoun used as the object of a preposition, the preposition is always at the end of the clause.

EXERCISE

15·4

Combine the pairs of sentences below with the relative pronoun that *or* whose. *Make any necessary changes.*

1. He found a puppy. The puppy needed a home.

   _____

2. Where did you put the groceries? I bought the groceries at the supermarket.

   _____

3. That's my car. My car has the convertible top.

   _____

4. There's the scientist. I told you about the scientist.

   _____

5. Do you know the woman? The woman's son is serving in the army.

   _____

6. They hired the lawyer. They got the best deal from the lawyer.

   _____

7. I need the map. The map has Cook County on it.

_____

8. I was introduced to the girl. John was dancing with the girl.

_____

9. Don't spend the money. I put the money on the dresser.

_____

10. Do you know the song? I'm playing the song on the piano.

_____

Rewrite the sentences that can be changed to the elliptical form. Be careful. Not all can be changed.

1. I lost the book that I got from Maria last week.

_____

2. We like the dress, which was probably designed in Paris.

_____

3. He read a sentence, which he can't understand at all.

_____

4. I have all the documents that I was speaking of.

_____

5. Will you give me some money, which I can use to buy new underwear?

_____

6. The champion, who is a native of Mexico, is touring the United States.

_____

7. He bought a used car that had been in an accident.

_____

8. Maria wants to use the umbrella that Mom bought last week.

_____

9. Do you understand the words that I wrote on this sheet of paper?

_____

10. I like Uncle Henry, from whom I received a beautiful gift.

_____

Complete each sentence with any appropriate relative clause.

1. Please show me the books _____ .

2. I met the actor _____ .

3. He bought a watch that _____ .

4. The boss, who _____ , is rather nice.

5. Where are the gifts _____ ?

6. This car, which _____ , is from Germany.

7. I have the DVD _____ .

Reflexive pronouns

Reflexive pronouns reflect back to the subject of a sentence. The English reflexive pronouns are: *myself, yourself, himself, herself, itself, ourselves, yourselves,* and *themselves*. Each one can only be used with its personal pronoun counterpart when that personal pronoun is the subject of the sentence:

Personal Pronoun	Reflexive Pronoun	A Sample Sentence
I	myself	I hurt myself again.
you	yourself	You can do it yourself.
he	himself	He enjoyed himself.
she	herself	She helped herself to some candy.
it	itself	It destroyed itself in a few seconds.
we	ourselves	We found ourselves in a strange city.
you	yourselves	You must clean yourselves up before dinner.
they	themselves	They accidentally burned themselves.

If the reflexive pronoun and the personal pronoun are not counterparts, then personal pronouns should be used in the sentence. Look at these examples:

Counterparts	Not Counterparts
I hurt myself again.	I hurt him again. I hurt them again.
He enjoyed himself.	He enjoyed it. He enjoyed them.
They harmed themselves.	They harmed me. They harmed her.

Remember that third-person singular and plural nouns will use the appropriate third-person singular and plural reflexive pronouns:

Marta bought herself a new car.
The boy cut himself.
The alien creature wounded itself with its own claws.
The men helped themselves to some beer.

EXERCISE

16·1

Rewrite each sentence appropriately with the subject personal pronouns given. Change to the appropriate reflexive pronoun.

1. I found myself in a difficult situation.

You (sing.) _____.

He _____.

She _____.

We _____.

They _____.

Amy _____.

2. We enjoyed ourselves at the party.

I _____.

You (pl.) _____.

He _____.

She _____.

They _____.

The boys _____.

3. He is going to be very proud of himself.

I _____.

My friends _____.

Mother _____.

They _____.

We _____.

Abdul and Ricky _____.

4. I just couldn't help myself.

You (pl.) _____.

He _____.

She _____.

We _____.

They _____.

The men _____.

EXERCISE

16·2

Replace the object personal pronoun in each sentence with the appropriate reflexive pronoun.

1. Jerry liked me in the new suit.

_____

2. They busied her with several different tasks.

_____

3. We were very proud of them.

_____

4. She is buying us a few new outfits.

_____

5. The children hurt me.

_____

6. I have to ask him what to do now.

_____

7. The young woman told you not to give in.

_____

8. He wants to find me something nice to wear.

_____

9. You've harmed no one but us.

_____

10. The lizard hid them under a rock.

_____

Using reflexive pronouns

To review, the personal pronouns have a form that is used when that form is in the objective case and is the *counterpart* of its personal pronoun. That form is called a *reflexive pronoun*. The reflexive pronouns look like this:

Subject Pronoun	Object Pronoun	Reflexive Pronoun
I	me	myself
you (singular)	you	yourself
he	him	himself
she	her	herself
it	it	itself
we	us	ourselves
you (plural)	you	yourselves
they	them	themselves
one	one	oneself

If the subject pronoun and the object pronoun refer to the same person, you should use the reflexive pronoun counterpart in the sentence. If the object pronoun refers to someone or something else, use its object pronoun form:

I suddenly saw **myself** in the mirror. (counterpart of *I*)
I suddenly saw **him** in the mirror. (different person)

We sometimes have to help **ourselves**. (counterpart of *we*)
We sometimes have to help **them**. (different persons)

Notice the difference between these pairs of sentences and the use of *him* and *himself*:

USING NOUNS: **Jim** accidentally hurt **Jim**.
USING PRONOUNS: **Jim** accidentally hurt **himself**.

USING NOUNS: **Jim** accidentally hurt **Michael**.
USING PRONOUNS: **Jim** accidentally hurt **him**.

EXERCISE
16·3

Rewrite each sentence, changing the italicized word or phrase to the appropriate reflexive pronoun.

1. She sometimes writes stories about *her friends*.

   _____

2. We really enjoyed *the party* very much.

   _____

3. My uncle cut *his little finger* with a sharp knife.

   _____

4. The ugly dragon hid *the bones* behind a pile of stones.

   _____

5. I described *the boys* honestly.

   _____

6. Would you recommend *this woman* for the job?

   _____

7. The girls saw *their reflection* in the still water of the pond.

   _____

8. He didn't recognize *the gentleman* in his new suit of clothes.

   _____

9. A young woman was admiring *the dress* in the store window.

   _____

10. Maria and Juan! You've hurt *him* again! Shame on you!

   _____

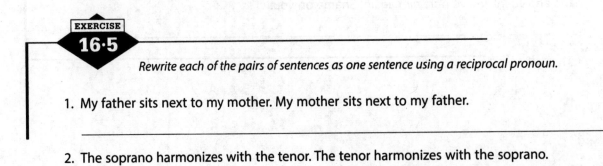

EXERCISE
16·4

Rewrite the following sentences with each of the pronouns given in parentheses. Use the appropriate reflexive pronouns.

1. John believes himself to be innocent.

a. (we) _____

b. (I) _____

c. (she) _____

d. (you plural) _____

2. She considers herself lucky.

a. (they) _____

b. (I) _____

c. (you singular) _____

d. (he) _____

Reciprocal pronouns

There are only two reciprocal pronouns: *each other* and *one another*. They are never used as the subject of a sentence, and they always refer to a plural antecedent. Their use is similar to how a reflexive pronoun is used, but they refer back to two or more persons or things in a plural antecedent. Look at these examples:

Maria helps Tom. Tom helps Maria. → Maria and Tom help **one another**.
or Maria and Tom help **each other**.
He loves her. She loves him. → They love **one another**.
or They love **each other**.
Two boys spoke with five girls. → They spoke with **one another**.
or They spoke with **each other**.
You saw my lesson. I saw your lesson. → You and I saw **one another's** lesson.
or You and I saw **each other's** lesson.

Notice how a possessive pronoun is changed to a possessive formed with an *apostrophe -s*: *my* lesson, *your* lesson = *one another's* lesson.

EXERCISE
16·5

Rewrite each of the pairs of sentences as one sentence using a reciprocal pronoun.

1. My father sits next to my mother. My mother sits next to my father.

_____

2. The soprano harmonizes with the tenor. The tenor harmonizes with the soprano.

_____

3. The boys danced with the girls. The girls danced with the boys.

_____

4. My boss spoke about the manager. The manager spoke about my boss.

_____

5. St. Paul is located near Minneapolis. Minneapolis is located near St. Paul.

_____

6. Barbara kissed Juan. Juan kissed Barbara.

_____

7. The lioness slept near the three cubs. The three cubs slept near the lioness.

_____

8. You respect me. I respect you.

_____

9. James sang for Maria. Maria sang for James.

_____

10. He likes her voice. She likes his voice.

_____

EXERCISE

16·6

Write three original sentences using the reciprocal pronouns in parentheses.

1. (one another)

a. _____

b. _____

c. _____

2. (each other)

a. _____

b. _____

c. _____

Possession

Nouns form **the possessive** in two ways: (1) they become the object of the preposition *of*, or (2) they add the ending *-'s* (apostrophe plus *-s*). Look at these examples:

the roar of a lion	a lion's roar
the color of the book	the book's color
the children of Mrs. Diaz	Mrs. Diaz's children
the prey of the wolves	the wolves' prey

(See Unit 12 regarding punctuation to review the rules for using the apostrophe.)
The possessive is used to show to whom or to what something belongs:

This is *Ginny's* car.
The kittens *of an alley cat* have a hard life.

EXERCISE
17·1

Change the italicized possessive phrase to a possessive ending in -'s.

EXAMPLE: The color of the car is red.
The car's color is red.

1. The center *of the storm* was just north of the city.

_____

2. The condition *of the victims* was very serious.

_____

3. I don't understand the behavior of *my classmates*.

_____

4. The equipment *of the lab* was outdated.

_____

5. The efforts *of each man* helped to make the project a success.

_____

6. The many illnesses *of the animals* were evidence of the filthy conditions.

   _____

7. The documents *of the young lawyer* were very impressive.

   _____

8. The room was filled with the scent *of the roses*.

   _____

9. A hunter captured the mother *of the little bear* cub.

   _____

10. We drove to the northern border *of the town*.

    _____

Possessive pronouns

Possessive pronouns are sometimes called *possessive adjectives*. No matter what you call them, their use is clear and simple. Just like reflexive pronouns, possessive pronouns have personal pronoun counterparts. Look at this table of pronouns to see the relationship:

Subject	Object	Possessive 1	Possessive 2
I	me	my	mine
you	you	your	yours
he	him	his	his
she	her	her	hers
it	it	its	its
we	us	our	ours
they	them	their	theirs

There is a difference in the use of the possessive pronouns 1 and 2. The possessive pronoun 1 always stands before a noun and modifies it. The possessive pronoun 2 replaces a possessive pronoun 1 and a noun, when the noun is understood. Look at these examples:

My gift is unusual.
Is this *your* brother?
Our friends live here.
His aunt is a doctor.
Her dress is very nice.

Which gift is *mine*? (my gift)
The seat on the right will be *yours*. (your seat)
These two dogs are *ours*. (our dogs)
His is a doctor. (his aunt)
Hers is very nice. (her dress)

Possessive pronouns tell to whom or to what something belongs.

Change the possessive pronoun 1 to a possessive pronoun 2 and omit the noun.

EXAMPLE: She has my book.
She has mine.

1. The car on the corner is my car.

   _____

2. Was this your house?

   _____

3. The invading soldiers searched their house.

   _____

4. Did Dee find her briefcase?

   _____

5. Our relatives have lived in Brazil for a long time.

   _____

6. His boss is fair with everyone.

   _____

7. These problems are entirely his problems.

   _____

8. I need your advice.

   _____

9. My landlord is going to raise the rent.

   _____

10. Their long conversations made no sense.

    _____

Change the italicized word or phrase to the possessive pronoun counterpart of the subject of the sentence.

EXAMPLE: He likes *the* new car.
He likes his new car.

1. The women want to visit *some* relatives in Europe.

   _____

2. She takes *the* children for a long walk.

_____

3. Do you have *the* tools in the truck?

_____

4. I sent *the* address and telephone number to the office.

_____

5. We want *this one*.

_____

6. The picture fell out of *the* frame.

_____

7. They spend *a lot of* time in Canada.

_____

8. Are you selling *these*?

_____

9. I left some papers in *the* apartment.

_____

10. Jose found *the* wallet under the bed.

_____

EXERCISE
17·4

Circle the boldface word that best completes each sentence.

1. Did you leave **yours/mine/your** keys on the desk?

2. Her brother met **his/her/their** wife in Paris.

3. This book is **our/his/her**, and that one belongs to Smita.

4. Where did they buy **theirs/blouse/its**?

5. I believe I forgot **mine/her/my** again.

6. My sister gave **mine/her/its** watch to me.

7. I saw your tickets, but where are **her/my/ours**?

8. **Hers/Theirs/His** uncle is coming to America to live.

9. The fox hurt **its/hers/front** foot in a trap.

10. May I have **hers/my/mine** dinner now?

Possessive pronouns

Just as nouns can be formed to show ownership or possession, so too can pronouns. Most nouns add an apostrophe plus an *-s* to show possession: *John's car, the woman's dress, a winter's night.* But pronouns form a completely new word. The following chart shows each subject pronoun and its possessive form.

Subject Pronoun	Possessive Pronoun 1	Possessive Pronoun 2
I	my	mine
you (singular)	your	yours
he, she, it	his, her, its	his, her, its
we	our	ours
you (plural)	your	yours
they	their	theirs
who	whose	whose

A possessive pronoun 1 is used to modify a noun. It is always used in a combination of the possessive pronoun and a noun or noun phrase. It shows to whom something belongs:

> I have books. = my books
> You have a car. = your car
> We have money. = our money
> Who has a funny hat? = whose funny hat

The third person possessive pronouns are used to replace possessive nouns:

> the young man's wallet = his wallet
> our daughter's party = her party
> the roach's nest = its nest
> my friends' new house = their new house

There is a difference in the use of the possessive pronoun 1 and 2. The possessive pronoun 2 *replaces a possessive pronoun 1 and a noun* when the noun is understood.

> This is **my glove**. = This is **mine**.
> Where is **your car**? = Where is **yours**?
> That was **his dinner**. = That was **his**.
> **Her dog** is smarter. = **Hers** is smarter.
> Did you meet **our friends**? = Did you meet **ours**?
> **Their son** is a sailor. = **Theirs** is a sailor.

EXERCISE 17·5

Rewrite each sentence, changing the possessive noun phrase to a possessive pronoun.

1. The pretty girl's brother goes to college.

   _____

2. Do you know Mr. Brown's niece?

   _____

3. The snake's hole was behind a large rock.

   _____

4. The birds' chirping woke me up early.

_____

5. She loved the ballerina's solo.

_____

6. I had to hold my mother's purse.

_____

7. The old sow's piglets slept in a cool pile of mud.

_____

8. Did you borrow your sister's skis?

_____

9. The strikers' demands were too much for the company.

_____

10. Where is the little puppies' bed going to be?

_____

EXERCISE
17·6

Fill in the blank with the possessive pronoun formed from the one in parentheses.

1. I wanted to dance with _____ (she) older sister.

2. Will you help me carry _____ (I) books up to the second floor?

3. They said _____ (you) father had been a colonel in the army.

4. _____ (We) tent was put up near a bend in the river.

5. Michael wanted to spend time at _____ (Maria and I) campsite.

6. I still haven't met _____ (they) parents.

7. _____ (Who) sailboat is that out on the lake?

8. I just can't get interested in _____ (he) novels.

9. _____ (It) roof has been replaced with cedar shingles.

10. Ms. Garcia wanted to borrow _____ (you and I) garden hose.

Prepositions

A **preposition** connects a certain word in a sentence to a noun or pronoun. But the meaning of prepositional phrases (preposition followed by a noun or pronoun) is varied. They tell where, when, why, how, or whose. Look at these examples:

where = in the garden
when = until Monday
why = because of the bad weather
how = by train
whose = of the bride

Here is a list of some commonly used prepositions.

about	behind	for	since
above	below	from	through
across	beside	in	to
after	between	of	under
along	by	off	until
around	despite	on	up
at	down	out	with
before	during	over	without

Compound prepositions consist of more than one word: *along with, because of, due to, in spite of, on account of, next to, on top of, together with,* and so on.

When a noun is used in a prepositional phrase, it does not change. But most pronouns do:

I → with me
you → to you
he → by him
she → without her
it → on it

we → from us
they → for them
the boys → to the boys
a girl → after a girl
my keys → over my keys

EXERCISE
18·1

Change the noun phrase in the prepositional phrase to the appropriate pronoun. Keep the same number and gender.

1. The man next to Jordan is a senator.

_____

2. Did they leave after the play?

_____

3. Evan was dancing with his aunt.

_____

4. Why did you leave the house without your wallet?

_____

5. Are there washers and dryers in the apartments?

_____

6. Juan had some nice wine for his guests.

_____

7. The man with Yvette is her new boyfriend.

_____

8. A large bear was coming toward the man.

_____

9. The letter from my parents made me very happy.

_____

10. In spite of all her problems, Tonya went on smiling.

_____

Note: Sometimes a prepositional phrase connected to the subject of a sentence can cause confusion. This is especially true when one of those elements is singular and the other is plural. Always remember that the subject—not the prepositional phrase—determines the form of the verb.

Singular Subject + Plural Object of the Preposition
The box of fresh cookies *was* torn open by their dog.
Each of you *has* a duty to help them.
One of the youngest candidates *needs* a lot more money.

Plural Subject + Singular Object of the Preposition
The musicians in the little band *were* given a new contract.
Several girls from our school *have* been awarded scholarships.

EXERCISE
18·2

Circle the boldface word that best completes each sentence.

1. One of the boys **are/is/were** a friend of mine.

2. The **woman/person/women** from our church are having a bake sale.

3. Each of the people at these meetings **want/have to/needs** to know the truth.

4. The box of chocolates **was/are/were** a gift from Thomas.

5. The students in this class **need/wants/has** more time to prepare.

6. Every one of you on the team **want/has/have** the chance to be a champion.

7. The magician, together with his assistants, **makes/are making/make** the rabbits disappear.

8. All of you in the third row **needs/need/was needed** to stand up.

9. Many tourists on this flight **doesn't/don't/does** have the proper visa.

10. A young teacher, along with several of her pupils, **find/are locating/captures** the robber.

Using prepositions

Prepositional phrases are formed using a preposition and its object (a noun or a pronoun). Prepositional phrases describe the relationship between the object of the preposition and another element of a sentence. In general, prepositional phrases describe relationships of place, time, and ownership.

> The dog is hiding **under the car**.
> They only rented that apartment **for a month**.
> The back door **of my house** is painted blue.

Following is a list of commonly used prepositions.

about	before	despite	of	to
above	behind	down	off	toward
across	below	during	on	under
after	beneath	for	out	until
against	beside	from	over	up
along	besides	in	since	with
among	between	into	through	within
around	beyond	like	throughout	without
at	by	near	till	

Compound prepositions

A **compound preposition** functions as a single preposition, but is composed of more than one word. Just like other prepositions, a compound preposition is followed by a noun or pronoun object.

Following is a list of common compound prepositions.

ahead of	in addition to	in regard to
as far as	in back of	in spite of
because of	in case of	instead of
by means of	in lieu of	next to
contrary to	in light of	out of

They solved the problem **by means of** a special algorithm.
In case of fire, do not use the elevators.
In spite of his hard work, the promotion went to Jane Anderson.
He ran **out of** the haunted house.

Whether simple or compound, prepositions function the same in sentences.

The preposition *between* expresses a choice involving two people or things, while the preposition *among* expresses a choice involving more than two people or things.

> She had to choose **between** going out or watching a movie at home.
> There is an enormous difference **between** love and hate.
> Just **between** you and me, I'd really like to go out with Juan's sister.

> The mood **among** the guests was quite festive.
> I have always counted you **among** my friends.
> **Among** the men in his squadron was a lad of only 19.

EXERCISE

18·3

In each sentence, underline the preposition(s), including compound prepositions, and their noun objects.

1. He would prefer a hybrid car instead of the truck.

2. If they are still swimming in the pool, then they will be late for dinner.

3. The clouds floated high above the hills.

4. Tell me about the book you read.

5. George ran into the room and quickly took a seat next to Helen.

6. Is she the one you spoke of?

7. I recently got a letter from him while he was away in Iraq.

8. Contrary to public opinion, the election is not a foregone conclusion.

9. Sitting among the students was a professor from the philosophy department.

10. Are you satisfied with this table? I can get you another by the window.

EXERCISE

18·4

Complete each sentence with an appropriate object for each preposition.

EXAMPLE   They had an argument with ___*their new neighbor*___ .

1. She spent a lot of time alone in _____.

2. They had to borrow some furniture from _____.

3. I must choose between _____.

4. We cannot leave before _____, but we'll arrive there around

    _____.

5. Does she know the way to _____?

6. In spite of _____, they set out on the mountain hike.

7. In light of _____, I feel you should retake the course.

8. Among _____, he saw many old friends.

9. I've always been interested in _____.

10. Because of _____, the game had to be canceled.

Noun and pronoun objects

The object of a prepositional phrase can be either a noun or a pronoun. In most cases, when a noun is replaced by a pronoun, the pronoun must be of the same number and gender as the noun.

Ms. Harper spoke **of her son** quite often.
Ms. Harper spoke **of him** quite often.

He sat **on the old mare** and looked out over the valley.
He sat **on her** and looked out over the valley.

In spite of the impending storm, they set off for the park.
In spite of it, they set off for the park.

She never received the gift **from Tom and me**.
She never received the gift **from us**.

He danced **with the same two girls** all evening.
He danced **with them** all evening.

However, if a prepositional phrase introduced by *in* indicates a location, a pronoun object sometimes cannot replace a noun object. Instead, it is more common to use an adverb, such as *here* or *there*. This is particularly true of cities and large regions.

She loved living **in Washington, D.C.**
She loved living **there**.

We haven't been **in this town** for very long.
We haven't been **here** for very long.

Compare the examples above with those below.

The woman sat comfortably **in a comfy chair**.
The woman sat comfortably **in it**.

Richard found 50 dollars **in the little box**.
Richard found 50 dollars **in it**.

Something similar occurs with the preposition *of* when it shows possession and, on occasion, with the preposition *by*. Although pronoun objects are quite acceptable following *of* and *by*, there is a tendency to use a possessive pronoun in place of the prepositional phrase.

The color **of the blouse** is bright red.
Its color is bright red.

The roar **of the huge lion** gave me chills.
Its roar gave me chills.

The quality **of his poems and short stories** was highly regarded.
Their quality was highly regarded.

The lecture **by Professor Helms** had an impact on us all.
His lecture had an impact on us all.

The raid on the house **by the police** was carried out in secret.

Their raid on the house was carried out in secret.

Although each of these sentences could have contained a prepositional phrase with a pronoun object, the tendency is to use a possessive pronoun instead of a prepositional phrase.

POSSIBLE   The raid on the house by them was unwarranted.

MORE LIKELY   Their raid on the house was unwarranted.

EXERCISE
18·5

Rewrite each sentence, changing the prepositional phrase to one with a pronoun object or to an appropriate adverb.

EXAMPLE   No students were allowed in the professors' lounge.

No students were allowed there.

1. We spent a lot of time in Brooklyn.

_____

2. They have been in Mexico for over three years.

_____

3. In the drawer, I found my sister's diary.

_____

4. City Hall has been located in this part of town for years.

_____

5. What are you hiding in those little sacks?

_____

Now, rewrite each sentence, changing the prepositional phrase to the appropriate possessive pronoun.

EXAMPLE   I met the brother of the governor of the state.

I met his brother.

6. Do you really like the smell of cabbage soup?

_____

7. The gowns of all three bridesmaids looked like flour sacks.

_____

8. A symphony by an old Viennese composer was recently found.

_____

9. They said the poems of Emily Dickinson are their favorites.

_____

10. The political goals of America are slowly changing.

_____

More than one prepositional phrase

Sentences are not limited to one prepositional phrase. Indeed, a series of prepositional phrases can occur in one sentence.

Look **in** the attic **in** a little box **on** the floor **behind** that old mattress.

Each prepositional phrase in this example gives further information about *where to look*.

Where should I look?	in the attic
Where in the attic?	behind that old mattress
Where behind the mattress?	on the floor
Where on the floor?	in a little box

Naturally, you cannot connect random prepositional phrases to form a sentence. They must make sense together and provide further information. Consider what might logically follow the prepositional phrases in these examples.

She spent the night in an old house . . .
She spent the night in an old house **located on a cliff near the Black River**.

The men worked on the roof . . .
The men worked on the roof **next to a chimney crumbling from years of neglect**.

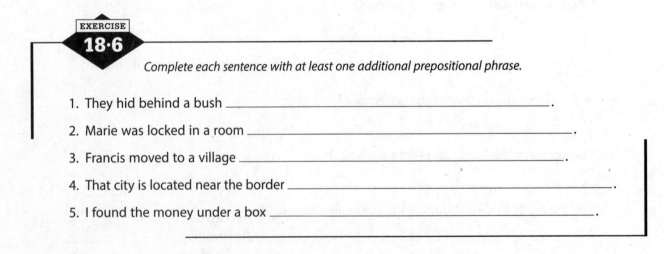

EXERCISE
18·6

Complete each sentence with at least one additional prepositional phrase.

1. They hid behind a bush _____.

2. Marie was locked in a room _____.

3. Francis moved to a village _____.

4. That city is located near the border _____.

5. I found the money under a box _____.

Prepositions that indicate location

Location can be thought of as the *area*, *point*, or *surface* of something. Certain prepositions indicate those locations. Here are some of the most commonly used ones:

above	in back of
along	in front of
among	in the middle of
at	near
behind	next to
below	on
beside	over
between	under
in	with

Most of these prepositions make sense in the same sentence, because they all indicate location:

The boy is **at** the table.
The boy is **behind** the table.
The boy is **beside** the table.
The boy is **next to** the table.
The boy is **under** the table.

Besides the verb *to be*, which is frequently used to show location, there are several other verbs that also indicate *where* someone or something is:

to be found	to remain
to be located	to sit
to be situated	to stand
to lie	to stay
to live	

Of course, there are many other such verbs. Those in the preceding list are among the ones used frequently. Look at these examples:

Is Guadalajara located **in** the east or west?
The center of the earthquake was situated **near** Los Angeles.
Shells like this can be found **along** the banks of the river.
John sits **in front of** me.
The girl was lying **on** a cot and resting.
A stranger stood **next to** us.
I have to remain **at** my workbench until noon.
You can stay **with** me.
We live **between** two large houses.

As long as you know the meaning of the prepositions, you can use them with relative accuracy. But in English, just like in all other languages, certain prepositions can only be used with certain verbs or phrases. And even if two or more prepositions can be used with the same phrase, there is a change in meaning—even if it's only a slight change.

Let's look at the prepositions *at* and *in*. They are used quite commonly and have a meaning that is easy to understand. In most cases, *at* is used to show that someone or something is positioned next to a horizontal or vertical surface:

at the table	at the door
at the computer	at the window
at the desk	at the blackboard

The preposition *in* indicates that someone or something is located *inside* something:

in the car	in the city
in the house	in the box
in the garden	in the center

These two prepositions, while having very distinct uses in a sentence, are also often used with the same phrases. But when they are, the meanings are different.

Use *at* to show that someone is *at* the location of his or her occupation, preoccupation, or some activity:

at school	at the store	at the hospital
at the movies	at the library	at the factory

With certain phrases, *in* can also be used:

in school	in the store	in the hospital
in the movies	in the library	in the factory

Notice the difference in meaning between the two prepositions:

at school = Someone is on the campus of the school, perhaps inside the building, or perhaps outside the building. This person is probably a student or teacher: "The chemistry teacher was **at school** until 7:00 P.M."

in school = Someone is inside the school building. This person is probably a student or teacher: "The injured student was **in school** again today."

Take note of yet another difference of meaning when the definite article *the* is added to the phrase:

at **the** school = Someone is on the campus of the school, perhaps inside the building, or perhaps outside the building. This person is *not necessarily* a student or teacher: "The landscaper was **at the school** to plant some new shrubs."

in **the** school = Someone is inside the school building. This person is *not necessarily* a student or teacher: "My father was **in the school** for a meeting."

There are several phrases that omit the definite article *the* when the preposition *at* is involved. Such phrases indicate that someone is *involved in the activity* described in the phrase:

He's **at work**. = He is working.
They're **at church**. = They're attending a religious ceremony.
The children are **at play**. = The children are playing.
She's **at home**. = She is staying in her house.
Tom's **at lunch**. = Tom is eating lunch. (also used with *breakfast*, *dinner*, and *supper*)
He's **at class**. = He is attending a class.

In general, *at* indicates that someone is involved in an activity at a location. *In* says that someone is inside that location:

The students are **at** school. (They are on campus somewhere.)
The students are **in** school. (They are in the building in their classes.)

Father is **at** the hospital. (Father is visiting. Or he may be a doctor or nurse.)
Father is **in** the hospital. (Father is a patient. Or he was outside. Now he's inside.)

Maria is **at** the factory. (She probably works there.)
Maria is **in** the factory. (She was outside. Now she's inside.)

Mom is **at** the store. (She is shopping there. Or perhaps she works there.)
Mom is **in** the store. (She was outside. Now she's inside.)

Be sure to distinguish between the prepositions *among* and *between*. Use *among* to say that you are in the company of more than just two people. Use *between* to say that you are in the company of only two people:

He sat **among** the members of the tribe and told them stories.
My sister sat **between** Jim and me.

Another pair of prepositions is often used to show "by means of what transportation" a person travels. It is common to use the preposition *by* to show the concept of traveling in a conveyance: *I went by car. We travel by plane. They go by train.* But *in* and *on* are also often used to show location on the forms of transportation:

We were **in the car** ready to leave for vacation.
They're **on a train** somewhere in Oregon.
What **bus** were you **on**?
Haven't you ever been **on a plane** before?

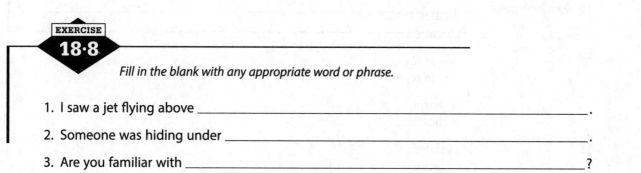

EXERCISE
18·7

Select the preposition that best completes each sentence.

1. A tiny rabbit was hiding **under/with/on** a bush.

2. Please don't sit **at/next to/over** me.

3. We saw several baby birds **at/behind/in** a nest in that tree.

4. There was nothing **below/with/among** the plane but empty space.

5. Father stays **on/above/at** the factory until 5:00 P.M.

6. An angry man stood directly **with/in the middle of/at** us.

7. John stayed **between/beside/among** me the entire time.

8. I saw Maria **in back of/above/among** the many people at the party.

9. There was a huge bug sitting **on/with/at** my bed!

10. I saw a stranger crouching **above/between/at** my car and the truck.

EXERCISE
18·8

Fill in the blank with any appropriate word or phrase.

1. I saw a jet flying above _____.

2. Someone was hiding under _____.

3. Are you familiar with _____?

4. My sisters both work at _____.

5. The frightened kitten hid in _____.

6. Someone stood behind _____.

7. Who was sitting among _____?

8. There's nothing in front of _____.

9. Gray clouds hovered over _____.

10. Have a seat next to _____.

11. He found his keys on _____.

12. I found a couple seats beside _____.

13. Let's set up our camp near _____.

14. We used to live between _____.

15. A puppy sat lazily in the middle of _____.

Write original sentences with the prepositional phrases given in parentheses. Use the prepositional phrase to show a location.

1. (on the train) _____

2. (at work) _____

3. (behind the dresser) _____

4. (next to her) _____

5. (in the hospital) _____

6. (with Maria) _____

7. (between them) _____

8. (over the mountains) _____

9. (in front of us) _____

10. (under a palm tree) _____

Prepositions that indicate movement or direction

The prepositions in this category do not suggest where someone or something is located. Instead, they describe someone's or something's movement or direction. Below is a list of some commonly used prepositions for this concept:

along	off
at	on
by	onto
from	out of
in	to
into	toward(s)

There are two forms of this preposition: *toward* and *towards*. Both are acceptable.

Certain verbs tell you that a preposition is being used to show location: *to be, to be located, to sit,* and many more. Certain other verbs tell you that a preposition is being used to show movement or direction. Here are some important ones:

to come	to journey
to drive	to jump
to fall	to return
to fly	to run
to go	to travel
to hurry	to walk

Just like prepositions that show location, a variety of prepositions that show movement or direction can be used in the same sentence. The basic sentence remains the same, but the preposition alters the kind of movement or direction involved. Look at these example sentences:

The women walked **along** the river.
The women walked **from** the river.
The women walked **into** the river.
The women walked **out of** the river.
The women walked **to** the river.
The women walked **toward** the river.

You need to be aware of the difference between *to* and *toward*. The preposition *to* says that someone *is going in the direction of a place and will arrive there soon*:

John is going **to** the park.

The preposition *toward* means that someone is going in the direction of a place but may decide to change direction:

John is going **toward** the park. (But he may decide to turn left and go to the bank instead.)

The prepositions *in* and *on* are used to show location. But they are also used to show movement or direction. Traditionally, only *into* and *onto* are used to show movement or direction, but many people today use *in* and *on* in place of them:

She runs **into** the house.	She runs **in** the house.
He fell **onto** the floor.	He fell **on** the floor.

If you consider the phrase *She runs in the house* literally, it means that *a girl is inside a house and running*. But English speakers know what is meant by this sentence from the context of the conversation where that sentence was used. So in casual speech you will hear both *in* and *into* and *on* and *onto* used interchangeably.

Select the preposition that best completes each sentence.

1. The children ran **in/toward/at** the gate.

2. The young couple strolled **along/out of/into** the beach.

3. The ball rolled **off/in/at** the table.

4. Is Thomas already **at/to/in** work?

5. I was hurrying **at/to/in** my desk.

6. Someone came running **into/onto/off** the room.

7. We slowly drove **off/at/by** their house.

8. Ms. Brown came **from/toward/at** England last year.

9. The poor girl fell **out of/onto/by** bed.

10. I dropped the tools **into/from/off** the box.

Fill in the blank with any appropriate word or phrase.

1. The cattle were heading toward _____.

2. Someone came out of _____.

3. Why were you going into _____?

4. My family frequently travels to _____.

5. Do you come from _____?

6. The carpenter fell off _____.

7. The burglar quietly climbed onto _____.

8. Maria wants to come into _____.

9. The men were walking along _____.

10. He came at _____ with a knife.

11. She drove by _____ without stopping.

12. What time did you come home from _____?

13. We're planning on traveling to _____.

14. The cat jumped into _____.

15. The woman moved cautiously toward _____.

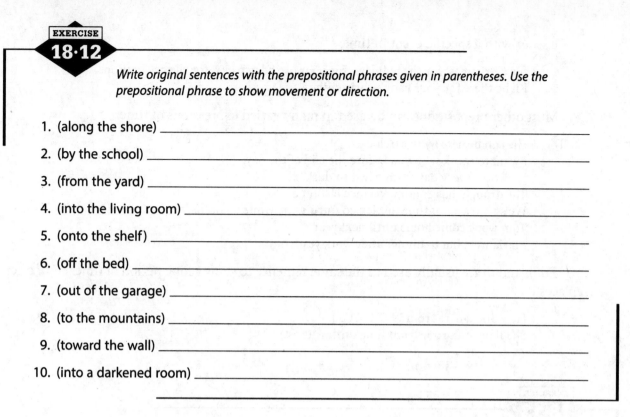

Write original sentences with the prepositional phrases given in parentheses. Use the prepositional phrase to show movement or direction.

1. (along the shore) _____

2. (by the school) _____

3. (from the yard) _____

4. (into the living room) _____

5. (onto the shelf) _____

6. (off the bed) _____

7. (out of the garage) _____

8. (to the mountains) _____

9. (toward the wall) _____

10. (into a darkened room) _____

Prepositions that indicate time

There are several prepositions that are used in expressions of time:

after	from
at	in
before	on
by	since
during	to
for	until

These prepositions are used with a variety of moments in time and in phrases that answer the question *when*. Some, such as *at*, *on*, *in* and *for*, have a limited use.

The preposition *at* is used primarily to point out an event in time or a time shown on a clock:

> **at** dawn, **at** dusk, **at** daybreak, **at** holiday time, **at** lunchtime, **at** midnight, **at** the end of the day, **at** 4:30 P.M., **at** 11:55 A.M.
> The soldiers finally got back **at** dawn.

On is used primarily with days of the week and dates:

> **on** Monday, **on** Tuesday, **on** Wednesday, **on** Thursday, **on** Friday, **on** Saturday, **on** Sunday, **on** June twelfth, **on** the fifteenth of May
> We're starting a new project **on** the first of the month.

Use *in* for a nonspecific time of a day, of a month, of a year, or of a season:

> **in** the morning, **in** January, **in** 2001, **in** summer
> We like going camping **in** autumn.

Use *for* with a specific event in time:

for Christmas, **for** the holidays, **for** your birthday party, **for** the celebration
I'll be there **for** your baby's christening.

Most other prepositions can be used in many varied expressions of time:

She can be here **by** five o'clock.
I want to speak with you **before** the end of the day.
He works every day **from** dawn **to** dusk.
The drought has continued **since** last June.
We spend a lot of time in Mexico **during** the winter months.
Tom won't come home **until** next year.
Maria went out to dinner **after** work yesterday.

From and *to* are usually used in the same sentence to show a long period of time. *Until* often replaces *to*:

He worked here **from** 1997 **to** 2002.
She'll be in Europe **from** June **until** August.

EXERCISE
18·13

Select the preposition that best completes each sentence.

1. They left the theater **on/before/until** the end of the film.

2. I should be home **during/for/by** ten o'clock.

3. She only works **from/at/for nine** to three.

4. We always have a picnic **on/in/to** the Fourth of July.

5. Do you always eat lunch **for/since/at** noon?

6. Bill has been sad **for/since/at** his fortieth birthday.

7. Aunt Jane came to town **in/on/for** Carmen's big party.

8. We do a lot of shopping **during/on/by** the holiday season.

9. It's coldest here from December **to/at/on** February.

10. I'm afraid that we'll have to wait **to/until/since** tomorrow.

EXERCISE
18·14

Fill in the blank with any appropriate word or phrase that expresses time.

1. The children were very noisy during _____.

2. We can expect Jim here for _____.

3. It's very rainy from May to _____.

4. I haven't seen you since _____ .

5. Can you stay with me until _____ ?

6. Tom works hard _____ morning to night.

7. They wanted to leave work before _____ .

8. The doctor gave him a checkup after _____ .

9. Try to get here by _____ .

10. His family usually stays at the lake in _____ .

11. The twins were born on _____ .

12. Dark shadows covered the ground at _____ .

13. They were living in Europe during _____ .

14. He's had a job in the city since _____ .

15. They want to start the marathon by _____ .

EXERCISE

18·15

Write original sentences with the prepositional phrases given in parentheses.

1. (from noon until midnight) _____

2. (by June) _____

3. (since the end of winter) _____

4. (in spring) _____

5. (on May tenth) _____

6. (after 11:00 P.M.) _____

7. (before next year) _____

8. (during his lifetime) _____

9. (after dark) _____

10. (at sunset) _____

Compound prepositions

When two or more words are strung together and end with *to, of,* or sometimes *from,* they are called *compound prepositions.* They function like all other prepositions. The only difference is that they are composed of more than a single word. Here is a list of the compound prepositions:

according to	in reference to
ahead of	in regard to
apart from	in spite of

because of	instead of
by means of	on account of
by way of	out of
in back of	up to
in front of	with respect to

Look at their use in a sentence and at the meaning that is derived:

Use in a Sentence	Meaning
According to Jim, the plan is perfect.	Jim's opinion
The project was completed **ahead of** schedule.	before expected, earlier than scheduled
Apart from a few complaints, everyone was satisfied.	except for a few complaints
Work stopped **because of** the storm.	the cause was the storm
The problem was solved **by means of** a complex formula.	by using a complex formula
Take a look at these examples **by way of** a contrast.	as a contrast
A stranger stood **in front of** me.	before me
No one was **in back of** us.	behind us
I gave this response **in regard to** his letter.	concerning his letter
We pointed out the law that is **in reference to** this crime.	concerning this crime
In spite of the blizzard, we drove all the way home.	not caring about the blizzard
Instead of a long dress, she chose a short one.	not choosing a long dress
He stayed in bed **on account of** his cold.	the cause was his cold
The girl suddenly ran **out of** the room.	from inside the room
The little boy stepped **up to** the microphone.	approached the microphone
With respect to all these losses, I have a few harsh words to say.	concerning all these losses

EXERCISE

18·16

Select the preposition that best completes each sentence.

1. Some men stood **in front of/instead of/up to** the store.

2. **Out of/By means of/According to** the forecast, it's going to rain today.

3. **By way of/Ahead of/In reference to** his remark, I just said, "Shame."

4. We stayed home **because of/out of/in regard to** the power outage.

5. Do you still live **with respect to/in back of/by way of** the shop?

6. There **ahead of/because of/on account of** us stood a large bison.

7. He quickly drove **by means of/out of/apart from** the driveway.

8. I was too nervous to walk **up to/in regard to/by way of** the president.

9. It happened **instead of/by means of/on account of** your carelessness!

10. She can't comment **in regard to/according to/up to** that matter.

EXERCISE
18·17

Fill in the blank with any appropriate word or phrase.

1. Please write a report in reference to _____.

2. In spite of _____, she continued to love him.

3. In regard to _____, I have a statement to make.

4. I bought a compact car instead of _____.

5. Who's waiting in front of _____?

6. The man was arrested on account of _____.

7. There were several tables and chairs in back of _____.

8. A strange smell came out of _____.

9. I sent her some flowers by way of _____.

10. A baby rabbit hopped up to _____.

11. You can get to the top of the mountain by means of _____.

12. With respect to _____, some changes have to be made.

13. Apart from _____, everyone else will be fired.

14. According to _____, we're in a heat wave.

15. I could see a winding road ahead of _____.

EXERCISE
18·18

Write original sentences with the prepositional phrases given in parentheses.

1. (ahead of time) _____

2. (because of an illness) _____

3. (in front of the factory) _____

4. (in reference to your last report) _____

5. (instead of a check) _____

6. (out of the clouds) _____

7. (with respect to his last wishes) _____

8. (according to the almanac) _____

9. (apart from a few friends) _____

10. (by means of the subway) _____

11. (in back of the garage) _____

12. (in spite of the darkness) _____

13. (on account of his riches) _____

14. (up to the river) _____

15. (in regard to these lies) _____

Prepositions that combine with other words

Adverbs modify verbs and answer the questions *where*, *when*, and *how* of the action of the verb:

> The sick girl remained **upstairs.** → Where did the sick girl remain?
> The books arrived **today.** → When did the books arrive?
> Bill ran **slowly.** → How did Bill run?

Often prepositions combine with another word to form a commonly used adverb. Prepositions in this form are frequently used as prefixes. Look at these examples:

Adverb	Meaning
by and by	soon
by and large	mostly, generally
downstairs	one floor below
indoors	in a building
inside	in the interior
outdoors	in the open air
outside	in the out-of-doors
underwater	beneath the surface of the water
up-country	toward the interior of the land
uphill	going up an incline
upstairs	one floor above
uptown	toward the center of the town

Sometimes the combination of a preposition and another word forms a noun:

Noun	Meaning
bylaw	an organization's rule
bypass	a detour
downfall	collapse, ruin
infield	the inner playing area in baseball
insight	understanding
outbreak	sudden or violent appearance
outgrowth	something that grows out of something else
outline	a preliminary or general plan
outlook	view, foresight

underarm	the area under the arm beneath the shoulder
underclassman	a freshman or sophomore in a school
underwear	garments worn under the clothes
upheaval	something rising up suddenly or violently
uproar	violent noise, tumult

At other times the combination of a preposition and another word results in a verb:

Verb	Meaning
install	establish or place in position
intone	recite in a monotone, give inflection
outdo	exceed, surpass
outline	draw the border, sketch
outlive	live longer than someone else
undergo	bear up under stress and survive
upgrade	raise to a higher level
uphold	raise, support, encourage
upset	overturn or disquiet someone

Adjectives are also formed in this way:

Adjective	Meaning
bygone	from a past time
down-and-out	poor or hopeless
downcast	looking downward or in low spirits
downhearted	discouraged, dejected
ingrown	having grown into the flesh
inland	land away from the sea
together	with each other, jointly
underage	not of legal age
undercover	secret, engaged in spying
upstanding	respectable, honest
up-to-date	modern, fashionable

The four preceding lists are only a small sampling of the many words that are derived from a preposition combining with another word. When you encounter such words, it is sometimes possible to analyze the meaning of the preposition and the meaning of the word with which it has been combined in order to determine the meaning of the new word. Consider these examples:

(**up** = rising upward + **grade** = level) = **to upgrade** (to raise to a higher level)
(**down** = going downward + **fall** = stumble) = **downfall** (collapse, ruin)

Keeping this in mind, you can sometimes guess the meaning of new words that are formed when a preposition is used as a prefix.

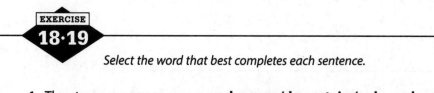

EXERCISE
18·19

Select the word that best completes each sentence.

1. The strange woman was an **undercover/downstairs/upheaval** agent.

2. The newly elected governor is a(n) **bygone/ingrown/upstanding** person.

3. She **underwent/upset/intoned** her voice with the anger she felt.

4. They decided to go **by and large/uptown/uphill** for dinner.

5. Did you follow our club's **insight/bylaws/outlook**?

6. Her views just aren't **up-to-date/underage/down-and-out**.

7. The hikers followed the creek **downstairs/up-country/by and by**.

8. The old man didn't want to **outline/outlive/outlook** his wife.

9. My aunt **underwent/installed/upheld** a serious operation last year.

10. His look was **upstanding/bygone/downcast** and his face quite sad.

EXERCISE

18·20

Fill in the blank with any appropriate word or phrase.

1. The new members refused to follow the bylaws _____.

2. Out in the street there was an uproar over _____.

3. While swimming underwater, he saw _____.

4. They were flying coach class but wanted to upgrade _____.

5. An underage girl came into _____.

6. The brothers were always trying to outdo _____.

7. The road uphill was _____.

8. There was a sudden outbreak of _____.

9. You need a technician to install _____.

10. The downhearted young man began to _____.

11. The couple lives downstairs from _____.

12. The underclassmen in _____ behaved badly.

13. I didn't mean to upset _____.

14. The undercover agent hid _____.

15. Within hours there was a total downfall of _____.

EXERCISE

18·21

Write original sentences with the words or phrases given in parentheses.

1. (outdoors) _____

2. (to a bypass) _____

3. (intone) _____

4. (ingrown toenail) _____

5. (by and large) _____

6. (insight) _____

7. (his underarms) _____

8. (underwear) _____

9. (outline) _____

10. (uphold the law) _____

11. (inland) _____

12. (uptown) _____

13. (upheaval) _____

14. (undergo) _____

15. (upstanding person) _____

Participial prepositions

This is a small category of prepositions but one that has some important uses. The present participial form of certain verbs, *although not true prepositions*, sometimes *have the characteristic of a preposition* and are used as one. Present participles are formed by adding *-ing* to the verb: *go → going, sing → singing, buy → buying*, and so on.

Only certain present participles can act as prepositions:

concerning	following
considering	regarding
excluding	

Their use as a preposition is different from their use as a verb form. Take careful note of the differences:

This is **concerning** to me. = participle used as an adjective

He often wrote me **concerning** this problem. = preposition (about this problem)

The club was **considering** buying new equipment. = present participle

The group spent hours **considering** this issue. = preposition (on this issue)

Why are you **excluding** our old friends? = present participle

We shall meet every Tuesday **excluding** the first Tuesday in May. = preposition (except the first Tuesday in May)

An old woman was **following** us. = present participle

The show will go on **following** one more rehearsal. = preposition (after one more rehearsal)

Do you have details **regarding** this case? = participle used as an adjective

She finally spoke up **regarding** her son's behavior. = preposition (about her son's behavior)

Rewrite each sentence, changing the italicized preposition to a participial preposition.

1. We'll need to put in a lot of time *on* this problem.

_____

2. I had a lot to tell *about* the crimes he had committed.

_____

3. I wanted to speak to her *about* our future together.

_____

4. Maria passed every test *except* the one in math.

_____

5. The picnic will go on as planned *after* the rainstorm.

_____

Write two original sentences with the words in parentheses. One should contain a present participle; the other should contain a present participle used as a preposition.

1. (concerning)

_____

_____

2. (considering)

_____

_____

3. (excluding)

_____

_____

4. (following)

_____

_____

Postpositive prepositions

This is another very small category of prepositions. They are derived from the shortened form of the preposition *toward*, which is *-ward*. *Postpositive* means that the prepositional form *-ward* occurs as a suffix. Notice how often another preposition acts as the prefix (*up, down, in, out*). Look at these examples:

backward	landward
downward	leeward
forward	outward
heavenward	seaward
homeward	upward
inward	windward

The points on a compass can also be combined with this suffix: *westward, eastward, northward, southward, southeastward.*

In each case, the word is adjectival or adverbial and means *in the direction of*. For example:

heavenward = in the direction of heaven
homeward = in the direction of home
seaward = in the direction of the sea

Two words that may be unfamiliar to you are *leeward* and *windward*. They do not conform precisely to the general meaning of this category of words. *Leeward* means *the direction in which the wind is blowing*. *Windward* means *the direction from which the wind is coming*.

Here are some sample sentences with each of these new words:

He walked **backward** without tripping.
When he looked **downward**, he saw a valley.
Tom moved **forward** a little in the crowded bus.
The balloons slowly rose **heavenward**.
Tomorrow I'm **homeward** bound!
You have to look **inward** to understand yourself.
The little boat drifted **landward**.
We sailed **leeward** into the sunset.
His **outward** appearance is good, but he's a nasty man.
Our ship moved **seaward** out of the little harbor.
When I looked **upward**, I saw the streaks of pink in the sky.
A steamer can travel **windward** with ease.
The troops marched **westward** toward the front lines.

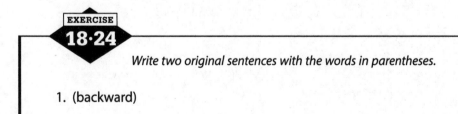

EXERCISE
18·24

Write two original sentences with the words in parentheses.

1. (backward)

_____

_____

2. (downward)

_____

_____

3. (homeward)

_____

_____

4. (inward)

_____

_____

5. (upward)

_____

_____

6. (windward)

_____

_____

7. (eastward)

_____

_____

More about prepositions

Words that require a specific preposition

Prepositions have a precise use. They cannot be used randomly but rather serve a particular function. As already discussed, some show a location. Others indicate a movement or a direction. In fact, there are some words and phrases that require a specific preposition in order to achieve the proper meaning. For example, you have to use the preposition *in* with the words *interested* or *interest*. Other prepositions make no sense:

> CORRECT: I'm very interested **in** computer technology.
> INCORRECT: Have you always been interested **about** classical music?
> CORRECT: She shows no interest **in** such things.
> INCORRECT: Tom has a great deal of interest **of** sports.

The same is true with many other words, most of which appear in verb phrases. Here is a list of commonly used expressions that require a specific preposition:

to ask for	to long for
to be alarmed by	to look after
to be capable of	to look at
to be generous with	to look for
to be interested in/interest in	to look forward to
to be sure of	to plead for/plea for
to beg for	to rely (up)on
to belong to	to speak about/of
to care about	to think about/of
to care for	to wait for
to depend (up)on	to walk up to
to dream about/of	to watch over
to forget about	to wish for
to hope for	to worry about
to listen to	*most passive structures* + by

Several phrases use the preposition *for* to complete their meaning. Whatever follows the preposition becomes the object of the preposition and forms a prepositional phrase. Look at the examples that follow:

> Juan *asked* **for** a second helping of potatoes. (ask for = request)
> The dog *begged* **for** a treat.
> Maria *is caring* **for** her sick mother. (care for = tend to)
> Jim really *cares* **for** Barbara. (care for = feel affection)
> The crowd *was hoping* **for** a win, but the team lost.
> Their family *longed* **for** a vacation in Europe.
> They spent hours *looking* **for** the lost kitten.

295

She *pleaded* with the judge **for** mercy.
The lawyer made a brilliant *plea* **for** justice in this case.
How long do we have *to wait* **for** a bus?
The little boy *wished* **for** a new bicycle.

There are many phrases that begin with *to be*. They usually include an adjective or a participle, and each one requires the use of a specific preposition:

The woman *was* suddenly *alarmed* **by** the threat of a storm.
I didn't think you *were capable* **of** such a terrible thing.
Mr. Garcia *is* always so *generous* **with** his time.
She's not *interested* **in** old movies.
I'm developing an *interest* **in** science.
How can you *be sure* **of** what to do next?

Phrases that require *to*:

That red car *belongs* **to** me. (belongs to = ownership)
Tom wants *to belong* **to** our sports club. (belong to = membership)
I *listened* **to** the speaker's remarks with great interest.
Everyone *is looking forward* **to** the start of vacation.
A beautiful woman *walked up* **to** me and shook my hand.

Phrases that require *about*:

My brother *cares* a lot **about** his girlfriend.
Last night I *dreamt* **about** our trip to Alaska.
She says she'll never *forget* **about** me.
You shouldn't *speak* **about** such things!
It seems I'm always *thinking* **about** food.
My parents still *worry* **about** my sister and me.

Phrases that require *on* or *upon*:

You can always *depend* **(up)on** us.
There's no one here that I can *rely* **(up)on**.

Phrases that require *of*. Notice that these phrases are often the same ones that use *about*:

The dog seemed to be *dreaming* **of** chasing a rabbit.
Someone *was speaking* **of** the new boss's bad temper.
Guess what I'm *thinking* **of**.

The verb *to look* forms two new expressions with the prepositions *after* (meaning "to care for") and *at*:

The men stayed home *to look* **after** the children.
They *were looking* upward **at** the stars in the sky.

When the verb *watch* is combined with the preposition *over*, it means "to tend to" and "to protect":

The shepherd *watched* **over** the nervous flock of sheep.

When an active sentence is changed to a passive sentence, the subject of the active sentence becomes the object of the preposition *by* in the passive sentence:

Active: A thief stole the wallet.
Passive: The wallet was stolen **by** the thief.

Here are a few more examples of sentences in the passive voice:

Active: A raging fire destroyed the house.
Passive: The house *was destroyed* **by** a raging fire.

Active: The proud father tucks the little girl into bed.
Passive: The little girl *is tucked* into bed **by** the proud father.

Active: The chief of police himself had warned them.
Passive: They *had been warned* **by** the chief of police himself.

Active: Will a new chef prepare dinner?
Passive: Will dinner *be prepared* **by** a new chef?

EXERCISE
19·1

Select the word that best completes each sentence.

1. I began to beg my father **of/about/for** more money.

2. She was being followed **by/to/for** a strange man.

3. Juanita also **depends/belongs/wishes** to our club now.

4. Don't you want to **watch/ask/care** for a little help?

5. I never stop worrying **for/of/about** my daughter.

6. I really care **by/at/for** her. I'm in love.

7. Tom has absolutely no interest **at/in/to** jazz.

8. It's difficult for them to forget **of/(up)on/about** the war.

9. I know I can **rely/hope/plead** on your honesty.

10. I **long/walk/dream** for a good night's sleep.

11. She was deeply hurt **to/over/by** his insults.

12. The child is hardly capable **of/for/(up)on** hurting anyone.

13. I'll **worry/wait/plead** for you in front of the theater.

14. You shouldn't be so generous **with/for/at** us.

15. Are you looking forward **for/at/to** the party?

EXERCISE
19·2

Fill in the blank with any appropriate word or phrase.

1. He became alarmed by _____.

2. You shouldn't worry about _____.

3. These women are very interested in _____.

4. I'm going to wish for _____.

5. Are you absolutely sure of _____?

6. The immigration officer walked up to _____.

7. Does this jacket belong to _____?

8. You're always thinking about _____.

9. How can I depend on _____?

10. The wounded soldier was pleading for _____.

11. Never forget about _____.

12. The barn was blown down by _____.

13. We need a guard to watch over _____.

14. You should listen to _____.

15. A large animal was looking at _____.

EXERCISE
19·3

Fill in the blank with the appropriate phrase. Choose from the phrases in this unit that require a specific preposition. Write all your sentences in the past tense.

EXAMPLE: My uncle *was interested in* American history.

1. The young man _____ me with a gift in his hand.

2. The orator _____ the importance of saving money.

3. I think this umbrella _____ to Aunt Norma.

4. I _____ the exam! I'm going to fail for sure!

5. If you needed anything, you always _____ me.

6. A police officer _____ the injured pedestrian.

7. Where were you? I _____ you for two hours!

8. Dad _____ me, but I knew how to take care of myself.

9. The boys _____ the missing child for several hours.

10. Jim _____ an extra ten dollars but got nothing.

EXERCISE
19·4

Write original sentences with the phrases given in parentheses.

1. (to be capable of) _____

2. (to look for) _____

3. (a passive structure 1 by) _____

4. (no interest in) _____

5. (to wish for) _____

6. (a plea for) _____

7. (to be sure of) _____

8. (to rely upon) _____

9. (to beg for) _____

10. (to look forward to) _____

11. (to care about) _____

12. (to hope for) _____

13. (to look after) _____

14. (to dream of) _____

15. (a passive structure + by) _____

Prepositions and phrasal verbs

This is a very large category of verbal expressions that use prepositions to change the meaning of a verb. It is different from the ordinary combination of a verb and a preposition because the verb-plus-preposition phrase as a whole acquires a completely new meaning and one that is often radically different from the original meaning of the verb.

Here are a few sentences with the verb *to come* used with its regular meaning. Each one has a prepositional phrase in it, but the meaning of *to come* is not changed:

> These young people **come from** Spain.
>
> He **came into** the room and sat down.
>
> **Come with** me, please.

Now look at these sentences with *to come* and a preposition. The meaning of the verb *to come* is changed:

> The man **came to** after a few minutes. (He regained consciousness.)
> Tom finally **came around** and signed the contract. (He changed his mind.)
> How did you **come up with** this idea? (How did you create this idea?)

Verbs that change their meaning when combined with one or more prepositions are called *phrasal verbs*. They are numerous in English and are an important element of grammar. It is essential to identify them and to be able to understand the new meanings that are derived by their formation. Let's look at some important phrasal verbs.

Ask

The regular verb *to ask* means "to pose a question" or "to make a request." That meaning is altered when the verb is combined with certain prepositions. In phrasal verbs those prepositions are sometimes called *particles*. You will notice that the particle-prepositions are often used as adverbs. The phrasal verb *to ask around* means "to seek information from a variety of sources." The particle *about* is sometimes used in place of *around*:

> I **asked around** about the new girl and learned she was from Poland.
> **Ask around** and you'll learn where you can rent a cheap apartment.
> **Ask about** and you'll discover where there's a nice place to eat.

The phrasal verb *to ask out* has changed its meaning again. It now means "to invite someone to go somewhere" or "to invite on a date." It suggests that someone is romantically interested in another person:

> John **asked** Maria **out**, but she refused.
> I was too shy **to ask** her **out**.
> The handsome man was **asked out** by his friend's cousin.

Be

You are already familiar with the verb *to be*. It shows the existence of someone or something (*They are here.*) or helps to describe a condition or quality (*I am old.*). It is an irregular verb and is the only English verb that has a complex conjugation in the present and past tenses:

Present		Past	
I am	we are	I was	we were
you are	you are	you were	you were
he, she, it is	they are	he, she, it was	they were

Its participle is *been*: *I have been*, *you have been*, *he has been*, and so on.

The verb *to be* is also used as an auxiliary with a present participle to show a continuing action:

> I am singing.
> You were writing.
> They have been studying.
> Tom will be working.

But the meaning of the verb is altered when it is used in certain phrases. Let's look at some examples of phrasal verbs formed from this verb.

The verb *to be in* has a very specific meaning. It says that someone is at home or available at the office:

> **I'm in** for the night.
> **Is** Dr. Jones **in** this afternoon?
> Tell my client that I won't **be in** until eight in the morning.

The opposite of *to be in* is *to be out*. It says that someone is not at home or not available at the office:

> John **is out** and won't be home until late.
> I believe Dr. Jones **is out** for the day. He'll be in the office at 8:00 A.M. tomorrow.

In the phrasal verb *to be on*, only the preposition *on* has been added, but the meaning is completely changed by it. This verb means that some apparatus, machinery, or equipment is functioning. It is the opposite of *to be off*:

> Press the green button, and the machine **is on**. Press the red button, and the machine **is off**.
> It's hot in here. **Is** the air conditioning **on**?
> The engine is so quiet that I can't tell if it **is on**.

Use *to be out of sight* to say that you can no longer see someone or something or that someone or something is no longer in your range of vision:

> He ran up the hill and **was** soon **out of sight**.
> In a couple more minutes the ship **will be out of sight**.
> The rocket **was out of sight** in just a matter of seconds.

The verb *to be with it* has two specific meanings. One describes a person who is very contemporary and in fashion. The other suggests that a person is in a good state of mind and is thinking properly:

> Mary has another new dress. She **is** always so **with it**.
> Your hairdo is old fashioned. Why can't you **be** more **with it**?
> John drank a lot last night and **isn't with it** today.
> I forget everything. **I'm** just not **with it** anymore.

Use *to be onto something* to say that someone is discovering something important or has an important idea. It also suggests that someone has found a clue that will help to solve a problem:

> What a great invention! **You're** really **onto something**!
> I read her article about stopping pollution. I think **she's onto something**.
> Look at the map I found. **We're** finally **onto something** that will help to find the treasure.

The verb *to be up to something* says that someone looks suspicious and has some kind of evil intentions. It is sometimes stated as *to be up to no good*:

> What's that man doing? I think **he's up to something**.
> I knew you **were up to something** when I saw you holding a shovel.
> Her children **are** always **up to no good**.

EXERCISE
19.5

Select the word or phrase that best completes each sentence.

1. It's cold. The heat **ask/on/is** probably off.

2. If you ask **around/with/out**, you'll get his address.

3. The old woman was **up to/onto/about** something again.

4. She was too timid to **be/ask/out of** Juan out.

5. The scientist knew she was **onto/out of/up** something.

6. My lawyer won't be **off/out of sight/in** until noon.

7. Your parents are so up-to-date and **onto something/with it/around**.

8. Why was the TV **on/out/up to something** all night?

9. The detective believed she was up **with it/to no good/and around**.

10. He wants to take a shower, but the water is **on/onto/off** again.

EXERCISE
19.6

Fill in the blank with any appropriate word or phrase taken from the phrasal verbs formed from ask *and* be.

1. I wanted to know who he was and _____ about him.

2. The jumbo jet was quickly _____.

3. The burglar was obviously _____ no good.

4. What time will Professor Gomez _____/in?

5. Did your nephew _____ my niece out?

6. Having found a clue, they knew they were _____.

7. If the fan _____, why is it so hot in here?

8. When he turned to look, her train was already out _____.

9. Use makeup! Color your hair! Try to be _____!

10. The dentist is _____ for the day.

Come

You're already familiar with this verb of motion that means "to approach, to move toward, or to arrive." Its conjugation is irregular and has these principal parts:

	Present	**Past**	**Present Perfect**	**Future**
you	come	came	have come	will come
he, she, it	comes	came	has come	will come

Four distinct meanings are derived from the phrasal verb *to come through (for) (with)*: (1) to endure or survive, (2) to be approved by some official body or institution, (3) to perform a helpful service for someone, and (4) to produce something that has been promised. Check these examples:

Somehow they **came through** the storm without a scratch.
Your loan **came through** and you'll receive a check in the mail.
Mom always **came through for** me whenever I had a problem.
Tom will never **come through with** the money he promised.

With the particle *to*, *come to* has a simple new meaning: to become conscious again or to wake up:

Her eyes opened and she slowly **came to**.
The old man fell asleep and never **came to** again.

The verb *to come up with* means "to find someone or something that someone needs." Look at these examples:

I'll try **to come up with** a piano player for your party.
She **came up with** another good idea.

The phrasal verb *to come upon* means "to happen upon someone or something." The particle *on* is sometimes used in place of *upon*:

When she **comes on** her brother, she'll have the shock of her life.
I **came upon** an interesting book in the library.

Get

This complicated verb has two basic meanings: "to receive" and "to become." But it is used in many other phrases and its meaning is altered each time. It's irregular and has these principal parts:

	Present	**Past**	**Present Perfect**	**Future**
you	get	got	have gotten	will get
he, she, it	gets	got	has gotten	will get

In this form, *to get back (at)* has two new meanings: (1) to return from someplace, and (2) using the preposition *at*, to seek revenge upon a person or group. Look at these examples:

When did you **get back** from Mexico?
He said he'd **get back at** you for lying about him.
The terrorist wanted **to get back at** the government.

To *get behind (in)* has two meanings: (1) to promote or support someone or some activity, and (2) using the preposition *in*, to be late or lagging behind in performing a task. Here are some examples:

You have **to get behind** your candidate, if you want him to win the election.
I'm **getting behind in** my work again.
If you **get behind in** your exercising, you'll put on weight again.

To *get in on* means "to participate in an event or to receive a share in something because of that participation." Some examples:

You'll need an invitation, if you want **to get in on** the conference.
I **got in on** the deal to sell farming equipment in Canada.

The phrase *to get into it* doesn't reveal what it means by the makeup of the words. Its new meaning is "to have an argument or a fight." Look at these examples:

John **got into it** with another driver over a parking space.
My parents always **get into it** over money.

In this form the phrasal verb *to get off* has two meanings: (1) often using the preposition *of*, to depart from your job, and (2) to have a person cleared of criminal wrongdoing. Some examples:

I **got off** early and came straight home.
What time will you **get off of** work tomorrow?
The clever lawyer **got** the burglar **off** with a small fine.
I'm innocent! You have **to get** me **off**!

Phrasal Verbs as Participles

The phrasal verbs *to get back*, *to get into*, and *to get off* can act as the participle in a passive voice sentence:

Her jewelry was never **gotten back**.
The room was **gotten into** by a clever thief.
The crook was **gotten off** by a shrewd lawyer.

With the particle *on*, *to get on (with)* has three meanings: (1) to cooperate and thrive with somebody, (2) often with the phrase *in years* it means to grow old, and (3) using the preposition *with*, to continue with something. Some examples:

The two former enemies seemed **to be getting on** without a problem.
My grandparents **are getting on in years**.
The crisis is over. Now we have **to get on with** our lives.

EXERCISE

19.7

Select the word or phrase that best completes each sentence.

1. Jim came through **with/for/up** me again.

2. Let's get on **to/with/back to** the meeting.

3. The drowsy woman came **to/onto/up with** very slowly.

4. The children came **upon/off/at** a little cottage in the woods.

5. I work all afternoon. I get **back at/into it/off at** 5:00 p.m.

6. Ms. Brown **came up/comes to/has come upon** with a wonderful slogan.

7. Hurry! You're **getting/got/coming** behind in your work.

8. How can I get **behind in/on with/in on** this deal?

9. The two boys got **back at/into it/up with** after school.

10. She got **back at/up with/on with** us for gossiping.

EXERCISE

19.8

Fill in the blank with any appropriate word or phrase taken from the phrasal verbs formed from come *and* get.

1. Start the music. Let's get _____ the show.

2. I don't want to stay in jail! Please _____ me off!

3. Mr. Brown finally _____ with our loan.

4. They were arguing over the accident and soon _____ it.

5. Maybe she'll come _____ if you give her some water.

6. Jim _____ an old magazine in the attic.

7. Did Maria get _____ the stock purchase?

8. We all _____ Ms. Brown, and she won the election.

9. The car dealer eventually came through _____ us.

10. I _____ at six. You can pick me up then.

Keep

This is an irregular verb that means "to retain, maintain, or cause to continue." Look at its principal parts:

	Present	Past	Present Perfect	Future
you	keep	kept	have kept	will keep
he, she, it	keeps	kept	has kept	will keep

Followed by a present participle, *to keep on (with)* means "to continue doing something." Using the preposition *with* followed by a noun or pronoun, it also means "to continue doing something." Look at these examples:

> The professor told the students **to keep on** studying.
> The professor told the students **to keep on with** their studies.

To keep out (of) has three meanings: (1) to stay outside a place, (2) to remain neutral about something as in "minding one's own business," and (3) to stop someone from entering a place:

> **Keep out!** This means you!
> I want you **to keep out of** my office when I'm working.
> **Keep out of** this! This is none of your business!
> I want you **to keep** Ms. Johnson **out of** our meeting.

Three new meanings are derived by using *to keep to (oneself)*: (1) to maintain an agreed-upon plan or promise, and (2) to remain withdrawn and alone. If you add *something* to the phrase (*to keep something to oneself*), it has a third meaning: "to maintain a secret." Some examples:

> If we **keep to** our original plan, we'll achieve our goals.
> The old woman **kept** more and more **to herself.**
> Please **keep** this information **to yourself**. Don't tell anyone.

The phrasal verb *to keep up (with)* also has three meanings: (1) to hold someone or something upright, (2) to prevent a person from falling asleep, and (3) using the preposition *with*, to remain equal with someone or something. Look at these examples:

> **Keep** him **up**. Don't let him fall.
> He's very sleepy, but somehow we have **to keep** Jim **up** until midnight.
> I can't **keep up with** you. Walk slower.

Kick

Kick is a regular verb and means "to strike with a foot." Look what happens to its meaning when it becomes a phrasal verb.

The phrasal verb *to kick off* means "to start something" and comes from the start of a football game, which is the *kickoff*. It has a colloquial meaning that is casual and somewhat crude: "to pass away or die." This second meaning is used without compassion:

> Let's **kick off** the meeting with a few words from Ms. Johnson.
> The poor old man **kicked off** during the night.

In this form the verb to kick out (of) means "to evict someone or eject something from a place":

> Maria **kicked out** her boyfriend last night.
> I **kicked** the boxes **out of** my way.

Knock

This verb is regular. It means "to strike, hit, or rap."

With the particle *down*, *to knock down* means "to hit someone or something to the ground." Here are some examples:

> The bully **knocked** me **down** and ran off laughing.
> The wind is going **to knock down** that old fence.

In this form the verb *to knock off (it, work)* derives a few new meanings: (1) to stop doing something, (2) using the pronoun *it* to make a rather rude meaning, "to cease a certain behavior," (3) as a slang expression, "to murder a person," and (4) using the noun *work*, "to conclude the day's work." As a noun—*knockoff*—the word means "an imitation." Some examples:

You can **knock off** digging. The plans have been changed.
Knock it off! Acting like that isn't funny!
The gangsters **knocked off** an old enemy.
My father usually **knocks off work** around 6:00 p.m.
He wanted a Rolex but bought a **knockoff** from a street vendor.

Look at the meanings that are derived for the verb *to knock out*: (1) to cause someone to become unconscious, (2) to develop or make something quickly, and (3) to cause something to stop functioning.

Bill hit the man so hard that he **knocked** him **out**.
That drink almost **knocked** me **out**.
The workers **knocked out** a prototype in a matter of hours.
A lightning strike **knocked out** the radio station.

Phrasal Verbs That Act as Nouns

The phrasal verbs to *kick off*, to *knock off*, and *to knock out* have a noun formation:

This party is the **kickoff** to a week of celebrating.
This isn't a Cartier. It's a **knockoff**.
The champ won the boxing match by a **knockout**.

EXERCISE
19.9

Select the word or phrase that best completes each sentence.

1. You run too fast. I can't keep **up with/to/out of** you.

2. With one blow, he knocked the man **on/out/it off**.

3. We have to **keep on/kick off/keep to** working until we're done.

4. The landlord kicked us **up with/off/out of** our apartment.

5. Knock **it/out/yourself** off. You're bothering me.

6. The carpenters **knocked down/kicked out of/kept up with** the wall in just a few minutes.

7. They kicked **out/out of/off** the parade with a patriotic march.

8. He was shot in the morning. He kicked **off/to/up with** in the afternoon.

9. What time do you knock **out/off/up with** work?

10. She's so lonely, yet she still keeps **up with us/off it/to herself**.

Fill in the blank with any appropriate word or phrase taken from the phrasal verbs formed from keep, kick, *and* knock.

1. The coach wanted them to _____ practicing.

2. Careful or you'll knock _____ the window!

3. How can we keep those kids _____ our yard?

4. You had better knock _____ before I get really angry.

5. If you keep _____ this road, you'll get there in an hour.

6. They had an argument, and she _____ him out.

7. The champ knocked his opponent ___, but he got up immediately.

8. If you pedal faster, you'll _____ with the other cyclists.

9. We'll _____ off the party with a few drinks.

10. What time do you _____ of work?

Put

To put is an irregular verb and means "to place or set." Its principal parts look like this:

	Present	Past	Present Perfect	Future
you	put	put	have put	will put
he, she, it	puts	put	has put	will put

The phrasal verb *to put down (for)* has four new meanings: (1) to cease holding someone or something up, (2) to ridicule or demean someone or something, (3) to write down, and (4) using the preposition *for*, to sign someone up to participate in something. Look at these examples:

I don't want you to carry me. **Put** me **down**!
I try very hard, but still you **put** me **down**. I can't do any better.
The stenographer **put down** every word the lawyer said.
Tim likes soccer. You can **put** him **down for** that.

In this form the verb *to put on* has three meanings: (1) to place on headgear or wear a certain garment, (2) to pretend, and (3) to tease someone. Some examples:

The woman **put on** a new hat and dress and went to the party.
He's not really sick. He's just **putting on**.
It can't be true! You're **putting** me **on**! Anna is married again?

This phrasal verb *to put out (oneself, of)* also has various new meanings: (1) to generate an abundance of something (often used as a noun: *output*), (2) to annoy a person, (3) using a reflexive pronoun, to allow oneself to be inconvenienced or to do a favor for someone, and (4) to eject someone or something from a place.

That new copy machine really **puts out**.
What's the total **output** of this department each month?
Professor Jones was really **put out** by all the silly questions.

I really **put** myself **out** for you. Is this the thanks I get?
Please **put** the dog **out**. I can't stand his barking.

To put up (with) has three new meanings: (1) to provide someone with housing (usually for one night), (2) to erect, and (3) using the preposition *with*, to tolerate someone or something:

It's storming. We had better **put** you **up** for the night.
We always **put up** the Christmas tree in early December.
I can't **put up with** your lying and cheating anymore.

Quiet

Quiet is a regular verb that means "to make calm or silent." As a phrasal verb, its meaning changes only slightly.

To quiet down means "to become calm or silent" or "to make someone calm or silent." Here are some examples:

As the grieving woman came in, the room suddenly **quieted down**.
Give the man a shot **to quiet** him **down**.

Rest

To rest is another regular verb. It means "to relax and enjoy an idle moment."

In the form to rest up (from), the meaning of the verb is not altered greatly. With the particle *up*, the suggestion is that the goal is to rest completely and not just for a moment. With the preposition *from*, you can tell what activity is avoided to provide rest:

You're exhausted. I want you **to rest up** and leave everything else to me.
I ache all over. I need **to rest up from** all this exercising.

EXERCISE
19.11

Select the word or phrase that best completes each sentence.

1. Put me **on/up/down** for the refreshments committee.

2. The baby is feverish and won't **put/quiet/rest** down.

3. I need to rest up **for/with/from** all this exercise.

4. Carmen **rest up/put on/put up with** his lies for many years.

5. You're so hospitable, but don't **put down/put up/put yourself** out.

6. He's so excited, but he needs to quiet **on/up/down**.

7. I **rested up/quieted down/put up with** all morning and went to work at noon.

8. She's not sick! She's just putting **out/off/on**!

9. It can't be true! Are you **put/down for/putting** me on?

10. The janitor was **quieted down/put up with/put out by** all the garbage in the hallway.

Fill in the blank with any appropriate word or phrase taken from the phrasal verbs formed from put, quiet, *and* rest.

1. Why don't you _____ ? You've had a long day.

2. You're never satisfied with my work. You always _____ me down.

3. Spend the night here. We can put you _____ .

4. When the class _____ down, I'll pass out the new material.

5. I love soccer. Put me _____ that team.

6. Tom _____ a dress and a wig for the Halloween party.

7. Anita can't put _____ his deceit any longer.

8. I think you should rest _____ that long trip.

9. He wished he could put his roommate _____ his house.

10. You can put the groceries _____ on that table.

Take

This is an irregular verb. It means "to receive, grasp, or accept." Look at its principal parts.

	Present	**Past**	**Present Perfect**	**Future**
you	take	took	have taken	will take
he, she, it	takes	took	has taken	will take

The combination of words *to take back (from)* has four meanings: (1) to return something, (2) to remind someone of something in the past, (3) to retract something that has been said or written, and (4) using the preposition *from*, to return something to the original owner from someone who had temporary possession of it. Some examples:

I **took** the tools I borrowed **back** to Jim.
Hearing that song **takes** me **back** to when I was still in college.
Take that **back**! You're lying!
She wants **to take back** the ring **from** me.

The phrasal verb *to take down (from)* has three new meanings: (1) to write something on paper, (2) to guide or transport someone or something to a place, (3) to dismantle or raze, and (4) using the preposition *from*, to remove someone or something from a high location. Look at these examples:

Take the phone number **down** for me: 555-0884.
Ms. Johnson **took** the reports **down** to the meeting.
If you don't know the way, I can **take** you **down** there.
They're going **to take down** the old movie palace.
Anna **takes** a box of letters **down from** the shelf.

To take in has three meanings: (1) to decrease the size of a garment, (2) to give someone shelter, and (3) to fool someone. Here are some examples:

> I've lost some weight. I need **to take** these pants **in**.
> My parents **took** the homeless man **in** for the night.
> Robert **took** me in with one of his silly schemes again.

Another phrasal verb can be used with three different prepositions. *To take off (after, for, of)* has a variety of meanings: (1) to remove a garment, (2) often using the word *day*, to stay home from school or work, (3) to leave the ground in flight, (4) using the preposition *after*, to run in the direction of someone or something, (5) using the preposition *for*, to depart for a place, and (6) using the preposition *of*, to remove from a place.

> The doctor asked me **to take off** my shirt.
> I felt ill, so I **took the day off**.
> The jet fighters **took off** in a matter of minutes.
> When he saw the prowler, Mike **took off after** him.
> Last night Jim and Maria **took off for** Vancouver.
> She **took** a spider **off of** the piano.

To take on has three meanings: (1) to accept, (2) to hire, and (3) to become emotional about something.

> You always **take on** too much work.
> If you **take on** Bill, he'll work as hard as two men.
> Anna often **takes on** about the death of her husband.

The verb *to take over (from)* has four new meanings: (1) to take control of a business, (2) to accept responsibility for something, (3) to deliver something, and (4) using the preposition *from*, to assume control of something from someone. Some examples:

> The corporation **took over** two smaller companies.
> Can you **take over** the Johnson account? They need someone like you.
> I **took** the CD player **over** to Maria's house.
> **We're taking over** the travel agency **from** Mr. Gomez.

Another phrasal verb with a variety of meanings is *to take up (with, on)*. It means (1) to raise the hem of a garment, (2) often using the preposition *with*, to discuss a person or issue, (3) to be involved in a special skill or hobby, (4) using the preposition *with*, to have an affair with someone, (5) using the preposition *on*, to agree to someone's proposal or offer. Look at these examples:

> That dress is too long. **Take** it **up** a couple inches.
> The committee **took up** the problem of recycling plastics.
> I need **to take up** the question of Jim's employment **with** you.
> My daughter **has taken up** stamp collecting.
> My ex-wife **is taking up with** a man from Texas.
> I'd like **to take** them **up on** their offer to buy my house.

Talk

Talk is a regular verb. It means "to speak or to converse."

With the particle *back*, *to talk back* means "to respond to someone rudely or disrespectfully." Some examples:

> The boy has no fear of **talking back** to his father.
> You shouldn't **talk back** to a teacher like that.

Phrasal Verbs That Act as Nouns

The verbs *to take down*, *to take off*, *to take over*, and *to talk back* have a noun formation. Nouns can often also act as adjectives.

> The wrestling match was over with two quick **takedowns**. (noun)
>
> **Takeoff** can be a dangerous time for an aircraft. (noun)
>
> The **takeoff** distance is 1,500 meters. (noun used as adjective)
>
> The **takeover** of our firm came as a surprise. (noun)
>
> We learned of the **takeover** bid too late. (noun used as adjective)
>
> **Talking back** to a parent is a terrible thing. (noun)

To talk someone into means "to convince someone of something":

> You'll never **talk** me **into** investing in that stock.
>
> Juan can **talk** anyone **into** anything.

The verb *to talk over* has two new meanings: (1) to discuss someone or something with another person, and (2) to use a microphone while speaking.

> We have **to talk over** Barbara's recent behavior.
>
> They're going **to talk** the matter **over** after lunch.
>
> My boss loves **talking over** a microphone.

Phrasal Verbs as Participles

The phrasal verbs *to take back*, *to take down*, *to take in*, *to take off*, *to take on*, *to take over*, *to take up*, and *to talk over* can act as the participle in a passive voice sentence:

> The books **are being taken back** by Tim.
>
> The drapes **have been taken down** for cleaning.
>
> They **were taken in** by his smooth talk.
>
> The vases **will be taken off** the shelf.
>
> The new girl **was taken on** last week.
>
> Why **was** this firm **taken over**?
>
> Your hemline should **be taken up** a bit.
>
> The matter **will be talked over** in a private meeting.

Select the word or phrase that best completes each sentence.

1. Ms. Brown will take over **from/off/on** Mr. Jones.

2. Let's sit down and talk this problem **into/over/back**.

3. I took everything **off of/down/back from** her apartment.

4. You shouldn't **talk back/take back/take over** to your mother!

5. You're not going to talk me **over/into/back** that again.

6. I'll take **down/off of/on** the curtains and wash them.

7. The shelter **takes over from/takes down/takes in** homeless people.

8. Take **on/over/off** your coat and relax.

9. That skirt is long. Let's take it **up/off/over from**.

10. My brother **takes over/took up/has taken in** with my ex-girlfriend.

Fill in the blank with any appropriate word or phrase taken from the phrasal verbs formed from take *and* talk.

1. A new company took _____ the factory.

2. His store is _____ several new employees.

3. _____ back to a teacher is terrible behavior.

4. In the summer the students took off _____ California.

5. Your waist is smaller. You should take _____ your pants.

6. I'd like to take you _____ your offer.

7. Anita _____ me into going to the dance with her.

8. The reporter took _____ every word I said.

9. You ought to _____ what you said to her.

10. No one talked it _____ with me.

Remember these separable phrasal verbs

Sometimes *particles* have two possible positions in a sentence with a phrasal verb when the direct object in the sentence is a noun: after the object or before the object. But when the object is a pronoun, it has only one position: after the object.

You encountered these separable phrasal verbs: *to kick off, to kick out, to knock down, to knock off, to knock out, to put down, to put on, to put up, to quiet down, to take back, to take down, to take in, to take off, to take on, to take over, to take up,* and *to talk over.* In these verbs the particles are *back, down, in, off, on, out, over,* and *up.* Look at these examples that show the position of the particle with nouns and pronouns:

He kicked his shoes **off**.
He kicked **off** his shoes.
He kicked them **off**.

We knocked the wall **down**.
We knocked **down** the wall.
We knocked it **down**.

Jim knocked the bully **out**.
Jim knocked **out** the bully.
Jim knocked him **out**.

Put that dress **on**.
Put **on** that dress.
Put it **on**.

I can't quiet the boy **down**.
I can't quiet **down** the boy.
I can't quiet him **down**.

We took the curtains **down**.
We took **down** the curtains.
We took them **down**.

John takes his shoes **off**.
John takes **off** his shoes.
John takes them **off**.

Their company took our company **over**.
Their company took **over** our company.
Their company took us **over**.

Let's talk the problem **over**.
Let's talk **over** the problem.
Let's talk it **over**.

She kicked the woman **out**.
She kicked **out** the woman.
She kicked her **out**.

I knocked his hat **off**.
I knocked **off** his hat.
I knocked it **off**.

I put the baby **down**.
I put **down** the baby.
I put her **down**.

We put a shelf **up**.
We put **up** a shelf.
We put it **up**.

Take what you said **back**!
Take **back** what you said!
Take it **back**!

Mom takes the old woman **in**.
Mom takes **in** the old woman.
Mom takes her **in**.

Did they take another man **on**?
Did they take **on** another man?
Did they take him **on**?

Take the hem **up**.
Take **up** the hem.
Take it **up**.

EXERCISE
19.15

Select the word or phrase that best completes each sentence.

1. Grandmother put on **it/an apron**.

2. We need to talk **it/these people** over.

3. I can't put up with **they/your insults**.

4. They'll kick off **them/the celebration** at ten o'clock.

5. We're going to take in **him/some boarders**.

6. The drug knocked **her/the doors** out.

7. Mr. Johnson took over **myself/our business**.

8. Put **we/the gun** down and turn around.

9. I'll measure the skirt, and you take **it/the hem** in.

10. We need to quiet **he/your mother** down.

Write three original sentences with the phrasal verbs in parentheses. Use the same noun in the first two and place the particle in the two different positions that are possible. Use a pronoun in the third sentence. Follow the example.

EXAMPLE: (TO PUT ON)

He put his gloves on.
He put on his gloves.
He put them on.

1. (to knock down)

_____

_____

_____

2. (to put up)

_____

_____

_____

3. (to take over)

_____

_____

_____

4. (to kick out)

_____

_____

_____

5. (to put down)

_____

_____

_____

6. (to take up)

_____

_____

_____

7. (to quiet down)

_____

_____

_____

8. (to knock off)

_____

_____

_____

You have had only a small sampling of phrasal verbs and the prepositions that help to form them. It is important to recognize phrasal verbs in order to determine their actual meaning. Frequently, someone who is learning English *assumes* the meaning of a sentence knowing the meaning of the basic verb in that sentence. But the verb could be a phrasal verb and, therefore, the meaning might escape the learner.

When you identify a phrasal verb in a sentence, look it up in a good dictionary. In the submeanings of the basic verb are often frequently used phrasal verbs. Here is a sample dictionary entry:

> **come** *verb* (**came, come, coming**) 1. to move to a place; to move here; to approach. 2. to arrive; to be present. –**to come about** 1. to happen or take place. 2. to turn to the opposite tack, as of a ship. –**to come to** 1. to revive; to regain consciousness. 2. to amount to

You will notice that *to come about* and *to come to* are both phrasal verbs, and the meaning of the phrases differ considerably from the meaning of the basic verb *come*. It is unwise to guess at the meaning of phrasal verbs. Rely on a good dictionary.

A variety of prepositional uses

You have encountered a wide variety of prepositions and learned how they are used. The following exercises will give you practice in identifying these varieties and in using them in context.

EXERCISE
19.17

Select the word or phrase that best completes each sentence.

1. We've been living in this house **because of/during/since/concerning** last March.

2. Coach is filled, but I can **to hope for/upgrade/agree with/into** you to first class.

3. The security guard **watched over/came up/agreed/agreed with** the new shipment of computers.

4. The electricity **gets on/on/came through with/has been off** for two days.

5. I often dream **about/for/on account of/off** my home in Ireland.

6. The frightened dog had been bitten **from/because/at/by** a snake.

7. The Constitution was finally ratified **by means of/by/at/on** this date.

8. I enjoy it here **along/at/in spite of/except** the bad weather.

9. There's a newspaper boy **of/at/on/onto** the front door.

10. We really look **at/forward to/with respect to/from** your next visit.

EXERCISE
19.18

Complete each sentence with any appropriate phrase.

1. Why do you spend so much time with _____?

2. Several fans came rushing up to _____.

3. Who asked for _____?

4. I usually get off _____.

5. I learned not to depend upon _____.

6. They should be in Detroit on _____.

7. The ship docked at _____.

8. Maria can't seem to forget about _____.

9. The sleek sailboat headed seaward and _____.

10. The new golf clubs belong to _____.

11. My relatives will return to New York in _____.

12. I haven't been in Europe since _____.

13. Did you remain in the United States during _____?

14. According to _____, there's going to be a storm today.

15. Somehow the new employee came up with _____.

16. The embarrassed girl decided to get back at _____.

17. Our flight arrived ahead of _____.

18. I don't like waiting for _____.

19. _____ upset the poor woman.

20. _____ in the pasture.

21. _____ was soon out of sight.

22. _____ wanted to belong to our fraternity.

23. _____ out of the conference hall.

24. Apart from my own parents, _____.

25. _____ toward the covered bridge.

Write an original sentence for each word or phrase in parentheses.

1. (onto) _____

2. (because of) _____

3. (after) _____

4. (homeward) _____

5. (concerning) _____

6. (to be interested in) _____

7. (to keep to oneself) _____

8. (at) _____

9. (in the middle of) _____

10. (out of sight) _____

11. (to be in) _____

12. (out of) _____

13. (instead of) _____

14. (by) _____

15. (down-and-out) _____

Capitalization

You are already aware that nouns fall into two general categories: proper nouns and common nouns. All nouns refer to persons, places, things, or ideas, but only certain nouns—proper nouns—are capitalized. All other nouns do not require capitalization (unless they occur at the beginning of a sentence). Let's look at the specifics that govern English **capitalization**.

A. The first word in a sentence is always capitalized. It does not matter if the sentence begins with a common noun or some other grammatical element.

> Terrell is my brother.
> The children are fast asleep.
> Are you going home now?
> When is that program on?

B. The first word in the title of any work of art (e.g., short story, article, book, TV program, film, painting, song, CD) is always capitalized. All the other words in the title are also capitalized, except for the articles, conjunctions, and prepositions. (However, if an article, conjunction, or preposition is the last word in a title, it must be capitalized.)

> "How to Buy a House"
> *The Adventures of Tom Sawyer*
> *Finding Nemo*
> "Take Me Out to the Ball Game"

C. The same rule applies to official names of businesses and institutions.

> The University of Illinois at Chicago
> Sears Roebuck and Company

D. First names, last names, initials, and personal titles of all kinds are always capitalized.

> Jason Kensington
> Ms. Alicia Jones
> Professor Rosa Morena
> Senator William Hayes
> General Dwight D. Eisenhower
> J. D. Powers

E. Titles that are not part of directly addressing the person who bears the title should not be capitalized. Compare the following:

I met a senator at the meeting.	Hello, Senator. How are you?
Is she the governor now?	It's good to see you, Governor Bejcek.
A captain entered the room.	Please sit down, Captain Bligh.

F. All days of the week, months of the year, and holidays are capitalized. Seasons and other categories of time are not.

Is it Monday already?	The weather is cooler in the fall.
My favorite month is June.	Where do you spend the winter?
She was born March 3, 2001.	How many years are in a decade?
Today is the Fourth of July.	The twentieth century was important.
I like Halloween.	It's a new millennium.

G. There are special rules for abbreviations for time. *B.C.* and *A.D.* are always capitalized. *B.C.* is used for eras or years that occurred *before Christ*. *A.D.* is used for eras or years that occurred *anno Domini* ("in the year of our Lord"), that is, beginning with the first year after Christ's birth. (B.C. follows the date; A.D. precedes the date.) A.M. and P.M. may or may not be capitalized. A.M. refers to the hours between midnight and noon, and P.M. refers to the hours between noon and midnight.

That happened in the fifth century B.C.
Columbus first landed in the New World in A.D. 1492.
They arrived exactly at 9:00 P.M.
I set my alarm for 7:35 A.M.

EXERCISE
20·1

Rewrite the words in each sentence that require capitalization.

1. john bought a new cadillac for his wife.

   _____

2. is colonel brubaker a friend of governor dassoff?

   _____

3. the president of the company was born on march tenth in the city of buffalo.

   _____

4. we stopped at a restaurant in chicago and ordered southern fried chicken.

   _____

5. in the summer the kids from whittier school play baseball at st. james park.

   _____

6. she invested some money last february with e. f. hutton in new york.

   _____

7. ms. assad met the general while he was touring the northern part of texas.

   _____

8. are mr. and mrs. cermak planning a large wedding for their daughter, britney?

   _____

9. ted bought us a coke and a hot dog for lunch.

_____

10. the students read *the adventures of huckleberry finn* in school last may.

_____

11. his sister was born on may tenth in cleveland memorial hospital.

_____

12. mia got up at precisely eight o'clock a.m.

_____

13. do you know the president of the corporation?

_____

14. if you see mayor yamamoto, tell him the governor has phoned again.

_____

15. we get the new york times every day but sunday.

_____

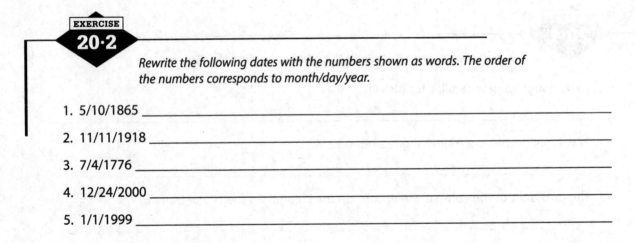

Rewrite the following dates with the numbers shown as words. The order of the numbers corresponds to month/day/year.

1. 5/10/1865 _____

2. 11/11/1918 _____

3. 7/4/1776 _____

4. 12/24/2000 _____

5. 1/1/1999 _____

Rewrite the following times as words and add A.M. or P.M. Look at the phrase in parentheses to help you decide which one.

6. 9:00 (in the morning) _____

7. 11:30 (in the evening) _____

8. 6:45 (at dawn) _____

9. 7:50 (at sunset) _____

10. 8:15 (during breakfast) _____

More on capitalization

To review, the first word of a sentence is always capitalized.

> **John** hurried to the drugstore.
> **She** always traveled with too much luggage.
> **Have** you spent a lot of time abroad?
> **Sometimes**, I wish I were a rock star.
> **Wealthy** people are not always intelligent people.

Proper nouns are always capitalized. If the proper noun is the name of a nation, the corresponding nouns referring to the nation's people and language are also capitalized.

> Proper names
> Joanna, Laurie, Paul, Sebastian, Tyler Johnson

Country	Nationality	Language
Germany	German	German
Spain	Spaniard	Spanish
Korea	Korean	Korean

Civil, military, religious, and professional titles, even when abbreviated, are capitalized when followed by a person's name.

> **Pope** Benedict XVI
> **President** Bill Clinton
> **Professor** Gibbons
> **Rabbi** Dahan
> **Dr.** Joanna Hughes
> **Ms.** Gloria Graham
> **Rev.** Lewis
> **Sir** Winston Churchill

When a person is addressed by his or her professional title, the title is capitalized.

> We beg you, **General**, to take our opinion into consideration.
> **Madam President**, I'd like to know what your budget proposal is.

The pronoun *I* is always capitalized. This is also true of the interjection *O*.

> Yesterday, **I** saw Megan in her wedding dress, and **O**, what a sight she was!

Geographical names are capitalized.

> the Allegheny Mountains
> the Champs-Élysées
> the Danube
> El Rastro
> Madrid
> the Mediterranean Sea
> the Mississippi River
> North Korea
> the Pacific Ocean
> the Sahara Desert
> the Tai Po River
> the Twin Cities
> Washington, D.C.

Religions, holy books, believers (as a group), holy days, and terms that refer to deities are capitalized.

Hinduism, Hindu, Brahman, Shiva
Islam, Koran, Muslim, Ramadan, Allah
Christianity, the Bible, Christian, Christmas, God

Names of organizations, institutions, government agencies, companies, as well as their abbreviations, acronyms, and shorter versions of their names, are capitalized.

the ACLU
Alpha Delta Kappa
Boy Scouts of America
the Red Cross
the FCC
NYPD
UNESCO
IBM
the Rand Corp.
the Yanks

Days of the week, months of the year, and holidays are capitalized. The seasons, however, are not usually capitalized.

Sunday
Monday
April
October
Veterans Day
Thanksgiving
summer
winter

Historical documents, events, periods, and cultural movements are capitalized.

Declaration of Independence
Magna Carta
World War II
the Renaissance
Cubism

However, ideologies and related terms not used as part of a proper-noun phrase are not capitalized.

IDEOLOGIES   democracy, democrat, democratic; communism, communist
PROPER NOUNS German Democratic Republic, Communist China

Names of trademarked merchandise are capitalized.

Adbusters
Adidas
Monopoly
Nike
Oreo
Post-it
Puffs
Velcro
Yahoo

Words derived from proper names are capitalized.

> Machiavellian
> Europeanization
> Americanized

The titles of poems, songs, movies, books, plays, and essays are capitalized. Articles, conjunctions, and prepositions are not capitalized unless they are the first word of the title. Prepositions are capitalized if they are the last word of the title.

> "The Second Coming"
> "Take the 'A' Train"
> *The Motorcycle Diaries*
> *The Grapes of Wrath*
> *Love's Labour's Lost*
> "How the Palestinian-Jewish Conflict Began"

The first word in quoted material is usually capitalized.

> She turned around and screamed, "Is there anybody out there!"
> A timid voice asked, "Is there more food, sir?"

The names of heavenly bodies, including the planets, are capitalized, but the words *earth*, *moon*, and *sun* are not.

> Andromeda Galaxy
> Milky Way
> Scorpio
> Jupiter

> The **earth** was parched and cracked; the drought had done its work.
> The **earth** is the third planet from the sun.

General compass directions are not capitalized unless they refer to specific geographical locations.

> Lyon is **south** of Paris.
> They walked in an **easterly** direction.
> The red team represents the **West**.
> They came from the **South**.
> They came from the **Southern** states.

The names of man-made objects, such as bridges, planes, spacecraft, ships, roads, monuments, and buildings, are capitalized.

> the Brooklyn Bridge
> the *Spirit of St. Louis*
> *Apollo 13*
> the *Santa María*
> Interstate 35
> the Lincoln Memorial
> the Museum of Natural Science
> the Sears Tower

EXERCISE 20.3

Rewrite each sentence, using correct capitalization.

1. teresa malcolm is president of the ford rotary club.

_____

2. in three weeks, we will be traveling through france, switzerland, and spain.

_____

_____

3. the night sky was so clear we could see the entire moon, venus, and jupiter.

_____

_____

4. as soon as he got home, patrick felt like putting on his new adidas swimsuit.

_____

_____

5. the second world war lasted nearly six years.

_____

6. the novel we bought at the airport was *the da vinci code*.

_____

7. i visited the empire state building when i was in new york.

_____

8. thelma and john saw the launch of the *uss enterprise*.

_____

9. the naacp is a prominent organization based in the united states.

_____

10. they told her, "we don't like the proposal you've written."

_____

_____

EXERCISE 20.4

Rewrite each sentence, using correct capitalization.

1. marilyn is the president of the ladies of grace at her church.

_____

2. some restaurants in los angeles serve americanized european food.

_____

3. members of all faiths gathered on campus to protest, including christians, jews, muslims, and hindus.

_____

_____

4. "the red wheelbarrow," by william carlos williams, is one of the most profound poems i've read.

_____

_____

5. they came from the eastern states in search of gold.

_____

6. we read *of mice and men* last week for class.

_____

7. the cia agent said he often works with fbi investigators, as well as with representatives of the faa.

_____

_____

8. a speaker from the national transportation safety board gave a presentation on the most common accidents that took place on interstate 66.

_____

_____

Subjunctive mood

The **subjunctive** is used in some limited but important ways. It is used to express a demand, suggestion, or request (*I suggest you be on time.*); to express a wish (*If only Jim were here.*); or to set a condition for a future action (*We would leave if the storm would let up.*). To understand these uses, you need to examine the subjunctive conjugations.

The present tense subjunctive is formed from the infinitive of a verb minus the particle word *to*. Notice that each pronoun requires the identical verb form:

Pronoun	to be	to go	to have	to work
I	be	go	have	work
you	be	go	have	work
he, she, it	be	go	have	work
we	be	go	have	work
they	be	go	have	work

The past tense subjunctive is formed from the plural past tense of either a regular or an irregular verb. Notice again that each pronoun requires the identical verb form:

Pronoun	to be	to go	to have	to work
I	were	went	had	worked
you	were	went	had	worked
he, she, it	were	went	had	worked
we	were	went	had	worked
they	were	went	had	worked

A third subjunctive conjugation is formed with the word *would* together with an infinitive, or *would have* plus a *past participle*. Look at these examples:

Indicative Sentences	Subjunctive Sentences
He is here.	He would be here.
She buys a book.	She would buy a book.
We have spoken.	We would have spoken.
I have played.	I would have played.

The present tense subjunctive is used to express a demand, suggestion, or request. In these instances, the subjunctive must be used in place of a regular present tense conjugation. Notice that it is optional to use the conjunction *that*. Consider these sentences:

She demanded you *be* on time tomorrow. (not *are*)
She demanded **that** you *be* on time tomorrow.

I suggested he *come* by for a visit. (not *comes*)
I suggested **that** he *come* by for a visit.

The judge requested the lawyer *have* the documents prepared. (not *has*)
The judge requested **that** the lawyer *have* the documents prepared.

This same structure is used with a few other similar verbs: *to command, to order, to propose*. The past tense subjunctive is often used to express a wish:

I wish Ahmed *were* my brother.
She wished she *had* enough money for a car.
If only my mother *worked* for him, too.
The children wish it already *were* Christmas.

Note that a wish can be expressed by beginning a sentence with *if* or *if only*.

You should be aware that *were* is sometimes avoided in casual conversation and is frequently replaced by the simple past tense verb *was* with singular subjects (e.g., *I wish Ahmed **was** my brother*.).

The subjunctive formed with *would* is used when there are two clauses in a sentence and one of them is an *if*-clause. This kind of sentence sets a condition in one clause for the action to occur in the second clause. The past tense subjunctive is used in the *if*-clause. The word *would* appears in the clause that does *not* begin with *if*. Some examples:

If Nadia *were* here, Mother *would be* very happy.
If I *had* a million dollars, I *would buy* a big house.
She *would travel* to Spain if her uncle *invited* her.
Mr. Perez *would learn* English if he *lived* in Texas.

These sentences mean that the action would happen in the present or the future if the conditions were right.

This would happen if these conditions were right.
She *would travel* to Spain if her uncle *invited* her.

The same format is required even if the verbs are structured like the present perfect tense (*I have gone, you have seen*, etc.):

If Nadia *had been* here, Mother *would have been* very happy.
Mr. Perez *would have learned* English if he *had lived* in Texas.

These sentences mean that the action would have happened in the past if the conditions had been right.

This would have happened if these conditions had been right.
Mr. Perez *would have learned* English if he *had lived* in Texas.

Combine the phrase in parentheses with the indicative sentence. Change the verb to the present tense subjunctive.

EXAMPLE: (I demand . . .) He gives me the money.
              I demand he give me the money.

1. (She demands . . .) Forrest returns home by 5:00 P.M.

   _____

2. (The man suggests . . .) You wear a shirt and tie to work.

   _____

3. (They requested . . .) I am a little more helpful.

   _____

4. (My father demanded . . .) We pay for the damage to the car.

   _____

5. (Did he suggest . . . ?) She comes in for an interview.

   _____

6. (Roger demands that . . .) The boy has enough to eat.

   _____

7. (Did Mother request that . . . ?) Her will is read aloud.

   _____

8. (He has suggested that . . .) We are trained for other jobs.

   _____

9. (Who demanded that . . . ?) The statue is erected on this site.

   _____

10. (Did he suggest . . . ?) The mayor finds a new assistant.

    _____

Complete each phrase below with any appropriate sentence.

1. He demands _____.

2. We suggest _____.

3. Dwayne requests _____.

4. I must demand that _____.

5. Will you suggest to him that _____?

EXERCISE

21·3

Rewrite the following sentences in the past tense subjunctive. Begin each one with the phrase I wish.

1. Becca is here today.

   _____

2. We are having a big party for Grandmother.

   _____

3. He has enough money to buy a condo.

   _____

4. My friends have come for a visit.

   _____

5. Darnell doesn't need an operation.

   _____

6. His uncle drives slowly.

   _____

7. I can borrow some money from you.

   _____

8. The weather is not so rainy.

   _____

9. They help me every day.

   _____

10. She wants to go on vacation with me.

   _____

EXERCISE

21·4

Combine the following phrases with the sentence shown in parentheses.

EXAMPLE: If you were here, . . . (I am happy.)

If you were here, I would be happy.

1. If Evelyn were older, . . . (Garrett asks her out.)

   _____

2. If I had more time, . . . (I go to the store.)

   _____

3. If you spoke louder, ... (He hears you.)

_____

4. If it were colder, ... (I turn on the heat.)

_____

5. If my brother came along, ... (He helps me wash the car.)

_____

6. She would make a cake if ... (It is Erin's birthday.)

_____

7. Gary would rent an apartment here if ... (He likes the neighborhood.)

_____

8. The boys would play soccer if ... (Someone has a soccer ball.)

_____

9. I would speak Spanish if ... (I live in Puerto Rico.)

_____

10. The doctor would come to our house if ... (The baby is sick.)

_____

EXERCISE
21·5

Rewrite the following sentences using the present perfect tense for the verbs.

EXAMPLE: He would buy a car if he had the money.

He would have bought a car if he had had the money.

1. She would sell me her bicycle if she bought a new one.

_____

2. If you came early you would meet my cousin.

_____

3. If only Karen were here.

_____

4. The children would play in the yard if it were not raining.

_____

5. If the lawyer found the document he would win his case.

_____

6. If only my mother were able to walk again.

_____

7. Juanita would travel to New York if she got the job.

_____

8. If he found the wallet he would give it to Rick.

_____

9. Jackie would want to come along if he had more time.

_____

10. If only they understood the problem.

_____

Hypothetical conditional

The sentences you will study in this unit have two parts: an *if* clause and a main clause. The *if* clause consists of a condition that is either slightly possible or impossible; the main clause states the consequences of the condition mentioned in the *if* clause.

> SLIGHTLY POSSIBLE: If he felt better, he would come with us.
> IMPOSSIBLE: If my aunt were still alive, she would be a hundred years old today.

To form a hypothetical conditional that refers to present or future time, use the simple past tense in the *if* clause; use a modal verb (either *would*, *might*, or *could*) and the base form of the main verb in the main clause.

> If he studied more, he would earn better grades.

In formal English, *were* is used in the *if* clause, even following the first- and third-person singular pronouns.

> If I were you, I would look for a job.
> If she **were** here, we could leave.

To form a hypothetical conditional that refers to past time, use the past perfect in the *if* clause; use *would have*, *might have*, or *could have* and the perfect/passive form of the main verb in the main clause.

> If they had asked earlier, I could have helped them.

EXERCISE
21·6

Complete each conditional sentence with the correct form of the verb in parentheses. Each sentence refers to either present or future time. In the main clause, use would *before the base form of the verb.*

1. If I _____ (be) the director, I _____ (change) the policy.

2. If you _____ (check) your e-mail more often, you _____ (know) about the assignments.

3. If we _____ (commute) together, the drive _____ (cost) less.

4. If he _____ (have) more time, he _____ (go) to the game with us.

5. If Emma _____ (visit) us on Thursday, she _____ (meet) my sisters.

6. If you _____ (mail) the package today, they _____ (receive) it by Friday.

7. If they _____ (lower) their prices, more people _____ (shop) there.

8. If we _____ (earn) more money, we _____ (buy) a new car.

9. If he _____ (exercise) more frequently, he _____ (be) healthier.

10. If my grandfather _____ (be) here, he _____ (tell) a joke.

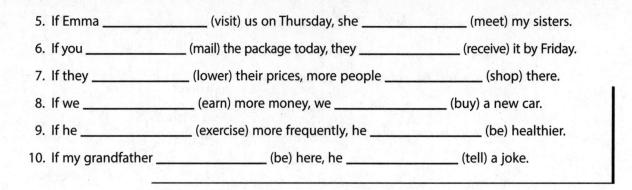

EXERCISE
21·7

Complete each conditional sentence with the correct form of the verb in parentheses. Each sentence refers to past time. In the main clause, use would have *before the perfect/passive form of the verb.*

1. If it _____ (rain), they _____ (cancel) the game.

2. If you _____ (be) on the roller coaster, you _____ (be) sick.

3. If I _____ (know) about the detour, I _____ (take) another route.

4. If she _____ (follow) the directions, she _____ (be) on time.

5. If I _____ (study) harder, I _____ (pass) the exam.

6. If he _____ (be) more productive, he _____ (receive) a promotion.

7. If they _____ (raise) tuition, the students _____ (protest).

8. If they _____ (repair) the car yesterday, we _____ (leave) today.

9. If you _____ (revise) your paper, your main points _____ (be) clearer.

10. If I _____ (be) the manager, I _____ (hire) Yoshi.

The subjunctive mood

To review, the English subjunctive mood has three forms. One is the infinitive of a verb with the omission of the particle word **to**: **(to) go**, **(to) be**, and so on. The second form is the past tense of a verb. In the case of the verb **to be**, only the plural past tense (**were**) is used in the subjunctive. The third form uses the auxiliary **would** followed by an infinitive or by **have** and a past participle. Let's look at these three forms:

Infinitive	Form 1	Form 2	Form 3
to be	be	were	would be/would have been
to come	come	came	would come/would have come
to go	go	went	would go/would have gone
to speak	speak	spoke	would speak/would have spoken

The infinitive form of the subjunctive is used in sentences that convey a suggestion, a request, a recommendation, or a proposal. Note that the conjunction **that** is optional in such sentences. For example:

I suggest she find another way to get to work.   *not* she finds
Would you recommend that **they be** allowed to stay here?   *not* they are

The past-tense form of the subjunctive is used to express a wish or a condition and is often combined with a subjunctive clause that includes either **would** plus an infinitive or **would have** plus a past participle:

- A wish

    If only Jack were here with us now.
    If you **could** just try to understand my perspective.
    If only he **had tried** a little harder.

- A condition

    If the rain let up, we would go out for a long walk.
    My son would have been here if he **had known** that you needed help.
    If you **were** my son, I would give you the same advice.

Notice that a "wish" statement often includes the word **only**.

In a conditional statement, the **if** clause sets the condition, and the accompanying clause is the "result" if the condition is met.

      condition   **result**

If she were well, she would pay us a visit.

EXERCISE
21·8

Complete each of the following sentences with any appropriate phrase.

1. I suggest _____ .

2. No one recommended she _____ .

3. The lawyer requested it _____ .

4. The mayor proposed that _____ .

5. Would you suggest that the law _____ ?

EXERCISE
21·9

Using the following verbs provided, write sentences that express a wish.

1. to find _____

2. to be _____

3. to be able to _____

4. to be seen _____

5. to have driven _____

Using the following pairs of verbs provided, write sentences that express a condition and a result; include a clause that begins with if.

EXAMPLE: to sing/to listen

If she sang in tune, I would listen to her song.

6. to bring/to eat

_____

7. permit/to love to chat

_____

8. have insisted/have not left

_____

9. to have to/to understand

_____

10. to be/to be

_____

Comparatives and superlatives

The **comparative** of an adjective or adverb describes a comparison of one person or thing with another person or thing. Most comparatives require an *-er* ending, for example, *taller, shallower*. If the adjective or adverb ends in a single consonant, that consonant is doubled before adding the ending: *mad → madder*. If an adjective or adverb ends in *-y*, change it to *-i* then add *-er*: *funny → funnier*.

The **superlative** of an adjective or adverb shows the greatest degree of the meaning of the adjective or adverb. Most superlatives end in *-est*: *tallest, shallowest*. If the adjective or adverb ends in a single consonant, that consonant is doubled before adding the ending: *mad → maddest*. If an adjective or adverb ends in *-y*, change it to *-i* then add *-est*: *funny → funniest*.

Both the comparative and the superlative are formed in another way by using *more* or *most*. The word *more* is placed in front of the adjective or adverb to form the comparative, and the word *most* is placed in front of the adjective or adverb to form the superlative: *more interesting/most interesting, more logical/most logical*. This formation is used primarily with words that are of two syllables or more and that come to English from French, Latin, or other foreign sources.

The other formation (*long, longer, longest*) is Anglo-Saxon in origin. Compare these lists of comparatives and superlatives:

Anglo-Saxon Origin		Foreign Origin	
bigger	biggest	more critical	most critical
finer	finest	more dangerous	most dangerous
grander	grandest	more dynamic	most dynamic
happier	happiest	more fruitful	most fruitful
jollier	jolliest	more harmonious	most harmonious
kinder	kindest	more hopeless	most hopeless
mightier	mightiest	more intense	most intense
poorer	poorest	more sensitive	most sensitive
smaller	smallest	more visible	most visible
thinner	thinnest	more willing	most willing

Note that words that end in *-ful*, *-less*, and *-ing* use *more* and *most* to form the comparative and superlative, even though such words do not have a foreign language origin.

There are a few irregular formations that must simply be memorized:

Positive	Comparative	Superlative
bad	worse	worst
far	farther/further	farthest/furthest
good	better	best
little (amount)	less	least
many	more	most
much	more	most
well	better	best

It is possible to use a comparative in a sentence without mentioning the person or thing with which another person or thing is being compared. Look at these examples:

> Jorge is a lot *taller*.
> My sister was *thinner* a few years ago.

In such sentences the person or thing compared is assumed. When stating the person or thing with which another person or thing is being compared, use the word *than*:

> Jorge is a lot taller *than* Michelle.
> My sister was thinner a few years ago *than* she is now.

The formation of both adjectives and adverbs in the comparative is identical. The difference is how they are used in a sentence:

> My car is faster than your car. (adjective)
> She runs faster than you do. (adverb)

With adverbs that end in *-ly*, both forms of comparative and superlative are possible:

> He spoke *quicker*./He spoke *more quickly*.
> He spoke *the quickest*./He spoke *the most quickly*.

The superlative adjective or adverb frequently is preceded by the word *the*:

> Lars is *the* strongest boy.
> She is *the* most beautiful girl here.

When the superlative is a predicative adjective and not followed by a noun, the word *the* can be omitted:

> Lars is strongest when he's not tired.
> She is most beautiful when she wakes up in the morning.

Comparative and superlative adverbs that are formed with *more* and *most* require the adverbial ending *-ly*:

> more willingly
> most capably

Rewrite each sentence with the italicized word changed to the comparative.

1. This freight train is moving *slowly*.

   _____

2. My *young* brother is a mathematician.

   _____

3. Where is the *old* man you told me about?

   _____

4. Fanny swims *well*, but she still cannot dive.

   _____

5. Hunter's cold is *bad* today.

   _____

6. They have *much* to do before the end of the day.

   _____

7. I think Robbie is *intelligent*.

   _____

8. The new employee is *careless* about his work.

   _____

9. She has *many* friends in the city.

   _____

10. This project is *critical* to the success of the company.

    _____

11. Clarice just can't speak *quietly*.

    _____

12. We have a *big* house out in the country.

    _____

13. Do you think that kind of language is *sinful*?

    _____

14. The inn is *far* down this road.

    _____

15. Your friend is *reckless*.

    _____

Use each set of words to write a sentence. Make a comparison using *than*.
(You may use different forms of the words listed.)

EXAMPLE: Maurice/Ingrid/speak/loudly
Maurice speaks louder than Ingrid.

1. cats/dogs/run/fast

_____

2. my brother/your sister/write/beautiful

_____

3. you/I/learn/quick

_____

4. Rashad/Steven/sell/many cars

_____

5. New York/Chicago/big

_____

6. Ginger/Fred/dance/well

_____

7. lake/sky/look/blue

_____

8. our team/your team/play/capable

_____

9. the husband/the wife/seem/jealous

_____

10. Mr. Espinosa/Ms. VanDam/have/little money

_____

Rewrite each sentence with the italicized word changed to the superlative.

1. Carlos is the *short* boy in the last row.

   _____

2. Paris is *beautiful*.

   _____

3. The white stallion runs *fast*.

   _____

4. Is Russia a *large* country in Europe?

   _____

5. Is this an *interesting* article?

   _____

6. They say that the CEO is *rich*.

   _____

7. Smoking is *bad* for your health.

   _____

8. The soprano sings *softly*.

   _____

9. The vice president spoke *brilliantly*.

   _____

10. Is the planet Pluto *far*?

    _____

11. Larry gets up *early*.

    _____

12. She is *systematic* about everything she does.

    _____

13. Brian is a *cute* boy.

    _____

14. Laura plays the violin *well*.

    _____

15. That book is *boring*.

    _____

Rewrite the words as a sentence. Form the adjective or adverb as a superlative and add any necessary words.

EXAMPLE: Dennis/jump/high
Dennis jumps the highest.

1. Melanie/funny/girl/in class

   _____

2. what/distant/planet

   _____

3. your/handwriting/bad

   _____

4. men/at the party/eat/much

   _____

5. Olive/smart/all/girls/in school

   _____

6. Mozart/compose/beautiful/music

   _____

7. grandmother/bake/delicious/cakes

   _____

8. pickpocket/steal/many/wallets

   _____

9. Raj/think/this symphony/boring

   _____

10. Janice/my/good/friend

    _____

Rewrite each sentence twice, first changing the adjective or adverb to the comparative and then to the superlative.

1. My coffee is hot.

   _____

   _____

2. Is this math problem difficult?

_____

_____

3. I feel well today.

_____

_____

4. Life in the jungle is dangerous.

_____

_____

5. This village is poor.

_____

_____

6. Mr. Hong always has little time.

_____

_____

7. The choir sang a merry song.

_____

_____

8. She wore a shabby dress.

_____

_____

9. Bert has many friends.

_____

_____

10. She can speak calmly about it.

_____

_____

Conjunctions

Conjunctions join words, phrases, and sentences together. First, let's look at some of the commonly used *coordinating conjunctions*: *and, but, or, nor, for, so,* and *yet.* Notice how they can combine words, phrases, or complete sentences:

Combined Words	Combined Phrases	Combined Sentences
Don *or* Norma	healthy again *yet* unable to work	We remained by the fire, *but* Lance went to the park to skate.
meat *and* potatoes		

Correlative conjunctions are also important. They consist of a pair of words that appear in different parts of the same sentence. The most commonly used are *both . . . and, either . . . or, neither . . . nor,* and *not only . . . but also* (sometimes stated as *not only . . . also*). Examples:

> *Both* Yoko *and* Marco have problems.
> *Either* you work hard *or* you leave.
> *Neither* the boys *nor* the girls wanted to end the game.
> You are *not only* a poor loser *but also* a bad soccer player.

Dependent (or subordinating) clauses consist of a subject and a verb. But these clauses usually cannot stand alone. Dependent clauses are preceded by *subordinating conjunctions* and are combined with an independent clause. The list of subordinating conjunctions is long. Here are some of the most commonly used:

after	before	since	until
although	even though	so that	when
as if	how	than	whenever
as long as	if	that	where
as though	now that	though	wherever
because	once	unless	while

Let's look at some example sentences:

> *After* she arrived, Alberto was the first to greet her.
> *Although* he was tired, he continued to run.
> I just don't know *how* you do it.
> *If* you don't pay your rent, you'll have to move.
> Bob doesn't know *where* she lives.

EXERCISE
23·1

Combine each pair of sentences with the appropriate coordinating conjunction:
and, but, or, nor, for, so, *or* yet.

1. That's my brother. The woman next to him is his wife.

   _____

2. We ran into the tent. Our clothes were already soaked by the storm.

   _____

3. Should we watch TV tonight? Should we go see a movie?

   _____

4. She began to cry. The book ended so sadly.

   _____

5. I hurried as fast as I could. I arrived home late as usual.

   _____

6. The red car was already sold. Kim bought the blue one.

   _____

7. Our dog likes to play in the yard. Our cat prefers to stay in the house.

   _____

8. Milo lives on Oak Street. His brother lives nearby.

   _____

9. Their credit was very poor. They decided to buy a piano anyway.

   _____

10. I love the snowy beauty of winter. I hate the heat of summer.

   _____

EXERCISE
23·2

Fill in the blanks with the appropriate correlative conjunctions: both . . . and,
either . . . or, neither . . . nor, *or* not only . . . but also.

1. _____ Maribeth _____ I will ever visit them again.

2. I want to buy _____ a new blouse _____ a new skirt.

3. They were already introduced to _____ Carol _____ her mother.

4. You _____ work too little _____ spend too much money.

5. _____ Father _____ Mother became ill during the cruise.

6. She wants _____ your help _____ your advice.

7. Reggie _____ broke his leg _____ bruised both arms.

8. It's always _____ too hot _____ too cold for you.

9. _____ the kitchen _____ the bathroom need to be cleaned.

10. _____ Cary _____ Kelly showed up at the party.

EXERCISE
23·3

Complete each sentence with a dependent clause to follow each subordinating conjunction.

1. She left for home after _____ .

2. When _____ , Pedro started to laugh.

3. I won't help you unless _____ .

4. Do you know where _____ ?

5. Once _____ , I was able to relax.

6. Chris closed the book before _____ .

7. You can stay up late as long as _____ .

8. While _____ , he relaxed under a tree.

9. I don't remember if _____ .

10. Now that _____ , they often go to the theater.

EXERCISE
23·4

Write two original sentences with each of the following conjunctions.

1. but _____

_____

2. unless _____

_____

3. neither . . . nor _____

_____

4. where _____

_____

5. how _____

_____

6. and _____

_____

7. not only . . . but also _____

_____

8. for _____

_____

9. when _____

_____

10. either . . . or _____

_____

Using conjunctions

Conjunctions connect words, phrases, and clauses. But not all conjunctions function in the same way. This unit describes the types of English conjunctions and how they are used in sentences.

Coordinating conjunctions

Coordinating conjunctions connect words or groups of words of the same grammatical type, such as verbs, nouns, and adjectives, or of the same grammatical structure, such as phrases and clauses. These are the coordinating conjunctions: *and, but, or, yet, for, so,* and *nor*.

If a coordinating conjunction connects more than two elements, it is generally placed between the last two elements of the series. The other elements are separated by commas.

> In order to find the treasure, you will need a compass, a shovel, a map,
>   **and** a lamp.
> He wanted to buy a hat, a pair of gloves, **or** some new boots.

Coordinating conjunctions can also connect other elements, such as infinitives and infinitive phrases.

> She wants to watch a movie **or** (to) listen to music.
> It's difficult to listen to him **and** to know that he is lying.

If a coordinating conjunction connects independent clauses, the conjunction is usually preceded by a comma. An independent clause is one that can stand by itself and make complete sense. If a coordinating conjunction connects independent clauses, it creates a **compound sentence**.

> She spoke to him harshly, **but** there was real pity for him in her heart.
> Tom was exhausted, **yet** he found enough strength to lead them out of the woods.

If the subject, verb, or auxiliary is the same in both clauses, the one in the second clause can be omitted. When this occurs, the comma can be omitted.

> He spoke slowly **but** [he] pronounced each word in anger.
> The men worked on the house **and** [worked] on the shed in the backyard.
> Someone is knocking at the door **and** [is] calling your name.

Conjunctions and their meaning

But and *yet* indicate a contrast between the elements they connect.

> His knee was hurting, **but** he finished the race anyway.
> The grape juice was bitter **yet** hydrating.

Or indicates a choice or offers alternatives between the elements it connects.

> On Sunday, we will go to the lake **or** to the river.
> He wants a new bicycle **or** some roller skates for Christmas.

Nor typically connects negative statements. Note that if an independent clause follows *nor*, its subject and verb are inverted.

> They did not fix my camera, **nor** did they fix my lens.
> She did not tell us where she was traveling to, **nor** did she tell us how long she would be gone.

The conjunction *for* is generally synonymous with *because*. *So* has a meaning similar to *therefore*. *For* and *so* can also express a cause-and-effect relationship.

> She could not think clearly, **for** her heart was so full of anger.
> They could not find the car keys, **so** they broke the window to get in.

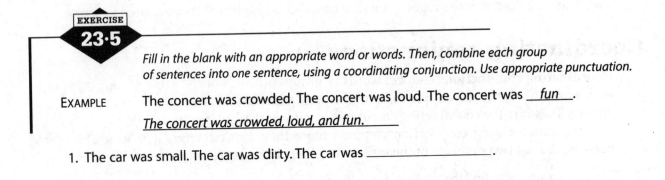

EXERCISE
23·5

Fill in the blank with an appropriate word or words. Then, combine each group of sentences into one sentence, using a coordinating conjunction. Use appropriate punctuation.

EXAMPLE   The concert was crowded. The concert was loud. The concert was ___fun___.
The concert was crowded, loud, and fun.

1. The car was small. The car was dirty. The car was _____.

   _____

2. The country lane was narrow. The country lane was long. The country lane was

   _____.

   _____

3. I dislike living downtown because of the noise. I dislike living downtown because of the

   crime. I dislike living downtown because of the _____.

   _____

4. The Dominican Republic has _____. The Dominican Republic has palm trees.

   The Dominican Republic has pretty beaches. The Dominican Republic has tropical birds.

   _____

   _____

   _____

5. I like to become acquainted with people from other countries. I like to become acquainted with customs from other countries. I like to become acquainted with _____ from other countries.

_____

_____

EXERCISE
23·6

Combine each group of sentences into one sentence, using a coordinating conjunction. Remember that using a coordinating conjunction allows you to omit repeated words.

EXAMPLE   Peter is staying home. Peter is sleeping.
Peter is staying home and sleeping.

1. Susan washed the dishes. Susan put the food away.

_____

2. Peter opened the door. Peter greeted the guests.

_____

3. Ralph is painting the garage door. Ralph is cleaning the brushes.

_____

4. Simon is generous. Simon is handsome. Simon is intelligent.

_____

5. Please try to make less noise. Please try to have some respect for others.

_____

6. She gave him chocolates on Monday. She gave him a CD on Tuesday. She gave him a bracelet on Wednesday.

_____

7. While we were in Los Angeles, we went to a concert. While we were in Los Angeles, we ate Mexican food. While we were in Los Angeles, we visited old friends.

_____

_____

8. I should have finished my project. I should have cleaned my car.

_____

9. He preferred to play poker. Sometimes he preferred to spend time in museums.

_____

10. I like water. I don't like soda.

_____

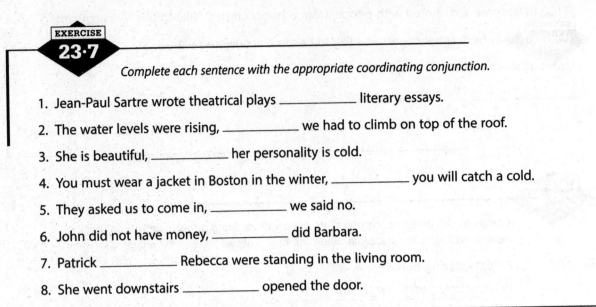

Complete each sentence with the appropriate coordinating conjunction.

1. Jean-Paul Sartre wrote theatrical plays _____ literary essays.

2. The water levels were rising, _____ we had to climb on top of the roof.

3. She is beautiful, _____ her personality is cold.

4. You must wear a jacket in Boston in the winter, _____ you will catch a cold.

5. They asked us to come in, _____ we said no.

6. John did not have money, _____ did Barbara.

7. Patrick _____ Rebecca were standing in the living room.

8. She went downstairs _____ opened the door.

Correlative conjunctions

Correlative conjunctions follow the same set of rules coordinating conjunctions do. Both types of conjunctions function in the same way, except that correlative conjunctions are composed of two parts. The most common of these conjunctions are *both . . . and . . .* , *not only . . . but also . . .* , *either . . . or . . .* , and *neither . . . nor . . . .*

When two subjects are connected by *not only . . . but also . . .* , *either . . . or . . .* , or *neither . . . nor . . .* , the subject that is closer to the verb determines whether the verb is singular or plural. However, when two subjects are connected with *both . . . and . . .* , the verb is always plural.

> **Not only** my sister **but also** my cousin is here.
> **Not only** my sister **but also** my parents are here.
>
> **Either** the cops **or** the robber was blamed for the victim's death.
> **Either** my sister **or** my parents were in attendance.
>
> **Neither** my sister **nor** my cousin is here.
> **Neither** my sister **nor** my parents are here.
>
> **Both** my sister **and** my cousin are here.
> **Both** the winter **and** the spring have been cold and damp.

These examples illustrate correlative conjunctions used with the subjects of the sentences. They can also be used to join objects in a sentence.

> He teased **both** my sister **and** my cousin.
> She bought **not only** a new blouse **but also** a new skirt.
> I spoke to **either** your wife **or** your daughter.
> We saw **neither** the crime **nor** the criminal.

Complete each sentence with is *or* are.

1. Both the coach and the player _____ present.

2. Neither the coach nor the player _____ present.

3. Not only the coach but also the players _____ present.

4. Not only the coach but also the player _____ present.

5. Either the players or the coach _____ using the weight room.

6. Either the coach or the players _____ using the weight room.

Combine each pair of sentences into one sentence, using a correlative conjunction.

1. She does not have a pen. She does not have a ruler.

   _____

2. The giant panda faces extinction. The white tiger faces extinction.

   _____

3. We could drive. We could take the bus.

   _____

4. She wants to buy a Honda. She wants to buy a Toyota.

   _____

5. We can fix dinner for them at home. We can take them to a restaurant.

   _____

6. Joseph is absent. Peter is absent.

   _____

7. Joe is not in class today. Pedro is not in class today.

   _____

8. You can have tea. You can have coffee.

   _____

9. Roger enjoys playing Nintendo. Sam enjoys playing Nintendo.

   _____

10. The President's press secretary will not confirm the story. The President's press secretary will not deny the story.

    _____

11. Coal is a nonrenewable natural resource. Petroleum is a nonrenewable natural resource.

   _____

12. Bird flu is a dangerous disease. Malaria is a dangerous disease.

   _____

13. Her parents don't know where she is. Her boyfriend doesn't know where she is.

   _____

14. According to the weather report, it will rain tomorrow. It will be windy tomorrow.

   _____

EXERCISE
23·10

Underline the conjunction(s) in each sentence.

1. He did not know whether he was on the right street or completely lost, for night was coming and the streets were getting dark.

2. She was hungry and wanted either a cup of water or a glass of lemonade.

3. The movie was not only interesting but beautiful, and it inspired me.

4. Neither argument nor begging would change the jury's verdict, but the defendant appealed the case.

5. Both the teacher and the students were eager to see the play, but unfortunately it was sold out.

Complete sentences are separated by a period, not a comma.

> It was very cold. He put on a sweater.
> We borrowed some money. We bought a used car.

However, you can use a comma before a coordinating conjunction to combine two sentences into a single sentence. If the subjects of the two sentences are identical, the subject of the second sentence can be omitted. In such a case, the comma is not used.

> It was very cold, **and** he put on a sweater.
> We borrowed money **and** bought a used car.

If the sentences are very short, the comma can be omitted.

> The concert ended **and** he left.

EXERCISE
23·11

Punctuate the following sentences, adding commas and periods and capitalizing letters where necessary. If a sentence needs no changes, mark it with an "X".

1. The men walked the boys ran.

2. Sylvia came to the meeting her brother stayed home.

3. Sylvia came to the meeting but her brother stayed home.

4. The professor spoke and the students listened.

5. The professor spoke the students listened.

6. His academic record was outstanding yet he was not accepted into Harvard.

7. Her academic record was outstanding she was not accepted into Harvard but she was not too unhappy about it.

8. We had to go to the grocery store for some milk and bread.

9. We had to go to the grocery store for there was nothing to eat in the fridge.

10. A barometer measures air pressure a thermometer measures temperature.

11. The Egyptians had good sculptors archeologists have found marvelous statues buried in the pyramids.

12. Murdock made many promises but he had no intention of keeping them he was known to be a liar.

13. I always enjoyed studying geography in high school so I decided to pursue it in college.

14. Cecilia is in serious legal trouble for she had no car insurance at the time of the accident.

15. Last night, Marie had to study for an exam so she went to a coffeehouse.

16. The team of scientists has not finished analyzing the virus yet their work will not be published until later this year.

17. You have nothing to fear for they are strong and united.

18. She threw the book out the window she had failed the exam again so she'd ruined her chances of bringing up her grade in the class.

19. Sophia struggled to keep her head above water she tried to yell but the water kept getting in her mouth.

20. The hurricane was devastating tall buildings crumbled and crashed to the ground.

21. It was a wonderful day at the park the children swam in the river collected rocks and insects and laughed all day the older kids played soccer the adults prepared the food supervised the children and played cards for a short while.

22. Caterpillars eat plants and can cause damage to some crops but adult butterflies feed primarily on flowers and do not cause any harm.

23. Both Jesse and I had many errands to do this morning Jesse had to go to the post office and the bookstore I had to go to the pharmacy the video store and the bank.

24. The butterfly is extraordinary it begins as an ugly caterpillar and turns into something colorful it almost looks like a piece of art.

Subordinating conjunctions

Subordinating conjunctions connect dependent, or subordinate, clauses to independent clauses. An independent clause can stand alone as a complete sentence. A dependent clause requires an independent clause to be correct or even to make sense. Furthermore, a dependent clause always begins with a subordinate conjunction.

Following is a list of the most common subordinating conjunctions.

after	because	if	unless
although	before	now that	until
as	even if	since	when
as if	even though	than	where
as though	except	though	while

They will head home **after** they finish eating.
She enjoyed talking to him, **because** he was so smart.
Tom will not join the team **unless** he can be the captain.

Several subordinating conjunctions express time relationships: *after, before, until, when,* and *while*. These conjunctions indicate when the action of the dependent clause takes place in relation to the action of the independent clause.

He was a doctor **before** becoming a veterinarian.
Pedro waited in line **while** Vanessa looked for a place to sit.

The subordinating conjunction *because* introduces a clause that provides a reason for something. It answers the question "why."

She loves the Doors, **because** they sing catchy songs.

The subordinating conjunctions *(ever) since* and *now that* express one of two things: an explanation or a time relationship.

They cannot go to Mexico, **since** they do not have enough money.
We have been eager to watch the movie **ever since** we saw the preview.
Now that they have enough money, they are going to Mexico.

Although, even though, and *though* express exception or indicate that a condition exists despite some other condition.

She liked her old apartment, **although** it was small and smelly.
I was good at volleyball, **even though** I was short.
I hated his choice of music, **though** his voice was quite good.

When it follows a negative statement, the conjunction *unless* expresses requirements or conditions.

She can't be part of the band **unless** she sings well.

The dependent *if* clause expresses a condition that must be met, and the independent clause describes what will happen when that condition is met.

He can be part of the band *if* he plays guitar or drums.

No punctuation is required before many subordinating conjunctions, especially those that express a time relationship, if the conjunction follows the independent clause.

Before he became a professional surfer, he was a skater.
He was a skater **before** he became a professional surfer.

The relative pronouns *who, whom, that, which,* and *whose* can also function like subordinating conjunctions, because they introduce dependent clauses.

The conjunction *than* may be used as a subordinating conjunction, often introducing an **elliptical clause**, that is, a clause in which information that is understood is omitted.

> You speak English far better **than** I [do].
> I like apple pie better **than** [I like] chocolate cake.

Colloquially, it is quite common to use *than* as a preposition.

> Cathy is more talented **than** him.
> My brother plays the piano better **than** me.

To be more precise, the verb in the dependent clause may be included, which requires *than* to be treated as a conjunction.

> Cathy is more talented **than he is**.
> My brother plays the piano better **than I do**.

EXERCISE 23·12

Complete each sentence with the appropriate subordinating conjunction.

1. I really liked my old apartment, _____ it was small and poorly lit.

2. You must buy a ticket _____ you can walk into the theater and watch a movie.

3. She will have to wait _____ the nurse calls her name to see the doctor.

4. He appreciates my mom's cooking skills, _____ she always makes good dishes.

5. They used to be friends _____ they had an argument.

6. Let's make a cake! You mix in the sugar _____ I beat the eggs.

7. They cannot cross the river, _____ they don't have a boat.

8. He was a great musician, _____ he was partly deaf.

9. The musician kept handing out his demo _____ he finally got signed by a music label.

10. She must be rich, _____ she wears a lot of expensive jewelry.

11. Everyone likes Sophia, _____ she is generous and friendly.

12. My father never answers his phone _____ I will try to call him.

13. Fortunately, the tennis tournament was over _____ the cold weather began.

14. You may have that puppy _____ you promise to take care of it.

15. Jason is older _____ she is by two weeks.

16. I'll finish cleaning the dishes _____ the news is over.

17. My dad was supportive of my academic choices _____ he had reservations.

18. The federal government will raise taxes _____ budget cuts can save enough money.

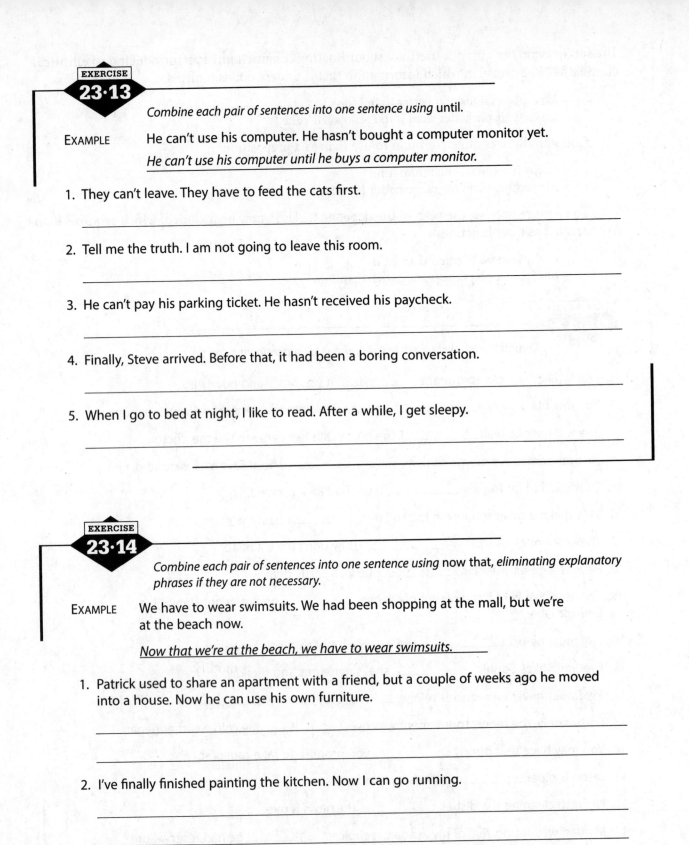

Combine each pair of sentences into one sentence using until.

EXAMPLE   He can't use his computer. He hasn't bought a computer monitor yet.

He can't use his computer until he buys a computer monitor.

1. They can't leave. They have to feed the cats first.

_____

2. Tell me the truth. I am not going to leave this room.

_____

3. He can't pay his parking ticket. He hasn't received his paycheck.

_____

4. Finally, Steve arrived. Before that, it had been a boring conversation.

_____

5. When I go to bed at night, I like to read. After a while, I get sleepy.

_____

Combine each pair of sentences into one sentence using now that, *eliminating explanatory phrases if they are not necessary.*

EXAMPLE   We have to wear swimsuits. We had been shopping at the mall, but we're at the beach now.

Now that we're at the beach, we have to wear swimsuits.

1. Patrick used to share an apartment with a friend, but a couple of weeks ago he moved into a house. Now he can use his own furniture.

_____

_____

2. I've finally finished painting the kitchen. Now I can go running.

_____

_____

3. They have to wear warm clothes. It's winter now.

_____

4. He just celebrated his 21st birthday. Now he can legally drink.

_____

5. Charles used to ride his bike to school, but last month he bought a Jeep. Now he can drive to school.

   _____

   _____

6. The civil war has ended. A new government is being formed.

   _____

   _____

7. It's been a long, hard month, but the project is finally over. We can relax.

   _____

   _____

8. Do you want to go swimming? The water has gotten warmer.

   _____

   _____

9. My best friend got married this morning. He's a married man now, so he has more responsibilities.

   _____

   _____

10. I can get a job as a translator. I know English now.

    _____

    _____

Adverbs that act as conjunctions

Conjunctive adverbs are also considered conjunctions, because they can be used to connect independent clauses. They also act as adverbs, because they modify one of the independent clauses.

Following is a list of the most commonly used conjunctive adverbs.

afterwards	for example	nevertheless	therefore
anyway	for instance	next	thus
besides	however	now	unfortunately
consequently	instead	otherwise	
eventually	later	still	
finally	likewise	then	

The car engine broke down; **consequently**, we did not finish the race.
I spent the day at the public library; **later**, I went for a walk to relax.
The thief lost his appeal; **therefore**, he was forced to go to prison.
She had a lot of bills this month; **unfortunately**, that means that she can't go on the trip with us.

Combine each pair of sentences into one sentence using a conjunctive adverb.

EXAMPLE   The young man was single for years. He met the girl of his dreams.

The young man was single for years; finally, he met the girl

of his dreams.

1. We stopped to visit our grandparents on our way to Oklahoma. We stayed with friends in Tulsa.

   _____

   _____

2. We had planned to go to the park today. The rain canceled our plans.

   _____

   _____

3. It was a difficult time for her. She learned a lot from the experience.

   _____

   _____

4. The hotel stayed vacant and abandoned for many years. The city council decided to tear it down.

   _____

   _____

5. They had a romantic walk along the river. They went back to the hotel to drink some champagne.

   _____

   _____

6. Mr. Williams cannot speak at the conference. Mr. Rogers will go in his place.

   _____

   _____

7. We enjoy all kinds of outdoor activities. We really like rock climbing.

   _____

   _____

8. The mall is already closed. You do not have any money to spend.

   _____

   _____

9. The essay must be written by Monday. You must not fall behind schedule.

   _____

   _____

10. Anna Nicole Smith was incredibly rich. She did not have a happy life.

_____

_____

11. They spent their entire afternoon shopping for clothes. They wore some of their purchases to the dance.

_____

_____

12. He likes seafood. He is allergic to oysters.

_____

Interrogatives

Interrogatives are words that ask a question. They are placed at (or near) the beginning of the sentence, and that sentence ends with a question mark. Some interrogatives are pronouns: *who, whom, whose, what,* and *which.* They can act as:

- the subject of a sentence
- a direct object
- the object of a preposition
- a possessive

Look at these examples:

Subject:	Who is standing on the corner?
	Whose is for sale? (The noun subject is understood.)
	What needs to be done?
	Which is for me?
Direct object:	Whom did you see last night?
	Whose did you borrow? (The noun object is understood.)
	What will they do?
	Which have you selected?
Preposition:	With whom was she dancing?
	About whose was he speaking? (The noun is understood.)
	To what are you referring?
	In which is it located?
Possessive:	Whose house burned down? (*Whose* modifies *house.*)

Other interrogatives act as adverbs: *how, when, where,* and *why.* Some examples:

Question	Possible Answer
How did he walk?	slowly
When was the party?	on Tuesday
Where are you going?	to the store
Why are you limping?	because my foot hurts

There are also some commonly used phrases that are a combination of *what, which,* and *how* and other words. Questions are formed with them like with other interrogatives:

what brand of, what kind of, what sort of, what about
which one, which way, which part of, which of you
how much, how many, how often, how about

Of course, these are not the only such combinations. They are examples. You will discover others that are formed similarly. Some example sentences:

> What kind of dress do you want to buy?
> What about your brother?
> Which one is for me?
> Which of you will help me?

Interrogative words can be used as conjunctions to combine two clauses. You encountered some of them in Unit 21 on conjunctions. But be careful! The sentence formed by using an interrogative as a conjunction is not necessarily a question when combined with another clause. It depends upon whether you are asking a question or making a statement:

Question	Statement
Do you know who he is?	Jill told me who he is.
Does she understand how it works?	I can't explain how it works.
Who told you where it was?	They couldn't discover where it was.
Can you tell me what kind of car this is?	I don't know what kind of car this is.

Notice the change in word order between a direct question and an interrogative clause combined with another clause. In direct questions the verb precedes the subject. In an interrogative clause the verb follows the subject.

Who **are** these people?	She asked me who these people **are**.
When **did** they **arrive**?	I don't know when they **arrived**.
How far **can** he **swim**?	They ask how far he **can swim**.

EXERCISE
24·1

Look at the italicized word or words in each sentence. Then, using the appropriate interrogative word, ask the question that relates to that word.

EXAMPLE: *Thomas* is a friend of his.

Who is a friend of his?

1. Lupita bought *a black* dress.

   _____

2. Panama is located *in Central America*.

   _____

3. She wanted to buy *a new hat and coat*.

   _____

4. Kevin decided to go *home*.

   _____

5. Kendall spent a lot of time talking *with his cousin*.

   _____

6. She started to laugh *because the movie was so funny*.

   _____

7. The man on crutches came down the steps *carefully*.

_____

8. The clock stopped *at precisely 10:42 A.M.*

_____

9. *Ms. Ewell* has worked for this company for years.

_____

10. *My sister's* husband is a firefighter.

_____

11. She should select *this* pair of gloves.

_____

12. There are *more than fifteen* people in the room.

_____

13. This dog is *a Chihuahua*.

_____

14. *The lion's presence* meant danger.

_____

15. Los Angeles is *either north or south* from here.

_____

EXERCISE
24·2

Circle the boldface word or phrase that best answers the question.

1. Whose car is in the driveway? **your/the girl/Nikki's**

2. What's crawling on the wall? **there/a bug/their house**

3. When can you pick the children up? **tomorrow/here/at your house**

4. What brand of car did you buy? **a Ford/foreign/a new one**

5. Which one of them took the money? **him/that man/theirs**

6. How long is this plank? **several/more than one/six feet**

7. Whom did he visit in Mexico? **the ocean/mountains/a friend**

8. Where is the village you come from? **for many people/near the sea/a little earlier**

9. How does your aunt feel today? **always/quickly/better**

10. Which part of the play didn't you understand? **the ending/of the actors/at the theater**

EXERCISE
24·3

Complete each sentence with any appropriate phrase.

1. I don't know why _____.

2. With whom were you _____?

3. He won't explain what kind of _____.

4. Whose parents _____?

5. What sort of man would _____?

6. Andi told me what _____.

7. It's hard to believe how _____.

8. The accident happened when _____.

9. How much _____?

10. Which one of you _____?

Using interrogative sentences

There are two types of interrogative sentences, and both types ask questions. The first type can be called a **yes-no** question, because the answer to such a question will begin with the affirmative word *yes* or the negative word *no*. Most questions of this type begin with a form of the auxiliary verb *do*.

> **auxiliary + subject + verb + predicate +?**
> Do + you + have + the books +?

Yes-no questions

If the verb in a **yes-no** question is the verb *to be* or the verb *to have*, the question is formed simply by placing the verb before the subject of the sentence.

> ***to be/to have* + subject + predicate +?**
> Is + she + the new student +?

This occurs in any tense. In the case of the perfect tenses or the future tense, it is the auxiliary of the verbs *to be* and *to have* that precede the subject. For example:

Present	**Is** she aware of the problem?
Past	**Was** there enough time to finish the exam?
Present perfect	**Have** you been here before?
Future	**Will** Professor Burns be today's lecturer again?

Present	**Have** you enough money for the tickets?
Past	**Had** he adequate notice?
Present perfect	**Has** your mother had the operation yet?
Future	**Will** the workers have some time off?

Auxiliaries

This kind of question structure, in which the verb precedes the subject, also occurs with numerous auxiliaries, such as the following:

be able to	ought to
can	shall/will
could	should
have	would
must	

auxiliary + subject + verb form + predicate +?
Should + we + help + them +?

Let's look at some example sentences:

Are you **able to** make out her signature?
Have you worked here for very long?
Ought she **to** have said that to her mother?

Notice in each example that the sentence contains a second verb. The initial verb is an auxiliary, and it is followed by an infinitive (such as *to work*) or by an elliptical infinitive, which omits the particle word (*to*); for example: *are you able to make, will you try*. With most auxiliaries, it is the tense of the auxiliary that determines the "time" of the action; for example: present (*can he speak*) and past (*could he speak*).

With the auxiliary *have*, however, its tense conjugation combined with a past participle (and not an infinitive) identifies the tense as either present perfect, past perfect, or future perfect:

Present perfect	has he spoken
Past perfect	had he spoken
Future perfect	will he have spoken

The auxiliaries *shall* and *will* identify the future tense and are followed by elliptical infinitives:

Shall I get you something for dinner?
Will you be staying the night?

In declarative sentences, most English speakers use *will*, although technically, *shall* should be used with singular and plural pronouns in the first person, and *will* should be used with the second and third persons. In questions, the rule is applied more strictly: *shall* with first-person singular and plural, and *will* with second- and third-person singular and plural.

	Singular	Plural
First	**Shall** I turn on the TV?	**Shall** we go to the movies tonight?
Second	Tom, **will** you help me with this?	Boys, **will** you please stop your arguing?
Third	**Will** she like this dress?	**Will** they be able to spend some time with us?

It is important to be knowledgeable about the other auxiliaries and how they function in the various tenses. Let's focus on two that can be conjugated like other verbs and form questions by placing the conjugated verb or its auxiliaries before the subject:

Present	**Is** she able to stand alone?
Past	**Was** she able to stand alone?
Present perfect	**Has** she been able to stand alone?
Future	**Will** she be able to stand alone?

Present	**Have** you a few extra dollars?
Past	**Had** you a few extra dollars?
Present perfect	**Have** you had a few extra dollars?
Future	**Will** you have a few extra dollars?

Compare *to be able to* and *have* with the following auxiliaries and what occurs with them in the various tenses:

◆ *Can* changes to *to be able to*

Present	**Can** Victor understand the problem?
Past	**Could** Victor understand the problem?
Present perfect	Has Victor **been able to** understand the problem?
Future	Will Victor **be able to** understand the problem?

◆ *Ought to* changes to *ought to have*

Present	**Ought** you to speak so harshly?
Past	*Ought to is not used in a past-tense question.*
Present perfect	**Ought** you **to have** spoken so harshly?
Future	*Ought to is not used in a future-tense question.*

◆ *Must* changes to *have to*

Present	**Must** he live alone?
Past	Did he **have to** live alone?
Present perfect	Has he **had to** live alone?
Future	Will he **have to** live alone?

◆ *Should* changes to *should have*

Present	**Should** they argue so much?
Past	*Should is not used in a past-tense question.*
Present perfect	**Should** they **have** argued so much?
Future	*Should is not used in a future-tense question.*

Questions with *do/did*

Verbs that are not auxiliaries form questions by beginning them in the present tense with *do* and in the past tense with *did*. The use of *do/did* does not occur in the other tenses. Let's examine a few cases in point:

Present	**Do** you enjoy her classes?
Past	**Did** you enjoy her classes?
Present perfect	Have you enjoyed her classes?
Future	Will you enjoy her classes?

Present	**Does** Thomas visit you often?
Past	**Did** Thomas visit you often?
Present perfect	Has Thomas visited you often?
Future	Will Thomas visit you often?

Since *have* is an auxiliary, it can be used in questions without *do/did*. Nevertheless, there is a tendency to add the extra *do/did* auxiliary both in speech and in writing.

Present	**Do** you have a few extra dollars?
Past	**Did** you have a few extra dollars?
Present perfect	Have you had a few extra dollars?
Future	Will you have a few extra dollars?

When using *have to* (which is much the same as *must* in meaning), you must use *do/did* in the present and past tenses.

Present	**Do** they have to work so many hours?
Past	**Did** they have to work so many hours?
Present perfect	Have they had to work so many hours?
Future	Will they have to work so many hours?

The auxiliaries *to want to* and *to like to* form their present- and past-tense questions with *do/did*. For example:

Present	**Does** Mom want to go shopping?
Past	**Did** Mom want to go shopping?
Present perfect	Has Mom wanted to go shopping?
Future	Will Mom want to go shopping?

Present	**Do** they like to listen to rap music?
Past	**Did** they like to listen to rap music?
Present perfect	Have they liked to listen to rap music?
Future	Will they like to listen to rap music?

You should be aware that while both *to want to* and *to like to* are auxiliary verbs, they are also used as transitive verbs, taking a direct object. When they are used as transitive verbs, the final *to* is omitted from the verb: *to want* and *to like*. Even when used as transitive verbs, they form their present- and past-tense questions with *do/did*.

do/did + subject + *want/like* + predicate +?

Does + she + like + him +?

Present	**Do** you want some help?
	Does she like pizza?
Past	**Did** you want some help?
	Did she like pizza?

EXERCISE

24·4

Rewrite the following questions in the missing tenses.

1. a. Present _____

    b. Past _____

    c. Present perfect _____

      Future <u>Will you be home for the holidays?</u>

2. a. Present _____

   Past <u>Did the arsonist burn down the bank?</u>

   b. Present perfect _____

   c. Future _____

3. a. Present _____

   b. Past _____

   Present perfect <u>Have you had to spend a lot of time studying?</u>

   c. Future _____

4. a. Present _____

   b. Past _____

   Present perfect <u>Have the workers done the job right?</u>

   c. Future _____

5.   Present <u>Can you really predict the outcome of the election?</u>

   a. Past _____

   b. Present perfect _____

   c. Future _____

EXERCISE
24·5

Write original questions with the following auxiliaries in the tense shown in parentheses.

EXAMPLE: can (past) <u>Could you see over the tall hedge?</u>

1. should (present perfect) _____

2. must (present) _____

3. want to (future) _____

4. have to (present) _____

5. have (future) _____

6. be able to (present) _____

7. will (future) _____

8. ought to (present perfect) _____

9. would (present) _____

10. must (present perfect) _____

*Using the phrases provided, first form a **yes-no** question. Then change the question by adding any appropriate auxiliary.*

EXAMPLE: to walk to work

Do you always walk to work?

Do you always have to walk to work?

1. to spend more than a hundred dollars

    a. _____

    b. _____

2. to arrive in the capital on time

    a. _____

    b. _____

3. to develop a new method

    a. _____

    b. _____

4. to remain calm

    a. _____

    b. _____

5. to consider the danger

    a. _____

    b. _____

6. to spell accurately

    a. _____

    b. _____

7. to prepare some lunch

    a. _____

    b. _____

8. to suggest a solution

    a. _____

    b. _____

9. to flee the storm

    a. _____

    b. _____

10. to pretend nothing is wrong

   a. _____

   b. _____

Progressive-form questions

Just as in a declarative sentence, verbs in a question can be formed in the progressive, which means that they are actions in progress or incomplete. Since the progressive form is composed of a conjugation of *to be* plus a present participle (*is going, was singing*), and *to be* never forms a question with *do/did*, all questions that have a progressive verb will begin with the verb *to be* or its auxiliaries.

> *to be* + subject + present participle (*-ing*) +?
> **Are** + you + working in the garden +?

For example:

Present	**Are** you planning on attending the party?
Past	**Was** she sleeping when the storm hit?
Present perfect	**Have** the men been working in the mine again?
Future	**Will** he be preparing for final exams?

Be aware that a verb in a *do/did* question will not require the auxiliary *do/did* when it is changed to its progressive form. For example:

Do you attend a state university?
Are you attending a state university?

Did the campers sleep in tents?
Were the campers sleeping in tents?

EXERCISE
24·7

Change each of the following sentences to a question. Then, in a second question, change the verb to the progressive form. Be sure to retain the tense of the original sentence.

EXAMPLE: Bill learned shorthand.

   Did Bill learn shorthand?

   Was Bill learning shorthand?

1. A plumber fixed the leaking pipes.

   a. _____

   b. _____

2. You couldn't work on that old car.

   a. _____

   b. _____

3. The judges have spoken about this for a long time.

a. _____

b. _____

4. Time goes by very fast.

a. _____

b. _____

5. Thunder rolled across the foothills.

a. _____

b. _____

6. You will take a series of exams.

a. _____

b. _____

7. Mr. Kelly has wanted to vacation there.

a. _____

b. _____

8. He's crazy.

a. _____

b. _____

9. The revelers have had a good time at the celebration.

a. _____

b. _____

10. I should sit nearer to her.

a. _____

b. _____

Questions using interrogative words

The second kind of question formation is one that begins with an interrogative word: *who, what, why, how, which,* or *when.* The rules that appy about the use of *do/did* in questions apply in the same way with questions that begin with an interrogative word. For example:

Can he understand you?	**How** can he understand you?
Do you like that man?	**Why** do you like that man?
Are you coming to the party?	**When** are you coming to the party?
Have you found the books?	**Where** have you found the books?

As you can see from these examples, **yes-no** questions and questions that begin with an interrogative word can be, for the most part, identical. Likewise, the choice of *do/did* in a question is the same in either type of question. This is possible because the interrogatives illustrated in the four examples are substitutes for adverbs, and since adverbs only modify, changes are not always needed in a question.

This is not the case, however, with *who* and *what*. These two interrogatives are actually pronouns that stand in place of a subject or an object in a sentence. In the following examples, an arrow (→) points out how a declarative sentence is changed to an interrogative sentence with *who* or *what*. For example:

Subject	The man is sick.	→	**Who** is sick?
Subject	A box is needed.	→	**What** is needed?
Object	They met the woman.	→	**Whom** did they meet?
Object	She broke the lamp.	→	**What** did she break?
Object	I spoke with him.	→	**With** whom did I speak?
Object	The boy sat on it.	→	**On** what did the boy sit?

In less formal style, *who* is often substituted for *whom*. This occurs even in writing, although in formal writing the appropriate use of *whom* should be applied.

Also, the placing of a preposition in front of *whom* or *what* is formal in style. In a less formal version, prepositions are placed at the end of the question and would look like this:

Who did you speak with?
What did the boy sit on?

If a possessive of *who* or *what* is required, use *whose* or *of what*.

I spoke with Tom's father.	With **whose** father did you speak?
The color of the book is red.	**Whose** color is red? (The color of **what** is red?)

EXERCISE

24·8

Use the underlined cue provided to determine which interrogative word applies; then write the appropriate question for the sentence.

EXAMPLE: John is a fantastic soccer player.

Who is a fantastic soccer player?

1. The attendant closed and locked the gates at seven sharp.

_____

2. They leave for Puerto Rico at the beginning of every February.

_____

3. Life isn't always easy to understand.

_____

4. Ms. Perez's two puppies got their shots today.

_____

5. They probably caught the flu from the boy who coughed through the lecture.

_____

6. We plan on getting to the match on the subway.

_____

7. That big bully threw the ball <u>on the other side of the fence.</u>

   _____

8. The girls should come home <u>right after the end of the movie.</u>

   _____

9. Andrea will dance with <u>the blond boy.</u>

   _____

10. They know about the change in plans, <u>because they received a fax from him today.</u>

   _____

EXERCISE
24·9

Write original sentences with the interrogatives provided.

1. why _____

2. how _____

3. whom _____

4. which _____

5. when _____

The interrogative *how* is often combined with other words to form new interrogatives. Just some of these are *how much, how many, how often, how old, how long,* and *how tall.* In sentences, they are used like this:

> **How much** does that magazine cost?
> **How often** do the girls work out?
> **How long** did you have to wait to see the doctor?
> **How tall** is the center on the basketball team?

EXERCISE
24·10

Form original questions with how *by combining it with the cues provided. Then give an appropriate answer to the question.*

EXAMPLE: many <u>How many players are there on a football team?</u>

   <u>There are eleven players on a football team.</u>

1. little

   a. _____

   b. _____

2. large

a. _____

b. _____

3. frequently

a. _____

b. _____

4. difficult

a. _____

b. _____

5. hot

a. _____

b. _____

6. strong

a. _____

b. _____

7. often

a. _____

b. _____

8. carefully

a. _____

b. _____

9. most

a. _____

b. _____

10. lazily

a. _____

b. _____

Negation

No is the opposite of *yes*. It is used as a negative response to a question. But there are other negative forms in English as well.

Simple **negation** occurs by placing *not* after the conjugated verb in a sentence. It is important to remember that it is the conjugated verb that determines the location of *not* and not the other verbal forms that may also be in a sentence.

> He **is not** at home today.
> We do **not** want to buy a car at this time.
> Marianne has **not** responded to my letter.

If the sentence is in the form of a question, *not* stands behind the subject:

> Can you **not** understand?
> How could he **not** have helped us?
> Will Martin **not** share his good fortune?

But in the case of a contraction with *not*, the two parts of the contraction are never separated. This is true whether the sentence is a statement or a question:

> He **isn't** at home today.   **Can't** you understand?
> We **don't** want to buy a car.   Why **couldn't** he help us?
> She **hasn't** answered yet.   **Won't** Martin share with us?

If the negated verb is not *to be*, *to have*, or other auxiliary (*can*, *should*, *must*, etc.), the negation is formed from the present or past tense of *do*, depending upon the tense of the verb:

> I am not   I do not speak
> she has not   she doesn't learn
> you shouldn't   you did not understand
> he can't   he didn't worry

Certain other negative words have two forms. One form begins with *no-* (except for *never* and *neither*), and the other consists of *not* followed by another word. When these words are not negative, they have a special positive form that often uses the word *some*. Look at the varieties that exist:

Formed with *no-*	Formed with *not*	Positive Form
none	not any	some
no one	not anyone (or anybody)	someone (or somebody)

Formed with *no-*	Formed with *not*	Positive Form
nothing	not anything	something
nowhere	not anywhere	somewhere
never*	not ever	ever
neither*	not either	either

Take note of the spelling.

Be aware of how the two forms are used differently:

I have **none** to give you.   I do **not** have **anything** to give you.
He spoke to **no one**.   He did **not** speak to **anyone**.
We want **nothing** from you.   We do **not** want **anything** from you.
She's **nowhere** to be found.   She's **not anywhere** to be found.
I'll **never** forgive you.   I will **not ever** forgive you.
He wants **neither** of them.   He does **not** want **either** of them.

When the negative word is removed from the sentence, the positive form replaces it:

Hector didn't dance with anyone. → Hector danced with someone.
The customer wants nothing. → The customer wants something.

Note: English never uses a double negative—for example, *doesn't want nothing*.

EXERCISE
25·1

Rewrite each sentence twice, first by adding not, *then by using a contraction of* not.

1. The boys were playing basketball at the park.

   _____

   _____

2. My sister is a concert pianist.

   _____

   _____

3. Are you well?

   _____

   _____

4. His nephew is learning Japanese.

   _____

   _____

5. Can they explain how this happened?

   _____

   _____

6. The judge ordered him sent to prison.

_____

_____

7. We will be traveling to Spain this summer.

_____

_____

8. Does Mr. Amin have our lawnmower?

_____

_____

9. My sister spends a lot of time in the library.

_____

_____

10. Judith understood the situation.

_____

_____

Rewrite each sentence by removing the negation. Use the appropriate positive form where necessary.

1. I haven't had enough time to work on this.

_____

2. Mark doesn't get to work on time.

_____

3. She didn't bring her dog along.

_____

4. Have you never been to New York City?

_____

5. Lin wasn't speaking with anyone.

_____

6. The children don't cooperate with the substitute teacher.

_____

7. They don't live anywhere in the city.

8. Couldn't the horse run faster?

_____

9. Marta didn't break the window.

_____

10. No, I don't like this kind of music.

_____

11. Chase isn't dancing with anyone.

_____

12. Can't you find anything you need?

_____

13. I haven't written the proposal for them.

_____

14. No, she doesn't spend her vacation with us.

_____

15. He got nothing interesting in the mail.

_____

EXERCISE

25·3

Write original sentences with the negative words in parentheses.

1. (not) _____

2. (never) _____

3. (no one) _____

4. (not anywhere) _____

5. (not anything) _____

6. (none) _____

7. (not ever) _____

8. (neither) _____

9. (nowhere) _____

10. (nothing) _____

Numbers

Numbers are generally used for specifying amounts and in mathematics: addition, subtraction, multiplication, and division. You have undoubtedly encountered them in many forms. Let's first review *cardinal numbers*:

0	zero	21	twenty-one
1	one	22	twenty-two
2	two	30	thirty
3	three	40	forty
4	four	50	fifty
5	five	60	sixty
6	six	70	seventy
7	seven	80	eighty
8	eight	90	ninety
9	nine	100	one hundred
10	ten	101	one hundred one
11	eleven	102	one hundred two
12	twelve	200	two hundred
13	thirteen	500	five hundred
14	fourteen	1,000	one thousand
15	fifteen	2,000	two thousand
16	sixteen	10,000	ten thousand
17	seventeen	11,000	eleven thousand
18	eighteen	20,000	twenty thousand
19	nineteen	100,000	one hundred thousand
20	twenty	111,111	one hundred eleven thousand one hundred eleven

Careful! English names for certain large numbers differ from those in other languages:

English	Number
million	1,000,000
billion	1,000,000,000
trillion	1,000,000,000,000

When numbers are used in equations, there are specific mathematical terms to be used. In addition, numbers are combined by either the word *plus* or the word *and*: five plus three, ten and nine.

In subtraction, the equation requires using the word *minus* (−): ten minus four.

In multiplication, the equation requires using the word *times* (×): six times three.

In division, the equation requires the phrase *divided by* (÷ or /): twenty divided by five.

If an equation has an equal sign (=) in it, it is stated as *equals* or *is*: two plus two equals four, six minus three is three.

If a number is a decimal, the decimal is expressed by the word *point*: 6.5 is said as "six point five"; 10.7 is said as "ten point seven."

The *ordinal numbers* are those that show a rank in a group or series. Most ordinals are formed by adding *-th* to the end of the number: *tenth*, *twentieth*, *sixty-seventh*, *hundredth*, and so on. But five ordinal numbers have special spellings which should be memorized:

1 = first
2 = second
3 = third
5 = fifth
12 = twelfth

Some example sentences with ordinal numbers:

We have three daughters, but Denise was our first.
The second seating for dinner is at 8:30 P.M.
She was born on the twenty-fifth of June.

Dates are expressed in two ways: *May fifth* or *the fifth of May*. When giving a date as a number, it is most common to give the month before the day: 9/11 = September eleventh, 6/12 = June twelfth. In many other languages, the day precedes the month. This can cause confusion, because to some people 6/12 means "the sixth of December." To English speakers it most commonly means "June twelfth." To avoid such confusion, it is wise to give dates in this form: June 12, 2005. Ordinals are also used to express fractions other than ½:

½ = one-half (not an ordinal)
¼ = one-fourth (**Note:** One-fourth is sometimes expressed as "one-quarter" or "a quarter.")
⅓ = one-third
³⁄₁₀ = three-tenths
¹⁴⁄₂₅ = fourteen twenty-fifths (Notice the plural formation of the ordinal when the accompanying number is greater than one.)

Years that precede 2000 are expressed in two parts: 1850 is said as "eighteen fifty," 1066 is said as "ten sixty-six." The years that follow 1999 are said another way:

2000	two thousand
2001	two thousand one, or twenty oh one
2002	two thousand two, or twenty oh two
2010	two thousand ten, or twenty ten
2022	two thousand twenty-two, or twenty twenty-two

When saying on what date an event occurred, the word *on* is optional:

The boy was born *on* May first.
The boy was born May first.

EXERCISE
26·1

Rewrite each equation in words.

1. 5 + 7 = 12

_____

2. 11 − 6 = 5

_____

3. 345 − 220 = 125

_____

4. 22 × 10 = 220

_____

5. 100 × 63 = 6,300

_____

6. 10,000 / 500 = 200

_____

7. 880 × 3 = 2,640

_____

8. 88,000 − 55,000 = 33,000

_____

9. 11.5 × 10 = 115

_____

10. 93.3 / 3 = 31.1

_____

Change the cardinal number in parentheses to the appropriate ordinal number.

1. Mr. Woo was born on the (2) _____ of October.

2. I'm sitting in the (4) _____ row.

3. My birthday was on the (21) _____ of July.

4. This is only the (3) _____ time we met.

5. The old woman died on her (100) _____ birthday.

6. They're celebrating their (30) _____ anniversary.

7. Who's the (5) _____ boy in line?

8. That was her (10) _____ phone call today.

9. Mr. Burton was their (1,000) _____ customer and won a prize.

10. Adam scored in the (99) _____ percentile.

11. I think I was (1) _____ in line.

12. Our seats are in the (12) _____ row.

13. Christmas Day is always on the (25) _____.

14. The old woman died on her (86) _____ birthday.

15. Our new car arrived on the (22) _____ of August.

Complete each sentence with the date shown in parentheses written as words. In each case the month precedes the day (e.g., 5/2 = May second).

1. (8/10) She was born on _____.

2. (10/12) He'll arrive on _____.

3. (11/11) The party will be _____.

4. (2/16/1999) He died on _____.

5. (4/1/2002) They met on _____.

6. (12/24) Christmas Eve is _____.

7. (7/4) Where will you spend _____?

8. (1492) Columbus arrived in the New World in _____.

9. (2/14/2004) The dance is _____.

10. (6/2) Was the baby born on _____?

Numbers

Whole numbers from one through ten are usually spelled out in sentences; whole numbers larger than ten are written as numerals. However, this is a style—not grammar—issue, and the main objective should be consistency.

> **Eight** in **ten** voters were disappointed.
> This hospital employs **437** nurses.

A number that begins a sentence is spelled out and capitalized.

> **Twenty-eight thousand** people crossed the border.

Very large numbers can be expressed in several ways.

> **30,000** political prisoners
> **30 thousand** political prisoners
> **thirty thousand** political prisoners

Numbers used in business documents or in legal writing are often spelled out and written as numerals to avoid confusion.

> The broker's profits are not to exceed **forty thousand (40,000)** dollars.

Uses of numbers

Numbers can be used to express time, dates, and periods of time.

> **3** P.M. ~ **3:00** P.M. ~ **three** o'clock in the afternoon
> July **23, 1976**
> the **seventeenth** century ~ the **17th** century
> the **'80s** ~ the **eighties** ~ the **1980s**

Numbers are used in addresses.

> **1949** Yucca Mountain Road
> **1600** Liberal Lane
> Chicago, IL **60601**

Numbers are used in decimals, percentages, pages and chapters of books, scenes in a play, temperature, geographic coordinates, money, and forms of identification.

> **0.0987, 20.75**
> **17** percent ~ **17%** ~ **seventeen** percent
> page **34**, chapter **45**
> Act **V**, Scene **III**, lines **108–110**
> **36°** C ~ **36** degrees Celsius
> latitude **45°** N
> **$5.30** ~ **five** dollars and **thirty** cents
> Queen Elizabeth **II**, Henry **VIII**
> Channel **8**
> Area **51**

Rewrite each sentence, using the numbers correctly. If the sentence is correct and no changes are required, mark an "X" in the blank.

1. An important date to remember is November seventeen 1959.

_____

2. The city paid $ thirty-four point seven million to build the tower.

_____

3. It took 5 out of 9 members to reach a consensus.

_____

4. In Europe, the nineteen seventies were marked by social and political change.

_____

5. Turn to page one hundred and nine, which should be chapter twelve.

_____

6. The morning temperature was forty-seven degrees Fahrenheit, or 8 degrees Celsius.

_____

7. The address listed in the phone book was 3465 Milkway Avenue.

_____

8. They drove down Interstate thirty-four to the lake.

_____

9. The Second Battle of Bull Run was fought from August twenty-eight to thirty, eighteen sixty-two.

_____

•27• Conversation: Introductions, opinions, descriptions

Introducing yourself and others

Conversation: Meeting at a party

TODD: Hi—you must be John's cousin Matt, **right?** From San Diego?

MATT: **Correct! I just got in** last night.

TODD: **I'm** Todd, John's roommate from Tech. **Glad to meet you. I can assure you that** I'm not anything like what John has told you.

MATT: **I'm happy to meet you, too**—and, yes—I have heard about you! Football player and **party animal extraordinaire**.

TODD: Football, yes—and **as a matter of fact**, I **do** like parties. **But tell me more about yourself** and **what you do** in San Diego.

MATT: Well, I'm more (of) a surfer than a football player. You know, San Diego has a fantastic coast—and we can surf all day and then party on the beach at night.

TODD: That sounds **awesome**. How long are you staying?

MATT: Well, I'll be here for two weeks. John has promised me a **nonstop schedule**— kind of **a mix** of sightseeing, meeting his friends, checking out **the local scene**, and—**hopefully**—camping in the mountains for **a couple of days**.

TODD: John's **a good guy**—and **you can be sure** he knows **the local scene**. He knows everybody in town. I'm sure he'll **show you a good time**. And his friends are here to help.

MATT: **Thanks so much**—I really appreciate that. I'm still a bit **jet-lagged** at the moment but should be **in good shape** by tomorrow. I'm **looking forward to** hearing what John **has in store** for me. . . .

TODD: Don't worry. We'll all take good care of you. And don't be surprised if we **show up on your doorstep** in San Diego one day, ready for surfing!

Improving your conversation

I'm Todd (Jones)

Simply using *I'm* and then saying your name is one way to introduce yourself. You could also say, for example, *My name's* Todd (Jones). It is customary to offer your right hand in a handshake to the other person. In very informal situations, you could just say Hi, *I'm* Todd, with no handshake.

To introduce one or more people other than yourself, say:

This is (my wife,) **Mary**. And **this is Susan**, **Bob**, **and Joe**.

To introduce more than one person and also tell how you know them, say:

These are my friends, **Susan and Bob.** And **this is Jim,** my coworker.

All of the people introduced would then shake hands. You could also say:

I want you to meet (my friends,) **Susan and Bob.**

Glad/happy to meet you

When you have been introduced to someone, it is customary to say *(I'm) glad/happy to <u>meet</u> you* or *It's nice to <u>meet</u> you.* The reply is *I'm happy to meet <u>you</u>* or *I'm happy to meet you, too.* (The underlined words are pronounced slightly louder than the others.)

Right?

Right? is an informal way to ask for confirmation that what you have just said is true. The answer can be *That's right!*

This train goes to Washington, **right?**	That's right.
You're from Panama, **right?**	That's right, I am.

Correct!

This is an informal answer to a question that asks for confirmation.

You're Matt, aren't you?	**Correct!**
This is Economics 101, **right?**	**Correct!**

If you want to tell your questioner that he or she is *not* correct, you can politely say this with, for example:

No, that's not **<u>right</u>**.
No, that's not **<u>correct</u>**.
No, I'm not <u>Matt</u>; I'm <u>Jim</u>.
No, she isn't my <u>sister</u>. She's my <u>cousin</u>.

(The underlined words in the examples should be spoken slightly louder than the other words in the sentence.)

To sarcastically indicate that something is *not* correct, *Yeah, right!* is used.

Dylan, I heard you just won the lottery jackpot!	**Yeah, right!** Where did you hear that nonsense?

Am, do, etc.

When a yes-or-no question using the verb *to be* is asked, the answer can be made emphatic by following it with a *tag*, in which, if the answer is *yes*, the verb is said a little louder than the other words. Affirmative tag answers are not contracted.

Are you unhappy?	Yes, I **<u>am</u>**.
Is he sick?	Yes, he **<u>is</u>**.
Are we winning?	Yes, we **<u>are</u>**.
Are they leaving?	Yes, they **<u>are</u>**.

When the answer is *no*, there are two ways to answer with a tag. The underlined words are the ones said a little louder. Negative tag answers are usually contracted. The full form makes them more emphatic.

Are you unhappy?	No, **I'm** <u>not</u>./No, I **am** <u>not</u>.
Is he sick?	No, **he's** <u>not</u>./No, he **isn't**./No, he **is** <u>not</u>.
Are we winning?	No, **we're** <u>not</u>./No, we **aren't**./No, we **are** <u>not</u>.
Are they leaving?	No, **they're** <u>not</u>./No, they **aren't**./No, they **are** <u>not</u>.

When an information question using any verb other than *to be* is asked, the answer can be made emphatic by following it with a tag, in which the verb is said a little louder than the other words.

Do you eat meat?	Yes, I **do**./No, I **don't**./No, I **do** <u>not</u>.
Does he like school?	Yes, he **does**./No, he **doesn't**./No, he **does** <u>not</u>.
Do we wait in line?	Yes, we **do**./No, we **don't**./No, we **do** <u>not</u>.
Do they live here?	Yes, they **do**./No, they **don't**./No, they **do** <u>not</u>.

As a matter of fact

As a matter of fact is a common expression that has a number of different meanings. In our example conversation it introduces a confirmation of what was previously said. It can go before the main clause or after the verb.

I heard you were looking for a job.	**As a matter of fact,** I <u>am</u>!
Your friend is very good-looking; is he single?	He <u>is</u>, **as a matter of fact**!

You can express the same meaning with *actually*, but put it after the verb.

I heard you were looking for a job.	I <u>am</u>, **actually**.
Your friend is beautiful, but I'll bet she's married.	She <u>is</u>, **actually**.

Just

This use of *just* indicates that something happened only a short time before. It can be used with the past tense or with the present perfect tense. For example:

Past tense	Present perfect tense
I **just** arrived.	I have **just** arrived.
They **just** finished.	They have **just** finished.
We **just** ate.	We have **just** eaten.
He **just** called.	He has **just** called.

To get in

To *get in* means to arrive and is usually used in the past tense.

What time did you **get in**?
They **got in** late last night.

Another way to say *to arrive*, when it refers to the future, is to **get there**.

I hope we **get there** on time.
She will **get there** by six.

To *get in* can also mean to be accepted by a school/college/university or other group with limited membership.

> He applied to that college and really hopes to **get in**.
> She didn't **get in** her first choice of sororities, but she **got in** another one, and she's happy.

I can assure you that . . . /you can be sure (that) . . .

These are common ways of saying that you believe something to be true, hoping to win the confidence of the person you are talking to.

> **I can assure you that** I will work hard.
> **You can be sure that** something interesting will happen.

Here is another way to express that you believe something to be true:

> **I promise you that** we won't leave until the work is done.

Party animal

Party animal is an informal expression used to characterize someone who spends a lot of time with friends or acquaintances for entertainment—either at home or in public places.

> My friend Eric will take you downtown on Saturday night; he's a real **party animal**, so you'll meet lots of people.

Extraordinaire

Extraordinaire is a word borrowed from French, pronounced in English "ek stra or d- NAYRE." It is used to exaggerate the meaning of the previous word.

> I'd like you to meet Marc—he's our pastry chef **extraordinaire**. You have to try his cheesecake!

What do you do?

The question *What do you do?* asks what one's job or occupation is. When you answer with a form of *to be*, you give a general job title. Note that the article *a* is always used when referring to only one person but is never used when referring to more than one person.

What do you do?	I'm a lawyer.
What does he do?	He's a painter.
What does she do?	She's a banker.
What do they do?	They're professors.

When the answer refers to someone who has a special title or position (i.e., is the only one in that position), use *the* instead of *a*.

What does he do?	He's the president of ABC Enterprises.
What do you do?	I'm the school secretary (the only one).

When you answer with another verb, you give more specific information about where you work.

What do you do?	I work for a large firm.
What does he do?	He drives a delivery truck.
What does she do?	She works at Atlas Bank.
What do they do?	They teach French at Loyola.

When a specific time or place is included in the question, the answer refers to how people spend their time, not just what their jobs are.

What do you do on weekends?   I relax and hang out with my friends.
What does she do at the beach?   She surfs, relaxes on the beach, and
goes to the boardwalk for fun.

Tell me about yourself

Tell me about yourself is a polite way to let someone know that you are interested in learning more about him or her. It is better than asking direct questions, as the person being asked can decide what to tell and what not to tell. For example:

Tell me about yourself.   Well, I'm twenty-seven, I have a degree
in mathematics, and I've been
working at SYZ Company for three
years. My parents are both
economists, and I have a sister who's
a nurse and two younger brothers.
They all live in Connecticut, where I
was born. I'm crazy about football
and have season tickets. I listen to
reggae, etc.

Tell me about yourself.   Well, I'm from a small town, and I
came here to work.

Awesome

Awesome is an expression that is used a lot—maybe too much!—to say that you think something is really good. Other ways to express the same thing include *great, fantastic, terrific, wonderful,* and *cool.*

So . . . how do you like it here?   It's **awesome**!
Did you like the movie?   It was **awesome**!
Thank you for taking me—
you're **awesome**!

Nonstop schedule

Nonstop schedule describes the activities of a very busy person, whether it be because of work, school, family responsibilities, or even social life.

I don't have time to see you this week, with my **nonstop schedule**.

Other ways to indicate nonstop activity are *around-the-clock* or *twenty-four-seven* (twenty-four hours a day, seven days a week).

I get telephone calls **around-the-clock**.
He works **twenty-four-seven**, so I hardly ever see him.

A mix

A *mix* refers to a combination of different elements, usually indicating variety.

There will be a good **mix** of music at the wedding, to keep the grandparents, the parents, and the young people happy.
We invited a **mix** of people—family, friends, coworkers, and neighbors.

Hopefully

Hopefully is a word inserted to indicate your wishes that something will happen. It can come in the middle of a verb phrase (will + *hopefully* + verb), before the subject, or at the end of a sentence.

I'll **hopefully** graduate in two years.
Hopefully, I'll graduate in two years.
I'll graduate in two years, **hopefully**.
If we leave right away, **hopefully** we'll arrive on time.

A couple of

A couple really means two; however, informally, it can mean more than that—but it does indicate a small number.

I'll see you in **a couple of** hours.	I'll see you sometime today.
It only costs **a couple of** dollars.	It costs less than five dollars.
He'll be home in **a couple of** months.	He'll be home before the end of the year.

A good guy

Calling someone *a good guy* is a common way to recommend a male as being understanding of someone's situation, helpful, or generous. A female with the same kind of recommendation would be called *understanding/helpful/generous*.

If you're looking for a used car, go see Sam Smith; he's **a good guy** and will probably give you a good price.
If you want a teaching job, call Mary Johnson; she's very **understanding** and will give you good advice.

The local scene

The **local scene** refers to the culture and range of entertainment offered in a particular area.

I'm moving to Springfield next month. What's the **local scene** like there?	Oh, it's great! There are lots of things to do at night and on weekends.

To show someone a good time

To *show someone a good time* means to make sure he or she is entertained.

If you come visit in December, we'll **show you a good time**. All our friends have parties in December!

Thanks so much

Thanks so much is a common way of expressing appreciation. Other ways to say this are *Thank you very much/Thanks a lot/I really appreciate this/You're a doll* (very informal)/*You're a sweetheart* (very informal).

The reply to any of these could be *You're welcome/No problem/I'm glad I could help you/Glad to help/Any time*.

Thanks so much for fixing my tire. **I really appreciate it.**	**No problem.**
Thank you very much for helping us.	**You're welcome. Any time.**

To be in good shape

To be *in good shape* means to be fit *financially* or *situationally*.

> My sister's husband has a good job, so they're **in good shape** financially.
> She has a good education and a lot of experience, so she's **in good shape** for the job market.

A similar expression, to be *in shape*, means to be *physically* fit.

> She exercises every day to stay **in shape**.
> You look great. How do you stay **in shape**?

To be looking forward to something

The expression *looking forward to* indicates that the speaker is very happy about a future event.

> I'm **looking forward to** seeing you on Saturday.
> She's really **looking forward to** going to college in the fall.

Another way to say this is with the expression, *can't wait to*.

> I **can't wait to** see you on Saturday.
> She **can't wait to** go to college in the fall.

To have in store for

The phrase *to have in store for* indicates an unknown situation that someone presents to someone else; it can be good or bad.

> Well, I'm going home, but I have no idea what my family will **have in store for** me.
> We're going shopping tomorrow to see what the designers **have in store for** us this season.
> He's been working there for years, but he never knows what's **in store for** him until he gets there.

To show up on someone's doorstep

To show up on someone's doorstep means to visit someone without notice. It doesn't necessarily mean that you plan to stay overnight—or longer—but it's possible.

> I was just getting ready to go out when my cousin **showed up on my doorstep**.

Related expressions are *drop in* and *drop by*, but these are used only for short visits—never an overnight stay.

> We were in town, so we decided to **drop in** to see you.
> Please **drop by** for a while. I miss seeing you.

To *show up*, on the other hand, is used negatively to indicate that someone often doesn't appear when expected.

> Pia said she was coming, but you never know if she'll **show up** or not.

Another meaning of *show up*, when used with a direct object, is to perform or seem better than someone else.

> Your singing was fantastic! You **showed up** all the other contestants.
> He will **show up** the competition with his fantastic speech.
> She **showed** us all **up** when she came in wearing that red dress!

Circle the most appropriate short answer for each question.

1. Is Larry coming tomorrow?
   a. Yes, he does.   c. Yes, he is.
   b. No, he doesn't.   d. No, he won't.

2. Do you like chocolate ice cream?
   a. No, I'm not.   c. Yes, I am.
   b. No, I don't.   d. Yes, she does.

3. Are we leaving at six?
   a. Yes, they are.   c. Yes, we are.
   b. Yes, they do.   d. No, we don't.

4. Is she a lawyer?
   a. No, she doesn't.   c. No, he doesn't.
   b. Yes, he is.   d. Yes, she is.

5. Are they here yet?
   a. No, they're not.   c. No, they do not.
   b. Yes, they're.   d. Yes, they do.

Match each remark in the first column with an appropriate response from the second column. Note: Some remarks have more than one appropriate response.

1. _____ Thank you!   a. As a matter of fact, no.

2. _____ I just got in from Chicago.   b. Awesome.

3. _____ Are you a doctor?   c. Glad I could help you.

4. _____ Tell me about yourself.   d. He's a cook.

5. _____ I'm a real party animal.   e. I am, actually.

6. _____ We're in good shape financially.   f. I hope I get in.

7. _____ You should go to college.   g. I'm a college student from Ohio.

8. _____ You're a doll.   h. No problem.

9. _____ Is this your doll?   i. No, I'm not.

10. _____ What does he do?   j. Then you can show us a good time.

                                               k. Welcome.

                                               l. Yeah, right!

                                               m. Yes, it is.

                                               n. You're welcome.

EXERCISE

27·3

Write a tag answer for each of the following questions.

1. Do you work twenty-four-seven?

_____

2. Are you from New York?

_____

3. Do your parents live in Los Angeles?

_____

4. Are you a student?

_____

5. Is your best friend studying English?

_____

EXERCISE

27·4

Write a yes-or-no question for each of the following answers.

1. _____

No, we don't.

2. _____

Yes, she is.

3. _____

No, they aren't.

4. _____

Yes, I do.

5. _____

Yes, he does.

6. _____

No, I'm not.

Match the words or expressions in the first column with words or expressions in the second column that have a similar meaning. Note: There may be more than one match for each expression.

1. _____ a party animal
2. _____ extraordinaire
3. _____ awesome
4. _____ a mix
5. _____ you're welcome
6. _____ nonstop
7. _____ hopefully
8. _____ in shape
9. _____ a couple of
10. _____ a good guy
11. _____ any time
12. _____ the local scene
13. _____ look forward to
14. _____ have in store for
15. _____ show up
16. _____ get in
17. _____ can't wait

a. twenty-four-seven
b. a combination
c. an understanding male
d. arrive
e. attend
f. be accepted
g. current events here
h. fantastic
i. glad to help you
j. have plans for someone
k. if we are lucky
l. no problem
m. physically fit
n. round-the-clock
o. someone who likes to have fun
p. two
q. expert
r. want to

Circle the most appropriate response to each remark.

1. Are you Sam's brother?
   a. No, I don't.
   b. That's correct.
   c. I can assure you.
   d. As a matter of fact.

2. I'm the president's brother.
   a. Actually!
   b. You're a doll!
   c. Yeah, right!
   d. You're welcome.

3. We're leaving at six tomorrow morning.
   a. Awesome.
   b. I'm in shape.
   c. Any time.
   d. No, I'm not.

4. I work all the time.
   a. Yes, you're a party animal.
   b. Yes, you got in.
   c. Yes, you have just arrived.
   d. Yes, you're busy twenty-four-seven.

5. Are you coming to my party?
   a. I'm looking forward to it.
   b. It's a mix.
   c. I'm in shape.
   d. I can assure you that.

Write a remark or question for each of the following responses.

1. _____

   She's a teacher.

2. _____

   You're welcome.

3. _____

   I can assure you that I'll show up on time.

4. _____

   I'm an engineer from Seattle, and I've been working here for six months.

5. _____

   I can't wait.

Fill each blank with the correct form of the indicated verb.

1. I can't wait to (see) _____ you next week.

2. We are looking forward to (see) _____ you next week.

3. Are you looking forward to (go) _____ on your vacation?

4. What are you looking forward to (do) _____ there?

5. I can't wait to (hear) _____ all about it.

Imagine you are introducing two of your friends to each other. Write what you would say and what each of your friends would say. Ask an English-speaking friend to check your answers.

_____

_____

_____

_____

_____

Write a conversation between two people, using at least eight of the expressions explained in this chapter. Ask an English-speaking friend to check your answers.

_____

_____

_____

_____

_____

_____

_____

_____

_____

Expressing opinions, likes, and dislikes

Conversation: Getting acquainted

LAUREN: Hi—you must be Sarah. I can **tell** from your picture. I'm Lauren. **Finally** we meet! **So** we're going to be **roomies** this semester!

SARAH: Yes, I recognize you from your photo, too! I'm so glad to meet you in person—and I see from your T-shirt that you **like** baseball. I'm a **big fan**, too!

LAUREN: Well, the T-shirt was a **going-away present** from my brother, who's a baseball player. Look on the back—it has a photo of all the players on his team. They **actually** won the city championship this summer.

SARAH: That's **awesome**. **I tell you**, I'm not very athletic, but I **love** to watch baseball, **even if** it's a **Little League** game. You **could say** I'm a professional spectator. What about you, do you play a sport?

LAUREN: Yes, I play tennis. **As a matter of fact**, I have a **scholarship**, and I'm going to play for the university. Now tell me, what else do you **like to do**?

SARAH: Well—what I **like** to do best is dance. I'm studying classical ballet, but I also **like to** dance to popular music.

LAUREN: **Cool.** We have a lot **in common**. I **like** to dance, too. Think you'll be **up for** checking out the local clubs this weekend?

SARAH: Oh, **yeah**. And the restaurants, too. **Speaking of which**—are you hungry? I'd **love** to **grab a bite** before it gets too late. I'm starving!

LAUREN: **Are you kidding me?** I'm always **up for** going out! How about trying the place up the street? I'm kind of hungry for a good hamburger.

Later:

SARAH: Lauren, **what do you think of** our room?

LAUREN: **To be honest with you**, I really **can't stand** that dark color on the walls. It's, **like**, really **depressing**. I prefer light colors. **Plus**, I'd **like** to change the rug and the bedspreads. Do you **like** them?

SARAH: No, I agree with you. They're **horrible**. With a couple of coats of paint and a few small changes, we'll make this room comfortable and cozy. Everybody will want to **hang out** here.

LAUREN: **Man**, I'm so relieved! I think we're really going to **get along**. I'm going to call my mom right now and tell her how **cool** my new **roomie** is.

Improving your conversation

Like

Like has a number of different meanings and uses. *What do you like?* asks what things a person finds pleasing.

Do you **like** ice cream?	Yes, I do./No, I don't.
What kind of ice cream do you **like**?	I **like** vanilla. My sister **likes** chocolate.

What do you *like to do?* asks what activities a person enjoys.

What do you **like to do** on weekends?	I **like to** relax and go out with friends.

Would you like . . . ? is a polite way of asking what someone wants.

What **would you like** for your birthday?	I **would like** a big party.
What **would you like** to do today?	I **would like** to go to the movies with you.

I'm/she's/he's/etc. like . . . is often inserted into a conversation to emphasize what someone is currently feeling or thinking. This is especially common among young people.

I'm **like** really mad at him.
She's **like** scared to death.
It's **like** the worst movie I've ever seen.

Love

Love, when it refers to a person or people, indicates deep affection. When love begins, there is often a feeling of great excitement, called *being in love*.

> Her husband **loves** her, but she is no longer **in love with** him.

Love, when it refers to a thing, indicates a thing or an activity that a person finds very pleasing.

Do you like ice cream?	Yes, I **love** it!/No, I don't **like** it.
Do you like to go shopping?	Yes, I **love** it!/No, I don't **like** to.
Would you like to dance?	I'd **love** to!/I'm sorry; I promised someone else.

What do you think of . . .?

What do you *think of* this? is a way of asking someone's opinion of something.

What do you **think of** the new teacher?	She's strict, but I **think** she's great. I **like** her.

Are you kidding me?

Are you kidding me? is an expression that indicates that something is so true—or untrue—that it doesn't need to be said.

Do you like to dance?	**Are you kidding me?** I'd rather dance than eat!
Would you like to go shopping tomorrow?	**Are you kidding me?** I have to study!

Up for

To be *up for* something means to want to do it.

Are you **up for** going to the movies with us?	Yes, I'd love to go.
I'm not really **up for** doing anything tonight. I'm too tired.	

Alternative expressions are to *feel like doing* something or to *be in the mood for* (doing) something.

Do you **feel like** going to a museum?	No, I'm not **in the mood for** (going to) a museum today.

Stand

To *stand* means to tolerate/to accept.

> It's pretty hot today, but I can **stand** it.
> He went home because he couldn't **stand** the hot sun.

Can't stand often means to not like.

> He says he **can't stand** his little sister, but we know it's not true.

Big fan

To *(not)* be a *(big) fan* indicates that someone does or does not like something.

> I like movies, but I'm not a **big fan** of science fiction.

Other ways of indicating something one likes include *awesome/cool/fantastic/great/amazing*.

> College is **awesome**. My professors are **cool**, the classes are **fantastic**, the nightlife is **great**, and my friends are **amazing**.

These words are interchangeable—all of them work in the positions of the others.

> College is **great/fantastic/cool/amazing**. My professors are **awesome/fantastic/amazing**, the classes are **awesome/cool/great/amazing,** the nightlife is **awesome/cool/fantastic/amazing**, and my friends are **awesome/cool/fantastic/great**.

Other ways of indicating dislike include *horrible/terrible/depressing/gross/disgusting*.

> I didn't like that show; I thought it was **horrible**. The plot was **depressing**, and the dancing was **gross**.

Going-away present

A *going-away present* is a gift customarily given to someone who is leaving for an extended period, perhaps to go to college, to move to another area, or to work in another place.

> They gave me a picture of everyone in the office as a **going-away present** when I left for my new job.

Tell

Tell is used in a number of expressions. It is followed by an object pronoun (*me/you/her/him/us/them*), the name of a person, or a word that refers to a person or people (friend[s], parent[s], etc.). *Tell me* is a way of asking someone to relate information.

> Call me and **tell me** about your classes.

After *tell me,* the subject-verb order of a question using the verb *be* is reversed.

> Who **is she**?   **Tell me** who **she is**.
> What **are you** doing?   **Tell me** what **you are** doing.

With all other verbs, the *do/does* is dropped, and the verb is conjugated normally.

> What **do you do**?   **Tell me** what **you do**.
> Where **do they go**?   **Tell me** where **they go**.
> When **does he get in**?   **Tell me** when **he gets in**.

Don't tell me indicates that you fear a certain answer.

> **Don't tell me** you're sick! (I'm afraid you're sick!)

I tell you indicates that you really mean what you are going to say.

> **I tell you**, the dorm is really gross!
> **I'm telling you**, it looks like rain.

Tell is used with *the truth*, with or without an object pronoun.

> He always **tells** (me) the truth.

Can tell indicates the ability to know something without being told. It is followed by a new clause with a subject and verb.

> I **can tell** (that) you had a good day by that smile on your face!
> **Can** you **tell** I've been crying?

Say

Say indicates making an utterance but without indicating that it is directed at any particular person.

> What did he **say**?   He **said** that he didn't know the answer.

Say to + an object pronoun or a person's name can be used to indicate information directed at a particular person or people.

> What did he **say to you?**/What did he **tell** you?

You *could/might say* indicates a suggested conclusion.

> You **could say** she's in love.
> You **might say** the cafeteria food is gross.

Speak

To *speak* means to use a language orally.

> They don't **speak** English at home.
> She lost her front teeth and **speaks** with a lisp.
> The teacher **spoke** for almost two hours.

Speaking of which is an expression that indicates that something mentioned reminds one of other information about it.

> I'm going to apply to the state university. **Speaking of which**, did you know Melissa is going there?
> Our state representative is up for reelection. **Speaking of which**, I heard she is coming to speak at our school next week.

Finally

Finally indicates relief that something long awaited has happened. It goes after a conjugated verb.

> I've been looking for my keys all day, and I've **finally** found them.

An expression with the same meaning is *at last*, which goes at the beginning or end of the clause.

> **At last** I've found them!
> I've found them **at last**!

So

So has many different uses. In the example conversation it introduces information that both people already know.

> **So** this is your new car. Will you take me for a ride?
> **So** you're getting married! Congratulations!

Actually/as a matter of fact

Actually and *as a matter of fact* often have the same function. They have many different uses. In the example conversation they indicate that a fact is a little surprising but of interest to the other person.

> So you're an Arabic teacher! I **actually** studied Arabic in college.
> I want you to meet my sister. **As a matter of fact**, she'll be here in a few minutes.

Even if

Even if can introduce a fact that seems a little hard to believe.

> I'm going to finish this paper **even if** I have to work on it all night.

Plus

Plus adds additional information that reinforces an opinion or argument.

> I like him. He's really nice. **Plus**, he's good-looking.

To be honest with you

The phrase *to be honest with you* introduces a statement that you think a person might not want to hear.

> Thank you for inviting me to the movies, but **to be honest with you**, I'm not really a big fan of horror movies.

Yeah

Yeah is an informal way of saying *yes*. It is pronounced with two syllables: "ye-uh."

Man

Man introduces something that the speaker feels strongly about. (It can be said to or by a male or a female.)

> **Man**, this course is really hard!
> **Man**, I wish I could take a week off!
> **Man**, your sister is beautiful!

Get along

Get along (with someone) means to live, work, or play with someone without problems or arguments.

> He's very easygoing. He **gets along** with everybody.
> Tom and his brother don't **get along**. They're always fighting.

Hang out

To *hang out* means to do something socially with one or more other people.

> We're going to **hang out** at Jess's house this afternoon. We'll probably just listen to music, maybe practice that new dance step.

Grab a bite

To *grab a bite* (to eat) means to get something to eat quickly.

> We're in a hurry to get there, so we'll just **grab a bite** to eat at a fast-food place.

Roomie

Roomie is an informal name for a person who shares a bedroom or home with you.

> How do you like your new **roomie**?

Scholarship

A *scholarship* is a prize or an award that provides money that enables someone to attend a private school or university.

I'm hoping to get a **scholarship** so I can go away to college next year.

Little League

Little League is an organization that teaches baseball to children, organizes them into teams, and arranges games and tournaments for them.

He just loves baseball. He's been playing it ever since he was in **Little League**.

EXERCISE 27·11

Write a question using like *for each of the following answers.*

1. _____

I'd love to have dinner with you.

2. _____

No, I don't like fast-food restaurants.

3. _____

We'd like to go to the mountains.

4. _____

I like to go skiing then.

5. _____

No, I'm not in the mood for doing that today.

6. _____

Cherries are my favorite.

7. _____

I don't know what he likes to do.

8. _____

No. She prefers vanilla.

9. _____

Yes, I love it!

10. _____

Yes, I'd love to!

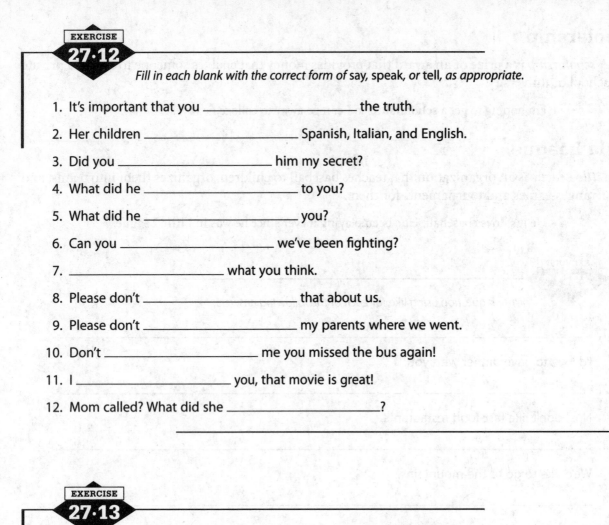

EXERCISE 27·12

Fill in each blank with the correct form of say, speak, *or* tell, *as appropriate.*

1. It's important that you _____ the truth.

2. Her children _____ Spanish, Italian, and English.

3. Did you _____ him my secret?

4. What did he _____ to you?

5. What did he _____ you?

6. Can you _____ we've been fighting?

7. _____ what you think.

8. Please don't _____ that about us.

9. Please don't _____ my parents where we went.

10. Don't _____ me you missed the bus again!

11. I _____ you, that movie is great!

12. Mom called? What did she _____?

EXERCISE 27·13

Change each question to a statement beginning with "Tell me . . . "

1. Where are you going?

   _____

2. What are they doing?

   _____

3. How do you get there?

   _____

4. When do you study?

   _____

5. Why is she crying?

   _____

6. What time do we leave?

   _____

7. Who are you texting?

_____

8. How much does it cost?

_____

Match the words or expressions in the first column with words or expressions in the second column that have a similar meaning. Note: There may be more than one match for each expression.

1. _____ great

2. _____ horrible

3. _____ can tell

4. _____ eat

5. _____ like a lot

6. _____ not argue

7. _____ not tolerate

8. _____ want to

9. _____ think of

10. _____ love

a. amazing

b. awesome

c. be a fan of

d. be in the mood for

e. be up for

f. can't stand

g. care about

h. cool

i. depressing

j. disgusting

k. fantastic

l. feel like

m. feel romantic about

n. get along with

o. grab a bite

p. gross

q. have an opinion about

r. know

Circle the word or expression that best completes each of the following sentences.

1. Why did you order this? You know I _____ this kind of food.
   a. don't get along with
   c. can't stand
   b. grab a bite with
   d. hang out with

2. She can afford to go to college. She has savings, _____ she got a scholarship.
   a. even if
   c. yeah
   b. plus
   d. finally

3. We are interested in buying the house we saw this afternoon. _____, it's much nicer than we expected.
   a. Actually
   c. Finally
   b. Plus
   d. Even if

4. Do you like your new roomie? Yeah, I _____ with her pretty well.
   a. hang out
   c. am honest
   b. stand
   d. get along

5. I just saw the movie that won the Academy Award for Best Picture. _____, what did you think of the dress the actress wore at the ceremonies?
   a. Are you kidding me?
   c. Speaking of which
   b. You might say
   d. I tell you

Circle the most appropriate response to each of the following questions or statements.

1. What did you think of her dress?
   a. Are you kidding me? It was gross.
   c. Actually, I'm not up for it.
   b. Man, I don't get along with it.
   d. I can tell you're honest with me.

2. Would you like to have dinner with me at the new Chinese restaurant?
   a. Plus, my roomie's going.
   c. To be honest with you, I can't stand Chinese food.
   b. Actually, I'm honest with you.
   d. You could grab a bite.

3. We're on the boat. Come over and hang out with us!
   a. I'm up for that.
   c. Speaking of which, I got the scholarship.
   b. I tell you, it's depressing.
   d. Plus, it's fantastic.

4. Man! I'm really hungry.
   a. Let's join Little League.
   c. You could say we don't hang out there.
   b. Let's grab a bite to eat.
   d. Speaking of which, I played in the Little League.

5. I've had a really bad day.
   a. That's awesome.
   c. I can tell.
   b. Even if it's raining.
   d. Even if you're tired.

Write an appropriate remark or question for each of the following responses.
Ask an English-speaking friend to check your answers.

1. _____

That's awesome.

2. _____

Speaking of which, I played in the Little League.

3. _____

I tell you, it's depressing.

4. _____

I'm not in the mood for that.

5. _____

As a matter of fact, I am.

6. _____

You might say it's a little difficult.

7. _____

Don't tell me you can't go!

8. _____

Finally!

Write a conversation between two people in which they ask each other and tell each other
what they like and what they like to do. Ask an English-speaking friend to check it for you.

_____

_____

_____

_____

_____

_____

_____

Answer the following questions. Ask an English-speaking friend to check your answers.

1. What do you like to do when you hang out with your friends?

   _____

2. What kind of restaurants do you like?

   _____

3. Are you usually up for going to your favorite restaurant, even if you're tired?

   _____

4. Where do you usually go to grab a bite to eat?

   _____

5. Is there anything you can't stand? Why?

   _____

Describing people, places, and things

Conversation: Talking about roommates

ERIC: **So**, Michael, what's your new roommate **like**?

MICHAEL: **Well**, if you have all day, **I'll** describe him for you. He's **quite the character**.

ERIC: I don't have all day, **dude**—but **basically**—do you get along with him?

MICHAEL: **Actually**, yeah—but that's only because we **hardly ever** see each other. The guy sleeps all day. Sometimes he gets up just to go to his classes, and **then** he comes back to the room and goes back to bed. **Then** **he'll** get up at midnight and study all night.

ERIC: **Really?** You don't eat together, **then**?

MICHAEL: **The truth is**, I don't even know when he eats, or where.

ERIC: **Then at least** he doesn't leave a mess in the kitchen.

MICHAEL: No! The guy is incredibly neat. He **actually** leaves the bathroom clean every day—and he doesn't seem to have dirty clothes. He's **like** a ghost.

ERIC: Man, I think you have the perfect roommate!

MICHAEL: **What about** yours? What's he **like**?

ERIC: **Well**, he's the exact opposite of yours. We're a lot **alike**, and we're together a lot. **I mean**, we have two classes together and we're in the same **fraternity**, so we're **really** good friends.

MICHAEL: **Sounds** to me **like** you have the ideal roommate!

ERIC: Well, yes—and no. Mine is a disaster in the house. **In the first place**, he always leaves a mess in the kitchen; he doesn't wash the dishes or take out the trash. **Plus**, he throws his clothes all over the place. **Not to mention** how he leaves the bathroom . . .

MICHAEL: **Come on**, Eric—he **sounds** a lot **like** you. **No wonder** you get along so well!

Improving your conversation

So

So has many different uses. In the example conversation, it is used to begin a question that is not surprising and may have even been expected.

> **So** how much do you want for the car? (You know I'm interested in buying it.)
> **So** when are we leaving? (We both know we are going somewhere together.)

Another use of **so** is to mean extremely.

> I can't wait to get there. I'm **so** excited.

To be like

Like asks for a description of a person, place, or thing.

What's his wife **like**? Is she nice?	Yes, she's very nice.
What's your new house **like**?	It's big, with four bedrooms and three baths.

To be *like* is also a slang (informal) expression that means to be thinking or telling your reaction.

> She comes home late, and **I'm like**, "Where have you been?"
> He told me I wasn't studying enough, and I **was like**, "What do you mean? I study for three hours every night!"
> The teacher told me I failed the math test, and I **was like**, "Oh man, my mom's going to be upset."

Look like, *smell like*, and *sound like* express similarity of appearance, smell, and sound.

> Mary **looks** (just/exactly) **like** her mother.
> This perfume **smells like** gardenias.
> When I talk to you on the phone, you **sound like** your dad.

These same combinations can also mean *seem like*, to indicate a guess about what is happening.

> It **looks like** (it's going to) rain.
> It **smells like** something's burning.
> It **sounds like** you're very upset.

When things are similar, they are said to *be*, *look*, *smell*, or *sound alike*.

> You guys **are** exactly **alike**—always getting into trouble.
> The twins **look alike**.
> These two roses **smell** (exactly) **alike**.
> You and your brother don't **sound** (at all) **alike**.

Will

Will—usually in contraction form (*'ll*)—is often used to make an offer to do something.

> I**'ll** go to the store for you.
> We**'ll** wash the dishes.

The same contraction can be used to emphasize that an activity is habitual.

> Sometimes when I'm alone I**'ll** go for a long walk.
> In the summer, he**'ll** stay up late every night playing poker with his friends.

Well

Well indicates that what you plan to say next may need a little explanation.

Did you write this letter?	**Well**, yes, but I was upset at the time, and I really didn't mean everything I wrote.
How are you?	**Well**, I'm OK now, but I've had a terrible week.

Dude

Dude is an informal, friendly way of calling a male friend or acquaintance instead of using his name.

> **Dude**, what time are we leaving tomorrow?

Basically

Basically indicates a summarized or generalized opinion.

What's your teacher like?	Well, **basically**, he's the worst teacher in the whole school.

Actually/the truth is

The terms *actually* and *the truth is* indicate that the speaker is telling the truth, even if it is surprising.

Do you like your new job?	**Actually**, yes—even though I work nine hours a day.

Another expression that means the same thing is *as a matter of fact*.

Are you moving?	**As a matter of fact**, I am!

Really

Really? is a way of asking if what was said was the truth.

I'm not going to study tonight.	**Really?** I thought you had a test tomorrow.

Really before an adjective means very.

> This movie is **really** good, but I'm **really** tired, so I'm going to bed.

Hardly ever

Hardly ever means almost never.

> You **hardly ever** call me anymore. Are you mad at me?

At least

At least indicates that a situation could be worse.

> Ooh, it's so cold outside today! Well **at least** it isn't raining.

What about . . . ?

What about . . . ? is a way to ask the same question about a different topic.

> Are you all going to the game?   Yeah, Jack and I are going.
> **What about** Joe?   No, he can't go.

I mean

I mean precedes further explanation of the previous information.

> She keeps her house really clean. **I mean**, she dusts and vacuums every day!

Other expressions that introduce further explanation include *in other words* and *that is*.

> He studies twenty-four-seven. **In other words**, he's a serious student.
> She's a real party animal. **That is**, she goes out every night.

In the first place

In the first place is used to present the first example of why you do or don't like something. *Second/in the second place* or *plus* can precede the next examples. A final example can be preceded by *not to mention that*.

> We're not happy in the suburbs.
> **In the first place**, it takes us almost two hours to get to work.
> **In the second place**, when we get home, we're exhausted.
> **Plus**, we spend so much on gas.
> **Not to mention** that the kids are in day care for more than ten hours!

Then

Then can introduce a logical conclusion.

> I've got my tickets, and my bags   **Then** you're all ready to go.
>   are packed.

Come on

Come on is a way to say that someone is exaggerating a little bit.

> I have to lose twenty pounds.   **Come on**, Alex, you're not that overweight!

It can also be used to ask for a reconsideration or change of mind.

I'm going to drive home.

Come on, dude, you've had too much to drink. Give me your keys!

Wonder

I wonder expresses an unanswered question or doubt. The subject-verb order is different from that of a question.

Where is Ellie?   **I wonder** where Ellie is.
Is Jon married?   **I wonder** if Jon's married.

No wonder indicates that something is obvious.

He's smart, energetic, well educated, and charming. **No wonder** you like him!

Quite the character

To be *quite the character* is to be unusual in some way.

She never stops talking but can always make you laugh.

Yeah, I hear she's **quite the character**.

He's really quiet and never talks to anybody, yet the girls all like him.

He must be **quite the character**.

Fraternity

A *fraternity* is an established social group made up of university men who often live together in a *frat* house. Fraternities are also known as *Greeks*, as they use Greek letters to form their names. Similar organizations exist for women and are called *sororities*.

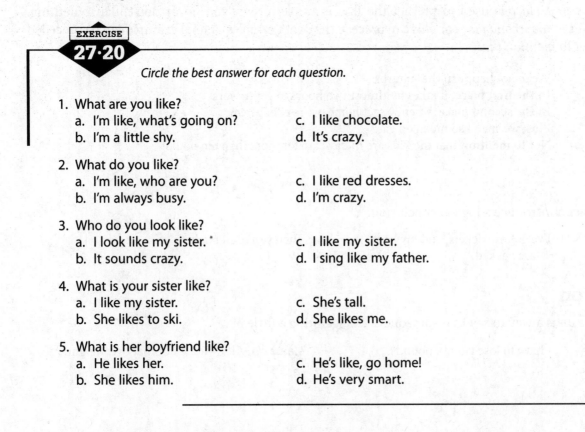

EXERCISE 27·20

Circle the best answer for each question.

1. What are you like?
   a. I'm like, what's going on?
   b. I'm a little shy.
   c. I like chocolate.
   d. It's crazy.

2. What do you like?
   a. I'm like, who are you?
   b. I'm always busy.
   c. I like red dresses.
   d. I'm crazy.

3. Who do you look like?
   a. I look like my sister.
   b. It sounds crazy.
   c. I like my sister.
   d. I sing like my father.

4. What is your sister like?
   a. I like my sister.
   b. She likes to ski.
   c. She's tall.
   d. She likes me.

5. What is her boyfriend like?
   a. He likes her.
   b. She likes him.
   c. He's like, go home!
   d. He's very smart.

EXERCISE
27·21

Write a question using like *for each of the following answers.*

1. _____

   He's very tall.

2. _____

   Yes, she does.

3. _____

   He's quite the character.

4. _____

   They like to play basketball.

5. _____

   She likes to play with dolls.

6. _____

   I'm honest.

EXERCISE
27·22

Match the words or expressions in the first column with those in the second column that have a similar meaning. Note: There may be more than one match for each expression.

1. _____ in general   a.   actually

2. _____ the truth is   b.   as a matter of fact

3. _____ almost never   c.   basically

4. _____ not to mention   d.   hardly ever

5. _____ next   e.   I mean

6. _____ it's no surprise that   f.   I wonder

7. _____ very   g.   I'm like

8. _____ in other words   h.   no wonder

9. _____ I don't know   i.   plus

10. _____ I'm thinking   j.   really

                                          k.   so

                                          l.   then

Match each question in the first column with an appropriate response from the second column.
Note: Some questions have more than one appropriate response.

1. _____ What is he like?

2. _____ What does he do?

3. _____ What does he like?

4. _____ Is he a singer?

5. _____ Does he play the piano?

6. _____ Is he in a fraternity?

7. _____ Does he call you a lot?

8. _____ When does he work?

a. Actually, he does.

b. Actually, he is.

c. Actually, he likes pizza.

d. Actually, he's really nice.

e. As a matter of fact, he doesn't.

f. As a matter of fact, he likes video games.

g. Hardly ever.

h. He doesn't have a job.

i. He looks like a movie star.

j. He's a carpenter.

k. He's a movie star.

l. He's awesome.

m. He's nice.

n. He's quite the character.

o. As a matter of fact, he is.

Circle the word or expression that best completes each of the following sentences.

1. Let's go home. I'm _____ tired.
   a. feel like
   b. basically
   c. really
   d. at least

2. We need another player for the team. _____ Tom?
   a. What about
   b. Actually
   c. As a matter of fact
   d. Hardly ever

3. It's a really hard course. _____ , I'm up all night studying.
   a. What about
   b. Then
   c. Hardly ever
   d. I mean

4. She talks a lot. _____ , she's on the telephone from the time she gets up 'til she goes to bed.
   a. So
   b. Then
   c. Plus
   d. Basically

5. This chair is _____ comfortable. I could sit here all day.
   a. so
   b. plus
   c. no wonder
   d. seems like

Circle the most appropriate response to each of the following questions or remarks.

1. Ben never showed up last night.
   a. Well, he hardly ever goes out.
   b. Come on, let's go out.
   c. At least he's sick.
   d. Actually, he's a party animal.

2. I don't think I'll go to the concert. It's too expensive.
   a. At least it costs $25.
   b. Come on, you have plenty of money.
   c. So you're going?
   d. I wonder if you have enough money.

3. What do you think of the new mayor?
   a. No wonder he is the mayor.
   b. I'll call him.
   c. What about Janice?
   d. At least he shows up at meetings.

4. There's a lot of traffic on Route 66.
   a. So where are we going?
   b. What about Route 95?
   c. Then we'll get there quickly.
   d. No wonder we like Route 66.

5. So, what do you like about your fraternity?
   a. In the first place, the guys are really cool.
   b. Dude, you're quite the character!
   c. I mean, she really likes her sorority.
   d. No wonder you're in a fraternity.

EXERCISE
27·26

The following statements explain why a friend does not like her apartment. Write in the words or expressions (e.g., in the first place, not to mention that, in the second place, plus) that introduce each statement.

I do not like my apartment.

1. _____, it's in a terrible location.

2. _____, it's way too small.

3. _____, the kitchen has really old appliances.

4. _____, there's a leak in the roof!

EXERCISE
27·27

Complete the following sentences in your own words to explain why you like or don't like something. Ask an English-speaking friend to check your answers.

What do you like or not like? _____

In the first place, _____.

Second, _____.

Plus, _____.

Not to mention that _____.

Write a conversation between you and a prospective roommate in which you describe yourself and ask him or her to do the same. Ask an English-speaking friend to check your answers.

_____

_____

_____

_____

_____

_____

_____

_____

_____

Conversation: Openers, appointments, needs

Striking up a conversation

Conversation: Running into a friend

NICOLE: Hi, Jen. **What's up?** I haven't seen you **for ages**.

JEN: Nicole! **Fancy running into you here**. Do you have time for a cup of coffee?

NICOLE: Sure. We really need to **catch up**. Do you work around here?

JEN: At the dress shop across the street. I'm a sales assistant **for the time being**, but I'm hoping they'll promote me to buyer after I have some experience **on the floor**.

NICOLE: Oh—I love that shop. Their clothes are so **trendy** and different from the **run of the mill**. You look fantastic—**I'll bet** their sales have gone up since you started working there.

JEN: Well—**I try! The thing is**, I enjoy the work, because I love the clothes, and I like helping people find what works for them. It's actually quite fulfilling.

NICOLE: Good for you. And I think the idea of becoming a buyer is great. **Before you know it**, you'll be working on your own designs. I remember how you **used to** dream of being a fashion designer.

JEN: Yeah, and I think this is **a step in the right direction**. Now, **what are you up to?** The last I heard, you were **about to** move across country. I hope you're back to stay!

NICOLE: As a matter of fact, I just got back a couple of months ago. I'm glad I went, because now I know I really want to be here. I'm working as a waitress right now but am hoping to get a teaching job. I've applied to most of the local school districts so **have my fingers crossed** I'll get something this fall.

JEN: What do you want to teach? I've heard **there are** openings for high school teachers in Howard County.

NICOLE: **No way!** I haven't even applied there. I'll do it **as soon as** I get home. Man, that'll be awesome if they need a biology teacher. Thanks for the **tip!** **Which reminds me**—waiting tables isn't all bad. On weekends I get pretty good **tips**. And **banking on** the info you just gave me, I think I'll follow you back to work and **splurge** on a new dress!

JEN: Great. I already have in mind some things for you to **try on**.

Later:

NICOLE: **Wow.** I love this one. I guess I'm **getting ahead of myself**, but I **have a feeling** this is just what I need for the interview with the principal.

JEN: And for the first day of school!

NICOLE: Thanks so much for your help. Now I'm really **pumped**! I'm so happy I **ran into** you today.

JEN: **Me, too.** Let's **make sure** we **get together** more often.

NICOLE: Yeah. I promise I'll **keep in touch**.

JEN: Take care, and **let me know** what happens. Bye for now.

NICOLE: Bye—and thanks again!

Improving your conversation

What's up?

What's up? is an informal way of asking people how they are. **What are you up to?** is a way to ask people what they have been doing lately.

Hey, Kim—**what's up?**   Oh, not much. How are you?
So, **what are you up to** these days?   Oh, just working, as usual. How about you?

Run into

Run into means to see someone by chance or in an unexpected place.

Fancy running into you here

Fancy running into you here means I didn't imagine I would see you. It is often said when you see people in places where you normally don't see them. Other expressions you could use in this situation are **fancy meeting you here** and **what a coincidence**.

For ages

For ages and **in ages** mean for a very long time.

How's Dan? I haven't seen him **for ages**.   Yes, it's been a long time. He's fine.

Before you know it

Before you know it means very quickly.

Oh, I'm so tired of school.   Calm down. **Before you know it**, you'll be finished and wishing you were back in school again!

As soon as

As soon as indicates that something will happen at the same time that something else happens.

We'll eat **as soon as** your dad gets home.
I'll call you **as soon as** I get the information.

Used to

Used to has several uses. **To be used to (something)** indicates a custom or habit.

At first it was difficult to live here, but now I **am used to** the cold weather.
I work the night shift, so I **am used to** staying up all night and sleeping during the day.

Used to (do) can indicate action that was once habitual but is no longer done, or a situation that was once true but no longer is.

> She **used to** live next door to us.
> He **used to** smoke.
> I **used to** be married to him.

Used to (do) can also indicate an action that was done routinely in the past.

> When we were little, we **used to** swim in the lake.
> When he was a kid, he **used to** ride his bike to school.

This meaning can alternatively be expressed with **would (always)** or a past tense verb.

> When we were little, we **would always** swim in the lake.
> When we were little, we **swam** in the lake.
> When he was a kid, he **would always** ride his bike to school.
> When he was a kid, he **rode** his bike to school.

Try

Try on means to put clothing, shoes, or accessories on to see if they fit or if you like them.

> I would never buy shoes without **trying** them **on** first.
> **Try** this dress **on**. Let's see how it looks.

Try out means to use a car or other equipment to see how well you handle it or if you like it.

> Your new camera looks awesome!   Would you like to **try** it **out**?

Try to/try and indicate an effort to do something that may not be easy.

> **Try to** be here before eight o'clock./**Try and** be here before eight o'clock.

Try + verb in -ing form (something) indicates a suggestion for solving a problem or problematical situation.

> I can't get the door open.   **Try turning** the key in the other direction.

I try is a way to express modesty after receiving a compliment.

> You are a good cook!   Thank you; **I try**.

There is/there are

There is is followed by a singular or non-count noun to indicate that it exists.

> **There is** a stop sign on the corner.
> **There is** milk in the refrigerator.
> **There is** too much pollution here.

There are is followed by a plural noun to indicate that more than one person, place, thing, or abstract notion exists.

> **There are** a lot of bikes on the road.
> **There are** too many people in this class.

Wow

Wow is a common way to express surprise.

Here is your exam.   **Wow!** I got an A.
This is where we'll be living for a while. **Wow**—it sure needs a lot of work!

I'll bet

I'll bet indicates sincere belief that what you are going to say is true, even though you have no proof.

What's Maria up to? **I'll bet** she's making a lot of money.

However, if you are replying to someone else's statement with **I'll bet**, this indicates that you do *not* believe it.

I hear Maria's making a lot of money.   **I'll bet.**

No way

No way is another expression that can mean two opposite things: definitely no or that's good news.

Are you going to Claudia's party?   **No way!** She hardly speaks to me.
We're going to the beach for a week.   **No way!** That sounds like a lot of fun!

On the . . .

To be **on the floor** means to be working as a salesperson in a store.

I'll bet you're tired after being **on the floor** all day.

To be **on the job** means to be working on a project that requires physical labor.

We're installing the electricity in   How long have you been **on the job?**
   the new building up the street.

Trendy

Trendy is an adjective that describes the latest fashions.

It looks like long skirts are **trendy** again this year.

Run of the mill

Run of the mill is a way to describe something very ordinary or nondescript. If used before a noun, it has a hyphen between each word; if used without a noun, there are no hyphens.

My shoes are comfortable but not trendy. They are quite **run of the mill**.
This book is quite interesting. It's not just a **run-of-the-mill** romance novel.

Tip

A **tip** is an extra payment made to a server, taxi driver, beautician, barber, or anyone else working to provide a service.

The waiter gave us great service, so he got a good **tip**.

A **tip** can also be a helpful suggestion.

The teacher told us to answer the easy questions first. That was a good **tip**.

The thing is

The thing is introduces an explanation for a situation.

Why aren't you ready for school?	**The thing is**, I can't find my backpack.
How does that guy keep his job? He never does anything.	**The thing is**, he's a friend of the boss's sister.

A step in the right direction

A step in the right direction refers to an action that will lead to success.

I'm so glad you've decided to go to college. That's definitely **a step in the right direction**.

Be about to

To **be about to** means to be going to do at that moment.

I can't talk anymore. We're **about to** leave for the airport.
Fasten your seat belt. The plane is **about to** take off.

Which reminds me

Which reminds me introduces new information that is remembered because of something that was just said. An alternative to this expression is **speaking of which**.

I'm about to go shopping for Halloween costumes for the kids—**which reminds me**—do you still have the witch hat you borrowed from me last year?
I heard that Brittany was in town. **Speaking of which**, did you know she was getting married?

Have one's fingers crossed

To **have one's fingers crossed** means to indicate strong desire or hope that something happens.

I **have my fingers crossed** that we'll win the game tonight.

Pumped

To be **pumped** means to be very excited and ready for an occasion or event. An alternative expression is **all fired up**.

The whole team is really **pumped** about the game tomorrow. We're ready to win.

Bank on

To **bank on** means to rely on, count on, or trust certain information.

Do you think our candidate will win the election?	You can **bank on** it. All the polls say he's ahead.

Splurge

To **splurge** means to spend more money than necessary on something, because you really want it.

She got a bonus at work, so she **splurged** on a first-class ticket.
Why don't we **splurge** and buy the beautiful sofa instead of the run-of-the-mill one?

Another expression that indicates spending a lot of money is **go overboard**.

It was their anniversary, so they **went overboard** and stayed at a five-star resort.

Get together

To **get together** means to meet.

They **get together** every week to discuss their research.

Keep in touch

To **keep in touch** means to continue to contact each other.

They have **kept in touch** for more than thirty years.

Catch up

To **catch up** can mean to find out the news of a friend you haven't seen in a while.

Let's get together for lunch tomorrow. We have a lot to **catch up** on!

It can also mean to reach someone who is ahead of you.

She's running so fast, we can never **catch up** with her.

Catch up can also mean to learn what the rest of the class learned when you weren't at school.

After being home sick for a week, Adrian had to work hard to **catch up** on his lessons.

Get ahead of oneself

To **get ahead of oneself** means to make plans based on something that may not happen. Another expression that has the same meaning is **to count one's chickens before they hatch**.

What? You just met him and you're already planning what to name your children? Aren't you **getting ahead of yourself**? You should never **count your chickens before they hatch**!

Have a feeling

To **have a feeling** about something is to think that it might be true or might happen.

They've never met, but I **have a feeling** they might like each other.

Make sure

To **make sure** means to follow all of the steps that will lead to a desired outcome.

Yes, you can take my car, but **make sure** you bring it back by four o'clock.

Let someone know

To **let someone know** means to tell a person information that he or she needs.

I'm not sure I can pick you up. I'll **let you know** as soon as I find out if my car is fixed.

Me, too

Me, too is a way of saying that you agree with something positive that someone has said or that you have an activity in common with someone else.

| I really like living in Springfield. | **Me, too**. |
| I'm going home now. | **Me, too**. |

Me, neither is used to express the same meanings after a negative statement.

| I really don't like living in Springfield. | **Me, neither**. |
| I'm not going home yet. | **Me, neither**. |

EXERCISE

28·1

Choose between There is *and* There are *to complete the following sentences.*

1. _____ only twenty-eight days in February.

2. _____ a lot of people in this city.

3. _____ a big pothole in this street.

4. _____ too many cars on the road.

5. _____ too much traffic here.

EXERCISE

28·2

Fill in each blank with the correct form of the indicated verb.

1. We're not used to (live) _____ in such a small space.

2. We used to (live) _____ in a big house.

3. He's fine now, but he used to (get) _____ into trouble all the time.

4. She used to (smoke) _____. I'm so glad she quit.

5. I can't get used to (get) _____ up so early.

6. I used to (stay) _____ up late every night.

7. Are you used to (work) _____ this hard?

8. I know that guy. He used to (go) _____ to my school.

9. They are used to (be) _____ cold in January.

10. It's hard to get used to (drive) _____ in traffic.

Circle the word or words that best complete each of the following sentences.

1. Always _____ your best.
   a. try to do   c. trying on
   b. try doing   d. trying out

2. I love these shoes. I'm going to _____.
   a. try buying them   c. try them on
   b. try them out   d. try

3. Before you buy any machine you should first _____.
   a. try buying it   c. try it out
   b. try it on   d. try it

4. You're a very good driver! Thanks, _____.
   a. I try to.   c. Try me.
   b. I try.   d. I'm trying to.

5. I can't get my finger to stop bleeding. _____ a bandage on it.
   a. Try to put   c. Try on
   b. Try out   d. Try putting

Match the words or expressions in the first column with those in the second column that have a similar meaning. Note: There may be more than one match for each expression.

1. _____ What a coincidence.   a. before you know it

2. _____ That's a wise decision.   b. Fancy meeting you here.

3. _____ I'll bet.   c. for ages

4. _____ I agree.   d. get ahead of yourself

5. _____ speaking of which   e. I don't think so.

6. _____ hopefully   f. I have my fingers crossed.

7. _____ count your chickens before they hatch   g. Me, neither.

8. _____ soon   h. No way!

9. _____ for a long time   i. Me, too.

10. _____ I don't agree.   j. That's a step in the right direction.

                                            k. What a surprise.

                                            l. which reminds me

                                            m. Wow!

Match the words or expressions in the first column with those in the second column that have a similar meaning. Note: There may be more than one match for each expression.

1. _____ be hopeful   a. be on the floor

2. _____ be all fired up   b. be on the job

3. _____ be accustomed to   c. be pumped

4. _____ see if something fits   d. be used to

5. _____ test something   e. catch up

6. _____ be working   f. get together

7. _____ spend a lot   g. go overboard

8. _____ meet   h. have a feeling

9. _____ write, call, or text   i. have your fingers crossed

10. _____ make up missed work   j. keep in touch

11. _____ get news   k. let someone know

12. _____ suspect   l. make sure

13. _____ not forget to do   m. splurge

                                   n. try it on

                                   o. try it out

                                   p. run into

Circle the most appropriate response to each question or remark.

1. What are you up to?
   a. I'm not used to wearing a suit.   c. I'm pumped up.
   b. I used to try.   d. I'm about to go on vacation.

2. I'm going back to school.
   a. Me, neither.   c. Don't get ahead of yourself.
   b. That's a step in the   d. Thanks for the tip.
      right direction.

3. Be sure to talk to my friend. He's in charge of the program.
   a. Thanks for the tip!   c. I'll run into him.
   b. I'll try it out.   d. I'm on the job.

4. Fancy meeting you here.
   a. Yes, what a coincidence.
   b. I haven't seen him for ages.
   c. Yes, it's a fancy restaurant.
   d. It's a run-of-the-mill restaurant.

5. It was great to see you again.
   a. I'll catch up with you.
   b. Be sure to keep in touch.
   c. Try to catch up.
   d. You're getting ahead of yourself.

EXERCISE

28·7

Match each remark in the first column with all of the appropriate responses from the second column.

1. _____ That was great service.

2. _____ What's up?

3. _____ This top is so trendy.

4. _____ I have a feeling she's pregnant.

5. _____ Let's get together soon.

6. _____ I have a little extra money.

7. _____ You can get a coupon online.

8. _____ He's on the job now.

9. _____ I'm pumped up about my date.

10. _____ Do you think he'll be there?

a. I have my fingers crossed!

b. I try!

c. I'll catch up with him later.

d. I'll keep in touch.

e. Let me know how it goes.

f. Let's splurge!

g. No way!

h. Not much.

i. Thanks for the tip.

j. Try it on!

k. Wow!

l. I have a feeling he will.

EXERCISE

28·8

Supply the following information in complete sentences. Ask an English-speaking friend to check your answers.

1. Write three things you used to do but don't do anymore.

   _____

   _____

   _____

2. Write three things that you are used to doing now that you weren't used to doing some years ago.

_____

_____

_____

3. Do you keep in touch with an old friend? How?

_____

4. What do you and your friends do when you get together?

_____

5. What are you pumped up about?

_____

_____

EXERCISE

28·9

Write a paragraph of five sentences in which you tell what you try to do every day. Ask an English-speaking friend to check your answers.

_____

_____

_____

_____

EXERCISE

28·10

Write a conversation between two old friends who run into each other in a shopping mall—seeing each other for the first time in five years. Use at least eight of the expressions described in this chapter. Ask an English-speaking friend to check your answers.

_____

_____

_____

_____

_____

_____

_____

Making dates and appointments

Conversation A: Making an appointment with a doctor

RECEPTIONIST: Drs. Manning and Sharp. How **can** I help you?

LISA: Hello. My name is Lisa Peterson. I'd like to make an appointment to see Dr. Sharp, hopefully sometime next week.

RECEPTIONIST: And what is it you want to see him about?

LISA: I need a complete physical for a new job I'm about to take.

RECEPTIONIST: Do you have a form that **has to** be filled out?

LISA: Yes, I do—and it looks like I'll need a pretty thorough exam.

RECEPTIONIST: **Can** you fax it to me? That way I'll know how much time to allot for your appointment.

LISA: Sure. **Can** you give me your fax number?

RECEPTIONIST: It's 202-739-5906.

LISA: Good. **I'll** fax it to you right away. **Will** you call me back when you get it?

RECEPTIONIST: **Right.**

Later:

RECEPTIONIST: Hello, Lisa. This is Dr. Sharp's office. I see you're going to need an hour-long appointment, and Dr. Sharp **won't be able** to do that for at least another month. **I could** give you an appointment with Dr. Manning next Thursday, **though**, **at** 1 P.M. **Would** you like to take that?

LISA: Um . . . yes, that sounds fine. Is there anything I **should** do to prepare for the exam?

RECEPTIONIST: Yes. I know this will be difficult, but you **mustn't** eat or drink anything after midnight the night before. **I wish I could** give you an appointment earlier in the day, but we don't have any other openings.

LISA: OK. But if there is a cancellation earlier in the day, please let me know. **I'd much rather** come in early in the morning.

RECEPTIONIST: **Of course.**

LISA: Thanks very much. Good-bye.

Conversation B: Changing a lunch date

LISA: Hi, Maria. It's Lisa. **Listen,** I'm not going to **be able** to have lunch with you next Thursday. I **have to** have a physical for my new job, and it's on Thursday at one o'clock—and it's in Alexandria. I'm really sorry. **Can** we make it another day?

MARIA: **No problem.** How about Friday **at** 12:30?

LISA: **Oh dear,** I **can't** do that, either. **Could** you do Wednesday?

MARIA: **Look,** we're going to have to make it the following week. We've **both** got **too much on our plates** right now. **Let's say** Thursday, the twenty-fourth, at one o'clock. OK?

LISA: **Perfect.** We'll have a lot to talk about by then!

Improving your conversation

In/on/at to indicate events

Events—dates, appointments, meetings, receptions, parties, concerts, classes, and so on—all have set days, times, and locations that are indicated by certain prepositions.

In indicates the month or year of an event.

> Her birthday dinner is **in** October.
> The celebration is **in** 2014.

On indicates the day or date of an event.

> The appointment is **on** Friday.
> Our classes are **on** Tuesdays and Thursdays.
> Her party is **on** August 13.

At indicates the time of an event.

> The reception is **at** ten o'clock.
> The concert is **at** 4:30.

Periods of the day are indicated as follows:

> **in** the morning
> **in** the afternoon
> **at** night

At indicates the location of an event or number in the street address.

> The movie is **at** the State Theater.
> The State Theater is **at** 405 S. Washington Street.

On indicates the name of the street in the address of the location.

> The movie is **at** the theater **on** State Street.

In indicates a location of an event where the address is already understood.

> The movie is **in** Theater A.
> The meeting is **in** the boss's office.

Modal auxiliaries

Following are explanations of the different uses of **modal auxiliaries**—verbs that modify other verbs in certain ways. They have the same conjugation in all forms.

> I/you/he/she/it/we/they   **will/can/may/might/could/would/should/must**

Will can indicate a prediction for the future. The negative form of **will** is **won't**.

> We **will** get fat if we eat too much candy.
> He **won't** be here long—he's leaving in a few minutes.

Will + **probably** indicates what is likely to happen.

> I **will probably** be home after midnight.
> She **probably won't** be with me.

Will is used to ask and accept favors.

> **Will** you lend me your pen?   Yes, I **will**.

Won't is used to refuse to do something.

> **Will** you lend me a thousand dollars?   No, I **won't**.

Can indicates ability. The negative form of **can** is **can't**.

> Present tense: She **can** cook like a pro. She **can't** sing, though.
> Past tense: She **could** cook when she was very young. She **couldn't** sing then, either.

An alternative way to indicate ability is **be able** to.

> She **is able** to cook.
> She **was able** to cook when she was young.
> She **will be able** to cook like a pro when she finishes culinary school.

Can also indicates permission.

> Present tense: He **can't** go to the movies with us. (His mother said no.)
> Past tense: He **couldn't** go to the movies with us.
> Future: He **won't be able** to go to the movies with us.

May is another way to ask for and give permission.

> **May** we sit here?   Yes, you **may.**/No, you **may not.**

May can also indicate possibility. Alternative ways to indicate this are **might** and **maybe** + **will**.

> It **may** rain tomorrow.
> It **might** rain tomorrow.
> **Maybe** it **will** rain tomorrow.

Could, in addition to being the past tense of **can**, also indicates a suggestion.

> How can I impress my boss?   You **could** wear a suit and tie to work.

Could is also a polite way to ask permission.

> **Could** I borrow a cup of sugar?   Of course, you **can/may**.

Should indicates direct or indirect advice.

> What **should** I wear to the interview?
> You **should** go home now.
> He **shouldn't** be here.
> Past tense: You **should have** gone home.

Ought to can be used to give direct or indirect advice. It is not used in a question or in negative form.

> What **should** I wear?   You **ought to** wear a suit.
> He **ought to** come to work on time.
> We **ought to have** been nicer to them.

Would is used with *if* to indicate how things could be different under different circumstances.

> If I were the teacher, I **would** make sure the children had fun while learning.

Would like is a polite way to say what you want.

> We **would like** three ice-cream cones.
> They **would like** donuts.

Would rather is a way to indicate preference. It is often contracted to **I'd, you'd, he'd, she'd, they'd**.

> She is teaching geometry, but she **would rather** teach algebra.
> I'm leaving now, but **I'd rather** stay here.

Would can also be a past tense marker, indicating repeated or habitual activity to describe the past.

> When we were little, we **would** go to my grandmother's house every Sunday for dinner.
> I **would** always play with my cousin, Bobby.
> Sometimes, we **would** get into trouble.

Must indicates probability. The negative form is not contracted for this meaning.

> He left at four o'clock, so he **must** be in Chicago by now.
> She doesn't answer her phone. She **must not** be home.

Must not indicates prohibition or strong advice. It is often contracted to **mustn't**.

> You **must not** put your feet on the table.
> You **mustn't** walk alone after dark.

Have to

Have to indicates obligation or necessity.

> Lee **has to** be at work by seven o'clock.
> Do you **have to** leave so early?   No, I **don't have to** leave. I thought you were ready for everyone to go home.

Supposed to

Supposed to indicates advice to follow a custom.

> We're **supposed to** be seated at our desks before the bell rings.
> You're not **supposed to** text during class.

Wish

To **wish** means to be sorry that something is not true. It is followed by a verb in the subjunctive mood. Present tense subjunctive forms are as follows:

The verb *be*: use **were** for all subjects (I, you, he, she, it, we, they).

> (You are not here.)   I **wish** you **were** here.
> (We are not in California.)   We **wish** we **were** in California.
> (He is not tall.)   He **wishes** he **were** tall.

All other verbs: use the past tense form.

> (She can't go to the concert.)   She **wishes** she **could go** to the concert.
> (I don't like to dance.)   I **wish** I **liked** to dance.
> (She doesn't study enough.)   We **wish** she **studied** more.

I wish! indicates that it would please you if something said were really true, even though you believe that it isn't true.

> You're the best student in the class.   **I wish!**

How about . . . ?

How about . . . ? is a way of making a suggestion.

> I want to go shopping.   **How about** going with me this afternoon?
> Do you have these shoes in size six?   No, but **how about** these? They're very similar.

Let's say

Let's say is a way of making a more forceful suggestion.

I want to go shopping.   **Let's say** you do your homework first.
Can you pick me up at 5 P.M.?   **Let's say** 5:30; I can't get there by 5.

Oh dear

Oh dear is an exclamation that indicates you wish something weren't true or hadn't happened.

Oh dear, I dropped my bag and my stuff is everywhere.
Oh dear, I said Friday and I meant Thursday. I'm so sorry.

Look

Look is an expression that indicates that you want the person you are speaking to to understand what you are going to say next.

You got here late!   **Look**, I said I was sorry.

Listen

Saying **listen** indicates that you want the person you are speaking to to pay attention to what you are going to say next.

You won't believe what I just heard   **Listen**, I don't want to hear any more gossip!
about Carrie.

Both

Both is used as a pronoun or adjective to refer to any two people, places, objects, or abstract notions.

I invited Todd and Carlos. I hope **both** of them can come.
We went to New York and Washington. **Both** are fascinating cities./They are **both** fascinating
cities./**Both** cities are fascinating.
I couldn't decide which shoes to buy, so I bought **both** pairs.

Though

Though can be used to mean however—indicating that there is an alternative answer.

Are you a good baseball player?   No, I'm good at hockey, **though**.
Is he in the band?   No, he does play the guitar, **though**.

Have too much on one's plate

To have too much on one's plate is an expression that indicates that someone is very busy—probably because of an unusual project or happening.

Look—I'd like to help you out, but we just moved to a new house, I'm learning a new job, and
I just **have too much on my plate** right now.

Right

Right indicates that you understand or agree with what was just said.

Am I supposed to wear a tie?   **Right.**

Yeah, right! is a sarcastic answer that indicates that what was said previously is ridiculous.

You're wearing a tie, of course.	**Yeah, right!** [Of course not!]
I got all As last semester.	**Yeah, right!** [I don't believe you.]

Perfect

Perfect indicates that you accept a suggestion or offer.

We can discuss this further at the meeting tomorrow.	**Perfect.**
Shall we meet in the cafeteria for lunch?	**Perfect.**

Of course

Of course indicates that what was said is agreed to or obvious.

Will you go over my homework with me?	**Of course.**
Do we have to work tomorrow?	**Of course!** It's not a holiday.

No problem

No problem can mean that a request is accepted.

Is it OK if I come in late tomorrow? I have a doctor's appointment.	**No problem.**

No problem can also be used as a reply to an expression of thanks. An alternative expression with the same meaning is **you're welcome**.

Thanks so much for fixing my flat tire.	**No problem.**	
Excuse me, you dropped your wallet.	Oh, thank you!	**You're welcome.**

EXERCISE
28·11

Fill in each blank with the appropriate preposition (in, on, at).

1. The game is _____ Fairfax High School, _____ the gymnasium, _____ Saturday _____ eight o'clock _____ the evening.

2. Our wedding is _____ November _____ Springfield Country Club.

3. The inauguration is _____ 2013 _____ the Capitol _____ Washington, D.C.

4. The dinner is _____ Friday _____ six o'clock _____ the evening _____ Emily's restaurant _____ the back room.

5. The show is _____ July 24 _____ one o'clock _____ the afternoon _____ the art gallery _____ Jefferson Avenue _____ Leesville.

Express the following using modal verbs or their alternatives.

1. (You are a student.) Ask your teacher for permission to leave the classroom.

   _____

2. (You are a teacher.) Tell your students that they are not allowed to leave the classroom.

   _____

3. Ask your friend if it is important for him to work today.

   _____

4. (You are the boss.) Tell your employee that she is obligated to work tomorrow.

   _____

5. (You are sick.) Ask your doctor for her advice about when to take the medicine she prescribed.

   _____

6. (You are a doctor.) Tell your patient that it is customary to take the medicine just before a meal.

   _____

7. (You are a police officer.) Tell a pedestrian not to jaywalk (cross the street in the middle of a block).

   _____

8. (You are a pedestrian.) Ask a police officer if it is necessary for you to wait for a green light before crossing.

   _____

9. (You are a waiter.) Ask your customer if he prefers his steak medium or well done.

   _____

10. Invite your friends to a party at your house on Saturday night.

   _____

11. Ask your brother to pick you up at the airport.

   _____

12. Tell your sister that you refuse to pick her up.

   _____

EXERCISE
28·13

Match the words or expressions in the first column with the words or expressions in the second column that have a similar meaning. There may be more than one match for each item.

1. _____ she prefers

2. _____ she wants

3. _____ she is able to

4. _____ she has permission to

5. _____ maybe she will

6. _____ she is advised to

7. _____ she probably isn't

8. _____ she probably doesn't

9. _____ she accepts

10. _____ she refuses

11. _____ she is advised not to

12. _____ she is not allowed to

13. _____ she is unable to

14. _____ maybe she won't

a. she can

b. she cannot

c. she is supposed to

d. she may

e. she may not

f. she might

g. she might not

h. she must not be

i. she mustn't

j. she ought to

k. she should

l. she shouldn't

m. she will

n. she won't

o. she would like

p. she would rather

q. she must not

EXERCISE
28·14

Fill in each blank with the correct form of the indicated verb.

1. I wish you (be) _____ here.

2. She wishes she (can) _____ go to school.

3. We wish they (will) _____ call us.

4. I wish we (have) _____ more time.

5. They wish I (do not) _____ spend my money on cars.

6. He wishes he (be) _____ back home.

7. Don't you wish it (be) _____ your birthday?

8. I wish I (can) _____ tell you the news.

9. I wish she (call) _____ me more often.

10. They wish she (live) _____ closer to their house.

Write a sentence using I wish *to indicate your dissatisfaction with the statement.*

1. You don't love me.

_____

2. My neighbors make a lot of noise.

_____

3. My mother isn't here.

_____

4. I'm not married.

_____

5. She can't stay here tonight.

_____

6. He won't move his car.

_____

7. She drives too fast.

_____

8. They come home late.

_____

9. I don't have enough money.

_____

10. Our house is too small.

_____

Circle the most appropriate response to each question or remark.

1. I wish we could take a vacation.
   a. Perfect.
   b. Yeah, right.
   c. Look—we can't afford it.
   d. Oh dear.

2. We'd rather go to the mountains than the beach.
   a. Listen—why don't you go to the mountains, and we'll go to the beach.
   b. Look—I'm tired.
   c. Perfect. Let's say we all go to the beach.
   d. Oh dear. Then we'll all go to the beach.

3. Can you help me with these packages?
   a. Oh dear, I can.
   b. Oh dear, I can't.
   c. Let's say no.
   d. Perfect.

4. Are you graduating in June?
   a. No problem!
   b. I wish!
   c. You have too much on your plate.
   d. I mustn't.

5. Why is your project late?
   a. No problem!
   b. Of course!
   c. I have too much on my plate!
   d. Right!

Match the words or expressions in the first column with those in the second column that have a similar meaning. There may be more than one match for each expression.

1. _____ Oh dear.
2. _____ Perfect.
3. _____ Of course.
4. _____ Let's say . . .
5. _____ Yeah, right.
6. _____ No problem.
7. _____ I wish.
8. _____ Look, . . .
9. _____ Listen, . . .
10. _____ Right.

a. How about . . .
b. I don't believe you.
c. I made a mistake.
d. It's OK with me.
e. No problem.
f. Of course not.
g. Pay attention.
h. That's a shame.
i. That's fine with me.
j. Too bad that's not true.
k. Understand this, . . .
l. Yes.
m. You don't need to ask.

Write a question or remark for each of the following responses. Ask an English-speaking friend to check your answers.

1. _____

Yeah, right.

2. _____

I wish!

3. _____

Of course!

4. _____

No problem.

5. _____

Right.

Write the details (name of event, day, date, time, location) of two events: one that you attended recently and one that you plan to attend in the near future. Ask an English-speaking friend to check your work.

Past event:

_____

_____

_____

Future event:

_____

_____

_____

Write a telephone conversation in which you make an appointment with a professional of some kind (doctor, lawyer, teacher, businessperson, etc.). Use at least eight of the expressions explained in this chapter. Ask an English-speaking friend to check your work.

_____

_____

_____

_____

_____

_____

_____

_____

_____

_____

Expressing wants and needs

Conversation: Looking for a new apartment

RECEPTIONIST: Good morning! How can I help you?

TED: **I'd like** to rent an apartment in this neighborhood and wonder if you can help me.

RECEPTIONIST: You **need** to talk to Shirley—she's our **go-to** agent for apartment rentals. Here, I'll take you to her office.

SHIRLEY: Hello, I'm Shirley. Have a seat and tell me what kind of apartment you're looking for. Is it just for you?

TED: Well, that depends on what's available. I'd really rather live alone, but if I don't see anything that works, I could share a bigger place with a friend of mine.

SHIRLEY: OK. First, tell me what you **have in mind**.

TED: The most important thing is the location. I want to be in the city, **preferably** in this neighborhood, so I can walk to the university and to the metro station. I don't have a car.

SHIRLEY: OK, then you **don't mind** if there's no parking space.

TED: Exactly. But I want a secure building. I also want it to have a living room, a dining room, one bedroom, and, of course, a modern kitchen and bathroom. I don't really **need all the bells and whistles**, but I would like to have a balcony.

SHIRLEY: And what is your budget? I mean, what monthly rent are you thinking about, including **utilities**?

TED: I'm hoping to find something for about $700 a month.

SHIRLEY: Look, I can tell you right now **there are no** decent apartments in this area under $1,200 a month—and **none** of them **have** dining rooms or balconies. There are modern, secure buildings that are actually near the metro—but they're at least six miles outside of the city.

TED: There's no way I'm going to live way out there. Do you think you could find a two-bedroom place closer in for, **say**, $1,400 a month? Something I could share with my friend?

SHIRLEY: Let me do a little research this morning and see what I can find. I'm not going to tell you that it's impossible, but I can't promise anything, either. Give me a couple of hours to see what's **out there**. If I find anything **worthwhile**, we can go **have a look** this afternoon. **In the meantime**, I **need** you to fill out this form so I have your contact information. As a matter of fact, both you and your friend will have to fill out an application in order to be approved as tenants. I'm assuming you want a one-year lease. Is that right? Oh, **one more thing**: you don't have a pet, do you?

TED: Yes, I'm willing to sign a one-year lease, and no, I don't have a pet. And I'll make sure my friend **gets rid of** his dog. He can leave it with his family—they have a place in the **country**. I'd better go give him a **heads-up** right now.

SHIRLEY: Good. Be sure both of you bring your financial and credit information with you.

TED: Right. We'll see you at noon, then. Thank you very much.

SHIRLEY: See you later.

Improving your conversation

Need

There are several words that indicate that something is required. To **need** is used to require urgent attention or action to prevent damage.

> I **need** a doctor. I'm really dizzy.
> We **need** to rest. We've been working for six hours.
> Flowers **need** water.

Need can also indicate a requirement dictated by someone else.

> I **need** six more credits in order to graduate.
> The children **need** to bring pencils and erasers to class.
> To be a taxi driver, you **need** to have a special driver's license.

To **have to** can indicate a personal need or an obligation to someone else.

> I **have to** get my car fixed.
> He **has to** work on Saturdays.
> You **have to** complete the prerequisites before you can take advanced courses.
> She was speeding and **has to** pay a $100 fine.

To **be required to** indicates you have to do something that is imposed by some sort of authority.

> The children are **required to** do their homework before watching television.
> The cadets are **required to** wear their uniforms to class.
> This warrant means you are **required to** allow the police to search your office.

A **requirement** is a standard imposed on someone by some sort of authority.

> Ability to speak another language is a **requirement** for this position.
> It's a **requirement** of the home owners' association that you keep your yard neat.

A **prerequisite** is proof of previous instruction or ability necessary for a certain job, course, or position.

> This course is open to beginners. There are no **prerequisites**.
> A master's degree in business is a **prerequisite** for this job.

Want

To **want** means to have a desire for something and indicates some belief that it will be attained.

> We **want** to move to a better neighborhood. (We're saving our money.)
> She **wants** to go to college. (She is trying to make good grades in high school.)
> He **wants** an ice-cream cone. (He is going to the ice-cream store/ordering ice cream.)

Would like indicates a desire that may or may not be possible to satisfy.

> **We'd like** a house with four bedrooms.
> **I'd like** to go on a vacation.
> **He'd like** to be able to visit his family at least once a year.

Mind

To **have in mind** means to have a good idea of the kind of thing you want.

> Sure, I'll help you decorate your living room. What kind of look do you **have in mind**?

To **have a mind to** means to be strongly considering an action.

> He stole money from me! I **have a mind to** report him.

To **mind** can mean to not be happy about something. This is the meaning used in the example conversation.

> I don't **mind** going to the store. I'm happy to do it.

To **mind** can mean to take charge of a store or shop.

> Thank you for **minding** the store while I had lunch.

To **mind** can also mean to babysit.

> Could you **mind** the children while I go to the store?

To **mind** can also mean to pay attention to.

> No, I won't babysit for your children, because they won't **mind** me.
> Don't **mind** her—she doesn't know what she's talking about.

To **make up your mind** means to decide.

> Do you want pizza or pasta? **Make up your mind!**
> I can't **make up my mind** between the SUV and the van.

To **change your mind** means to have a different idea or opinion than before.

> I was going to paint the dining room red, but I **changed my mind** and painted it blue.

Never mind means to disregard what was said. **Forget it** is another way of expressing this.

> What did you say?   **Never mind**—it wasn't important.

Mind is also a noun that refers to the brain.

> At the age of ninety-five, her body is weak, but her **mind** is still perfect.

A **mind reader** is someone who knows what someone else is thinking.

> How was I supposed to know you had a headache? I'm not a **mind reader**.

There is and there are

There is indicates that something exists, and is followed by a singular noun.

> **There is** a gas station up ahead.

There are indicates that more than one thing exists, and is followed by a plural noun.

> **There are** several gas stations about three miles down the road.

Words that indicate that nothing exists—such as **zero**, **no**, and **not any**—are followed by a plural noun.

> We have exactly **zero** applications for the position.
> There are **no** heart specialists in this area.
> She doesn't have **any** brothers or sisters.

Likewise, the pronoun that takes the place of these words, **none**, is followed by a plural verb.

> We have three teachers to contact, but **none** (of them) **are** available this week.

Have a look

To **have a look** means to make a short investigation.

> I lost my earring yesterday. Do you think it might be at your house?   I'll **have a look** and see if I can find it.

Get rid of

To **get rid of** means to make sure to no longer have something.

> The car used too much gas, so we **got rid of** it. We sold it last week.
> You should **get rid of** that suit. It doesn't look good on you.

Preferably

Preferably indicates someone's first choice.

> I'd like to buy a new car, **preferably** one that doesn't use much gas.

Go-to

Go-to is an expression used as an adjective to describe a person, place, or object that people depend on or "go to first" for what they need.

> You need a handyman? Call Ron—he's my **go-to** person for everything that goes wrong in the house.
> I love Cherrydale Hardware. It's my **go-to** store for supplies.

Worthwhile

Worthwhile describes something that has value in terms of time, money, experience, or purpose.

> The translation course is intensive, but it is really **worthwhile**.
> Cancer research is a **worthwhile** cause.

Out there

Out there is an expression that refers to the real world, at the present time.

> Go out and have fun! There are a lot of nice people **out there**.
> I'm always careful walking at night. You never know what dangers are **out there**.

Utilities

Utilities include the services necessary for the functioning of a house or apartment, including those for water and sewage, heating, air-conditioning, electricity, and sometimes trash collection.

> Some apartment buildings include the cost of **utilities** in the monthly rent, and some don't.

All the bells and whistles

The expression **all the bells and whistles** refers to the most modern, up-to-date—usually expensive—features of homes and other buildings that are either new or recently remodeled.

> The apartment has **all the bells and whistles**—a soaking tub with jets, multiple showerheads, granite countertops and stainless-steel appliances in the kitchen, energy-efficient appliances, and many more exclusive features.

Country

Country can refer to a nation.

> What **country** are you from?   I'm from Colombia.

Country can also refer to the areas that are distant from cities, often where there are farms.

> We like to go to the **country** on weekends, to get some peace and quiet.

A heads-up

A **heads-up** is a warning that something is going to happen, so that the other person will be ready.

> Hey, Mom—I'm bringing a friend home for dinner and wanted to give you **a heads-up**.

Say

Say can introduce an example of a possibility.

> I'm sure you can get someone to pick you up. Why don't you ask, **say**, Rosita or Laura?
> Why don't you paint this room a brighter color, **say**, yellow or green?

In the meantime

In the meantime indicates a period of time between two events. Another word with the same meaning is **meanwhile**.

It will be a big help if you go to the store and get what we need for dinner. **In the meantime,** I'll set the table.

Joey had to go away for six months. **In the meantime,** Julie went to classes and learned to cook.

One more thing

One more thing is an expression used at the end of a series of remarks. It could be something important that you almost forgot to say or a question that you almost forgot to ask.

OK, now, go to school. Mind the teacher, try to finish all your work, and don't pick fights with the other kids. **One more thing:** don't forget to thank the teacher for helping you with your math!

So, doctor, I'll take the medicine you gave me and go to physical therapy. **One more thing—** when do you think I'll be able to go back to work?

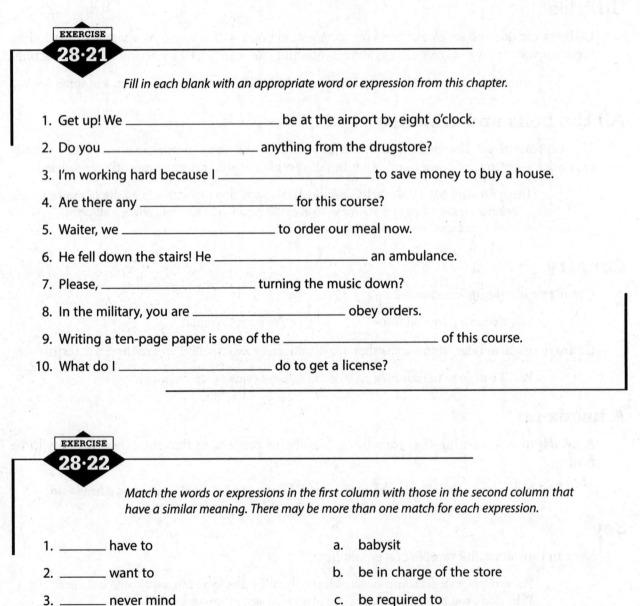

EXERCISE

28·21

Fill in each blank with an appropriate word or expression from this chapter.

1. Get up! We _____ be at the airport by eight o'clock.

2. Do you _____ anything from the drugstore?

3. I'm working hard because I _____ to save money to buy a house.

4. Are there any _____ for this course?

5. Waiter, we _____ to order our meal now.

6. He fell down the stairs! He _____ an ambulance.

7. Please, _____ turning the music down?

8. In the military, you are _____ obey orders.

9. Writing a ten-page paper is one of the _____ of this course.

10. What do I _____ do to get a license?

EXERCISE

28·22

Match the words or expressions in the first column with those in the second column that have a similar meaning. There may be more than one match for each expression.

1. _____ have to
2. _____ want to
3. _____ never mind
4. _____ not care
5. _____ not be bothered
6. _____ have a new opinion

a. babysit
b. be in charge of the store
c. be required to
d. change your mind
e. forget it
f. have a good mind

7. _____ be intelligent

8. _____ mind

9. _____ decide

g. have a mind to

h. need to

i. not mind

j. pay attention to

k. would like to

l. wouldn't mind

m. make up your mind

Circle the most appropriate response to each question or remark.

1. There are no decent men for me to date.
   a. Come on! There are lots of worthwhile men out there.
   b. Give me a heads-up.
   c. Make up your mind.
   d. Never mind. He's our go-to person.

2. The utilities will cost us a fortune.
   a. It's a prerequisite.
   b. Have a look at the basement.
   c. Still, the house is worthwhile.
   d. It's out there.

3. Why don't you consider a trip to, say, the Caribbean or Hawaii?
   a. It's not a requirement.
   b. One more thing, it's in the country.
   c. I need a heads-up.
   d. I wouldn't mind that.

4. He's our go-to mechanic.
   a. I need to talk to him.
   b. Get rid of the car.
   c. I have a mind to drive home.
   d. This is worthwhile.

5. This house has all the bells and whistles.
   a. I don't see any bells.
   b. It's out there.
   c. I'll mind them.
   d. But it's in the country.

Write a question or remark for each of the following responses. Ask an English-speaking friend to check your work.

1. _____

   Give me a heads-up.

2. _____

   It's definitely worthwhile.

3. _____

Preferably, in the country.

4. _____

Let's have a look.

5. _____

We wouldn't mind.

6. _____

I've changed my mind.

7. _____

How about, say, a ring or a necklace?

8. _____

None of them are here.

9. _____

She's our go-to travel agent.

10. _____

Get rid of it.

Write a word or expression from this chapter for each definition.

1. to babysit

_____

2. to investigate

_____

3. to feel like doing

_____

4. zero

_____

5. to throw out

_____

6. to warn

_____

7. to have value

_____

8. between now and then

_____

9. to have a new opinion

_____

10. heat, electricity, water

_____

11. Oh, I almost forgot . . .

_____

12. not the city

_____

13. trusted source

_____

14. for example

_____

15. forget it

_____

16. the brain

_____

17. obligatory

_____

18. requirement for beginning

_____

19. modern features

_____

20. in today's world

_____

Answer the following questions in complete sentences. Ask an English-speaking friend to check your answers.

1. What do you want to accomplish in the next five years?

   _____

   _____

   _____

2. What do you need to do to reach your goals?

   _____

   _____

   _____

3. What are you required to do at work/at school/at home?

   _____

   _____

   _____

4. What do you have to do this week?

   _____

   _____

   _____

5. What would you like to do this weekend?

   _____

   _____

   _____

6. What chores do you not mind doing?

   _____

   _____

   _____

Conversation: Future events, narration, electronic communication

Talking about future events

Conversation A: Scheduled events

RAJ: What time does the movie **start**?

INES: It **starts** at 7:30 and **ends** at 9:45.

RAJ: Good, we can go on the bus, and get back home before it's too dark. Is there a bus stop near your house?

INES: Yes. It **stops** on the corner every fifteen minutes.

RAJ: Perfect. I'm looking forward to seeing this movie.

Conversation B: Plans for the very near future

JENNY: What are you **doing** tomorrow?

PAULA: I'm going to the beach with my family for a week. We're leaving early—at 6 A.M.

JENNY: Oh, nice! So I guess you're **planning** to go to bed early tonight.

PAULA: Yeah, I'm **gonna** pack my bag and try to **hit the sack** by nine o'clock.

JENNY: **Good luck with that!** What are you taking?

PAULA: I always **pack light** for the beach—a bathing suit, a couple of pairs of shorts, some T-shirts, a hat, and lots of sunscreen. How about you? What are you doing next week?

JENNY: I'm **going to** stay home and **catch up on** some unfinished projects.

PAULA: Like what?

JENNY: Oh, I have a long list! First I'm **going to** clean up my office, pay bills, write letters, and **take care of a bunch of** paperwork. Then I'm **going to** redecorate my bedroom—paint the walls and get new curtains.

PAULA: Wow. What color are you **going to** paint it?

JENNY: It's a very light blue. I've already picked it out and bought the paint.

PAULA: Cool.

Conversation C: Long-term plans

EMMA: What do you think **you'll** do when you finish college?

KIM: Oh, **I'll probably** stay in the city and look for work here. Then I'll go back home on holidays.

EMMA: I love that idea, but **I'll probably** go closer to home to get a job. I like being close to my family and old friends. **Still**, life in the big city is certainly tempting!

KIM: Well, **maybe** you could find a job in a big city closer to home.

EMMA: Yeah, that would be a good **happy medium**.

KIM: **On the other hand**, **since** you like to travel, you could possibly get a job in another country—do something exotic.

EMMA: You're right. I **might** get really bored just doing **the same old thing**. I'd learn a lot **overseas**—even **pick up** another language. It's definitely something to think about.

KIM: Well, I guess we don't have to decide now, since we're still in our **freshman** year!

Conversation D: Predictions for the more distant future

TEACHER: What will the world be like fifty years from now?

ANDY: **Just think!** People **will** be living on Mars.

EMILY: **I'll bet** cars **will** be replaced by little helicopters, so you'll be able to fly ahead in traffic.

HOLLY: There **won't** be any more wars.

JULIE: Women **will** make more money than men.

STACEY: **No way!** Women **will** stay home and the men **will** do all the work.

JOE: There **will** be a better form of government.

ZACK: People **will** have forgotten how to talk and **will** only communicate electronically.

HEATHER: There **won't** be any disease, and people **will** live to be 150 years old.

COURTNEY: That **will** be horrible. It **will** be so crowded!

ANDY: That's why people **will** be living on Mars!

Improving your conversation

No one can say for sure what will happen in the future, yet we often talk about it. Future events can be described in several different ways, depending on how probable it is that they will happen.

Scheduled events

The present tense is used to talk about the future. It is used to give the time of scheduled events (99 percent probability).

> The flight **leaves** at four o'clock this afternoon.
> The movie **starts** at five o'clock, so don't be late.

The present tense is also used to tell what normally happens and is expected to be the same in the future (99 percent probability).

> The stores **open** at ten o'clock tomorrow morning.
> The children **go** back to school in September.
> Class **ends** at 3:15.
> The train **stops** near our building every hour.

I'll bet

The present tense is used after the expression **I'll bet**, meaning I'm pretty sure it will happen.

> **I'll bet** she wins the election.
> **I'll bet** he calls me as soon as he gets home.

Going to

To be **going to** is used to indicate events planned for the near future (95 percent probability).

> We're **going to** move to our new house next month.
> They're **going to** get married in June.

In informal conversation, **going to** is often pronounced "**gonna**."

> I'm **gonna** go see my grandmother this afternoon.

The present progressive (**basic verb** + **-ing**) can be used as an alternative to **going to** (95 percent probability).

> We're **moving** to our new house next month.
> They're **getting** married in June.
> We're **planning** to go to the game tomorrow.
> I'll be **doing** homework after school.

Will probably

Will probably + **basic verb** is used to indicate about a 75 percent probability of happening.

> She'll **probably** be late.
> We'll **probably** leave early.

Probably won't + **basic verb** is used to indicate about a 25 percent probability of happening.

> He **probably won't** come with me.
> You **probably won't** like this movie.

May/might

May or **might** + **basic verb** can be used to express about a 50 percent possibility of something happening.

> He **may** be late, because he has to work until 6.
> She **might** be late, too.
> I **might** come over tomorrow. It depends on what time I get home.

Maybe

Maybe also expresses about a 50 percent possibility of something happening. Unlike **may** and **might**, it is placed before the subject.

> **Maybe** they'll be late.
> **Maybe** I'll come over tomorrow.

Will

Will + **basic verb** is tricky, as it can indicate both very high and very low probability. It is used to make a promise (99 percent probability).

> I'**ll** be here at six tomorrow morning.
> We'**ll** call you as soon as we arrive.

It is also used to predict the more distant future (10 percent probability).

> My baby **will** be a doctor when he grows up.
> You **will** get married and have a bunch of children.

Won't

Won't + **basic verb** indicates a very low probability that something will happen.

> He **won't** be at the wedding.
> We **won't** be able to see you in such a big crowd.

Hit the sack

Hit the sack is a very informal way to say to go to bed and sleep.

> Man, I was exhausted last night. I **hit the sack** as soon as I got home.

Pack light

To **pack light** means to prepare only a very small suitcase or carry-on for traveling.

> Be sure to **pack light**, because we'll have to carry our bags part of the way.

Catch up on

To **catch up on** means to do or learn something that you didn't do earlier.

> When we're at the beach, I plan to **catch up on** some important reading.

Take care of

To **take care of** can mean to perform a task.

> I was going to call a plumber, but my husband said he would **take care of** it.
> Will you mow the lawn for me?   Sure, I'll **take care of** it.

Take care of can also mean to attend to a child or other person needing supervision.

> They're looking for someone to **take care of** her ninety-year-old mother during the day.

Pick up

To **pick up** means to grasp something that is on a lower surface.

> I broke the glass and had to **pick up** all the pieces.

It can also mean to lift.

> This box is too heavy. We can't **pick** it **up**.

Pick up can also mean to meet and give a ride to someone.

> You can go with us. We'll be glad to **pick** you **up**.

To **pick up** can also mean to learn easily.

> I don't think you can **pick up** Italian just by going to Venice on a vacation.
> Of course, you will **pick up** a few useful phrases.

Happy medium

To reach a **happy medium** means to agree by accepting some parts of one argument and some parts of the opposing argument.

> His style was modern, and hers was traditional. They reached a **happy medium** by buying an old house and putting in modern furniture.

A verb with the same meaning is to **compromise**.

> The only way to keep everybody happy is to **compromise**.

A bunch of

A (**whole**) **bunch of** means a lot of. Alternative expressions include **quite a few** and **a number of**.

> A **whole bunch of** friends are coming over tonight.
> She has **quite a few** admirers.
> There are still **a number of** tickets available.

The same old thing

The **same old thing** is a way to indicate that activities are routine.

> What are you up to these days? Oh, you know, the **same old thing**—working, taking care of the kids, going to school at night.

On the other hand

On the other hand is an expression that introduces an argument that is contrary to—or opposite to—a previously mentioned argument.

> Well, we could use our savings to buy the house. **On the other hand**, we could use the money to visit your family in Ethiopia.

Since

Since can mean because, usually indicating that something is convenient.

> I don't have an appointment for a haircut, but **since** I was in the neighborhood, I stopped by to see if you had time for me.
> I was going to go home early today, but **since** you're here, I'll do your hair.

Since can also indicate the beginning of a time period.

> She's been studying English **since** last September.
> I've been waiting for you **since** four o'clock.

Still

Still has several meanings. In the example conversations, it introduces information that the speaker feels is contrary to the previous information, indicating a dilemma.

> I'd love to buy the house. **Still**, it's important to go visit my family.

Overseas/abroad

Overseas refers to places on the other side of the ocean. **Abroad** refers to all countries except the one you are in.

> We lived **overseas** for a number of years.
> Many college students have the opportunity to study **abroad**.

Freshman

Freshman refers to a student in the first year of high school or college. It can also be another name for the first year. Second-year students are called **sophomores**; third-year students are **juniors**, and fourth-year students are **seniors**.

> She may look like a **freshman**, but actually she's in her **senior** year.
> This is the biggest **freshman** class we've ever had.

Senior (citizen) can also refer to a person who is sixty years old or more.

> He's a **senior** in high school, and his grandmother is a **senior**.

Just think

Just think is an expression that introduces a fantasy or real plan the speaker is excited about.

> **Just think!** We could get married and have children.
> **Just think!** This time tomorrow we'll be in Rome!

Good luck with that

Good luck with that is an expression indicating that the speaker doesn't think the previous statement is very likely to happen.

> They told me I'd win $500 if I wrote the best essay.

> **Good luck with that.** They told the same thing to all the elementary school students in the whole city.

No way

No way indicates that something is impossible, unbelievable—or even wonderful.

> Are you going to major in chemistry?

> **No way!** There's **no way** I'm going to spend four years working in a laboratory.

> John and Mary are getting married next month.

> **No way!** They were fighting the last time I saw them.

> I'm going to Denmark for two weeks.

> **No way!** Lucky you!

Fill in each blank with the most appropriate word or words.

1. When you grow up, you _____ rich and famous.
   a. are being
   b. are
   c. will be
   d. were

2. Can you join us tomorrow? That's impossible because we _____ sightseeing.
   a. went
   b. are going
   c. will go
   d. go

3. Don't be late. The show _____ at 6:30.
   a. will start
   b. is starting
   c. started
   d. starts

4. Will you go to the party with me on Friday night? I can't. I _____.
   a. study this weekend
   b. will stay in
   c. am going to stay in
   d. might

5. I'm not sure what to do. _____
   a. Maybe I'll take the job.
   b. I'll take the job.
   c. I won't take the job.
   d. I'm taking the job.

6. Is your brother going to the circus with you? _____
   a. No. He doesn't go.
   b. No. Maybe he doesn't go.
   c. No. He won't go.
   d. No. He is going.

Match the words and expressions in the first column with those in the second column that have a similar meaning. Note: There may be more than one match for each expression.

1. _____ go to bed
2. _____ pack light
3. _____ catch up on
4. _____ take care of
5. _____ pick up
6. _____ reach a happy medium

a. attend to someone
b. compromise
c. do
d. do something you didn't do earlier
e. give a ride to
f. hit the sack
g. learn a little
h. learn something you missed
i. lift
j. take a small suitcase

Circle the word or expression that best completes each of the following sentences.

1. Our mayor is an excellent politician. _____, he's not exactly a good administrator.
   a. Just think   b. No way   c. On the other hand

2. I'll probably take his course. _____, I've heard he's a hard grader.
   a. Still   b. Just think   c. No way

3. It's great to have a holiday. _____, otherwise we'd be at the office right now.
   a. Just think   b. No way   c. Still

4. I'm exhausted. I'll probably _____ as soon as I get home.
   a. hit the sack   b. pack light   c. reach a happy medium

5. I'm going to ask the teacher to give me an A in this course. _____!
   a. Still   b. Just think   c. Good luck with that

Fill in each blank with an appropriate word or expression that is explained in this chapter.

1. There aren't very many jobs available. _____, I'm going to keep looking.

2. He's seventy-five, so he gets a _____ discount.

3. We're so bored. It seems like every day we do _____.

4. Maybe if I got a job _____, I could pick up another language.

5. There will be _____ new students next year.

6. I heard the _____ class is going to be the biggest one ever.

7. You have a lot of airport changes on this trip. You really should _____.

8. She's staying at home tonight to _____ some reading.

9. I tried to pay for the dinner, but he insisted on _____ it.

10. He wants an apartment, and she wants a house. They could _____ by buying a townhouse.

Write a question or remark for each of the following responses. Ask an English-speaking friend to check your work.

1. _____

   I'll take care of it!

2. _____

   I'll take care of her!

3. _____

   Still, I'm not sure it's a good idea.

4. _____

   We could pick up a little Arabic.

5. _____

   On the other hand, it's very expensive.

6. _____

   Just think! We'll be having so much fun!

7. _____

   She won't go.

8. _____

   Good luck with that!

9. _____

   No way!

10. _____

   That sounds like a good happy medium.

Write a letter to a friend in which you tell of your plans for today and tomorrow and of your hopes and dreams for the future. Use all of the future expressions explained in this chapter. Ask an English-speaking friend to check your work.

_____

_____

_____

_____

_____

_____

_____

_____

_____

_____

Narrating a story

Conversation: A traffic accident

JACK: Hey, buddy, what happened to you? Don't tell me you broke your leg!

SAM: No, it's not that drastic. I just twisted my ankle. Still, it hurts a lot, and walking with these crutches is a **pain in the neck**.

JACK: So when did it happen?

SAM: It was the night of the basketball championship. And **the worst thing** is that we lost the game and all hopes of winning our title back.

JACK: What a **bummer**! Sit down here for a minute and tell me all about it.

SAM: Well, it all happened last Thursday. It was **pouring down rain** and also freezing. I was in a hurry to get to the gym early to **chill out** a bit before the game. I was all **stressed out** about the game when I left home, but I got in the car and started to drive toward the gym. **All of a sudden** my phone rang—it was my girlfriend. She was **all excited** about the game and wanted to **wish** me good luck. I started to get **pumped up** and ready for the game. My girlfriend and I kept on talking when I suddenly **realized** that the cars in front of me were stopped, and I was going a little fast. I slammed on the brakes, but it was **too** late. The street was wet, and I hit the car that was stopped **in front of** me. That hard braking caused me to twist my ankle. I could hardly get out of the car to talk to the other driver because my ankle hurt so much. **To tell you the truth**, I was so **freaked out** I didn't know what to do. I was thinking about the game, my girlfriend, my teammates—it never occurred to me that I wouldn't be able to play that night. **Finally** a **cop** came and made me sign some **papers**; then an ambulance took me to the hospital. They took some X-rays to see if my ankle was broken or not. **Thank goodness** it wasn't broken, but **the upshot** was that I wasn't going to play basketball that night. And now I'm **stuck with** these crutches.

Improving your conversation

The example dialogue is very informal and uses only a few of the traditional markers that indicate the order of events in a narration.

First/second/next/then/after that

In a more formal or longer narration, chronological order can be made clearer with the use of expressions such as **first**, **second**, **next**, **then**, and **after that**. The last event in the series is preceded by **finally**.

> **First**, I got into the car and started to drive toward the gym.
> **Second**, I had an accident.
> **Then** I realized that I had twisted my ankle.
> **After that**, they took me to the hospital.
> **Finally**, I went to the game on crutches and watched my team lose.

Note that each of these expressions is followed by a comma (or pause, when speaking), with the exception of **then**. **Second** can be replaced with **then**, **next**, or **after that**, which are interchangeable.

> This is what happened at the meeting this afternoon. **First**, we discussed the budget; **second**, the chairman announced the new position in Human Services. **Next** we talked about the problems in Customer Service. **After that**, we had a short coffee break, and **then** we had a chance to ask questions. **Finally**, we adjourned.

Finally

Finally can also indicate relief or joy that something long awaited or expected has happened.

> After three long days on the road, I **finally** got to San Antonio.
> **Finally** you're here! We expected you two hours ago.

Thank goodness

Thank goodness and **thank God** are other ways to express relief, joy, or satisfaction.

> **Thank goodness** you arrived safely. Now we can celebrate.

Thank goodness and **thank God** (but not **finally**) can also express appreciation.

> We have enough money to live on, **thank God**.
> All of the children are healthy, **thank goodness**.

To top it all off

Sometimes a series of events are meant to tell a convincing story. **To top it all off** is an expression that is used to introduce a final event that adds weight to the sum of the previous events. Other expressions with the same function are **for the frosting on the cake** and **as if that weren't enough**.

> **First**, my alarm didn't go off, and I woke up an hour late. **Then** I spilled coffee all over my suit and had to change clothes. **After that**, I got in the car and noticed that it was completely out of gas. **Finally**, I had to wait in a long line to get gas. And **to top it all off**, when I left the gas station, I was in the middle of a huge traffic jam.

All of a sudden

Events that interrupt a narration can be preceded by **all of a sudden, suddenly, before I knew it, out of nowhere, out of the blue,** and **just like that**—all of which mean without warning.

> We were enjoying our picnic, when **all of a sudden**, it began to rain cats and dogs.
> They were taking a test, when **suddenly** the fire alarm went off.
> I stepped on a slippery rock, and **before I knew it**, I was on the ground.
> He was driving down the street, and **out of nowhere**, a car approached from the left.
> I was watching TV the other night, when **out of the blue** I got a call from an old friend whom I hadn't seen in ages.
> I was feeling a little depressed, and **just like that**, my favorite song came on the radio and cheered me up.

The best thing and the worst thing

The best thing and **the worst thing** indicate that what follows is the most or least desirable aspect of an issue.

> **The best thing** about this school is that it has wonderful students. They are all eager to learn.
> **The best thing** you can do at this point is be patient.
> **The worst thing** about this apartment is the location. It's not convenient to anything.

The upshot

The upshot of an issue is its result or outcome. This is often used to avoid telling a complete story or explaining an issue in detail.

> I'm not going to give you all the details. **The upshot** is that Caitlyn has left town and won't be back.

An expression that has a similar function is **the bottom line**.

> I just had a long conversation with the chairman of the company. **The bottom line** is that I've been promoted.

> I don't have time to hear your whole story—what's **the bottom line?**

> **The bottom line** is that I got fired and I'm looking for a new job.

Paper

Paper has a number of meanings. **Paper** is the most common material used for writing, printing, and cleaning, and it is in many manufactured goods. In this function, it is a non-count noun and is not made plural.

> This book is made of **paper**.
> We need to conserve **paper** in order to protect our forests.

Paper can also be a count noun, and can be made plural, when it means document.

> We need to fill out a whole bunch of **papers** when we go to the doctor.

Paper is also a count noun when it means essay, written composition, or thesis.

> I have two research **papers** to write, so I will probably spend the weekend in the library.

A **paper** can refer to the newspaper. **The paper** can mean today's newspaper.

> She went down to the newsstand to buy a **paper**.
> Have you read **the paper** yet? The news is amazing!

Bummer

A **bummer** is an item of bad news or bad luck.

> Snow again! What a **bummer**! Now our flight will be canceled.

For serious occasions or tragedies, **a shame** would be a better expression.

> I'm so sorry to hear about your dad's illness. What **a shame**!

Pain in the neck

A **pain in the neck** can refer to anything or any person that is annoying.

> I wish my sister would stop banging on the door. She really is a **pain in the neck**.
> I lost my Internet connection again. What a **pain in the neck**!

Cop

Cop is a slang term that means police officer.

> There are **cops** stationed along the turnpike, waiting for speeders.

To **cop out on someone** has nothing to do with the police; it means to stop participating in an activity in which other people are counting on you. It indicates that the speaker is unhappy with this decision.

> We had five players for the basketball team, but Steve **copped out**, and now we can't play a proper game.
> Sandy promised to drive me to the game, but he **copped out on me** at the last minute, so now I'll have to take the bus.

Pouring down rain

To be **pouring down rain** means to be raining heavily. An alternative expression is **raining cats and dogs**.

> The kids can't play outside; it's **pouring down rain**.
> I had to pull the car off to the side of the road because it was **raining cats and dogs**.

Pumped up

To be **pumped (up)** means to be excited. An alternative expression is to be **all excited**.

> We are both **pumped up** for the concert this weekend.
> She is **all excited** about her date with you. Where are you guys going?

Stressed out

To be **stressed out** means to be very tense, nervous, or worried about something.

> She has two sick children at home and is trying to work at the same time. No wonder she is **stressed out**!

Another way to express this feeling is to say that something **stresses you out**.

> Having two sick children at home really **stresses me out**.

Freaked out

To **freak out** or be **freaked out** means to be extremely scared, angry, or excited. Also, something can **freak you out**.

> He **freaked out** when he saw his brother driving his new car.
> She is **freaked out** because she has three exams tomorrow.
> That car speeding toward us really **freaked me out**.

Creeped out

To be **creeped out** means to be disgusted or frightened by something. Also, something can **creep you out**.

> Those pictures of dead bodies really **creeped me out**.
> It **creeps me out** that he just sits there and never says a word.

Another way to indicate disgust is to be **grossed out**.

> It really **grosses me out** when the kids have food fights.

Stuck with

To be **stuck with** means to have to cope with an uncomfortable or undesirable situation.

> My brother went out with his friends, and I'm **stuck with** looking after my little sister.

Chill out

To **chill out** means to relax or calm down.

> Come on over! We're just **chillin' out** on the back patio.
> Oooh! I'm so mad I could scream!   **Chill out**, babe. It's not worth getting upset over.

Realize

To **realize** means to be aware of, to already know.

> I'm sorry I yelled at you. I **realize** that I was wrong.

Wish

To **wish** means to be sorry that something isn't true. It is followed by a clause with a subjunctive verb.

> [You are not here.] I **wish** you were here.
> [I can't go with you.] I **wish** I could go with you.

Wish is also used in formal greetings.

> We **wish** you a happy New Year.
> I **wish** you the best of luck.

To tell you the truth

To tell you the truth precedes information that may surprise the listener.

> Did you enjoy your trip?   **To tell you the truth**, it wasn't that great.

Too

Too has a number of meanings. It can mean also.

> I went home early, and Jon did, **too**.

It can mean excessively.

> She is way **too** thin. I'm afraid she's anorexic.

It can mean so extreme that there is a negative result.

> He has **too** much free time. He gets into trouble.
> She's **too** nice. It creeps me out.

In front of

In front of indicates the location of something in relation to something else. It can mean facing something else.

> The teacher sat in a chair **in front of** her students and read them a story.

It can mean ahead of, facing in the same direction as, something else.

> There were three cars **in front of** mine, waiting for the light.
> I had to stand in line, and there were a lot of people **in front of** me.

It can mean within someone's eyesight, facing in any direction.

> There is a car parked on the street **in front of** your house.

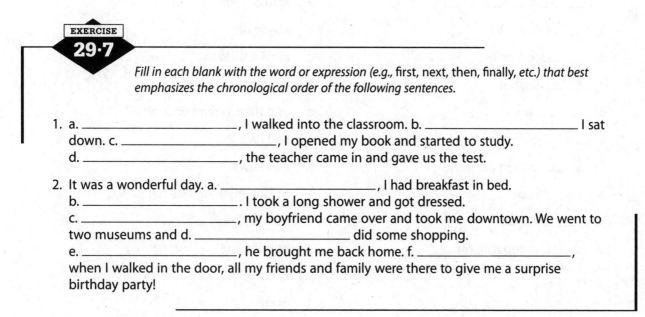

EXERCISE
29·7

Fill in each blank with the word or expression (e.g., first, next, then, finally, etc.) that best emphasizes the chronological order of the following sentences.

1. a. _____, I walked into the classroom. b. _____ I sat down. c. _____, I opened my book and started to study. d. _____, the teacher came in and gave us the test.

2. It was a wonderful day. a. _____, I had breakfast in bed. b. _____. I took a long shower and got dressed. c. _____, my boyfriend came over and took me downtown. We went to two museums and d. _____ did some shopping. e. _____, he brought me back home. f. _____, when I walked in the door, all my friends and family were there to give me a surprise birthday party!

EXERCISE
29·8

Circle the word or expression that most appropriately completes each sentence.

1. After five years of studying, he _____ got his degree.
   a. just like that
   b. suddenly
   c. finally
   d. after that

2. It's been dry all summer long, and now, _____ it's pouring down rain.
   a. thank goodness
   b. before you know it
   c. the bottom line is
   d. to top it all off

3. She was going to help us, but she _____.
   a. was pumped up
   b. chilled out
   c. copped out
   d. realized

4. I wanted to go with them, but I was _____.
   a. all excited
   b. a pain in the neck
   c. a bummer
   d. too late

5. The insects in that horror movie really _____.
   a. creeped me out
   b. chilled me out
   c. gave me a pain in the neck
   d. rained cats and dogs

EXERCISE
29·9

Match the words and expressions in the first column with those in the second column that have a similar meaning. Note: There may be more than one match for each expression.

1. _____ after that
2. _____ first
3. _____ suddenly
4. _____ upshot
5. _____ paper
6. _____ bummer
7. _____ pain in the neck
8. _____ cop
9. _____ in front of
10. _____ to top it all off

a. across from
b. ahead of
c. all of a sudden
d. annoying
e. as if that weren't enough
f. bad luck
g. bad news
h. before anything else happened
i. before I knew it
j. bottom line
k. document
l. essay
m. facing
n. for the frosting on the cake

o. in sight of

p. just like that

q. material to write on

r. newspaper

s. next

t. out of nowhere

u. out of the blue

v. police officer

w. result

x. second

y. then

EXERCISE

29·10

Write an appropriate question or remark for each of the following responses. Ask an English-speaking friend to check your answers.

1. _____

What a bummer!

2. _____

He's a real pain in the neck.

3. _____

Thank goodness, we're all safe.

4. _____

I finished writing it last night, thank God.

5. _____

Yeah, that's the bottom line.

6. _____

It was right out of the blue.

Match the words or expressions in the first column with those in the second column that have a similar meaning. Note: There may be more than one match for each expression.

1. _____ be pumped up

2. _____ be stuck with

3. _____ be raining cats and dogs

4. _____ be freaked out

5. _____ be stressed out

6. _____ chill out

7. _____ realize

8. _____ be creeped out

9. _____ wish

10. _____ cop out

a. be all excited

b. be angry

c. be aware of

d. be disgusted

e. be frightened

f. be grossed out

g. be in an unfortunate situation

h. be nervous

i. be pouring down rain

j. be scared

k. be sorry that something isn't true

l. be surprised

m. be tense

n. be worried

o. calm down

p. feel enthusiastic

q. know

r. not participate as promised

s. relax

t. stop worrying

Write an appropriate question or remark for each response. Ask an English-speaking friend to check your work.

1. _____

That really creeps me out.

2. _____

You need to chill out.

3. _____

They copped out on me.

4. _____

I realize that.

5. _____

No wonder you're stressed out!

EXERCISE
29·13

Form sentences beginning with I wish *to indicate your regret that the previous information is not true.*

1. You are not here.

_____

2. I can't get a promotion at this company.

_____

3. She is always stressed out.

_____

4. He doesn't know my e-mail address.

_____

5. They never come to see me.

_____

EXERCISE
29·14

Circle the most appropriate answer for each question or remark.

1. How was your interview?
   a. It was pouring down rain.
   b. It was the worst thing.
   c. It was out of nowhere.
   d. To tell you the truth, it stressed me out.

2. What's the matter?
   a. I'm stuck with the job of collecting money.
   b. I have a pain in the neck.
   c. To tell you the truth, that's the upshot.
   d. The best thing is that she copped out.

3. My dog died yesterday.
   a. What a pain in the neck.
   b. What a shame.
   c. It's raining cats and dogs.
   d. To top it all off, I'm chilling out.

4. Tell me what happened.
   a. I'm out of paper.
   b. That creeps me out.
   c. The upshot is that I'm single again.
   d. It's a good paper.

5. A strange person calls me in the middle of the night and then hangs up.
   a. That chills me out.   c. That creeps me out.
   b. That grosses me out.   d. That's a cop-out.

EXERCISE
29·15

Have you ever been freaked out? Write four or five sentences to describe what happened.
Ask an English-speaking friend to check your work.

_____

_____

_____

_____

_____

EXERCISE
29·16

Write a narration that describes something that happened recently in your life. Use at least
eight of the words or expressions explained in this chapter. Ask an English-speaking friend to
check your work.

_____

_____

_____

_____

_____

_____

_____

_____

_____

Electronic conversation

While face-to-face conversations are still considered to be the best ones, people everywhere are depending more and more on electronic devices for communication. Apart from the fixed telephone, which has been around since 1876—and is still going strong—conversations are now also carried on through cell phones, e-mail, and other electronic devices.

E-mail

E-mail (electronic mail) enables written conversations that are either typed on a computer or cell phone keyboard or entered on a touch screen on a cell phone or other electronic device. These messages are then sent to the desired recipient via the Internet. In order to use **e-mail**, you need to have an **e-mail address**, and you need to know the **e-mail address** of the person with whom you wish to communicate.

E-mail addresses can be assigned by the company that provides an Internet connection or through companies that issue subscriptions through the Internet. An **e-mail address** begins with a series of numbers or letters (of the individual's choosing), followed by the symbol @ (pronounced "at"), and then followed by the name of the provider, a period (pronounced "dot"), and finally a suffix of two or three more letters that indicates the domain—the type of organization that is providing the **e-mail account**. Here are some examples of these final domain letters:

com	commercial (the most widely used suffix; preferred by businesses)
edu	education (for schools, colleges, and universities)
gov	government (for government organizations)
net	network (most commonly used by Internet service providers)
org	organization (primarily used by nonprofit groups and trade associations)

The suffix can alternatively indicate the name of the source country. For example:

au	Australia
es	Spain
mx	Mexico
uk	United Kingdom

IM

An **IM** is an "instant message," designed to get the immediate attention of the person contacted. Electronic devices give an audible signal when an **IM** is received.

Texting

Texting is the practice of sending written messages from one cell phone to another, using the receiver's telephone number.

Texters often leave out the vowels in words or make up abbreviations in order to communicate faster. For example:

cd	could
cls	class
cn	can
hv	have
prnts	parents
sndy	Sunday
tchr	teacher
wd	would

Tweeting

Tweeting is the practice of sending written messages to the general public through a commercial website, called twitter.com. Messages are limited to 140 characters. Important or famous people often use this to keep their constituents, clients, or fans informed of what they are doing or thinking.

Acronyms

Acronyms are combinations of letters that are used as abbreviations to replace words and expressions. **Acronyms** and other symbols are commonly used in **e-mail**, **texting**, and **tweeting**. They may be in all capital (uppercase) letters, all lowercase letters, or a combination of the two. There are really no rules!

Following is a list of commonly used **acronyms** and other symbols:

☺, :)	I'm happy.
☹, :(	I'm unhappy.
@	at
2nite	tonight
4	for/four
411	information [traditionally a telephone number to call to get help finding a telephone number]
4ever	forever
4U	for you
911	emergency; call me [traditionally the contact number for the police or fire department]
ABT2	about to
AKA	also known as (another name for someone or something)
asamof	as a matter of fact
ASAP	as soon as possible
AWOL	absent without leave (not being where one is supposed to be) [traditionally a military expression]
AYS	are you serious? (really?)
BBB	boring beyond belief
B/C	because
B4	before
B4N	bye for now
BFF	best friends forever
BTDT	been there, done that (I don't need to do it again)
BTW	by the way
BYOB	bring your own beer/bring your own bottle
CEO	chief executive officer [traditionally used to indicate the person in charge of a company]
DIY	do it yourself
DOA	dead on arrival [traditionally used by hospital emergency rooms]
DUI	driving under the influence (of alcohol or drugs) [traditionally used by police departments]

DWI	driving while intoxicated (by alcohol or drugs) [traditionally used by police departments]
ETA	estimated time of arrival [traditionally used in airports and train and bus stations]
EZ	easy
FAQ	frequently asked questions
FF	friends
FSBO	for sale by owner [traditionally used in the real estate industry]
FYI	for your information
GAL	get a life (don't be so boring!)
GO	get out (that's unbelievable!)
GR8	great!
HAND	have a nice day
IM	instant messaging
IMO	in my opinion
ISO	in search of (looking for)
L8R	later
LOL	laugh out loud (what you sent me was funny!)
LTR	long-term relationship
MIA	missing in action [traditionally a military term]
MYOB	mind your own business
N/A	not applicable [traditionally used in formal applications]
NP	no problem
NTW	not to worry (don't worry!)
NW	no way
OBO	or best offer [traditionally used in "for sale" ads]
OK	okay
OMG	oh my God! (also spelled "omigod")
OTC	over the counter (medicine that can be purchased without a doctor's prescription)
OTL	out to lunch (not focused/lacking good judgment)
PC	politically correct (avoiding the use of stereotypes or negative attacks in public)
PC	personal computer
PDA	public display of affection (kissing and hugging in public)
PDQ	pretty damn quick [traditionally a military term]
PLZ	please
POV	point of view (opinion)
PS	postscript [traditionally used after a signature in a letter to add one more message]
R&R	rest and relaxation [traditionally a military term]
RSVP	*répondez s'il vous plaît* (please reply to this invitation)
RUS	are you serious? (really?)
SO	significant other (the other person in a romantic relationship)

SOW	speaking of which
SRO	standing room only [traditionally used in the theater]
TBA	to be advised/announced
TBD	to be determined
TGIF	thank goodness it's Friday
TLC	tender loving care [traditionally used for nurses]
TTYL	talk to you later
TX	thanks
U	you
U2	you, too
UR	you are
W/	with
W/O	without
W8	wait
XOXO	kisses and hugs [traditionally used in written letters: *X* = a kiss; *O* = a hug]
Y	why
YR	yeah right

EXERCISE

29·17

"Translate" each of the following messages.

1. Cn U cm ovr asap?

_____

2. AYS? im @schl. BBB

_____

3. its OVR btwn us. sory

_____

4. lol UR crzy

_____

5. im :(w/o U

_____

6. me2

_____

7. CU L8r

_____

8. OMG shes OTL

_____

Write a text message conversation between you and a good friend. Use at least ten acronyms, symbols, or other abbreviations. Ask an English-speaking friend to check your work.

_____

_____

_____

_____

_____

_____

_____

_____

_____

_____

·30· Some Important Contrasts

As you study English and become more and more proficient, you will become aware that there are native speakers who say things that break the rules of good grammar. The more you know about English, the more you'll discover that this is true. Natives in all languages speak at different levels of competency. Some speak with great grammatical accuracy. Others are more casual or just careless and disregard the rules for good language.

The following eight pairs of words demonstrate where natives frequently make errors. By being aware of these words, you can make a choice for yourself about how you wish to speak English: speaking and writing accurately, or conforming to casual or careless habits.

Bad and badly

It is obvious that *bad* is an adjective and *badly* is an adverb. However, some native English speakers use *bad* exclusively as both an adjective and an adverb. The problem probably derives from the fact that *bad* seems like an adverb when it follows a linking verb (*to be*, *to become*, *to seem*, *to appear*, etc.):

That's too bad.
She looks bad this morning.

You can review linking verbs in Unit 5 on verbs.

You might hear someone say, "That little boy reads and writes *bad*." However, in this usage an adverb is required. The sentence should be, "That little boy reads and writes *badly*." Let's look at some examples of how *bad* and *badly* should be used correctly:

You're a bad dog.	(adjective modifying *dog*)
In bad weather we stay at home.	(adjective modifying *weather*)
Your cut isn't so bad.	(adjective following linking verb *is*)
His reply sounded bad.	(adjective following linking verb *sounded*)
You have a badly broken wrist.	(adverb modifying participle *broken*)
They played badly today.	(adverb modifying verb *played*)

Good and well

This pair of words is misused in much the same way as *bad* and *badly* and for some of the same reasons. But there is extra confusion involved with *good* and *well* because the word *well* can be either an adjective or an adverb, depending upon its usage. *Well* is the adverbial form of *good*, and it is also a word that means *not ill* when used as an adjective.

Good is the opposite of *bad* and is an adjective. Notice how the adjectival and adverbial meanings of this word are used:

Adjective	Adverb
Miguel is a *good* soccer player.	Miguel plays soccer *well*.

If *good* means "kind," you can use *kindly* as its adverbial part:

Adjective	Adverb
David is a *good* man.	He always speaks so *kindly* of them.

But when *well* is used with a linking verb, it is an adjective. You might hear someone say, "I don't feel *good*." That usage is incorrect, for the meaning here is "not ill." The correct usage is "I don't feel *well*."

But that is not the end of the story of *good* and *well*. They both can follow linking verbs, and they both are in that instance considered adjectives. However, their meanings are different:

Sentence with Linking Verb	Meaning
She looks *good*.	She doesn't look bad.
She looks *well*.	She doesn't look ill.
They are *good*.	They aren't bad. **OR** They aren't unkind.
They are *well*.	They aren't ill.

Few and a few

The difference between the words in this pair is not great. It is correct to say, "Few men are strong enough." You can also say, "A few men are strong enough." But there is a slight difference in implication between the sentences. Let's look at some examples that will demonstrate this difference:

The Sentence	The Implication
Few people saw this movie.	Not many people went to see this movie. (There is a negative implication here.)
A few people saw this movie.	Some people saw this movie but not a lot. (The implication is more positive.)
Few students understood him.	He was hard to understand. (There is a negative implication here.)
A few students understood him.	Some of the students did understand him. (This implication is more positive.)
She has few friends.	She has almost no friends. (There is a negative implication here.)
She has a few friends.	She has some friends but not a lot. (This implication is more positive.)

Use *few* to imply a negative point of view about something. Use *a few* to show a more positive point of view.

Fewer and less

Many people misuse these two words. But their usage is quite simple: Use *fewer* to modify plural nouns and use *less* to modify singular (and often collective) nouns. *Fewer* is the comparative of *few*, and *less* is the comparative of *little*. Some examples:

Plural Nouns	Singular Nouns
I have fewer books.	I have less money.
We need fewer jobs to do.	She has less time than usual.
Fewer and fewer friends came to visit.	Mom has less and less patience with him.

Now let's compare the *positive* and *comparative* forms of these words:

Positive	Comparative
He has few ideas.	He has fewer ideas than you.
February has few days.	February has fewer days than March.
I have little time.	I have less time now than a year ago.
She has little pain.	She has less pain today than yesterday.

Lay and lie

Many English speakers confuse these two verbs. *Lay* is a transitive verb and takes a direct object. *Lie* is intransitive and does not take a direct object but is often followed by a prepositional phrase showing a location.

He lays the baby on the bed.	(transitive/direct object = baby)
Where did you lay my book?	(transitive/direct object = book)
Hamburg lies on the Elbe River.	(intransitive/prepositional phrase with *on*)
Your coat is lying over the railing.	(intransitive/prepositional phrase with *over*)

Confusion arises between these two verbs because of their conjugations. Compare them in all the tenses and take particular note of the past tense of *to lie*:

	to lay	to lie
Present	he lays	he lies
Past	he laid	he lay
Present Perfect	he has laid	he has lain
Past Perfect	he had laid	he had lain
Future	he will lay	he will lie
Future Perfect	he will have laid	he will have lain

If there is any difficulty deciding whether to use *lay* or *lie*, substitute *put* for the verb. If it makes sense, use *lay*. If it doesn't, use *lie*.

He *puts* the baby on the bed. (makes sense) → He *lays* the baby on the bed.
She *puts* on the bed and sleeps. (makes no sense) → She *lies* on the bed and sleeps.

Little and a little

This pair of words is similar to *few* and *a few*. *Little* has a negative implication. *A little* shows a more positive point of view. Some examples:

The Sentence	The Implication
Little is known about him.	Not much is known about him.
	(There is a negative implication here.)

A little is known about him.	Something is known about him but not a lot.
	(This implication is more positive.)
She does little work.	She doesn't work much.
	(There is a negative implication here.)
She does a little work.	She does some work but not much.
	(This implication is more positive.)
He says little.	He doesn't say much.
	(There is a negative implication here.)
He says a little.	He says something but not much.
	(This implication is more positive.)

Than and then

In rapid conversation these words are rarely confused, even though they sound so much alike. But in writing they must be distinguished. *Than* can be used as a preposition or a conjunction and stands between two elements that are being compared: Marisa is taller *than* Anthony. She runs faster *than* you do.

The word *then* has two major functions: (1) it can be used as an adverb and answers the question *when*, or (2) it can be a conjunction and combines two clauses with the meaning "and as a consequence or thereafter." Let's compare these two functions:

Adverb	Conjunction
We were in Mexico then, too.	I found the book then returned to my room.
Then I decided to go to college.	She slapped his face, then she ran down the street.

Who and whom

These two words are used frequently, and often misused. *Who* is the form used as the subject of a question:

> *Who* sent you?
> *Who* knows the man over there?

Whom is used as a direct object, indirect object, or the object of a preposition:

> direct object → *Whom* did you meet at the party?
> indirect object → (*To*) *Whom* will you give an invitation?
> object of preposition → With *whom* was he sitting?

Refer to Unit 22 on interrogatives for a review of *who* and *whom*.

It is important to remember that many native speakers of English avoid *whom* and use *who* exclusively. Compare these sentences:

Standard English	Casual English
Whom did they arrest?	Who did they arrest?
From whom did you get the gift?	From who did you get the gift? **OR**
	Who did you get the gift from?

When speaking or writing formally, you should use the standard forms of *who* and *whom*. In casual letters or conversation you can be the judge and avoid *whom*.

Circle the better of the two boldface words.

1. Today was a very **bad/badly** day at work.

2. The patient isn't doing **good/well** this morning.

3. He's an awful man. **Few/A few** people like him.

4. Tori has known **fewer/less** happiness in her later years.

5. Does your dog always **lay/lie** in that corner?

6. She's very ill, but we still have **little/a little** hope.

7. I believe this knife is sharper **than/then** that one.

8. **Who/Whom** will you invite to dinner?

9. Her ankle is **bad/badly** swollen.

10. The condition of the wall looks **good/well** again.

11. I'm not poor. I have **few/a few** dollars to give him.

12. You know **fewer/less** about her than I do.

13. If you **lay/lie** that on the shirt, you'll wrinkle it.

14. **Little/A little** kindness won't do him any harm.

15. I grabbed an umbrella **than/then** rushed out the door.

16. A long massage always feels **good/well**.

17. I know **fewer/less** men in this club than you.

18. Did you **lay/lie** my new skirt on the ironing board?

19. Why do you treat your pet so **bad/badly**?

20. You think you're smarter **than/then** I am.

Rewrite each sentence in standard English.

1. The little boy acted very bad in class today.

   _____

2. Don't you feel good?

   _____

3. Omar has less friends than his brother.

   _____

4. Mom is laying down for a while.

_____

5. Kris is prettier then Hilda.

_____

6. Who did you send the letter to?

_____

7. Were you in Europe than, too?

_____

8. I laid on the floor and played with the dog.

_____

9. Johnny plays good with the other children.

_____

10. Her voice sounds badly today.

_____

EXERCISE

30·3

Using the words in parentheses, write original sentences in standard English.

1. (bad)

_____

2. (badly)

_____

3. (good)

_____

4. (well)

_____

5. (few)

_____

6. (a few)

_____

7. (fewer)

_____

8. (less)

_____

9. (to lay)

_____

10. (to lie)

_____

11. (little)

_____

12. (a little)

_____

13. (than)

_____

14. (then)

_____

15. (who)

_____

16. (whom)

_____

Phrasal verbs

Phrasal verbs are verbs that are combined with other words—prepositions and adverbs—to form a new meaning, often a meaning that is radically different from the meaning of the verb alone. Because there are hundreds of such constructions, this chapter illustrates only a sampling of high-frequency verbs that form commonly used phrasal verbs.

common verb + adverb and/or preposition

to hold + up (to rob)

When an adverb, a preposition, or a combination of both is attached to a verb, the conjugation of the verb is not altered. It is the meaning and, therefore, the use of the verb that is changed. Let's look at the common verb *to come* to see how its meaning changes in a few phrasal verb forms:

to come to	*to regain consciousness*
to come up to	*to approach*
to come up with	*to create, or to discover*

Compare the use of these three phrasal verbs with a standard verb in the following examples:

When Jane **came to**, she didn't know where she was.
When Jane **regained consciousness**, she didn't know where she was.

I **came up to** the weary horse and patted its nose.
I **approached** the weary horse and patted its nose.

How did you **come up** with so much money?
How did you **find** so much money?

In order to deal with phrasal verbs effectively, a student of English should have a dictionary that specializes in phrasal verbs. This is an important tool for identifying phrasal verbs and for understanding their meanings and uses.

Be

Many phrasal verbs are formed from the verb *to be*. Let's look at three of them: *to be in* or *out*, *to be with it*, and *to be up to something*.

The phrasal verb *to be in*, as noted in Chapter 8, conveys that a person is at home or in the office, while *to be out* means a person is away from home or away from the office. In addition, *to be out* can indicate that someone is "out" having fun. For example:

> Little Michael **is in** for the day and taking a nap.
> What time will Dr. Schultz **be in**?
>
> Why **were** you **out** so late last night?
> My dentist **is out** for the day.

The second phrasal verb under this heading, *to be with it*, suggests fashionability or awareness of the latest trends. Used in the negative, it can mean that someone is not up to date or not in touch with pop culture.

> Andrea has another new dress. She**'s always so with it**.
> Poor Bill still can't dance. He**'s just not with it**.

To be up to something (sometimes *to be up to no good*) conveys that someone looks suspicious and has some kind of evil intentions.

> What's that man doing? I think he**'s up to something**.
> I knew you **were up to something** when I saw you holding a shovel.
> Her children **are always up to no good**.

With this phrasal verb, it is usual to follow the word *something* with an appropriate adjective; for example: *I think he's up to something illegal.* When adding an adjective in this manner, it is also possible to change *something* to *anything* when the sentence is negated: *I don't think they're up to anything wrong.*

Break

Among the phrasal verbs that can be formed with the verb *to break* are *to break down* and *to break up*. The use of the words *up* and *down* may suggest that these are opposites, but that is not the case.

The phrasal verb *to break down* has two meanings: (1) to stop working (such as in reference to a mechanical device); and (2) to give in to one's emotions or someone's demands. For example:

> How often does this computer **break down**?
> The day had been awful, and she **broke down** and cried.
> We questioned the thief for hours, and he finally **broke down** and confessed.

The phrasal verb *to break up* carries the sense of causing someone to laugh aloud. It suggests that the actions or words in question were so funny that the person could not control his or her amusement.

> Maria's joke **broke everyone up**.
> The clown's silly antics always **broke the audience up**.

The same construction has a radically different meaning and use when followed by the preposition *with*. It means that one person is ending a romantic relationship with another person: *to break up with someone.*

> After five months of dating, she knew she had **to break up with Tom**.
> He no longer loved her. It was time **to break up**.

Breeze

The phrase *to breeze through* refers to the ability to carry out a task with ease or dispatch.

> Don **breezed through** his workday and set off for his date with Tina.
> No one ever **breezes through** Professor Chang's exams.

Count

Do not confuse the usage *to count* (*on*)—that is, in the sense of to calculate by using one's fingers—with the phrasal verb *to count on*, which means *to rely on*. The preposition *upon* sometimes replaces *on* in the phrasal meaning.

> The little boy **counted** on his fingers.
> I know I can **count on** you for your support.
> You shouldn't have **counted on** Jim to give you any help in moving.

EXERCISE

31·1

Using each phrasal verb provided, write two original sentences.

EXAMPLE: to be in

Mr. Cane won't be in until after two P.M.

I have to stay in this evening and do some studying.

1. to be out

a. _____

b. _____

2. to be with it

a. _____

b. _____

3. to be up to something/no good

a. _____

b. _____

4. to break down

a. _____

b. _____

5. to break up (with)

a. _____

b. _____

6. to breeze through

    a. _____

    b. _____

7. to count on

    a. _____

    b. _____

Cut

The verb *cut* can be combined with the preposition *out: to cut (something) out.* Meanings of this phrasal verb include (1) to stop doing something; (2) to eliminate or cast out someone or something; and (3) to clip out or excise a shape from something. Here are some examples:

> **Cut that out!** You're being too noisy!
> Why **cut me out?** I spent as much time on the project as anyone.
> Maria **cut out a cartoon** from the newspaper.
> I'll **cut a recipe out of** the magazine.

This kind of phrasal verb is special in that the object of the verb can either precede or follow the preposition *out* if that object is a noun. Pronouns can only precede the preposition. Don't forget that prepositions in phrasal verbs can serve as adverbs:

> **noun direct object + preposition**
>
> I cut **an interesting article + out** for you.
>
> **preposition + noun direct object**
>
> I cut **out + an interesting article** for you.
>
> **pronoun direct object + preposition**
>
> I cut **it + out** for you.

This flexibility occurs with many phrasal verbs—but *not with all*. This characteristic is identified in reference to other phrasal verbs in the remainder of this chapter as the "flexible position" of a preposition. Be aware that many of these prepositions are not functioning as prepositions in these sentences; they are functioning as adverbs. In the phrasal verb *to call (someone) up*—meaning either to phone someone or to conscript someone for military service—*up* is used as an adverb. Consider the following sentence:

> They **called up my brother** to serve two years in the army.

In this sentence, the words *up my brother* do not constitute a prepositional phrase. Instead, *up* modifies the verb *call*, and *my brother* is a direct object.

Drop

When *to drop* is combined with *in*, the new phrasal verb means to stop at someone's home for a short visit. To specify what person is being visited, the preposition *on* is added. Here are some examples:

> My parents **dropped in** last night around eight.
> When you're in town, please **drop in on us**.
> I never **drop in on Michael** unexpectedly.

End

When *up* is added to the verb *to end*, the phrase takes on either of two distinct meanings: (1) to reach completion or termination; or (2) when the preposition *with* is added, to find oneself in the company of someone or in possession of something—usually a result that is unwanted or unpleasant. Let's look at some examples:

> These meetings won't **end up** until tomorrow after two P.M.
> Professor Hill **ended the lecture up with** a few words of advice.
> After her date with Jim, Maria **ended up with** a bad cold.
> I wanted to dance with Martin! How did I **end up with** Michael?

Sometimes *to end up with* is stated as *to wind up with*. They mean the same thing:

> He **ended up with** no money at all.   He **wound up with** no money at all.

The preposition in this phrasal verb has a flexible position around the object:

> She **ended up the discussion** with a little joke.
> She **ended the discussion up** with a little joke.
> She **ended it up** with a little joke.

Follow

When *to follow* is combined with *up*, and sometimes *on*, the phrasal verb means to examine something that has been done, or to evaluate how someone has performed. Some examples:

> I'll **follow up on** Maria's progress with a report.
> The detective decided to **follow up** the new clue.
> The reporter was **following up on** the strange story.

When the preposition *up* is used without *on* in this phrasal verb, *up* has a flexible position around the object:

> We should **follow that report up**.
> We should **follow up that report**.
> We should **follow it up**.

Fool

The verb *to fool* is synonymous with *to deceive*. However, when *around* is attached to the verb, new meanings emerge: (1) it means to hang about idly; (2) when the preposition *with* is added, it means to do something wasteful or useless; and (3) when used with the preposition *on* instead, it means to be unfaithful. Here are some examples:

> There was nothing else to do, so we just **fooled around** in the park.
> Why are you **fooling around with** that old radio?
> If you're **fooling around on** me, I want you to tell me now.

Get

Several phrasal verbs are formed with the verb *to get*. Two that are worth discussion are *to get away (with)* and *to get at*.

When *to get away* is used alone, it means to escape or to move away from a location. The addition of the preposition *with* changes the meaning: the new phrase means to carry out an evil act without punishment. Look at these examples:

> The prisoner dug a tunnel from his cell and tried to **get away**.
> **Get away** from the window. It's drafty there.
> He thought he **got away with** his crime, but he was arrested last week.

Get at has three meanings: (1) to put one's hands on or attack someone; (2) to hint at something; and (3) to begin discussing something. Some examples:

> The bully was trying to **get at** me, but my friends held him back.
> I don't understand. What are you **getting at**?
> It's time we finally **get at** the heart of the matter and solve this problem.

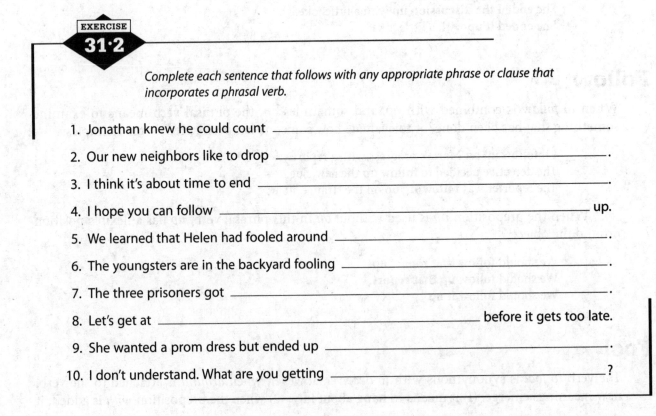

EXERCISE

31·2

Complete each sentence that follows with any appropriate phrase or clause that incorporates a phrasal verb.

1. Jonathan knew he could count _____.

2. Our new neighbors like to drop _____.

3. I think it's about time to end _____.

4. I hope you can follow _____ up.

5. We learned that Helen had fooled around _____.

6. The youngsters are in the backyard fooling _____.

7. The three prisoners got _____.

8. Let's get at _____ before it gets too late.

9. She wanted a prom dress but ended up _____.

10. I don't understand. What are you getting _____?

Have

Have is another high-frequency verb that can form numerous phrasal verbs. One that bears analysis is the phrase *to have something against*. This combination of words means to harbor an attitude of disrespect or dislike. Some examples:

> What do you **have against** me? I never did anything to you.
> Anna **had something against** Bob and let him know it.
> I **have nothing against** apple pie. I just don't want any.

Notice that with the third example, *something* changes to *nothing* in the negative. When this phrase is negated with *not*, the word *anything* is used: *I don't have anything against apple pie.*

When *have* is combined with *on* another meaning is derived. It is synonymous with *wear*. For example:

> Why do you **have** that old shirt **on**?
> When the postman came to the door, I didn't **have** anything **on**.
> I love the blouse you gave me. I **have** it **on** right now.

Lay

The phrasal verb *to lay off* (*of*) has two meanings: (1) often followed by the preposition *of*, it means to stop bothering or harassing someone; (2) used without *of*, it means to end a person's employment. The latter meaning is sometimes accompanied by the preposition *from*. The following examples illustrate the variants:

> **Lay off** (**of**) me! You have no right talking to me like that!
> Tom just won't **lay off** (**of**) the man who scratched his new car.
> Business was bad, and the boss had **to lay the men off** (from their jobs).

The preposition *off* in this phrasal verb has a flexible position around the object:

> Mr. Jones **laid the whole staff off**.
> Mr. Jones **laid off the whole staff**.
> Mr. Jones **laid everyone off**.

Lead

When the verb *to lead* is followed by the preposition **on**, the phrase has the normal meaning of to continue to lead, but when a direct object is included, its meaning becomes to tantalize someone—often with the idea of love or romance. These examples shed further light:

> **Lead on**, sir. These men will follow you anywhere.
> Are you just **leading me on**? I can't believe your story is true.
> The woman was **leading Bill on**. She just wanted his money.

The preposition *on* in this phrasal verb has a flexible position around the object:

> Why are you **leading on** that nice young man?
> Why are you **leading that nice young man on**?
> Why are you **leading him on**?

Let

Combining the verb *let* with the preposition *down* yields a phrasal verb that means to disappoint someone. It can also have the meaning of to ease up in an activity. Consider these examples:

Don't **let me down**. Please lend me the money.
John knew he was **letting her down** when he couldn't help her move.
Don't **let down** now. You've got only a mile left to go in the marathon.

The preposition *down* in this phrasal verb has a flexible position around the object:

We can't **let down Uncle Bill**.
We can't let **Uncle Bill down**.
We can't **let him down**.

When the verb *let* is followed by *on*, the phrase means to be obvious or to provide knowledge or information. Add the preposition *about* to cite the topic of the information. To cite the recipient of the information, add the preposition *to*. Here are some examples:

Don't **let on** that you know me.
You mustn't **let on to** Robert **about** the accident we had.
She didn't **let on to** me **about** it, but I guessed the truth.

Make

The verb *to make* has a variety of uses and can form many phrasal verbs. Here, just a salient few are considered.

To make of has three primary meanings: (1) to interpret someone or something; (2) to make a success of oneself; and (3) in the construction *to make something of it*, to invite someone to fight. Here are examples:

I don't know what **to make of** this note from Karen. What does it mean?
John has **made something of** himself and has become rich in the process.
Yes, I took your books! Do you want **to make something of it**?

Followed by the preposition *up*, the verb *to make* produces a few new meanings: (1) to fabricate or lie; (2) to apply cosmetics; (3) often with the pronoun *it* and using the preposition *to*, to compensate a person for something; and (4) accompanied by the preposition *with*, to reconcile.

I confess. I **made the whole story up**.
Two women were **making the bride up** for her wedding.
Tom promised **to make it up to me**, but nothing ever happened.
Robert **made up with Carmen**, but she was still angry.

The preposition *up* in this phrasal verb has a flexible position around the object:

John **made up another excuse**.
John **made another excuse up**.
John **made it up**.

If you use the preposition *for* with *to make up*, the phrasal verb means to compensate for something that was done.

I hope this check will **make up for** the problem you had with our product.
You can't **make up for** such bad behavior.

When *to make up* is used with the object *the bed*, the reference is to putting fresh sheets and coverings on a mattress. With that meaning, the preposition *up* again has a flexible position around the object:

Let's **make up the bed**.
Let's **make the bed up**.
Let's **make it up**.

EXERCISE
31·3

Fill in each blank in the following sentences with the appropriate form of the missing phrasal verb. Use the definition provided in parentheses to choose each verb.

EXAMPLE: The police officer came <u>up</u> to me and asked for my identification.

1. They're going _____ the entire advertising department. (end employment)

2. I hope my sister doesn't _____ that I got in at two A.M. (be obvious, provide information)

3. I can't understand why Phillip _____ you. (harbor an attitude of disrespect)

4. My boss just doesn't know what _____ this report. (interpret)

5. Although he's still angry, I finally _____ my ex-boyfriend. (become friends again)

6. Little Billy _____ a silly story about why he was late again. (fabricate)

7. All your apologies cannot _____ for the way you treated me. (compensate)

8. He can't restrain himself from _____ having bought a new house. (be obvious)

9. I wish that horrid man would just _____ me. (stop bothering)

10. I think it was cruel of you to _____ Jake _____. (tantalize with the idea of love)

Pass

When the verb *pass* is followed by *away*, a new meaning is produced: *to die*. This expression is often used in place of *to die* in order to blunt the reality and impart a tone of compassion. When the verb *pass* is followed by the phrase *off as*, the meaning of the phrasal verb is to represent that someone or something is different from what it really is. Some examples:

Old Mrs. Jarvis **passed away** last night.
The man tried to **pass the pretty girl off** as his daughter.
The crooked dealer thought he could **pass off an old chair** as an antique.

The preposition *off* in this phrasal verb has a flexible position around the object:

> He **passed off a forgery** as the real thing.
> He **passed a forgery off** as the real thing.
> He **passed it off** as the real thing.

Set

With the addition of the preposition *back*, the verb *to set* has three new meanings: (1) followed by the preposition *from*, to move something away from other things; (2) to change the time on the clock to an earlier time; and (3) to cause a temporary failure or delay.

> I **set** the stack of books **back from** my work space. I needed more room to write.
> Tomorrow we have **to set all the clocks back** an hour.
> The broken equipment **set us back** a whole week in completing the job.

When *to set* is followed by *off*, it has four primary new meanings: (1) to anger someone; (2) to cause something to explode or go off; (3) followed by the preposition *on*, to depart for a journey; and (4) followed by the preposition *for*, to depart for a specific destination. Some examples:

> Jim's cruel remark really **set Anna off**. She began to scream at him.
> The bomb was **set off** by a remote detonator.
> The next morning we **set off on** the short trip to Sun Valley.
> After breakfast the tourists **set off for** Las Vegas.

The preposition *off* in this phrasal verb has a flexible position around the object:

> That **set off my boss**.   Who **set off the alarm?**
> That **set my boss off**.   Who **set the alarm off?**
> That **set him off**.   Who **set it off?**

Stand

When *to stand* is combined with *for*, the phrasal verb has two meanings: (1) to symbolize something; and (2) to tolerate something. Look at these examples:

> The American flag **stands for** freedom and democracy.
> I won't **stand for** your rude behavior any longer.

Take

When *to take* is combined with *back*, it has three meanings: (1) to return something; (2) to trigger a memory of something; and (3) to retract something.

> I **took the tools I borrowed back** to Jim.
> Hearing that song **takes me back** to when I was still in college.
> **Take that back!** You know that's not true!

The adverb *back* in this phrasal verb has a flexible position around the object:

> Mark won't **take back the money**.
> Mark won't **take the money back**.
> Mark won't **take it back**.

Another phrasal verb is formed with *to take* and the preposition *up*. It has four primary meanings: (1) to raise the hem of a garment; (2) sometimes using the preposition *with*, to discuss a subject; (3) to be involved in an activity; and (4) followed by the preposition *on*, to agree to a proposal. Here are examples of each:

That dress is too long. **Take it up** a couple inches.
The committee **took up** the problem of recycling plastics.
I need **to take up** the question of Jim's employment with you.
My daughter has **taken up** stamp collecting.
I'd like to **take them up** on their offer to buy my house.

The preposition *up* in this phrasal verb has a flexible position around the object:

My cousin **took up the piano**.
My cousin **took the piano up**.
My cousin **took it up**.

Walk

The verb *to walk* when followed by *out* means to leave, or to exit. When the preposition *on* is added, the meaning is altered: to abandon something or to jilt someone.

Why did you **walk out on** the last act of the play?
I don't understand why she **walked out on** Jim. Does she have a new boyfriend?

Warm

When *to warm* is followed by *up*, it means to make something warm by placing it over a heat source or that something is becoming warm. When the preposition *to* is added to this phrase, a different meaning results: to become comfortable with a person or situation.

It will start **warming up** around the middle of April.
As soon as I met Jake, I **warmed up to** him right away.
At first I thought the idea was silly, but I soon **warmed up to** it.

Water

When you add *down* to the verb *to water*, the phrase conveys that a liquid is being diluted, or that someone's efforts are being reduced in effectiveness.

The bartender **watered down** the whiskey to reap a few more dollars.
If you **water down** that solution any further, it won't clean anything.
Congress hoped to **water down** a strict old law.
The committee **watered down** the chairman's powers.

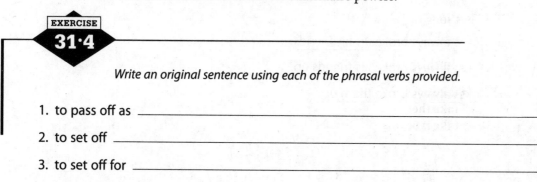

EXERCISE
31·4

Write an original sentence using each of the phrasal verbs provided.

1. to pass off as _____

2. to set off _____

3. to set off for _____

4. to stand for _____

5. to take back _____

6. to take up _____

7. to walk out _____

8. to walk out on _____

9. to warm up to _____

10. to water down _____

Other parts of speech

If a phrasal verb is transitive, it can be used to form the passive voice. The verb in the phrasal verb is formed as a past participle and is introduced by the auxiliary *to be*. For example:

> The two brothers **were cut out** of the will.
> The stew still has **to be warmed up**.

Many phrasal verbs can be used as nouns. In some cases, they are combined as one word by means of a hyphen, and in other instances they are written as one word.

> The children played on the floor with the **cutouts**.
> After a hard winter, we're hoping for a quick **warm-up**.

In addition, nouns and past participles formed from phrasal verbs can act as adjectives:

◆ Nouns as adjectives

> The **getaway** car was a black SUV.
> We'll present a **follow-up** report tomorrow.

◆ Participles as adjectives

> The **laid-off** workers began to plan a protest.
> I can't eat **watered-down** soup.

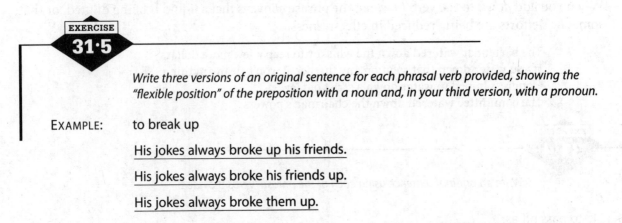

EXERCISE 31·5

Write three versions of an original sentence for each phrasal verb provided, showing the "flexible position" of the preposition with a noun and, in your third version, with a pronoun.

EXAMPLE: to break up

His jokes always broke up his friends.

His jokes always broke his friends up.

His jokes always broke them up.

1. to break down

   a. _____

   b. _____

   c. _____

2. to follow up

   a. _____

   b. _____

   c. _____

3. to lay off

   a. _____

   b. _____

   c. _____

4. to lead on

   a. _____

   b. _____

   c. _____

5. to let down

   a. _____

   b. _____

   c. _____

6. to pass off

   a. _____

   b. _____

   c. _____

7. to set off

   a. _____

   b. _____

   c. _____

8. to warm up

   a. _____

   b. _____

   c. _____

9. to water down

    a. _____

    b. _____

    c. _____

10. to make up

    a. _____

    b. _____

    c. _____

EXERCISE 31·6

Fill in each blank in the sentences that follow with the missing preposition, adverb, or combination of both.

1. How could that woman just walk _____ her husband and children?

2. Ms. Fleming tried to pass herself _____ only thirty years old.

3. Judge Mills won't be _____ until ten.

4. He decided to water _____ his remarks before he gave the speech.

5. I think you should get _____ from that grumpy dog.

6. Who set _____ the bomb?

7. She doesn't like Bob. She can't warm _____ him.

8. Your child should take _____ the violin.

9. You have to find a way to make _____ these bad grades.

10. He knows all the hottest clubs. He's really _____ it.

Review 1

EXERCISE

R1·1

Look at the italicized word or phrase in each sentence and decide how it is used. Then write subject, direct object, indirect object, object of a preposition, *or* predicate nominative *in the blank.*

1. _____ Mark bought *his grandmother* a dozen yellow roses for her birthday.

2. _____ Will *the tourists* from Greece have any trouble reading the menu?

3. _____ Maria was writing a story *about him* for her English class.

4. _____ I need to get *a new tire* for my car.

5. _____ We need to decide *what kind of books* to buy for the children.

EXERCISE

R1·2

Write a sentence using the word in parentheses in the form specified. For example:

(my brother/direct object)   *I gave my brother my old bicycle.*

1. (these people/subject) _____

2. (she/indirect object) _____

3. (the puppies/predicate nominative) _____

4. (we/direct object) _____

5. (your parents/object of a preposition) _____

Fill in the blank with either the definite article or the indefinite article, whichever makes better sense.

1. What time does _____ bus arrive?

2. I think I lost _____ directions.

3. Mark found _____ cell phone under a tree in the park.

4. Let's take _____ subway to Central Park.

5. _____ girls and boys participate in many sports.

If the noun in italics is singular, rewrite the sentence with that word in the plural. If it is in the plural, rewrite the sentence with that word in the singular.

1. The girls like playing with *the puppies*. _____

2. Does John have *a son*? _____

3. I want to buy *lamb chops*. _____

4. *A raccoon* is hiding under our porch. _____

5. My neighbors gave me *the key* to their house. _____

Circle the adjective that makes the most sense in the sentence.

1. Jim needed a **tall / blue / this** shirt for his new suit.

2. The movie we saw was very **sad / regular / handsome**.

3. There was a **beautiful / silly / right** sunset last night.

4. Their new apartment has **careful / quick / spacious** rooms.

5. Mr. Garcia's son is quite **long / handsome / annual**.

6. The little girl's behavior is **true / early / terrible**.

7. The **misty / tall / sudden** man is Professor Jones.

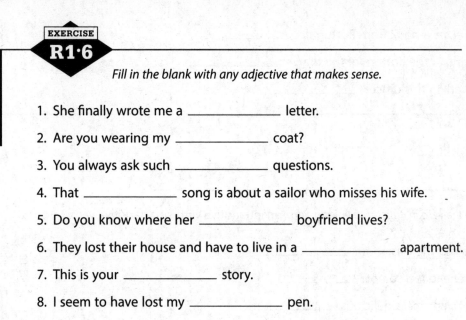

EXERCISE R1·6

Fill in the blank with any adjective that makes sense.

1. She finally wrote me a _____ letter.

2. Are you wearing my _____ coat?

3. You always ask such _____ questions.

4. That _____ song is about a sailor who misses his wife.

5. Do you know where her _____ boyfriend lives?

6. They lost their house and have to live in a _____ apartment.

7. This is your _____ story.

8. I seem to have lost my _____ pen.

EXERCISE R1·7

Circle the pronoun that best completes the sentence.

1. Miguel wanted **you / I / his** to visit him next week.

2. She was crying so we told **her / us / him** a cheerful story.

3. My sister visited **me / I / her** in Miami last week.

4. Is this yours? I found **you / them / it** on the floor.

5. The postcards you sent were beautiful. I loved **yours / them / its**.

6. When will **I / them / us** be able to see you again?

7. Please give **you / us / he** a check by tomorrow.

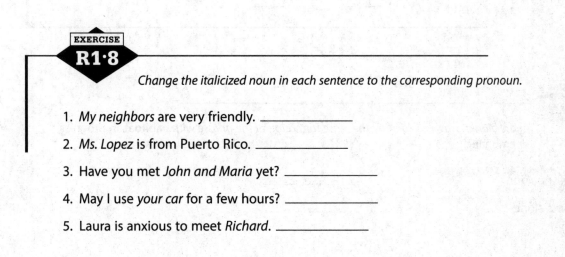

EXERCISE R1·8

Change the italicized noun in each sentence to the corresponding pronoun.

1. *My neighbors* are very friendly. _____

2. *Ms. Lopez* is from Puerto Rico. _____

3. Have you met *John and Maria* yet? _____

4. May I use *your car* for a few hours? _____

5. Laura is anxious to meet *Richard*. _____

6. Juan sent *Jean and me* a book from Portugal. _____

7. *The money* was lying at the bottom of the drawer. _____

8. Do *her brothers* work in this office? _____

EXERCISE
R1·9

Identify the verb in italics as a linking verb, an intransitive verb, *or a* transitive verb.

1. The little boy *ran* into the classroom. _____

2. Why does her forehead *feel* so hot? _____

3. The turkey in the oven *smells* delicious. _____

4. I *tasted* the sour milk and felt ill. _____

5. Can you *speak* a little French? _____

EXERCISE
R1·10

In the blanks provided, write the simple past tense and the past participle of each verb.

Example	<u>Past Tense</u>	<u>Past Participle</u>
find	*found*	*found*
1. go	_____	_____
2. like	_____	_____
3. be	_____	_____
4. give	_____	_____
5. throw	_____	_____

EXERCISE
R1·11

In the blanks provided, identify the tense formation of the phrase with habitual, in progress, *or* emphatic.

1. he is speaking _____

2. I stood alone _____

3. she did go home   _____

4. they do the dishes   _____

5. were you working   _____

Change each sentence by adding the auxiliary provided in parentheses. Maintain the tense of the original sentence.

1. We wash the car every Saturday. (must) _____

2. The children sing sweetly. (to be) _____

3. The patient gets out of bed for a while. (to be able to) _____

4. Bill broke the mirror accidentally. (to have) _____

5. The boys prepare supper tonight. (to be supposed to) _____

6. Have you filled out the application? (to be able to) _____

7. Jean painted her mother's portrait. (to want to) _____

8. Are you funny? (to be) _____

9. We will visit them at Christmas. (to need to) _____

10. My aunt will drive to Los Angeles. (to have to) _____

Rewrite the active voice sentence in the passive voice. Maintain the tense of the original sentence.

1. Mark kisses his grandmother. _____

2. Three men painted the old church white. _____

3. They have arrested three people. _____

4. I will buy a cottage on the lake. _____

5. My uncle is making a delicious soup. _____

EXERCISE R1·14

Rewrite the passive sentence in the tense described in parentheses.

1. Several men are forced into the back of the truck. (simple past) _____

2. Magazines are sold here every day. (present perfect) _____

3. The little girl is spoiled by grandfather. (future) _____

4. Are the women interrogated? (past perfect) _____

5. His prize mare is awarded the grand prize. (simple past) _____

EXERCISE R1·15

Circle the verb form that best completes the sentence.

1. I wish that the rainstorm **ends / would end / end** soon.

2. She would have been so happy if Tom **had been / was / will be** here.

3. I demanded that Jack **gives back / return / would send** it to me.

4. Mr. Keller suggests he **was / were / be** more punctual.

5. If Larry **came / come / will come** to the party, we'd have more fun.

6. My uncle requested that his will **is / would / be** read at the memorial.

7. I would bake an apple pie if Mary **were / was / is** back from the Middle East.

8. He wishes they **help / would help / are helping** him scrub the floor.

9. **When / Would / If** Carmen were here, she'd know what to do.

10. Stefan **was / would / were** study with me if I asked.

EXERCISE R1·16

In the blank provided, write how, where, *or* when, *depending upon the meaning of the italicized adverb. If the adverb is functioning as an adjective or adverb modifier, write* modifier.

1. The children ran *into the family room* to play a video. _____

2. John drove *home* and went straight to bed. _____

3. That was an *extremely* difficult play to understand. _____

4. Her car pulled up to his house *at noon*. _____

5. Laura smiled *warmly* at the handsome man. _____

6. Tom had a *rather* silly look on his face. _____

7. His father had a *very* bad temper. _____

8. Little Jimmy cried *loudly* on the floor. _____

Fill in the blank with an appropriate adverb.

1. His sister is a _____ smart student.

2. Where did you learn to play the guitar so _____?

3. This article is _____ boring.

4. The train _____ arrived.

5. Mr. Brown is a _____ talented artist.

6. She went _____ to bed.

7. With any luck they will get here _____.

Form a contraction with the combination of words provided.

1. he is not   _____

2. we would   _____

3. they have   _____

4. I should not   _____

5. who has   _____

6. it is   _____

7. we were   _____

8. he does not   _____

9. I am   _____

10. she will   _____

If the noun in boldface is singular, change it to the plural, and if it is plural, change it to singular.

1. The **factory** is old. _____

2. He chased the little **mouse**. _____

3. His **feet** are big. _____

4. Where is your **brother**? _____

5. The **wife** sits on the sofa. _____

6. The **leaves** are falling already. _____

7. I met the **women** in Toronto. _____

8. Did he use a **veto**? _____

9. I found the sharp **knives**. _____

10. Did they find the old **ox**? _____

What punctuation mark completes the sentence correctly?

1. Mr. Johnson _____ please have a seat _____

2. Watch out _____ You're in danger _____

3. How old is your grandmother _____

4. _____ This is going to be a problem _____ " he said.

5. The man_____s name is Thomas _____

6. I have the evidence_____ it will prove his innocence _____

7. Add these to your grocery list _____ milk _____ eggs _____ and bread.

8. Bob asked, _____ Where is the bank _____ "

9. Well _____ you came home on time today _____

10. He spoke with an M.D _____ at one.

EXERCISE
R1·21

Restate the verb in parentheses as an infinitive *or a* gerund, *whichever completes the sentence appropriately.*

1. (make) I quit smoking _____ you happy.

2. (read) The best book _____ is *Catcher in the Rye*.

3. (live) I don't enjoy _____ in this building.

4. (get) He was arrested for _____ drunk.

5. (bore) This is a very _____ film.

6. (show) Tom sent me a check _____ his appreciation.

7. (hike) Do they really like _____?

8. (end) The _____ was so sad that I cried.

9. (visit) The store _____ is Macy's.

10. (chirp) The _____ birds sound so happy.

EXERCISE
R1·22

Combine the two sentences, making the second one a relative clause with the pronoun that.

1. This is the jacket. The jacket belonged to Maria. _____

2. What is the country? Max came from the country? _____

3. Did you meet the woman? I met the woman in Madrid. _____

4. I found the money. He hid the money in the attic. _____

Combine the two sentences with a form of who *or* which.

5. He learned another language. It is a difficult task. _____

6. Where's the box? I put the books in the box. _____

7. I spoke with the boy. His sister is a police officer. _____

Restate the sentence, omitting the relative pronoun.

8. This is the gentleman, to whom I gave my passport. _____

9. Is that the hat, in which he carried the message? _____

10. That's the girl that I really like. _____

Restate each sentence with the new subjects provided.

He really enjoyed himself.

1. I _____

2. She _____

3. They _____

Restate each sentence with the new subjects provided.

He was happy with himself.

4. You _____

5. We _____

6. Who _____?

7. The twins _____

Restate each sentence with the new subjects provided.

He couldn't help himself.

8. I _____

9. Tina _____

10. John and Mike _____

Restate the sentence with possession formed with of *to possession formed with -'s or -s'.*

1. The health of the woman was good. _____

2. The end of the storm was a relief. _____

3. The buzzing of the bees scares her. _____

4. Are the pups of the German shepherd healthy? _____

5. I don't like the behavior of that child. _____

Restate the sentence with possession formed with -'s or -s' to possession formed with of.

1. The boys' shouting disturbed him.   _____

2. Are those elks the lion's prey?   _____

3. The town's western border is Main Street. _____

4. The victim's condition grew worse.   _____

5. Where are the doctor's instruments?   _____

Omit the noun in boldface and restate the sentence appropriately.

1. Is the car down the street your **car**?   _____

2. Tom wanted my **keys**.   _____

3. His **sister** danced with everyone.   _____

4. **The snake's** nest was behind a rock.   _____

5. Jane found our **computer** in the basement. _____

Change the word in boldface to the appropriate possessive pronoun.

1. John took **the** dog for a walk.   _____

2. The photograph slipped out of **the** frame. _____

3. **Some** students made Mr. Connelly proud. _____

4. I rarely spend **a lot of** time sleeping. _____

5. Will you visit **some** friends in Washington? _____

Look at the italicized word or phrase in each sentence. Decide how it is used, then write subject, direct object, indirect object, object of a preposition, or predicate nominative in the blank.

1. _____ I like dancing with *Maria*.

2. _____ Do you have *enough money* for the movies?

3. _____ Is *your sister* staying home tonight?

4. _____ My aunt sent *my mother* a beautiful bouquet.

5. _____ My older brother became *a teacher*.

6. _____ Uncle John is *a major* in the Air Force.

7. _____ *That e-mail* is from a friend in Spain.

8. _____ Tom wants to buy *a piano*.

9. _____ I lend *my cousin* twenty dollars.

10. _____ The young couple sits beside *the river*.

Fill in the blank with either the definite or indefinite article, whichever makes the best sense.

1. We greeted _____ tourists as they entered the room.

2. Where are _____ keys to this door?

3. Do you see _____ bus or a streetcar coming?

4. She has _____ difficult puzzle for you.

5. Do you want to order a pizza or _____ French fries?

6. What time does _____ plane land?

7. _____ teacher's name is Ms. Johnson.

8. Is that _____ rabbit hiding under the bush?

9. She really liked _____ story I wrote.

10. Can you read _____ sign over the entrance?

EXERCISE
R1·30

Circle the boldface adjective that makes the most sense in the sentence.

1. Jack found a **long / several / wrong** board behind the garage.

2. The new school has a **large / young / quick** gymnasium.

3. The **former / boring / last** train leaves at 10:00 P.M.

4. That woman is very **long / old / final**.

5. We were watching a **careful / funny / gray** movie.

6. There was a **green / sad / empty** snake hiding in the shade.

7. That driver is just too **same / careless / red**.

8. I hope you can visit us at our **new / short / tall** apartment.

9. After the race, the athletes were **big / thirsty / simple**.

10. That **long / green / handsome** man is my cousin.

EXERCISE
R1·31

In the blank provided, write the word or phrase in bold as its appropriate pronoun.

1. I gave **Tom** a few extra dollars. _____

2. We found **these beautiful dishes** in France. _____

3. I hope you can send **my wife and me** a postcard. _____

4. My son never eats **broccoli**. _____

5. **Mr. Garcia** is the new manager of the store. _____

6. I'd like to introduce you to **Anna Keller**. _____

7. Are **the children** still asleep? _____

8. **A large rock** is in the middle of the driveway. _____

9. **The whole team** went out for pizza. _____

10. Do **Paul and I** have to do the dishes tonight? _____

Rewrite each sentence in the past tense, present perfect tense, and the future tense.

1. I have a job in the city.

   _____

   _____

   _____

2. Do you like working for him?

   _____

   _____

   _____

3. My mother wants to buy a new TV.

   _____

   _____

   _____

4. He pins a medal on my chest.

   _____

   _____

   _____

5. Your husband needs to get more exercise.

   _____

   _____

   _____

6. Ashley does not drive.

   _____

   _____

   _____

7. The children are learning to write.

   _____

   _____

   _____

8. Are you well?

_____

_____

_____

9. The man often breaks a dish.

_____

_____

_____

10. Are your sons living together?

_____

_____

_____

Rewrite each sentence with the auxiliaries provided in parentheses. Keep the same tense as the original sentence.

1. I borrow some money from her.

   (to have to)

   _____

   (to need to)

   _____

2. We shall drive to New Orleans.

   (to be able to)

   _____

   (to have to)

   _____

3. You help your neighbors.

   (can)

   _____

   (ought to)

   _____

4. The boys were a little lazy.

(can)

_____

(might)

_____

5. The smallest children do not play here.

(should)

_____

(must)

_____

6. Do they work long hours?

(to have to)

_____

(to want to)

_____

7. I didn't perform in the play.

(to want to)

_____

(could)

_____

8. Jean leaves for Hawaii on Tuesday.

(should)

_____

(may)

_____

9. Will you stay with relatives?

(to have to)

_____

(to be able to)

_____

10. Mr. Patel doesn't live in the suburbs.

(to want to)

_____

(should)

_____

Rewrite the following active sentences as passive sentences. Keep the same tense.

1. Our broker will sell the house.

   _____

2. Did your company build the new jetliner?

   _____

3. My aunt is baking a cake.

   _____

4. I located the island on this map.

   _____

5. An earthquake destroys the village.

   _____

6. Tom has written the e-mail incorrectly.

   _____

7. Robert is carrying the baby into the nursery.

   _____

8. No one saw the accident.

   _____

9. Dr. Patel was examining the sick child.

   _____

10. Won't a mechanic repair the car?

   _____

Fill in the blank with an appropriate subjunctive form of the verb in parentheses.

1. I demand that he _____ an I.D. right now. (to show)

2. She would be grateful if you _____ to help her. (to try)

3. If only my parents _____ here! (to be)

4. Thomas wishes he _____ enough money to take a vacation. (to have)

5. The lawyer suggested the woman _____ the document. (to sign)

6. If Mary _____ late, she wouldn't be able to meet the new student.
   (to arrive)

7. Ms. Nguyen would have learned English if she _____ here longer. (to live)

8. If only the man _____ been more careful. (to have)

9. If Tim had found the money he would _____ the bills. (to pay)

10. I recommended that you _____ allowed to live here a bit longer. (to be)

Appropriately place the adverb in parentheses in the sentence. If the word in parentheses is an adjective, change it to an adverb and place it appropriately in the sentence.

1. They never arrive. (punctual)

_____

2. Your brother is a talented gymnast. (rather)

_____

3. A little puppy followed Jimmy. (home)

_____

4. The sergeant called the soldiers to attention. (harsh)

_____

5. Does your cousin sing? (good)

_____

6. The boys ran into the classroom. (fast)

_____

7. She was sleepy and went home. (too)

_____

8. The man's voice was strong. (quite)

_____

9. Jane ran the race rapidly. (so)

_____

10. John stepped before the judge. (brave)

_____

EXERCISE
R1·37

In the blank provided, write the words in bold as a contraction.

1. We **must not** waste any more time. _____
2. **He would** really like this movie. _____
3. **I have** never seen such beautiful mountains. _____
4. **Did** you **not** get your homework done? _____
5. **They are** spending too much time at the mall. _____
6. **Who has** been using my laptop? _____
7. **I am** exhausted! _____
8. Tom **will not** be going to the dance. _____
9. **She will** find full-time work. _____
10. **It is** too cold today. _____

EXERCISE
R1·38

Change each noun in the following sentences to its plural. Make any necessary changes to the verbs and articles.

1. Your best friend has always been your wife.

   _____

2. The man has a painful broken tooth.

   _____

3. A goose is paddling in the pond.

   _____

4. That child is hiding in the box.

   _____

5. The woman's foot was swollen.

   _____

6. The person who caught the mouse is no hero.

   _____

7. The deer was grazing in the field.

   _____

8. Where is the leaf for the table?

   _____

9. This lady wants to buy a fork and a knife.

_____

10. The ox roamed alongside the river.

_____

EXERCISE
R1·39

Place a period, an exclamation point, or a question mark at the end of each sentence.

1. Did you have enough time to finish the project _____

2. Shut up now _____

3. My son turns ten years old tomorrow _____

4. Bob was asking whether I knew about the accident _____

5. Why did you break that lamp _____

Rewrite each sentence and place commas where they are needed.

6. Jane set the books pens and documents on my desk.

_____

7. No it happened on June 28 2009.

_____

8. Grandfather dozed in a chair but grandmother worked in the kitchen.

_____

9. By the way you need flour butter and eggs for this recipe.

_____

10. My son was born on June 10 and my daughter on November 21 of the following year.

_____

EXERCISE
R1·40

Look at each sentence and decide how the infinitive or gerund is used. Then write noun, verb, adverb, or adjective in the blank provided.

1. _____ My parents were *sitting* in the backyard.

2. _____ A swiftly *flowing* river can be dangerous.

3. _____ The car *to buy* should get good gas mileage.

4. _____ *Jogging* is great exercise.

5. _____ My youngest son doesn't like *swimming*.

6. _____ I bought her a necklace *to show* my love to her.

7. _____ We are *traveling* to Canada tomorrow.

8. _____ The *ending* of the movie was very sad.

9. _____ Bill was sent home from school for *cheating*.

10. _____ *To vote* is a citizen's obligation.

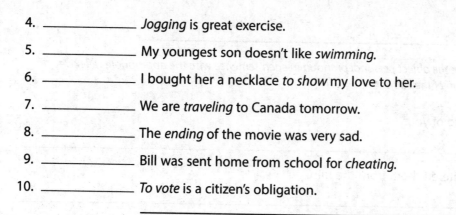

EXERCISE R1·41

Combine the following pairs of sentences by changing the second sentence to a relative clause. Use that as the relative pronoun.

1. I haven't used the new pen. Tom bought me the new pen.

_____

2. They visited the city. Grandfather was born in the city.

_____

3. Have you met the athletes? I told you about the athletes.

_____

4. Maria showed me the math problem. She cannot understand the math problem.

_____

5. Bob has a good memory. His memory always serves him well.

_____

Follow the same directions. Use who, whom, or whose as the relative pronoun.

6. This is the man. The man's wife is a concert pianist.

_____

7. Let me introduce the guests. I told you about the guests yesterday.

_____

8. I was speaking with the young couple. The young couple's first child was born a week ago.

_____

9. She danced with the man. The man wrote a cookbook.

_____

10. Todd likes the girl. He met the girl at our party.

_____

Replace the object personal pronoun in each sentence with the appropriate reflexive pronoun of the subject.

1. I was really proud of you.

   _____

2. The squirrel sheltered them from the rain.

   _____

3. She found him something good to eat.

   _____

4. I don't like her in that dress.

   _____

5. How did you injure him?

   _____

6. The two boys forced us to finish the race.

   _____

7. We are going to buy him some ice cream.

   _____

8. Robert always pampered me.

   _____

9. I had to ask him how that happened.

   _____

10. The little girl always liked me in a pink dress.

    _____

Change the italicized possessive phrase to a possessive ending in -'s.

EXAMPLE   The color *of the car* is red.
              The car's color is red.

1. Do you have a picture of the father *of the bride*?

   _____

2. This is the largest parking lot *of the city*.

   _____

3. The office *of my doctor* is on the second floor.

_____

4. The value *of this factory* has gone up.

_____

5. The owner *of the puppies* could not be found.

_____

Follow the same directions but change the italicized phrase to a possessive made with of.

EXAMPLE   *The car's* color is red.
            <u>*The color of the car is red.*</u>

6. *The flowers'* scent filled the living room.

_____

7. *The nation's* wealth comes from oil.

_____

8. How do you explain *the children's* bad grades?

_____

9. The judge could not understand *the document's* meaning.

_____

10. Rabbits are often *the wolves'* prey.

_____

EXERCISE
R1·44

Circle the boldface word that best completes each sentence.

1. Did your girlfriend leave **my / her / hers** in her room?

2. The twins were visiting **ours / mine / their** relatives in Boston.

3. This bed is mine, and that one is **his / your / her**.

4. **Our / Yours / Mine** uncle was a ship captain.

5. No one in the classroom understood **one / her / theirs** lecture.

6. The injured pup licked **its / hers / theirs** paw.

7. Did you bring along **your / mine / ours** sleeping bag?

8. I think you took **my / your / mine** by accident.

9. Jim found his passport, but where is **our / hers / their**?

10. Julie wants to borrow **hers / yours / my** car again.

EXERCISE
R1·45

Circle the boldface word that best completes each sentence.

1. Two of the girls **was / is / are** new to our class.

2. Who is that sitting **next to / between / about** Ms. Garcia?

3. The **man / friend / men** I work with have been with the company for a year.

4. Several students **on / in / out** this class forgot about the test.

5. I have several gifts for **he / your / them**.

6. This letter **below / from / since** the mayor was a surprise.

7. I won't go to the party without **she / you / they**.

8. **Three / Several / One** of the actors wins an award.

9. An unfamiliar dog was running **off / toward / during** the child.

10. Only one **from / of / by** the boys will be chosen for the team.

EXERCISE
R1·46

Rewrite the words in each exercise that require capitalization.

1. maria was born on july fifteenth in chicago, illinois.

_____

2. we like to spend every sunday with our grandparents in the city.

_____

3. will professor johnson give another speech on tax reform?

_____

4. during the winter jack often goes skiing in the mountains of colorado.

_____

5. ms. patel rarely drinks coffee or tea in the morning.

_____

6. when he visited the united states, he stayed at the hilton hotel in new york.

_____

7. there was a terrible accident on main street on october first.

_____

8. the reporter wanted to speak to the president but was stopped by captain wilson.

_____

9. everyone in the tenth grade liked reading *to kill a mocking bird*.

_____

10. governor shaw announced plans for new highways around the state.

_____

_____

Rewrite each sentence twice, first changing the adjective or adverb to the comparative and then to the superlative.

1. Our neighbors are rich.

_____

_____

2. They walked in the darkness carefully.

_____

_____

3. I have little patience with him.

_____

_____

4. Tina didn't feel well yesterday.

_____

_____

5. The tea was hot.

_____

_____

6. Tom ran slowly.

_____

_____

7. John and Ashley are my good friends.

_____

_____

8. The boys ate many cookies.

_____

_____

9. Was the play boring?

_____

_____

10. That man's language is bad.

_____

_____

Complete each sentence with an appropriate clause.

1. The older dog likes to sleep a lot, but _____.

2. When _____, I often went to a

Broadway show.

3. My neighbor said that _____.

4. Jose and his wife live on the third floor, and _____.

5. If you lose your driver's license, _____.

6. _____, so I stay out of the hot sun.

7. Did the woman ask you where _____?

8. Do you want to go shopping, or _____?

9. While I was living in Mexico, _____.

10. He had no idea how _____.

*Look at the italicized word or phrase in each sentence. Then, using the appropriate
interrogative word, ask the question that relates to that word.*

EXAMPLE   *The car* won't start again.

          What won't start again? _____

1. Guatemala is located in *Central America.*

_____

2. *Ms. Keller's* cat is hiding in the attic.

_____

3. I should try on *that* dress.

_____

4. He saw *more than twenty* injured people there.

_____

5. The next train arrives *in the early morning.*

_____

6. John's parents began to cry *because they were so proud of him.*

_____

7. *The woman standing on the corner* is waiting for a bus.

_____

8. You saw *several girls* playing soccer in the park.

_____

9. The angry look in his eyes meant *danger.*

_____

10. The hallway is *about ten feet long.*

_____

_____

EXERCISE

R1·50

Rewrite each sentence twice, first by adding not, *then by using a contraction of* not.

1. The girls were chatting in the living room.

_____

_____

2. I am home before 7:00 P.M.

_____

_____

3. Are they coming to the dance?

_____

_____

4. Ashley spoke with Mr. Barrett about it.

_____

_____

5. Have the twins done their homework?

_____

_____

6. Does that woman see the car coming?

_____

_____

7. Tom will be spending the winter in Colorado.

_____

_____

8. Can you understand the lecture?

_____

_____

9. His fiancée sent his ring back.

_____

_____

10. Would you like to sit in the shade for a while?

_____

_____

EXERCISE
R1·51

Complete each sentence with the date or number shown in parentheses written as words. In the case of months and days, the month precedes the day (e.g., 5/2 —May second).

1. Tomorrow is (6/30) _____.

2. How much is (15 + 6) _____?

3. The man died on (11/5) _____.

4. Who's the (3) _____ man in line there?

5. Her birthday was (10/2) _____.

6. The party is on the (12) _____ of this month.

7. How much is (210 − 50) _____?

8. How much is (6.5 × 10) _____?

9. This is my (1) _____ driver's license.

10. Jack was their (500) _____ customer and won a prize.

Circle the boldface word that best completes each sentence.

1. The blade on the long sword is sharper **than / then** on the short one.

2. It's a difficult text. **Few / Little / A few** people understand it.

3. John had a **bad / well / badly** time at school today.

4. You can **lay / laid / lie** the baby on the bed.

5. Only **much / a little / few** is known about the woman.

6. The patient had **laid / lie / lain** on his side for an hour.

7. That man talks a lot but says **less / little / fewer**.

8. A restful night's sleep is always **good / well**.

9. There are **few / less / fewer** people in the audience tonight than last night.

10. **Who / Whom** was supposed to meet Aunt Mary at the station?

Review 2

EXERCISE

R2·1

Underline the entire auxiliary verb in each sentence.

1. We have to go grocery shopping.

2. He has to be able to run five miles in less than half an hour.

3. He is able to speak Persian.

4. He should be working a lot harder if he wishes to pass the exam.

5. I had better see a dermatologist.

6. She is my friend, so I am going to have to tell her.

7. I am going to write a novel based on our family.

8. I had better be able to pass this driving test.

EXERCISE

R2·2

Correct the error in each sentence.

1. Is impossible to learn Arabic quickly.

   _____

2. Eating everything, we decided to go to a restaurant.

   _____

3. Paul finished to work early today.

   _____

4. They have succeeded in to becoming rich.

   _____

5. I am tired of work so hard just to make money.

   _____

6. They look forward to meet you.

_____

7. I am going to try to prevent you from to drink too much.

_____

8. Shannon is interested in learn more about Artificial Intelligence.

_____

9. To go willingly is to shown courage.

_____

10. They wanted come earlier, but their flight was delayed.

_____

11. Laura hopes going to Iceland next year, even if she knows it's so cold there.

_____

12. Are you enjoy yourself?

_____

EXERCISE
R2·3

Complete each sentence with the appropriate tense of the verb in parentheses.

1. ADRIAN: Hi, Loretta. _____ (you + meet) my close friend Kerry?

   LORETTA: No, I don't believe I _____ (ever + have) the pleasure of making his acquaintance.

   ADRIAN: Well, let me introduce you!

2. BETH: Wait! What _____ (you + do)?

   ADRIAN: I _____ (try) to pull out whatever _____ (jam) the blender.

   BETH: You really should not _____ (put) your hand in there while it's still plugged in. You _____ (probably + hurt) yourself.

3. ADRIAN: There's Loretta.

   BETH: Where?

   ADRIAN: She _____ (sit) on that bench in the shade.

   BETH: Oh yes, I _____ (see) her now.

   She _____ (certainly + look) focused. Let's go bother her anyway.

4. KERRY: What_____(be) wrong with Adrian?

   BETH: While he_____(run), his shoelaces _____(come) untied and he_____(fall).

   KERRY: I_____(not + believe) it!_____(be) you serious?

   BETH: Yes. I'm not kidding you. I wish I_____(be), but I'm not.

   KERRY: Poor Adrian, he_____(seem) to_____ (suffer) quite a bit too.

5. PAUL: _____(you + take) an Economics component this semester?

   PATRICIA: No, I_____(not + be).

   PAUL: _____(you + ever + take) it?

   PATRICIA: Yes, I_____(have).

   PAUL: When_____(you + take) it?

   PATRICIA: In 2006.

   PAUL: Who_____(teach) the class back then?

   PATRICIA: Dr. Bumshelgell.

   PAUL: I_____(take) his class next semester._____ (be) he a good professor?

   PATRICIA: When I_____(take) the class, he_____ (be) very pleasant to work with. His class_____(be) very difficult to pass, but it's well worth it.

6. DANIEL: I_____(spend) some time in Prague last month.

   I_____(never + be) there before.

   JESSE: What_____(you + do) while you were there?

   DANIEL: My girlfriend and I_____(drive) around, randomly stopping in places we_____(think) looked interesting.

7. The weather_____(be) terrible lately. It_____(rain) off and on for a whole week, and for two days the temperature _____(drop) below ten degrees. It_____(be) in the low 40s right now. Just yesterday, the sun_____(shine) and the weather was as pleasant as can be. It almost seems like the weather _____(change) all the time, and one never_____ (know) what to expect. At this point, I_____(be) ready for anything. When I wake up tomorrow morning, maybe everything_____ (freeze).

8. BRIAN: I _____ (go) to a concert last night.

GREGORY: _____ (it + be) any fun?

BRIAN: I _____ (not + do) think so, but Patricia

_____ (enjoy) it quite a bit.

GREGORY: Who _____ (you + see)?

BRIAN: Postal Service. I _____ (never + see) them perform live before.

GREGORY: Oh! I _____ (see) them in concert, too.

I _____ (go) to their concert when they were on tour a couple

of years ago. I _____ (think) it _____ (be)

a great show!

BRIAN: Well, I _____ (not + think) so.

EXERCISE
R2·4

Underline the entire auxiliary verb in each sentence.

1. It's the end of spring break, so Peter is going back to school next week.

2. We should open the window.

3. Allison is going to Austin next weekend.

4. We don't have to paint all the kitchen walls tonight.

5. Are we supposed to get there before nightfall?

6. Josh should have to pay for all the groceries.

7. Patricia is going to open a vintage record store next month.

8. Since last week, I have been running every morning.

9. Bureaucrats should be able to stay polite at all times.

10. He has been playing the drums all morning.

EXERCISE
R2·5

Complete each sentence with an appropriate form of the verb in parentheses.

1. Her mother recommended that they _____ (stay) inside until it stopped snowing.

2. She really wanted her room _____ (paint) in the same color as her sister's.

3. It was such a long train ride that our friend suggested that we _____ (take) a few games with us.

4. This table should _____ (move) to the living room, that way more people can sit around it.

5. His aunt recommends that they not _____ (eat) too much sugar before going to sleep.

6. The drivers recommend that the bus route _____ (cancel) until that road is repaired.

7. His father asks that she _____ (be) cautious while driving her brother's new car.

8. It is very important that students _____ (teach) and then _____ (test) so that they can improve.

9. She demanded that she _____ (allow) to see her husband, even if he was still asleep.

10. It is important that he_____ (not + be) late for his job interview.

11. Their teacher requested that the students _____ (practice) their English as often as possible.

12. My parents requested that I _____ (not + allow) to stay at the party after midnight.

13. The artist made sure that his brush _____ (be) clean before painting.

14. It is important that you _____ (meet) with me tomorrow in the morning.

15. It is imperative that they _____ (read) to as often as they can.

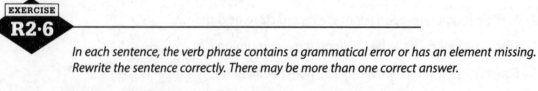

EXERCISE
R2·6

In each sentence, the verb phrase contains a grammatical error or has an element missing. Rewrite the sentence correctly. There may be more than one correct answer.

EXAMPLE   Mike has visit Philadelphia twice this past month.
           Mike has visited Philadelphia twice this past month.

1. Kenji been studying Portuguese.

   _____

2. Juan has live in Madrid for two years.

   _____

3. He has to came back to meet us here.

   _____

4. My father, Raoul, who studied Mathematics with my uncle, looking for a job.

_____

5. After work, Anjali will going to the pub.

_____

6. Last week, Mark was able to visited the president's office.

_____

7. The soil is dry. They will not are able to plant vegetables there.

_____

8. He doesn't likes his neighbors, because they're too noisy.

_____

9. They didn't had any problems with the rental car.

_____

10. I have been learned a lot since I began doing my exercises.

_____

11. Are you think of buying another car soon?

_____

12. She was visited many monuments when she was in Rome.

_____

13. I didn't saw a single beautiful sunset.

_____

14. He couldn't forgot her after the love affair.

_____

15. He always attempting to catch the students cheating.

_____

16. Sometimes when I cross the street, I don't looked to see if a car is coming.

_____

17. I've thinking about it for a long time now.

_____

18. I feel my English grammar might improving.

_____

19. Mrs. Gilmore was sad, because her son had to went back to the front lines.

_____

20. All my friends can helps me become a better person.

_____

Each sentence may have a noun or pronoun with an error in number. Write the corrected word in the blank. If the sentence is correct, mark an "X" in the blank.

1. Some of us wanted to be talented musicians, and others wanted to be famous painter.

   _____

2. Good professors like graduate students to be outspoken in their class.

   _____

3. Each person should make up his or her own mind.

   _____

4. The 50 states of the United States all have their own law.

   _____

5. When he was elected, the president did what he had promised: He gave more power to the syndicates and more power to the worker themselves.

   _____

6. Talented people who come to Europe to study should then return to their countries to help improve their society.

   _____

7. I like to travel, because it helps me understand the custom of other countries.

   _____

Rewrite each sentence, correcting the grammatical error(s), if any. If the sentence is correct, mark an "X" in the blank.

1. Hello you. How are you?

   _____

2. It's such a nice city to visit. There is so many things to do.

   _____

3. One should always look after one's family.

   _____

4. Some will study in Germany; other, instead, will studied somewhere else in Europe.

   _____

5. I am in love with you and want us to stay together. Whichever you go, I will follow you.

   _____

6. I am not sure of what will wrong with Nancy but somethings is bothering her.

   _____

7. I wasn't here but mom told me somebody called you last night.

   _____

8. It won't be a party just for friends. Anybodies who wants to come are welcome.

   _____

9. It's unlikely the train will leave on time. Many of the passengers knows that.

   _____

10. Some work in the evenings, but much work in the daytime.

    _____

11. No one understands me other than my closest friend.

    _____

12. I asked Peter where they were going this summer and he tell me they is traveling to Paris.
    It seems like everyone are visiting France this year.

    _____

    _____

13. I'm sorry, no one speak Mandarin here.

    _____

14. Karen doesn't like going out with Eric. He generally drink quite a lots.

    _____

EXERCISE

R2·9

Complete each sentence by supplying the missing preposition.

1. Everyone is _____ schedule, so the project won't be completed on time.

2. Such behavior is _____ her.

3. We walked and walked _____ hours.

4. She has earned a place _____ the best heart surgeons in Switzerland.

5. He was named _____ a character of a movie his parents loved.

6. Let's meet _____ Saturday. Does that work for you?

7. Christian and Isabel are going to Costa Rica _____ September.

8. She's working _____ setting up the office.

9. I'm getting _____ the subway as we speak.

10. I'm going _____ vacation next month.

11. Catherine is free _____ five o'clock on.

12. Charles and her were both born _____ June.

13. Don't they know right _____ wrong any longer?

14. That man has spent his entire life _____ politics.

15. You can use your credit card, but you can also pay for it _____ cash.

16. They have always lived _____ privileged people.

17. Seth just got _____ the plane.

18. The temperature has been _____ normal the entire summer.

19. She always takes a walk _____ Mondays.

20. I live _____ the train station.

21. Our office is only a few blocks _____ here.

22. He thinks highly _____ her artistry.

23. There are _____ two hours to go before we reach Brisbane.

24. The garage is right _____ the corner from here.

25. I'll go to the theatre _____ meeting them for dinner, not after.

26. The construction runs all _____ the street.

27. We try to get in bed _____ eleven every night.

28. We'll see him _____ the afternoon.

EXERCISE
R2·10

Complete each sentence, supplying the missing auxiliary verb form.

1. Sherlock will _____ meeting with his associate soon to discuss his theory.

2. Watson knew that he should _____ looking harder for clues.

3. The murderer could _____ tried to keep his prints off the doorknob.

4. They _____ captured the murderer by April 6.

5. He could not understand how the police might _____ found out where he lived.

6. Inspector Pretz pushed Jack into the prison cell, because he _____ not want to take any risks.

7. Now when I see Watson, I just tell him, "You are a genius!" because he could _____ found a way to solve the mystery.

8. When Sherlock Holmes _____ working on a case, he tries to use every little bit of information he can get his hands on.

Each item should be a complete, grammatical sentence. If it is, mark an "X" in the blank. If it contains an error, describe the error, and then write a correct, grammatical sentence based on the item.

1. Teaching math to smart students.

   _____

2. Listen!

   _____

3. If you want to observe what is taking place.

   _____

4. Last week, she began writing her new book.

   _____

5. The European Union.

   _____

6. I already ran three miles

   _____

7. before I walked in, I rang the bell, hoping someone would open the door.

   _____

8. Many different photographs in that dusty, black book.

   _____

9. Has many children.

   _____

10. Open the garage before you leave.

    _____

11. The Panama Canal can be a dangerous zone.

    _____

12. Writing complete sentences is easy.

    _____

13. If your friend is a lawyer, doesn't have to worry about finding a job.

    _____

14. Madrid it is the capital of Spain.

    _____

15. Also, he very smart, quiet, and polite.

    _____

Complete each sentence with the appropriate answer, (a), (b), or (c).

EXAMPLE   They started leaving _____.

        (a) one after the other
        (b) one than
        (c) themselves

They started leaving *one after the other.*   (a)

1. One of the office managers is from Peru; _____ are from here.
    (a) one
    (b) the others
    (c) they

2. Don't trust them. Whatever _____ say, it is simply not true!
    (a) anyone
    (b) one
    (c) they

3. The richer you become, the more _____ are expected to be generous.
    (a) you
    (b) one
    (c) yourself

4. They call _____ almost daily.
    (a) each other
    (b) every other
    (c) anyone

5. The dominoes started falling _____.
    (a) one another
    (b) one after the other
    (c) every other

6. They call each other _____ day.
    (a) one after the other
    (b) one another
    (c) every other

7. The older one becomes, the more _____ is supposed to eat healthier food.
    (a) you
    (b) one
    (c) the other

Each item should be a complete, grammatical sentence. If it is, mark an "X" in the blank. If it is not, write one or more correct sentences based on the item.

EXAMPLE   To cook that much rice. She'll need more water.
To cook that much rice, she'll need more water.

1. When I was younger. I thought the earth was flat.

   _____

2. My ambition is to become a pilot.

   _____

3. My favorite color was red. Because it reminded me of my sister.

   _____

4. He hates horror movies. Because he gets scared immediately.

   _____

5. Now I realize that dreaming is not enough.

   _____

6. She is back it's the end of spring semester at UCLA.

   _____

7. To paint this wall. You need a special brush.

   _____

8. Elvis is over there. With Tupac and Biggie and they look happy.

   _____

9. You will get a free subscription in addition you will receive a free towel. A matching bathrobe, a sticker, and a silver pen.

   _____

   _____

10. Once you have done all your stretching. Run for two miles or so.

    _____

11. As soon as you get there, make sure you take a right.

    _____

12. When the water is boiling. Put the pasta in the pot.

    _____

13. After the sun comes up can begin hiking up the mountain.

    _____

EXERCISE R2·14

Complete each sentence by using the appropriate subordinating or coordinating prepositions.

1. We're running late so I'll can you _____ we get there.

2. _____ we may not succeed, we'll try again.

3. Please send me a message _____ you leave.

4. _____ that is the case, what should we do?

5. Richard always goes to the theatre _____ he likes it.

6. I am not bored, _____ am I tired.

7. The wine is too cold _____ delicious.

8. Daniel _____ Patrick should pay for that, not you.

9. _____ I like classical music, I cannot listen to Mozart's compositions anymore.

10. Beth is not well, _____ she's not joining us for coffee.

11. Einstein really liked physics _____ really liked art.

12. Our summers are very warm, _____ everyone knows.

13. I tripped on the sidewalk _____ I ran to try and catch the bus.

14. Carl and Lisa decided to go out _____ they had finished dinner.

15. _____ she finds programming easy, she prefers to study anything but computer science.

EXERCISE R2·15

Complete each sentence with an appropriate form of the verb in parentheses.

EXAMPLE   I hope that Catherine ___*drives*___ (drive) carefully, because the roads are slippery.

1. I recommend that Pablo _____ (promote) to a managerial position.

2. We demand that you _____ (give) us the location of the treasure.

3. She requested that we not _____ (knock) on her door after midnight.

4. Mrs. Taylor insists that he _____ (be) careful with his new watch.

5. It was such a sunny day outside that my mom suggested we _____ (have) lunch in the park.

6. It is essential that hate crimes _____ (study) and eventually _____ (stop).

7. I request that I _____ (allow) to leave the room.

8. The students recommended that the finals _____ (postpone) until the end of summer.

9. The plastic surgeon requested that he _____ (remain) in his house until the infection has healed.

10. He insisted that the puppy _____ (name) after his dead cat.

11. Their coach recommended that they _____ (take) a week off.

12. I suggest that all citizens _____ (write) a letter to the president.

13. It is crucial that I _____ (meet) with you tomorrow.

14. It is essential that he _____ (talk) to the professor about his assignment.

15. It is necessary that all of you _____ (join) him at five o'clock sharp.

16. The theater director insisted that his stage _____ (be) perfect.

17. It is very important that no one _____ (admit) backstage without a pass.

18. It is essential that they _____ (not + be) late to their meeting.

19. It is essential that he _____ (return) home immediately.

20. She specifically asked that I _____ (not + tell) anyone about the treasure.

EXERCISE R2·16

Turn each sentence into a negative one and an interrogative one, changing the verb into the right tense:

EXAMPLE   They're traveling to Europe.

<u>Haven't they traveled to Europe?</u>

1. He fixed the garage door.

_____

2. John gets her sense of humor.

_____

3. British people say that.

_____

4. She speaks to the doctor.

_____

5. You do it.

_____

Rewrite each sentence, correcting the error in subject-verb agreement.

1. The private and public sectors in Africa needs to work closely together.

_____

_____

2. It is undeniable that armed conflict make things worse.

_____

3. They sit on the bench and feel that the judge condemn them for no apparent reason.

_____

4. Many families in this area who doesn't own houses feels that they should get interest-free loans.

_____

_____

Complete each passive sentence with the correct form of one of the verbs listed below.

build	expect	offer	spell
cause	frighten	order	surprise
confuse	invent	report	surround
divide	kill	schedule	wear

EXAMPLE   An island ___*is surrounded*___ by water.

1. A necklace _____ around your neck.

2. The telephone _____ by the American scientist Alexander Graham Bell.

3. Is *sitting* really _____ with a double *t*?

4. Even though it took almost 20 years, the bridge _____ by next month.

5. I doubt the train will be coming in late. The monitor announced that it

   _____ to arrive on time.

6. I still can't understand the math problem. Yesterday in class, I _____
   by the professor's explanation.

7. The children _____ in the middle of the night, because a squirrel managed to get inside their tent. They thought it was a monster.

8. Last week, she _____ a job at a local record store, but she had already decided to work as a waitress.

9. In spite of his knee injury, he _____ to play in the championship game.

10. The plane crash _____ in the newspapers last week.

11. They read about the hunter who _____ by the wild animal.

12. He enlisted in the army, but he _____ to return home because of a back injury.

13. Nathalie's house burned down. The fire _____ by lightning.

14. The team is too big, so it _____ into two smaller teams.

EXERCISE
R2·19

Rewrite each sentence, correcting the grammatical error(s), if any. If the sentence is correct, mark an "X" in the blank.

1. When we get older, you can do a lot of thing.

   _____

2. Pedro ate a few piece of cheese with his enchilada.

   _____

3. He read some book at the public library before they closed.

   _____

4. Last year, I gave him *Star Wars* and *Indiana Jones* for Christmas, but I don't know if he ever watched those movie.

   _____

   _____

5. There are too many person in this car.

   _____

6. My little sister is only three year old, but she seems older.

   _____

7. We had not been to Portugal in six year.

   _____

8. He is an intelligent and gifted 30-year-old actor.

   _____

9. If you want to form your own opinion, you should read many news articles and watch many kind of documentaries.

_____

_____

10. In addition to the art gallery, there are a lot of beautiful place to visit.

_____

EXERCISE R2·20

Complete each sentence with the appropriate reflexive, reciprocal, or relative pronouns.

1. That is a nation _____ influence over international affairs has been greatly reduced.

2. Counting on others is great but one should always look after _____.

3. The situation will work _____ out, even if by times it seems unlikely.

4. It doesn't matter what others think, she considers _____ to be skilled and hardworking.

5. The song, _____ style is very jazzy, has been playing on the radio a lot.

6. The novel _____ I read yesterday was more interesting than the one I read a few weeks ago.

7. My car, _____ is brand new, is always giving me problems.

8. They are the couple _____ are coming to our wedding.

9. We tried to do it _____, but couldn't. In the end, we had to hire a plumber.

10. They seem to only worry about _____, so it makes it difficult to become their friends.

11. I feel rather nervous about hiking alone. I'm not sure I can do it by _____.

12. The woman _____ plays Nala in the *Lion King* musical is my sister.

13. The jacket _____ I bought yesterday is much too tight, I have to return it.

14. My cousin and his fiancée really adore _____.

15. She always does things _____!

16. I love the piano piece _____ you performed last night.

17. Those _____ believe in him will soon find out that they have been duped.

18. They bought only _____ they absolutely needed.

19. Do you live by _____?

20. _____ is really shocking is that they didn't even mention a word about the accident.

21. To _____ did you speak to earlier on the phone?

22. The shelf on _____ I place these books is rather old and dusty.

EXERCISE
R2·21

Rewrite each sentence, correcting the grammatical error(s).

1. She will going to Dallas to visit her brother.

_____

2. Patrick has know me since I was six years old.

_____

3. He been living in Lisbon for years but we still keeping in touch via e-mail.

_____

4. When I get to Peter's house, he will have to opens the front door.

_____

5. I soon noticed that Paul didn't drove very well. Among other things, he didn't respected the speed limit on the highways.

_____

_____

6. Paul knows that he should taking driving classes.

_____

7. If he were move back home he could helped his mom more, and he could to take care of her on a daily basis.

_____

_____

8. Vanessa should to do her shopping at Trader Joe's.

_____

9. I taking the GRE next month and I am quite nervous.

_____

Complete each sentence with the appropriate form of the verbs listed below.

EXAMPLE   The movie _____ when you called me, so I couldn't answer. (begin)

The movie   _had begun_   when you called me, so I couldn't answer.

1. We _____ the house when you got there. (leave)

2. When we arrived, the band _____ playing. (just + finish)

3. Yes, she _____ it long before you asked her to. (already + do)

4. It looks like they _____ the apartment before we arrived. (already + clean)

5. While he _____ out yesterday, she came to visit.

Rewrite each sentence, correcting the grammatical error(s), if any. If the sentence is correct, mark an "X" in the blank.

1. In terms of transportation, cars are a basic parts of modern life.

_____

2. The automobile have made it possible for people to travel many mile from their home.

_____

3. Research has made great progress in the field of microbiology.

_____

4. Students study more than they used to, and learn about more thing than they used to.

_____

5. Life expectancy is much greater than it was a hundred year ago.

_____

EXERCISE
R2·24

Rewrite each sentence, correcting the error in subject-verb agreement.

1. She is having so much fun at the live show but still think the ticket was too expensive.

   _____

2. It's going to storm tonight so it's likely the heavy rain will makes driving more difficult.

   _____

3. Many people who don't vote during the recent elections now feels that they should have taken the time to do it.

   _____

4. It is definitely her grandma's secret ingredient that make that cake taste so good.

   _____

5. In case of an emergency landing, the airline crew and the passengers on the airplane needs to remain calm.

   _____

   _____

6. She wait in line at the grocery store and wish it would go faster.

   _____

   _____

EXERCISE
R2·25

Make a complete sentence by matching the parts in the two columns.

1. _____ Once the movers were here, we had

2. _____ We weren't sure about buying a new television, but they got us

3. _____ My teacher

4. _____ Although he cooked, I also had him

5. _____ She didn't feel like it but her parents got

a. wash the dishes.

b. to reconsider.

c. got me to learn more vocabulary.

d. her to clean up her room.

e. them to empty the garage.

Rewrite each sentence, correcting the grammatical error(s), if any. If the sentence is correct, mark an "X" in the blank.

1. The ten districts in this city has decided to build more modern-looking buildings.

   _____

2. Some cities in Argentina surprise tourists with its architecture.

   _____

3. Often, the term "third-world country" make people think of crime and poverty.

   _____

4. Technology has been crucial in modern society.

   _____

5. The graduate courses are very difficult; you feel like everyone else understand and you don't.

   _____

   _____

6. Study a lot, and you will get many of the answer right.

   _____

7. If a student don't understand the answer to his or her question, he or she should feels comfortable enough to ask again.

   _____

   _____

8. All students have to take the two part of the exam.

   _____

9. These drill cannot prove the ability of the nurses, because the nurses simply executes certain emergency procedures.

   _____

   _____

10. There are two kind of people in this company: honest persons and greedy persons.

    _____

11. There are many problem at my office, but one problem is the lack of motivation.

    _____

12. Any person whose parents are seriously sick worry about their health.

    _____

13. You can find many kind of people working in our offices.

    _____

14. Italian ice cream are so delicious. I'm pretty sure you'll like it.

   _____

15. When I first came to this hotel, I didn't like the food, but now I like them very much.

   _____

16. That was the first time I bought my own furniture. I enjoyed picking them out, and I felt like an adult.

   _____

17. The people who shares my apartment are friendly, but they're messy.

   _____

18. There are six freshly planted tree on my street.

   _____

19. If you drive when you're too tired, he might cause an accident.

   _____

20. I left my wallet and my keys on the counter. When I came back, I couldn't find it anymore.

   _____

21. Everyone want to be successful and be in good healths.

   _____

22. Count the money again before you put them in the envelope.

   _____

23. Every people should help improve their neighborhood.

   _____

   _____

EXERCISE R2·27

Complete each passive sentence with the correct form of one of the verbs listed below.

separate   drive   build   bake   fire   offer   design

decide   begin   bother   complete   divided   cause

EXAMPLE   Countries are   *separated*   by frontiers.

1. The car must _____ around the block at least once a week, otherwise the battery might die.

2. The Taj Mahal palace in India _____ by Emperor Shah Jahan. Its construction _____ in 1632 and was _____ in 1643.

3. She _____ by all the noise the neighbors made. She had forgotten to close the windows before going to sleep.

4. This class has too many students, so it _____ into 3 different groups.

5. Can a cake really _____ without flour or sugar?

6. They heard about all the people who _____ by the company.

7. The dress worn by Michelle Obama at the President's inauguration _____ by Jason Wu.

8. The policemen and the ambulances were still blocking the street when I got back home. The accident _____ by a drunk driver.

9. A few days ago, Tina _____ a managerial position, but she had already _____ she wanted to get a new job somewhere else.

EXERCISE
R2·28

Rewrite each sentence, correcting the grammatical error(s), if any. If the sentence is correct, mark an "X" in the blank.

1. I had not seen my best friend in over twenty year.

_____

2. There are not enough person to play this game.

_____

3. In spite of his sore back, he still managed to win the championship.

_____

4. When you're off work, you are able to accomplish more personal task.

_____

5. This record player was made thirty year ago, but it still work perfectly.

_____

6. Her writing is rich and sophisticated for a 19-year-old writer.

_____

7. If Pierre wants to learn how to cook, he should try out many recipe and try different type of food.

_____

8. Henry added a few spoon of sugar to his cup of tea.

_____

9. This is not the only beautiful building in Madrid; there are many other architectural landmark across the city.

_____

10. He rented some movie at the video store before they closed for the day.

_____

_____

Complete each passive sentence by supplying the missing preposition.

1. Victor is done _____ working late at night; he is going to try changing his work schedule.

2. She was introduced _____ my wife many years ago.

3. Is she worried _____ his health?

4. Are you involved _____ theatre or music?

5. He is married _____ Julie.

6. We are filled _____ joy and could not be happier he finally graduated.

7. Peter and Maria are related _____ my ex-wife, can you believe that?

Rewrite each sentence, correcting the grammatical error(s), if any. If the sentence is correct, mark an "X" in the blank.

1. My mother never forgets to put her house keys in her purse before she leaves the house.

_____

_____

2. Christine enjoys walking along the river. She likes that he's so peaceful.

_____

3. My boyfriend's mother is an attorney. He works for important people.

_____

4. If you want to purchase gloves, you can buy them online.

_____

5. He needed a coffee table and a couch, but he decided he could live without it.

_____

6. My cousins are all younger than I, but she is taller than I am.

_____

7. Japan is a small country. They have a long history.

_____

8. Many person in the world are learning English. This person wants to improve his language skills and get a better job.

_____

_____

9. If the tourists go to Puerto Rico, you should visit Old San Juan. You ought to try the food too, because they're delicious.

_____

_____

10. All his ideas comes from dreams, and he tries to make this dream reality.

_____

11. Mrs. Hutchinson put his jacket back on.

_____

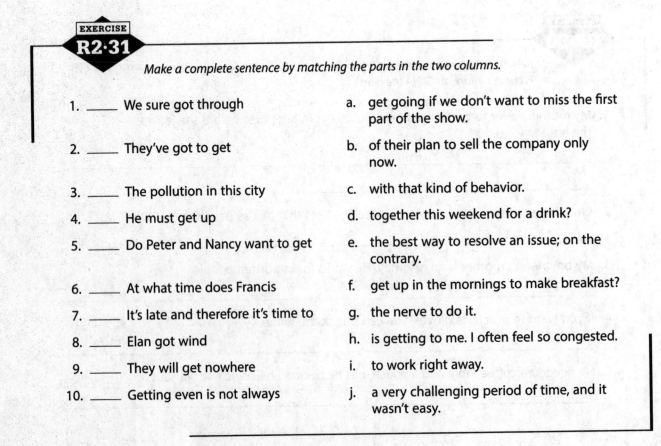

EXERCISE
R2·31

Make a complete sentence by matching the parts in the two columns.

1. _____ We sure got through

2. _____ They've got to get

3. _____ The pollution in this city

4. _____ He must get up

5. _____ Do Peter and Nancy want to get

6. _____ At what time does Francis

7. _____ It's late and therefore it's time to

8. _____ Elan got wind

9. _____ They will get nowhere

10. _____ Getting even is not always

a. get going if we don't want to miss the first part of the show.

b. of their plan to sell the company only now.

c. with that kind of behavior.

d. together this weekend for a drink?

e. the best way to resolve an issue; on the contrary.

f. get up in the mornings to make breakfast?

g. the nerve to do it.

h. is getting to me. I often feel so congested.

i. to work right away.

j. a very challenging period of time, and it wasn't easy.

Rewrite each sentence, correcting the grammatical error(s).

1. This government has been running by Cardinal Richelieu since 1626.

   _____

2. I'm quite exciting to see her again.

   _____

3. I am so happy. Finally, I was pass the exam.

   _____

4. They're not sure if the problem will be work out by tomorrow.

   _____

5. I'm interesting in advance technology.

   _____

6. The other colors have to be change.

   _____

7. We need to love someone and be love.

   _____

8. This question can be decide by taking into account all the information we've gathered.

   _____

9. I like the people there, because they're very educate.

   _____

10. I like the way math is teaching in her class.

    _____

11. This store is locate on the third floor of the mall.

    _____

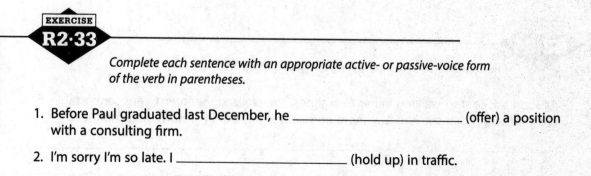

Complete each sentence with an appropriate active- or passive-voice form of the verb in parentheses.

1. Before Paul graduated last December, he _____ (offer) a position with a consulting firm.

2. I'm sorry I'm so late. I _____ (hold up) in traffic.

   It _____ (take) me an hour to get here instead of half an hour.

3. According to a recent survey, out of every euro a German spends on groceries, 30 cents

   _____ (spend) on fruits and vegetables.

4. I was supposed to take my math test yesterday, but I _____

   (not + admit) into the testing room, because they _____

   (already + begin) the test.

5. Only two of us _____ (work) in the laboratory this morning when

   the explosion _____ (occur).

6. It's ten o'clock, so the mail should be here soon. The mailman _____
   (generally + deliver) our mail before noon.

7. According to the cover of *The Economist*, solar energy _____ (use)
   extensively by the end of this century.

8. Paul _____ (study) Spanish here for the last two years. His spoken

   Spanish _____ (finally + get) better, but he still needs to improve

   his spelling.

9. Right now, tickets to the concert _____ (sell) at the counter. If you
   want to go to the concert, you should hurry up and buy some tickets before it's too late.

10. John is a hero. His name will go down in history. He _____
    (never + forget).

11. When you _____ (arrive) at the bus station tomorrow morning,

    you _____ (meet) by my sister. She _____

    (wear) a red shirt and a black skirt. She _____ (stand) near the main

    entrance. I'm sure you will be able to find her.

12. Today _____ (be) a terrible day. First, I _____
    (lose) my car keys. Then, I _____ (drop) my glasses on the floor

    while I _____ (walk) and they _____ (break).
    Finally, my car _____ (steal).

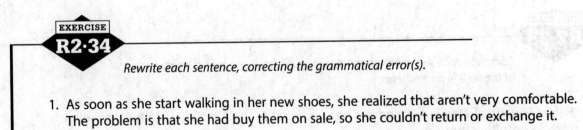

EXERCISE
R2·34

Rewrite each sentence, correcting the grammatical error(s).

1. As soon as she start walking in her new shoes, she realized that aren't very comfortable.
   The problem is that she had buy them on sale, so she couldn't return or exchange it.

   _____

   _____

2. Susan was upset that her grades is so low. She knows that she should studying more often.

_____

_____

3. It is so windy and rainy this morning. When I get home, I will have to closed the windows and make sure the floor and furniture is still dry.

_____

_____

4. Matt has move to Iceland but we still talking on the phone every other week. We also try to see ourselves twice a year. I still miss him very much

_____

_____

5. Charles and I have be friends since we were children. I meet him in kindergarten and a few years later, his family move to our neighborhood.

_____

_____

6. He having minor surgery next month and is worried about it.

_____

_____

7. Sebastien should have his hair to done at my local hairdresser; I'm sure he would liked the place and the service.

_____

_____

8. The first time Jessica went to the pool with her son Mark, she noticed that he couldn't swam very well.

_____

_____

9. They leaving their daughter Cara with a baby sitter for the first time since she was born. I hope it go well because if not, they never leave the house again.

_____

_____

Complete each sentence with an appropriate active- or passive-voice form of the verb in parentheses.

1. The Amazon rainforest needs to be protected, because almost 20 percent of the planet's oxygen _____ (produce) there.

2. Did you see that terrible car accident on the highway? Several of my friends _____ (see) it, including one who _____ (interview) by a police officer.

3. In Europe, certain prices _____ (control) by the government. Other prices _____ (determine) by the market.

4. I am so mad! Earlier today, the wind _____ (blow) my cap off. I tried to catch it, because it was autographed by A-Rod and it _____ (cost) a lot of money.

5. Right now, Alice is in the hospital. She _____ (treat) for a really bad sunburn on her forehead.

6. Frostbite occurs when the skin _____ (expose) to extremely cold weather. It mostly _____ (affect) hands, feet, noses, and ears.

7. Some researchers claim that Napoleon did not die of natural causes, but that he _____ (poison) instead.

8. The government used to finance this school. Today, it _____ (support) by the generous donations of alumni.

9. Charles was demoted this morning. He _____ (tell) that he was being relieved of his duties as general manager, because he wasn't making enough money for the company.

10. The game _____ (probably + lose) by the opposing team tomorrow. We're a lot better than they are.

11. In 1989, photographs of Neptune _____ (send) back to earth by *Voyager 2*.

12. The World Health Organization hopes that a human vaccine for Ebola _____ (develop) soon. Vaccines _____ (already + test) successfully on monkeys.

Rewrite each sentence, correcting the grammatical error(s).

1. Elizabeth got back into his car; she was not looked forward to the long drive back home.

   _____

   _____

2. The Chicago Bulls is a great team. They have won many championships.

   _____

   _____

3. Most of Susy's neighbors are richer than her, but we are more selfish than she is.

   _____

   _____

4. If you want to get a better job, you're going to have to quit yours.

   _____

   _____

5. If his family decides to purchase that house, she should make sure to carefully inspecting it first. She should have the plumbing checked as well, because they'll cost a lot of money to repair.

   _____

   _____

   _____

6. Most of their money come from their investment, but the stock market is been unreliable.

   _____

   _____

7. Pierre generally can't begin his days without a coffee and a croissant. Today they were running late for work so he thought it would be best to skip it.

   _____

   _____

8. Samantha decided to buy a Tesla car, but they told her she'd had to wait for six months.

   _____

   _____

9. Pedro's sister is a professional tennis player. He's won many tournaments and travel to many countries.

   _____

   _____

10. I always forget to lock the car door when I park it in the garage.

         _____

         _____

11. Greg really enjoys running in the park early in the morning. He find it peaceful, enjoys the he's clean, and often sees fish swam in the pond.

         _____

         _____

EXERCISE R2·37

Underline the entire auxiliary verb in each sentence.

1. Are they meant to get here before or after midnight?

2. Karen should have to make sure all of the children are on the bus before it leaves.

3. Lady Gaga and Khaled are planning to release their new video in the next few days.

4. Since her last doctor's visit, she has been eating less meat.

5. She is going to cancel all of her magazine subscriptions next year.

6. He doesn't have to finish all of his homework today.

7. Frank is going to buy a scooter next week.

8. It's the beginning of summer, so Bill is going to get a part-time job.

9. His father has been marinating the fish and the vegetables all day.

10. Sarah's kale salads and desserts are so delicious; she should be able to open her own

    little restaurant.

11. I should have to pay for what I have done, even if it was an accident.

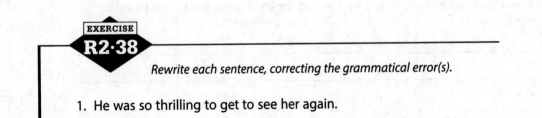

EXERCISE R2·38

Rewrite each sentence, correcting the grammatical error(s).

1. He was so thrilling to get to see her again.

         _____

2. Tyler is interesting in trying out yoga.

   _____

3. She was so proud. At last, her son was pass his driving test.

   _____

4. The way we live have to change if we want to reduce global warming.

   _____

5. The library is locate inside the main building on campus.

   _____

6. The chess club has been managing by students since 1984.

   _____

7. We need to respect others and be respect.

   _____

8. The decision can be overrule only if there isn't a majority.

   _____

9. They appreciate their neighbors, because they is kind, not too noisy, and well manner.

   _____

EXERCISE R2·39

Complete each sentence with an appropriate active- or passive-voice form of the verb in parentheses.

1. Jenna was meant to speak at the conference this morning, but she

   _____ (not + board) on her flight because the airline crew

   _____ (already + close) the airplane door. She didn't make it to the

   gate in time.

2. Until tonight, the store _____ (offer) a 50% discount on everything.

   If you want to buy your jacket for less, you should try to make it there before it closes.

3. Alex _____ (practice) the drums on his own for a few months. His

   technique _____ (definitely + improve) but he still needs help on

   his form.

4. I'm sorry I wasn't there when you came by the house. I had just

   _____ (pick up) by Carol.

5. It was just Laura and I _____ (cry) at the cinema last night, when the main character _____ (lose) his life in the final scene. I guess people are embarrassed to cry in public!

6. Before Karen took her final test last week, she _____ (ask) to review all of her lessons.

Rewrite each sentence, correcting the grammatical error(s), if any. If the sentence is correct, mark an "X" in the blank.

1. She must play The Beatles. Who else could it have been?

    _____

2. He may nap, so do not bother him.

    _____

3. They should gone to the supermarket with you.

    _____

4. You mayn't do that.

    _____

5. We can have water in order to survive.

    _____

6. Paul told me last week that they had not go to the gym last month.

    _____

7. They willn't come till much later.

    _____

8. Long should they live!

    _____

9. Would Margaret come in?

    _____

10. If Shawn and Mary should help, they would.

    _____

11. I can run faster when I was younger.

    _____

12. Should they be excused?

_____

13. She cans do it too.

_____

Complete each sentence with the appropriate tense of the verb in parentheses.

1. Traffic on our road _____ (be) terrible this week, I hope they finish the construction soon. It _____ (be + take) us so much longer to get to work in the mornings.

2. What a manageable winter it's been so far. It _____ (snow) for a few hours each day and earlier this week it _____ (freeze) over the course of an afternoon, but it _____ (not + be) that cold. Today _____ (be) sunny so _____ (spend) time outside has been pleasant.

3. We _____ (go) to get some groceries yesterday, but we _____ (forget) to pick up a few tomatoes and some lettuce. _____ (it + be) possible for us to make a salad with what we have?

4. I _____ (spend) a few hours at the park this afternoon. It's beautiful. I (not + be) there before and regret _____ (not + realize) it before today.

5. Jeremy _____ (fall) while riding his bike this past weekend, and he has _____ (be + rest) since. It was nothing serious, he just _____ (scrape) his knee. It could _____ (be) worse but thankfully, he _____ (be + wear) his helmet. He _____ (sleep) when you called, that's why he didn't answer his cellphone.

Rewrite each sentence, correcting the grammatical error(s).

1. This team formation is not working. The players has to be switch out and replace.

   _____

   _____

2. Becky are tired from a long day of work but when her husband arriving home they decided to go out anyways

   _____

   _____

3. Honestly, I'm not sure if the package will be deliver by next week. Maybe I have chosen a faster shipping option.

   _____

   _____

4. they went to play outside even though it was rather cold. Rachel, his mother, was glad they did because she needed clean up the living room.

   _____

   _____

5. Our organization is dedicate to saving animals when they are been abandoned. We try their best to keep them safe and fed until they're eventually adopt.

   _____

   _____

6. Carla appreciates the way Paul is helping it with the suitcases. They're actually not that heavy, she just enjoy that he are being a gentleman.

   _____

   _____

7. I can't believe you forget the keys on the counter and slam the door shut. ah why did you do that

   _____

   _____

8. Sophie is feeling so proud. At last, she was receive a raise at work, and next month she was promoted to a managerial position.

   _____

   _____

9. Stayed calm is important shouting is not. People tend to are more receptive to kindness. No one like being screamed at.

   _____

   _____

10. Bill is fascinating by the sharks at the aquarium. The way it moving back and forth in the water tank is hypnotized.

_____

_____

11. They've been look for her all over the place. shes here isnt she

_____

_____

12. Frank's issue can only be resolve once he is taken all of the elements into consideration.

_____

_____

13. I must completing this form before the counter closes in half an hour. give me that pen right away

_____

_____

14. That restaurant's apple pie are so amazing. We guarantee you'll want some more!

_____

_____

15. please stay on the line she said. This was his third time calling customer service and it kept putting him hold.

_____

_____

EXERCISE R2·43

Each item should be a complete, grammatical sentence. If it is, mark an "X" in the blank. If it is not, write one or more correct sentences based on the item.

1. To wash this stain. You'll need a powerful detergent.

_____

2. Shawn is playing over there. With his two cousins and they are having fun.

_____

3. After we wake up in the morning can meet them for breakfast.

_____

4. Once our name is called step up to the window and picks up your order.

_____

5. Patricia will get a monthly gym membership in addition to the classes she will have access to the pool. The sauna, their tanning salon, and the Zumba classes.

_____

6. As soon as Peter gets home, don't forget to hand him the car keys.

_____

7. They are leaving tomorrow it's the beginning of his summer break.

_____

8. Lucy doesn't like drawing. Because she claims she has no talent for it.

_____

9. My dream is to live somewhere close to the beach.

_____

10. When I was living in New York. I assumed it has been the greatest city in the world.

_____

11. His favorite cartoon were *The Smurfs*. Because it reminded him of his childhood.

_____

12. Today Paul and Tina realize that working hard isn't enough to be happy.

_____

EXERCISE
R2·44

Rewrite each sentence, correcting the grammatical error(s), if any. If the sentence is correct, mark an "X" in the blank.

1. You will notice many kind of student attending our English classes.

_____

2. There are many way of writing it, but the right way is the best of way.

_____

3. All airplane pilot have to score high points on the two section of the flight simulation.

_____

4. There are two kind of chocolate in this cake: white chocolates and milk chocolates.

_____

5. Eight out of ten engineers has confirmed that the bridge is safe to use.

_____

6. A couple of magicians in the show startled the audience with its tricks.

_____

7. Science has been key in the evolution of mankind.

_____

8. Mathematics is a confusing class to me; it seems like most students does well on the quizzes, but I don't.

_____

_____

9. In my experience, using the dictionary as often as possible give students the opportunity to learned new words.

_____

_____

10. There are three kind of people in this world: good persons, bad persons, and persons who don't care.

_____

_____

11. The DJ was playing four newly released song on the radio this morning.

_____

12. The movies Wes Anderson makes is so fun to watch, he's a great director. I'm guessing you'll really like his work.

_____

_____

13. If Shauna and Coy sleep on their international flight, it might feel less tired the next day.

_____

14. French cuisine are so simple and minimal, yet the flavors is often so rich and complex.

_____

15. Everyone who care about her country should vote.

_____

16. Weigh the flour and the sugar again before you mix it in with the eggs.

_____

17. The three new employees shares the office that is in the corner.

_____

18. She forgot her umbrella and her hat in the taxi. She called the taxi company later that afternoon; can you believe they found it?!

_____

_____

19. Most people wish to lives a long and happy life.

_____

20. At first, I didn't like going to the opera, but now I appreciate them a lot more.

_____

EXERCISE
R2·45

Each item should be a complete, grammatical sentence. If it is, mark an "X" in the blank. If the item contains an error, describe the error, and then write your own correct, grammatical sentence based on the item.

EXAMPLE   Has many cars.

This item contains an error because it is a sentence fragment:
Drake has many cars.

1. The World Cup.

_____

_____

2. Last year, he began to work on his garden.

_____

_____

3. Edmond Dantès he is the hero of the novel *The Count of Montecristo*.

_____

_____

4. If she wants to feel rested.

_____

_____

5. Close the door on your way out.

_____

_____

6. Helping children to share.

_____

_____

7. Running long distances is difficult.

_____

8. Have they already fixed all these problems

_____

_____

9. after they were done eating, they cleaned up the kitchen.

_____

_____

10. different fun rides in that loud, crowded amusement park.

_____

_____

11. Not only she kind, she also very generous.

_____

_____

12. Patience takes effort.

_____

_____

13. If you're not lying, don't have to be worried.

_____

_____

14. Pay attention!

_____

_____

APPENDIX A
Irregular past tense and past participle forms

Following are common verbs that have irregular past tense forms. Usually the past participle forms are the same as the past tense forms. Those that are *not* are in bold type.

Verb	Past tense	Past participle
be	was/were	**been**
beat	beat	**beaten**
become	became	**become**
begin	began	**begun**
bend	bent	bent
bet	bet	bet
bite	bit	**bitten**
bleed	bled	bled
blow	blew	**blown**
break	broke	**broken**
bring	brought	brought
build	built	built
buy	bought	bought
catch	caught	caught
choose	chose	**chosen**
come	came	**come**
cost	cost	cost
cut	cut	cut
dig	dug	dug
do	did	**done**
draw	drew	**drawn**
drink	drank	**drunk**
drive	drove	**driven**
eat	ate	**eaten**
fall	fell	**fallen**
feed	fed	fed

Verb	Past tense	Past participle
feel	felt	felt
fight	fought	fought
find	found	found
fit	fit	fit
fly	flew	**flown**
forget	forgot	**forgotten**
forgive	forgave	**forgiven**
freeze	froze	**frozen**
get	got	**gotten**
give	gave	**given**
go	went	**gone**
grow	grew	**grown**
hang	hung	hung
have	had	had
hear	heard	heard
hide	hid	**hidden**
hit	hit	hit
hold	held	held
hurt	hurt	hurt
keep	kept	kept
know	knew	**known**
lay	laid	laid
lead	led	led
leave	left	left
lend	lent	lent
let	let	let
lie	lay	**lain**
light	lit	lit
lose	lost	lost
make	made	made
mean	meant	meant
meet	met	met
pay	paid	paid
put	put	put
quit	quit	quit
read	read (pronounced "red")	read (pronounced "red")
ride	rode	**ridden**
ring	rang	**rung**
rise	rose	**risen**
run	ran	**run**
say	said	said
see	saw	**seen**

Verb	Past tense	Past participle
sell	sold	sold
send	sent	sent
set	set	set
shake	shook	**shaken**
shoot	shot	shot
show	showed	**shown**
shrink	shrank	**shrunk**
shut	shut	shut
sing	sang	**sung**
sit	sat	sat
sleep	slept	slept
speak	spoke	**spoken**
speed	sped	sped
spend	spent	spent
spin	spun	spun
spread	spread	spread
stand	stood	stood
steal	stole	**stolen**
sting	stung	stung
strike	struck	struck
sweep	swept	swept
swim	swam	**swum**
take	took	**taken**
teach	taught	taught
tear	tore	torn
tell	told	told
think	thought	thought
throw	threw	**thrown**
understand	understood	understood
upset	upset	upset
wake up	woke up	**woken up**
wear	wore	worn
win	won	won
write	wrote	**written**

APPENDIX B
Short tag questions and answers

Present tense

Be

Questions	Affirmative answers	Negative answers
I am, **am I not?** (formal) I am, **aren't** I? (informal) I'm not, **am** I?	Yes, you **are.**	No, you **aren't.** No, you **aren't.** No, you **aren't.** No, **you're not.**
You are, **aren't** you? You aren't, **are** you?	Yes, I **am.**	No, **I'm not.** No, **I'm not.**
He is, **isn't** he? He isn't, **is** he? (she)	Yes, he **is.** (she)	No, he **isn't.** No, **he's not.** (she)
There is, **isn't** there? There isn't, **is** there?	Yes, there **is.**	No, there **isn't.** No, **there's not.**
We are, **aren't** we? We aren't, **are** we?	Yes, we **are.**	No, we **aren't.** No, **we're not.**
They are, **aren't** they? They aren't, **are** they?	Yes, they **are.**	No, they **aren't.** No, **they're not.**
There are, **aren't** there? There aren't, **are** there?	Yes, there **are.**	No, there **aren't.**

Modal verbs

Questions	Affirmative answers	Negative answers
Can I can, **can't** I? I can't, **can** I? (you/he/she/it/we/they)	Yes, you **can.** (I/you/he/she/it/we/ they)	No, you **can't.** (I/you/he/she/it/we/ they)
Could I could, **couldn't** I? I couldn't, **could** I? (you/he/she/it/we/they)	Yes, you **could.** (I/you/he/she/it/we/ they)	No, you **couldn't.** (I/you/he/she/it/we/ they)

Questions	Affirmative answers	Negative answers
May (permission) I can, **can't** I? I can't, **can** I? (you/he/she/it/we/they) **May (possibility)** I will, **won't** I? I won't, **will** I? (you/he/she/it/we/they)	Yes, you **may**. (I/you/he/she/it/we/they) Yes, you **may**. (I/you/he/she/it/we/they)	No, you **may not**. (I/you/he/she/it/we/they) No, you **may not**. (I/you/he/she/it/we/they)
Might I will, **won't** I? I won't, **will** I? (you/he/she/it/we/they)	Yes, you **might**.	No, you **might not**.
Must I have to, **don't** I? I don't have to, **do** I? We have to, **don't** we? You have to, **don't** you? He has to, **doesn't** he? (she/it) They have to, **don't** they?	Yes, you **do**. Yes, I **do**. Yes, he **does**. (she/it) Yes, they **do**.	No, you **don't**. No, I **don't**. No, he **doesn't**. (she/it) No, they **don't**.
Should I should, **shouldn't** I? I shouldn't, **should** I? (you/he/she/it/we/they)	Yes, you **should**. (I/you/he/she/it/we/they)	No, you **shouldn't**. (I/you/he/she/it/we/they)
Would I would, **wouldn't** I? I wouldn't, **would** I? (you/he/she/it/we/they)	Yes, you **would**. (I/you/he/she/it/we/they)	No, you **wouldn't**. (I/you/he/she/it/we/they)

Pattern for all other verbs

Questions	Affirmative answers	Negative answers
I do, **don't** I? I don't, **do** I? We do, **don't** we? You do, **don't** you? He does, **doesn't** he? (she/it) They do, **don't** they?	Yes, you **do**. Yes, I **do**. Yes, he **does**. (she/it) Yes, they **do**.	No, you **don't**. No, I **don't**. No, he **doesn't**. (she/it) No, they **don't**.

Present perfect tense
Pattern for all verbs

Questions	Affirmative answers	Negative answers
I have, **haven't** I? I haven't, **have** I? (you/we/they)	Yes, you **have**. (I/we/they)	No, you **haven't**. (I/we/they)
He has, **hasn't** he? He hasn't, **has** he? (she/it)	Yes, he **has**. (she/it)	No, he **hasn't**. (she/it)

Past tense
Be

Questions	Affirmative answers	Negative answers
I was, **wasn't** I? I wasn't, **was** I? We were, **weren't** we?	Yes, you **were**.	No, you **weren't**.
You were, **weren't** you? You weren't, **were** you?	Yes, I **was**. Yes, we **were**.	No, I **wasn't**. No, we **weren't**.
He was, **wasn't** he? He wasn't, **was** he? (she/it)	Yes, he **was**. (she/it)	No, he **wasn't**. (she/it)
There was, **wasn't** there? There were, **weren't** there?	Yes, there **was**. Yes, there **were**.	No, there **wasn't**. No, there **weren't**.

Modal verbs

Questions	Affirmative answers	Negative answers
Can I could, **couldn't** I? I couldn't, **could** I? We could, **couldn't** we? We couldn't, **could** we? You could, **couldn't** you? You couldn't, **could** you?	Yes, you **could**. Yes, I **could**. Yes, we **could**.	No, you **couldn't**. No, I **couldn't**. No, we **couldn't**.
Could I could have, **couldn't** I? I couldn't have, **could** I? We could have, **couldn't** we? We couldn't have, **could** we? You could have, **couldn't** you? You couldn't have, **could** you? He could have, **couldn't** he? He couldn't have, **could** he? (she/it/they)	Yes, you **could have** (**could've**). Yes, you **could have**. Yes, we **could have**. Yes, I **could have**. (she/it/they)	No, you **couldn't have**. No, I **couldn't have**. No, we **couldn't have**. No, he **couldn't have**. (she/it/they)

Questions	Affirmative answers	Negative answers
May **permission** (same as **could**) **possibility** I may have, **right**? I may not have, **right**? We may have, **right**? You may have, **right**? You may not have, **right**? He may have, **right**? He may not have, **right**? (she/it/they)	Yes, you **may have.** Yes, I **may have.** Yes, we **may have.** Yes, he **may have.** (she/it/they)	No, you **may not have.** No, I **may not have.** No, we **may not have.** No, he **may not have.** (she/it/they)
Might I might have, **right**? I might not have, **right**? We might have, **right**? We might not have, **right**? You might have, **right**? He might have, **right**? He might not have, **right**? (she/it/they)	Yes, you **might have.** Yes, I **might have.** Yes, he **might have.** Yes, he **might have.** (she/it/they)	No, you **might not have.** No, I **might not have.** No, he **might not have.** No, he **might not have.** (she/it/they)
Should I should have, **shouldn't** I? I shouldn't have, **should** I? We should have, **shouldn't** we? You should have, **shouldn't** you? You shouldn't have, **should** you? He should have, **shouldn't** he? He shouldn't have, **should** he? (she/it/they)	Yes, you **should have** (**should've**). Yes, I **should have.** Yes, we **should have.** Yes, he **should have.** (she/it/they)	No, you **shouldn't have.** No, I **shouldn't have.** No, we **shouldn't have.** No, he **shouldn't have.** (she/it/they)

Questions	Affirmative answers	Negative answers
Will I would, **wouldn't** I? I wouldn't, **would** I? We would, **wouldn't** we? We wouldn't, **would** we?	Yes, you **would**.	No, you **wouldn't**.
You would, **wouldn't** you? You wouldn't, **would** you? He would, **wouldn't** he? He wouldn't, **would** he? (she/it/they)	Yes, I **would**. Yes, we **would**. Yes, he **would**. (she/it/they)	No, I **wouldn't**. No, we **wouldn't**. No, he **wouldn't**. (she/it/they)
Would I would have, **wouldn't** I? I wouldn't have, **would** I? We would have, **wouldn't** we? We wouldn't have, **would** we?	Yes, you **would have** (**would've**).	No, you **wouldn't have**.
You would have, **wouldn't** you? You wouldn't have, **would** you?	Yes, I **would have**. Yes, we **would have**.	No, I **wouldn't have**. No, we **wouldn't have**.
He would have, **wouldn't** he? (she/it/they)	Yes, he **would have**. (she/it/they)	No, he **wouldn't have**. (she/it/they)

Pattern for all other verbs

Questions	Affirmative answers	Negative answers
I did, **didn't** I? I didn't, **did** I? (you/he/she/it/we/they)	Yes, you **did**. (I/you/he/she/it/we/they)	No, you **didn't**. (I/you/he/she/it/we/they)

Past perfect tense
Pattern for all verbs

Questions	Affirmative answers	Negative answers
I had, **hadn't** I? I hadn't, **had** I? (you/he/she/it/we/they)	Yes, you **had**. (I/you/he/she/it/we/they)	No, you **hadn't**. (I/you/he/she/it/we/they)

Future tense

Pattern for all verbs

Questions	Affirmative answers	Negative answers
I will, **won't** I? I won't, **will** I? (you/he/she/it/we/they)	Yes, you **will**. (I/you/he/she/it/we/they)	No, you **won't**. (I/you/he/she/it/we/they)

Future perfect tense

Pattern for all verbs

Questions	Affirmative answers	Negative answers
I will have, **won't** I? I won't have, **will** I? (you/he/she/it/we/they)	Yes, you **will have**. (I/you/he/she/it/we/they)	No, you **won't have**. (I/you/he/she/it/we/they)

Answer key

1 Nouns

1·1 1. proper 2. common 3. proper 4. proper 5. common 6. common
7. proper 8. common 9. proper 10. common

1.2 1. glass 2. Rocky Mountains 3. Mexico 4. flowers 5. bus
6. the store 7. New York Times 8. Roberto 9. Professor Romano
10. my books

1.3 1. direct object 2. subject 3. direct object 4. predicate noun 5. indirect object
6. indirect object 7. subject 8. predicate noun 9. direct object 10. direct
object

1.4 Sample Answers:
1. He likes my sister. 2. I want a new car. 3. Did you meet Jackie?
4. I gave the children some candy. 5. I fed a puppy some meat.
6. He sent Grandfather a gift.

1.5 1. The girl does not trust the boys.
2. Father often misplaces his wallet.
3. She always gives the landlord the rent money.
4. Anita wants to sell her new computer soon.
5. She buys her grandchildren the toys.
6. You must visit Ms. Johnson in New York.
7. They like their new house so much.
8. She can give little Johnny the present.
9. He needs to see Dr. Lee today.
10. She throws Michael the ball.

1.6 *Answers may vary.*
1. They were eating an Italian specialty.
2. They have worked in Austin for two years.
3. We purchased it last week.
4. The salad is awful.
5. It looks comfortable.
6. Mrs. Robinson went to the theater.

1.7 1. Children
2. Water
3. Prague
4. The furry, clean, calm cat
5. The furry, clean, calm, black cat
6. The furry, clean, calm, black cat with a scar
7. The big, ugly, dirty, brown bear with long ears and large claws
8. She
9. Peter
10. Lending money and giving too much advice

2   Definite and Indefinite Articles

2.1   1. a   2. the   3. a   4. the   5. —   6. the **OR** an   7. the   8. The **OR** A   9. the   10. a

2.2
1. They gave us oranges.
2. I like the books very much.
3. Do you often visit the farms there?
4. Rabbits are hiding behind it.
5. Katrina likes to play with the kittens.
6. Montel has a dog and a cat.
7. I want to buy the rose.
8. There is a gift for you.
9. Can you hear the baby crying?
10. Do you have a brother or a sister?

3   Adjectives

3.1   1. late   2. little   3. young   4. fast   5. funny   6. handsome   7. early   8. terrible   9. white   10. short

3.2
1. The song from Mexico was sad.
2. The story about a clown is funny.
3. The waiter out of work is careless.
4. The snake from Egypt is ugly.
5. The woman from Spain is beautiful.

3.3   Sample Answers:

1. beautiful   2. chocolate   3. interesting   4. young   5. good   6. old . . . thick   7. new   8. difficult   9. little   10. strange

3.4
1. We had never arranged a surprise party for them.
   We had rarely arranged a surprise party for them.
2. The soprano from France never sang at the Met.
   The soprano from France rarely sang at the Met.
3. Grandfather was never in a good mood.
   Grandfather was rarely in a good mood.
4. My brother could never fix his own car.
   My brother could rarely fix his own car.
5. They will never go to Alaska in the winter.
   They will rarely go to Alaska in the winter.

3.5   1. hard   2. best   3. beautiful, happy   4. fast, good   5. humid   6. beaming, radiant   7. hurriedly   8. rarely   9. loudly   10. finally   11. often   12. biweekly   13. seriously   14. indoors   15. regularly   16. still   17. perhaps

3.6   *Sample answers are provided.*   1. a. busy b. Monday was always a busy day.   2. a. strange b. He made a strange noise and fainted.   3. a. dead b. The dead flowers had been severely frostbitten.   4. a. excellent b. This candidate has excellent credentials.   5. a. old-fashioned b. She wore an old-fashioned dress and a bonnet.   6. a. tired b. She had a tired look on her face.   7. a. happy b. Everyone wished her happy birthday.   8. a. nervous b. The nervous man turned out to be a thief.   9. a. wonderful b. We had a wonderful time in the park.   10. a. sad b. The sad look on her face made me want to cry.

3.7   *Sample answers are provided.*   1. a. The CD player is broken again. b. This is my new CD player. c. When did you buy this CD player?   2. a. Young children shouldn't see this movie. b. Their young children are well behaved. c. These young children shouldn't be punished.   3. a. A yacht is only for the rich. b. Is your yacht a sailing vessel? c. Who owns that large yacht?   4. a. The new lobby has to be repainted. b. Our new lobby looks fantastic. c. I've never been in that new lobby in the Foster Building.   5. a. Where are the new pillows? b. Whose pillows are on the floor? c. These pillows are very soft.   6. a. I spend a lot of time with friends and relatives. b. Her friends and relatives are very nice. c. I never got to meet those friends and relatives.   7. a. The grammar of this language is difficult. b. Your grammar is quite good. c. I don't understand this grammar and its rules.   8. a. Do you understand the mathematical formula I showed you? b. Whose mathematical formula is this? c. I can't trust this mathematical formula.   9. a. The calendar was a great invention. b. My weekly calendar is up to date. c. This calendar is from four years ago.   10. a. This is an unusual painting. b. His most unusual painting is on the other wall. c. That unusual painting is too strange for my taste.

3·8 *Sample answers are provided.*   1. Each student needs a valid enrollment card.   2. Some residents are going to boycott the meeting.   3. This is his first attempt at driving a car.   4. I dropped by to see the elderly man every third day.   5. Are there eleven players on a football team?   6. There haven't been many complaints today.   7. I'll place very few demands on you.   8. Have you been introduced to our daughter?   9. I tried to get tickets in the fifth row center.   10. You're making too much noise.

3·9 *Sample answers are provided.*   1. a. What wristwatch is from Switzerland? b. A Rolex is from Switzerland. 2. a. What blanket is warmer? b. A woolen blanket is warmer.   3. a. What set of towels will look best in the bathroom? b. The yellow towels will look best in the bathroom.   4. a. What length should these boards be? b. These boards should be two meters long   5. a. Which writing implements are older? b. The quill and inkwell are older.   6. a. Which path is more dangerous? b. The path along the cliff is more dangerous. 7. a. Which breakfast menu do you prefer? b. I prefer the continental breakfast menu.   8. a. Whose passport and visa is that on the desk? b. That passport and visa belong to the man from Honduras.   9. a. Whose Cuban relatives are moving to Maryland? b. Juanita's Cuban relatives are moving to Maryland. 10. a. Whose coin purse is that on the table? b. That's Mrs. Timm's coin purse on the table.

3·10 *Sample answers are provided.*   1. I'm a real fan of Elizabethan literature.   2. That judge had served in the divorce court for years.   3. Where is the Kennedy presidential library located?   4. I'll meet you at the recreation center at two P.M.   5. I lost my chemistry book.   6. The faculty lounge is off-limits to students.   7. The White House press corps met in a conference room.   8. The movie theater was packed. 9. How long is baseball season?   10. I always enjoy a Jack London novel.

3·11 *Sample answers are provided.*   1. to be watered   2. to play   3. to admire   4. to spend   5. to write 6. They have new plans to develop.   7. Is there an easier way to clean up?   8. Ms. Johnson still has several exams to grade.   9. In his case, there is nothing to defend.   10. She is the only woman to be praised so enthusiastically.

4   Personal Pronouns

4.1   1. you   2. him   3. She   4. it   5. me   6. us   7. We   8. they   9. us   10. them 11. you   12. I   13. it   14. us   15. her

4.2   1. They   2. it   3. us   4. they   5. She   6. her   7. They   8. it   9. him   10. it

4.3   Sample Answers:
1. My friend and I   2. the music   3. the books   4. My aunt   5. Craig   6. the teacher 7. the girls   8. The radio   9. Elizabeth   10. the members

4.4   1. I sent it to my friends.   2. She is giving them to us.   3. Trey sold it to her.   4. I didn't buy it for Ella.   5. My brother will bring them to me.

4.5   1. me   2. you   3. him   4. her   5. it   6. us   7. them   8. us   9. us   10. him

4.6   1. it   2. them   3. it   4. her   5. him   6. us   7. them

4.7
1. **She** has to go home at five o'clock.
2. When do **you** leave on your trip?
3. **They** were frightened during the storm.
4. **I** am planning on early retirement.
5. Why are **you** crying?
6. **Who** wants to arrange a surprise party for **her**?
7. **He** was sound asleep.
8. **What** needs to be repaired right away?
9. Where does **she** go every afternoon?
10. **They** earn a very good salary.

4.8
1. **She** is such a sweet child.
2. **They** just can't seem to get along.
3. Where did **they** find a place to rest?
4. **We** spent a week camping in the mountains.
5. **It** burned down last night.
6. Where is **he** from?
7. **They** roared overhead.
8. Why is **she** laughing?
9. Does **it** still hurt?
10. **We** can help you today.

4.9
1. Yes, I do. No, I don't.
2. Yes, she is. No, she isn't.
3. Yes, they have. No, they haven't.
4. Yes, he was. No, he wasn't.
5. Yes, you are. No, you aren't.
6. Yes, we are. No, we aren't.
7. Yes, she should. No, she shouldn't.
8. Yes, I can. No, I can't.
9. Yes, he should. No, he shouldn't.
10. Yes, they will. No, they won't.

4.10
1. Why would the police want to arrest **us**?
2. My uncle visited **me** in Chicago.
3. Did the doctor ask **you** about the accident?
4. John caught **him** stealing a bicycle.
5. Can you join **us** for dinner?
6. I just can't believe **it**!
7. How can I reach **you** after you move?
8. The boys watched **her** all afternoon.
9. You can help **us** clean up the kitchen.
10. **Whom** should I call about a leaky faucet?

4.11
1. My sister liked **him** a lot.
2. Can you understand **it**?
3. I bought **them** at the mall.
4. When did you first meet **us**?
5. I spent **it**.
6. We used to visit **them** regularly.
7. I'd like to introduce **her**.

4.12
1. He won't sell **him** the car.
2. Did you bring **her** a gift?
3. I loaned **them** a hundred dollars.
4. Please give **her** a copy of the will.
5. I'm going to buy **them** some new pajamas.
6. James sent **her** a bouquet of roses.
7. She wrote **him** several letters.

4.13
1. I wanted to give **you** something nice.
2. Please send **her** a telegram with the news.
3. They brought **us** breakfast in bed.
4. Can you lend **me** a few dollars until tomorrow?
5. You ought to write **him** a letter every week.
6. She'll buy **you** new socks and underwear.
7. Mr. Brown gave **us** a lecture on politics again.
8. I'm sending **them** the directions to our new house.
9. Tell **me** a story.
10. Who bought **us** these tools?

4.14
1. They were asking questions about **you**.
2. I received several letters from **her**.
3. From **whom** did you borrow the money?
4. **What** were they all laughing about?
5. Someone threw a rock at **me**.
6. This problem has nothing to do with **you**.
7. That shirt really looks good on **him**.
8. A crow was flying directly over **them**.
9. An old woman came up to **us**.
10. Those stories were written by **us**.

4.15
1. Three of the girls wanted to dance **with** me.
2. The artist painted a wonderful portrait **of** her.
3. **To** whom did you send the manuscript?
4. A little bird was sitting **on** it. (**near** it, **by** it, **with** it)

5. What did you put it **in**? (**near, on**)
6. I entered the building right **after** him.
7. There's a new bank **near it**. (**by** it)
8. The frightened dog came slowly up **to** us.

4.16
1. The magician showed **it to us**.
2. Don't give **them to the children**.
3. I can't lend **it to you**.
4. Who sent **it to your cousin**?
5. Tom is going to buy **it for them**.
6. The lawyer did **it for him**.
7. The lonely soldier wrote **them to his girlfriend**.
8. She gave **it to me**.
9. Uncle Robert bought **it for us**.
10. Do you send **it to them** every week?

4.17
1. The judge sent **them to them**.
2. Why did you show **it to her**?
3. I can't lend **it to him**.
4. Dr. Brown gave **them to her (him)**.
5. Show **it to her (him)**.
6. They're going to buy **them for him**.
7. Will you save **it for her**?

4.18
1. **They** were standing on the corner and laughing.
2. Someone threw **it** through that window!
3. Bill wants to buy **it** for her.
4. You shouldn't speak about **him** in that terrible way.
5. Where did you buy **it**?
6. Ms. Smith has moved out of **it**.
7. Do you know **them**?
8. **We** were on our way to the party when **it** happened.
9. I bought **them** for you.
10. Do you want to go **there** with **us**?
11. **She** has been elected chairperson of the committee.
12. **He** hates **them**.
13. Put **them** in the attic, please.
14. Is **he** the new boss?
15. We love **it**.

4.19 Sample Answers:
1. They met **me** in Chicago. Someone gave **me** ten dollars. Maria danced with **me**.
2. Do you know **her**? I sent **her** some flowers. I was thinking of **her**.
3. Mother introduced **us** to them. Jim bought **us** a hot dog. They got a letter from **us**.
4. The girl kissed **them**. Tom sent **them** a telegram. Did you speak with **them**?
5. **Whom** would you elect mayor? To **whom** did you give permission? From **whom** did they get these gifts?

4.20
1. I found **this** puppy behind a bush.
2. She thought **these** magazines were interesting.
3. **That** tall building is the city hall.
4. Would you like some of **these** nuts?
5. **Those** dark clouds mean a storm is coming.
6. **That** town is about two hundred miles from here.
7. Why do **those** people make so much noise?
8. I bought **this** necklace on sale.
9. **That** swing set is just for children.
10. **Those** boys played soccer all afternoon.

4.21
1. He has three brothers. **Each** served in the navy for three years.
2. I bought seven tickets. **All** were purchased at a discount.
3. The children didn't like her, and **none** would play with her.
4. **Nobody** put in enough time on the project.
5. **Everything** he said turned out to be a lie.
6. Many of them enjoyed the concert. **Others** went home early.

7. They invited a hundred guests. **Several** are already in the reception hall.

8. The two girls took part in the competition, but **neither** had a chance of winning.

9. **Anyone** found without proper identification will be arrested.

10. **Much** has been said about the problem, but nothing has been done.

4.22
1. **Who** would like to order some dinner?
2. **What** did she find in the drawer?
3. **Whose** is the fastest horse in the race?
4. **What** were they discussing?
5. **What** were several women talking about?
6. **Whom** did we meet while traveling in Mexico?
7. **Who** spent a lot of time in the mountains?
8. **What** do they prefer?
9. **What** slithered across the road?
10. From **whom** did they receive several letters?

4.23
1. **Five** were playing in the mud.
2. I have **eleven** in that drawer.
3. **Two** are friends of mine.
4. **One** came from Ms. Garcia.
5. There were **five** on the table a moment ago.
6. The new sales clerk sold her **eight**.
7. **Three** applied for the same job.
8. There were at least **fifty** scattered about the floor.

4.24
1. **You** must have strength to carry on.
2. Should **you** always be on time for **your** lessons?
3. If **you lose your** wallet, **you** should report that to the police.
4. **You** ought to try to stay in shape.
5. When **you drink** too much, **you get** drunk
6. **You** have little choice when it comes to love.
7. **You** should always behave **yourself**.
8. How can **you** be so mean to her?
9. If **you have** too much time on **your** hands, **you need** to find a job.
10. When **you have** humility, **you** also **have** respect.

4.25
1. **One** might **get** into a lot of trouble. **You** might **get** into a lot of trouble.
2. If **one speaks** slowly, **one is** better understood. If **you speak** slowly, **you are** better understood.
3. **One ought** to consider taking the train there. **You ought** to consider taking the train there.
4. Should **one** criticize **one's** own mistakes? Should **you** criticize **your** own mistakes?
5. **One learns** slowly when **one is** very young. **You learn** slowly when **you are** very young.
6. In time, **one accepts one's** limitations. In time, **you accept your** limitations.
7. If **one carries on** like a fool, **one** will be considered a fool. If **you carry on** like a fool, **you** will be considered a fool.
8. When **one gets** a little too heavy, **one** should begin to exercise. When **you get** a little too heavy, **you** should begin to exercise.

4.26
Sample answers are provided.   1. a. It was annoying, because I really needed them. b. Did you read about them in a local newspaper? c. No, I found their description in a flyer.   2. a. My son saw it from his bedroom window. b. I heard my neighbors speaking of it yesterday. c. Its path of destruction was a mile wide. 3. a. They always begged us for food. b. They just have to be with us constantly. c. Our solution was to leave them in the yard at mealtime.   4. a. My father bought me the airline ticket. b. Do you have time to go with me? c. My hotel reservation is for two people.   5. a. What prevented you from going? b. A man at the party asked about you. c. I suppose it was your brother.   6. a. Lots of other things made him laugh as well. b. As soon as you start telling a joke to him, he starts to giggle. c. His sense of humor is very good.   7. a. Did a doctor see her? b. Yes, he was with her about an hour. c. Her condition isn't good.

4.27
Sample answers are provided.   1. which greatly frightened the inhabitants   2. which was a fantastic experience   3. who used to play football at Notre Dame   4. about whom I told you earlier   5. which I found in an old textbook   6. who looked a lot friendlier   7. that has a powerful battery   8. whom you punched   9. who waited on me earlier   10. that Mr. Keller sent you

4.28
Sample answers are provided.   1. a. , near which a giant castle stood. b. , which they located an inn in. c. that a stranger directed them to. d. no one had ever heard of before.   2. a. from whom he had received the property. b. , whom he had completely relied upon. c. who he had given a down payment to. d. his wife had

told him about.   3. a. , upon which lay a large shaggy dog. b. , which the cat liked to sleep under. c. that she had been looking for. d. her husband was sleeping on.   4. a. about whom so much had been written. b. , whom she yearned for in her dreams. c. that she had been interested in since grade school. d. Jane had told her about.   5. a. at which smokers are allowed. b. , which people just argue and complain in. c. that only members can participate in. d. you can learn as much from in a memo.

4.29 *Sample answers are provided.*   1. a. I'll come by for a visit this weekend. b. This is hard to tolerate.   2. a. That restaurant is quite good. b. That is the last straw!   3. a. Are these CDs yours? b. These belong to my cousin.   4. a. Those steaks were delicious. b. Those made me sick to my stomach.

4.30 *Sample answers are provided.*   1. a. In the spring she refreshed herself with a daily walk. b. Why did she buy herself another ring?   2. a. You rarely groom yourself properly. b. You soon gave yourself another reward for the job you had done.   3. a. At dinner we had to serve ourselves. b. We ordered ourselves a large, sweet dessert.   4. a. I angrily reproached myself for those terrible words. b. I pretended to tell myself a similar story.   5. a. They fed themselves on tasty sandwiches. b. They gave themselves wine and snacks and forgot about their guests.   6. a. Tom was interested only in his grandfather. b. Tom was interested only in himself.   7. a. Did you think about the wounded soldier? b. Did you think about yourselves? 8. a. At this moment I thought about the poor flight attendant. b. At this moment I thought about myself. 9. a. Ms. Brown was talking to the young dancer. b. Ms. Brown was talking to herself.   10. a. John and Laura arranged a party for their guests. b. John and Laura arranged a party for themselves.

4.31 *Sample answers are provided.*   1. Much was said, but there was little action.   2. Is either of these cars still for sale?   3. Each is allowed only one piece of luggage.   4. Neither of the girls won a prize. 5. One is a friend of mine; the other is a complete stranger.   6. Everybody loves Raymond.   7. No one understands why they're arguing.   8. Few of them have any knowledge on the subject.   9. Many still believe that global warming is a myth.   10. Each of the contestants has to sing a song.

4.32 1. William himself tried to free the car from the muddy rut.   2. Several of the men themselves heard the strange sounds in the attic.   3. I myself longed to return to my homeland.   4. Ms. Thomas and I ourselves were rather good dancers.   5. The administration itself is responsible for our improved economy. 6. Nancy herself broke down in tears upon hearing the news.   7. You yourself (yourselves) tried to get some help for them.   8. He himself felt ashamed for what had happened that day.   9. They themselves attempted to exploit the situation.

5   Verbs

5.1   1. I can't see you. The light (shine) in my eyes. **is shining**
The light (shine) against the paintings on the wall. **shines**
2. The kids (play) in the living room. **are playing**
The kids (play) indoors when it rains. **play**
3. The company (publish) my first novel. **is publishing**
The company (publish) works by new authors. **publishes**
4. Bad news always (spread) faster than good news. **spreads**
The news (spread) all over town. **is spreading**
5. We (gain) weight as we get older. **gain**
We (gain) weight on this trip. **are gaining**
6. The board (make) the final decision on hiring. **makes**
The board (make) a bad mistake. **is making**
7. Conflicts about immigration always (divide) communities. **divide**
The conflict on immigration (divide) the community into factions. **is dividing**
8. The garage always (check) the oil. **checks**
The mechanic (check) the oil now. **is checking**
9. John (smile) whenever he thinks about what you said. **smiles**
John (smile) at what you just said. **is smiling**
10. We (walk) every chance we get. **walk**
We (walk) to the park. Want to come along? **are walking**

5.2   1. Not OK   2. OK   3. Not OK   4. OK   5. Not OK   6. Not OK   7. OK   8. OK   9. Not OK 10. OK   11. OK   12. Not OK   13. OK   14. Not OK   15. OK

5.3   1. OK habitual   2. OK assertion   3. Not OK   4. OK assertion   5. OK habitual   6. Not OK 7. Not OK   8. OK habitual (also assertion)   9. Not OK   10. OK assertion

5.4   1. (1) making assertions   2. (3) commenting on present-time actions   3. (1) making assertions 4. (1) making assertions   5. (3) commenting on present-time actions   6. (2) describing habits

7. (2) describing habits   8. (1) making assertions   9. (1) making assertions   10. (2) describing habits
11. (3) commenting on present-time actions   12. (1) making assertions   13. (2) describing habits
14. (1) making assertions   15. (1) making assertions

5.5   1. OK   2. Not OK   3. OK   4. Not OK   5. Not OK   6. OK   7. Not OK   8. OK   9. OK
10. OK

5.6   1. If I <u>see</u> him, I <u>will</u> say hello.

2. Until they <u>save</u> some more money, they <u>will have</u> trouble paying for it.

3. We definitely <u>will accept</u> if they <u>offer</u> us the job.

4. As soon I <u>get</u> home, I <u>will start</u> dinner.

5. We <u>will watch</u> a movie after we <u>finish</u> eating.

6. Once I <u>get</u> my check, I <u>will look</u> for a new apartment.

7. The game still <u>will be played</u>, even if it rains.

8. We <u>will go</u> ahead as planned, even though there <u>are</u> some objections.

9. Unless there <u>is</u> a problem, we <u>will meet</u> you in Denver tomorrow.

10. I <u>will try</u> to visit them next time I <u>go</u> to Phoenix.

5.7   1. (6)   2. (5)   3. (4)   4. (5)   5. (1)   6. (1)   7. (2)   8. (7)   9. (3)   10. (1)   11. (6)
12. (2)   13. (3)   14. (7)   15. (4)

5.8   1. If I were you, I <u>would</u> watch what I <u>ate</u>.

2. If I were you, I <u>would</u> talk only about what I <u>knew</u>.

3. If I were you, I <u>would</u> remind them what they <u>agreed</u> to pay.

4. If I were you, I <u>would</u> be worried about where I <u>parked</u> my car.

5. If I were you, I <u>would</u> start working only when I <u>had</u> enough light to see what I <u>was</u> doing.

5.9   1. What <u>did</u> you think about it?

2. <u>Would</u> you join us for lunch?

3. <u>Could</u> you stop by my office before you leave?

4. <u>Would</u> you be free this evening?

5. <u>Might</u> I make an alternative proposal?

5.10   1. Prediction   2. Prediction   3. Intention   4. Intention   5. Prediction   6. Intention
7. Prediction   8. Intention   9. Prediction   10. Intention

5.11   1. Everyone <u>stays</u> with friends until the water recedes. Not OK

2. They <u>move</u> out of the apartment at the end of the month. OK

3. I <u>wax</u> the car as soon as the water dries. Not OK

4. We <u>help</u> the public radio fund-raising program Saturday from noon till 4:00. OK

5. Loretta <u>presents</u> the keynote at this year's conference. OK

6. They <u>sell</u> their house as soon as they get a reasonable offer. Not OK

7. The course <u>covers</u> that material in the last week. OK

8. Because of global warming, some insurance companies <u>raise</u> their flood insurance rates next year.
Not OK

9. The contractor <u>lays</u> the carpet as soon as he can get the pad installed. Not OK

10. I <u>teach</u> that class next semester. OK

5.12   1. Immediate future action   2. Scheduled or fixed future event   3. Normal expectations   4. New
information   5. Immediate future action   6. Scheduled or fixed future event   7. Scheduled or fixed
future event   8. Normal expectations   9. Immediate future actions   10. New information

5.13   1. Careful, you <u>are about to sit</u> in a wet chair.

2. The tournament <u>begins</u> this Saturday.

3. I <u>am going to need</u> to rent a car. (Note: <u>am needing</u> is ungrammatical because *need* is a stative verb.)

4. I <u>will turn</u> the lights off when I leave the building.

5. We <u>are about to replace</u> the countertops in the kitchen.

6. They <u>will launch</u> a search for the overdue hikers.

7. The news <u>comes</u> on at 10:00 tonight.

8. The storm <u>is about to hit</u> the coast with heavy rains.
9. The aides <u>will handle</u> all the registration details.
10. He <u>is trying/is going to try</u> a totally new approach.

6   More about Verbs

6·1
1.	eat	habitual action
2.	carries	habitual action
3.	speak	fact
4.	produces	fact
5.	make	custom
6.	watches	habitual action
7.	says	custom
8.	begins	future time
9.	live	fact
10.	grow	fact
11.	wear	custom
12.	shake, meet	custom

6·2   The correct subjects and verbs are provided. Other parts of the sentence may vary.
1. She always **makes** strawberry pies for the Fourth of July.
2. I **take** the garbage out every Tuesday night.
3. It **gives** me a headache.
4. They **come** to our house on Labor Day.
5. I **use** my computer every day.
6. He **leaves** in ten minutes.
7. They **like** the theater.
8. She **writes** poetry and short stories.
9. We **listen** to the baseball games on KXLE.
10. It **contains** something fragile.
11. It **starts** at 9:00.
12. He **understands** the theory.

6·3
1. He **does not go** to school every day.
2. My roommate **does not like** snakes.
3. You **do not know** my family.
4. The owner **does not open** the store every day at 8:00.
5. We **do not help** our neighbors.
6. My friends **do not send** me letters.
7. I **do not feel** tired.
8. She **does not speak** five different languages.
9. They **do not study** in the library.
10. We **do not listen** to pop music.
11. They **do not grow** tomatoes in their backyard.
12. This car **does not run** well.

6·4   1. am   2. are, am   3. are   4. is   5. is   6. are   7. are   8. am   9. is   10. is   11. is   12. are

6·5   1. is   2. are   3. are   4. is   5. are   6. is   7. is   8. are   9. are   10. is   11. is   12. is

6·6   1. worked   2. waited   3. remembered   4. needed   5. missed   6. sold   7. went   8. met   9. cut   10. wore

6·7   1. lived   2. have lived   3. have studied   4. studied   5. traveled   6. have traveled   7. have worked   8. worked   9. has built   10. built

6·8
1. He **did not come** to work on time.
2. My roommate did not like the movie.
3. She **did not understand** the problem.
4. We **did not take** a wrong turn.
5. The students **did not need** help with the homework.
6. The driver **did not blame** me for the accident.
7. I **did not listen** to the directions.
8. She **did not earn** a degree in economics.

9. He **did not calculate** the taxes.

10. They **did not complain** about the weather.

6.9 1. was 2. were 3. were 4. was 5. was 6. were 7. was 8. were 9. was 10. was

6.10 1. was 2. were 3. was 4. was 5. were 6. were 7. was 8. was 9. were 10. was

6.11 1. answer 2. Have 3. Open 4. be 5. Finish 6. Call 7. Bake 8. Meet
9. Turn 10. Drive

6.12
1. Do not be
   Don't be late!
2. Do not run
   Don't run on the deck of the pool.
3. Do not forget
   Don't forget your homework.
4. Do not lie
   Don't lie to me.
5. Do not shout
   Don't shout at us.
6. Do not drink
   Don't drink the water.
7. Do not start
   Don't start the car yet.
8. Do not blame
   Don't blame me.
9. Do not boil
   Don't boil the water too long.
10. Do not break
    Don't break anything.

6.13 *Sample answers are provided.* 1. Keep away from me! 2. Give me that! 3. Get out! 4. Don't be a jerk! 5. Hurry up! 6. Leave me alone! 7. Don't excite the dog! 8. Hang on tight! 9. Pour me a Coke! 10. Have a heart!

6.14 *Sample answers are provided.* 1. a. Please enjoy the rest of the trip. b. Enjoy the rest of the trip, please.
2. a. Please find the capital of Ireland on the map. b. Find the capital of Ireland on the map, please.
3. a. Please remember to take your receipt. b. Remember to take your receipt, please. 4. a. Please choose a partner for the rumba. b. Choose a partner for the rumba, please. 5. a. Please explain this sentence to me. b. Explain this sentence to me, please. 6. a. Please remain in your assigned seats. b. Remain in your assigned seats, please. 7. a. Please pretend that none of this happened. b. Pretend that none of this happened, please.
8. a. Please join in the fun. b. Join in the fun, please. 9. a. Please follow my instructions. b. Follow my instructions, please. 10. a. Please hurry down to dinner. b. Hurry down to dinner, please.

6.15 *Sample answers are provided.* 1. a. Let's spend about two hundred dollars. b. Let the girls spend about two hundred dollars. 2. a. Let's send Jim a text. b. Let Maria send Jim a text. 3. a. Let's send them another e-mail. b. Let the boss send them another e-mail. 4. a. Let's report the burglary to the police. b. Let Mr. Snyder report the burglary to the police. 5. a. Let's repair the rickety steps. b. Let the boys repair the rickety steps. 6. a. Let's try to signal the boat struggling in the swift current. b. Let Captain Jones try to signal the boat struggling in the swift current. 7. a. Let's send for the paramedics. b. Let my wife send for the paramedics. 8. a. Let's drive to the edge of the cliff. b. Let the stuntman drive to the edge of the cliff.
9. a. Let's put up a privacy fence. b. Let the neighbors put up a privacy fence. 10. a. Let's solve the difficult equation. b. Let John solve the difficult equation.

6.16 1. a. How about sitting down under a shady tree? b. Why don't you sit down under a shady tree? c. Why don't we sit down under a shady tree? 2. a. How about coming to an understanding about this matter? b. Why don't you come to an understanding about this matter? c. Why don't we to come to an understanding about this matter? 3. a. How about letting them work it out for themselves? b. Why don't you let them work it out for themselves? c. Why don't we let them work it out for themselves? 4. a. How about granting her permission to take the trip? b. Why don't you grant her permission to take the trip? c. Why don't we grant her permission to take the trip? 5. a. How about singing a song for Grandma? b. Why don't you sing a song for Grandma? c. Why don't we sing a song for Grandma? 6. a. How about refraining from using such language? b. Why don't you refrain from using such language? c. Why don't we refrain from using such language? 7. a. How about fertilizing the fields with dung? b. Why don't you fertilize the fields with dung? c. Why don't we fertilize the fields with dung? 8. a. How about opening a business on State

Street? b. Why don't you open a business on State Street? c. Why don't we open a business on State Street? 9. a. How about registering to vote in the next election? b. Why don't you register to vote in the next election? c. Why don't we register to vote in the next election? 10. a. How about trying to behave a little better? b. Why don't you try to behave a little better? c. Why don't we try to behave a little better?

6·17 *Sample answers are provided.* 1. Please pass me the butter. 2. Let's get together and play poker tomorrow night. 3. Let the boys take a couple laps around the track to warm up. 4. Please, refrain from chatting so others can concentrate on their studies! 5. How about helping me translate this article into English? 6. Why don't you find a good job and settle down? 7. Why don't we spend more time with the children? 8. Let's work out together at the gym tomorrow. 9. Please keep your dog on a leash. 10. Why don't you fax a copy of the contract to me?

6.18 1. will 2. should 3. may 4. must 5. can 6. would 7. May 8. must 9. may 10. will 11. should 12. Can 13. may 14. would

6.19 1. are going to 2. ought to 3. used to 4. have to 5. is able to 6. used to 7. ought to 8. have to 9. are able to 10. is going to

6.20 1. was going to 2. ought to 3. had to 4. was able to 5. was going to 6. ought to 7. had to 8. were able to

6.21 1. might [modal], be able to [semi-modal]
2. are going to [semi-modal], be able to [semi-modal]
3. might [modal], have to [semi-modal]
4. are going to [semi-modal], have to [semi-modal]
5. will [modal], have to [semi-modal]

7 Auxiliary Verbs

7.1 1. had checked past perfect 2. has delayed present perfect 3. will have closed future perfect 4. had gone past perfect 5. have started present perfect 6. had gotten past perfect 7. have maintained present perfect 8. will have finished future perfect 9. had anticipated past perfect 10. will have armed future perfect

7.2 1. I have asked them to provide more information.
2. Surely the lake will have frozen by now.
3. We had told them about what they said.
4. They will have cleared customs by now.
5. The court has ruled on many similar cases over the years.
6. Before they moved in, they had repainted the entire apartment.
7. They will have invited more people than they have space for.
8. Fortunately, we had adjusted the insurance before the accident happened.
9. Surely, he has retired by now.
10. His announcement will have attracted a lot of attention.

7.3 1. Continuously ongoing state (stative) 2. Intermittent action (dynamic) 3. Continuously ongoing state (stative) 4. Intermittent action (dynamic) 5. Intermittent action (dynamic) 6. Continuously ongoing state (stative) 7. Intermittent action (dynamic) 8. Continuously ongoing state (stative) 9. Intermittent action (dynamic) 10. Intermittent action (dynamic)

7.4 1. Noncontinuous 2. Continuous 3. Continuous 4. Noncontinuous 5. Noncontinuous 6. Noncontinuous 7. Continuous 8. Continuous 9. Noncontinuous 10. Continuous

7.5 1. Emphatic 2. Neutral 3. Emphatic 4. Emphatic 5. Neutral 6. Emphatic 7. Neutral 8. Emphatic 9. Neutral 10. Emphatic

7.6 1. Emphatic: The senator has refused to retract his statement.
Neutral: The senator refused to retract his statement.
2. Emphatic: A big tree has fallen in the backyard.
Neutral: A big tree fell in the backyard.
3. Emphatic: A reporter has revealed the source of the money.
Neutral: A reporter revealed the source of the money.
4. Emphatic: They have told me what happened.
Neutral: They told me what happened.
5. Emphatic: I have turned down the offer.
Neutral: I turned down the offer.
6. Emphatic: We have bought a new car.

Neutral: We bought a new car.

7. Emphatic: I have found my car keys.
   Neutral: I found my car keys.
8. Emphatic: The CEO has seen the new sales figures.
   Neutral: The CEO saw the new sales figures.
9. Emphatic: Our flight has been canceled.
   Neutral: Our flight was canceled.
10. Emphatic: The game has ended in a tie.
    Neutral: The game ended in a tie.

7.7 1. Neutral expectation 2. Affirmative expectation 3. Affirmative expectation 4. Neutral expectation 5. Affirmative expectation 6. Neutral expectation 7. Neutral expectation 8. Affirmative expectation 9. Affirmative expectation 10. Neutral expectation

7.8
1. Affirmative expectation: Has the Coast Guard warned boaters about the storm?
   Neutral: Did the Coast Guard warn boaters about the storm?
2. Affirmative expectation: Has the paint dried?
   Neutral: Did the paint dry?
3. Affirmative expectation: Has the committee adopted the proposal?
   Neutral: Did the committee adopt the proposal?
4. Affirmative expectation: Has he bought the tickets?
   Neutral: Did he buy the tickets?
5. Affirmative expectation: Has the garage checked the battery?
   Neutral: Did the garage check the battery?
6. Affirmative expectation: Have you stayed there before?
   Neutral: Did you stay there before?
7. Affirmative expectation: Has she kept the receipts?
   Neutral: Did she keep the receipts?
8. Affirmative expectation: Have they responded to our offer?
   Neutral: Did they respond to our offer?
9. Affirmative expectation: Have you gotten enough to eat?
   Neutral: Did you get enough to eat?
10. Affirmative expectation: Have they started to work?
    Neutral: Did they start to work?

7.9
1. We revised the estimates that we had made earlier.
   more recent past-time event   older past-time event
2. He went into the hospital after his temperature had reached 103 degrees.
   more recent past-time event   older past-time event
3. They had patented the device before they put it on the market.
   older past-time event   more recent past-time event
4. I tried to get tickets, but they had already sold out.
   more recent past-time event   older past-time event
5. We fell into bed utterly exhausted as soon as we had eaten.
   more recent past-time event   older past-time event
6. The sun came out for the first time in days after the storm had finally passed.
   more recent past-time event   older past-time event
7. I knew the answer as soon as she had asked the question.
   more recent past-time event   older past-time event
8. I had picked up a cold when I was traveling.
   older past-time event   more recent past-time event
9. We had lived there some time before we met them.
   older past-time event   more recent past-time event
10. The bakery stopped making the cake that everyone had liked so much.
    more recent past-time event   older past-time event

7.10
1. Before we started driving, we had adjusted the car seats.
2. Before everyone finished eating, the waiter had started clearing the dishes.
3. By the time we cut the cake, the ice cream had already melted.
4. When we first moved in, the house had been empty for years.
5. Before I noticed the dirty glasses, we had already finished setting the table.
6. Before the position was approved, he had advertised the job opening.
7. Long before we got on the road, the sun had risen.

8. Before the soldiers arrived, the rebels had already abandoned the fort.
9. By the time we got our tents set up, the rain had stopped.
10. Even before I reached the door, I had heard the loud music.

7.11
1. Normal order: We had taped all the windows and doors before we started painting.
   Inverted: Before we started painting, we had taped all the windows and doors.
2. Normal order: John had already swum competitively before he went to college.
   Inverted: Before he went to college, John had already swum competitively.
3. Normal order: Everyone had put on protective headgear before they went bicycle riding.
   Inverted: Before they went bicycle riding, everyone had put on protective headgear.
4. Normal order: I had skipped lunch because I had an important conference call at noon.
   Inverted: Because I had an important conference call at noon, I had skipped lunch.
5. Normal order: The lawyers had totally revised their strategy before court reconvened after lunch.
   Inverted: Before court reconvened after lunch, the lawyers had totally revised their strategy.
6. Normal order: The cook had rubbed the roast with herbs before he put it in the oven.
   Inverted: Before he put it in the oven, the cook had rubbed the roast with herbs.
7. Normal order: He had hesitated noticeably before he answered the question.
   Inverted: Before he answered the question, he had hesitated noticeably.
8. Normal order: They had drained a lot of water out of the reservoir before the heavy rains came.
   Inverted: Before the heavy rains came, they had drained a lot of water out of the reservoir.
9. Normal order: The company had analyzed the proposal carefully before they invested money in it.
   Inverted: Before they invested money in it, the company had analyzed the proposal carefully.
10. Normal order: They had gotten extra car insurance as soon as their son was old enough to drive.
    Inverted: As soon as their son was old enough to drive, they had gotten extra car insurance.

7.12
1. As soon as the plane had landed, I called them on my cell phone.
2. Even before he had finished asking me the question, I knew the answer.
3. Even before we had found our seats, our team scored.
4. After the sun had come out, we hung the clothes on the line.
5. After we had passed the qualifying exam, we could declare a thesis topic.
6. Even before we'd had a chance to talk about it, I had to come up with a plan.
7. After we had reboarded the bus, we looked for better seats.
8. After the Civil War had ended, General Lee became a college president.
9. After they had repaired it, it functioned much better.
10. After we had sat on the tarmac for an hour, the plane finally took off.

7.13
1. Normal order: They were eligible to play professional football when their class had graduated from college.
   Inverted: When their class had graduated from college, they were eligible to play professional football.
2. Normal order: The airlines instituted a new policy after there had been a near collision on the tarmac.
   Inverted: After there had been a near collision on the tarmac, the airlines instituted a new policy.
3. Normal order: He was arrested after he had lied to the grand jury under oath.
   Inverted: After he had lied to the grand jury under oath, he was arrested.
4. Normal order: Ralph quit his job and moved to Florida after he had won the lottery.
   Inverted: After he had won the lottery, Ralph quit his job and moved to Florida.
5. Normal order: The cloth shrunk badly after it had gotten wet.
   Inverted: After it had gotten wet, the cloth shrunk badly.
6. Normal order: The protesters were arrested after they had disrupted a city council meeting.
   Inverted: After the protestors had disrupted a city council meeting, they were arrested.
7. Normal order: The witness was excused from testifying after she had invoked her right against self-incrimination.
   Inverted: After the witness had invoked her right against self-incrimination, she was excused from testifying.
8. Normal order: Someone called the fire department after the residents had been alerted by the smell of smoke.
   Inverted: After the residents had been alerted by the smell of smoke, someone called the fire department.
9. Normal order: The meetings were better attended after they had started serving refreshments.
   Inverted: After they had started serving refreshments, the meetings were better attended.
10. Normal order: The dog chewed up all the furniture after they had left for work that morning.
    Inverted: After they had left for work that morning, the dog chewed up all the furniture.

7.14
1. Completed: The two companies will have merged by the end of the fiscal year.
2. Happening: I think that they will make me an offer soon.

3. Completed: They will have traced the source of the leak in a few hours.
4. Happening: The carpets will fade quickly if they are not protected from the sun.
5. Completed: Surely any message they sent will have reached us by now.
6. Completed: Hurry, or they will have sold all the good seats by the time we get our orders in.
7. Happening: The doctor will prescribe a different medication after seeing what happened.
8. Completed: Her heirs will have gained control of their estate when they turned 18.
9. Completed: The chair will have cut off discussion after two hours.
10. Completed: The police will have informed him of his rights the moment he was arrested.

7·15 1. have built   2. have eaten   3. have lent   4. have spoken   5. has fallen   6. have known
7. have sold   8. has rained   9. have kept   10. has spent   11. have cut

7.16 1. had attended   2. had held   3. had sold   4. had met   5. had felt   6. had hit   7. had sat
8. had run   9. had snowed   10. had been

7.17 1. arrived, had left   2. had finished, went   3. had assigned, completed   4. was, had worked
5. wore, had given   6. revised, had written   7. had knocked, entered   8. knew, had taken
9. read, had received   10. celebrated, had passed

7.18 1. Our company is sponsoring a number of charity auctions. **Present progressive**
2. We were just admiring your garden. **Past progressive**
3. Our pets will be going to the vet for their annual shots. **Future progressive**
4. I am translating some technical manuals into Spanish. **Present progressive**
5. The kids will be staying overnight at a friend's house. **Future progressive**
6. Am I interrupting anything? **Present progressive**
7. They will be completing their training in June. **Future progressive**
8. I was falling asleep at my desk so I took a little walk to wake up. **Past progressive**
9. I don't know why they are blaming me for what happened. **Present progressive**
10. Remember, they will be relying on you. **Future progressive**

7.19 1. You will be wasting your time if you do that.
2. I am making some coffee; would you like some?
3. The polls were leaning toward the incumbent candidate.
4. I will be teaching part-time next year.
5. The heat was killing all of our shade plants.
6. Their flight will be arriving at 9:45.
7. They are referring the whole matter to their legal department.
8. I thought that they were dealing with the situation very well.
9. We will be discussing that issue at our next meeting.
10. His doctor is treating the infection with a new antibiotic.

7.20 1. The sausages weigh two pounds. **Stative**
The butcher weighs the sausages. **Dynamic**
Present progressive: **X** The sausages are weighing two pounds.
Present progressive: The butcher is weighing the sausages.
2. College graduates pile up a lot of debt. **Dynamic**
College graduates owe a lot of money. **Stative**
Present progressive: College graduates are piling up a lot of debt.
Present progressive: **X** College graduates are owing a lot of money.
3. Bill has a broken toe. **Stative**
Bill has some friends over to celebrate his promotion. **Dynamic**
Present progressive: **X** Bill is having a broken toe.
Present progressive: Bill is having some friends over to celebrate his promotion.
4. The children appear to be ready to go. **Stative**
The situation changes by the minute. **Dynamic**
Present progressive: **X** The children are appearing to be ready to go.
Present progressive: The situation is changing by the minute.
5. The kids always turn their bedroom into a playground. **Dynamic**
The kids' bedroom resembles the scene of a natural disaster. **Stative**
Present progressive: The kids are always turning their bedroom into a playground.
Present progressive: **X** The kids' bedroom is resembling the scene of a natural disaster.
6. Her new hairstyle suits her very well. **Stative**
Her new hairstyle takes a lot of time to maintain. **Dynamic**
Present progressive: **X** Her new hairstyle is suiting her very well.
Present progressive: Her new hairstyle is taking a lot of time to maintain.

7. Everyone <u>tells</u> me to be careful. **Dynamic**
Everyone <u>needs</u> to be careful. **Stative**
Present progressive: Everyone <u>is telling</u> me to be careful.
Present progressive: **X** Everyone <u>is needing</u> to be careful.

8. The public <u>doubts</u> what the congressman is claiming. **Stative**
The public <u>agrees</u> with what the congressman is claiming. **Dynamic**
Present progressive: **X** The public <u>is doubting</u> what the congressman is claiming.
Present progressive: The public <u>is agreeing</u> with what the congressman is claiming.

9. A big payment <u>comes</u> due at the end of the month. **Dynamic**
A big problem <u>exists</u> in our cash flow. **Stative**
Present progressive: A big payment <u>is coming</u> due at the end of the month.
Present progressive: **X** A big problem <u>is existing</u> in our cash flow.

10. The students <u>discussed</u> how to thank you. **Dynamic**
The students <u>appreciate</u> all that you have done for them. **Stative**
Present progressive: The students <u>are discussing</u> how to thank you.
Present progressive: **X** The students <u>are appreciating</u> all that you have done for them.

7.21   1. The chest <u>contains</u> extra blankets and pillows **whenever it gets cold. Stative**
We <u>take</u> out extra blankets and pillows **whenever it gets cold. Dynamic**
Present progressive: **X** The chest <u>is containing</u> extra blankets and pillows **whenever it gets cold.**
Present progressive: We <u>are taking</u> out extra blankets and pillows **whenever it gets cold.**

2. I <u>resolved</u> the issue **in a minute. Dynamic**
Everyone <u>recognizes</u> the issue **in a minute. Stative**
Present progressive: I <u>am resolving</u> the issue **in a minute.**
Present progressive: **X** Everyone <u>is recognizing</u> the issue **in a minute.**

3. We <u>track</u> the paths of protons **when we are in the lab. Dynamic**
Atoms <u>consist</u> of protons **when we are in the lab. Stative**
Present progressive: We <u>are tracking</u> the paths of protons **when we are in the lab.**
Present progressive: **X** Atoms <u>are consisting</u> of protons **when we are in the lab.**

4. They <u>seem</u> to be reliable **all the time. Stative**
We <u>check</u> on their reliability **all the time. Dynamic**
Present progressive: **X** They <u>are seeming</u> to be reliable **all the time.**
Present progressive: We <u>are checking</u> on their reliability **all the time.**

5. He <u>finds</u> out what the answer is **on Wednesday. Dynamic**
He <u>understands</u> what the answer is **on Wednesday. Stative**
Present progressive: He <u>is finding</u> out what the answer is **on Wednesday.**
Present progressive: **X** He <u>is understanding</u> what the answer is **on Wednesday.**

6. The new shoes <u>fit</u> well **every weekend. Stative**
I <u>wear</u> the new shoes **every weekend. Dynamic**
Present progressive: **X** The new shoes <u>are fitting</u> well **every weekend.**
Present progressive: I <u>am wearing</u> the new shoes **every weekend.**

7. We <u>buy</u> a new car **next week. Dynamic**
A new car <u>costs</u> more than we can afford **next week. Stative**
Present progressive: We <u>are buying</u> a new car **next week.**
Present progressive: **X** A new car <u>is costing</u> more than we can afford **next week.**

8. The children <u>love</u> their new school **in the fall. Stative**
The children <u>enter</u> their new school **in the fall. Dynamic**
Present progressive: **X** The children <u>are loving</u> their new school **in the fall.**
Present progressive: The children <u>are entering</u> their new school **in the fall.**

9. Their new apartment <u>looks</u> like their old place **when they move in. Stative**
They <u>plan</u> to remodel their new apartment **when they move in. Dynamic**
Present progressive: **X** Their new apartment <u>is looking</u> like their old place **when they move in.**
Present progressive: They <u>are planning</u> to remodel their new apartment **when they move in.**

10. Everyone <u>helps</u> to rearrange the layout of our office **every Monday morning. Dynamic**
Everyone <u>dislikes</u> the layout of our office **every Monday morning. Stative**
Present progressive: Everyone <u>is helping</u> to rearrange the layout of our office **every Monday morning.**
Present progressive: **X** Everyone <u>is disliking</u> the layout of our office **every Monday morning.**

7.22   1. The baby **is** hungry all the time.   **X**
2. Fortunately, we **have** a laptop at our disposal.   **X**
3. I <u>am supervising</u> a new construction project.   OK

4. The estimate **includes** all taxes and fees.   **X**

5. The kids are mowing the backyard this afternoon.   OK

6. I **hate** the fact that we are having so much trouble.   **X**

7. I don't think it is harming anyone.   OK

8. The ceremony is beginning at 4 p.m.   OK

9. They **all like** the company's new logo.   **X**

10. The heavy rain is ruining everyone's gardens.   OK

7.23

1. The babysitter **is warming** the kids' dinner in the oven.

2. The kids **want** to watch TV until bedtime.

3. Their approval **means** a lot to us.

4. I told the waiter that we **are celebrating** a birthday.

5. George **knows** where the restaurant is.

6. The children **are quarreling** again.

7. We **are soaking** all of our dirty hiking clothes in the washing machine.

8. The purse **belongs** to that young lady over there.

9. The tire **seems** a little flat to me.

10. The flowers in the garden **are blooming**.

8   The past progressive tense

8.1

1. **X**   *Stative*   We ~~were knowing~~ all along that the job would be difficult.

2. OK   *Dynamic*   Because of the kitchen repairs, we were eating out a lot.

3. OK   *Dynamic*   Clearly, all of the politicians were avoiding the issue.

4. **X**   *Stative*   Frank ~~was~~ always ~~possessing~~ a great sense of humor.

5. OK   *Dynamic*   The kids were sleeping in a tent in the backyard.

6. **X**   *Stative*   The orchestra ~~was consisting~~ of a string section and some woodwinds.

7. OK   *Dynamic*   I was training everyone in the office to use the new accounting software.

8. OK   *Dynamic*   The government was encouraging everyone to get flu shots.

9. **X**   *Stative*   After it started raining, the kids ~~were wanting~~ to go home.

10. **X**   *Stative*   Everyone ~~was needing~~ to take a break because of the heat.

8.2

1. The cold weather threatened to ruin the entire crop.

2. The country was slowly emerging from financial chaos.

3. During the whole time, I was trying to get a word in edgewise.

4. The company rapidly expanded into Asian markets.

5. As it turned out, the police were recording the entire conversation.

6. The heavy truck traffic was damaging the road surfaces.

7. The company represented some of the firms in the industry.

8. All the noise was frightening the children.

9. The kids were swimming at the pool in the community center.

10. Their lawyer advised them not to say anything about what happened.

8.3

1. I was listening to the radio on the way to work.
Confirmation: On the way to work, I was listening to the radio.

2. Everybody was completely on edge after what happened.
Confirmation: After what happened, everybody was completely on edge.

3. The water was flooding the lower fields after all the heavy rains.
Confirmation: After all the heavy rains, the water was flooding the lower fields.

4. They were performing at schools around the state <u>during the fall</u>.
   Confirmation: <u>During the fall</u>, they were performing at schools around the state.
5. The police were still questioning witnesses <u>even after the trial started</u>.
   Confirmation: <u>Even after the trial started</u>, the police were still questioning witnesses.
6. The wind was blowing faster than 100 miles an hour <u>during the worst of the storm</u>.
   Confirmation: <u>During the worst of the storm</u>, the wind was blowing faster than 100 miles an hour.
7. The manager was interviewing ski instructors <u>over the Thanksgiving break</u>.
   Confirmation: <u>Over the Thanksgiving break</u>, the manager was interviewing ski instructors.
8. She was working on her master's degree <u>then</u>.
   Confirmation: <u>Then</u> she was working on her master's degree.
9. I was just quitting for the night <u>when the alarm sounded</u>.
   Confirmation: <u>When the alarm sounded</u>, I was just quitting for the night.
10. Things were looking pretty bad for our candidate <u>before we got the new poll results</u>.
    Confirmation: <u>Before we got the new poll results</u>, things were looking pretty bad for our candidate.

8.4
1. Step 1: I <u>was reading</u> a book on my Kindle
   Step 2: I <u>was reading</u> a book on my Kindle while everyone else relaxed by the pool.
   Step 3: While everyone else relaxed by the pool, I <u>was reading</u> a book on my Kindle.
2. Step 1: When he <u>was undergoing</u> surgery
   Step 2: My father suffered a minor stroke when he <u>was undergoing</u> surgery.
   Step 3: When he <u>was undergoing</u> surgery, my father suffered a minor stoke.
3. Step 1: The troops <u>were storing</u> ammunition
   Step 2: The troops <u>were storing</u> ammunition when the big explosion happened.
   Step 3: When the big explosion happened, the troops <u>were storing</u> ammunition.
4. Step 1: They <u>were shutting</u> the door
   Step 2: They <u>were shutting</u> the door after the horse was stolen.
   Step 3: After the horse was stolen, they <u>were shutting</u> the door.
5. Step 1: The campers <u>were packing</u> up all their gear
   Step 2: The campers <u>were packing</u> up all their gear when the storm finally broke.
   Step 3: When the storm finally broke, the campers <u>were packing</u> up all their gear.
6. Step 1: While you <u>were talking</u> on the phone
   Step 2: I got all the dishes done while you <u>were talking</u> on the phone.
   Step 3: While you <u>were talking</u> on the phone, I got all the dishes done.
7. Step 1: The fund <u>was investing</u> in Swiss francs
   Step 2: The fund <u>was investing</u> in Swiss francs whenever the dollar was overvalued.
   Step 3: Whenever the dollar was overvalued, the fund <u>was investing</u> in Swiss francs.
8. Step 1: Every time they <u>were doing</u> their homework
   Step 2: We would make the kids give us their cell phones every time they <u>were doing</u> their homework.
   Step 3: Every time they <u>were doing</u> their homework, we would make the kids give us their cell phones.
9. Step 1: The birds <u>were building</u> nests
   Step 2: The birds <u>were building</u> nests whenever they could find a protected place.
   Step 3: Whenever they could find a protected place, the birds <u>were building</u> nests.
10. Step 1: When we <u>were flying</u> in or out of Newark
    Step 2: Our flights were always late when we <u>were flying</u> in or out of Newark.
    Step 3: When we <u>were flying</u> in or out of Newark, our flights were always late.

8.5
1. **X**   Stative
   I ~~will be seeing~~ about it and let you know what I find out.
2. OK   Dynamic
   The electrician <u>will be rewiring</u> the kitchen on Monday.
3. **X**   Stative
   Their children ~~will be looking~~ just like them.
4. **X**   Stative
   They ~~will not be minding~~ it if we park in their driveway.
5. OK   Dynamic
   The committee <u>will be counting</u> votes tomorrow.
6. **X**   Stative
   The team ~~will be deserving~~ its reputation if they can win today.
   Dynamic

7. OK   The kids <u>will be playing</u> on the swings all afternoon.

                           Stative
8. **X**   The dinner ~~will not be including~~ dessert or beverage.

                           Dynamic
9. OK   The company <u>will be expanding</u> its online information system.

               Dynamic
10. OK Ruth <u>will be playing</u> tennis this afternoon with some of her friends.

8.6
1. The principal will be judging the spelling competition <u>at 1 p.m.</u>
   Confirmation: <u>At 1 p.m.</u> the principal will be judging the spelling competition.
2. They will be living in Spain <u>until the end of the summer.</u>
   Confirmation: <u>Until the end of the summer,</u> they will be living in Spain.
3. We will be continuing the discussion <u>after everyone finishes dinner.</u>
   Confirmation: <u>After everyone finishes dinner,</u> we will be continuing the discussion.
4. We will be closing down the beach house <u>after Labor Day.</u>
   Confirmation: <u>After Labor Day,</u> we will be closing down the beach house.
5. The sales staff will be showing the apartment <u>as soon as it is vacant.</u>
   Confirmation: <u>As soon as it is vacant,</u> the sales staff will be showing the apartment.
6. Department heads will be meeting with the CFO <u>every Monday morning.</u>
   Confirmation: <u>Every Monday morning,</u> department heads will be meeting with the CFO.
7. They will be expecting us to begin discussions <u>the minute we get off the plane.</u>
   Confirmation: <u>The minute we get off the plane,</u> they will be expecting us to begin discussions.
8. I will be teaching Accounting 101 <u>in the winter quarter.</u>
   Confirmation: <u>In the winter quarter,</u> I will be teaching Accounting 101.
9. They will be getting married <u>after she graduates.</u>
   Confirmation: <u>After she graduates,</u> they will be getting married.
10. Maintenance will be replacing all the old carpets <u>over the holidays.</u>
    Confirmation: <u>Over the holidays,</u> maintenance will be replacing all the old carpets.

8.7
1. Everyone <u>will be rushing</u> to get their taxes in before the April 15 deadline.
2. This last payment <u>will fulfill</u> the terms of the contract.
3. Everyone <u>will be checking</u> their roofs for damage as soon as this terrible wind lets up.
4. The governor <u>will announce</u> the winners of the state awards at the banquet.
5. On the first day of school all the kids <u>will be clinging</u> to their parents.
6. Henry <u>will be editing</u> the white paper before we send it out for review.
7. Everyone <u>will notice</u> that Pat is gone.
8. They <u>will be fishing</u> until it gets too dark to bait their hooks.
9. I <u>will grab</u> a bite at the cafeteria before I go to the meeting.
10. All the rivers <u>will be overflowing</u> their banks after all this rain.

8.8
1. He <u>had been scoring</u> nearly half of the team's goals.
   Past perfect progressive
2. The painters <u>will have been stripping</u> off all the old paint.
   Future perfect progressive
3. They <u>had been washing</u> all the dishes by hand during the power outage.
   Past perfect progressive
4. I <u>have been smelling</u> gasoline for days.
   Present perfect progressive
5. She <u>will have been studying</u> English since she was in elementary school.
   Future perfect progressive
6. Fortunately, I <u>had been keeping</u> a good record of all our building expenses.
   Past perfect progressive
7. The wild pigs <u>had been reproducing</u> at a rapid rate.
   Past perfect progressive
8. Apparently, they <u>have been posing</u> as reporters.
   Present perfect progressive

9. She <u>will have been administering</u> the fund for more than 20 years.

  Future perfect progressive

10. The doctor <u>has been prescribing</u> an antifungal drug for me.

  Present perfect progressive

8.9

  Dynamic
1. OK They <u>have been waiting</u> for a final decision for months.

  Stative
2. **X** Their decision to get married <u>~~will have been pleasing~~</u> to both families.

  Dynamic
3. OK My uncle <u>will have been fishing</u> every day this summer.

  Dynamic
4. OK They were warned that they <u>had been exceeding</u> their budget.

  Stative
5. **X** He <u>~~had been recognizing~~</u> some old friends.

  Stative
6. **X** I'm afraid that I <u>~~have been lacking~~</u> enough money to do it.

  Dynamic
7. OK They <u>have</u> certainly <u>been putting</u> up with a lot lately.

  Stative
8. **X** Henry <u>~~had been loving~~</u> pistachio ice cream ever since he was a child.

  Stative
9. **X** My old suits <u>~~had been fitting~~</u> me again after I had lost all that weight.

  Dynamic
10. OK The government <u>had been exerting</u> a lot of pressure on them to reform.

8.10
1. Present perfect: I <u>have made</u> a reservation for dinner at that new restaurant.
2. Present perfect progressive: Grandfather <u>has been telling</u> that story ever since I was a child.
3. Present perfect: Jackson <u>has injured</u> his leg again.
4. Present perfect: The dean <u>has recommended</u> her for promotion.
5. Present perfect progressive: Beginning with the Industrial Revolution, the climate <u>has been</u> steadily <u>warming</u>.
6. Present prefect: The reception <u>has been</u> canceled because of the storm.
7. Present perfect progressive: My cousin <u>has been restoring</u> old cars as long as I have known him.
8. Present perfect: The company <u>has started</u> a new internship program you might be interested in.
9. Present perfect: Remind me who he is. I <u>have forgotten</u> his name.
10. Present perfect progressive: It seems as though it <u>has been raining</u> forever.

8.11
1. was being   2. was ringing   3. was waiting, was dreaming   4. were living   5. was taking, was studying   6. was putting   7. was knocking, was getting   8. was raining   9. were going   10. were cleaning

8.12
1. complete action   2. action in progress   3. action in progress   4. complete action   5. action in progress   6. complete action   7. complete action   8. action in progress   9. action in progress   10. complete action

8.13
1. He **was not attending** a conference.
2. They **were not laughing**.
3. I **was not complaining** about the work.
4. She **was not helping** us.
5. Ted **was not studying** last night.
6. They **were not paying** attention.
7. I **was not talking** to myself.
8. You **were not speaking** loud enough.
9. They **were not doing** their homework.
10. We **were not trying** hard.

8.14
1. had been working   2. had been discussing   3. had been studying   4. had been increasing   5. had been playing   6. had been raining   7. had been watching   8. had been writing   9. had been studying   10. had been working

8.15 1. The supervisor **had not been assigning**
      2. The weather **had not been improving**
      3. Jodi and I **had not been following**
      4. They **had not been checking**
      5. She **had not been ignoring**
      6. You **had not been getting**
      7. I **had not been exercising**

8.16 1. He **hadn't been expecting**
      2. **It'd been changing**
      3. **We'd been hoping**
      4. They **hadn't been looking**
      5. **She'd been lying**
      6. You **hadn't been joking**
      7. **I'd been thinking**

8.17 1. will commute   2. will require   3. will give   4. will visit   5. will be   6. will announce
      7. will leave   8. will complete   9. will call   10. will expand

8.18 1. They'll believe   2. I'll deliver   3. You'll like   4. It'll end   5. He'll help   6. She'll introduce
      7. We'll sit

8.19 1. He **will not finish** by tomorrow.
      2. You **will not have** a lot of fun there.
      3. She **will not know** the answer.
      4. We **will not ignore** the problem.
      5. They **will not keep** your secret.
      6. He **will not lie** to you.
      7. I **will not need** help with my homework.
      8. Marian **will not be** alone.
      9. I **will not mention** your name.
     10. They **will not be** late.

8.20 1. He **won't finish** by tomorrow.
      2. You **won't have** a lot of fun there.
      3. She **won't know** the answer.
      4. We **won't ignore** the problem.
      5. They **won't keep** your secret.
      6. He **won't lie** to you.
      7. I **won't need** help with my homework.
      8. Marian **won't be** alone.
      9. I **won't mention** your name.
     10. They **won't be** late.

8.21 1. is going to be   2. are going to build   3. is going to buy   4. am going to cancel   5. are going
      to climb   6. are going to celebrate   7. is going to call   8. is going to come   9. is going to deliver
     10. are going to elect

8.22 1. is going to   imminent action
      2. will   commitment
      3. am going to   imminent action
      4. is going to   imminent action
      5. will   commitment

8.23 1. Taxes **are not going to increase**
      2. It **is not going to snow**
      3. We **are not going to go**
      4. He **is not going to listen**
      5. She **is not going to travel**
      6. You **are not going to have**
      7. I **am not going to forget**

8.24 1. **He's not going to come** OR **He isn't going to come**
      2. **It's going to rain**
      3. **I'm going to clean**
      4. **They're not going to believe** OR **They aren't going to believe**
      5. **She's not going to call** OR **She isn't going to call**

6. **You're going to do**

7. **I'm not going to cook**

8.25   1. will be representing   2. will be leaving   3. will be following   4. will be waiting   5. will be watching   6. will be producing   7. will be providing   8. will be snowing   9. will be wearing   10. will be opening

8.26   1. They **will not be appearing**

2. It **will not be starting**

3. We **will not be reading**

4. He **will not be arriving**

5. She **will not be staying**

6. You **will not be living**

7. I **will not be making**

8.27   1. He **won't be joining**

2. **It'll be affecting**

3. **I'll be treating**

4. They **won't be needing**

5. She **won't be arriving**

6. **you'll be flying**

7. I **won't be thinking**

8.28   1. will have left   2. will have written   3. will have introduced   4. will have flown   5. will have eaten

8.29   1. You **will not have rested**

2. they **will not have eaten**

3. We **will not have finished**

4. Mark **will not have slept**

5. She **will not have saved**

8.30   1. **they'll have completed**

2. he **won't have finished**

3. **you'll have recovered**

4. They **won't have made**

5. **She'll have given**

8.31   1. will have been living   2. will have been discussing   3. will have been practicing   4. will have been playing   5. will have been working

8.32   1. they **will not have been talking**

2. the subways **will not have been running**

3. they **will not have been producing**

4. the dance troupe **will not have been performing**

5. she **will not have been working**

8.33   1. they **won't have been working**

2. **they'll have been broadcasting**

3. **we'll have been renting**

4. **they'll have been returning**

5. he **won't have been assisting**

9   Passive voice

9.1   1. Glenda is being kissed by Stuart.

2. She was being spoiled by her parents.

3. My eyes are being tested in the clinic.

4. They were being arrested for a crime.

5. Monique is being awarded a medal.

6. The treasure was being buried on an island.

7. The dog is being punished again.

8. Was the old barn being burned down?

9.2   1. We have been punished by Father.

2. The men have been taken prisoner.

3. She has been thanked by the happy tourists.

4. I have been beaten by a robber.

5. The car has not been washed again.

6. Tony has been examined by the doctor.
7. They have been surrounded by the enemy.
8. Has your sister been fired from her job?
9. Has the baby been carried to his bedroom?
10. She has been congratulated by her boss.

9·3
1. The cottage was destroyed by a storm.
2. Was the New World discovered by Columbus?
3. Our house will be bought by them.
4. The cakes have been baked by my grandmother.
5. The bread is being cut by Phil.
6. The newspapers were being sold by Sergio.
7. Has the money been taken by Iris?
8. The baby will be kissed by her.
9. Is the fence being built by Max?
10. The map was forgotten by her brother.

9·4
1. A hundred dollars was found by Maria.
2. The Preamble to the Constitution will be memorized by the students.
3. Were the tickets purchased by you?
4. Some ancient ruins have been discovered by them.
5. The room is being measured by Bill.

9·5
1. A thousand cars were manufactured at that plant.
2. Theories about that are being developed.
3. That painting will be bought today.
4. The opening of the new store has been postponed.
5. His work is not respected.

9·6
1. A new design for the logo has been suggested by Kevin.
2. The formula is going to be explained by the professor.
3. People at the bar are served by bartenders.
4. A speech is being prepared by Noam Chomsky.
5. Marie will be invited to the party by Alex.
6. The novel *American Gods* was written by Neil Gaiman.

9·7
1. will have been   2. is   3. is being   4. has been   5. is going to be   6. will be   7. had been

9·8
1. Every professional school in New York teaches technical skills.
2. TF1 is broadcasting the ping-pong tournament.
3. X
4. Keats wrote this poem. García Lorca wrote the other one.
5. X, Later, Arabs produced paper in Baghdad.
6. X
7. X

9·9
1. My purse was stolen by someone.
2. X
3. My fork was borrowed by Gabriel at lunch.
4. This antique sewing machine was made in 1834 by someone.
5. X
6. The plants were being watered by Steve when I walked into the garden this morning.
7. The president is going to be judged by the jury on the basis of his testimony.
8. When was the atomic bomb invented by America?
9. X
10. Is a reunion being organized by Maureen this week?
11. The Bible has been translated into many languages by professionals.

9·10
1. should be told
2. should have been driven
3. should clean OR should have cleaned
4. must be kept
5. couldn't be convinced
6. couldn't open
7. may be offered
8. may not offer

9. may have already been offered
10. may have already hired
11. must have been surprised
12. should have been sent
13. should be sent
14. had better clean
15. had better be cleaned
16. has to return OR will have to return
17. have to be returned OR will have to be returned OR had to be returned
18. ought to be divided
19. ought to have been divided

9·11 *Answers may vary.*
1. may be
2. can be seen
3. must be put
4. should not get
5. should not be encouraged
6. ought to be postponed
7. might be misunderstood
8. can't be explained
9. must be married
10. must have been left
11. will be displeased
12. has to be pushed
13. should be built
14. ought to be saved
15. has to be done
16. should be elected

9·12   1. disappointed   2. exciting   3. interested   4. gratifying   5. confusing   6. confused
7. excited   8. excited

9·13   1. is broken   2. is closed   3. was closed   4. is made   5. is shut   6. are bent, are folded   7. is
finished   8. are turned   9. is not crowded   10. is hidden   11. is torn   12. are gone   13. is set,
are finished, are lit   14. is made, is vacuumed, are washed   15. was stuck   16. is stuck

10   Adverbs

10.1   1. walked timidly   2. quietly sat down   3. rather angrily   4. entered the classroom noisily OR noisily
entered   5. too boring   6. talked harshly   7. followed the pretty girl home   8. very smart
9. plays the piano well   10. coldly stared

10.2   Sample Answers:
1. He very neatly stacked the books on the shelf.
2. You sing well.
3. She spoke sadly about the tragedy.
4. You're too weak.
5. He said it rather quickly.
6. I was there yesterday.
7. She never lied to me.
8. The man expressed his beliefs quite strongly.
9. You wrote that too carelessly.
10. She played the song so beautifully.

10.3   *Sample answers are provided.*   1. The children ran out of the school with joy.   2. The baritone could sing
better than the soprano.   3. His brother lounged lazily on the sofa and watched TV.   4. Michael showed
them his new car with great pride.   5. She acted responsibly after arriving at the accident site.   6. The
woman muttered weakly that she was ill.   7. The professor congratulated the students on their progress
with a bit of sarcasm.   8. The eight-year-old pianist played the piece beautifully.   9. Little James recited
the poem capably and took a bow.   10. Ellen slapped the man and screamed with rage.

10·4   *Sample answers are provided.*   1. a. During the storm, the puppy huddled under the bed. b. The puppy
huddled under the bed during the storm.   2. a. Yesterday, Tina found a wallet. b. Tina found a wallet

yesterday.   3. a. On the weekend, I usually go hiking. b. I usually go hiking on the weekend.   4. a. Soon I'll be able to play the guitar. b. I'll be able to play the guitar soon. or I'll soon be able to play the guitar. 5. a. Next Friday, we're going to a soccer match. b. We're going to a soccer match next Friday.   6. a. In time, Maria became a physician. b. Maria became a physician in time.   7. a. After Paul gets here, we can play cards. b. We can play cards after Paul gets here.   8. a. In June, they were finally married. b. They were finally married in June.   9. a. Last year, I took a course at the college. b. I took a course at the college last year.   10. a. Before I studied English, I didn't understand a word anyone said. b. I didn't understand a word anyone said before I studied English.

10·5   *Sample answers are provided.*   1. We always supported our troops fighting overseas.   2. Larry sometimes had to work on the weekend.   3. I never planned to take art courses at the college.   4. Do you often work at the new plant in the suburbs?   5. Martin always renews his subscription to this magazine.   6. We usually drink coffee with breakfast.   7. Did your parents always live in Europe? 8. My sister and I often baked a cake or cookies.   9. Jim and Ellen seldom went to a dance.   10. Have you never thought of becoming a doctor?

10·6   *Sample answers are provided.*   1. George was in a highly emotional state.   2. What you suggest is totally irrelevant.   3. I feel I can recommend you highly to my manager.   4. Mr. Jones spoke immensely proudly of his gifted daughter.   5. The weekend sale was hugely successful.   6. The women wept profoundly.   7. You behaved really stubbornly.   8. You have a really stubborn nature   9. These claims are entirely false.   10. Your statement is only partially true.

10·7   *Sample answers are provided.*   1. a. I studied there for an hour. b. A stork was nesting on the roof.   2. a. They played outside in the cold. b. They bought the house next door.   3. a. We sat anywhere there was a free seat. b. The portrait hung over the mantle.   4. a. Why did you sleep upstairs? b. The mouse had a home in a small box.   5. a. The miners worked underground for ten hours. b. A strange man lived beyond the river in the hills.   6. a. I think the museum is somewhere in that direction. b. The girls spread out a blanket under a leafy tree.

10·8   1. a. Surely, you don't believe his story. b. You surely don't believe his story.   2. a. Undoubtedly, the man is a genius. b. The man undoubtedly is a genius.   3. a. Personally, I feel I can place my trust in this woman. b. I personally feel I can place my trust in this woman.   4. a. Presumably, Mr. Lee has a wonderful new job in Boston. b. Mr. Lee presumably has a wonderful new job in Boston.   5. a. Cleverly, Daniel found a seat next to the pretty girl from Korea. b. Daniel cleverly found a seat next to the pretty girl from Korea.

10·9   *Sample answers are provided.*   1. Clearly, they usually don't care what anyone thinks.   2. Foolishly, he left on a hike last week during a storm.   3. Bravely, they entered the very gloomy cemetery. 4. Fortunately, I sometimes have a brief moment of brilliance.   5. Personally, I think you're a really nice person.   6. a. I quickly ran to the window and saw Bill. b. Fortunately, I ran to the window and saw Bill. c. I ran to the window and suddenly saw Bill.   7. a. Wisely, Juanita destroyed the strange object. b. Juanita immediately destroyed the strange object. c. Juanita destroyed the very strange object.   8. a. After she fainted, they carried her into the living room. b. They carefully carried her into the living room. c. They carried her into the living room around five o'clock.   9. a. Presumably, the old men sat around the little table. b. The extremely old men sat around the little table. c. The old men sat silently around the little table. 10. a. Her left leg is seriously broken. b. Her left leg is once again broken. c. Her left leg is broken in two places.

11   Contractions

11.1   1. You've   2. I'm   3. He'd   4. They're   5. It's   6. She'll   7. Who's   8. He's   9. We've 10. I'll   11. She's   12. Who'd   13. You're   14. They've   15. It's

11.2   1. mustn't   2. can't   3. won't   4. couldn't   5. aren't 6. Didn't   7. wasn't   8. don't   9. Isn't 10. shouldn't

11.3   Sample Answers:
  1. He hasn't left for work yet.
  2. You mustn't do that.
  3. I shouldn't help you.
  4. You needn't be so rude.
  5. Weren't you at the game yesterday?
  6. I've been here a long time.
  7. He'll help us.

8. They're very good friends.
9. You'd like my brother.
10. She's quite ill again.

12 Plurals

12.1   1. houses   2. wives   3. oxen   4. foxes   5. teeth   6. mice   7. fezzes   8. persons/people
9. candies   10. vetoes   11. deer   12. factories   13. leaves   14. universities   15. juries

12.2   1. The boys are chasing the little mice.
2. His brothers are putting the pots in the boxes.
3. Do the teachers know the men?
4. The heroes of the stories were children.
5. My friends want to buy the knives, spoons, and dishes.
6. Geese are flying over the fields.
7. The clumsy persons/people hurt my feet.
8. The poor women have broken teeth.
9. We saw wild oxen in the zoos.
10. The ugly witches wanted the trained wolves.

13 Punctuation

13.1   1. She took a book from the shelf and began to read.
2. Do you like living in California?
3. She asked me if I know her brother.
4. Sit down and make yourself comfortable.
5. Shut up!
6. How many years were you in the army?
7. I can't believe it's storming again! OR.
8. When did they arrive?
9. Watch out!
10. Her little brother is about eight years old.

13.2   1. Ms. Muti, please have a seat in my office.
2. She bought chicken, ham, bread, and butter.
3. By the way, your mother called about an hour ago.
4. Paul was born on May 2, 1989, and Caroline was born on June 5, 1989.
5. No, you may not go to the movies with Rich!
6. Well, that was an interesting discussion.
7. The men sat on one side, and the women sat on the other.
8. Oh, the dress, hat, and gloves look beautiful on you, Jane.
9. It happened on April 5, 1999.
10. Yes, I have a suitcase and flight bag with me.

13.3   1. There are some things you need for this recipe: sugar, salt, and flour.
2. She understood the meaning of the story: Thou shalt not kill.
3. Peter is an excellent swimmer; he coaches a team at our pool.
4. This document is important; it will prove his innocence.
5. Add these names to the list: Irena, Helen, Jaime, and Grace.

13.4   1. She asked, "Why do you spend so much money?"
2. I learned that from "Tips for Dining Out" in a restaurant magazine.
3. Rafael said, "Elena's grandfather is very ill."
4. "This is going to be a big problem," he said sadly.
5. Kurt will say, "I already read 'The Ransom of Red Chief' in school."

13.5   1. The geese's eggs are well hidden.
2. She can't understand you.
3. Is Mr. Hancock's daughter still in college?
4. The two girls' performance was very bad.
5. Ms. Yonan's aunt still lives in Mexico.
6. She met several M.D.'s at the party.

7. Do you know Mr. Richards?
8. The women's purses were all stolen.
9. He won't join the other Ph.D.'s in their discussion.
10. It isn't right to take another man's possessions.

13.6
1. Blake, will you please try to understand my problem?
2. They went to England, Wales, and Scotland.
3. Someone stole my money! **OR.**
4. She asked, "When is the train supposed to arrive?"
5. Mr. Wilson's son wants to buy a house in Wisconsin.
6. I have the following documents:a will, a passport, and a visa.
7. Grandmother died September 11, 1999.
8. Jack is a pilot;he flies around the world.
9. Well,I can't believe you came home on time.
10. Are you planning another vacation?

13·7
1. The city council requested that Gov. Madison allocate more funds to the development of children's playgrounds.
2. Richard told his parents, "I enjoy having dinner before eight o'clock, because it gives me enough time to finish my homework before going to sleep."
3. Meet them at Whole Foods for breakfast.
4. Nathan said to his professor, "I can't be done with my paper by Monday."
5. I thanked Mrs. Bronco for giving us a ride to school this morning.
6. Sgt. Pepper was called to the conference room for an important membership meeting.

13·8
1. *The comma is used to separate the dependent clause from the main clause.*
2. *Commas are used to separate the elements of the address and to separate the date from the year.*
3. *The comma is used to separate the two independent clauses.*
4. *The comma is used to separate large numbers into smaller groups of digits.*
5. *The comma is used to separate the interrupting words* as promised *from the rest of the sentence.*
6. *The comma is used to separate the persons addressed from the rest of the sentence.*
7. *The comma is used to separate items in a series.*

13·9
1. Taylor asked, "How are we supposed to cook this with no oven?"
2. She packed two blouses, a black skirt, and a new business suit.
3. According to the U.S. Census Bureau, the world population reached 6,500,000,000 on February 25, 2006.
4. Dear Mrs. Dimple,
5. The Persian Gulf War officially ended on February 28, 1991.
6. They were so excited by the soccer game, which went into three overtimes, that they hardly noticed the afternoon go by.
7. Marie, Catherine, and Chris are all going to the theater together.
8. IBM, not Apple, will build a fast computer.
9. If you've never been to the craft show, there will be selected sales and bargain bins.
10. She will be participating, won't she?
11. Yes, I think there is enough time for you to pick it up and get back home before dinner.
12. If I could get a nickel for every time he lies, I would be a billionaire.
13. He had intended to stay home, but he decided instead to go running.

13·10
1. The computers at my job have large monitors, loud speakers, CD burners, DVD players, and all sorts of other useful hardware; are equipped with the most recent software; and have the most sophisticated firewall.
2. Peter was amazed by the talent of the opposing team's poetry skills; at the same time, he knew his team could win the poetry contest.
3. Greg was the first to run out of the burning house; however, Elizabeth was the one who made it to a pay phone to call the fire department.
4. Each of us had enough time to get in the hotel's swimming pool; nevertheless, we were all there on business.
5. There are moments when one needs to think about a situation calmly and for a long time; likewise, there are moments when one needs to make decisions quickly and instinctively.
6. Gina said, "Let's work as a group"; Peter said, "We should work individually instead"; and Andrew said, "Let's split the team, and while some can work as a group, others can work individually."
7. Karen has been painting the kitchen for three hours; all the while, she has been cooking and playing with the dogs.

13·11
1. She told me what her favorite colors were: blue, red, and light olive green.
2. Dear Madam President:
3. It is 5:30 A.M.; why are you calling me so early?
4. There are three main ingredients in a cake: sugar, flour, and eggs.
5. It was time for the lawyer to make his closing statement: "My client is an honest man, a hardworking man, a good husband, and he should not be sitting in this court today."
6. Nixon said: "Looting and pillaging have nothing to do with civil rights. Starting riots to protest unfair treatment by the state is not the best of solutions."
7. John has five trophies on his bookshelf: Four of them are from basketball tournaments.
8. The professor made an interesting statement during class: "We have not yet addressed the topic of social revolutions, which is a key component of our present argument."

13·12
1. Are you serious?
2. Get out of here now!
3. What do you think of the president's decision to go to war? his views on foreign policy? his thoughts on the economy?
4. Quickly! What are you waiting for?
5. Are you in a hurry?
6. When were you going to tell me?
7. Super!
8. That's so cool!
9. Do you think the corporation will apologize for unjustly firing those employees? taking away their retirement? not providing them with a severance package?
10. Are you out of your mind!

13·13
1. *The sentence refers to each person's painting methods, so 's is added to each name.*
2. Cassettes *is plural, not possessive, so it has no apostrophe.*
3. It's *has an apostrophe, because it is the contraction of* it is. Its walk *has no apostrophe, because* its *is possessive, referring to the dog's walk.*
4. The 1990s *is plural, not possessive, so it has no apostrophe.*
5. The Doors *is plural and possessive, so it has an apostrophe.*
6. *Because the two individuals own the car as a couple, 's is added to the second person's name only.*

13·14
1. The sergeant's boots were always the shiniest of all.
2. She really likes that about the '80s.
3. A doctor's quick intervention can save a life.
4. There are times when the UN's presence has prevented armed conflict.
5. Who's winning today?
6. X
7. X
8. Natalie's new bicycle is red and yellow.
9. The Cutlips' cat wandered into our garage this morning.
10. Her mother's and father's wills were drafted by the lawyer.

13·15
1. I met a woman who said she could make "magic potions."
2. From what I hear, Joseph said the turning point in the novel is when Carlito tells his cousin, "You should have never worked with Francisco in the first place; he's not to be trusted."
3. She read "The Palm-Tree" and was very moved by the poem.
4. What do you think of John Coltrane's tune "My Favorite Things"?
5. The morning newspaper mentioned that there might be "snow tonight with a chance of hail and strong winds."
6. His father asked him, "What would you like to do this summer, work or travel?"
7. As Patrick walked away, she hesitated and then screamed, "Will you go out with me?"
8. X (*Book titles are italicized.*)
9. We analyzed the play *The Flies* by Jean-Paul Sartre and his famous essay "Americans and Their Myths." (*Titles of plays are italicized.*)
10. The song "Organ Donor" is best qualified as "groundbreaking."
11. The photographer encouraged the model by telling her, "You're doing really well, but I want you to relax a little more. When the camera is pointed at you, just imagine someone is saying to you, 'You're the only one that can do this,' and I want you to believe it!"

13·16
1. Eric could not figure out how to get out of the maze—how silly and useless he felt!
2. The touchdown scored by the Patriots was an 83-yard play.
3. They were once considered wishy-washy.

4. Carla was about to close the front door and thought to herself—do I have everything I need in the bag?
5. The tight-lipped receptionist told the reporters nothing.
6. She detests animal testing, so she never buys Yves Saint-Laurent products.
7. Thirty-two of the 52 figure skaters missed at least one of their jumps.
8. The Security Council voted against three crucial resolutions—an armed attack, a forced embargo, and unified retaliation.

13·17
1. *The Skibby Chronicle* [published anonymously in the 1530s but now believed to be the work of Poul Helgesen] describes Danish history from 1047 to 1534.
2. As members of the book club, we had to read *The Stranger* (Albert Camus [1913–1960]) and discuss the novelist's concept of the absurd.
3. According to historical accounts, the first bridge over the Chattahoochee River there [Columbus, Georgia] was built by John Godwin in 1832–33.
4. They were told there was a heavy load of work that they would have to deal with during the semester: They would have to (1) take two three-hour exams, (2) read 13 books, and (3) write a 50-page essay.
5. Thomas Hart Benton (1888–1975) finished his famous *Indiana Murals* in 1932.
6. Some scholars argue that Michelangelo (noted Italian painter and inventor [1475–1564]) was the quintessential Renaissance man.

14 Infinitives and gerunds

14.1
1. adverb   2. noun   3. adjective   4. adverb   5. noun

14.2
1. adjective   2. verb   3. adjective   4. noun   5. noun   6. noun   7. adjective   8. verb
9. noun   10. noun

14.3
1. having   2. being surprised   3. having mentioned   4. trying   5. having been invited   6. eating
7. having been chosen   8. reviewing   9. having been   10. being treated   11. stopping   12. being given   13. playing   14. damaging   15. being introduced

14.4 The verbs and possible gerunds are provided. Other parts of the sentence may vary.
1. I **enjoy visiting** my relatives.
2. I **have avoided writing** letters.
3. I **dislike doing** chores on the weekend.
4. I **liked being told** the story about the three little pigs.
5. I **miss seeing** my friend Judy.

14.5
1. to be working   2. to pay   3. to have earned   4. to have fainted   5. to be hired   6. to help
7. to have been leaked   8. to be networking   9. to have received   10. to be given   11. to meet
12. to stay   13. to turn in   14. to move   15. to close

14.6 The verbs and infinitives are provided. Other parts of the sentence may vary.
1. I **plan to go** to the park.
2. I **intend to be** right here.
3. I **need to buy** a new notebook.
4. I **want to have** a pizza.
5. I **expect to study** chemistry.

14·7
1. him to exercise   2. us to attend   3. my sister to ride   4. me to turn   5. people to touch
6. Brent and me to be   7. local artists to hang   8. the protesters to leave   9. me to rethink
10. employers to provide   11. Robyn to major   12. everyone to conserve

14.8
1. infinitive: to rain   no significant change in meaning
2. infinitive: to bring   memory to perform action
3. gerund: quitting   memory of action
4. infinitive: to talk   no significant change in meaning
5. gerund: going   vivid depiction
6. infinitive: to clean up   hypothetical occurrence
7. gerund: returning   memory of action
8. gerund: throwing   vivid depiction
9. infinitive: to make   no significant change in meaning
10. infinitive: to take   potential occurrence

14·9 *Answers may vary.*
1. drawing, practicing, sleeping late, juggling
2. hunting, kayaking, skiing, weightlifting

15 Relative pronouns

15.1
1. I found the money that belonged to Jack.
2. She has a good memory that always serves her well.
3. This is the woman that I told you about.
4. I have a document that proves my innocence.
5. They want to visit the country that Marsha comes from.
6. This is the doctor who saved my life.
7. Do you know the musician whom I met in Hawaii?
8. She likes the gentleman whom I was telling her about. OR She likes the gentleman about whom I was telling her.
9. I visited the sisters whose father had recently died.
10. Jerod noticed the stranger at whom all the neighbors were staring. OR Jerod noticed the stranger whom all the neighbors were staring at.
11. Pablo threw away the picture which the boys had found.
12. I live in the house in which my grandfather was born.
13. He bought a suit which is navy blue.
14. Anna has a new hat which I like very much.
15. He wanted to paint the bench on which a man was sitting. OR He wanted to paint the bench which a man was sitting on.

15.2 Sample Answers:
1. ... about whom they wrote so much.
2. ... that is located in Asia.
3. ... whom you invited.
4. ... in which I placed the eggs?
5. ... that was so funny.
6. ... whom you told me about.
7. ... whose book was published.
8. ... whom my uncle had worked for.
9. ... blouse that has dark purple buttons.
10. ... whose passports were lost.

15.3
1. He was in the city I visited last year.
2. Did you finally meet the woman I was telling you about?
3. Ron sold the house he was born in.
4. My father lost the checkbook he kept his credit card in.
5. Did you find the ball I threw over the fence?
6. That's the pretty girl I wrote this poem for.
7. I don't know the people he gave the flowers to.
8. The hat the magician pulled a white rabbit from was empty.
9. She forgot the tickets she had placed next to her briefcase.
10. They live in a tiny village we finally located on a map.

15.4
1. He found a puppy **that** needed a home.
2. Where did you put the groceries **that** I bought at the supermarket?
3. That's my car **that** has the convertible top.
4. There's the scientist **that** I told you about.
5. Do you know the woman **whose** son is serving in the army?
6. They hired the lawyer **that** they got the best deal from.
7. I need the map **that** has Cook County on it.
8. I was introduced to the girl **that** John was dancing with.
9. Don't spend the money **that** I put on the dresser.
10. Do you know the song **that** I'm playing on the piano?

15.5
1. I lost the book I got from Maria last week.
2. We like the dress, which was probably designed in Paris. (no change)
3. He read a sentence he can't understand at all.
4. I have all the documents I was speaking of.
5. Will you give me some money I can use to buy new underwear?
6. The champion, who is a native of Mexico, is touring the United States. (no change)
7. He bought a used car that had been in an accident. (no change)

8. Maria wants to use the umbrella Mom bought last week.
9. Do you understand the words I wrote on this sheet of paper?
10. I like Uncle Henry, from whom I received a beautiful gift. (no change)

15.6 Sample Answers:
1. Please show me the books **that you have for sale**.
2. I met the actor **who studied in Berlin**.
3. He bought a watch that **keeps perfect time**.
4. The boss, who **graduated from Harvard**, is rather nice.
5. Where are the gifts **that you received from Martha**?
6. This car, which **was recently repainted**, is from Germany.
7. I have the DVD **that came out just last month**.

16   Reflexive pronouns

16.1
1. You found yourself in a difficult situation./He found himself in a difficult situation./She found herself in a difficult situation./We found ourselves in a difficult situation./They found themselves in a difficult situation./Amy found herself in a difficult situation.
2. I enjoyed myself at the party./You enjoyed yourselves at the party./He enjoyed himself at the party./She enjoyed herself at the party./They enjoyed themselves at the party./The boys enjoyed themselves at the party.
3. I am going to be very proud of myself./My friends are going to be very proud of themselves./Mother is going to be very proud of herself./They are going to be very proud of themselves./We are going to be very proud of ourselves./Abdul and Ricky are going to be very proud of themselves.
4. You just couldn't help yourselves./He just couldn't help himself./She just couldn't help herself./We just couldn't help ourselves./They just couldn't help themselves./The men just couldn't help themselves.

16.2
1. Jerry liked himself in the new suit.
2. They busied themselves with several different tasks.
3. We were very proud of ourselves.
4. She is buying herself a few new outfits.
5. The children hurt themselves.
6. I have to ask myself what to do now.
7. The young woman told herself not to give in.
8. He wants to find himself something nice to wear.
9. You've harmed no one but yourself (yourselves).
10. The lizard hid itself under a rock.

16.3
1. She sometimes writes stories about **herself**.
2. We really enjoyed **ourselves** very much.
3. My uncle cut **himself** with a sharp knife.
4. The ugly dragon hid **itself** behind a pile of stones.
5. I described **myself** honestly.
6. Would you recommend **yourself** for the job?
7. The girls saw **themselves** in the still water of the pond.
8. He didn't recognize **himself** in his new suit of clothes.
9. A young woman was admiring **herself** in the store window.
10. Maria and Juan! You've hurt **yourselves** again! Shame on you!

16.4
1. John believes himself to be innocent.
   a. We believe ourselves to be innocent.
   b. I believe myself to be innocent.
   c. She believes herself to be innocent.
   d. You believe yourselves to be innocent.
2. She considers herself lucky.
   a. They consider themselves lucky.
   b. I consider myself lucky.
   c. You consider yourself lucky.
   d. He considers himself lucky.

16.5
1. My father and mother sit next to one another.
2. The soprano and the tenor harmonize with one another.
3. The boys and the girls danced with each other.

4. My boss and the manager spoke about each other.
5. St. Paul and Minneapolis are located near one another.
6. Barbara and Juan kissed one another.
7. The lioness and the three cubs slept near one another.
8. You and I respect each other.
9. James and Maria sang for each other.
10. They like one another's voices.

16.6 Sample Answers:
1. (one another)
   a. They love one another.
   b. The boys and girls wouldn't play with one another.
   c. Bob and Jim fought one another after school.
2. (each other)
   a. We stared at each other.
   b. Tom and I often helped each other.
   c. They cared for each other's dogs.

17 Possession

17.1
1. the storm's center
2. the victims' condition
3. my classmates' behavior
4. the lab's equipment
5. each man's efforts
6. the animals' many illnesses
7. the young lawyer's documents
8. the roses' scent
9. the little bear cub's mother
10. the town's northern border

17.2
1. The car on the corner is mine.
2. Was this yours?
3. The invading soldier searched theirs.
4. Did Dee find hers?
5. Ours have lived in Brazil for a long time.
6. His is fair with everyone.
7. These problems are entirely his.
8. I need yours.
9. Mine is going to raise the rent.
10. Theirs made no sense.

17.3
1. The women want to visit their relatives in Europe.
2. She takes her children for a long walk.
3. Do you have your tools in the truck?
4. I sent my address and telephone number to the office.
5. We want ours.
6. The picture fell out of its frame.
7. They spend their time in Canada.
8. Are you selling yours?
9. I left some papers in my apartment.
10. Jose found his wallet under the bed.

17.4 1. your   2. his   3. his   4. theirs   5. mine   6. her   7. ours   8. His   9. its   10. my

17.5
1. **Her** brother goes to college.
2. Do you know **his** niece?
3. **Its** hole was behind a large rock.
4. **Their** chirping woke me up early.
5. She loved **her** solo.
6. I had to hold **her** purse.
7. **Her** piglets slept in a cool pile of mud.
8. Did you borrow **her** skis?

9. **Their** demands were too much for the company.
10. Where is **their** bed going to be?

17.6
1. I wanted to dance with **her** older sister.
2. Will you help me carry **my** books up to the second floor?
3. They said **your** father had been a colonel in the army.
4. **Our** tent was put up near a bend in the river.
5. Michael wanted to spend time at **our** campsite.
6. I still haven't met **their** parents.
7. **Whose** sailboat is that out on the lake?
8. I just can't get interested in **his** novels.
9. **Its** roof has been replaced with cedar shingles.
10. Ms. Garcia wanted to borrow **our** garden hose.

18 Prepositions

18.1
1. The man next to him is a senator.
2. Did they leave after it?
3. Evan was dancing with her.
4. Why did you leave the house without it?
5. Are there washers and dryers in them?
6. Juan had some nice wine for them.
7. The man with her is her new boyfriend.
8. A large bear was coming toward him.
9. The letter from them made me very happy.
10. In spite of all of them, Tonya went on smiling.

18.2
1. is 2. women 3. needs 4. was 5. need 6. has 7. makes 8. need
9. don't 10. captures

18·3
1. instead of, truck
2. in, pool; for, dinner
3. above, hills
4. about, book
5. into, room; next to, Helen
6. of, one
7. from, him; in, Iraq
8. Contrary to, opinion
9. among, students; from, department
10. with, table; by, window

18·4 *Answers may vary.*
1. her lovely garden
2. their sister
3. a chocolate éclair and a banana split
4. noon, sundown
5. the old monastery
6. the threat of a storm
7. your poor showing on the exam
8. the visitors to the museum
9. origami
10. the electrical storm

18·5
1. We spent a lot of time there.
2. They have been there for over three years.
3. In it, I found my sister's diary.
4. City Hall has been located here for years.
5. What are you hiding in them?
6. Do you really like its smell?
7. Their gowns looked like flour sacks.
8. His OR Her symphony was recently found.
9. They said her poems are their favorites.
10. Its political goals are slowly changing.

18·6   *Answers may vary.*
1. next to a school for the blind
2. beneath the first floor of a hotel
3. on the outskirts of Paris
4. of the state of Indiana
5. in the closet of his bedroom

18.7
1. A tiny rabbit was hiding **under** a bush.
2. Please don't sit **next to** me.
3. We saw several baby birds **in** a nest in that tree.
4. There was nothing **below** the plane but empty space.
5. Father stays **at** the factory until 5:00 p.m.
6. An angry man stood directly **in the middle of** us.
7. John stayed **beside** me the entire time.
8. I saw Maria **among** the many people at the party.
9. There was a huge bug sitting **on** my bed!
10. I saw a stranger crouching **between** my car and the truck.

18.8   Sample Answers:
1. I saw a jet flying above **the Rocky Mountains**.
2. Someone was hiding under **a large bush**.
3. Are you familiar with **the new family down the block**?
4. My sisters both work at **the new mall**.
5. The frightened kitten hid in **an old shoe box**.
6. Someone stood behind **the door and listened**.
7. Who was sitting among **the honored guests at the conference**?
8. There's nothing in front of **the broken-down SUV**.
9. Gray clouds hovered over **the dark forest**.
10. Have a seat next to **my mother-in-law**.
11. He found his keys on **the backseat of the car**.
12. I found a couple seats beside **the manager of the team**.
13. Let's set up our camp near **the bank of the river**.
14. We used to live between **the Miller family and old Mrs. Jones**.
15. A puppy sat lazily in the middle of **the freshly painted floor**.

18.9   Sample Answers:
1. We were on the train for over five hours.
2. I spend much too much time at work.
3. There was a mouse hiding behind the dresser.
4. Please take a seat next to her.
5. The elderly man is in the hospital again.
6. I like dancing with Maria.
7. I stood between them and stopped the fight.
8. An eagle was gliding over the mountains.
9. An angry bear stood up in front of us.
10. Grandfather slept under a palm tree.

18.10
1. The children ran **toward** the gate.
2. The young couple strolled **along** the beach.
3. The ball rolled **off** the table.
4. Is Thomas already **at** work?
5. I was hurrying **to** my desk.
6. Someone came running **into** the room.
7. We slowly drove **by** their house.
8. Ms. Brown came **from** England last year.
9. The poor girl fell **out of** bed.
10. I dropped the tools **into** the box.

18.11   Sample Answers:
1. The cattle were heading toward **a distant watering hole**.
2. Someone came out of **a dark corner of the room**.
3. Why were you going into **my private office**?
4. My family frequently travels to **the countryside of Mexico**.
5. Do you come from **Canada or the United States**?

6. The carpenter fell off **the steep roof**.
7. The burglar quietly climbed onto **the porch and reached for the window**.
8. Maria wants to come into **the dining room for a moment**.
9. The men were walking along **one of the beams of the building**.
10. He came at **his frightened victim** with a knife.
11. She drove by **our house** without stopping.
12. What time did you come home from **the rock concert?**
13. We're planning on traveling to **South America next year**.
14. The cat jumped into **my sister's lap**.
15. The woman moved cautiously toward **the open door**.

18.12   Sample Answers:
1. A little boy wandered along the shore.
2. The retired teacher drove by the school again.
3. She ran from the yard shouting.
4. Michael bolted into the living room and fell on the floor.
5. I threw a magazine onto the shelf.
6. The puppy fell off the bed.
7. The young driver slowly pulled out of the garage.
8. We've never traveled to the mountains.
9. The rabbit hopped toward the wall.
10. She was afraid of going into a darkened room.

18.13   Sample Answers:
1. They left the theater **before** the end of the film.
2. I should be home **by** ten o'clock.
3. She only works **from** nine to three.
4. We always have a picnic **on** the Fourth of July.
5. Do you always eat lunch **at** noon?
6. Bill has been sad **since** his fortieth birthday.
7. Aunt Jane came to town **for** Carmen's big party.
8. We do a lot of shopping **during** the holiday season.
9. It's coldest here from December **to** February.
10. I'm afraid that we'll have to wait **until** tomorrow.

18.14   Sample Answers:
1. The children were very noisy during **the long meeting**.
2. We can expect Jim here for **your birthday party**.
3. It's very rainy from May to **August**.
4. I haven't seen you since **you were a little girl**.
5. Can you stay with me until **I finish this report?**
6. Tom works hard **from** morning to night.
7. They wanted to leave work before **their shift ended**.
8. The doctor gave him a checkup after **a long illness**.
9. Try to get here by **dusk**.
10. His family usually stays at the lake in **the summer months**.
11. The twins were born on **September fifth**.
12. Dark shadows covered the ground at **daybreak**.
13. They were living in Europe during **their youth**.
14. He's had a job in the city since **he came back from Mexico**.
15. They want to start the marathon by **twelve thirty**.

18.15   Sample Answers:
1. Her shift is from noon until midnight.
2. I hope to graduate by June.
3. We've been planting shrubs since the end of winter.
4. Tom returns home in spring.
5. The parade was on May tenth.
6. Quiet hours begin after 11:00 p.m.
7. I hope to finish the course before next year.
8. He's had many different jobs during his lifetime.
9. Uncle James got home after dark.
10. We usually sit on the porch at sunset.

18.16
1. Some men stood **in front of** the store.
2. **According to** the forecast, it's going to rain today.
3. **In reference to** his remark, I just said, "Shame."
4. We stayed home **because of** the power outage.
5. Do you still live **in back of** the shop?
6. There **ahead of** us stood a large bison.
7. He quickly drove **out of** the driveway.
8. I was too nervous to walk **up to** the president.
9. It happened **on account of** your carelessness!
10. She can't comment **in regard to** that matter.

18.17 Sample Answers:
1. Please write a report in reference to **the latest sales figures**.
2. In spite of **his odd behavior**, she continued to love him.
3. In regard to **recent events**, I have a statement to make.
4. I bought a compact car instead of **a large SUV**.
5. Who's waiting in front of **that newsstand?**
6. The man was arrested on account of **several unpaid tickets**.
7. There were several tables and chairs in back of **the conference room**.
8. A strange smell came out of **the trash barrel**.
9. I sent her some flowers by way of **thanks for a great evening**.
10. A baby rabbit hopped up to **my foot and sniffed**.
11. You can get to the top of the mountain by means of **the aerial tramway**.
12. With respect to **our company's low morale**, some changes have to be made.
13. Apart from **two senior managers**, everyone else will be fired.
14. According to **the latest weather report**, we're in a heat wave.
15. I could see a winding road ahead of **us in the hills**.

18.18 Sample Answers:
1. Fortunately the bus arrived ahead of time.
2. She cancelled the trip because of an illness.
3. The strikers marched in front of the factory.
4. I have some comments in reference to your last report.
5. I paid with cash instead of a check.
6. A small plane flew out of the clouds.
7. With respect to his last wishes, a memorial service will be held tomorrow.
8. There will be a drought according to the almanac.
9. Apart from a few friends in Chicago, he knows no one in Illinois.
10. Travel is easiest by means of the subway.
11. You'll find a wheelbarrow in back of the garage.
12. In spite of the darkness, the carpenter continued his work.
13. He was only respected on account of his riches.
14. The hikers came up to the river.
15. I have something to say in regard to these lies.

18.19
1. The strange woman was an **undercover** agent.
2. The newly elected governor is an **upstanding** person.
3. She **intoned** her voice with the anger she felt.
4. They decided to go **uptown** for dinner.
5. Did you follow our club's **bylaws?**
6. Her views just aren't **up-to-date**.
7. The hikers followed the creek **up-country**.
8. The old man didn't want to **outlive** his wife.
9. My aunt **underwent** a serious operation last year.
10. His look was **downcast** and his face quite sad.

18.20 Sample Answers:
1. The new members refused to follow the bylaws **of our organization**.
2. Out in the street there was an uproar over **a minor traffic accident**.
3. While swimming underwater, he saw **the outline of a boat**.
4. They were flying coach class but wanted to upgrade **to business class**.
5. An underage girl came into **the little tavern**.
6. The brothers were always trying to outdo **one another**.

7. The road uphill was **too steep for our little car**.
8. There was a sudden outbreak of **measles in our area**.
9. You need a technician to install **such complicated equipment**.
10. The downhearted young man began to **regret his decision to live alone**.
11. The couple lives downstairs from **a retired opera singer**.
12. The underclassmen in **our high school** behaved badly.
13. I didn't mean to upset **her relatives**.
14. The undercover agent hid **a package in a hollow tree trunk**.
15. Within hours there was a total downfall of **morale among the workers**.

18.21 Sample Answers:
1. The kids like playing outdoors.
2. This road leads to a bypass.
3. Dad intoned his words like a religious chant.
4. That ingrown toenail looks infected.
5. By and large, she's quite a nice person.
6. I have some further insight into the affair.
7. His underarms were wet with perspiration.
8. I bought some new underwear.
9. He drew up an outline for the manuscript.
10. The police are there to uphold the law.
11. There are several villages farther inland.
12. You have to go uptown to find a large bank.
13. The government fell because of an upheaval of the population.
14. I can't undergo another operation.
15. She's the most upstanding person in the legislature.

18.22
1. We'll need to put in a lot of time **considering** this problem.
2. I had a lot to tell **concerning** the crimes he had committed.
3. I wanted to speak to her **regarding** our future together.
4. Maria passed every test **excluding** the one in math.
5. The picnic will go on as planned **following** the rainstorm.

18.23 Sample Answers:
1. I had the reports that were concerning your work here. He spoke for several minutes concerning the company's future.
2. I've been considering all your suggestions. He did a good job considering his lack of skill.
3. This club has been excluding women for years. He visited all the dealerships excluding the ones that sell foreign cars.
4. Someone is following us! He took a long shower following the two-hour workout.

18.24 Sample Answers:
1. The pup fell over backward. He walked backward toward the door.
2. When I looked downward, I saw the footprints. The eagle swooped downward and targeted a rabbit.
3. Tomorrow we're homeward bound. The tourists eagerly headed homeward.
4. She looked inward for a reason for her behavior. Inwardly, he knew he couldn't believe the boy.
5. With a glance upward, he saw the missing package on a shelf. With an upward thrust, he knocked the man off his feet.
6. The lions moved windward so as not to leave a scent. Sailing vessels have difficulty sailing windward.
7. The refugees hiked eastward. An eastward wind meant that a storm was coming.

19 More about prepositions

19.1
1. I began to beg my father **for** more money.
2. She was being followed **by** a strange man.
3. Juanita also **belongs to** our club now.
4. Don't you want to **ask** for a little help?
5. I never stop worrying **about** my daughter.
6. I really care **for** her. I'm in love.
7. Tom has absolutely no interest **in** jazz.
8. It's difficult for them to forget **about** the war.
9. I know I can **rely** on your honesty.
10. I **long** for a good night's sleep.

11. She was deeply hurt **by** his insults.
12. The child is hardly capable **of** hurting anyone.
13. I'll **wait** for you in front of the theater.
14. You shouldn't be so generous **with** us.
15. Are you looking forward **to** the party?

19.2   Sample Answers:
1. He became alarmed by **the patient's condition**.
2. You shouldn't worry about **unimportant things**.
3. These women are very interested in **computer science**.
4. I'm going to wish for **a brand new car**.
5. Are you absolutely sure of **the doctor's diagnosis?**
6. The immigration officer walked up to **the last applicant in line**.
7. Does this jacket belong to **anyone here?**
8. You're always thinking about **other people**.
9. How can I depend on **a man like Jim?**
10. The wounded soldier was pleading for **release from his pain**.
11. Never forget about **what happened to me**.
12. The barn was blown down by **a sudden northern gale**.
13. We need a guard to watch over **the shipment that just came in**.
14. You should listen to **your elders**.
15. A large animal was looking at **me from out of the brush**.

19.3   1. The young man came up to me with a gift in his hand.
2. The orator **spoke about** the importance of saving money.
3. I think this umbrella **belonged** to Aunt Norma.
4. I **forgot about** the exam! I'm going to fail for sure!
5. If you needed anything, you always **depended (relied) on** me.
6. A police officer **cared for** the injured pedestrian.
7. Where were you? I **waited for** you for two hours!
8. Dad **worried about** me, but I knew how to take care of myself.
9. The boys **looked for** the missing child for several hours.
10. Jim **begged (pleaded) for** an extra ten dollars but got nothing.

19.4   Sample Answers:
1. You're capable of better work than this.
2. She was looking for her keys.
3. The tree was struck by lightning.
4. I have no interest in that man.
5. It's silly to wish for things.
6. The mother made a plea for her son's life.
7. I'm sure of what I saw.
8. You know you can rely upon my word.
9. The pup sat up and begged for the bone.
10. Anita is looking forward to her date with Jim.
11. I don't care about ancient history.
12. Barbara hoped for a chance to be on the team.
13. The flight attendant looked after the passengers' needs.
14. I dream of becoming a jet pilot.
15. They were motivated by their greed.

19.5   1. It's cold. The heat is probably off.
2. If you ask **around**, you'll get his address.
3. The old woman was **up to** something again.
4. She was too timid to **ask** Juan out.
5. The scientist knew she was **onto** something.
6. My lawyer won't be **in** until noon.
7. Your parents are so up-to-date and **with it**.
8. Why was the TV **on** all night?
9. The detective believed she was up **to no good**.
10. He wants to take a shower but the water is **off** again.

19.6   1. I wanted to know who he was and asked around about him.
2. The jumbo jet was quickly **out of sight**.

3. The burglar was obviously **up to** no good.
4. What time will Professor Gomez **be** in?
5. Did your nephew **ask** my niece out?
6. Having found a clue, they knew they were **onto something**.
7. If the fan **is on**, why is it so hot in here?
8. When he turned to look, her train was already out **of sight**.
9. Use makeup! Color your hair! Try to be **with it**!
10. The dentist is **out (in)** for the day.

19.7
1. Jim came through for me again.
2. Let's get on **with** the meeting.
3. The drowsy woman came **to** very slowly.
4. The children came **upon** a little cottage in the woods.
5. I work all afternoon. I get **off** at 5:00 P.M.
6. Ms. Brown **came up** with a wonderful slogan.
7. Hurry! You're **getting** behind in your work.
8. How can I get **in on** this deal?
9. The two boys got **into it** after school.
10. She got **back at** us for gossiping.

19.8
1. Start the music. Let's get on with the show.
2. I don't want to stay in jail! Please **get** me off!
3. Mr. Brown finally **came up** with our loan.
4. They were arguing over the accident and soon **got into** it.
5. Maybe she'll come **to** if you give her some water.
6. Jim **came upon** an old magazine in the attic.
7. Did Maria get **in on** the stock purchase?
8. We all **got behind** Ms. Brown, and she won the election.
9. The car dealer eventually came through **for** us.
10. I **get off** at six. You can pick me up then.

19.9
1. You run too fast. I can't keep up with you.
2. With one blow, he knocked the man **out**.
3. We have to **keep on** working until we're done.
4. The landlord kicked us **out of** our apartment.
5. Knock **it** off. You're bothering me.
6. The carpenters **knocked down** the wall in just a few minutes.
7. They kicked **off** the parade with a patriotic march.
8. He was shot in the morning. He kicked **off** in the afternoon.
9. What time do you knock **off** work?
10. She's so lonely, yet she still keeps **to herself**.

19.10
1. The coach wanted them to keep on practicing.
2. Careful or you'll knock **out** the window!
3. How can we keep those kids **out of** our yard?
4. You had better knock **it off** before I get really angry.
5. If you keep **to** this road, you'll get there in an hour.
6. They had an argument, and she **kicked** him out.
7. The champ knocked his opponent **down**, but he got up immediately.
8. If you pedal faster, you'll **keep up** with the other cyclists.
9. We'll **kick** off the party with a few drinks.
10. What time do you **knock off** of work?

19.11
1. Put me down for the refreshments committee.
2. The baby is feverish and won't **quiet** down.
3. I need to rest up **from** all this exercise.
4. Carmen **put up with** his lies for many years.
5. You're so hospitable, but don't **put yourself** out.
6. He's so excited, but he needs to quiet **down**.
7. I **rested up** all morning and went to work at noon.
8. She's not sick! She's just putting **on**!
9. It can't be true! Are you **putting** me on?
10. The janitor was **put out by** all the garbage in the hallway.

19.12
1. Why don't you rest up? You've had a long day.
2. You're never satisfied with my work. You always **put** me down.
3. Spend the night here. We can put you **up**.
4. When the class **quiets** down, I'll pass out the new material.
5. I love soccer. Put me **down for** that team.
6. Tom **put on** a dress and a wig for the Halloween party.
7. Anita can't put **up with** his deceit any longer.
8. I think you should rest **up from** that long trip.
9. He wished he could put his roommate **out of** his house.
10. You can put the groceries **down on** that table.

19.13
1. Ms. Brown will take over from Mr. Jones.
2. Let's sit down and talk this problem **over**.
3. I took everything **back from** her apartment.
4. You shouldn't **talk back** to your mother!
5. You're not going to talk me **into** that again.
6. I'll take **down** the curtains and wash them.
7. The shelter **takes in** homeless people.
8. Take **off** your coat and relax.
9. That skirt is long. Let's take it **up**.
10. My brother **took up** with my ex-girlfriend.

19.14
1. A new company took over the factory.
2. His store is **taking on** several new employees.
3. **Talking** back to a teacher is terrible behavior.
4. In the summer the students took off **for** California
5. Your waist is smaller. You should take **in** your pants.
6. I'd like to take you **up on** your offer.
7. Anita **talked** me into going to the dance with her.
8. The reporter took **down** every word I said.
9. You ought to **take back** what you said to her.
10. No one talked it **over** with me.

19.15
1. Grandmother put on an apron.
2. We need to talk **it** over.
3. I can't put up with **your insults**.
4. They'll kick off **the celebration** at ten o'clock.
5. We're going to take in **some boarders**.
6. The drug knocked **her** out.
7. Mr. Johnson took over **our business**.
8. Put **the gun** down and turn around.
9. I'll measure the skirt and you take **it** in.
10. We need to quiet **your mother** down.

19.16 Sample Answers:
1. She knocked the thief down. She knocked down the thief. She knocked him down.
2. Help put the tents up. Help put up the tents. Help put them up.
3. Norma took the company over. Norma took over the company. Norma took it over.
4. The fireman kicked the window out. The fireman kicked out the window. The fireman kicked it out.
5. She puts the baby down for a nap. She puts down the baby for a nap. She puts her down for a nap.
6. Let's take the old carpet up. Let's take up the old carpet. Let's take it up.
7. Can you quiet the kids down? Can you quiet down the kids? Can you quiet them down?
8. Don't knock the vase off. Don't knock off the vase. Don't knock it off.

19.17
1. We've been living in this house since last March.
2. Coach is filled, but I can **upgrade** you to first class.
3. The security guard **watched over** the new shipment of computers.
4. The electricity **has been off** for two days.
5. I often dream **about** my home in Ireland.
6. The frightened dog had been bitten **by** a snake.
7. The Constitution was finally ratified **on** this date.
8. I enjoy it here **in spite of** the bad weather.
9. There's a newspaper boy **at** the front door.
10. We really look **forward to** your next visit.

19.18 Sample Answers:
1. Why do you spend so much time with **such rude people?**
2. Several fans came rushing up to **the rock star**.
3. Who asked for **a Coke and a hamburger?**
4. I usually get off **at half past eight**.
5. I learned not to depend upon **anyone but myself**.
6. They should be in Detroit on **New Year's Day**.
7. The ship docked at **5:00 P.M.**
8. Maria can't seem to forget about **her ex-boyfriend**.
9. The sleek sailboat headed seaward and **then set a course for Bermuda**.
10. The new golf clubs belong to **the boss's wife**.
11. My relatives will return to New York in **two weeks**.
12. I haven't been in Europe since **the fall of 2002**.
13. Did you remain in the United States during **the gas crisis?**
14. According to **the local newspaper**, there's going to be a storm today.
15. Somehow the new employee came up with **a very clever idea**.
16. The embarrassed girl decided to get back at **the boy who played a trick on her**.
17. Our flight arrived ahead of **schedule**.
18. I don't like waiting for **food deliveries**.
19. **The dog's snarling** upset the poor woman.
20. **Lazy cattle were grazing** in the pasture.
21. **The giant dirigible** was soon out of sight.
22. **The captain of the soccer team** wanted to belong to our fraternity.
23. **A disruptive visitor was shown** out of the conference hall.
24. Apart from my own parents, **no one came to see me in the play**.
25. **The horse and carriage clattered** toward the covered bridge.

19.19 Sample Answers:
1. Throw a log onto the fire.
2. We crashed into a tree because of a deer.
3. I don't know what I want to do after college.
4. We were heading homeward when we decided to go to Las Vegas instead.
5. He was making some notes concerning the debate about pollution.
6. Are you interested in botany?
7. Jim likes keeping to himself.
8. Someone was standing at the window and looking in.
9. Don't interrupt me when I'm in the middle of a sentence.
10. He went over the top of the hill and was out of sight.
11. Is my attorney in today?
12. She jumped out of the closet and startled him.
13. I'll have a cheeseburger instead of the pizza.
14. This portrait was painted by Rembrandt.
15. The poor man was down-and-out and had no place to go.

20 Capitalization

20.1
1. John, Cadillac
2. Is, Colonel Brubaker, Governor Dassoff
3. The, March, Buffalo
4. We, Chicago
5. In, Whittier School, St. James Park
6. She, February, E. F. Hutton, New York
7. Ms. Assad, Texas
8. Are, Mr., Mrs. Cermak, Britney
9. Ted, Coke
10. The, The Adventures, Huckleberry Finn, May
11. His, May, Cleveland Memorial Hospital
12. Mia, A.M.
13. Do
14. If, Mayor Yamamoto
15. We, New York Times, Sunday

20.2

1. May tenth, eighteen sixty-five
2. November eleventh, nineteen eighteen
3. July fourth, seventeen seventy-six
4. December twenty-fourth, two thousand
5. January first, nineteen ninety-nine
6. nine A.M.
7. eleven thirty P.M.T
8. six forty-five A.M.
9. seven fifty P.M.
10. eight fifteen A.M.

20·3

1. Teresa Malcolm is president of the Ford Rotary Club.
2. In three weeks, we will be traveling through France, Switzerland, and Spain.
3. The night sky was so clear we could see the entire moon, Venus, and Jupiter.
4. As soon as he got home, Patrick felt like putting on his new Adidas swimsuit.
5. The Second World War lasted nearly six years.
6. The novel we bought at the airport was *The Da Vinci Code*.
7. I visited the Empire State Building when I was in New York.
8. Thelma and John saw the launch of the *USS Enterprise*.
9. The NAACP is a prominent organization based in the United States.
10. They told her, "We don't like the proposal you've written."

20·4

1. Marilyn is the president of the Ladies of Grace at her church.
2. Some restaurants in Los Angeles serve Americanized European food.
3. Members of all faiths gathered on campus to protest, including Christians, Jews, Muslims, and Hindus.
4. "The Red Wheelbarrow" by William Carlos Williams is one of the most profound poems I've read.
5. They came from the Eastern states in search of gold.
6. We read *Of Mice and Men* last week for class.
7. The CIA agent said he often works with FBI investigators, as well as with representatives of the FAA.
8. A speaker from the National Transportation Safety Board gave a presentation on the most common accidents that took place on Interstate 66.

21 Subjunctive mood

21.1

1. She demands Forrest return home by 5:00 P.M.
2. The man suggests you wear a shirt and tie to work.
3. They requested I be a little more helpful.
4. My father demanded we pay for the damage to the car.
5. Did he suggest she come in for an interview?
6. Roger demands that the boy have enough to eat.
7. Did Mother request that her will be read aloud?
8. He has suggested that we be trained for other jobs.
9. Who demanded that the statue be erected on this site?
10. Did he suggest the mayor find a new assistant?

21.2 Sample Answers:

1. . . . she be on time.
2. . . . you stay here tonight.
3. . . . I help him out.
4. . . . he behave himself.
5. . . . he forget about this?

21.3

1. I wish Becca were here today.
2. I wish we were having a big party for Grandmother.
3. I wish he had enough money to buy a condo.
4. I wish my friends had come for a visit.
5. I wish Darnell didn't need an operation.
6. I wish his uncle drove slowly.
7. I wish I could borrow some money from you.
8. I wish the weather were not so rainy.
9. I wish they helped me every day.
10. I wish she wanted to go on vacation with me.

21.4   1. . . . Garrett would ask her out.
2. . . . I would go to the store.
3. . . . he would hear you.
4. . . . I would turn on the heat.
5. . . . he would help me wash the car.
6. . . . it were Erin's birthday.
7. . . . he liked the neighborhood.
8. . . . someone had a soccer ball.
9. . . . I lived in Puerto Rico.
10. . . . the baby were sick.

21.5   1. She would have sold me her bicycle if she had bought a new one.
2. If you had come early, you would have met my cousin.
3. If only Karen had been here.
4. The children would have played in the yard if it had not been raining.
5. If the lawyer had found the document, he would have won this case.
6. If only my mother had been able to walk again.
7. Juanita would have traveled to New York if she had gotten the job.
8. If he had found the wallet, he would have given it to Rick.
9. Jackie would have wanted to come along if he had had more time.
10. If only they had understood the problem.

21.6   1. were, would change
2. checked, would know
3. commuted, would cost
4. had, would go
5. visited, would meet
6. mailed, would receive
7. lowered, would shop
8. earned, would buy
9. exercised, would be
10. were, would tell

21.7   1. had rained, would have canceled
2. had been, would have been
3. had known, would have taken
4. had followed, would have been
5. had studied, would have passed
6. had been, would have received
7. had raised, would have protested
8. had repaired, would have left
9. had revised, would have been
10. had been, would have hired

21.8   *Sample answers are provided.*   1. this plan be rejected   2. give up all her rights   3. remain a matter for the court   4. a committee be formed to look into the situation   5. be changed for your personal needs

21.9   *Sample answers are provided.*   1. If only we found a solution to the problem.   2. If only it weren't true.
3. If only Jim were able to return home for a while.   4. If only the sign weren't seen by so many people.
5. If only I had driven a little faster.   6. If Sarah brought home a pizza, the kids would eat nothing else.
7. If you would permit me to sit with you for a while, I would love to chat about your travels.   8. If you had insisted on my staying longer, I would not have left so early.   9. She would have to agree with you if she understood your motives.   10. I would be grateful if you were a bit kinder to my sister.

22   Comparatives and superlatives

22.1   1. This freight train is moving slower. OR This freight train is moving more slowly.
2. My younger brother is a mathematician.
3. Where is the older man you told me about?
4. Fanny swims better, but she still cannot dive.
5. Hunter's cold is worse today.
6. They have more to do before the end of the day.

7. I think Robbie is more intelligent.
8. The new employee is more careless about his work.
9. She has more friends in the city.
10. This project is more critical to the success of the company.
11. Clarice just can't speak quieter. OR Clarice just can't speak more quietly.
12. We have a bigger house out in the country.
13. Do you think that kind of language is more sinful?
14. The inn is farther down this road.
15. Your friend is more reckless.

22.2
1. Cats run faster than dogs.
2. My brother writes more beautifully than your sister.
3. You learn quicker than I do.
4. Rashad sells more cars than Steven.
5. New York is bigger than Chicago.
6. Ginger dances better than Fred.
7. The lake looks bluer than the sky.
8. Our team plays more capably than your team.
9. The husband seems more jealous than the wife.
10. Mr. Espinosa has less money than Ms. VanDam.

22.3
1. Carlos is the shortest boy in the last row.
2. Paris is the most beautiful.
3. The white stallion runs the fastest.
4. Is Russia the largest country in Europe?
5. Is this the most interesting article?
6. They say that the CEO is the richest.
7. Smoking is the worst for your health.
8. The soprano sings the softest.
9. The vice president spoke the most brilliantly.
10. Is the planet Pluto the farthest?
11. Larry gets up the earliest.
12. She is the most systematic about everything she does.
13. Brian is the cutest boy.
14. Laura plays the violin the best.
15. That book is the most boring.

22.4
1. Melanie is the funniest girl in class.
2. What is the most distant planet?
3. Your handwriting is the worst.
4. The men at the party ate the most.
5. Olive is the smartest of all the girls in school.
6. Mozart composed the most beautiful music.
7. Grandmother baked the most delicious cakes.
8. This pickpocket stole the most wallets.
9. Raj thinks this symphony is the most boring.
10. Janice is my best friend.

22.5
1. My coffee is hotter./My coffee is the hottest.
2. Is this math problem more difficult?/Is this math problem the most difficult?
3. I feel better today./I feel the best today.
4. Life in the jungle is more dangerous./Life in the jungle is the most dangerous.
5. This village is poorer./This village is the poorest.
6. Mr. Hong always has less time./Mr. Hong always has the least time.
7. The choir sang a merrier song./The choir sang the merriest song.
8. She wore a shabbier dress./She wore the shabbiest dress.
9. Bert has more friends./Bert has the most friends.
10. She can speak more calmly about it./She can speak the most calmly about it.

23 Conjunctions

23.1
1. That's my brother, and the woman next to him is his wife.
2. We ran into the tent, but our clothes were already soaked by the storm.

3. Should we watch TV tonight, or should we go see a movie?

4. She began to cry, for the book ended so sadly.

5. I hurried as fast as I could, but (**OR** yet) I arrived home late as usual.

6. The red car was already sold, so Kim bought the blue one.

7. Our dog likes to play in the yard, but our cat prefers to stay in the house.

8. Milo lives on Oak Street, and his brother lives nearby.

9. Their credit was very poor, but (**OR** yet) they decided to buy a piano anyway.

10. I love the snowy beauty of winter, but I hate the heat of summer.

23.2
1. Neither . . . nor
2. either . . . or
3. both . . . and
4. not only . . . but also
5. Neither . . . nor/Both . . . and
6. both . . . and/neither . . . nor
7. not only . . . but also
8. either . . . or
9. Neither . . . nor/Not only . . . but also
10. Neither . . . nor/Both . . . and

23.3 Sample Answers:
1. She left for home after she graduated from college.
2. When she told another joke, Pedro started to laugh.
3. I won't help you unless you make some effort.
4. Do you know where Stephan put his wallet?
5. Once the kids were in bed, I was able to relax.
6. Chris closed the book before he got to the end.
7. You can stay up late as long as you get up on time tomorrow.
8. While I weeded the garden, he relaxed under a tree.
9. I don't remember if I turned off the coffee pot.
10. Now that they live in the city, they often go to the theater.

23.4 Sample Answers:
1. I like the beach, but the water is cold. She's smart, but she's vain.
2. I'll quit unless you pay me more. We're going home unless the weather gets better.
3. Neither the husband nor the wife understood me. I want neither your time nor your money.
4. Do you know where she lives? I found out where you hid the money.
5. I don't know how you knew that. Tell me how I can fix the car.
6. He is my friend and helps me with everything. Alex is a mechanic, and Minnie is a teacher.
7. She's not only bright but also talented. I not only fell down but also tore my shirt.
8. I fought in the battle, for it was the right thing to do. The children were tired, for they had been busy all day.
9. He has no idea when the movie starts. This dog always knows when it's dinner time.
10. Either you find a job, or you find a new place to live. The songs were either too loud or too soft.

23.5 *Sample answers are provided.*
1. red, The car was small, dirty, and red.
2. muddy, The country lane was narrow, long, and muddy.
3. pollution, I dislike living downtown because of the noise, crime, and pollution.
4. kind people, The Dominican Republic has kind people, palm trees, pretty beaches, and tropical birds.
5. foods, I like to become acquainted with people, customs, and foods from other countries.

23.6
1. Susan washed the dishes and put the food away.
2. Peter opened the door and greeted the guests.
3. Ralph is painting the garage door and cleaning the brushes.
4. Simon is generous, handsome, and intelligent.
5. Please try to make less noise and have some respect for others.
6. She gave him chocolates on Monday, a CD on Tuesday, and a bracelet on Wednesday.
7. While we were in Los Angeles, we went to a concert, ate Mexican food, and visited old friends.
8. I should have finished my project and cleaned my car.
9. He preferred to play poker or spend time in museums.
10. I like water, but not soda.

23.7 1. and 2. so 3. but 4. or 5. but 6. nor 7. and 8. and

23.8   1. are   2. is   3. are   4. is   5. is   6. are

23.9   1. She has neither a pen nor a ruler.
2. Both the giant panda and the white tiger face extinction.
3. We could either drive or take the bus.
4. She wants to buy either a Honda or a Toyota.
5. We can either fix dinner for them at home or take them to the restaurant.
6. Not only Joseph but also Peter is absent. or Both Joseph and Peter are absent.
7. Neither Joe nor Pedro is in class today.
8. You can have either tea or coffee.
9. Both Roger and Sam enjoy playing Nintendo.
10. The President's press secretary will neither confirm nor deny the story.
11. Both coal and petroleum are nonrenewable natural resources.
12. Both bird flu and malaria are dangerous diseases.
13. Neither her parents nor her boyfriend knows where she is.
14. According to the weather report, not only will it rain tomorrow but it will also be windy.

23.10   1. whether, or, for, and
2. and, either, or
3. not only, but, and
4. Neither, nor, but
5. Both, and, but

23.11   1. The men walked. The boys ran.
2. Sylvia came to the meeting. Her brother stayed home.
3. Sylvia came to the meeting, but her brother stayed home.
4. X
5. The professor spoke. The students listened.
6. His academic record was outstanding, yet he was not accepted into Harvard.
7. Her academic record was outstanding. She was not accepted into Harvard, but she was not too unhappy about it.
8. X
9. We had to go to the grocery store, for there was nothing to eat in the fridge.
10. A barometer measures air pressure. A thermometer measures temperature.
11. The Egyptians had good sculptors. Archeologists have found marvelous statues buried in the pyramids.
12. Murdock made many promises, but he had no intention of keeping them. He was known to be a liar.
13. I always enjoyed studying geography in high school, so I decided to pursue it in college.
14. Cecilia is in serious legal trouble, for she had no car insurance at the time of the accident.
15. Last night, Marie had to study for an exam, so she went to a coffeehouse.
16. The team of scientists has not finished analyzing the virus yet. Their work will not be published until later this year.
17. You have nothing to fear, for they are strong and united.
18. She threw the book out the window. She had failed the exam again, so she'd ruined her chances of bringing up her grade in the class.
19. Sophia struggled to keep her head above water. She tried to yell, but the water kept getting in her mouth.
20. The hurricane was devastating. Tall buildings crumbled and crashed to the ground.
21. It was a wonderful day at the park. The children swam in the river, collected rocks and insects, and laughed all day. The older kids played soccer. The adults prepared the food, supervised the children, and played cards for a short while.
22. Caterpillars eat plants and can cause damage to some crops, but adult butterflies feed primarily on flowers and do not cause any harm.
23. Both Jesse and I had many errands to do this morning. Jesse had to go to the post office and the bookstore. I had to go to the pharmacy, the video store, and the bank.
24. The butterfly is extraordinary. It begins as an ugly caterpillar and turns into something colorful. It almost looks like a piece of art.

23.12   1. although
2. before
3. until
4. because
5. before
6. while
7. since

8. even though
9. until
10. since OR because
11. because
12. when OR whenever
13. before OR when
14. if
15. than
16. after OR as soon as OR when
17. even though OR although
18. unless

23.13 *Sample answers are provided.*
1. They can't leave until they feed the cats.
2. I am not going to leave this room until you tell me the truth. OR Until you tell me the truth, I am not going to leave this room.
3. He can't pay his parking ticket until he receives his paycheck.
4. It had been a boring conversation until, finally, Steve arrived. OR Until Steve finally arrived, it had been a boring conversation.
5. When I go to bed at night, I like to read until I get sleepy.

23.14 *In these answers, the dependent clause beginning with* Now that *precedes the independent clause; however, it could also follow the independent clause.*
1. Now that Patrick moved into a house, he can use his own furniture.
2. Now that I've finally finished painting the kitchen, I can go running.
3. Now that it's winter, they have to wear warm clothes.
4. Now that he's 21, he can legally drink.
5. Now that Charles has a Jeep, he can drive to school.
6. Now that the civil war has ended, a new government is being formed.
7. Now that the project is finally over, we can relax.
8. Now that the water has gotten warmer, do you want to go swimming?
9. Now that my best friend is married, he has more responsibilities.
10. Now that I know English, I can get a job as a translator.

23.15 *Answers may vary.*
1. We stopped to visit our grandparents on our way to Oklahoma; afterwards/later/then, we stayed with friends in Tulsa.
2. We had planned to go to the park today; however/unfortunately, the rain canceled our plans.
3. It was a difficult time for her; still/however/nonetheless, she learned a lot from the experience.
4. The hotel stayed vacant and abandoned for many years; finally/eventually, the city council decided to tear it down.
5. They had a romantic walk along the river; afterwards/later, they went back to the hotel to drink some champagne.
6. Mr. Williams cannot speak at the conference; instead/therefore, Mr. Rogers will go in his place.
7. We enjoy all kinds of outdoor activities; for example, we really like rock climbing.
8. The mall is already closed; besides/anyway, you do not have any money to spend.
9. The essay must be written by Monday; otherwise, you fall behind schedule.
10. Anna Nicole Smith was incredibly rich; however, she did not have a happy life.
11. They spent their entire afternoon shopping for clothes; afterwards/later, they wore some of their purchases to the dance.
12. He likes seafood; however, he is allergic to oysters.

24   Interrogatives

24.1
1. What kind of dress did Lupita buy?
2. Where is Panama located?
3. What did she want to buy?
4. Where did Kevin decide to go?
5. With whom did Kendall spend a lot of time talking?
6. Why did she start to laugh?
7. How did the man on crutches come down the steps?
8. When did the clock stop?

9. Who has worked for this company for years?
10. Whose husband is a firefighter?
11. Which pair of gloves should she select?
12. How many people are in the room?
13. What breed is this dog?
14. What meant danger?
15. Where is Los Angeles from here?

24.2 1. Nikki's   2. a bug   3. tomorrow   4. a Ford   5. that man   6. six feet   7. a friend
8. near the sea   9. better   10. the ending

24.3 Sample Answers:
1. . . . you said that.   2. . . . speaking at the meeting?   3. . . . problems he has.   4. . . . brought the food to the picnic?   5. . . . do such a thing?   6. . . . you were planning to do.   7. . . . they managed to escape.
8. . . . a car pulled in front of me.   9. . . . did you have to pay for it?   10. . . . is going to help us?

24.4 1. a. Are you home for the holidays? b. Were you home for the holidays? c. Have you been home for the holidays?   2. a. Does the arsonist burn down the bank? b. Has the arsonist burned down the bank? c. Will the arsonist burn down the bank?   3. a. Do you have to spend a lot of time studying? b. Did you have to spend a lot of time studying? c. Will you have to spend a lot of time studying?   4. a. Do the workers do the job right? b. Did the workers do the job right? c. Will the workers do the job right?
5. a. Could you really predict the outcome of the election? b. Have you really been able to predict the outcome of the election? c. Will you really be able to predict the outcome of the election?

24.5 *Sample answers are provided.*   1. Shouldn't you have been a little more polite to him?   2. Must you play your drums so late at night?   3. Won't Ms. Anderson want to meet the author, too?   4. Does that woman have to smoke so much?   5. Will you have another cup of tea? or Will you have arrived by Friday?
6. Is the parking attendant able to drive a stick shift?   7. Will the others join us for dinner tonight?
8. Ought he to have been so mean to her?   9. Would you take a job in another part of the country?
10. Have you ever had to study so hard before?

24.6 *Sample answers are provided.*   1. a. Did Tom really spend more than a hundred dollars? b. Did Tom really have to spend more than a hundred dollars?   2. a. Have they arrived in the capital on time? b. Have they been able to arrive in the capital on time?   3. a. Did the scientist finally develop a new method? b. Could the scientist finally develop a new method?   4. a. Do the children try to remain calm? b. Should the children try to remain calm?   5. a. Do you sometimes consider the danger involved in this? b. Shouldn't you sometimes consider the danger involved in this?   6. a. Do the second-graders spell accurately? b. Can the second-graders spell accurately?   7. a. Will Maria prepare some lunch? b. Will Maria try to prepare some lunch?   8. a. Did the judge suggest a solution? b. Did the judge want to suggest a solution?   9. a. Will they flee the storm? b. Will they be able to flee the storm?   10. a. Does he always pretend nothing is wrong? b. Must he always pretend nothing is wrong?

24.7 1. a. Did a plumber fix the leaking pipes? b. Was a plumber fixing the leaking pipes?   2. a. Couldn't you work on that old car? b. Couldn't you be working on that old car?   3. a. Have the judges spoken about this for a long time? b. Have the judges been speaking about this for a long time?   4. a. Does time go by very fast? b. Is time going by very fast?   5. a. Did thunder roll across the foothills? b. Was thunder rolling across the foothills?   6. a. Will you take a series of exams? b. Will you be taking a series of exams?   7. a. Has Mr. Kelly wanted to vacation there? b. Has Mr. Kelly been wanting to vacation there?   8. a. Is he crazy? b. Is he being crazy?   9. a. Have the revelers had a good time at the celebration? b. Have the revelers been having a good time at the celebration?   10. a. Should I sit nearer to her? b. Should I be sitting nearer to her?

24.8 1. What did the attendant close and lock at seven sharp?   2. When do they leave for Puerto Rico?
3. What isn't always easy to understand?   4. Whose two puppies got their shots today?   5. From whom did they probably catch the flu?   6. How do we plan on getting to the match?   7. Where did that big bully throw the ball?   8. When should the girls come home?   9. With which boy will Andrea dance?
10. Why do they know about the change in plans?

24.9 *Sample answers are provided.*   1. Why do you always contradict me?   2. How do you spell the applicant's last name?   3. With whom was the young man arguing?   4. Which airline flies directly to Frankfurt?   5. When did you decide to become a physician?

24.10 *Sample answers are provided.*   1. a. How little were the newborn pups? b. Each of the pups weighed less than eight ounces.   2. a. How large is the mayor's new house? b. The mayor's new house is a gigantic mansion.   3. a. How frequently do you get an oil change? b. I get an oil change every four thousand miles.
4. a. How difficult did you find the GRE? b. I found the GRE less challenging than I expected.   5. a. How

hot was it in Miami yesterday? b. It was over ninety-five degrees yesterday.   6. a. How strong must a person be to become a mountain climber? b. A person should be in good condition and have a developed body to become a mountain climber.   7. a. How often do you travel abroad? b. I travel abroad about two times a year.   8. How did the worker carry the dynamite? The worker carried the dynamite carefully. 9. How many of the children went to the zoo? Most of the children went to the zoo.   10. How did John work today? John worked lazily today.

25   Negation

25.1
1. The boys were not playing basketball at the park./The boys weren't playing basketball at the park.
2. My sister is not a concert pianist./My sister isn't a concert pianist.
3. Are you not well?/Aren't you well?
4. His nephew is not learning Japanese./His nephew isn't learning Japanese.
5. Can they not explain how this happened?/Can't they explain how this happened?
6. The judge did not order him sent to prison./The judge didn't order him sent to prison.
7. We will not be traveling to Spain this summer./We won't be traveling to Spain this summer.
8. Does Mr. Amin not have our lawnmower?/Doesn't Mr. Amin have our lawnmower?
9. My sister does not spend a lot of time in the library./My sister doesn't spend a lot of time in the library.
10. Judith did not understand the situation./Judith didn't understand the situation.

25.2
1. I have had enough time to work on this.
2. Mark gets to work on time.
3. She brought her dog along.
4. Have you ever been to New York City?
5. Lin was speaking with someone.
6. The children cooperate with the substitute teacher.
7. They live somewhere in the city.
8. Could the horse run faster?
9. Marta broke the window.
10. Yes, I like this kind of music.
11. Chase is dancing with someone.
12. Can you find something you need?
13. I have written the proposal for them.
14. Yes, she spends her vacation with us.
15. He got something interesting in the mail.

25.3 Sample Answers:
1. I do not understand.   2. They never help me.   3. No one saw the accident.   4. It's not anywhere to be found.   5. He does not have anything for you.   6. None of your work is correct.   7. He has not ever been in Europe.   8. She bought neither purse.   9. The thief was nowhere to be seen.   10. Uma knows nothing about math.

26   Numbers

26.1
1. Five plus seven is twelve.
2. Eleven minus six is five.
3. Three hundred forty-five minus two hundred twenty equals one hundred twenty-five.
4. Twenty-two times ten equals two hundred twenty.
5. One hundred times sixty-three is six thousand three hundred.
6. Ten thousand divided by five hundred is two hundred.
7. Eight hundred and eighty times three equals two thousand six hundred and forty.
8. Eighty-eight thousand minus fifty-five thousand is thirty-three thousand.
9. Eleven point five times ten is one hundred fifteen.
10. Ninety-three point three divided by three equals thirty-one point one.

26.2 1. second   2. fourth   3. twenty-first   4. third   5. one hundredth   6. thirtieth   7. fifth   8. tenth   9. one thousandth   10. ninety-ninth   11. first   12. twelfth   13. twenty-fifth   14. eighty-sixth   15. twenty-second

26.3
1. August tenth
2. October twelfth
3. November eleventh

4. February sixteenth, nineteen ninety-nine
5. April first, two thousand two
6. December twenty-fourth
7. July fourth
8. fourteen ninety-two
9. February fourteenth, two thousand four
10. June second

26·4
1. An important date to remember is November 17, 1959.
2. The city paid $34.7 million to build the tower.
3. It took five out of nine members to reach a consensus.
4. In Europe, the 1970s were marked by social and political change.
5. Turn to page 109, which should be chapter 12.
6. The morning temperature was 47 degrees Fahrenheit, or 8 degrees Celsius.
7. X
8. They drove down Interstate 34 to the lake.
9. The Second Battle of Bull Run was fought from August 28 to 30, 1862.

27 Conversation: Introductions, opinions, descriptions

27.1 1. c 2. b 3. c 4. d 5. a

27.2 1. c, h, n 2. b, k 3. a, e, g, i, l 4. g 5. b, j, k 6. b, l 7. f, l 8. c, h, n
9. a, m 10. d

27.3 1. Yes, I do./No, I don't. 2. Yes, I am./No, I'm not. 3. Yes, they do./No, they don't.
4. Yes, I am./No, I'm not. 5. Yes, he (or she) is./No, he (or she) isn't.

27.4 Answers will vary, but questions should begin as follows. 1. Do you . . . ?
2. Is she . . . ? 3. Are they . . . ? 4. Do you . . . ? 5. Does he . . . ? 6. Are you . . . ?

27.5 1. o 2. q 3. h 4. b 5. i, l 6. a, n 7. k 8. m 9. p 10. c 11. i, l
12. g 13. r 14. j 15. d, e 16. d, f 17. r

27.6 1. b 2. c 3. a 4. d 5. a

27.7 These are possible answers. 1. What does she do? 2. Thank you. 3. Don't be late!
4. Tell me about yourself. 5. We finish tomorrow.

27.8 1. see 2. seeing 3. going 4. doing 5. hear

27.9 Answers will vary.

27.10 Answers will vary.

27.11 1. Would you like to have dinner with me/us? 2. Do you like fast-food restaurants? 3. Where would you like to go on your vacation? 4. What do you like to do on weekends/in the winter/etc.? 5. Do you feel like _____ing?
6. What kind of fruit do you like? 7. What does he like to do? 8. Does she like chocolate ice cream?
9. Do you like _____? 10. Would you like to _____?

27.12 1. tell 2. speak 3. tell 4. say 5. tell 6. tell 7. Say 8. say 9. tell
10. tell 11. tell 12. say

27.13 1. Tell me where you're going. 2. Tell me what they're doing. 3. Tell me how you get there. 4. Tell me when you study. 5. Tell me why she's crying. 6. Tell me what time we leave. 7. Tell me who you're texting. 8. Tell me how much it costs.

27.14 1. a, b, h, k 2. i, j, p 3. r 4. o 5. c, g 6. n 7. f 8. d, e, l 9. q 10. c, g, m

27.15 1. c 2. b 3. a 4. d 5. c

27.16 1. a 2. c 3. a 4. b 5. c

27.17 Answers will vary.

27.18 Answers will vary.

27.19 Answers will vary.

27.20 1. b 2. c 3. a 4. c 5. d

27.21 1. What's he like? 2. Does she like _____? 3. What's he like? 4. What do they like to do? 5. What does she like to do? 6. What are you like?

27.22 1. c   2. a, b   3. d   4. i   5. l   6. h   7. j, k   8. e   9. f   10. g

27.23 1. d, i, l, m, n   2. h, j, k   3. c, f   4. b, o   5. a, e, g   6. b, o   7. a, e, g   8. e, g, h

27.24 1. c   2. a   3. d   4. d   5. a

27.25 1. a   2. b   3. d   4. b   5. a

27.26 1. In the first place   2. Second/In the second place   3. Plus   4. Not to mention that

27.27 Answers will vary.

27.28 Answers will vary.

28 Conversation: Openers, appointments, needs

28.1 1. There are   2. There are   3. There is   4. There are   5. There is

28.2 1. living   2. live   3. get   4. smoke   5. getting   6. stay   7. working   8. go   9. being   10. driving

28.3 1. a   2. c   3. c   4. b   5. d

28.4 1. b, h, k   2. j   3. e, h   4. i   5. l   6. f   7. d   8. a   9. c   10. e, h

28.5 1. i   2. c   3. d   4. n   5. o   6. a, b   7. g, m   8. f, p   9. j, k   10. e   11. e   12. h   13. l

28.6 1. d   2. b   3. a   4. a   5. b

28.7 1. b, i   2. h   3. j, k   4. a, g, k   5. d   6. f   7. i   8. c, i   9. a, e   10. a, g, l

28.8 Answers will vary.

28.9 Answers will vary.

28.10 Answers will vary.

28.11 1. at, in, on, at, in   2. in, at   3. in, at, in   4. on, at, in, at, in   5. on, at, in, at, on, in

28.12 1. May/Can I leave?   2. You mustn't/must not leave.   3. Do you have to work today?   4. You have to work tomorrow.   5. When should I take the medicine?   6. You're supposed to take the medicine just before a meal.   7. You can't/mustn't jaywalk./You're not supposed to cross here.   8. Do I have to/Am I supposed to/Are you supposed to wait for a green light?   9. Would you rather have your steak medium or well done?   10. Will/Can/Could you come to a party at my house on Saturday night?   11. Will/Can you pick me up at the airport?   12. No, I won't pick you up.

28.13 1. p   2. o   3. a   4. a, d   5. d, e, f, g   6. j, k   7. h   8. q   9. m   10. n   11. l   12. b, e, q   13. b   14. d, e, f, g

28.14 1. were   2. could   3. would   4. had   5. didn't   6. were   7. were   8. could   9. called   10. lived

28.15 1. I wish you loved me.   2. I wish my neighbors didn't make so much noise.   3. I wish my mother were here.   4. I wish I were married.   5. I wish she could stay here tonight.   6. I wish he would move his car.   7. I wish she didn't drive so fast.   8. I wish they didn't come home so late.   9. I wish I had enough/more money.   10. I wish our house were bigger./I wish we had a bigger house./I wish we lived in a bigger house.

28.16 1. c   2. a   3. b   4. b   5. c

28.17 1. c, h   2. d, e, i   3. d, e, i, l, m   4. a   5. b, f, j   6. d, e, i, l   7. j   8. k   9. g   10. l

28.18 Answers will vary.

28.19 Answers will vary.

28.20 Answers will vary

28.21 1. have to   2. need/want   3. want   4. prerequisites   5. would like   6. needs   7. would you mind   8. required to   9. requirements   10. need to/have to

28.22 1. c, h   2. g, k   3. e   4. i, l   5. i, l   6. d   7. f   8. a, b, j   9. m

28.23 1. a   2. c   3. d   4. a   5. d

28.24 Answers will vary.

28.25 1. to mind   2. to have a look   3. to have a mind to   4. none   5. to get rid of   6. to give a heads-up   7. to be worthwhile   8. in the meantime/meanwhile   9. to change your mind   10. utilities

11. One more thing   12. the country   13. go-to person/place   14. say   15. never mind
16. the mind   17. required   18. prerequisite   19. all the bells and whistles   20. out there

28.26 Answers will vary.

29 Conversation: Future events, narration, electronic communication

29.1 1. c   2. b   3. d   4. c   5. a   6. c

29.2 1. f   2. j   3. d, h   4. a, c   5. e, g, i   6. b

29.3 1. c   2. a   3. a   4. a   5. c

29.4 1. Still   2. senior   3. the same old thing   4. overseas   5. a whole bunch of   6. freshman
7. pack light   8. catch up on   9. taking care of   10. reach a happy medium/compromise

29.5 Answers will vary.

29.6 Answers will vary.

29.7 1. a. First   b. Then   c. After that/Next   d. Finally   2. a. First   b. Then   c. Next/After that
d. then   e. Finally   f. For the frosting on the cake/To top it all off/As if that weren't enough

29.8 1. c   2. a   3. c   4. d   5. a

29.9 1. s, x, y   2. h   3. c, i, p, t, u   4. j, w   5. k, l, q, r   6. f, g   7. d   8. v   9. a, b, m, o   10. e, n

29.10 Answers will vary.

29.11 1. a, p   2. g   3. i   4. b, e, j, l   5. h, m, n   6. o, s, t   7. c, q   8. d, f   9. k   10. r

29.12 Answers will vary.

29.13 1. I wish you were here.   2. I wish I could get a promotion at this company.   3. I wish she weren't
always stressed out.   4. I wish he knew my e-mail address.   5. I wish they would come to see me.

29.14 1. d   2. a   3. b   4. c   5. c

29.15 Answers will vary.

29.16 Answers will vary.

29.17 1. Can you come over as soon as possible?   2. Are you serious? I'm at school. Boring beyond belief.
3. It's over between us. Sorry.   4. Laugh out loud. You're crazy.   5. I'm unhappy without you.
6. Me, too.   7. See you later.   8. Oh my God. She's out to lunch.

29.18 Ansrs wl vry. :)

30 Some Important Contrasts

30.1 1. bad   2. well   3. Few   4. less   5. lie   6. a little   7. than   8. Whom   9. badly   10. good
11. a few   12. less   13. lay   14. A little   15. then   16. good   17. fewer   18. lay   19. badly   20. than

30.2 1. The little boy acted very badly in class today.
2. Don't you feel well?
3. Omar has fewer friends than his brother.
4. Mom is lying down for a while.
5. Kris is prettier than Hilda.
6. To whom did you send the letter?
7. Were you in Europe then, too?
8. I lay on the floor and played with the dog.
9. Johnny plays well with the other children.
10. Her voice sounds bad today.

30.3 Sample Answers:
1. This is a bad situation.   2. They played badly today.   3. She's a very good mother.   4. I don't feel well.
5. I have few reasons to doubt you.   6. We have a few things to discuss.   7. There are fewer boys than girls.
8. She has less time now.   9. I'll lay it on the table.   10. He was lying on the floor.   11. There is so little
money left.   12. I have a little time to spare.   13. You're younger than Barry.   14. I got up then took a
shower.   15. Who is that stranger?   16. Whom will the boss promote?

31 Phrasal verbs

31·1 *Sample answers are provided.* 1. a. I'll be out until suppertime. b. I was out with Tina last night. 2. a. That handsome guy is really with it. b. Buy some new clothes and get with it. 3. a. The man in the red jacket seems to be up to something. b. Those kids are up to no good again. 4. a. Uncle Jake broke down and cried. b. I saw tears in her eyes and knew she was breaking down. 5. a. The comedian broke up the audience. b. I have to break up with you. 6. a. We breezed through lunch and hurried back to work. b. Anna breezes through every test. 7. a. You can count on me for about twenty dollars. b. Don't count on Hal for any help.

31·2 *Sample answers are provided.* 1. on his brother 2. in unannounced 3. up this conversation 4. this story 5. on her husband 6. with the lawn mower 7. away during the night 8. the problem 9. with a skirt and blouse 10. at

31·3 1. to lay off 2. let on 3. has something against 4. to make of 5. made up with 6. made up 7. make up 8. letting on 9. lay off of 10. lead / on

31·4 *Sample answers are provided.* 1. She tried to pass off the piece of glass as a gem. 2. Someone set off the fire alarm! 3. It's time we set off for home. 4. What do these symbols stand for? 5. I was wrong. I take back what I said. 6. You ought to take up knitting. 7. At six I walked out into the evening air and hurried home. 8. You can't just walk out on me. 9. I'll never warm up to your mother. 10. Did you water down this coffee?

31·5 *Sample answers are provided.* 1. a. Tom broke down her silence. b. Tom broke her silence down. c. Tom broke it down. 2. a. I'll follow up the story. b. I'll follow the story up. c. I'll follow it up. 3. a. They laid off our department. b. They laid our department off. c. They laid us off. 4. a. He's just leading on the girl. b. He's just leading the girl on. c. He's just leading her on. 5. a. We let down Dad. b. We let Dad down. c. We let him down. 6. a. He passed off the watch as a Rolex. b. He passed the watch off as a Rolex. c. He passed it off as a Rolex. 7. a. They set off a firecracker. b. They set a firecracker off. c. They set it off. 8. a. I'll warm up the coffee. b. I'll warm the coffee up. c. I'll warm it up. 9. a. Don't water down my martini. b. Don't water my martini down. c. Don't water it down. 10. a. The beautician made up her face. b. The beautician made her face up. c. The beautician made it up.

31·6 1. out on 2. off as 3. in 4. down 5. away 6. off 7. up to 8. up 9. up for 10. with